Introduction to Biological Psychology

Introduction to Biological Psychology

Third Edition

Philip M. Groves
University of California–San Deigo

George V. Rebec
Indiana University–Bloomington

Based upon previous editions by
Philip M. Groves and Kurt Schlesinger

wcb
Wm. C. Brown Publishers
Dubuque, Iowa

Book Team

Editor *James M. McNeil*
Developmental Editor *Sandra E. Schmidt*
Production Editor *Mary Jean Gregory*
Designer *Barbara J. Grantham*
Visual Processor *Joyce E. Watters*
Permissions Editor *Mavis M. Oeth*
Photo Research Editor *Shirley Charley*
Product Manager *Marcia H. Stout*

wcb

Chairman of the Board *Wm. C. Brown*
President and Chief Executive Officer *Mark C. Falb*

wcb group

Wm. C. Brown Publishers, College Division

Executive Vice-President, General Manager *G. Franklin Lewis*
Editor in Chief *George Wm. Bergquist*
Director of Production *Beverly Kolz*
National Sales Manager *Bob McLaughlin*
Production Editorial Manager *Colleen A. Yonda*
Manager of Design *Marilyn A. Phelps*
Photo Research Manager *Faye M. Schilling*

Cover Image: A computer-assisted three-dimensional reconstruction of the human brain looking up at its ventral surface. This shows the brain stem (yellow), cerebellum (pink), and cerebral hemispheres (red). (Illustration courtesy of Dr. Robert B. Livingston, Laboratory for Quantitative Morphology, Department of Neuroscience, School of Medicine, University of California at San Diego, La Jolla, California.)

This book is dedicated to Gould P. and Eleanor Groves and to George M. and Nadine Rebec.

Contents

Preface

Introduction to Biological Psychology, 3d edition, is designed for the first course in the college curriculum that deals with the biological or physiological bases of behavior. Although offered primarily in psychology departments, this course is really an interdisciplinary endeavor, combining concepts in the physical and natural sciences with the basic principles of behavior. Thus, in writing this book, we have tried to explain the essential details of anatomy, physiology, biochemistry, and pharmacology within the context of behavioral processes. Moreover, whenever possible, we present the basic biology of human behavior, a topic to which we all can relate. In doing so, however, we do not overlook the results of animal experiments nor do we oversimplify research findings. We do our best to present all of the relevant information and to weave it into the story of each chapter. Our goal is to offer a text that provides a solid, self-contained introduction to the field.

Students will find a rich reward in reading this book. They will have a better understanding of the biological factors that guide and regulate behavior, including their own. They also will have a better appreciation of the biomedical advances that have become a routine feature of daily news reports. And most importantly from our point of view, they will come to appreciate what the field of biological psychology—and the people who work in it—are all about.

Neuroscience has made great strides in the past decade, and research continues to reveal new ideas and information about the biology of behavior. The third edition of this text has been revised extensively to incorporate these new discoveries. But the revision process is more than just an update. Entire chapters have been rewritten in order to discuss research topics in an insightful, narrative form.

Biological psychology is more than a list of anatomical terms or arcane chemical reactions. These are but the vocabulary of a far more interesting story—the story of how the brain controls behavior. Each chapter summarizes the insights that we have gained into this still unfolding mystery.

Many new approaches to research on the brain and behavior also are described in this edition, including such advances as computer imaging of the brain, radioligand receptor mapping and imaging, computer-assisted three-dimensional reconstruction of the brain from serial sections, and immunocytochemical techniques. The application of these new methods of studying and visualizing the brain is described and shown in new figures included in many of the chapters in this edition. New techniques, such as computer-assisted three-dimensional reconstruction of the brain, are illustrated in new color illustrations in this edition of the book and on its cover. The book is designed to present a thoroughly modern introduction to the field.

The important issue of the use of animals in brain research also is addressed in this edition. We hope to make it clear that those who vandalize research laboratories and steal research animals are woefully misguided. Brain research is devoted to the alleviation of human suffering brought about by the tragedy of mental illness and brain disease. Without animal research, we would have no hope of reducing the scope of this enormous human burden.

The fifteen chapters contained in this edition have been written to achieve a continuity of length, topic coverage, depth and breadth, as well as a continuity of style. An extensive study guide designed specifically for this text provides further basic science information relevant to the needs of students taking an introductory course in this field; it also provides substantial study aids for mastering the material in the text. A companion manual for the instructor also is available.

All test questions found in the instructor's manual are available on wcb TestPak, a free, computerized testing system. Instructors can either use the call-in/mail-in service or can use an Apple IIe, Apple IIc, or IBM-PC to create their own tests. Also, a set of color transparencies and a supplementary slide set incorporating images not found in the text are available to the instructor adopting this edition.

We are indebted to a large group of talented and expert reviewers who have read and criticized every chapter in this edition. Their comments have made an enormous contribution to the current version of this text, although we hasten to emphasize that any inaccuracies or flaws in this edition are ours alone. It is a pleasure to acknowledge the invaluable assistance of Anthony R. Caggiula, University of Pittsburgh; J. Timothy Cannon, University of Scranton; Leo M. Chalupa, University of California, Davis; Alice H. Cydell, San Diego City College; Linda J. Enloe, Idaho State University; Gabriel P. Frommer, Indiana University; Thomas W. Gardiner, Indiana University; Gordon K. Hodge, University of New Mexico; Laverne C. Johnson, San Diego Naval Health Research Center; Duane G. McClearn, Elon College; and John Simpson, University of Washington.

The authors gratefully acknowledge the support for brain research received from the Office of Naval Research, the National Institute of Mental Health, the National Institute on Drug Abuse, and the National Science Foundation.

We offer a special thanks to James M. Tepper and Stephen Young of the Department of Psychiatry, University of California at San Diego, and Thomas W. Gardiner of the Department of Psychology, Indiana University, Bloomington, for their valuable assistance. We appreciate their critical remarks and many suggestions.

The many people at Wm. C. Brown also deserve our sincere gratitude for their thorough and competent job of producing this edition of the text. Sandy Schmidt and Jim McNeil have been especially helpful in shepherding the entire project to completion. A special thanks goes to Mary Jean Gregory for helping to make the final manuscript a better organized and more coherent product. We also thank Mary Blackwood for her careful preparation of the manuscript.

Finally, we are most grateful to the students and faculty who have given the field of biological psychology its life and meaning. Their interest and devotion to scholarship make all of our efforts worthwhile.

Philip M. Groves
George V. Rebec

Introduction to Biological Psychology

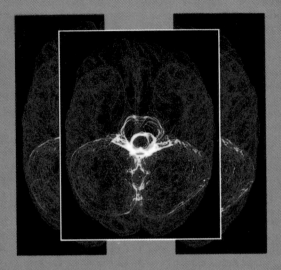

Outline

Introduction

Biological psychology combines an interest in behavior with the machinery that makes it possible. This machinery includes glands, muscles, and other organs regulated and controlled by the nervous system. At the center of this regulation and control is the brain, the only object in the universe that we truly know from the inside.

Although biological psychology is young as an interdisciplinary science, interest in the brain and behavior is as old as antiquity. In the fifth century B.C., the Greek philosopher Alcmaeon of Crotona recognized the brain as the seat of human intellectual capacities. But this view was not widely accepted in the ancient world. The Egyptians attributed no special powers to the contents of the head. When they entombed their dead leaders, they preserved the intestines and other internal organs, but not the brain. They used a special spoon to scoop it out through the nose. For the Assyrians and the ancient people of Israel, the liver, with its rich connections to the blood supply, represented the seat of all that is human. Aristotle, too, ignored the brain. He pointed to the active, pulsating heart as the center of sensory experience and behavior. Only very gradually, over a period spanning hundreds of years, did the importance of the brain in sensation, thought, and action become widely accepted.

Models of the Brain

In this chapter, we will describe some of the most important conceptual developments that forged the link between brain and behavior. In most cases, concepts of brain function originated with the physical and engineering sciences. Throughout history, new developments

Chapter

1

Historical Concepts and Lessons Learned

in these sciences were regarded as possible keys to understanding the brain. Any new technological achievement that came along—the telephone, the camera, the radio, the hologram, the computer—was used as a model of how the brain works. To begin our study, therefore, it will be useful to survey some of the efforts that have been made to relate technological advances in other fields to an understanding of the brain. We know of no better way to introduce the fundamental concepts—the logic—of brain research.

The Royal Fountains

In seventeenth-century Europe technological creations often appeared first in the form of toys built for the amusement of royalty. Among such devices displayed before the court of Louis XIV were animated statues, or automata, the limbs of which were moved by hydraulic power. When a visitor in the courtyard stepped on a hidden plate, cylinders powered by water pressure were set in motion, and the statues, which were connected to this hydraulic system, began to move. The first theory of how the nervous system controls behavior originated with a comparison of animal motion with the motion of these ingenious statues.

This first theory was developed by René Descartes, a French philosopher and mathematician. For Descartes, the nervous system was really a hydraulic system consisting of hollow tubes that led to muscles made up of empty bladders. The fluid that flowed through this hydraulic system was known as the **animal spirit** (from the Latin *anima,* meaning life). Descartes suggested that this spirit was stored in the hollow chambers of the brain, and during movement, it flowed through the hollow tubes

and inflated the muscles. According to Descartes, animals are the automata of God's courtyard.

Descartes also believed that animal movements are caused by external events. Something outside the organism activates the senses, which in turn causes the animal spirit to flow. No thinking is required. Animals, Descartes maintained, have no rational soul, though he believed firmly that humans do. Nevertheless, he recognized that even many human movements do not require conscious thought. Simple movements, like withdrawing your foot from a fire, require no deep thinking. According to Descartes's model, shown in figure 1.1, sensory information from the foot reaches the brain, which then "reflects" the animal spirit to the muscles to cause movement. The concept of **reflex,** a simple movement that requires no thought, was born.

For those movements that do require thought, Descartes had to devise a way for the

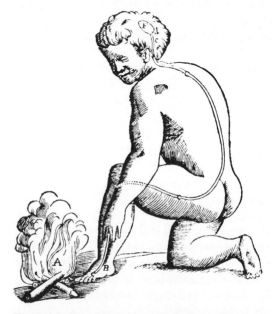

Figure 1.1 Descartes's concept of reflex action.

rational soul to control the animal spirit. He searched for an area in the brain where such an interaction could take place and settled on the **pineal gland,** a small organ near the center of the brain. Descartes saw the pineal as a gate that controlled the flow of the animal spirit. When reason demanded a particular movement, it would tilt the pineal in a certain direction and thereby allow the animal spirit to flow from the brain into the appropriate muscles.

Descartes's hydraulic model of the nervous system seems laughable today, but considering the physiological information available in the seventeenth century, you would have to agree it was a very plausible model. In fact, as you soon will see, his description of simple reflexes had a major impact on the brain sciences in the twentieth century. But perhaps the greatest feature of Descartes's model was that it could be tested experimentally. It generated certain predictions about how the nervous system works, and physiologists could devise experiments that tested these predictions. One obvious prediction of Descartes's model was that muscles should increase in volume when they contracted; muscles, you will recall, were thought to swell with the animal spirit during contraction. The prediction failed. When a person flexes an arm in a container of water, the water level does not rise, indicating that muscles are not expanded by an animal spirit. Other investigators found that frog muscles still could contract when they were separated from the rest of the body, obviously ruling out the flow of animal spirit from the brain. Moreover, tubes implanted in contracting muscles collected no fluid. By the end of the seventeenth century the hydraulic model collapsed, and the animal spirit was replaced by another seemingly magical substance—electricity.

Nervous Energy and Electricity

When the Enlightenment dawned in the eighteenth century, electricity captured everyone's imagination. It was known as the electric fluid in those days, and everyone was fascinated by it. Benjamin Franklin plucked sparks from the air by flying kites in thunderstorms, and the Abbé Jean Nollet, an entertainer for the court of France, plucked them from small boys. The Abbé's demonstration involved suspending a boy on silken ropes from a ceiling and then applying a static charge to his feet. When a brass plate was brought close to the boy's face, sparks flew from his nose. Electricity seemed to be an extraordinarily dramatic and powerful substance, suitable perhaps to be the active principle of the brain. This thought occurred to more than one eighteenth-century philosopher.

The early investigators of electricity, however, were handicapped by their primitive devices for generating, storing, and measuring it. Electricity was generated by machines designed to produce charge by friction on a revolving disk. It was stored in a Leyden jar, a primitive electronic capacitor invented around midcentury, and was measured by the metallic leaf electroscope or spark gap. Several scientists used such devices to study the torpedo fish (an electric ray) and the electric eel. By the last quarter of the century, it was believed that these animals could generate electricity at will and did so through the power of their nerves. Toward the end of the century, Luigi Galvani observed, as others had done before him, that a frog's leg could be made to twitch when one of its nerves was touched by a charged body. The leg would twitch spontaneously and incessantly if it was suspended from an iron railing by brass hooks in such a way that a circuit was made between two dissimilar metals

Figure 1.2 Galvani provoking contractions from the leg muscles of a frog by means of electricity.

and the leg itself (fig. 1.2). From these observations, Galvani concluded that the normal movements of the leg must be produced by electricity—**animal electricity**—derived from nervous tissue.

But Galvani's experiment was flawed. After much acrimonious dispute, physicist Allesandro Volta demonstrated that in Galvani's experiment electricity was derived not from animal tissues but from an external source. In the case of the frog's leg in contact with two dissimilar metals, the source of electricity was not the frog's tissues, but rather the contact between the iron railing and the brass hooks. When dissimilar metals make contact through a salt solution, which is what the frog's body

is, an electrical current results. By identifying the source of electricity in these experiments, Volta invented the voltaic pile, or battery. Galvani, meanwhile, may have set up his experiment improperly, but he was on the right track. His suspicion that nervous energy is electrical in character soon would be vindicated.

As mentioned before, a major problem in early investigations was that instruments to measure animal electricity were not sensitive enough. This problem finally was overcome with the invention of the **galvanometer,** based upon the discovery that electrical current flowing through a wire deflected a compass needle. Around 1840, an Italian professor of physics at Pisa, Carlo Matteucci, made numerous measurements on animal tissues with the galvanometer. He observed that electrical current flowed between the surface of a muscle and its end. A few years later, Émil du Bois-Reymond confirmed Matteucci's discovery. Although neither Matteucci nor du Bois-Reymond clearly described the source of the electrical current that flows between the surface of a muscle and its end, we now know that it was an injury current caused by a difference in electrical potential across the cell membrane. When inactive, an excitable cell (muscle or nerve cell) shows a difference in electrical potential across its membrane of about 0.07 volts, the inside of the cell being negative with respect to the outside. Each cell, therefore, is like a miniature battery: the negative terminal being the inside surface of the membrane and the positive terminal the outside surface. When the membrane is punctured or cut so that a conducting pathway exists, electrical current flows from the outside (positive terminal) to the inside (negative terminal) of the cell. This presumably is the current that Matteucci and du Bois-Reymond observed in excised muscle.

du Bois-Reymond was able to demonstrate similar injury currents in nerves, and he also noted that when nerves and muscles were stimulated electrically and became active, the injury current decreased. It was as if during activity the outside surface of these cells became less positive (or more negative) relative to the inside when they responded to a stimulus. du Bois-Reymond named this change in electrical potential a negative variation. We now call it an **action potential,** and as you will see in later chapters, it forms the basis for communication in the nervous system. du Bois-Reymond must have sensed the impact that his discovery would make on brain research when he said proudly, "If I do not greatly deceive myself, I have succeeded in realizing in full actuality . . . the hundred years' dream of physicists and physiologists, to wit, the identity of the nervous principle with electricity" (Brazier 1959, 22).

An action potential, or nerve impulse as it sometimes is called, is a very brief event, lasting only a few thousandths of a second. Hermann von Helmholtz (fig. 1.3), one of the first and greatest biological psychologists of the nineteenth century, succeeded in measuring how fast this impulse travels along a nerve fiber. Until Helmholtz came along, it was commonly assumed that electrical activity in nerves travels at the same speed as electricity in wires, which approaches the speed of light. Helmholtz found instead that action potentials travel much slower. In fact, they move along a nerve fiber at speeds of less than 50 meters per second—certainly nowhere near the speed of light. That brief instant after you smash your thumb with a hammer and before you feel the pain represents the time it takes for action potentials to travel along the pain pathway from your hand to your brain. This

Figure 1.3 H. von Helmholtz.

delay means that nerves do not function exactly like electrical wires and, as you will see in later chapters, the action potential is far more complex than a simple pulse of electricity.

Localization of Function

The discovery of action potentials and their movement along nerve fibers raised another fundamental question about the operation of the nervous system. How could different nerves carry different types of information if all the messages were conveyed by action potentials? How, for example, could the optic nerve, which links the eyes to the brain and conveys visual information, send the same type of impulses as the auditory nerve, which is responsible for the sensation of sounds? Johannes Müller, a German physiologist and mentor of Helmholtz, reasoned that although all messages reach the brain as action potentials, the brain perceives them differently. Thus, the brain interprets impulses arriving from the optic nerve as visual sensations, whereas impulses traveling along the auditory nerve are interpreted as sound. This idea has become known as Müller's **doctrine of specific nerve energies,** and you can observe it every time you rub your eyes. Pressure on the eyeball activates the optic nerve, and you perceive a shower of light even though there really is no light. The brain simply interprets the action potentials that arrive from the optic nerve as light, even if the action potentials were caused by pressure from your finger.

Specific nerves travel to specific areas of the brain, suggesting that different areas of the brain have different functions. An area of the brain that receives information from the optic nerve, for example, deals with visual sensations and must perform a different function than an area that receives auditory information. Thus, we can think of the brain not as a homogenous mass of tissue, but as a complex organ with different parts performing different functions.

But the brain is responsible for many different functions, and in the early part of the nineteenth century a lively debate arose as to whether all functions of the brain were localized in specific areas or whether some functions were distributed widely throughout the brain. Sir Charles Bell, an English physiologist, began the debate by noting that the brain could be divided into its two most easily distinguishable parts—the **cerebrum** and the **cerebellum.** As shown in the sketch of a human brain in figure 1.4, the cerebrum includes the

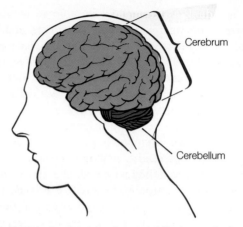

Figure 1.4 A schematic diagram of the human brain illustrating the expansive cerebrum and the cerebellum.

cerebral hemispheres, which cover most of the rest of the brain, whereas the cerebellum pokes out from behind the cerebrum at the back of the head. Bell observed that the cerebrum was quite small in lower mammals and that it attained its greatest mass in humans. From this observation, Bell concluded that the cerebrum is the seat of "higher mental activity." As for the cerebellum, Bell found that movements could be produced when the cerebellum of an animal was touched with a probe; similar movement could not be obtained when the cerebrum was touched. Thus, Bell concluded that the role of the cerebellum was to control movement of the muscles. With these observations, Bell laid the groundwork for future investigations of brain function, and as you will see in later chapters, we still associate the cerebrum with "higher mental activity" and the cerebellum with movement, although we now know that such a distinction is a gross oversimplification.

Bell's most important discovery, however, was revealed with the 1811 publication of a paper that some historians believe marks the beginning of modern neuroscience. This paper focused on the spinal cord rather than on the brain, but it made a lasting contribution to the debate over localization of function within the nervous system. Bell observed that spinal nerves, the fibers that enter and exit the spinal cord and carry sensory and motor information, divide into two roots: a dorsal root and a ventral root. Touching the ventral root produces movement, but touching the dorsal root does not. Bell concluded, therefore, that sensory and motor fibers were distinct and that motor information left the spinal cord by way of the ventral root, whereas sensory information entered the cord by way of the dorsal root. At approximately the same time though working independently, François Magendie, a member of the Academy of Sciences of Paris, made the same discovery. Today, this discovery is known as the **Bell-Magendie Law.** Along with Müller's doctrine, it helped to establish that different parts of the nervous system did indeed perform different functions.

Meanwhile, in Germany, Franz Joseph Gall began to take a very extreme position on the issue of localization of function. So extreme was his position, in fact, that he became one of the most controversial figures in early nineteenth-century science. Gall believed that the cerebrum is the seat of higher mental activity and argued that every type of mental function had its own specific location within the cerebrum. Curiosity, for example, resided in one area of the cerebrum, sense of humor in another, and so on. Gall also believed that the extent to which these functions were expressed in a given individual corresponded to bumps or grooves on the skull. Thus, Gall and his followers claimed that by studying the shape of someone's skull, they could determine that person's intelligence and personality. This practice became known as

phrenology, and a phrenological map of the skull devised by Gall is shown in figure 1.5. Note how very specific functions were linked to very specific areas. People were diagnosed as saints or sinners simply on the basis of the shape of their skulls.

For this reason, government edicts prohibited the practice of phrenology. But it flourished instead. The idea that you could predict someone's personality so easily had tremendous popular appeal. Moreover, there was no hard evidence to contradict Gall's basic tenet of extreme localization of function within the cerebrum. However, almost forty years after phrenology was introduced, the first contradictory evidence did appear. Distinguished French neurophysiologist Pierre Flourens invented the ablation technique, a procedure for removing specific parts of the brain. This technique enabled him to study the behavior of animals. From his findings, Flourens was convinced that although the cerebrum was responsible for higher mental functions, they were not localized in specific areas. In 1864 he wrote ". . . not only do all perceptions, all volitions, in a word, all intellectual faculties reside exclusively in this organ, but they reside there coextensively and without being separable from each other" (Flourens 1864, 249). In addition, it became apparent that phrenologists were only guessing at what the bumps on a person's skull could mean. When confronted with people whose personality did not fit the contour of their skulls, phrenologists invented other explanations and began to modify their maps to fit the personalities of the individuals they were examining. Disillusioned, many followers of phrenology turned to other nonscientific movements that claimed to have even more direct ways of understanding human nature. Phrenology gradually faded away.

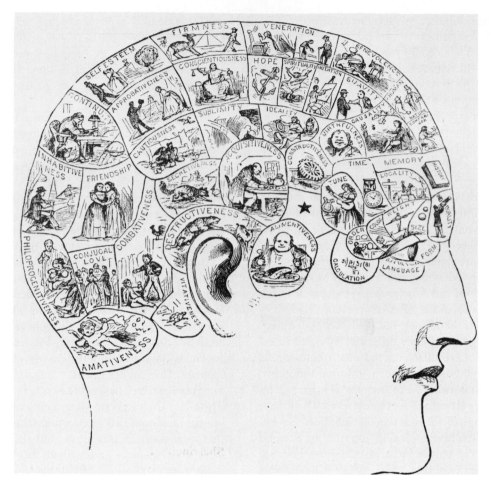

Figure 1.5 A phrenology map based on the system developed by Gall. Phrenologists claimed that psychic functions were localized in the cerebral cortex where the tissue responsible for each function produced a characteristic bump on the skull. Personality was deduced by mapping the bumps and ridges on a person's head.

The debate over localization of function, however, did not end with Flourens or the fall of phrenology. Indeed, in 1861 the debate swung decidedly in the direction of extreme localization of function. In that year at a meeting of the Paris Anthropological Society, Paul Broca presented the brain of one of his patients as evidence of localization of function. While the patient was alive, he seemed normal in most respects though he could not speak. In fact, he was known as Tam because it was the only word he had been able to utter for more than thirty years. During a post-mortem examination of Tam's brain, Broca identified a lesion in the third frontal convolution of the left cerebral hemisphere. It was not long before this small area became known as Broca's speech area. Broca's findings provided strong evidence of the localization of at least one intellectual trait; namely, the power of speech.

Other evidence soon followed. John Hughlings Jackson, while working with epileptic patients who exhibited motor convulsions, guessed at the existence of discrete motor areas in the cerebral hemispheres. His guess was verified when other investigators, using electrical stimulation in animals, demonstrated discrete movements while stimulating what today is called the motor cortex. The brain stimulation technique is used in some forms of neurosurgery, and even now doctors are able to use it to demonstrate localization of function (fig. 1.6).

From this and other evidence, the concept that certain parts of the brain are important in mediating specific behaviors evolved. In addition, because mental illness is manifest in behavioral symptoms, the idea that the brain is important in various types of mental disorders also began to gain credence. Clinical case studies of patients who had suffered some type of brain damage were used to support this idea.

The debate over whether or not specific functions are localized in specific regions of the brain continues. Whether, for example, particular memories are contained in particular parts of the brain or in a particular group of nerve cells is a topic of modern research. These and other issues in the study of brain and behavior will be discussed throughout this book.

The Enchanted Loom

When the twentieth century arrived, Descartes's hollow tubes had given way to nerve cells or neurons, and it appeared that the cellular logic of the nervous system was known. But Descartes's notion of reflex, a simple movement that requires no thought, still was used to explain how the nervous system worked. To English physiologist Sir Charles

THE FAR SIDE By GARY LARSON

© 1986 Universal Press Syndicate   6-19

"Whoa! *That* was a good one! Try it, Hobbs — just poke his brain right where my finger is."

Figure 1.6 A lighter look at brain stimulation experiments.

Sherrington (fig. 1.7) this was not enough. He emphasized the integrative activity of the nervous system—its ability to control behavior by integrating or bringing together different kinds of information.

For Sherrington, the reflex was simply the basic unit of this integrative process. To explain how the nervous system controlled behavior, therefore, Sherrington tried to define the laws that governed the interaction of simple reflexes. In so doing, he recognized the importance of inhibition. Movement itself would be impossible if we could not inhibit certain muscles while exciting others. Thus, Sherrington proposed that behavior is not simply

Figure 1.7 Sir Charles Sherrington.

the stringing together of simple reflexes, but the integration of powerful excitatory and inhibitory influences in the nervous system. Each neuron, he argued, receives excitatory and inhibitory inputs from other neurons. By integrating these inputs, each neuron "decides" whether or not to send its own signal. For those neurons that control the muscles, the outcome determines whether or not a certain behavior is performed. This decision-making process is repeated over and over again as each neuron constantly integrates its inputs. In one of his more poetic moments, Sherrington (1940) likened the activity of individual neurons to little points of light, making the brain ". . . an enchanted loom where millions of flashing shuttles weave a dissolving pattern, always a meaningful pattern, though not ever an abiding one . . ." (p. 413).

The concept of neuronal integration is still the guiding principle of most brain research. After World War II, however, the brain sciences confronted another issue, the beguiling notion of psychic energy.

Energizing the Brain

To understand what happened in the brain sciences after World War II, it is best to return to the nineteenth century and the laboratory of French psychiatrist Charles Fere. He was interested in measuring the effect of music on grip strength using a device called a dynamometer. Ordinarily, a person's grip strength remains more or less constant from day to day. But Fere found that grip strength could be enhanced momentarily by the presentation of certain musical notes and melodies. Loud notes and happy melodies, for example, produced the greatest increase in grip strength. This was called the dynamogenic effect after the device used to measure it, and a general activation or energizing of the nervous system came to be known as **dynamogenesis.**

This notion of an energizing principle arose in the latter part of the nineteenth century when steam locomotives and other displays of the power of physical energy captured the imagination (fig. 1.8). In fact, the science of thermodynamics developed out of an attempt to explain exactly how the steam engine transformed energy from heat into work. Of course, we all know that living organisms do not operate like steam engines, but if there was physical energy that could be explained by thermodynamic principles, then was it so unreasonable to suggest that there is also a form of psychic energy that powered the brain and guided behavior? Indeed, psychologists intrigued by Fere's concept of dynamogenesis tried to explain behavior in terms of psychic

Figure 1.8 In an indirect way, the steam locomotive became the impetus for yet another model of the brain.

or nervous energy. They sought some quantity in the brain that energizes behavior. As you will see, calling upon energy to explain behavior and brain function played a fundamental role in revolutionizing brain research in the middle of the twentieth century.

Evidence for an Energizing System

In 1949, an Italian physiologist, Guiseppe Moruzzi, and an American anatomist, Horace Magoun, coauthored a report that had an enormous impact upon brain research. They had been studying a structure in the brain stem called the **reticular formation** (so called because of its networklike, or reticular, appearance). If you were to make a clay model of the brain, you would start with an elongated mass of clay—the reticular formation—and then the known structures and systems would be laid on or embedded in this primordial core. Thus,

the reticular formation appeared to occupy a strategic position among all other brain structures, but no one was sure of its function. Moruzzi and Magoun discovered that the reticular formation seemed to control the general level of excitability of the entire nervous system. Stimulation of the reticular formation produced alert wakefulness, even in a lightly anesthetized or sleeping animal, and also increased the excitability of certain reflexes.

Subsequent experiments seemed to show that all sensory systems communicated with the reticular core, and that this same core sent fibers to virtually all parts of the nervous system. Thus, there appeared to be an anatomical basis for Fere's dynamogenesis. Every stimulus not only activates specific sensory systems, but also sends impulses to the reticular formation, and activation of the reticular formation energizes the entire nervous system. Indeed, the level of activity in the reticular formation appeared to represent the psychological energy level of the brain. At that time in history, it was possible to think that by measuring the electrical activity of the reticular formation a pure measure of psychic energy could be obtained. Moreover, because consciousness itself depended upon a certain level of reticular activation, there was the hope that brain science finally was on its way to a physiology of consciousness.

A revolution had occurred. It no longer was sufficient to describe the brain in terms of simple reflex arcs chained together according to specific laws. What appeared to be required instead was a discussion of the dynamogenic effects of a stimulus. In some shape or form, the concept of dynamogenesis was incorporated into most psychological theories of the twentieth century, even before the discovery of the importance of the reticular formation. But when the discovery was made, it concretized thought so that even those brain scientists who were unable or unwilling to deal with vague abstractions could enjoy the benefits of incorporating a dynamogenic mechanism into their models of the brain.

The notion of an energizing system in the brain seemed simple enough, but sometimes even the simplest ideas have surprising consequences. As you will see in the next section, an ingenious study designed to examine the functions of the reticular formation went awry, and brain research took another unexpected turn.

A Simple Idea Leads to Unexpected Results
The possible existence of an energizing system in the brain opened up new avenues for explaining the operation of the brain. Consider one view of brain function that was emerging in the early 1950s: Suppose that you are entertaining various hypotheses about how to respond to some problematic situation, first considering one plan for action, then another, and so on. Suppose further that one of these plans (or the cerebral activity representing it) happens to be dominant at a moment when your reticular formation undergoes, for whatever reason, a significant increase in activity so that your brain is energized. This energizing effect will facilitate the plan that was being entertained at that moment. Thus, the plan you have in mind the moment your brain is energized is the plan that you are most likely to carry out.

Two young investigators at McGill University in Montreal, James Olds and Peter Milner (fig. 1.9), attempted to test this hypothesis using laboratory animals. The idea behind their experiment went something like this: A rat, coming to the choice point of a maze, commonly engages in what is called "vicarious trial and error." The rat, in other words, looks in one direction and then in another until it finally makes a decision to follow one of the maze paths. If it really were true that the reticular formation energized the rest of the brain and this energization facilitated thought, then stimulating the reticular formation when the rat turned in one direction, say to the right, would facilitate the tendency to turn right, and the animal then would turn in that direction. If this procedure were repeated many times, then any stimuli associated with turning right eventually would cause this energizing effect. Thus, whenever the animal looked right, it would experience stimuli that had acquired an energizing, or dynamogenic, power. This should facilitate the right-going response, and the animal should run consistently to the right arm of the maze.

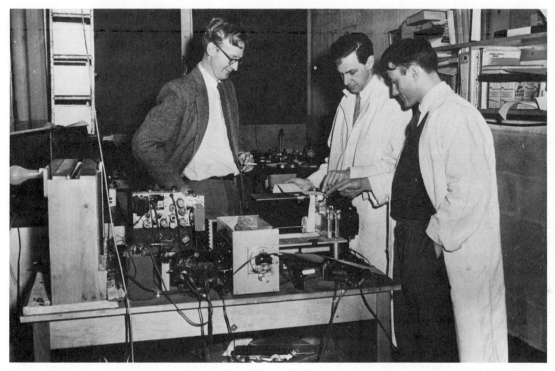

Figure 1.9 (From right to left) James Olds, Peter Milner, and Seth Sharpless recording brain waves from a rat in a study of pleasure areas of the brain. Circa 1955.

To test their idea, Olds and Milner tried to place stimulating electrodes in the reticular formation of a rat. After they performed the surgery and began the experiment, the animal behaved exactly as Olds and Milner had predicted. The rat consistently went to the place at which it received stimulation. In fact, the rat behaved as if it actually were "seeking" the electrical stimulation and kept coming back for more. Olds and Milner, however, were not very skilled at placing electrodes in the brain (as few people were in those days). When the experiment was completed, they learned that the electrodes had missed their target. They were not in the reticular formation at all but in a completely different structure several millimeters away, the septal area.

What Olds and Milner had stumbled onto was one part of a large circuit in the brain that appeared to mediate positive reinforcement. Activation of this circuit was very rewarding, and animals would learn to activate this circuit themselves, stimulating their own brains in some cases more than two thousand times an hour. Thus, the rat was not turning right because Olds and Milner had activated some form of psychic energy, but because the stimulation was reinforcing. Presumably, it felt good, and the rat wanted more. As you will see in later chapters, parts of this reward system are very sensitive to some widely abused drugs, including cocaine, and may hold the key for understanding certain forms of drug addiction.

Important discoveries often are made in this way—by a fortunate meld of half-formed ideas and half-developed experimental techniques in the hands of alert and open-minded investigators. In a long, arduous, and well-designed series of experiments, Olds mapped out the areas of the brain from which rewarding or self-stimulating effects could be obtained. (These areas are described in the chapter on emotional behavior.) And what became of the reticular formation? The original idea that this area served as a psychic energizer was much too simple. Indeed, the reticular formation has turned out to be a far more complex and organized structure than anyone in the early 1950s could have imagined. You will encounter the reticular formation again in many chapters of this book.

Chemistry of the Brain

Another significant event that occurred in the 1950s was the introduction of drugs to treat major mental illnesses. In 1955, the year that widespread drug therapy began, over 500,000 patients were residing in state mental hospitals in the United States. By 1975, just twenty years later, that number had declined to less than 200,000, and in the 1980s, fewer than 150,000 mental patients required hospitalization. As you will see in chapter 15, drugs are not a cure for psychosis, nor are they free of side effects, some of which can be very debilitating. But for many thousands of persons suffering from schizophrenia, clinical depression, and other major mental diseases, drugs offer a second chance of living in society, free of the chains and straitjackets that confined psychotic patients only fifty years ago.

Research on the drugs used to treat major mental illness uncovered an astounding amount of information about the chemistry of the brain. It soon became obvious that the brain was not just a bundle of electrically active nerve cells, but a veritable storehouse of chemicals as well. When imbalances in these chemicals were correlated with specific changes in behavior, the chemical revolution in the brain sciences began.

This revolution, however, just like all other ways of thinking about the brain, had its roots far back in history. For centuries, Egyptian scholars attributed specific mental abilities to chemical substances, or humors, in the body. Even Descartes, who described the flow of an animal spirit in the nervous system, was following the authority of Galen, an ancient physician and writer. Galen, one of the few early Greeks to recognize the brain as the seat of thought, described a series of cavities in the brain, now known as **ventricles,** which he thought contained a fluid that was the source of all intellect. He also attributed delirium to the action of a yellow bile and melancholy to an overabundance of black bile (melancholy itself is derived from the Greek, meaning "black bile").

Even during the Enlightenment, however, chemistry was scarcely more than alchemy. Thus, scholars who spoke of chemical changes in the brain did not have a good model on which to base their speculations. Moreover, apart from the ventricles, there were no visible structures in the brain that might even contain chemical substances, not to mention a place where they might act. Indeed, many anatomists, even late in the nineteenth century, thought that nerve cells were connected physically. The predominant idea at the time was that nerve cells formed a continuous network, or syncytium.

We now know that the nervous system is not a syncytium. The great Spanish neuroanatomist Santiago Ramon y Cajal demonstrated that although nerve cells are packed closely together there is no physical connection between them. Instead, they are separated by a tiny space through which they communicate. Sherrington called this space, or junction, between nerve cells a **synapse** (from the Greek meaning a union or joining). The process by which one nerve cell communicates with another across the synapse is referred to as **synaptic transmission,** and involves the release of chemicals. Each nerve cell acts as a little gland. The terminals of the cell secrete a chemical substance, the **neurotransmitter,** which leaks from the nerve ending, diffuses across the synapse, and acts on the next nerve cell, either exciting or inhibiting it. A nerve impulse enhances this process. When an action potential arrives at the nerve ending, much more neurotransmitter leaks out, causing an even greater excitatory or inhibitory effect on the next cell. The 1921 discovery of synaptic transmission represents a pivotal event in the history of brain science, and the definitive experiment that first demonstrated this process is described in chapter 6.

The discovery of synaptic transmission made chemical models of the brain possible. However, it was not until the introduction of drugs to treat mental illness in the 1950s and the subsequent wave of drug abuse that began in the 1960s that such models became extremely relevant. At the same time, technological advances made it possible to visualize neurotransmitters in nerve endings and to map specific chemical pathways in the brain. In a twenty-year span, scientists went from maps of the brain that included only three neurotransmitters to maps that now list more than three dozen. A revolution had occurred not only in the treatment of psychiatric disorders but also in the way the operation of the brain was perceived. Understanding the chemistry of the brain promised to be every bit as exciting and complex as understanding its electricity.

At this point in the history of brain science, the revolution continues. During the past two decades, breakthroughs in brain chemistry have been nothing short of remarkable. Treatments for most major neurological and mental disorders now involve some manipulation of brain chemistry. But still we must be careful. By no means do we understand how the brain operates, and we can be sure that it does not operate on chemicals alone. The brain is not some kind of pease porridge hot mixed together in the stewpot of the skull. The chemicals found in the brain are no more important than its anatomy or its physiology. In the midst of a chemical revolution, it is easy to overlook this point, and we all need to be reminded of it.

Nevertheless, the chemistry of the brain and its influence on behavior remain a central topic in the present era of biological psychology. As you will see in this text, many contemporary brain scientists look to chemistry for models of brain function. When combined with a knowledge of the brain's anatomy and physiology, such models may prove to be the most powerful yet in helping us to understand how the brain works.

Using Animals in Research

When we learn of breakthroughs or discoveries in the brain sciences, we think of the human brain and how it applies to human behavior. Indeed, the ultimate goal of brain research is to understand how this enormously complex organ works and to use this knowledge for the benefit of humankind. Much of our current knowledge about the brain, however, has come from research on animals, though some people would argue that such research is irrelevant for understanding the human brain. They assume that the cognitive capacities of humans are fundamentally different from those of animals. Some argue further that animal research is cruel and that animals suffer unspeakable torture at the hands of heartless investigators.

Such objections are shortsighted and wrong. Consider the argument that the intellectual capacity of humans is so much greater than that of a monkey or a rat that any comparison between humans and animals is useless. Humans, the argument goes, can do things that no laboratory animal can ever do, so how can anything we learn about animal brains apply to human brains? In reality, the brains of all mammals share the same basic organization and contain the same basic structures. Among primates, brains are remarkably similar. In fact, there is little qualitative difference between the structure of a human brain and that of a chimpanzee. Even many aspects of brain function in rats are similar to those in humans. Damage to certain parts of the rat cerebrum produces the same behavioral impairments in humans who have suffered similar damage.

This does not mean that monkeys and rats are miniature versions of humans dressed up in furry suits. Clearly, they are not. Brains of different species are adaptations to different ecological niches. Consider the duck-billed platypus, a primitive mammal that relies on touch receptors in its expanded bill-like snout to look for food in muddy water. Its brain is organized like that of all mammals, but it is relatively small—a reflection of its primitive life-style. The nerve that carries tactile information from the snout to the brain, however, is enormous as are the brain regions that process this information (enormous, of course, with respect to other brain regions in the platypus). This is not surprising considering how important the snout is for the survival of this animal. Similarly, the areas of the brain that process olfactory information in all animals that survive because of a keen sense of smell are unusually large.

By studying the brains of animals we can learn a great deal about how the human brain functions. This will enable us to make intelligent decisions about the cause and treatment of neurological disorders that plague millions of people. In fact, some questions of brain function can be addressed in primitive species. Consider very basic questions about the operation of nerve cells. How do they generate action potentials? What is responsible for the difference in electrical charge between the inside and outside of these cells? The answers, which we discuss in the early chapters of this book and which lay the foundation for all subsequent work on the brain, came largely from research on the squid. We are not saying that the squid thinks like a human or even a mammal, but the basic building block of all brains, nerve cells, operate according to the same principles in all species. No one yet has found a nerve cell in a rat, monkey, or human that does not operate according to the same principles as squid nerve cells.

The rationale for selecting a certain species for study depends primarily on the nature of the question being asked. When neurophysiologists chose the squid to study nerve cells, for example, they picked an animal having

ColorPlate1

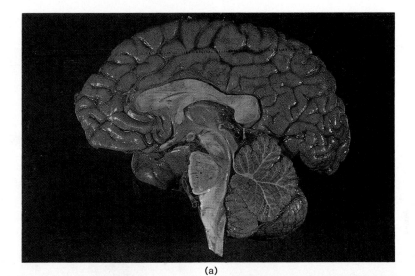

(a)

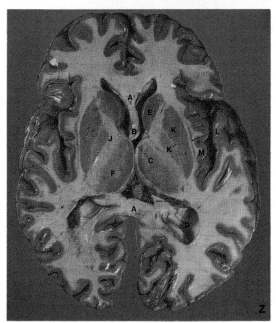

(b)

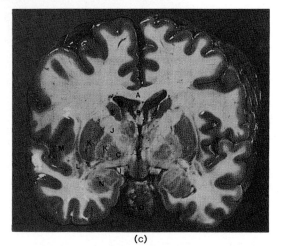

(c)

Color Plate 1   The human brain showing a midsaggital section in (a), a horizontal section in (b), and a frontal section in (c). Various structures identified with letters correspond to the following: A—the corpus callosum; B—the fornix; C—the fornix; D—the lateral ventricle; J—the internal capsule; K—the putamen; K+—the globus pallidus; L—the claustrum; M—the insula; N—the amygdala; P—the lateral geniculate nucleus. It is instructive to identify the structures in (a) that correspond to the diagram of the midsaggital section of the human brain in figure 4.11b.
(Yokochi, C. and Rohen, J. W.: *Photographic Anatomy of the Human Body,* Second edition. © Igaku-Shoin, Ltd., 1978.)

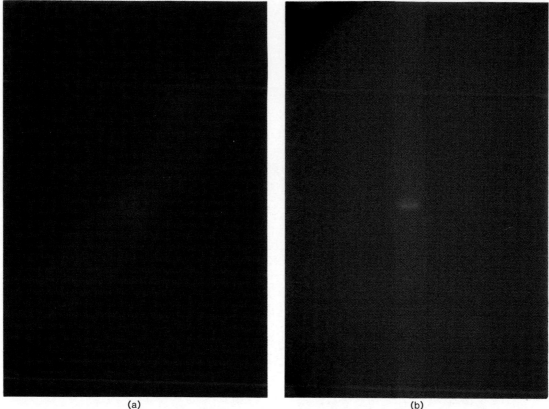

(a)　　　　　　　　　　　　　　　　(b)

Color Plate 2 Examples of immunocytochemistry. In (a), antibodies were raised against the purified sodium channel and attached to a fluorescent marker. When a myelinated peripheral nerve was stained, intense immunoreactivity was seen at nodes of Ranvier as shown. A similar procedure was used in (b) to localize the enzyme sodium-potassium ATPase, the critical enzyme for the sodium-potassium pump of the neuronal cell membrane. Intense immunoreactivity can be seen at the nodes of Ranvier showing that the sodium-potassium pump is localized to this site. Faint immunoreactivity can also be observed along the outer membrane of the Schwann cells making up the myelin sheath. (c) Amacrine cells of the pigeon retina have been stained with a fluorescent compound following their localization with an antibody directed against the peptide enkephalin. (d) A ganglion cell in the pigeon retina stained with a fluorescent compound after localization with immunocytochemistry directed against the catecholamine neurotransmitter synthetic enzyme tyrosine hydroxylase. Such evidence shows that covert patterns of connectivity in the retina or elsewhere can be revealed using immunocytochemical identification for specific biochemical markers. (Micrographs [a] and [b] courtesy of Mark Ellisman, Department of Neuroscience, School of Medicine, University of California at San Diego, La Jolla, CA. Micrographs [c] and [d] courtesy of Dr. Harvey Karten, Departments of Neuroscience and Psychiatry, School of Medicine, University of California, San Diego, La Jolla, California.)

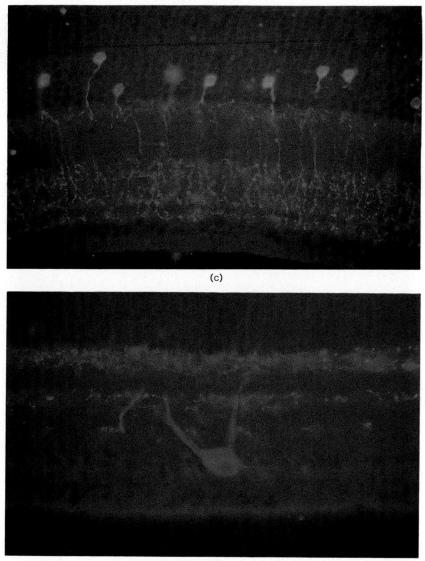

(c)

(d)

Color Plate 3   (a) An image of the noradrenergic nucleus locus coeruleus in the rat brain showing the histofluorescent reaction. Reacted with formaldehyde vapor or glyoxylic acid, norepinephrine is a fluorescent green when exposed to ultraviolet light as explained in chapter 4. (b) A computer-assisted three-dimensional reconstruction of the patchy staining pattern seen when the caudate nucleus of the cat brain is stained using immunocytochemistry. This reveals the distribution of the peptide enkephalin. Patchy zones are stained in individual sections as shown in figure 9.28. When all of the patches are drawn into the computer from many serial sections, the three-dimensional, networklike structure of enkephalin staining becomes apparent.
([a] Courtesy of Floyd Bloom, Director of Preclinical Neuroscience and Endocrinology, Scripps Clinic and Research Foundation, La Jolla, California. [b] Courtesy of Maryann Martone, Department of Neurosciences, School of Medicine, University of California at San Diego, La Jolla, California.)

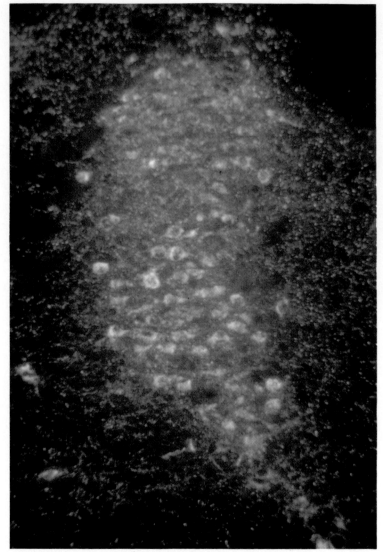

(a)

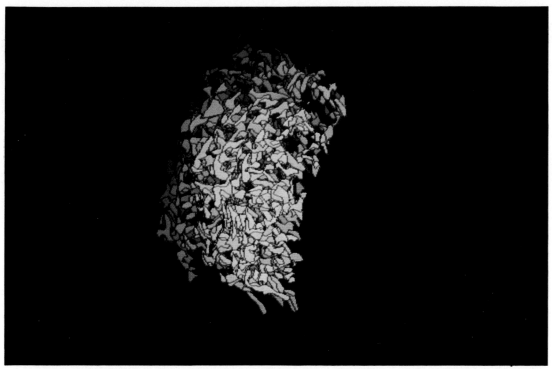

(b)

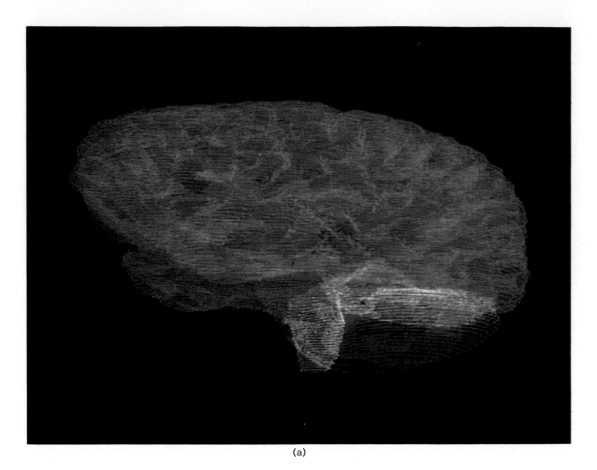

(a)

Color Plate 4 Computer-assisted three-dimensional reconstructions of the human brain and certain structures within it. (a) The entire human brain is reconstructed with the frontal lobes to the left and viewed from the side. This reconstruction shows the cerebral hemispheres (green), the brain stem (yellow), and the cerebellum (purple). (b) The human brain stem and certain limbic system structures are depicted. The angle of view is rotated toward the observer when compared to (a). Illustrated are the brain stem (green) with hypothalamus (blue), as well as the hippocampus

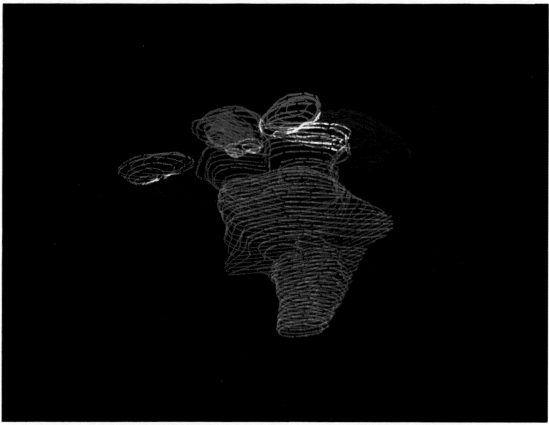

(b)

(purple) and amygdalae (pink), both of which are viewed without the surrounding cerebral hemispheres and temporal lobes in which they are embedded. (c) The cerebral ventricles of the human brain (blue) from the same angle of view as in (b) and (d). From this angle of view also, certain structures of the basal ganglia are shown: the substantia nigra (blue); the caudate nucleus (green); and the putamen (ivory) without the surrounding cerebral hemispheres.
(Illustrations courtesy of Dr. Robert B. Livingston, Laboratory for Quantitative Morphology, Department of Neuroscience, School of Medicine, University of California at San Diego, La Jolla, California.)

(Continued)

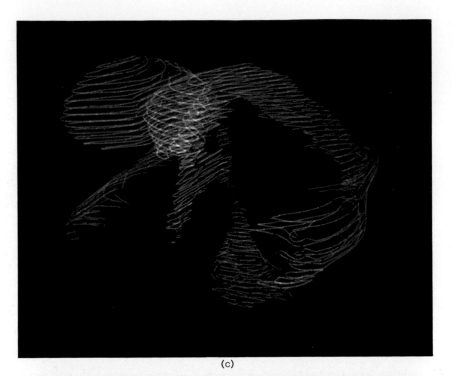

(c)

(d)

nerve fibers that were large and easily accessible. A similar rationale applies to investigators who study learning and memory in snails and sea slugs. These animals have very simple nervous systems, making it relatively easy to identify neural changes that may occur during the learning process. Once such changes are documented, investigators will have a much easier time developing a hypothesis on the neural mechanisms underlying learning and memory in more complex animals, even humans. The knowledge to be gained has implications for mental retardation, learning disabilities, and even senile dementia in the elderly. Rats and mice often are used in experiments because more is known about the brains of rodents than of any other mammals; new findings obtained from these animals can easily be related to previous knowledge.

Another goal of animal research is to develop models of human disorders. In this case, animals become substitutes for humans, and it is important to show that the condition produced in animals mimics the human condition. If it does, then various manipulations can be performed on animals in an attempt to identify the cause of the disorder and, ultimately, to arrive at an effective treatment. Such research has been particularly successful in the study of Parkinson's disease, a debilitating movement disorder caused by the degeneration of neurons in specific areas of the brain. Drugs now provide an effective relief for this disease, which only three decades ago was considered untreatable. In fact, most of the drugs on the market today, from those used to treat epilepsy to those used to treat mental disease, were identified by testing their effects on the behavior of animals. Unfortunately, drugs are not a cure, and almost all of them have serious side effects. Thus, research continues in order to develop more effective treatments with fewer dangerous complications.

Advances in the brain sciences are impossible without animal research. This is just as true today as it was in the eighteenth century. Computer simulations and mathematical models have added a new dimension to brain research, helping to resolve some fundamental issues at the cellular and molecular levels. But by themselves computers and mathematics cannot be expected to provide an explanation of how the brain works; at this stage, too little is known of the complex circuitry of the brain and how it controls behavior. Research on animals remains one of the most important means by which inquiry in biological psychology proceeds.

Yet no one in the brain sciences studies animals simply for the sake of studying animals. Researchers, for example, do not operate on the brains of animals because of an intrinsic interest in animal surgery. Their goal is to increase the pool of knowledge about the brain and, in so doing, to develop cures and treatments for the many brain disorders that afflict millions of people each year and take an increasing toll on our collective economic and emotional lives.

Because of its importance, animal research must be performed with care and concern. The humane treatment of animals is essential, not only because it is expected, but also because sick or tortured animals do not provide meaningful data. Moreover, guidelines exist that prevent researchers from performing unnecessarily cruel experiments on animals. Ethical review committees, which spend many hours reviewing experimental procedures, have been established at major research institutions. Journals in which scientists publish their findings require justification of any procedure that may be harmful to research animals and reserve the right to reject papers that fail to comply. Agencies that provide research funds have established strict guidelines for the care and treatment of animals; research proposals that fail to meet these guidelines are rejected. In short, science itself demands that animals be treated humanely.

As long as some groups hold that no experiments on animals are justified—regardless of the potential benefit to humans and regardless of how humanely the animals are treated—emotional outbursts and hysterical attacks can be expected from people on both sides of the issue. Such an outcome is unfortunate, but it seems inevitable. Emotional arguments, after all, attract the most public attention, and it is the public that ultimately will decide the issue. Our hope is that the decision—whatever it is—is made in full knowledge of the consequences that it will have for brain research.

Modern Technical Innovations in Brain Research

The previous sections of this chapter have revealed that advances in the more established physical and engineering sciences have profoundly affected how we study and understand the brain. It is generally true that new discoveries about the brain follow the development of new techniques for studying it. As in the past, many new techniques have often developed from increased understanding and technical advances in other scientific disciplines. Powerful methods for studying the biochemical anatomy of the nervous system have been developed, for example, by taking advantage of our increased understanding in the field of immunology. Consider the method of immunocytochemistry, which, when applied to nerve cells, is used to identify neurons having specific biochemical or neurochemical identities.

Similarly, advances in cellular biology have led to histochemical techniques, such as the histofluorescence technique for identifying the locations of neurons containing certain neurotransmitters. More recently, biological techniques, such as the use of the plant enzyme horseradish peroxidase and other products derived from plants, have provided major advances in the ability to visualize neurons and to trace their connections in the nervous system. Intracellular injection of horseradish peroxidase allows the researcher to label a single neuron from which neurophysiological data have been obtained and to analyze the structure and connections of this neuron with both light and electron microscopy. These new methods and their applications are discussed in chapters 3 and 4. Some results are illustrated in color plates 2 and 3.

The fusion of nuclear physics and medicine has led to the development of exciting new methods for visualizing the activity of the living human brain. It is now possible to measure blood flow and brain metabolism while subjects are performing a specific behavior by using positron emission tomography (the PET scan). These techniques have produced important and sometimes surprising new evidence regarding the localization of function in the brain. These methods are discussed in chapter 4. Some results are depicted in color plates 7 and 8.

Advances in engineering and computer science have resulted in the availability of powerful, high-speed computer systems that have become indispensable to the modern neuroscientist. In addition to serving as a model for understanding information processing by the brain, computers are used for the collection, analysis, and interpretation of neurophysiological, neuroanatomical, and biochemical data. Advanced computer graphics have enabled the researcher to create three-dimensional reconstructions of the brain or anatomical structures within it that have previously only been viewed in the two-dimensional image of a single section on a microscope slide or in a photomicrograph. Computer-assisted three-dimensional reconstructions are illustrated on the cover of this text and in color plates 3, 4, and 5. The ability to color code and visualize variations in drug or neurotransmitter receptor distribution, electrical activity of the brain, blood flow, and brain metabolism (see color plates 6, 7, and 8) have made it possible to correlate these dynamic measures of brain activity with their anatomical location and distribution. Images such as those illustrated in color plates 2 through 8 provide new evidence and new insight regarding the anatomy and function of the brain in humans and other animals.

We are in a time of accelerating technical progress and can anticipate the further development of remarkable techniques for studying the brain. It is now possible to obtain images of single atoms using the electron microscope, and recent advances in molecular biology have begun to unravel the genetic machinery that controls the development and function of neurons and other cells. In the coming years, we will see a continuation of this explosive era of technical achievement that will lead to an increased understanding of the brain and how it operates.

What to Expect
in the Pages Ahead

The long history of interest in the brain is reflected in the vocabulary used to describe it. As you read this book and learn about the brain, you will encounter many terms having roots in archaic languages. You will learn of

chemicals and chemical reactions that seem to comprise a foreign tongue. But the use of strange-sounding words is not intended to confuse you nor to impress you. They are the words of a multidisciplinary science, and we have done our best to explain them and the concepts they convey as clearly as possible. The brain is a complex organ, and although it may seem in some parts of your reading that everything there is to know about the brain is known already, the simple truth is very little is known. Yet, as you progress from chapter to chapter, you cannot fail to notice that most of our knowledge about the brain is of very recent origin, dating from the early 1960s. Given this fact, it is surprising that we know so much.

Summary

Biological psychology is the interdisciplinary study of the brain and behavior. Interest in the brain as the organ of behavior dates back to the early Greeks (fifth century B.C.), but remains a frontier in science and philosophy today. Since World War II, our knowledge of the brain has grown enormously. Yet much of the conceptual basis for the study of brain and behavior originated from concepts in the more ancient and fundamental sciences of physics and engineering. Technological advances in these fields often have been used as models for understanding the brain and its relations to behavior.

One of the most influential theories of the integrative power of the nervous system—the doctrine of reflex action—developed from the work of Descartes, who compared the animated hydraulic statues of seventeenth-century Europe to the simple movements of animals and humans. Descartes believed that special fluids—**animal spirits**—were set in motion in the ventricles of the brain by external stimuli, and then flowed through hollow nerve fibers to the muscles to produce movement. This hypothesis stimulated experimentation on the nervous system, and although research soon showed it to be wrong, it had a significant impact on brain research well into the twentieth century.

In the eighteenth century, the concept of animal spirits was replaced by the discovery of a seemingly magical substance, electricity. During the next one hundred years, the development of sensitive instruments revealed the existence of an electrical potential across cell membranes, and the basic electrical properties of the nervous system were discovered, including the **action potential,** or nerve impulse. The movement of electrical pulses along nerve fibers raised another issue: How could nerves that carry different information use the same means of communication with the brain? Müller argued in his **doctrine of specific nerve energies** that although all action potentials are essentially the same, the brain perceives them differently. This suggests that areas of the brain that receive information from different nerves have different functions. Consistent with this idea, Bell and Magendie discovered that nerves carrying sensory and motor information were separate and distinct.

From these and related findings, a debate arose as to how localized individual functions were part of the nervous system. Gall, the founder of **phrenology,** took the extreme view that very specific behaviors were controlled by very specific areas of the brain. Phrenologists believed that a person's intellect and personality could be determined by the shape of the skull, which they thought reflected the growth

or atrophy of specific brain areas. Using animals, Flourens provided experimental evidence to refute the phrenologists' claims. Although the hemispheres of the brain mediated higher mental functions, they were not localized in specific areas, but coexisted throughout the hemispheres. Other investigators found evidence to the contrary, and some functions, such as speech, soon were believed to be localized. The debate over localization of function continues in modern research.

Early in the twentieth century, Sherrington continued the tradition of Descartes and studied simple reflexes. But Sherrington recognized that even a simple reflex represents the integration of powerful excitatory and inhibitory influences in the nervous system. This emphasis on neuronal integration continues to exert a strong influence on brain research, but after World War II the brain sciences also confronted the beguiling notion of psychic energy. The **reticular formation,** a mysterious structure in the brain stem, appeared to have the ability to excite the entire nervous system. Soon it was thought that the level of activity in this structure represented the psychological energy level of the brain. In the 1950s, Olds and Milner attempted to test this hypothesis by placing stimulating electrodes in the reticular formation of rats. They missed their target, and discovered instead a new phenomenon: a brain circuit that appeared to mediate pleasure. Their research had far-reaching implications, especially on later work with the neurobiology of drug addiction. Subsequent research also showed that the reticular formation was far more complex than a simple psychic energizer.

Another significant event that occurred in the 1950s was the recognition that chemicals in the brain may play a significant role in controlling behavior. The **synapse,** a point of functional contact between nerve cells, had been discovered earlier in the century, and it was known that transmission across the synapse was chemical in nature. In the 1950s, drugs that altered this chemical process were used successfully to treat major mental illnesses, and a focus on brain chemistry began that continues today.

It is generally true that new discoveries about the brain follow the development of new techniques for studying it. As in the history of our field, new techniques have often come from advances in other fields such as immunology, cell biology, molecular biology, computer science, engineering, and physics. Many important new insights have developed as a result of these advances.

Advances in the brain sciences depend on animal research. The basic similarities between the brains of animals and humans have allowed investigators not only to learn some very basic principles about the operation of the brain, but also to treat a wide variety of neurological disorders that afflict millions of people. Future research will continue to depend on the use of animals, though the very nature of the scientific process demands that all subjects be treated humanely.

Suggested Readings

Blakemore, C. 1977. *Mechanics of the mind.* New York: Cambridge University Press. *An easy-to-read account of the history of the brain sciences from ancient times to the present. The book also contains a wealth of outstanding illustrations.*

Fearing, F. 1970. *Reflex action: A study in the history of physiological psychology.* Cambridge, MA: M.I.T. Press. *This book has become a classic account of the history of the reflex arc doctrine and its importance to research in the field of brain and behavior. Also available in paperback.*

Miller, N. E. 1985. The value of behavioral research on animals. *American Psychologist* 40: 423–40. *This article outlines in detail the arguments in favor of using animals in behavioral research. Subsequent issues of this journal contain additional articles on the same topic.*

Uttal, W. R. 1978. *The psychobiology of mind.* Hillsdale, NJ: Lawrence Earlbaum Associates. *Intended for the serious student, this book explores the historical and philosophical perspectives of the relationship between the brain and the mind.*

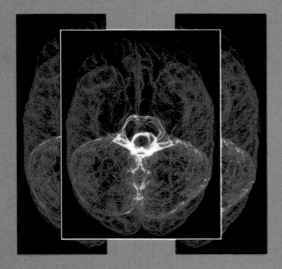

Outline

Introduction

Most of this book is concerned with behavior and how behavior is determined by the brain and related organ systems of the body. It will become apparent that the structure and function of the brain are inextricably linked to, indeed they form the essential basis for, the behavior of organisms. Further, the structure and function of the brains of humans and other animals must be determined in part by the program of development established by the genetic makeup of the species and each individual. Evolutionary forces acting on the genetic diversity inherent in populations of organisms have shaped our brains and behavior to be what they are today. In light of this, the structure of the brain is a little like the structure of a face. Each face is unique, but each has certain features in common with all others. Each brain is unique, yet the process of evolution has given rise to many different species of organisms each adapted to its specific niche in the world, but with many groups bearing a remarkable similarity to one another. Thus, with the exception of their size and the differential development and elaboration of the cerebral cortex, the brains of mammals such as the rat, cat, monkey, and human have a remarkable resemblance in structure and function. Because of this, studies of the brains and the behavior of animals have provided essential and fundamentally important information regarding the operation of the human brain.

In this chapter we describe the theory of evolution and the means by which the evolution of organisms is possible. That is, we discuss the genetic mechanisms that underlie inheritance. Behavior contributes to the formation and maintenance of species of organisms, and, like the structure and function of

Chapter

2

Behavioral Genetics and Evolution

the brain, is determined jointly by heredity and environment. Overwhelming evidence exists to show that behavior is determined in part by the genetic makeup of the individual, even though in most instances we cannot yet specify the detailed mechanisms by which genes have their effect on specific behaviors.

The field of behavioral genetics is concerned with the degree and nature of the heritable causes of behavior. Voluminous research in this field on animals as well as humans establishes that all behaviors are determined jointly by the interaction of hereditary and environmental factors. Although the degree of hereditary versus environmental influence on a particular behavioral pattern cannot be specified for a single individual, studies of populations of organisms provide a means for assessing the relative contributions of the genetic and environmental factors that determine behavior. As we explore the role of genetics and environment in determining behavior, the essential place of animal models and the study of animal brains and behavior will be emphasized. We can begin by outlining Darwin's theory of evolution and the importance of behavior to the evolution of organisms. We will describe abundant evidence from behavioral genetics research for the importance of both heredity and environment in determining the behavior of organisms.

Darwin, Evolution, and Behavior

The era of "modern" biology is often said to have begun in 1859, the publication date of Charles Darwin's epoch-making work *On the Origins of Species by Means of Natural Selection, or the Preservation of Favoured Races in the Struggle for Life*. In this monumental work, Darwin presents the theory of **biological evolution,** justly called one of the cornerstones

of modern science because it represents one of the great unifying theories in biology.

As background for our discussion of behavior and evolution, it is necessary to sketch the theory of evolution, which, as described by Darwin, consists of two parts. The first part involves three ideas: (1) **species** evolve slowly from preexisting forms; (2) evolutionary changes underlie the formation of new species; and (3) new forms are not created *de novo* in each instance. To support these ideas Darwin marshaled an overwhelming body of evidence. For example, he pointed out that the fossil record left behind by both plants and animals strongly suggests that organisms evolve slowly in time. If you examine geological strata carefully, you often find that fossils in more recent layers resemble those in older layers with only very slight modifications. When you put the entire fossil record together, a picture emerges indicating that species have evolved slowly in time and that contrary to the hypothesis of catastrophic extinction followed by repeated creation, no evidence of new creation can be found. Darwin also compared the morphology of living forms and was struck by their resemblance. For example, a human's hand, a cat's paw, and even a bird's wing are all remarkably similar. It seemed as if existing forms were changed slightly to fit new requirements. Finally, Darwin pointed to the results of domestication, evidence that impressed him enormously. This, he argued, was living proof of evolution. Where were German shepherds, Arabian horses, garden tomatoes, and other domesticated plants and animals even a few thousands years ago? They had obviously evolved from preexisting forms; there simply is no evidence of their sudden creation. Darwin argued that living species can be changed, even changed rapidly, as human beings put plants and animals to their use.

In the second part of his theory, Darwin presented a mechanism by which he explained how it is that species evolve from existing forms. Darwin called this mechanism **natural selection.** The idea of natural selection occurred to Darwin, or so the story goes, quite suddenly as he was reading Malthus's book, *An Essay on the Principle of Population,* which was written in 1798. The book's major theme is biological waste: a single tree may produce millions of seeds, but few grow into adult trees; a single fish may produce thousands of eggs, but few hatch and mature to become adults. If the full reproductive capacity of any species were realized, populations would steadily increase. This is not the case, and populations remain relatively stable over very long periods of time. What determines which organisms survive and which do not? One possibility is that the process is **random.** If this were true, evolutionary progress would not be possible. However, if some organisms are more **fit** (that is, better able to locate food, to find a mate, to avoid predation, and so forth), then the potential for change exists. This became Darwin's **principle of selection,** for which Spencer coined the term **survival of the fittest.** Survival of the fittest often evokes an image of a violent struggle for survival. This is not at all what Darwin had in mind. **Fitness,** in the Darwinian sense, refers to the number of offspring an individual leaves to the next generation, organisms that themselves survive to reproductive age.

Darwin was quite explicit in pointing out that behavioral traits can contribute to the fitness of an organism; behavioral traits can have fitness value. In one of his other books, *The Descent of Man and Selection in Relation to Sex,* Darwin devotes an entire chapter to the discussion of behavior and how it may contribute to fitness. In some instances, the relationship of behavior to fitness is quite obvious,

as in the case of behavioral sequences that determine the reproductive success of an organism. In other instances, the relationship between a given behavioral pattern and fitness is more subtle and complex. However, there is no doubt that many behaviors contribute to fitness, and in the next section of this chapter we will describe some behaviors that make this point quite explicitly.

Fitness and Behavior

Social Dominance

DeFries and McClearn (1970; 1972) have reported the results of several experiments in which they demonstrate that the reproductive success of dominant and subordinate male mice is quite different. In these experiments, male and female mice were housed together in specially constructed living quarters called **triad units.** An example of one such unit is illustrated in figure 2.1. These units were constructed of standard mouse laboratory cages connected to one another by a Y-shaped piece of plastic. This arrangement allowed the mice

Figure 2.1 The triadic living arrangement used by DeFries to study social behavior in mice.

free access to all parts of the apparatus and to the food and water in all of the cages.

At the beginning of these experiments, three female and three male mice were placed into each of twenty-two such living arrangements. They were left there for two weeks. The mice were observed during this interval and the paternity of the resulting offspring was determined. During the course of the experiment, the following observations were made. Upon being placed into these living quarters, the male animals began to fight with each other almost immediately. Within a day or so this fighting ended and a stable social heirarchy was established in which one of the male mice emerged as the dominant animal. Of the sixty-one litters produced by these animals, 92 percent (fifty-two litters) were sired by the dominant male mice. In each of several replications of this study, over 90 percent of the litters were sired by the dominant male animals. It seems quite obvious that the behaviors that render one animal dominant over others confer a great selective advantage on that animal.

Similar observations have been made in animals of other species. LeBouef (1974), for example, studied male-male competition in California elephant seals. These large mammals congregate on beaches during the breeding season. Here, great battles between competing males occur, the winners acquiring the choice of breeding territories. Having acquired a breeding territory, the males gather large numbers of female elephant seals into harems that are jealously guarded by the dominant male. An example of a battle between two adult male elephant seals is shown in figure 2.2.

The results of LeBouef's observations are that the largest and most aggressive male elephant seals sire an overwhelming number of offspring. Thus, the competition between male animals results in selection for aggressiveness and size since animals that possess these traits

Figure 2.2 Two elephant seal bulls threatening each other. If these threats do not suffice, huge battles between these large animals often ensue. These battles are for control of breeding territories and females, some of which can be seen in the foreground.

are most successful in winning breeding territories and mating with large numbers of females.

These examples illustrate that behaviors, such as those determining social dominance, can have a profound influence on the reproductive success and, therefore, the fitness of organisms. There are numerous other examples that illustrate this same important principle.

Darwin was not aware of the underlying genetic mechanisms by which evolution was possible. It was not until several decades later that breeding experiments that had been carried out by an obscure Augustinian monk would reveal the underlying principles that govern inheritance and the processes of evolutionary change. The era of modern genetics, by which these mechanisms came to be understood, is often traced to the work of the Austrian monk and naturalist Gregor Johann Mendel, who lived from 1822 to 1884.

The Experiments of Gregor Mendel

Mendel engaged in breeding experiments on common varieties of garden pea, pollinating plants that have seven different and easily identifiable characteristics. These traits included the size of the plants (e.g., tall versus dwarf plants), the color of the seed (yellow versus green), the seed texture (smooth versus wrinkled), and so forth. As it turned out, the garden pea was ideally suited for the classic experiments that Mendel carried out because of two important features of his work with this plant. First, the traits studied by Mendel were **dichotomous,** meaning that the characteristics could be classified into two mutually exclusive categories. That is, plants were either tall or dwarf and measurement of these two traits was therefore simple and straightforward in this respect. Second, his experiments were begun

by crossing **true-breeding** plants. This meant that breeding two identical plants always produced offspring that were exactly like the parental plants. Thus, when true-breeding tall plants were self-pollinated, all of the resulting offspring were tall plants. These two perhaps accidental features of Mendel's experiments led ultimately to Mendel's two laws that formed the basis of the modern science of genetics. These are the **law of segregation** and the **law of independent assortment.**

Mendel began his pioneering experiments by crossing plants that differed from each other by only one trait. For example, true-breeding tall plants were crossed with true-breeding dwarf plants. When he examined the offspring of such a mating, termed the F_1 **hybrid** generation, he noted that all of the plants were tall. Mendel called the trait that appeared in the F_1 hybrid generation the **dominant** trait and the one that did not appear in any of the F_1 hybrids the **recessive** trait. The experiment was continued by cross-pollinating two F_1 hybrids. In this way, a second generation was produced that is termed the F_2 generation. He noted that in the F_2 generation, both tall and dwarf plants were seen. When Mendel calculated the number of tall versus dwarf plants in the F_2 generation, he noted that the ratio of these two traits was always three tall plants to every one dwarf plant. Mendel also noted that in plants of the F_2 generation, the dwarf plant always bred true, whereas when one of the tall plants bred true, the other two tall plants did not.

To explain these results, Mendel hypothesized that each of the parental plants contained two "factors" and that only one of these factors was passed on to the offspring from each parent plant, as drawn schematically in figure 2.3. We now refer to these factors as **genes,** and the dominant or recessive forms of the gene are called **alleles.** Further, he rea-

genotype (jen'o-tīp)

Diagrammatic illustration of the
results of Mendel's experiment

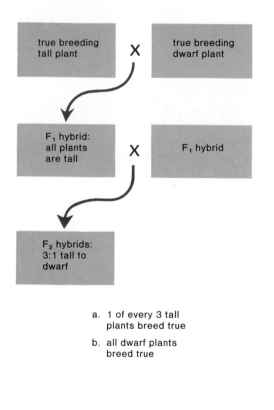

a. 1 of every 3 tall
   plants breed true

b. all dwarf plants
   breed true

Mendel's model to explain the
results of his breeding experiment

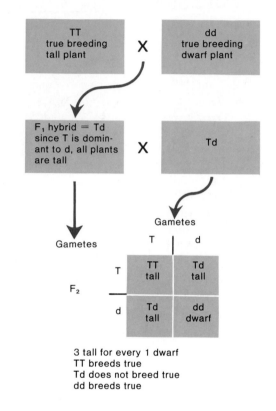

3 tall for every 1 dwarf
TT breeds true
Td does not breed true
dd breeds true

Figure 2.3 Mendel's classic experiment that resulted in the formulation of the *law of segregation*. The left-hand side of the diagram illustrates the actual results of the experiment: beginning with true-breeding tall plants and true-breeding dwarf plants. Mendel obtained only tall plants in the F_1 hybrid generation. When two such F_1 hybrid plants were crossed, both tall and dwarf plants were obtained. The ratio was 3 tall plants : 1 dwarf plant. The right-hand side of the diagram illustrates Mendel's explanatory model, which is discussed in the text.

soned that in true-breeding plants these two factors were identical. If the capital letter T represents the allele of the true-breeding tall plant, then the two factors that Mendel hypothesized can be represented as TT. In a dwarf plant, the two factors can be represented by the letter d, in which case the two factors inherited by the dwarf plant are dd. Thus, in true-breeding plants the genetic identity of the plants, or **genotype,** will be either TT, a true-breeding tall plant, or dd, a true-breeding dwarf plant. Since each parent passed only one of these factors to its offspring, the result of crossing a tall plant with a dwarf plant would lead to an F_1 hybrid generation in which each plant had the genotype Td. Since the gene represented by T was expressed as a dominant trait, all of the F_1 hybrid plants were tall.

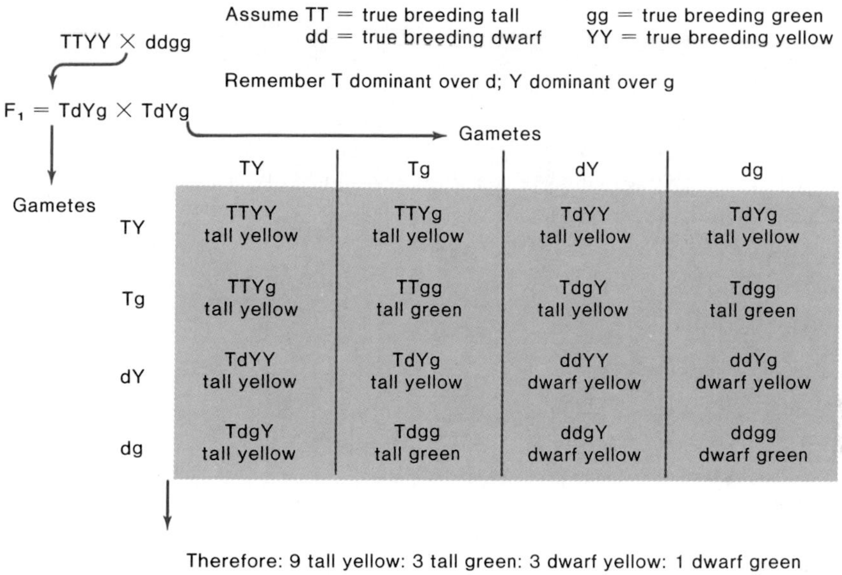

Assume TT = true breeding tall   gg = true breeding green
dd = true breeding dwarf   YY = true breeding yellow

TTYY $\times$ ddgg

Remember T dominant over d; Y dominant over g

F_1 = TdYg $\times$ TdYg

Gametes

Gametes		TY	Tg	dY	dg
	TY	TTYY tall yellow	TTYg tall yellow	TdYY tall yellow	TdYg tall yellow
	Tg	TTYg tall yellow	TTgg tall green	TdgY tall yellow	Tdgg tall green
	dY	TdYY tall yellow	TdYg tall yellow	ddYY dwarf yellow	ddYg dwarf yellow
	dg	TdgY tall yellow	Tdgg tall green	ddgY dwarf yellow	ddgg dwarf green

Therefore: 9 tall yellow: 3 tall green: 3 dwarf yellow: 1 dwarf green

Figure 2.4 The results of an experiment that led to the formulation of Mendel's *law of independent assortment*. Here, true breeding parent plants that differed in two traits (tall and dwarf and green and yellow) were crossed. All of the F_1 hybrid plants were tall and yellow. However, in the F_2 cross, four types of plants were recovered and in the ratio of 9:3:3:1. This experiment illustrates that the genes that mediate these two characteristics were inherited "independently" of each other.

When two F_1 hybrids were crossed, however, a different pattern of traits was observed in the F_2 generation. Since the F_1 hybrids each had the genotype *Td,* and since each plant could pass only one factor to its progeny, such a cross produced three types of plants: *TT, Td,* and *dd*. These occurred in the proportions 1:2:1. Since *T* was dominant, both *TT* and *Td* were tall plants. Because of this, three tall plants were produced for every one dwarf plant. Further, the one tall plant having a *TT* genotype will breed true as will the dwarf *dd* since they can pass on to their offspring only one type of gene. The other two tall plants resulting from crossing the F_1 hybrids have the genotype *Td* and can, therefore, pass either gene *T* or gene *d* to their offspring, thus not breeding true. The results of this classic experiment led to the formulation of Mendel's law of segregation, in which the two factors hypothesized by Mendel are segregated and only one of the factors is passed by each parent to its offspring. There is no mixture or blending of the two genes.

The principle underlying Mendel's law of independent assortment was derived from experiments in which plants that differed from each other in more than one trait were crossed. Such an experiment is illustrated in figure 2.4, where true-breeding tall yellow plants (*TTYY*) are first crossed with true-breeding dwarf green plants (*ddgg*). Since tall is dominant over dwarf and yellow is dominant over green, all of the offspring of this mating (*TYgd*) were tall, yellow plants. When two of the F_1 hybrids were crossed, however, four types of plants appeared in the offspring—tall yellow, tall green, dwarf yellow, and dwarf green—as illustrated in figure 2.4 in the ratio of 9:3:3:1. This numerical result showed that the two genes that underlie size and color do not influence the way

mitosis   (mi-to′sis)
diploid   (dip′loid)
meiosis   (mi-o′sis)

that each trait is passed on to the next generation and are, therefore, inherited independently of one another. We will see that this pattern of transmission of genetic material occurs during the process of cell division and that the **gametes,** or sex cells (the sperm and egg), result from a special kind of cell division that governs the transmission of Mendel's factors, or genes.

Chromosomes and the Genetic Material, DNA

Mendel published the results of his plant hybridization experiments in 1866, but his findings and interpretations were disregarded and all but forgotten for many years. However, around the turn of the century, the structure and function of cells came under intense scrutiny and experimental analysis. Cells were seen to reproduce by dividing, each daughter cell receiving its own nucleus. Further, during the process of cell division tiny rodlike structures within the nucleus of the parent cell were recognized and termed **chromosomes.** During the process of cell division, these structures can be

made visible under the light microscope, and it was noticed that they exist in pairs, which was consistent with Mendel's hypothesis of two separate factors being involved in the process of genetic transmission. Intense study of the process of cell division revealed that there are two types of cell division. In one, termed **mitosis** and illustrated schematically in figure 2.5, the number of chromosomes first doubles and, at a later phase of the process when the nucleus divides, each daughter cell receives a full complement of chromosomes. The number of chromosomes is characteristic of each species of organism. Human beings, for example, have twenty-three pairs of chromosomes in all of the cells of the body, while fruit flies have only four pairs of chromosomes. The number of chromosomes possessed by each cell is termed the **diploid** number and is characteristic for each species of organism. Since human beings possess twenty-three pairs of chromosomes, the diploid number of chromosomes is forty-six.

A second kind of cell division is characteristic of the sex cells, or gametes, and is termed **meiosis** (fig. 2.6). During the process

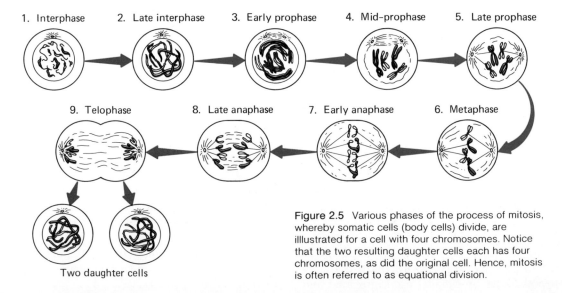

1. Interphase   2. Late interphase   3. Early prophase   4. Mid–prophase   5. Late prophase

9. Telophase   8. Late anaphase   7. Early anaphase   6. Metaphase

Two daughter cells

Figure 2.5 Various phases of the process of mitosis, whereby somatic cells (body cells) divide, are illlustrated for a cell with four chromosomes. Notice that the two resulting daughter cells each has four chromosomes, as did the original cell. Hence, mitosis is often referred to as equational division.

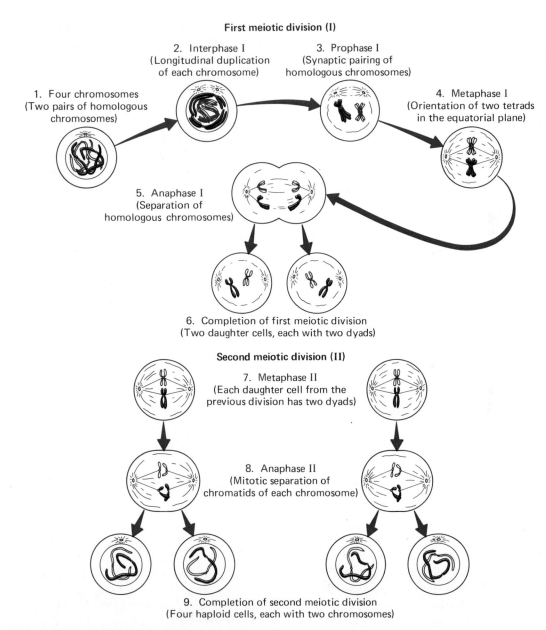

First meiotic division (I)

2. Interphase I
(Longitudinal duplication
of each chromosome)

3. Prophase I
(Synaptic pairing of
homologous chromosomes)

1. Four chromosomes
(Two pairs of homologous
chromosomes)

4. Metaphase I
(Orientation of two tetrads
in the equatorial plane)

5. Anaphase I
(Separation of
homologous chromosomes)

6. Completion of first meiotic division
(Two daughter cells, each with two dyads)

Second meiotic division (II)

7. Metaphase II
(Each daughter cell from the
previous division has two dyads)

8. Anaphase II
(Mitotic separation of
chromatids of each chromosome)

9. Completion of second meiotic division
(Four haploid cells, each with two chromosomes)

Figure 2.6 Different phases of meiosis, the process
by which germ cells divide, are illustrated. Two
successive cell divisions, the first and second meiotic
divisions, are required to produce four cells, each with
one-half (the haploid number) of the chromosomes in
the original cell. Meiotic division is often therefore
called reductional division.

haploid   (hap'loid)
zygote   (zi'gōt)
homologous   (hō-mal'o-gus)
deoxyribonucleic acid   (de-ok"se-ri"bo-nu-kla'ik)

nucleotides   (nu'kle-o-tīds)
adenine   (ad'e-nīn)
cytosine   (si'to-sin)
guanine   (gwan'in)
thymine   (thi'min)

of meiosis, as seen in figure 2.6, the number of chromosomes received by each gamete is only one-half the full complement, termed the **haploid** number. When fertilization occurs, the sperm and egg combine to form the **zygote,** each contributing the haploid number of chromosomes so that the full complement of chromosomes, the diploid number characteristic of the species, is reestablished.

In 1903, American geneticist Walter Sutton published a work entitled *The Chromosomes in Heredity* in which he accurately recognized that Mendel's factors, or genes, were located on chromosomes and that the transmission of Mendel's factors involved the transmission of the chromosomes to the progeny in cell division. This theory came to be known as the **chromosomal theory of heredity.**

It soon was discovered that many genes do not obey Mendel's law of independent assortment, as occurs when two genes are located on the same chromosome, a situation termed **linkage.** Two genes that are located on the same chromosome are referred to as linked genes, and their inheritance does not obey the law of independent assortment. It was also discovered that linkage is never complete and that the degree of linkage may vary from slightly less than 100 percent to about 50 percent. The basis for linkage is that during meiosis two chromosomes in a pair, termed **homologous chromosomes,** may exchange material. This process is confirmed by microscopic observations and is termed crossing-over.

Thomas Morgan, the great American geneticist, discovered while working with fruit flies that a systematic relationship exists between the rate of crossing-over of any two genes located on homologous chromosomes and the distance that separates them on the chromosome. The closer together any two genes

are, the lower the frequency of crossing-over between them. Conversely, the greater the distance between two genes on a chromosome, the higher the frequency of crossing-over. These principles, coupled with important methodological advances, soon allowed geneticists to map the relative positions of genes on a chromosome, each gene occupying a definite position, or **locus,** on a given chromosome. Morgan published the results of his work in 1919 in a volume entitled *The Mechanisms of Mendelian Heredity.* With the publication of this work, the chromosomal theory of heredity was firmly established.

It now is recognized that the chromosomes are comprised, in part, of the genetic material **deoxyribonucleic acid,** or DNA. The chemical structure and function of DNA is well known and under intensive study. (The chemical structure of DNA is illustrated in figure 2.7.) DNA is a very large molecule made up of two chains that wind around each other. DNA is a polymer, being composed of repeating units called monomers that are linked together to form long chains. Two such chains are connected to each other to form the famous DNA double helix, the DNA structure first revealed in 1953 by Watson and Crick, who later shared the Nobel prize for this important achievement. The monomers that form the DNA chains are known as deoxyribonucleotides, or more simply, **nucleotides.** A single strand of DNA is composed of many such nucleotides. As shown schematically in figure 2.7, each nucleotide in the DNA chain is made up of three components—a base, a sugar (deoxyribose), and a phosphate group. There are four different bases in DNA; namely, **adenine, cytosine, guanine,** and **thymine.**

As described, DNA exists in nature in the form of two intimately associated chains that wrap around each other to form a double

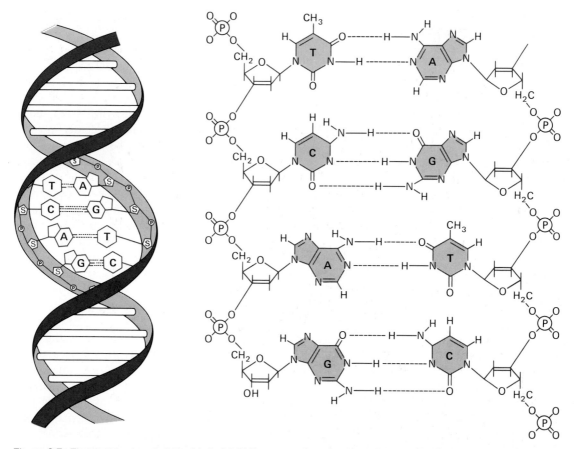

Figure 2.7 The double-stranded (double helix) DNA molecule is shown diagrammatically. Note that the phosphate and sugar form the backbone of the molecule. The bases are attached by hydrogen bonds, three between the cytosine (C) and guanine (G) and two between the adenine (A) and thymine (T). The shape of the double helix is also shown.

helix (fig. 2.7). Each DNA chain is many thousands of nucleotides long. To form the double-helix structure, the bases in each chain bond to one another in a specific way. The bonds between bases are always hydrogen bonds in which two atoms share, or bond with, a single hydrogen atom, represented in figure 2.7 by the chemical symbol H. It is apparent from the examples shown in figure 2.7 that only certain types of bases bond with each other to form the DNA molecule: adenine always bonds with thymine, and cytosine always bonds with guanine. The order of these bases along the DNA molecule codes the information contained within the DNA, as we will discuss shortly.

The double-stranded structure of DNA suggests the way in which the molecule duplicates itself so as to transmit the genetic information to a new generation (fig. 2.8). The double-stranded molecule of DNA, the "old"

ribonucleic acid   (ri″bo-nu-kla′ik as′id)

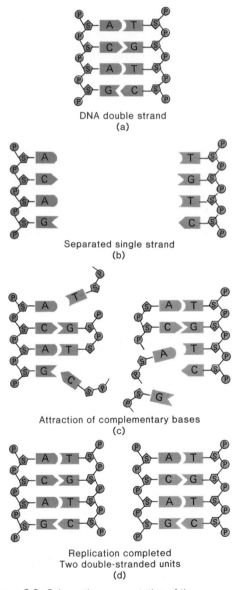

DNA double strand
(a)

Separated single strand
(b)

Attraction of complementary bases
(c)

Replication completed
Two double-stranded units
(d)

Figure 2.8 Schematic representation of the
mechanism involved in the duplication of DNA.

molecule that is about to duplicate itself, separates into two strands by breaking the hydrogen bonds between the bases. The individual strands then attract new nucleotides that become attached to each separated strand of DNA. In this way, two new molecules of DNA have been synthesized, both exact copies of the original molecule.

The basic difference between molecules of DNA is the order of the different bases along the long chain of the molecule. The order of these bases constitutes the genetic code: different sequences contain different messages or information. The DNA code is a triplet code, which means that three of the bases on the DNA molecule code for a particular amino acid. Since the approximately twenty amino acids are the basic building blocks of proteins, the information carried by the DNA molecule is used ultimately to determine what varieties of proteins can be manufactured by the cell. The control of protein synthesis occurs because the message along the DNA molecule is copied onto another similar molecule, **ribonucleic acid,** or RNA. This constitutes the process of **transcription.** RNA then controls the process of protein synthesis, which is termed **translation.** Thus, we can see that DNA has essentially two functions. One is to code for the synthesis of more DNA, the process of **duplication.** The other is to code for the synthesis of RNA, the process of transcription, and because of this it ultimately controls the synthesis of proteins, the process of translation. These processes can be diagrammatically represented as follows:

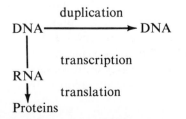

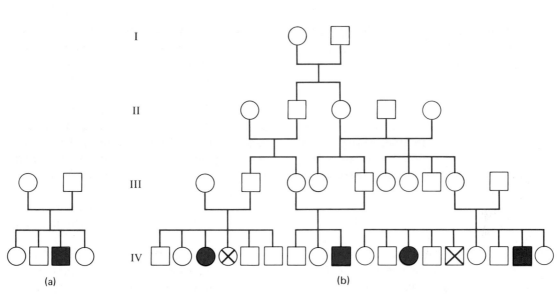

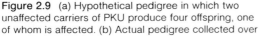

I

II

III

IV

(a)   (b)

Figure 2.9   (a) Hypothetical pedigree in which two unaffected carriers of PKU produce four offspring, one of whom is affected. (b) Actual pedigree collected over four generations in which PKU appeared. This heritable disease is discussed more fully in the text.

We will have more to say about the processes involved in protein synthesis in the next chapter. Here it is important to reiterate the functions of DNA. One is to provide the code for the synthesis of more DNA. The other is to provide the code for the synthesis of proteins. Although these are the only functions of DNA, it will become clear that our genetic makeup can profoundly affect behavior. That is, DNA can affect behavior. However, it is essential to recognize that there are no genes for behavior, and given its two functions, DNA can influence behavior only through indirect, complex, and still poorly understood ways.

Single Genes and Behavior

In many organisms, even a single gene can affect behavior in a profound way as we now understand from observations of both animals and humans. One example shows clearly that a single gene can have a definite impact on human behavior. **Phenylketonuria** is caused by a single recessive gene.

Phenylketonuria

Phenylketonuria is a heritable disease that is passed on by unaffected carriers to one-fourth of their offspring. In other words, the disease is caused by a single recessive gene. Consider the pedigree (ancestral line) illustrated in figure 2.9*a*. In such a pedigree, affected individuals (in our example individuals who suffer from PKU) are depicted by solid symbols and unaffected individuals by open symbols. Females are represented by circles and males by squares. The lines joining the individuals represent familial relationships: horizontal lines join parents, and progeny are listed below. The tyrosine   (tī-rō-sēn)

phenylalanine hydroxylase   (fen″il-al′ah-nīn hi-drok′si-lās)

phenylpyruvic acid   (fen″il-pi-ru′vik as′id)

melanin   (mel′ah-nin)

pattern of inheritance illustrated here is characteristic of the transmission of a single recessive gene from two unaffected individuals to an offspring who is affected. Say that the genotype of the female is *Pp* and that she mates with a male who is also *Pp*. This union will produce an affected PKU individual (*pp*) one time out of every four. In other words, one in four offspring from such a union can be expected to be genotypically *pp* and therefore to be phenylketonuric.

Next, consider figure 2.9*b*, which is an actual pedigree of a family in which PKU occurred. The pedigree represents four successive generations. In the fourth generation, affected individuals were produced in three marriages, one of which was a union between cousins. Individuals marked with an X represent probable cases of PKU that occurred in individuals who died too young to make positive identification possible. These unions produced a total of eighteen children, four with definite cases and two with probable cases of PKU. Since the odds are one in four of having the disease, and assuming the parents to be carriers of the disease, we would expect 4.5 cases of PKU. Statistical analysis of these data reveals that there is no significant difference between 4.5 (our expectations based on our genetic hypothesis) and 6 (our actual empirical result). Therefore, we conclude that PKU is transmitted as a single recessive gene. In reality, of course, we would not make such a positive prediction based on data from a single pedigree. However, many families have been studied that result in the same conclusion.

Just as we know the genetic basis of PKU, so do we know the effects of the gene that causes it. PKU individuals cannot properly metabolize the amino acid **phenylalanine.**

In normal individuals, phenylalanine is converted to another amino acid, **tyrosine.** This metabolic step is controlled by the enzyme (a protein) **phenylalanine hydroxylase.** The phenylketonuric individual lacks this enzyme, or more specifically, lacks the gene that normally codes for the enzyme. Instead, PKU individuals accumulate large quantities of phenylalanine in their blood that they then convert to abnormal phenylalanine metabolites such as **phenylpyruvic acid.** The **metabolism** of phenylalanine in a normal person and in a PKU person are illustrated schematically in figure 2.10.

Having discussed the inheritance of PKU and the biochemical disturbance that causes it, we come to the symptoms associated with the disease, which are varied and include the following. 1. Severe mental retardation is common, and the majority of affected individuals have very low IQ test scores, usually less than 30. Only approximately 1 percent of untreated PKU individuals have IQ scores greater than 70. 2. A very high percentage of PKU individuals suffer from convulsive disorders. 3. Victims tend to have other signs of neurological dysfunction such as exaggerated reflexes and postural abnormalities. 4. These individuals have short life spans, and many die before they reach age thirty. 5. PKU individuals are frequently of fair complexion with blond hair and blue eyes, due to the fact that PKU individuals produce only small amounts of **melanin,** a dark skin pigment.

It is apparent that many of these symptoms are caused by brain disturbances. For example, convulsions are produced by abnormal neural activity in the brain, and the mental retardation responsible for the low IQ test scores is due to a brain abnormality. However, the

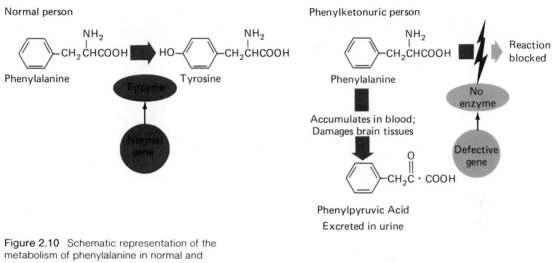

Figure 2.10 Schematic representation of the metabolism of phenylalanine in normal and phenylketonuric individuals.

disease can be thought of as a liver abnormality since phenylalanine hydroxylase is a liver-specific enzyme. How is it, then, that a liver abnormality can produce central nervous system effects? How do we get from a gene to mental retardation? We do not yet know the answer, although several interesting hypotheses have been proposed. For example, it may be that high levels of circulating phenylalanine or abnormal phenylalanine metabolites (such as phenylpyruvic acid) are injurious to the developing nervous system. At this time, scientific knowledge does not permit critical distinction between these and other hypotheses, although a good deal of research has been and continues to be devoted to this question.

A treatment for PKU has been developed on the basis of our understanding of the biochemical disturbance in affected individuals. When early identification of the abnormally high accumulation of phenylalanine in the blood is made, affected individuals are placed on a special diet that is very low in phenylalanine but enriched with other essential amino acids. The results of this treatment have been very encouraging as shown in figure 2.11. Individuals treated early with the special diet showed significantly higher IQ (intelligence quotient) or DQ (developmental quotient) scores than older siblings who had not received treatment or those who received the new treatment at an older age.

The example of PKU illustrates the important effect that even a single gene can have on behavior: Profound mental retardation and other disturbances of behavior occurred in affected individuals. It shows further that an understanding of the genetic and biochemical basis for this affliction led to the development of a rational therapy that so far appears to be a successful one. It is true that other similar disorders are yielding to continued research efforts.

karyotype   (kar′e-o-tīp)
autosomes   (aw′to-sōmz)

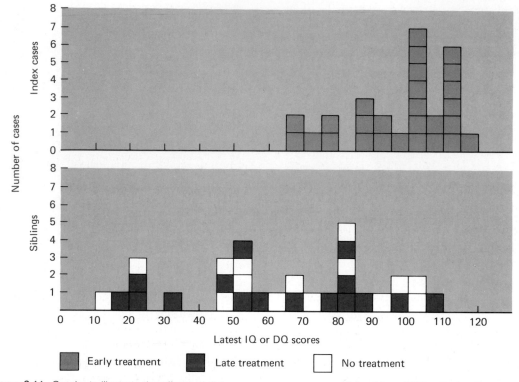

Figure 2.11 Graphs to illustrate the effects of dietary treatment on the IQ test scores of patients with phenylketonuria. The data presented here compare the results from several studies in which either IQ or DQ scores were obtained from PKU patients who were not placed on the diet, were placed on the diet early in life, or were placed on the diet late in life.

Chromosomes and Behavior

If single genes can affect behavior, and we have already seen that this is the case, then it is not surprising that whole chromosomes, or more specifically abnormalities associated with whole chromosomes, also can have behavioral consequences. In this section we will consider the behavioral effects of chromosomal abnormalities associated with accidents of meiosis.

The human chromosomes can be viewed in cultured cells, a process termed **karyotyping.** During a specific phase of cell division, the chromosomes of these cultured cells can be made visible for photographing. The resulting pictures allow for classification of chromosomes according to their size and the position of attachment during this phase of cellular division. The resulting **karyotype** looks like the one depicted in figure 2.12, showing a normal human karyotype with examples of the sex chromosomes for both a male and female. Note that there are twenty-two pairs of **autosomes** and one pair of sex chromosomes, a pair of X chromosomes for the female but one X and one Y chromosome for the male.

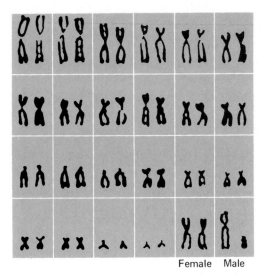

Female   Male

Figure 2.12 This figure illustrates the normal male and normal female human karyotypes. Both sexes have twenty-two pairs of autosomes and one pair of sex chromosomes. Normal human females have two X chromosomes; normal human males have one X and one Y chromosome. Human chromosomes are usually classified according to the so-called Denver classification system, which is based on the size of the various chromosomes and the location of the centromere, the point of attachment of the mitotic spindle. According to this system group A contains the three largest chromosomes (chromosomes 1, 2, and 3); group B contains chromosomes 4 and 5; Group C contains chromosomes 6 through 12 and the X chromosomes; group D includes chromosome pairs 13, 14, and 15; Group G contains the smallest chromosomes, namely, chromosomes 21, 22, and the Y chromosome.

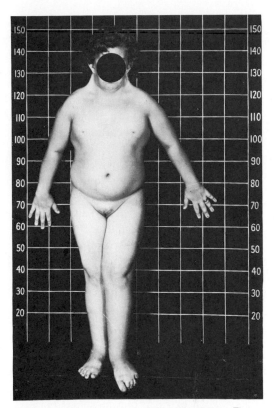

Figure 2.13 A patient with Turner's syndrome. These patients have the normal number of autosomes (twenty-two pairs), but lack one of the X chromosomes. The characteristics of Turner's syndrome are described in the text.

Turner's Syndrome

Turner's syndrome occurs approximately once in every three thousand live female births. Genetically, the disease is characterized by the absence of one of the two X chromosomes. In other words, individuals with Turner's syndrome have the normal number of autosomes (twenty-two pairs) but lack one X chromosome. The karyotypes of these individuals show only forty-five chromosomes instead of the normal forty-six. People afflicted with Turner's syndrome are female and show poor sexual development. In addition, these patients are of short stature and have a characteristically "webbed" neck. Some of the features of this **phenotype** can be seen in figure 2.13.

Early research on patients with Turner's syndrome suggested that these individuals were mentally retarded; it appeared as if their scores on standard IQ tests were quite low.

Subsequent research, however, has failed to substantiate these early findings. The incidence of these individuals in institutions is not higher than it is in the population at large, though patients with Turner's syndrome do suffer from a particular cognitive deficit. When tested on a standard IQ test, they do poorly on questions involving perceptual organization. Research by Money (1968), for example, indicates that the cognitive defect that Turner's patients exhibit is restricted to tasks requiring spatial abilities. Their full-scale IQ test scores, however, are not significantly different from those of the general population.

An interesting example of research concerning another abnormality of the sex chromosomes is the XYY condition in males.

Males with Extra Y Chromosomes

Although human males with an XYY genotype were first described in 1961, the condition did not receive widespread attention until Jacobs and his associates reported a correlation between extra Y chromosomal material and aggressive behavior in human males (Jacobs et al. 1965). These investigators karyotyped 197 prisoners who had been institutionalized because of "dangerous, violent, or criminal propensities." Nine of the individuals they examined were found to have extra Y chromosomal material and another three had chromosomal abnormalities involving the autosomes. These investigators also noted that the individuals with extra Y chromosomes were quite tall; on average, individuals with extra Y chromosomes were found to be seventy-three inches tall as compared with an average height of sixty-seven inches for prisoners with normal karyotypes. An example of

a karyotype of an XYY male is shown in figure 2.14.

The incidence of XYY males in the general population has been estimated to be approximately 1 in 1,000. Shah (1970), who has summarized the results of eighteen studies of institutionalized males, reports that among prisoners this incidence is much higher, approximately 2 percent. Thus, although these estimates are only approximate values, it seems clear that the incidence of extra Y chromosomes is much greater in institutionalized males than in the population at large. The question is whether or not extra Y chromosomes tend to render human beings more aggressive, though perhaps other reasons explain the high incidence of this chromosomal abnormality among prisoners. For example, it is possible that the excessive height in XYY males makes life adjustments more difficult. Individuals with this genotype have also been described as having poor coordination, a condition that might also make adjustment more difficult.

The most extensive study on XYY individuals has been reported by Witkin and his associates (Witkin et al. 1976). They did report an elevated crime rate in people with extra Y chromosomes. However, these individuals had not committed more violent crimes. Thus, Witkin and his associates conclude that XYY males are not more aggressive than other prisoners. Nevertheless, the higher incidence of criminal behavior in XYY males needs to be explained. These investigators also found that XYY males had lower IQ scores as estimated from Army selection tests and educational attainment. Thus, the elevated crime rate in XYY males might be related to low intelligence.

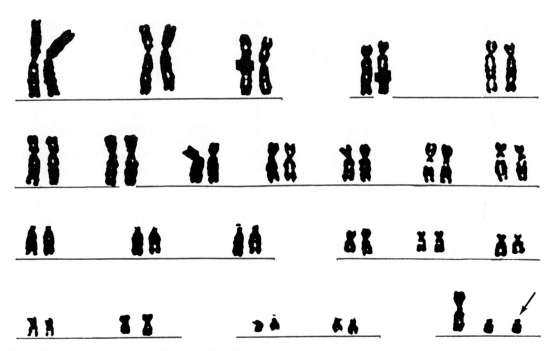

Figure 2.14 A karyotype of an XYY male. Note the extra Y chromosome indicated by the arrow.

Klinefelter's Syndrome

Klinefelter's syndrome also results from an accident of meiosis. Genetically, patients with Klinefelter's syndrome possess an extra X chromosome, their karyotype being XXY (they have forty-seven chromosomes instead of the normal forty-six). This condition occurs between one and two times per one thousand live male births. The incidence of Klinefelter's disease is somewhat higher in children born to older women.

Phenotypically, these individuals are characterized by underdeveloped testes. Behaviorally, approximately half of the individuals afflicted with this disease are mentally retarded. The incidence of Klinefelter's patients is higher among institutionalized individuals than in the population at large. The averge IQ test score of Klinefelter's patients has been reported to be between 80 and 85; the average in the normal population is approximately fifteen to twenty IQ points higher.

Trisomy 21

A karyotype of an individual suffering from trisomy 21 is shown in figure 2.15. Examination of the karyotype reveals that patients suffering from this disease have forty-seven chromosomes; more specifically, they have

polygenic   (pol″e-jēn′ik)
isogenic   (i′sō-jēn″ik)
homozygous   (ho″mo-zi′gus)
heterozygous   (het″er-o-zi′gus)

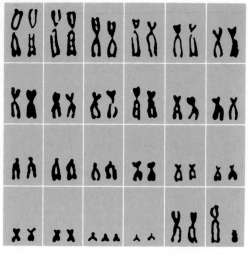

Female   Male

Figure 2.15 Karyotype of a patient with Down's syndrome (trisomy 21). Note the abnormal number of autosomes; this patient has three chromosomes 21, instead of the normal complement of two. The consequences of this chromosomal anomaly are discussed in the text.

three chromosomes number twenty-one instead of the usual complement of two. The incidence of trisomy 21 is approximately one in six hundred live births, and is considerably higher in children born to older women. Various estimates have been made, and it seems probable that the incidence of this disease would be about half if women over forty years of age did not have children.

Many different phenotypes are associated with trisomy 21, including a high incidence of leukemia and susceptibility to all types of respiratory infections. For these reasons, patients with trisomy 21 show a very high mortality rate, particularly in infancy.

Characteristic of this disease are epicanthal folds—small folds of skin over the inner corners of the eyes. By far the most serious effect associated with trisomy 21 is severe mental retardation. Average IQ test scores of patients institutionalized because of trisomy 21 are approximately 25. For this reason, most patients with trisomy 21 need to be institutionalized.

Behaviors Typically Are Influenced by Many Genes

Most behavior, of course, is not determined by single genes or single chromosomes; rather, it is affected by many genes. Such behaviors are said to be **polygenically** determined. In **polygenic systems,** many genes influence the expression of a trait, each single gene having only a small and cumulative effect. Many methods have been used to study behaviors that are polygenically determined, of which the most common methods in behavioral genetics are **inbred strain comparison studies** and **selective breeding experiments.**

Inbreeding and Strain Comparison Studies

Strains of animals are produced by **inbreeding,** a genetic technique that is technically defined as the mating of animals who are related to each other more closely than by chance. This can be accomplished by mating brother with sister, offspring with parent, first cousin with first cousin, and so forth. Regardless of the particular inbreeding schedule that is used, the effects are always the same. Systematic inbreeding will eventually produce populations of **isogenic** animals. This means that the animals in the population are genetically identical in the same sense that monozygotic twins (identical twins; one-egg twins) are genetically identical. Inbreeding also produces animals that are **homozygous** at each locus. Thus, considering only the *A* locus, inbred animals may be genetically either *AA* or *aa,* but not **heterozygous** *Aa.* Inbred animals are used in two ways in behavioral research: to investigate genetic influences and to investigate environmental influences. Behavior can be compared in two or more inbred strains, and provided that the animals of the various strains have been reared in identical or nearly identical environments, strain differences can be taken as *prima facie* evidence that the behavior being studied is determined at least in part by genetic factors. Why must this statement be qualified by saying "at least in part"? Because all behaviors are determined jointly by hereditary and environmental factors, a point illustrated in the following examples.

Aggression

Ginsburg and Allee (1942) performed a classic strain comparison study in which they investigated aggressive behavior in three inbred strains of mice. For the purpose of their experiment they defined aggression as the tendency of animals to initiate and sustain fights with animals of the same species. Using this definition, they measured aggression in C57BL, C3H, and BALB/c (designations identifying the three strains) mice. Large strain differences in aggressive behavior were observed; C57BL mice initiated many more fights than did C3H animals, which in turn were more aggressive than BALB/c mice. These strain differences were statistically significant and, as we have just said, are *prima facie* evidence that the trait in question is determined at least in part by genetic factors.

Continuing the experiment, Ginsburg and Allee next exposed mice from the three strains to either "victory" or defeat" experiences by contriving situations in which the outcome of a fight was predetermined. The results were quite clear: defeat experiences tended to make animals less aggressive, whereas victory experiences made the mice

more aggressive. It is most important to note that mice could be made either more or less aggressive by experience, but only with respect to the average level of aggression of the group from which the animals came. In other words, BALB/c mice could be made more aggressive by victory experiences, but they were never more aggressive than C3H mice that had not been trained at all. This work illustrates clearly that aggression in mice is determined by both genetic and environmental factors.

Locomotor Activity

This behavior has been intensively investigated through the use of strain-comparison studies. Locomotor activity, often measured as grid crossings in an arena or "open field," has been studied extensively, in part because it can be measured easily. McClearn (1959) measured locomotor activity in six inbred strains of mice, testing this behavior in four different situations. He observed large strain differences in this behavior, differences that were consistent in all four situations. For example, C57BL mice were very active, whereas mice of strain A/Jax were inactive, regardless of the particular apparatus used.

A/Jax mice happen to be albino animals, which are deficient in pigmentation, and a survey of the research literature shows that albino mice are always less active than mice from pigmented strains. Could it be that albinism, the expression of which depends on a single gene, influences locomotor activity? The answer to this question is yes. Consider how tests for locomotor activity have often been given. Animals are placed into a novel environment that is brightly lighted. Can it be that the level of illumination in these situations influences locomotor behavior of albino animals? McClearn (1960) tested this possibility by testing pigmented and albino animals in arenas that were either brightly lighted (the usual condition) or dimly illuminated by red light. Albino animals were more active in red light than in bright light, but they were not more active in either condition than pigmented mice.

These classic examples illustrate the important and recurring point that behavior is always determined jointly by genetic and environmental factors. In the case of aggressive behavior, strain differences provide *prima facie* evidence for a genetic influence on this behavior, but the experience of each organism (e.g., whether they have experienced victory or defeat) markedly affects the expression of the behavioral phenotype. In the instance of locomotor activity, the activity of albino animals is significantly influenced by the ambient light present in the test environment. It is perhaps equally important to note that in both of these examples as well as in those to follow the phenotypes are complex and can be affected by a variety of genetic and environmental factors.

Selective Breeding

The second technique used extensively by behavioral geneticists to study polygenically determined behaviors is **selective breeding.** Basically, the procedure involves the mating of organisms of a like character. As a result, a breed of animals or plants, which differ on the average from the original (or base) population, is obtained. For example, you can test horses for their speed of running a certain distance. If the fastest horses are then mated, over a number of generations one would expect to obtain a breed of fast racehorses. You could

also start with a population of chickens, measure the length of their shanks, and breed the birds with the longest legs. If this procedure continues for a number of generations, you would obtain a population of birds with large drumsticks.

It is very important to understand that the animals that are selected for reproduction in a selective breeding experiment are chosen on the basis of some phenotypic trait rather than because they possess this or that gene(s). Since traits are determined both by environmental and by genetic factors, an organism's phenotype is not a perfect index of its genotype and vice versa. However, if phenotypic differences are determined even in part by genetic factors, a selective breeding experiment carried out over a number of generations will then result in establishing lines of animals that differ on the average from the animals that constituted the original population. In the following section, we will consider two such selective breeding experiments for a behavioral trait.

The Tryon Experiment

In a classic example of selective breeding, Robert Tryon (1940) selectively bred for **maze-bright** and **maze-dull** rats. He began his experiments by testing a large number of rats obtained from a variety of sources. These were tested for their ability to learn a complex, automated, seventeen-unit T-maze, using food deprivation to motivate the animals and giving food to reward them. The correct solution of the maze depended on the utilization of spatial cues. In order to run through the maze without errors, the rats had to remember from trial to trial first to turn right, then right again, then left, right, left, left . . . until the maze was solved. In testing the original population

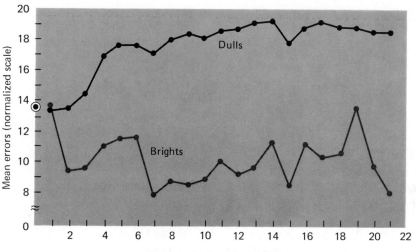

Figure 2.16 The results of Tryon's selective breeding experiment performed over twenty-one generations. The results are plotted in terms of mean number of errors made by the animals as a function of number of selected generations.

Tryon found that some rats made many errors in learning the maze, other rats made a few errors, and most made an average number of errors. Tryon than mated those animals that made few errors (which he called maze bright) with each other and those animals that made many errors (which he called maze dull) with each other. In due course, these matings produced offspring that were tested again, and males from the bright line, which made few errors, were mated with females from the bright line, which made few errors. Conversely, females from the dull line, which made many errors, were mated with males from the dull line, which also made many errors. And so the experiment went for twenty-one generations, with the results illustrated in figure 2.16.

As is evident from figure 2.16, Tryon was successful in his experiment, and two lines of rats were produced that differed in their ability to learn the maze. In fact, after just seven generations, Tryon had established two lines of animals that differed from each other so substantially that their distribution of error scores no longer overlapped. In other words, after seven selected generations, the dullest animal in the bright line was making fewer errors than the brightest animal from the dull line.

Are Tryon's maze-bright rats generally bright in that they can learn any task more quickly than the maze-dull rats, or are the results more specific to the type of maze used by Tryon and to the motivational condition he employed? Searle (1949) performed an experiment aimed at answering precisely this question. He tested animals in a wide variety of mazes and found that maze-bright animals were better *only* in situations that involved spatial cues and hunger motivation. Maze-bright rats did not do better in mazes in which visual cues were necessary, nor when the motivation was to escape from water. These results proved that Tryon had bred for a very special kind of rat, one which readily learns spatial cues when it is hungry. He had not selected for a "generally bright" animal. This fact is hardly surprising, and an analogy might help to make this clear. Wheat selected to grow well in Kansas might not be the correct variety to grow in Canada, or vice versa. Similarly, rats selected to do well in a seventeen-unit T-maze cannot be expected to be good learners in general. Even so, Tryon's maze-bright and maze-dull rats have been used in countless other experiments and represent an important resource for many other scientific investigations.

Selective Breeding for Alcohol-related Behaviors

The behavioral response to alcohol has been investigated extensively in behavior genetics research. There is considerable evidence that alcoholism in humans, for example, is partly familial and that a significant genetic contribution to this disorder is very likely (Schuckit 1985). Studies of animal behavior have attempted to produce an animal model of alcoholism, and it has been shown that many behaviors related to alcohol consumption in mice vary in different strains and can be affected by a program of selective breeding (Wimer and Wimer 1985). It has been known for many years, for example, that various inbred strains of mice will differ dramatically in their preference for alcohol. When given a choice, animals of some strains will prefer to drink substantial quantities of alcohol while others will drink only water. In addition to strain differences in alcohol preference, this phenotype has also been the subject of selective breeding experiments showing that preference for alcohol can be influenced substantially by selective breeding.

For example, mice have been selectively bred for the time they are asleep following a sleep-inducing dose of alcohol (McClearn and Kakihana 1981). Called the Colorado Long and Short Sleep lines, these two selectively bred lines of mice show considerable divergence in their "sleep time" following equivalent doses of alcohol, providing clear evidence for a genetic influence on this behavioral response to alcohol. Another phenotype that presumably reflects the behavioral sensitivity to alcohol is the severity of withdrawal symptoms following the development of alcohol dependence. This phenotype is defined by a variety of measures thought to reflect the severity of the withdrawal reaction following the development of alcohol dependence. The animals are given alcohol via a forced liquid diet or by ethanol vapor inhalation. In one series of experiments, mice were selected on the basis of the severity of seizures that occur following withdrawal from the alcohol (Crabbe et al. 1983). These lines of animals are termed the Withdrawal Seizure Prone and Withdrawal Seizure Resistant lines, and their behavior during withdrawal from alcohol dependence illustrates considerable heritability. Importantly, some of the measures of withdrawal show independent genetic control, illustrating that the cluster of alcohol-related behaviors that have been studied in such experiments are not all determined by the same underlying genotype. This is likely to be the case with a human phenotype as complex as alcoholism.

Other Selective Breeding Experiments

A recent review indicates that there are many behavioral phenotypes that have been used for selective breeding experiments (Wimer and Wimer 1985). In many instances, these programs of selective breeding attempt to produce models of human disease for further scientific study. In other instances, selective breeding is used to dissect the control of normal behavior in animals. One of the longest-running selective breeding experiments, for example, is concerned with the activity levels of mice in an open field. Performed at the University of Colorado's Institute for Behavioral Genetics, mice have been selected on the basis of high- and low-activity levels in an open-field apparatus (DeFries and Plomin 1978). After more than thirty generations, the result of selection is so dramatic that the low activity line is very nearly motionless in the open field while those selected for high activity are extremely active.

Other behavioral phenotypes that have been studied by selective breeding include other measures of learning, activity, "emotionality" or "nervousness," susceptibility to various types of seizures, and many others. All of these selective breeding experiments prove the same point; namely, that many different types of behaviors have a genetic component. More importantly, however, such experiments provide the material on which questions regarding the mechanisms that mediate behavior and that interrelate gene with behavior can be studied. The use of animals selectively bred for the induction of seizures, for example, provides appropriate experimental subjects to study how seizure disorders are produced in the brain and how they might be controlled and eventually cured. Studies of mice that have been selectively bred for their sensitivity or preference for alcohol provide animal models for the investigation of alcoholism, including how the preference for alcohol is determined and how the brain is affected in such animals. The investigation of polygenically determined behaviors in humans has profited greatly from this arsenal of methods, ideas, and experimental models developed in behavior genetics research.

The Heritability of Psychotic Disorders

One of the great goals of biological psychology and the neurosciences is to understand the substrates of mental illness and how to alleviate the suffering of the millions of individuals afflicted with serious disorders of mood and rationality. There can be little doubt that severe mental disorders, such as **schizophrenia,** are familial diseases. With respect to schizophrenia, for example, the incidence of this disorder in relatives of schizophrenic patients is much higher than the incidence in the general population. Further, as shown in figure 2.17, the closer the biological relationship of an individual to an affected patient, the greater the likelihood that the individual will display psychotic symptoms. In other words, the risk of schizophrenia to the relatives of a schizophrenic increases markedly with the degree of "genetic relatedness," the risk being highest between monozygotic twins when one twin is affected (Nicol and Gottesman 1983). These are twins who develop from a single fertilized egg and are, therefore, genetically identical. Given the orderly and clear relationship of the probability of getting the disease to the degree of genetic

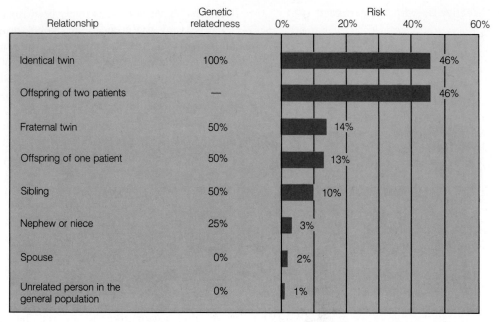

Relationship	Genetic relatedness	Risk
Identical twin	100%	46%
Offspring of two patients	—	46%
Fraternal twin	50%	14%
Offspring of one patient	50%	13%
Sibling	50%	10%
Nephew or niece	25%	3%
Spouse	0%	2%
Unrelated person in the general population	0%	1%

Figure 2.17 Lifetime risks of developing schizophrenic are largely a function of how closely an individual is genetically related to a schizophrenic and not a function of how much the environment is shared. The observed risks, however, are much more compatible with a multifactorial polygenic theory of transmission than with a Mendelian model or one involving a single major locus.

relatedness between individuals, a genetic influence in the development of this and other psychotic disorders now seems well established. The results of numerous twin-comparison studies of schizophrenics indicate that the **concordance** for schizophrenia between identical twins probably lies somewhere between 40 and 70 percent. This degree of concordance means that if one identical twin has schizophrenia there is a 40–70 percent chance that the other twin will also show symptoms of the disease.

One difficulty with the twin-comparison method is that it is virtually impossible to separate genetic factors from environmental factors in ways that satisfy all critics. Heston (1970), however, reported on an experiment in which genetic and environmental factors are more or less clear cut. Heston (1970) identified forty-seven children born to schizophrenic mothers who were given up for adoption during the first month of life. As control subjects, fifty children born to nonschizophrenic mothers and also given up for adoption during the first month of life were identified. These individuals were studied extensively as adults. All ninety-seven subjects were given a psychiatric interview and tested in various ways, and extensive biographical material was obtained. The results of this study are summarized in table 2.1

These data are fairly unambiguous in implicating genetic factors as contributing to the expression of schizophrenia. In every

Table 2.1 Summary of Heston's Adoption Study

Category	Control Subjects	Experimental Subjects
Number of subjects	50	47
Number diagnosed as schizophrenic	0	5
Number with mental deficiency (IQ less than 70)	0	4
Number with antisocial personalities	2	9
Number with neurotic disorders	7	13
Number incarcerated in penal or psychiatric institutions	2	11

Note: Control subjects represent persons born to normal mothers, and experimental subjects, persons born to schizophrenic mothers.

From Heston, L. L., "The Genetics of Schizophrenia and Schizoid Disease" in *Science,* Vol. 167, pp. 249–256, Fig. 7, 16 January 1970. Copyright © 1970 by the American Association for the Advancement of Science. Reprinted by permission.

category, individuals born to schizophrenic mothers and raised in foster homes show more abnormal behavior than do individuals born to nonschizophrenic mothers. It is difficult to explain these data on environmental grounds. The only possibility is that the prenatal environment and the first month of life were different in these two groups of individuals. Yet, compelling evidence comes from many different studies of identical and dizygotic twins, as summarized in table 2.2. Clearly, the weight of evidence shows the concordance is highest in identical twins and strongly suggests a genetic factor is at work in the development of schizophrenia.

Genetic factors also contribute substantially to the expression of manic-depressive psychosis, a serious disorder of mood. Twin studies of manic-depressive psychosis yielded concordance rates among monozygotic twins that range from 33 to 96 percent and concordance rates in dizygotic twins between 9 and 67 percent (Kringlen 1967).

Table 2.2 Concordance for Schizophrenia in Twin Studies

Investigator	Year	Country	Concordance in Monozygotic Twins No. Affected	Total No.	Percent	Concordance in Dizygotic Twins No. Affected	Total No.	Percent
Kallmann	1946	United States	120	174	69	53	517	10
Slater	1953	United Kingdom	24	37	65	10	112	9
Inouye	1961	Japan	33	55	60	2	17	12
Tienari	1963	Finland	0	16	0	2	21	10
Kringlen	1966	Norway	19	50	38	13	94	14
Gottesman & Shields	1966	United Kingdom	10	24	42	3	33	9
Fischer	1966	Denmark	3	10	30	0	8	0

From *Introduction to Behavioral Genetics* by G. E. McClearn and J. C. DeFries. W. H. Freeman and Company. Copyright © 1973.

In summary, it seems fair to state that all of these studies present a convincing case for the involvement of genetic variables in psychotic disorders. This evidence further suggests that biological factors contribute importantly to the cause of these disorders. We will explore the biological basis for psychotic disorders again in chapter 15.

It is important to note that the concordance for schizophrenia even between individuals who are genetically identical is far from being 100 percent. In the case where there is concordance for schizophrenia between genetically identical individuals, there may be considerable variation in the severity of their schizophrenic illness. An interesting case that illustrates this important principle is that of four monozygotic quadruplet sisters who have been observed and studied by scientists at the National Institute of Mental Health for over two decades (Mirsky et al. 1985). These four genetically identical sisters are all schizophrenic, but differ quite dramatically in the severity of their illness. This means that environmental influences must contribute to the development and severity of schizophrenia and that like other behavioral phenotypes discussed throughout this chapter, schizophrenia represents a product of the combined influence of heredity and environment. It is very important here to understand that by environment, we do not simply mean "learning," but rather all influences that can affect the organism that are not genetic. These might include the early biochemical environment and other influences on the developing brain as well as other, clearly biological events. Other examples of "environmental" influences that appear to be significant in the development or severity of schizophrenia are those summarized recently by Mirsky and Duncan-Johnson (1985) from the results of long-standing research efforts conducted at the National Institute of Mental Health. These investigators note, for example, that ". . . [O]ur current data lead to the conclusion that in children at genetic risk for schizophrenia, noxious familial influences, such as intrusive, punitive parental behavior and negative expectations, greatly increase the likelihood of the expression and/or the severity of the disorder."

The Nature-Nurture Question

Since ancient times, some thinkers have argued that behavior is the product of genetics, whereas other authorities have maintained that behavior is determined solely by experience. Is a person aggressive because she comes from aggressive stock, or is a person aggressive because he was conditioned to be so by his experience? When put in this way, the question has no answer because all behaviors, as we have seen throughout this chapter, are the joint products of hereditary and environmental influences. However, by studying populations of organisms, it is possible to assess the degree to which variations in behavior between individuals are due to genetic variation within a population and, by contrast, how much variability is due to environmental factors. An example of one of many statistical techniques developed to assess the degree of genetic and environmental influence on a particular phenotype within a population is the coefficient of genetic determination.

The Coefficient of Genetic Determination

We have repeatedly stated that behavior is the joint product of genes, the environment, and their interaction. We have also stated that the variability in the behavior of a population of animals is caused by both genetic and environmental factors. Let us call the variability in behavior in a population of animals V_P for total phenotypic variability. Let us further say that the portion of V_P determined by genetic differences in the animals of the population is V_G, and the portion caused by environmental differences is V_E. Then we can say:

$$V_P = V_G + V_E \quad \text{(Equation 1)}$$

It should now be apparent why animals from inbred strains are useful in experiments in which one tries to determine how much of the variability in a given behavior is due to genetic factors. Remember that animals from inbred strains are isogenic; therefore, it follows that the variability in behavior in these animals must be due to V_E, since by definition V_G is equal to zero in these animals. Given that this is the case, then you should be able to estimate the proportion of total phenotypic variability due to genetic factors, a statistic referred to as the coefficient of genetic determination, or sometimes as heritability. The coefficient of genetic determination can also be defined as:

$$\frac{V_G}{V_G + V_E} = \text{coefficient of genetic determination}$$

(Equation 2)

How do we calculate this statistic and what does it mean? The data from an experiment performed by DeFries and Hegmann (1970) in which they measured locomotor activity in two inbred strains of mice and in animals derived from subsequent generations are given in table 2.3.

As we have already said, the variability in behavior observed in inbred strain A, inbred strain B, and the first generation hybrid is due

Table 2.3 Locomotor Activity in Two Inbred Strains of Mice and Derived Generation

Genotype	Locomotor Activity
Strain A	Average activity score = 4.67 Variability = 6.33
Strain B	Average activity score = 15.73 Variability = 4.86
F_1 hybrid	Average activity score = 14.52 Variability = 11.25
F_2 hybrid	Average activity score = 11.97 Variability = 16.15

to environmental factors. Therefore, our best estimate of V_E is the average variability in these three populations,

$$\frac{6.33 + 4.86 + 11.25}{3} = 7.48$$

An estimate of the variability due to genetic variation in the population (V_G) can be obtained by subtracting the estimate of variability due to environment (V_E) from the total variability that is measured in the F_2 hybrid where both genetic and environmental variation can contribute to the measured phenotype:

$$V - V_E = V_G$$
$$\text{or}$$
$$16.15 - 7.48 = 8.67$$

Since we now have estimates of V_E and V_G, we can apply equation 2 and solve for the coefficient of genetic determination, which in our example is

$$\frac{8.67}{8.67 + 7.48} = 0.54$$

This number indicates that 54 percent of the variability in locomotor behavior as measured in the F_2 hybrid generation is due to genetic variation between members of this population. Such an estimate will vary considerably depending upon the conditions under which the variability is measured, the particular samples of individuals in the population that are included, and other factors.

The question regarding the degree of hereditary and environmental influence over behavior cannot be answered for a single individual. By studying populations of animals and humans, however, the important questions regarding the nature and degree of genetic and environmental influences on behavior and the biological processes that underlie the behavior of organisms will continue to yield to scientific understanding.

Summary

In this chapter we have discussed how organisms have evolved and the mechanisms underlying the genetic transmission of information from one generation to the next. Darwin's theory of evolution, for which an overwhelming body of evidence has been accumulated, suggests that plants and animals evolved slowly in time. The examination of geological strata, for example, supports the view that in most instances organisms changed slowly from one age to the next and that catastrophic extinction and recreation is an unlikely explanation of the evidence. The similarity in the form of living organisms, the results of domestication of plants and animals, and other evidence provides a compelling case for the theory of biological evolution, which is considered one of the great unifying theories in biological science. Darwin identified the process of "natural selection" as the mechanism underlying the evolution of organisms. He reasoned that some individuals were better able to survive and reproduce than others, and the characteristics that made these individuals more successful could then be transmitted to the next generation. Success in mating represents a key to the evolutionary process. This was referred to as fitness by Darwin and was later called "survival of the fittest." We described several examples that illustrate the importance of behavior for the fitness of organisms, such as those behaviors that determine dominance in male mice and elephant seals.

The genetic mechanisms underlying evolution were unknown to Darwin, although the work of Gregor Mendel, an Augustinian monk doing experiments on the inheritance of various characteristics of the common garden pea, initiated what ultimately became a revolution in understanding the mechanisms of inheritance. Mendel formulated the **law of segregation** and the **law of independent assortment** on the basis of the transmission of parent-plant traits, such as plant height, seed color, and seed texture, to their progeny. He hypothesized that each parent plant passed one of two factors to the offspring. Later experiments showed that Mendel's factors were genes.

Over the first half of the twentieth century, it became known that genes exist on **chromosomes** in the nuclei of cells and that the transmission of genetic information occurs by the process of cell division. **Meiosis** is the form of division by which the sperm and egg each possess one half of the normal number of chromosomes, termed the **haploid** number. When fertilization occurs, the sperm and egg combine genetic material to restore the normal complement of chromosomes to the resulting organism, the **diploid** number, which in human beings is forty-six chromosomes consisting of twenty-three pairs. The chromosomes contain the genetic material **deoxyribonucleic acid,** or DNA. Each molecule of DNA contains four bases: **adenine, cytosine, guanine,** and **thymine.** The order of bases along the length of the molecule contains the genetic information and governs the process of duplication of DNA as well as the information determining the many proteins that are manufactured by cells.

There are many examples in which the genetic makeup of individuals clearly affects behavior. One example is **phenylketonuria** in humans, an inherited disorder in which a single gene is missing and the consequences of which include severe mental retardation. Other disorders illustrate that abnormalities of the chromosomes can also have profound effects on human behavior, including **Turner's syndrome, Klinefelter's syndrome,** and **trisomy 21.** Although many examples of single genes or single chromosomes affecting behavior exist, most behavior is determined by many genes, or, polygenically. Techniques in behavior genetics research that address the polygenic influence on behavior include **inbreeding,** in which a strain of organisms is produced by mating individuals who are genetically related. Inbreeding leads to a strain of animals that are isogenic, meaning that all individuals in the population are genetically identical.

Studying inbred strains has revealed that many behavioral **phenotypes** involve genetic determinants, including such phenomena as aggressive behavior, locomotor activity, alcohol consumption, susceptibility to seizures, and many others. All of these examples of behavior illustrate further that no behavior is determined solely by **genotype,** but rather that all behavior represents the joint influence of genetic and environmental factors. Selective breeding for behavioral phenotypes, such as learning ability in selected mazes, alcohol consumption, locomotor activity, and many others, provides additional evidence for a genetic influence on behavior.

Behavior genetics research illustrates the important influence that genetic factors have in determining the behavior of organisms and provides biological material for further studies of the links between gene and behavior. An important goal of such research is to understand the genetic influence responsible for illness and disease. Psychotic disorders, alcoholism, and many other disorders of human behavior illustrate that the combined influence of genes and environment must determine behavior. Even though we cannot specify the relative contribution of genes and environment to behavior in a single individual, by studying populations of organisms, statistical methods can be employed to determine the relative contribution of genes and environment to the expression of behavior. As we have seen throughout this chapter, a definitive answer to the age-old Nature-Nurture controversy is that all behavior is determined jointly by heredity and environment.

Suggested Readings

Fuller, J. L., and W. R. Thompson. 1978.
Foundations of behavior genetics. St.
Louis: C. V. Mosby.
*This is a revision of the first, and therefore
classic, textbook in behavioral genetics
(the first edition was published in 1960).
The book reviews most of the research in
this field prior to its date of publication.*
Gottesman, I. I., and J. Shields. 1982.
Schizophrenia: The epigenetic puzzle.
Cambridge: Cambridge University Press.
*This book outlines the compelling evidence
suggesting that severe mental disorders
such as schizophrenia are determined in
part by genetic factors.*

Plomin, R. J., J. C. DeFries, and G. E. McClearn.
1980. *Behavioral genetics.* San Francisco:
W. H. Freeman.
*This book provides a modern introduction
to the field of behavioral genetics. Both
human behavioral genetics and research
utilizing mice are emphasized. The book
offers a particularly good introduction to
quantitative methods used in this field.
The book is also noteworthy for its
detailed discussion of behavior and
evolution.*
Thiessen, D. D. 1972. *Gene organization and
behavior.* New York: Random House.
*A short introduction to behavioral genetics,
this book is especially useful in that it
reviews areas of research—for example,
habitat selection—in some detail.*

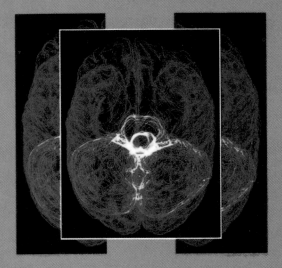

Outline

Introduction

All living matter is composed of cells and the products of cellular activity. In complex organisms, such as humans, cells are organized into tissues and organs that are designed to carry out specific functions. The nervous system, which underlies all aspects of behavior, is a tissue made up of mostly two categories of cells—neurons and neuroglia. There are many (probably more than one million) different types of nerve cells that are organized into a highly complex organ called the brain. It can now be stated that the brain is the tissue that makes possible awareness, thought, and all behavior ranging from the relatively simple motor skills involved in brushing one's teeth to the remarkable and creative achievement of composing a symphony. In order to understand the biological basis of behavior, which depends upon the integrated activity of literally billions of nerve cells, it is essential to begin with the structure and function of individual cells. In this chapter we describe some of the structures and biological processes that are carried out by nerve cells and provide the biological basis for behavior.

We begin with a discussion of cellular structures and processes that are found in all cells. Later, we describe the unique properties of nerve cells.

Chapter

3

Structure and Function of Nerve Cells

The Structure and Composition of Cells

From an historical point of view we should note that the term **cell** was first used by Robert Hooke in 1665 to describe the structure of cork. Hooke did not actually observe any cells; rather, he recognized the cavities of the cellulose walls of this tissue. Similar observations were soon made on other plant cells. In 1674, Leeuwenhoek, the father of microscopy, was the first person to recognize "free" cells by using a simple arrangement of magnifying lenses—a simple microscope. He even described some of the internal organization of cells. Most importantly, he described the nucleus in some types of cells. Beginning with Leeuwenhoek and continuing well into the early nineteenth century, many other biologists studied cells and their structure. All of this research culminated in the work of the botanist Schleiden (1838) and the zoologist Schwann (1839), who are credited with first postulating the cell theory in its modern form; that is, they recognized the cell as the fundamental unit of life. Today, this theory forms the basis of all the diverse branches of the biological sciences.

Individual cells vary greatly in both size and shape. Table 3.1 illustrates the fact that cells exist in an amazing array of sizes. Some are quite large—for example, the ostrich egg—while others, such as filter-passing viruses, are exceedingly small. Most cells, however, are very small, and it is for this reason that they are referred to as marvels of miniaturization. Consider that a human sperm with a mass of only 10^{-9} gram (0.000000001 g) contains fully

Table **3.1** The Variety in Cells

Mass of Cell in Grams	Type of Cell
100	Ostrich egg
0.0001	Striate muscle cell
0.00001	Human ovum
0.000001	Large sensory nerve cell
0.000000001	Human sperm
0.00000000001	Anthrax bacillus
0.000000000000001	Filter-passing virus

Data adapted from Giese, A. C., *Cell Physiology.* © 1968 W. B. Saunders Co., Philadelphia. Reprinted by permission.

half of the genetic material necessary to produce a human being. Larger cells, which appear to be an exception to this rule, contain large amounts of nutritive material.

Cells also differ greatly in shape. Certain muscle cells, for example, are spindle shaped; the cells that form the outer layer of the skin, **epithelial** cells, are shaped like cubes; and blood cells are disklike. The shapes of various kinds of cells are illustrated in figure 3.1.

All cells are made up of ions and molecules. These particles aggregate to form **subcellular structures,** or **organelles** (little organs) as they are sometimes called. All of these organelles, arranged in particular and varying configurations, constitute cells. In multicellular forms, cells cluster together to form tissues, and different tissues aggregate to form organs that function in such a way as to constitute the living plant or animal. An example of a "typical" animal cell is shown in figure 3.2, in which the shape and some of the internal organization of a **eukaryotic cell** are illustrated. Eukaryotic cells are those that contain a **nucleus.** The other type of cell now

Shape of cell	Type of cell	Example	Illustration of shape
Cuboidal	Epithelial cell	Epidermis (outer layer or skin)	
Spindle	Muscle	Smooth muscle	
Cell body with long fiber	Nerve	Sensory and motor neurons	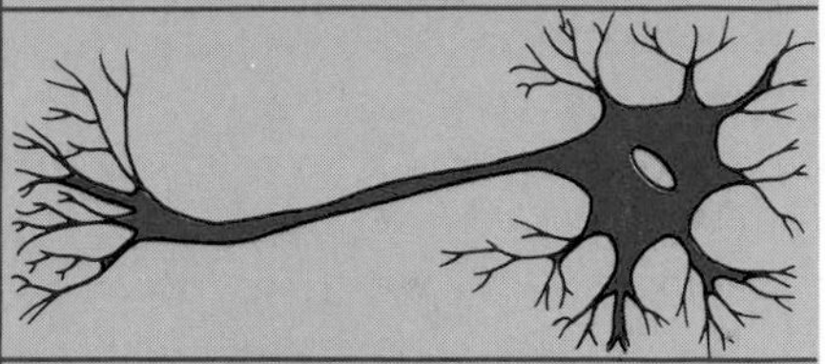
Disk	Blood	Red blood cell	
Flagellated	Gamete	Sperm	

Figure 3.1 The various shapes of cells. Note particularly the shape of the nerve cell. It consists of a cell body with a long fiber. As we shall see subsequently, this is only one type of nerve cell. Other kinds of nerve cells assume very different shapes.

recognized is the **prokaryotic cell,** which lacks a nucleus. The bacteria and the blue-green algae are prokaryotic cells. All other plant and animal cells contain a nucleus and are, therefore, eukaryotes.

Different types of cells contain different types and numbers of certain organelles and basic constituents. However, all eukaryotic cells contain a nucleus, and all cells are bounded by the **cell membrane,** sometimes referred to as the **plasma membrane,** which separates the cell from the extracellular space.

The molecular composition of an "average" animal cell is given in table 3.2. Notice that cells are largely composed of water. This aqueous phase is very similar to salt water, a fact that reflects the evolutionary origins of life in the seas. All of the structures in the cell are either dissolved or suspended in this liquid medium. The interior of cells, however, is not simply a bag of liquid, but rather is organized into compartments. Many long, tubelike processes called **microtubules,** fine **filaments** and

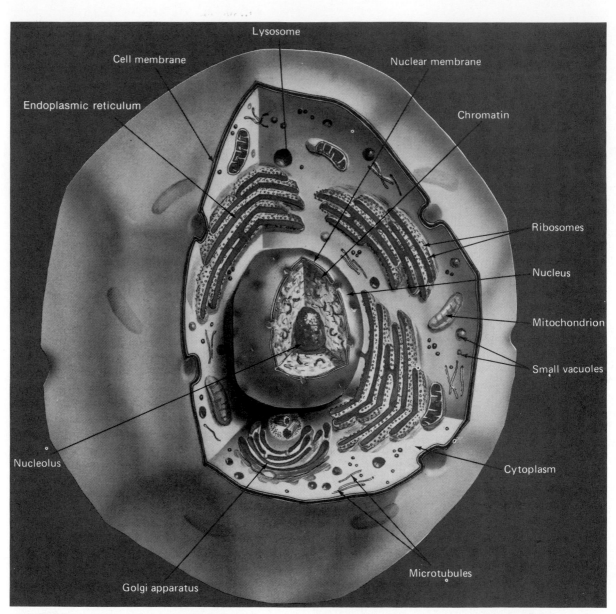

Lysosome

Cell membrane

Nuclear membrane

Endoplasmic reticulum

Chromatin

Ribosomes

Nucleus

Mitochondrion

Small vacuoles

Nucleolus

Cytoplasm

Microtubules

Golgi apparatus

Figure 3.2 An example of an idealized animal cell. This diagram represents the modern conception of the structure of a typical animal cell based on observations made with the electron microscope. Some of the subcellular structures contained within such a cell are illustrated. Visible are such structures as the nucleus, the nucleolus, the nuclear membrane, the endoplasmic reticulum, the Golgi apparatus, the mitochondria, the lysosomes and the cellular or plasma membrane.

Table 3.2 Composition of an Average Animal Cell

Substance	Percent
Water	85
Protein	10
Nucleic acids	1.1
DNA	0.4
RNA	0.7
Lipids (fats)	2
Other organic materials	0.4
Inorganic materials	1.5

fibers of different sizes, and a very fine, ubiquitous network termed the **microtrabecular** network, which interconnects all other cellular organelles, can be seen throughout the cell (Ellisman and Porter 1980). All of these processes constitute part of the "skeleton" of the cell, or **cytoskeleton.** They are involved in maintaining the structural integrity of the cell, the movement of materials within the cytoplasm, affecting changes in cell shape, as well as other dynamic properties of the living cell.

Techniques for Studying Cellular Structure and Function

Biological psychologists use a wide range of techniques in their studies. These include a host of behavioral procedures, anatomical techniques, histological techniques, and biochemical assays.

Microscopy

The unaided human eye has a resolving power of approximately 100 micrometers (a micrometer, or μm, is equal to one-millionth of a meter). **Resolving power** is the physical distance between two points necessary for them to be discriminated. Most cells have a diameter of approximately 0.5–40 microns, and are therefore too small to be seen with the unaided eye. Since this is the case, microscopes must be used to view these cells.

Three attributes of microscopes are particularly important in cellular studies: magnification, resolution, and contrast. **Magnification** simply means increasing the apparent size of an object until the eye can see it. **Resolution**, as we have already indicated, is the ability to discriminate two or more close objects from each other. **Contrast** is the degree of differences between the lightest and darkest parts of an image. All of these elements are essential in order to detect cellular and subcellular structures.

Basically, one can distinguish between two kinds of microscopes—light microscopes and electron microscopes. In the main, these instruments differ in the degree of resolution they achieve. Although light microscopes with very high magnification have been built, their resolving power is very limited. The resolving power of light microscopes is approximately 0.2 microns, or approximately 500 times greater than that of the unaided eye. This degree of resolution is still too small to distinguish between certain parts of cells. On the other hand, the electron microscope has a resolving power of approximately 10 angstrom units (an angstrom unit, Å, is equal to ten-billionths of a meter), or approximately 10,000 times that of the unaided eye. A microscope's resolution capability is directly related to the wavelength of the source of illumination. Because a beam of electrons has a much shorter

Figure 3.3 An electron microscope such as this is used to observe the fine structure of cells. Details of cellular structure can be magnified as much as several hundred thousand times.

wavelength than visible light, it is possible to see objects with the electron microscope that are much smaller than the wavelength of visible light. Since 1945, when Porter, Claude, and Fullam (1945) first viewed cells under the electron microscope (fig. 3.3), cellular and subcellular structures have been studied in great detail.

Fixation and Staining

In order to prepare tissue for microscope observation, it is necessary to harden the tissue by **fixation** and then to stain it so as to achieve the appropriate contrast. Most tissues are quite soft. The brain, for example, has the consistency of soft custard. Therefore, it is often very difficult to prepare slides for microscopic viewing without first hardening the tissue. The first procedure used to harden brains for further study was to boil them thus utilizing the same principles as are involved in boiling an egg. Today, other modern techniques for fixation of tissue are available. The most commonly used chemical reagents used for fixation are aldehydes. Aldehydes harden tissue and have other desirable properties as well. For example, they destroy enzymes that promote deterioration of the tissue and alter the structure and biochemical composition of the brain (Hayat 1986).

Most fixative agents are employed as follows: First, the animal that is being studied is sacrificed, usually by injection with an overdose of a barbiturate. The thoracic cavity is quickly exposed and the fixative is injected into the general circulation. The tissues are thus hardened. Next, the desired tissue, say the brain, is carefully dissected free. It can then be embedded into a block of paraffin to be cut into thin sections. These thin sections can then be mounted directly onto slides to be viewed under the microscope or they can be stained for subsequent observation. Alternatively, the dissected tissue can be frozen quickly and cut into thin slices in this hardened state. Cutting tissue into thin sections is a difficult art that requires considerable practice. The instruments used to cut tissues into such thin sections are called **microtomes,** of which many varities have been developed.

Staining tissue allows the microscopist to develop the contrast essential for seeing the details of cells, particularly nerve cells. Unfortunately, no single stain is appropriate for visualizing all the details of nerve cells. Probably the most common single staining technique employed in studies of the nervous system is to encrust the tissue with a heavy metal, such as silver or mercury. Nerve cells have a great affinity for silver, and this technique, invented by biologist Camillo Golgi and hence referred to as the **Golgi method,** has been used with great success to view normal nerve cells. Studies have shown that degenerating nerve cells have an even greater affinity for silver than do normal nerve cells so this technique has been useful in distinguishing degenerating from normal cells (Heimer 1970). There are other methods for tracing degenerating nerves, one of which is referred to as the **Weigert method.** This method depends on the fact that after a nerve is injured, the myelin sheath that surrounds the nerve cells degenerates. The Weigert stain reveals this lack of myelin.

Many different parts of nerve cells can be stained using special techniques or agents, such as methyl blue or neutral red. These dyes have a special affinity for nucleic acids and, therefore, stain the nucleus of the cell as well as the nucleic acid–rich portions of the cell interior.

Nerve cells react in a special way with silver salts, such that the entire nerve cell becomes stained a dark brown or black. The Golgi stain, mentioned previously, is such a stain. It has a still mysterious and useful property. Although it stains entire nerve cells, it only stains a tiny fraction of the cells in a given region. If all of the nerve cells were stained, individual cells could not be seen because they are so densely packed. Staining only a small

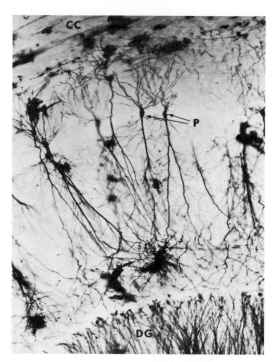

Figure 3.4 Cells and their dendrites and axons in the pyramidal cell layer of the hippocampus of the rat stained with the Golgi stain. Pyramidal cells (P) are also illustrated. Most of the fiber processes shown are dendrites. Also shown are the corpus callosum (CC) and a region below the pyramidal cell layer, the dentate gyrus (DG).

percentage, however, allows visualization of entire individual neurons even though they exist in a dense network or population of cells. The famous neuroanatomist Santiago Ramon y Cajal, who shared the Nobel prize with Golgi in 1906, used Golgi's method to carry out his remarkable description and characterization of the nervous system. "His microscopic preparations, and especially his drawings, are works of precision and art that have never been surpassed" (Jasper and Sourkes 1983). An example of nerve cells stained by the Golgi method is given in figure 3.4. It should be

Figure 3.5 The electron micrograph illustrates various features of a nerve cell, of which only about one-fourth of the cell body can be seen in this picture. At the top of the picture is the dark nucleolus embedded within the nucleus of the cell, which is bounded by the nuclear membrane. A portion of the cytoplasm of the cell that surrounds the nucleus and contains mitochondria (mit.), elements of the Golgi apparatus (go), endoplasmic reticulum (Er), lysosomes (lys), and other organelles is visible. The cell membrane separates the cell from its surrounding environment, and thin layers of processes from glia can be seen coating the cell. The surrounding neuropil is busy with various axons, dendrites, and glia passing to and fro. Dendrites of other neurons can be seen in cross section (Den), each of which is limited by a cell membrane and contains various organelles. A small group of unmyelinated axons can also be seen cut in cross section (axons) and two, larger myelinated axons are also visible.

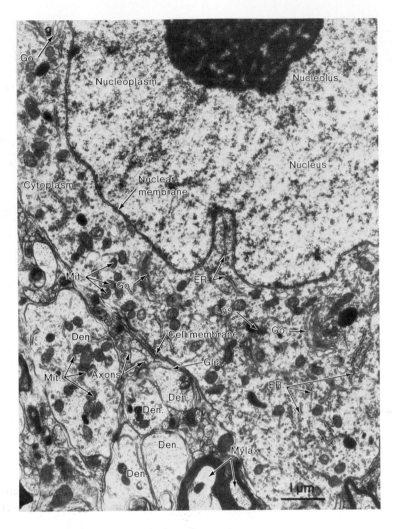

pointed out that the fine structure of nerve cells and their organelles, and especially the functional connections between them, cannot be seen with the light microscope. These small structures can only be viewed using the electron microscope. Various features of a nerve cell and its surroundings in the brain as seen through the electron microscope are illustrated in the electron micrograph shown in figure 3.5.

Cellular Structure

The cells of higher organisms, as already indicated, are composed of a nucleus and cytoplasm. These two structures are separated from each other by the nuclear membrane, and both contain many identifiable organelles (Porter and Bonneville 1973). It will be useful to refer to these various organelles and features of the cell as depicted in the schematic diagram of the animal cell in figure 3.2 and the electron micrograph illustrating them in figure 3.5.

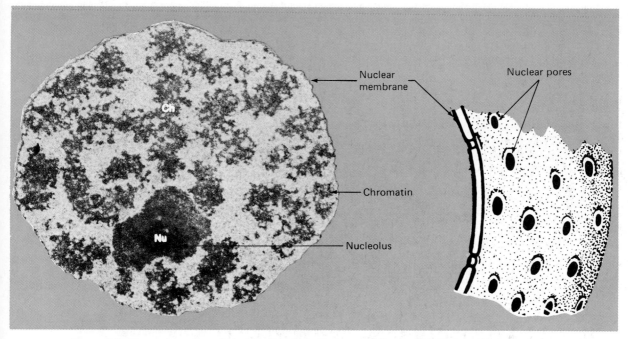

Figure 3.6 The nucleus of a cell showing its principal components: the nuclear membrane, nucleolus, and chromatin (the genetic material). On the right, a schematic diagram shows the surface of the nuclear membrane. This illustrates its porous nature, which allows for the passage of materials into and out of the nucleus.

Nucleus

Nuclei from different cells vary in a number of ways. First, the shape of the nucleus varies in different cells (in round or cubical cells it is typically spherical). Second, the size of the nucleus varies, although it is roughly proportional to the amount of cytoplasm present in a given cell. Third, the location of the nucleus within a cell varies in different cells.

Figure 3.6 is an **electron micrograph** of the nucleus of a cell. The nucleus, as can be seen, contains several structures. One of the nuclear structures is the **nucleolus** (plural, nucleoli). Nucleoli are seen as round, dense bodies and are packed with granular material called **ribonucleic acid,** or **RNA.** It is believed that the nucleoli are the sites at which certain types of RNA are made.

Another structure within the nucleus, seen in figure 3.6 as dense granular patches distributed throughout the nucleus, is **chromatin.** Chromatin is composed of **deoxyribonucleic acid,** or **DNA.** DNA is a large molecule that contains the genetic information carried by the cell. In most cells, DNA is bound to proteins in structures termed **chromosomes,** although these thin, rodlike structures cannot be seen except during a specific phase of cell division. Since mature nerve cells do not divide, the chromosomes themselves cannot be seen in the nuclei of nerve cells. Instead, they appear as the patches of chromatin shown in figure 3.6.

The spaces between these various nuclear structures are filled entirely with a colloidal suspension—large molecules suspended in solution. Collectively, these are referred to as the **nucleoplasm.**

The nucleus is totally enclosed within the nuclear membrane. This two-layered structure is interrupted in many places by small pores through which the nucleolus and the cytoplasm exchange materials.

Cytoplasm

All of the structures and substances located outside the nucleus but inside the cell are referred to collectively as the cytoplasm of the cell.

Mitochondria

The **mitochondria** are subcellular structures found in relative abundance in the cytoplasm of all cells. Electron microscopic observation of the mitochondria shows that their organization is complex. The internal organization of the mitochondria is illustrated in the electron micrograph and the sketch provided in figure 3.7.

Figure 3.7*b* shows that the mitochondrion is enclosed within a two-layered membrane. The inner membrane is characterized by many infoldings known as **cristae,** whose function is to provide a membrane surface on which chemical reactions can occur. These reactions supply the cell with energy. In fact, mitochondria are often referred to as the power station or powerhouse of cells.

Endoplasmic Reticulum

Much of the cell cytoplasm contains an extensive network of fine membranes that are called the **endoplasmic reticulum.** It was first believed that the endoplasmic reticulum was restricted to that region of the cytoplasm near the nucleus. Further studies, however, have revealed that the endoplasmic reticulum can

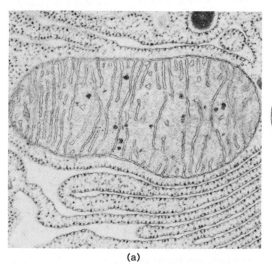

(a)

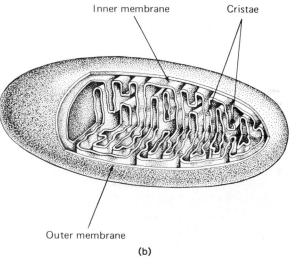

Inner membrane   Cristae

Outer membrane

(b)

Figure 3.7 (a) Electron micrograph of mitochondrion showing the two-layered membrane enclosing it and its characteristic enfoldings or cristae. (b) Three-dimensional drawing to illustrate the structures shown in (a).

occur throughout the cytoplasm of the cell. In most cells, two different varieties of endoplasmic reticulum can be distinguished. One of these consists of a network of smooth membranes throughout the cytoplasm. This network provides passageways through the cell for the movement of materials here and there, membrane surfaces where chemical reactions can occur, and membrane-bound compartments, or cavities, called **cisternae** for the segregation of cellular materials. In a second type of endoplasmic reticulum, the membranes are studded with tiny, dark organelles called ribosomes that, as will be described next, are involved in the synthesis of proteins. This type of endoplasmic reticulum has a rough appearance in the electron microscope and is, therefore, appropriately called the **rough endoplasmic reticulum.** Sometimes the rough endoplasmic reticulum occurs in large stacks, where layer upon layer of ribosome-studded membrane can be seen (fig. 3.8). In the light microscope, this stacked rough endoplasmic reticulum can be identified as a large clump, which is sometimes termed the **Nissl substance** or **Nissl body.**

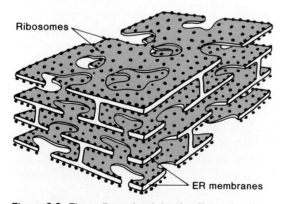

Figure 3.8 Three-dimensional drawing illustrating the rough endoplasmic reticulum. A collection of these membranes is referred to as a Nissl body or Nissl substance.

Ribosomes

First described by Palade (1953), **ribosomes** consist of RNA attached to proteins. It is now recognized that ribosomes are the site of protein synthesis in cells. (Protein synthesis and the role of ribosomes in this process are discussed in a subsequent section of this chapter.) Many ribosomes attach to the endoplasmic reticulum, giving it a rough, or studded, appearance as we have just described.

Golgi Apparatus

Another type of membranous structure found in some types of cells is the **Golgi apparatus** (see fig. 3.9), so named after its discoverer, Camillo Golgi, who first observed this structure in nerve cells in 1898. Golgi was able to observe the structure because of its selective staining with certain types of dyes—silver salts, for example. Electron microscopic examination has shown that the Golgi apparatus is very similar to and continuous with the endoplasmic reticulum. It resembles the smooth endoplasmic reticulum because it lacks ribosomes. Research has revealed some of the possible functions of the Golgi apparatus (Neutra and LeBlond 1969). Proteins that are synthesized on the ribosomes of the endoplasmic reticulum are stored in its cisternae and in the other spaces of the endoplasmic reticulum. After the proteins have been stored, and as a result of the action of certain mechanisms that are not yet understood, stored proteins break away and move toward the Golgi apparatus where they are concentrated by removal of water and are then packaged. Once concentrated and wrapped, the proteins leave the Golgi apparatus as vacuoles that may migrate to the cell membrane and be released into the extracellular space (fig. 3.9).

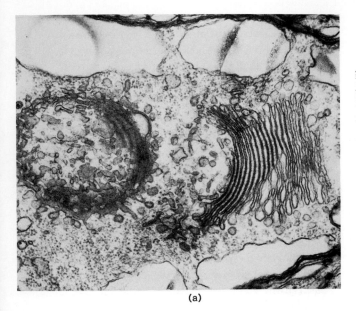

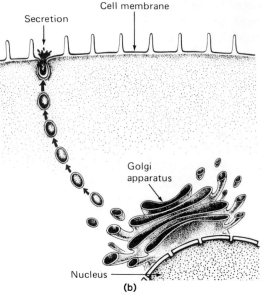

(a)

(b)

Figure 3.9 (a) An electron micrograph of a Golgi apparatus magnified about 40,000 times; the Golgi apparatus consists of membranous sacs that are continuous with the endoplasmic reticulum.

(b) Portions of the Golgi apparatus function in packaging proteins, which are then moved to the cell membrane and released as a secretion.

Lysosomes

The Golgi apparatus is also capable of packaging digestive enzymes, which are then released into the cytoplasm as **lysosomes** (DeDuve 1963). The enzymes contained in lysosomes can digest, or lyse, many substances, particularly large molecules, within the cell. The lysosomes provide each cell with its own small digestive system. Once the lysosomes have produced their metabolic effects, they fill with waste products and migrate toward the cell membrane, from which they are secreted into the extracellular space. The lysosomes of white blood cells engulf and digest invading bacteria. It is for this reason that the white blood cell count increases during infection.

The Cell Membrane

The structure of the cell membrane and other similar membranes such as the one surrounding the nucleus, and their chemical composition have been the subject of intensive investigation (see Fox 1972). The cell membrane surrounds the entire cell, and when viewed in the electron microscope at high magnification, it seems to possess three distinct layers—two dark lines that are separated by a lighter space (fig. 3.5). The membrane consists of **lipids** (fats) and **proteins.** The dark lines in the electron micrograph have been interpreted to be the dense ends of lipid molecules. The light areas have been interpreted to be the lighter parts of lipid molecules. The schematic diagram depicted in figure 3.10 shows the structure of the cell membrane

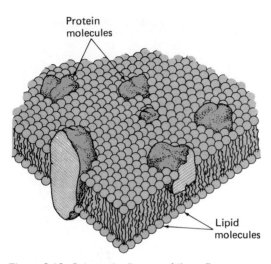

Protein
molecules

Lipid
molecules

Figure 3.10 Schematic diagram of the cell membrane.

clearly (Singer and Nicolson 1972). It consists of a double layer of lipid molecules that is very much like a delicate bubble made of oil. Embedded in the layer of lipid molecules are large proteins that may protrude from one side of the membrane or may penetrate it completely to protrude from both sides of the membrane. Other membranes of the cell—for example those surrounding other organelles such as the mitochondria or the membranes of the endoplasmic reticulum—are of this same basic design.

In the preceding sections of this chapter we discussed some of the subcellular organelles that can be found in most cells. Next, we will briefly review these structures and list some of the basic functions that they mediate.

Nuclear Organelles
In the nuclei of most animal cells we can identify the following structures: (1) the **chromosomes,** (2) **nucleoli,** and (3) **nuclear membranes.** As we mentioned in chapter 2, the chromosomes, consisting of DNA and proteins, contain the genetic material. DNA controls nearly all aspects of cellular metabolism; more specifically, DNA codes for the synthesis of proteins, both in a qualitative and quantitative sense. Since all enzymes are proteins, the types of molecules synthesized by a particular cell, as well as the numbers of molecules manufactured, are crucial in determining the metabolism of cells. The nucleolus is important in that it is the site of synthesis of a certain type of RNA; namely, ribosomal RNA, which is produced in the nucleoli. Finally, the nuclear membrane functions not only as an envelope that maintains the integrity of the nucleus, but also functions to control the transport of cytoplasmic material into and out of the nucleus.

Cytoplasmic Organelles
Many different structures can be identified within the cytoplasm of cells. The cytoplasmic organelles include the (1) **mitochondria,** (2) **endoplasmic reticulum,** (3) **ribosomes,** (4) **Golgi apparatus,** (5) **vacuoles,** and (6) **cellular,** or **plasma, membrane.** The mitochondria are organelles that are important as sites of energy synthesis within cells. As we have seen, the mitochondria have a complex structure, and most of the energy produced in cells comes from chemical reactions that occur along the membranes of the internal mitochondrial partitions. The endoplasmic reticulum consists of extended membranous networks that provide a surface area for many different types of chemical reactions. The endoplasmic reticulum also serves as a channel of communication between the cytoplasm and the nucleus and between different parts of the

cytoplasm. The ribosomes are the sites of protein synthesis in cells. When they are located on the endoplasmic reticulum, their appearance identifies this area as rough endoplasmic reticulum. (We will discuss the process of protein synthesis in a subsequent section of this chapter.) The Golgi apparatus functions as the site of synthesis of certain secretory products produced by cells. The lysosomes, for example, are synthesized by the Golgi apparatus. The vacuoles within cells serve many diverse functions; they are used to store and transport various types of cellular material, for example. Finally, the cellular membrane is a complex structure with many functions: it serves to control the transport of materials into and out of cells and in nerve cells, it is especially important in mediating neural conduction. The structural integrity and arrangement of the cellular interior is partly dependent on the cytoskeleton.

Protein Synthesis

As we have indicated several times, DNA controls the synthesis of proteins. More specifically, DNA controls the synthesis of RNA in a process called **transcription.** RNA, in turn, controls the synthesis of proteins, a process known as **translation.** The study of these processes is termed molecular biology or molecular genetics. This modern field has seen a tremendous growth within the past decade, and it is now possible in certain instances to alter the genetic material so that new or different products are manufactured by the cell. In the following section, we introduce the basic principles by which the genetic machinery of the cell works.

The genetic material, DNA, is found on chromosomes that are located within the

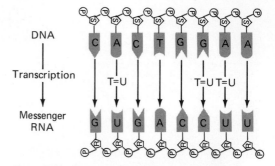

Figure 3.11 The process of transcription illustrated diagrammatically. Note that transcription of RNA involves only a single strand of the DNA molecule. Apparently, the same strand is always transcribed. Note further that thymine becomes uracil during the process.

nucleus. Proteins, on the other hand, are synthesized in the cytoplasm on the rough endoplasmic reticulum as we described earlier. For this reason, the control of protein synthesis requires the action of an intermediary molecule—RNA. The RNA molecule is synthesized using DNA as a template, as described in chapter 2, and it resembles the latter except for three differences: (1) RNA contains the sugar **ribose** instead of the deoxyribose found in DNA; (2) one of the bases in RNA is **uracil** instead of thymine found in DNA; and (3) RNA is single stranded. This type of RNA, DNA-like RNA, carries the information coded on the DNA into the cytoplasm and is therefore called messenger RNA (mRNA). The process by which DNA controls the synthesis of RNA, transcription, is illustrated diagrammatically in figure 3.11.

In describing protein synthesis it is important to remember that proteins consist of long chains of amino acids. The process of translation occurs as follows. First, the information-rich mRNA molecule is transported to the cytoplasm. Here mRNA associates with

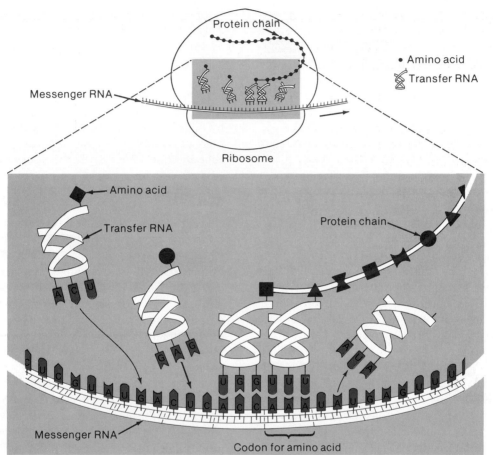

Figure 3.12 Schematic drawing to show the steps in control of protein synthesis in cells. The details of protein synthesis are described in the text. Note that protein synthesis occurs in the cytoplasm on ribosomes and that it requires the integrated action of messenger RNA, transfer RNA, and amino acids. In addition, several enzymes are required for the process as is energy in the form of ATP.

the ribosomes found on the endoplasmic reticulum. The ribosomes themselves are structures made of a second type of RNA—ribosomal RNA manufactured in the nucleoli—and proteins. This association between mRNA and the ribosomes results in the formation of a new structure called a **polyribosome,** or more simply a **polysome.** These polysomes are the real sites of protein synthesis.

Protein synthesis (fig. 3.12) is a complex process requiring the coordinated action of several mechanisms in which three classes of RNA—messenger RNA, ribosomal RNA, and transfer RNA (tRNA)—must all participate. Protein synthesis begins with transcription; next, the mRNA attaches to ribosomes and several other processes occur simultaneously.

In one process, a molecule of tRNA recognizes and attaches itself to one of the more than twenty amino acids. Transfer RNA is a molecule that contains a code on both of its ends. One end recognizes and attaches to one of the twenty amino acids. The other end recognizes a specific sequence of three bases on the messenger RNA molecule, termed a **codon.**

Amino acids recognized by tRNA are brought to the polysomes and attached to one another in specific sequences. The particular sequence depends on the mRNA code. Once the amino acids are aligned in sequence, they attach to each other and form long chains that are called **polypeptides.** These polypeptides attach to each other to form proteins. The differences in the many types of proteins that cells synthesize depend on the sequential arrangements of the amino acids in their structure. This structure ultimately depends on the base sequences in the DNA molecules that are being transcribed.

Proteins serve many purposes in all types of cells. For example, they function as organic catalysts—enzymes—that control the rates at which chemical reactions occur in cells. All enzymes are proteins. Proteins also have a structural function. The cell membrane, for example, consists in part of protein molecules. Proteins have very complex molecular shapes and participate in the cell's recognition of other molecules.

One of the important questions in molecular biology is how translation is regulated. Since all cells contain the same chromosomes and thus the same DNA, every cell has the theoretical potential to manufacture all of the proteins coded for by the DNA. But obviously all cells do not manufacture every protein (Sutcliffe et al. 1984). Thus, cells of the liver are very different in structure and function from those of the kidney or brain, in part because of the different proteins manufactured by these cells. It is now possible to alter the genetic machinery of certain types of cells, such as bacteria, so that selected gene products can be produced. A significant advance of this kind is the production of the insulin needed by diabetic individuals. Many other applications of modern molecular biological knowledge promise additional benefits for society.

Cellular Respiration

All cells require energy to carry out their many functions. Respiration is the word used to describe those processes by which a cell converts the energy found in molecules such as carbohydrates, lipids, and proteins into usable energy. In other words, cellular respiration describes those processes utilized by cells to convert chemical energy into metabolically useful energy. This metabolically useful energy is required for cells to perform work.

The major parts of the respiratory process occur in specialized cytoplasmic organelles, the mitochondria. The molecules from which cells derive energy all converge on the mitochondria; these organelles contain all the enzymes necessary to catalyze those chemical reactions involved in the formation of metabolically useful energy. Most of these chemical reactions occur on the cristae, the internal membranes of the mitochondria.

The formation of metabolically useful energy in cells depends in the first place on the sun. It is solar energy that enables certain plants to manufacture primary organic molecules that are used as fuels by other organisms. The chemical bonds in these molecules contain energy, and it is the breaking up of these bonds that releases the energy necessary for metabolic work. In large measure, metabolically useful energy is derived from the breaking up of carbon-to-carbon bonds.

Cells require energy all the time. They constantly destroy large molecules in a process that we shall refer to as catabolism. In order to balance catabolism, cells constantly manufacture, or synthesize, large molecules. Both processes, catabolism and synthesis, require energy. It is the food we consume that provides the raw material for both of these processes. Foods serve both as the building material used to synthesize molecules and as the fuel that cells burn to produce energy.

Now, if the food were just burned, then all the energy produced during catabolism would be lost as heat. In point of fact, cells do lose approximately 50 percent of the energy in foods as heat. The remainder of the energy in foods, however, is "trapped" in a form that is useful. For this to happen, cells require some type of "energy-trapping" mechanism. All cells have such a mechanism in the form of a reversible chemical reaction that changes one type of molecule, **adenosine diphosphate** (ADP), into **adenosine triphosphate** (ATP). This reaction can be represented as follows:

$$ADP + phosphate + energy \longrightarrow ATP$$

The energy is stored in the ATP molecule in the form of a high-energy phosphate bond. When this bond is broken and ATP is converted back into ADP, the energy is released and becomes available for use by the cell. ATP is the major product of respiration, and it is an energy-rich compound. It is ATP that is formed inside mitochondria, and these molecules are transported to all parts of the cell that require energy. In obtaining energy, the reaction just described is reversed: ATP is broken down, energy is released, and ADP and phosphates are

again formed. Thus, ATP is a molecule with a dual purpose: It is used to trap energy *and* to transport energy to different parts of the cell.

The process of cellular respiration involves three distinct phases. Two of these phases involve the breakdown of molecules that are used as fuels, and the third involves the trapping, or transfer, of energy. We refer to these three phases as (1) **hydrogen transfer,** (2) **fuel breakdown,** and (3) **energy transfer.** All of these three processes occur simultaneously, but let us say that respiration begins when a fuel molecule such as glucose, a carbohydrate, is broken down into two smaller fragments. The chemical reaction involved in this process is referred to as oxidation, and these reactions liberate hydrogen atoms. Therefore, it is necessary that the released hydrogen atoms be accepted by other atoms or molecules. These other atoms or molecules are called **acceptors.** If oxygen functions as the acceptor, water is formed. In any event, oxidation involves the transfer of hydrogen atoms, and this step in the respiratory process is referred to as hydrogen transfer. The second phase of oxidation involves the further breakdown of fuel molecules into smaller and smaller constituents until only single carbon fragments remain. This phase of the process is called fuel breakdown, which also involves acceptors, and the single carbon fragments are combined with oxygen to become carbon dioxide (CO_2) that we expire. Finally, the last phase in cellular respiration is the transfer of energy released from the breaking of chemical bonds to the ADP/ATP system described previously.

Let us briefly consider what happens when we metabolize a single glucose molecule to carbon dioxide and water. This process yields a total of thirty-eight molecules of ATP.

Thirty-six of these ATP molecules are produced by chemical reactions that require oxygen. It is for this reason that oxygen is essential for most animals, and it is especially important for cells with very high metabolic rates such as nerve cells. We refer to these processes as **aerobic** (oxygen-requiring) **metabolism,** and properly speaking, we call this oxidative metabolism of carbohydrates cellular respiration. Two molecules of ATP are produced through chemical reactions that do not require oxygen, or **anaerobic metabolism.** The steps in this process are called **glycolysis.** Much less energy is produced through anaerobic metabolism. However, at certain times glycolysis becomes very important. For example, when you actively exercise particular muscle groups, the oxygen supplied by breathing is insufficient. Under these conditions, glycolysis supplies the extra energy, but at a cost. An oxygen debt is built up that must be repaid through rapid breathing or panting. Further, during glycolysis lactic acid accumulates in the tissue, which contributes to muscle fatigue. Lactic acid must then be removed from the tissue. Protein synthesis and cellular respiration are fundamentally important to cells and will take on added significance as we describe the biological processes that underlie behavior.

Nerve Cells

We have noted in previous sections of this chapter that cells have a wide range of shapes and sizes. Nowhere is this remarkable variety more evident than in the nervous system (Palay and Chan-Palay 1977) (fig. 3.13). A number of properties distinguish nerve cells from other kinds of cells. One such property is that differentiated (adult) nerve cells usually do not divide, although one very interesting and important exception to this general rule occurs in

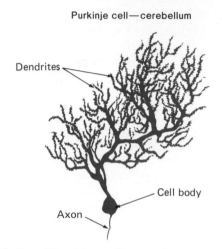

Purkinje cell—cerebellum

Figure 3.13 Four different types of nerve cells are drawn from tissue stained with the Golgi method. Note the remarkable variety of sizes and shapes of these cells. Different portions of each type of cell are labeled.

the brains of certain adult songbirds (Nottebohm 1984). In these birds, a new song is sung each year, the variation due to the growth and differentiation of new nerve cells in a specific nucleus in the bird's brain.

There are two principal categories of cells in the nervous system: the nerve cells, or **neurons,** and the nonneural cells, called **neuroglia.** In the human brain, it has been estimated that there are well over ten billion nerve cells and probably more than 10 times that number of glial cells. In this section, we will discuss the principal features of the morphology (shape) of neurons and neuroglia. Figure 3.14 is an actual photograph taken through the light microscope illustrating a nerve cell from the thalamus of the rat brain. The three principal components of the cell can be identified in this photograph: the **soma,** or cell body; dendrites; and axon (indicated by the arrow).

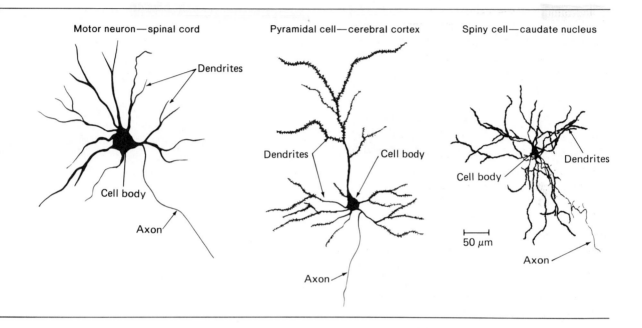

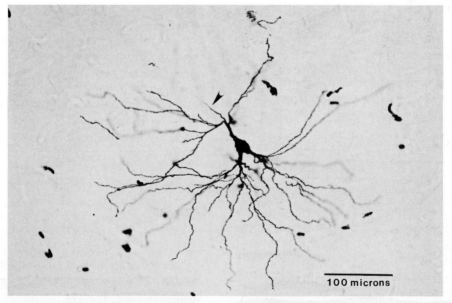

Figure 3.14 Photomicrograph of a nueron from the motor thalamus of a rat brain intracellularly labeled with horseradish peroxidase. The soma and dendrites are darkly stained, and the arrow points to the proximal region of the axon.

The Soma

The nerve cell body contains the nucleus of the nerve cells, and the cytoplasm surrounding the nucleus houses the many systems of organelles described in previous sections and illustrated in the electron micrograph shown in figure 3.5. For example, the Golgi apparatus of the nerve cell occurs within the soma typically surrounding the nucleus and often spreads out to invade the dendrites that extend from the cell body. Numerous mitochondria and other inclusions are found throughout the cytoplasm of the soma as well as throughout the cytoplasm contained in the dendrites and axons of neurons, although these are most numerous in the soma (see fig. 3.5). These organelles carry out the various metabolic and other activities of the nerve cell as we have discussed for other types of cells.

The Dendrites

Two types of processes extend away from the soma of the neuron. The nerve cell typically has numerous **dendrites** that radiate outward from the soma and may form the intricate and highly organized characteristic shape of the nerve cell, the *dendrite tree.* Note, for example, the complex and beautiful dendritic tree of the **Purkinje cell** of the cerebellum in figure 3.13 and of the thalamic neuron in figure 3.14.

At one level, it can be said that the neuron is specialized to receive, integrate, and transmit information; and the shape of the neuron reveals important clues as to how nerve cells accomplish this task. The dendrites, of which there are typically many emanating from a single cell body, are the receiving portion of the nerve cell and serve the important function of information collecting. The information is then channeled toward the cell body. The means by which this function occurs will be the subject of some discussion in this chapter and will be considered in more detail in chapters 4 and 5. Among the interesting features of the dendrites is the fact that their surface area is typically many times greater than that of the cell body. The dendrites, therefore, expand the surface over which incoming messages may be received and processed by the neuron. In some types of neurons (for example, the Purkinje cell, pyramidal cell, and spiny cell depicted in figure 3.13), the dendrites are laden with small, fingerlike appendages termed **spines,** which further expand the area of the dendrites and serve as special points where inputs from other cells are directed. The spines can be seen more clearly in the high-magnification, light-microscopic photographic montage of a spiny neuron dendrite from the caudate nucleus of the rat brain shown in figure 3.15. Note that the first 20 microns of dendritic length are relatively spine-free, but after this point the dendrite is heavily laden with spines. Each spine consists of a spherical head region and a shaft, or neck, connecting it to the parent dendrite. The head region is typically the point where input from another neuron is directed, although information may also be transmitted to the spine shaft.

The Axon

The **axon** of the nerve cell, of which there is only one, extends from the cell body or from a large dendrite near the soma. The point at which the axon joins the cell body or dendrite is called the **axon hillock.** Axons are like a fine cylindrical tube and are usually much thinner

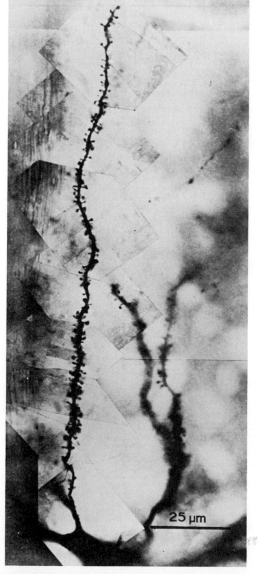

Figure 3.15 Photomicrographic montage of a spine-laden dendrite from a medium spiny neuron from the rat caudate nucleus. The initial 20 microns of the dendrite are relatively spine-free, and the spine density increases to a maximum at about 60 μm from the cell body.

than dendrites, which are usually fairly large at their base and taper as they radiate outward from the cell body. Another important difference between the axon and dendrites is that only a single axon emanates from the nerve cell, although it may sometimes branch to give off a number of **collaterals.** These are destined to carry information away from the cell body to other cells nearby or at a distance. Indeed, the axon of a nerve cell may travel long distances to reach its destination. In a human, for example, the axon of an individual cell may extend from the top of the brain to the base of the spinal cord, a distance of over 3 feet! In a giraffe, the same cell type may be over 10 feet long. Thus, an extremely important and revealing fact about the axon is that it is like a long, fluid-filled cable that is specialized to carry information away from the cell body to other cells. The axon is specialized to carry information in the form of tiny electrical impulses called **action potentials,** which travel from the cell body along the surface of the axon to its destination. When the action potential reaches the end of the axon, the information that it conveys is transferred to another cell by a chemical signal set in motion by the arrival of the nerve impulse. Having just emphasized the fact that axons can convey information over very long distances, we should now point out that not all axons are very long. Indeed, some axons are quite short and in some of these information is conveyed down the axon not by means of action potentials but by passive **electrotonic** conduction, a process that will be discussed in greater detail in chapter 5.

Another dimension along which axons vary greatly is diameter. Some axons have a diameter of approximately 20 micrometers (type A fibers) whereas others may have diameters of less than 1 micrometer (type C fibers). Fibers of intermediate thickness are referred to as type B fibers. There is an important relationship between the diameter of the axon and the rate at which the action potentials flow down its length. The greater the diameter of the axon, the greater is the velocity at which it conducts action potentials. Conduction velocity in large-diameter, type-A fibers may be as great as 100 meters/second, whereas conduction velocity in small type-C fibers may be as slow as 1 meter/second or less.

The conduction of information by the axon is its most important function; many other processes that occur in the soma and dendrites of nerve cells are not carried out by the axon. For example, axons do not contain the machinery to synthesize proteins. Proteins that are needed by the axon are manufactured in the soma and are transported into and along the interior of the axon. The movement of molecules as well as small organelles such as mitochondria along the axon is another very important function of the axon. This process is called **axonal transport.** Various substances are constantly being transported away from the cell body to the distant reaches of the axon, while others move along the axon toward the soma. These two processes are known as **anterograde** and **retrograde transport,** respectively (Fink and Gainer 1980). Materials are also transported within dendrites, and the general picture that is only now beginning to emerge is that there is a constant movement of molecules and organelles between all parts of the nerve cell and also between neighboring cells. The rate at which transport occurs may be as high as 1 millimeter per hour or as low as 1 millimeter per day.

The Synapse

When axons reach their destinations, they typically branch into a number of fine collaterals that end in small swellings called **synaptic endfeet,** or **synaptic terminals.** These synaptic terminals represent the end of the axon and it is at these small swellings that information, which has been carried to this point by the axon, is transferred from one cell to another. This transfer occurs at the points of functional contact between neurons. This form of chemical communication also occurs between nerve cells and muscle cells where the synapse is called the **neuromuscular junction.** With respect to any given synapse, we always distinguish between two cells: the cell that is sending the message—the **presynaptic cell**—and the cell destined to receive the information—the **postsynaptic cell.** The actual synapse is formed by the synaptic terminal of the presynaptic cell coming very close to the dendrites or soma of the postsynaptic cell. As we have already noted, the presynaptic cell transmits its message by secreting a chemical substance that is detected by the postsynaptic cell. The chemical substances used by neurons for this purpose are thought to be stored in special organelles known as **synaptic vesicles.** These synaptic vesicles appear as simple spherical objects seen in the presynaptic neuron and are thought to be filled with the chemical transmitter molecules or neurotransmitter. These and other details of the anatomy of the synapse are illustrated in figure 3.16.

Synaptic vesicles and other types of vesicles vary along several dimensions, including their size. Since there are many different types of neurotransmitter substances (as we will discuss in greater detail in chapters 4 and 5), different-sized synaptic vesicles have been

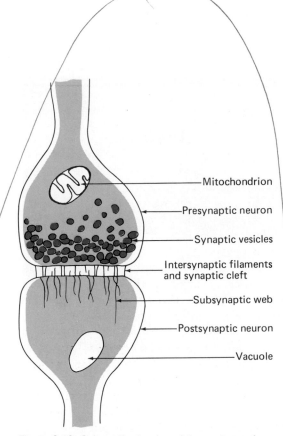

Mitochondrion

Presynaptic neuron

Synaptic vesicles

Intersynaptic filaments and synaptic cleft

Subsynaptic web

Postsynaptic neuron

Vacuole

Figure 3.16 Schematic drawing of the anatomy of a synapse. Notice the synaptic vesicles in the presynaptic terminal. Compare this diagram with the electron micrographs of the synaptic region shown in figure 3.17.

nervous system as well as in the brain. They are sometimes seen in the soma, dendrites, and elsewhere, but are especially numerous in some types of synaptic endings. The third type of vesicle is between 800 and 900 angstroms in diameter, is spherical, and is characterized by an electron-dense core. Finally, there exist yet larger vesicles, between 1,200 and 1,500 angstroms in diameter, that appear to contain large droplets. These vesicles are thought to be filled with certain classes of hormones.

Several different classes of synapses are shown in figure 3.17. These pictures illustrate many of the interesting features characteristic of these structures. When the synapse is between the axon terminal of one cell and the dendrite of another cell it is called an **axodendritic** synapse. Synapses made by an axon terminal onto the cell body of a neuron are termed **axosomatic.** Many other sites where synaptic contacts are made have also been characterized. In certain cases, synaptic contacts may even occur between the dendrites of two nerve cells, a special arrangement termed a **dendrodendritic** synapse.

As shown in figure 3.16, the synapse consists of two portions: a presynaptic portion, which includes the synaptic terminal; and a postsynaptic portion, which is typically the surface of a dendrite or cell body of another cell. In this process of **synaptic transmission,** the chemical transmitter substance is released from the synaptic terminal, a reaction triggered by the arrival of the action potential. Release is thought to occur by means of **exocytosis,** a process during which the small, spherical synaptic vesicles fuse with the membrane of the synaptic terminal to dump their contents into the small, narrow space that occurs between the terminal and the postsynaptic cell. Thus, for each synaptic vesicle that

postulated to contain different neurotransmitters. One system for classifying different synaptic vesicles was developed by Palay (1967), who described four kinds of vesicles. The first type is the most common synaptic vesicle and is approximately 200–400 angstrom units in diameter. It is spherical and has a clear center. These kinds of vesicles are found in many locations, including the neuromuscular junction where they are thought to contain **acetylcholine,** one kind of neurotransmitter. The second type of vesicle is between 400 and 800 angstroms in diameter. It is also spherical and has an electron-dense core. These types of vesicles are found in certain locations in the autonomic

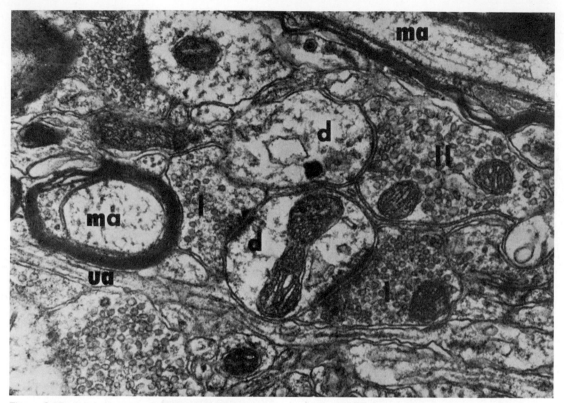

Figure 3.17 An electron micrograph showing the substantia nigra of a rat's brain. Type I and type II synapses are illustrated in which the synaptic endings make symmetric (type I) or asymmetric (type II) synaptic contact with dendrites (d). Each synapse contains one or two mitochondria as well as numerous synaptic vesicles. The two labeled dendrites are approximately 1.5 m in diameter. Also illustrated are two myelinated axons (ma), one seen in longitudinal section (above) and one in cross section (below) . A small, unmyelinated axon (ua) is also shown.

fuses with the membrane of the presynaptic ending, a small amount of vesicle membrane is added to the terminal membrane. This added amount of membrane is later recaptured by the terminal by a process in which a small amount of terminal membrane buds off into the interior of the synaptic ending. In this way, the membranes of synaptic vesicles are "recycled" by the presynaptic cell (Heuser and Reese 1979).

The small gap that occurs between the presynaptic ending and the postsynaptic cell is termed the synaptic cleft. It is typically only 20–30 nanometers wide, and is formed by the close apposition of the membrane of the presynaptic ending and the membrane of the postsynaptic cell. The chemical transmitter molecules diffuse across the synaptic cleft to attach to specialized receptors located on the surface of the postsynaptic membrane. It is the interaction between the transmitter molecules and the receptors that affects the postsynaptic, or receiving, cell. The means by which this influence occurs will be the subject of subsequent chapters.

The cross sections through synapses, shown in the electron micrograph in figure 3.17, illustrate several other interesting properties of synapses. For example, the membranes of synaptic terminals and the postsynaptic dendrite typically appear quite different from regions of membranes where synaptic contact does not occur. The presynaptic and postsynaptic membranes may show prominent thickenings that appear "fuzzy" and darker than surrounding membranes. Further, synaptic endings may exhibit quite a range in the shapes and sizes of the synaptic vesicles contained within them, as we have seen already.

As shown in the electron micrograph of the substantia nigra of the rat brain in figure 3.17, two synapse types or categories are commonly seen in the mammalian brain, which Gray designated type I and type II synapses (Gray 1959). These two characteristic types of synaptic contact may be differentiated on the basis of the appearance of the membranes that form the synaptic contact. For type I synapses, sometimes termed asymmetric, the membrane of the postsynaptic neuron appears to be comparatively dense and thick. For type II synapses, the presynaptic and postsynaptic membranes are approximately equal in density and thickness when viewed in the electron microscope. For this reason, type II synapses are often termed symmetric synapses. It is now recognized that these two categories of synapses are frequently associated with synaptic function. In those cases where the synaptic function has been ascertained by neurophysiologic methods, type I synapses are associated with an excitatory action, while type II synapses are found to exert inhibition.

Presynaptic Dendrites

We normally think of the dendrite of a neuron as postsynaptic. That is, the dendrite is considered the receiving station, with axon terminals forming synapses on the dendrites, which are termed axodendritic synapses. However, it is now known that some dendrites appear to release neurotransmitter and function in other ways that make them **presynaptic** structures as well (e.g., Rall et al. 1966; Shepherd 1974). In some instances, dendrites appear to form synapses with other dendrites, termed dendrodendritic synapses. Such structures have been revealed by the electron microscope in the retina, olfactory bulb, and many other places in the brain. As yet only a few functions have been attributed to neurotransmitter released from dendrites. For example, dendrites may use this mechanism to affect nearby blood vessels. Dendrites may form electrotonic synapses with other dendrites in which chemical transmission does not occur, but rather the two cells are "electrically coupled" to one another.

Another suggestion is that in some neurons, neurotransmitter may be released from the cell's dendrites in order to control its own impulse activity or the firing activity of its close neighbors. Such a process has been suggested for dopaminergic neurons in the brain. These neurons release dopamine from their dendrites, which appears to inhibit the occurrence of action potentials of the same neuron from which the dopamine was released as well as other dopaminergic neurons with which the cell makes dendrodendritic synapses (Groves et al. 1975; 1976; Wilson, Groves, and Fifkova 1977). An illustration of a dendrodendritic synapse between dopaminergic dendrites in the rat brain is shown in figure 3.18.

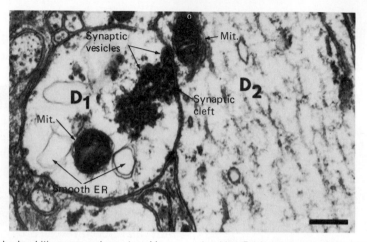

Figure 3.18 A dendrodendritic synapse is captured in this electron micrograph. The presynaptic dendrite (D_1), appearing in cross section, contains a large cluster of "synaptic vesicles," which appear very dark because they have been labeled with a substance to make them easily identifiable. The postsynaptic dendrite (D_2) has been sectioned longitudinally. Note the narrow "synaptic cleft" separating the dendrites at the dendrodendritic synapse. Each dendrite contains a mitochondrion (Mit.). Pieces of the smooth endoplasmic reticulum (smooth ER) can be seen in one of them. Calibration line is equal to 0.25 micrometers.

Neuroglia

We have noted that there are two principal cell types in the nervous system: the neurons and the nonneural cells of the nervous system, the neuroglia. Glia are far more numerous (by a factor of ten or more) than neurons. Although glial cells also have complex shapes, the morphology and functions of neuroglia are quite different from those of neurons. These cells do not have axons and their dendrites are not specialized to receive and transmit information. Instead, they serve a supporting function in the nervous system, acting in part to facilitate the information-carrying function of neurons and to serve nerve cells in other ways that optimize the capabilities of the nerve cells to perform their role. This section will review the types of neuroglia found in the nervous system.

Three different types of neuroglia occur in the brain. These include **astrocytes, oligodendrocytes,** and **microglia.** In addition, the **Schwann cell,** which occurs in the peripheral nervous system (that is, those parts of the nervous system found outside the brain and spinal cord), will be described. Examples of two oligodendrocytes and an astroglia are illustrated in the drawings shown in figure 3.19. These cells are not specialized to receive and transmit information. Instead, they serve a supporting function in the nervous system, acting in part to facilitate the information-carrying function of neurons and to serve nerve cells in other ways that optimize their capabilities to perform their role. This section will review the types of neuroglia found in the nervous system.

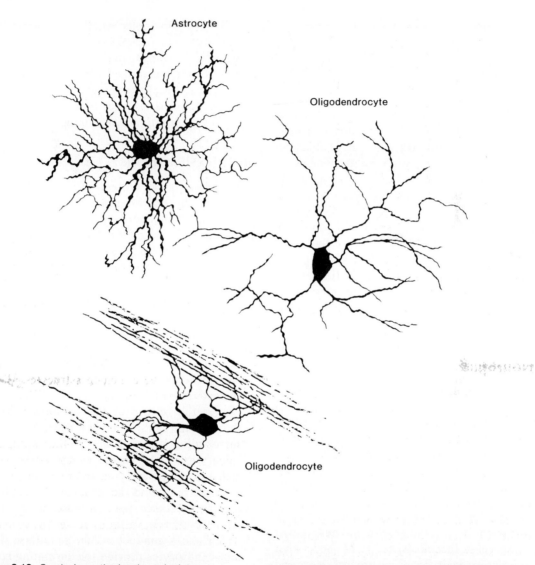

Astrocyte

Oligodendrocyte

Oligodendrocyte

Figure 3.19 Semischematic drawings depict neuroglia from the rat brain stained with the Golgi method. The astrocyte sends out many processes that surround the nerve cells and may also form end-feet that are apposed to blood vessels that participate in the blood-brain barrier. In the example at the bottom, the oligodendrocyte sends out many processes, each forming an individual segment of myelin around a single axon. The direction of the axons in this fiber bundle is easily seen by the parallel array of many myelin segments that are associated with each of many axons.

Astrocytes

Astrocytes are glial cells that surround nerve cells. Two different types of astrocytes can be differentiated in the brain. The two are **protoplasmic astrocytes,** which occur around cell bodies and dendrites of nerve cells, and **fibrous astrocytes,** which are more often found in areas where there are large numbers of axons coursing through the brain matter. The astrocyte is typically a small cell with hundreds of complex, branching processes extending from the central cell body. These processes literally fill the spaces between nerve cells and provide an extensive layer that separates the nerve cells and their processes from one another.

Speculations concerning the functions of astrocytes abound, although in comparison to the properties of neurons, surprisingly little is known about the role of glia in the brian. It is known, for example, that these glial cells do not generally receive any synapses from nerve cells, although they may possess receptors that make them responsive to chemical substances secreted by nerve cells or hormones secreted by various endocrine glands. They participate in regulating the extracellular environment in the brain, especially the concentrations of various substances—for example, potassium and chloride ions dissolved in the fluid bathing the nerve cells (Newman 1986). It has been thought for many years that astrocytes play an important part in the growth and nutrition of nerve cells. Indeed, it has been shown that neurons grown in tissue culture live longer and appear to grow better when astrocytes are present (Banker 1980). Glial cells also participate in the structural organization of the brain during development and may even direct the formation and shapes of the dendritic tree of individual nerve cells. Another important feature of astrocytes is the formation of endfeet, or small swellings, that surround the blood vessels coursing through the brain. These astrocytic endfeet are apparently involved in the regulation of substances that cross the brain blood vessels into nervous tissue.

Oligodendrocytes and Schwann Cells

Oligodendrocytes represent the second variety of glial cells that occur in large numbers in the brain and spinal cord. At least one important function of these cells has been described and is being studied extensively. These glial cells form the **myelin sheath** that surrounds the axons of many nerve cells. A schematic diagram illustrating this process is shown in figure 3.20.

As we have already mentioned, information is conducted along the axon of a nerve cell by means of small electrical impulses termed action potentials, which travel down the axon to reach the synaptic terminals and trigger the release of chemical neurotransmitter substances. A myelin sheath is found surrounding many axons in the brain and spinal cord; it also occurs around axons in peripheral nerves carrying information to and from the brain and the spinal cord. Myelin is a fatty substance that, because of its insulating properties, vastly increases the speed at which axons conduct action potentials. The oligodendrocytes provide this insulating coat. In the brain, the processes extending from the oligodendrocytes wrap around the axons of nerve cells, insulating them from one another with layer upon layer of myelin. This myelin sheath is not a continuous coating of the axon, but rather consists of individual segments separated by small gaps called the **nodes of Ranvier** (see color plate 2). When located within

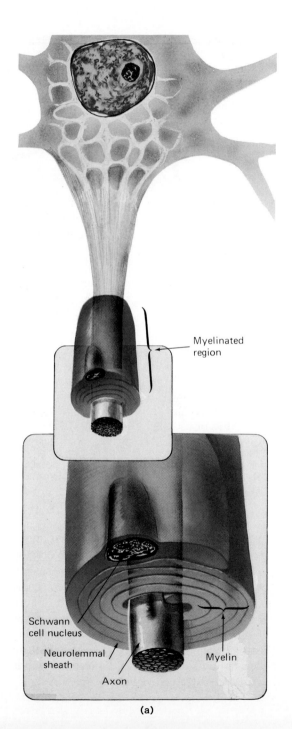

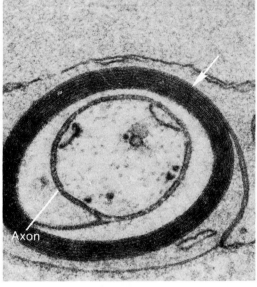

(b)

Figure 3.20 (a) A schematic illustration of the myelin sheath (neurolemmal sheath) that surrounds axons in the central and peripheral nervous system. In this case, a Schwann cell surrounds an axon of a peripheral nerve with many layers of myelin. In the brain, this process is done by oligodendrocytes. (b) An electron micrograph showing the axon and its myelin sheath in cross section.

a large bundle of nerve cells in the brain, a single oligodendrocyte may send out many processes, each of which wraps around an axon to form a single segment of myelin. An oligodendrocyte of this type is illustrated in figure 3.19, where it lies within a large bundle of axons. The direction of the axons, even though they have not been stained, is easily discerned. On both sides of the oligodendrocyte, individual processes wrap around individual axons, forming a parallel array of myelin segments, each surrounding a different axon. In regions of the brain where there is not such a concentration of myelinated axons, the processes of the oligodendrocytes radiate outward to provide myelin to axons scattered among the neuronal environment around them, as shown in figure 3.20.

In peripheral nerves, which carry information toward and away from the brain and spinal cord, individual segments of myelin are formed by Schwann cells that wrap themselves around the axon in layer upon layer, each Schwann cell forming the many layers contained within an individual segment of myelin. This is shown in figure 3.20. Each Schwann cell wraps itself around only a single axon and forms only a single segment of the myelin sheath. The Schwann cells, like the segments of myelin in the brain, are separated from each other at the gaps that occur between them, the Nodes of Ranvier.

Microglia

The third prominent type of glial cell is the **microglia.** This cell type occurs much less frequently in the nervous system under normal conditions, but is found in very large numbers when an insult to the brain or a disease process occurs. The major function of microglia is

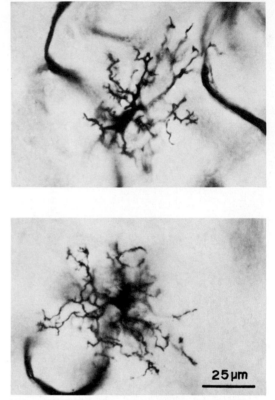

Figure 3.21 Two microglia have been photographed with the aid of the light microscope and the Golgi stain. They appear very dense because they possess so many slender, processes radiating from the central cell body. Both are located near blood vessels.

phagocytosis, in which diseased and dying remnants of tissue are removed from a region of injury or disease. These tiny cells, several of which are depicted in the light microscopic pictures in figure 3.21, are able to move through the brain to the site of an injury. They engulf the debris left from injured or dying tissue, packaging it in large vacuoles that can then be used to release the unwanted debris across nearby blood vessels.

Summary

The biological psychologist wishes to understand the biological processes that underlie the behavior of organisms. Since all living matter is made up of cells and cell products, it is important to understand how cells function and especially to know the principles that govern the cells of the nervous system. Cells come in a variety of sizes and shapes, but **eukaryotic cells** (that is, those having a **nucleus**) have many processes and structures in common. For example, eukaryotic cells are comprised of about 85 percent water, while the rest of the cell is composed of mostly proteins, lipids, and other organic and inorganic materials.

Each cell is bounded by the **cell** or **plasma membrane,** which separates it from the external environment. Each cell has a nucleus that directs cellular development and function. Much about the structure of cells has been discovered with the aid of light and electron microscopes. When cells are fixed and stained to achieve contrast, images from the light and electron microscopes have revealed that mammalian cells possess numerous **organelles.** The nucleus, for example, contans the **chromosomes** composed of deoxyribonucleic acid, or DNA. The **nucleolus** is an important organelle contained within the nucleus. The **nuclear membrane** separates the nucleus from the cytoplasm of the cell, with small nuclear pores for communication between the **nucleoplasm** and the **cytoplasm.** Within the cytoplasm are numerous organelles. **Mitochondria,** for example, occur throughout the cytoplasm. These are small, sausage-shaped organelles where cellular respiration occurs, which supplies the cell with energy. **Ribosomes** are small, dark organelles where protein synthesis occurs. The smooth endoplasmic reticulum is a network of membranes throughout the cell. It creates passageways through the cell and membranes on which chemical reactions occur. The **rough endoplasmic reticulum** is so called because it is studded with ribosomes and appears rough compared to the smooth endoplasmic reticulum. The **Golgi apparatus** is specialized to package various cellular biochemical products for transport and secretion.

The process of **protein synthesis** takes place at the ribosomes. Directed by the DNA inside the nucleus, the genetic code is transcribed onto the RNA molecule. Subsequently, this information directs translation of the code into the sequence of amino acids that make up the newly manufactured protein molecule. All enzymes are proteins and control the rates of chemical reactions in cells. Without enzymes, chemical reactions would be too slow to maintain life. The principle source of energy in cells is derived from **cellular respiration,** including the three phases of **hydrogen transfer, fuel breakdown,** and **energy transfer.** Generally, energy is stored in the energy-rich molecule **adenosine triphosphate,** or ATP. **Respiration** refers to those processes by which cells convert the energy in the foods we consume to metabolically useful chemical energy.

While all of the processes of metabolism and respiration occur in nerve cells, the structure of nerve cells offers a special clue to nerve cell function. Nerve cells typically consist of three major portions. The **soma,** or cell body, contains the nucleus of the nerve cell. Extending from the soma are the **dendrites,** which are the information-collecting areas of the cell. The **axon** emanates from the cell to carry the information collected by the nerve cell to other neurons with which it makes synaptic contact.

Substances can be transported along the axon either away from the cell body, termed **anterograde transport,** or toward the cell body, termed **retrograde transport.** The **synapses** thus formed secrete chemical messengers, or **neurotransmitters,** from their storage sites in the synaptic ending, the **synaptic vesicles.** Neurotransmitter is secreted into the narrow space, or **synaptic cleft** formed by the membranes of the synapse, consisting of the presynaptic and postsynaptic membranes.

Another major class of cells comprising the nervous system are the **neuroglia. Astrocytes** are glial cells that surround nerve cells. These are of two types: protoplasmic and fibrous astrocytes. **Oligodendrocytes** and **Schwann cells** form the myelin sheath. Oligodendrocytes surround many neuron axons in the brain, and Schwann cells surround peripheral nerves. The **microglia** are small glial cells whose major function appears to be phagocytosis, the process of removing diseased or dying remnants of cells from nervous tissue.

Suggested Readings

Mader, S. S. 1987. *Inquiry into life.* 5th ed. Dubuque, IA: Wm. C. Brown Publishers.
This is a basic textbook in biology that provides an extended discussion of cells and other basic concepts from biology appropriate for further reading by beginning students in biological psychology.

Nauta, W. J. H. and M. Feirtag. 1986. *Fundamental neuroanatomy.* New York: W. H. Freeman.
This is an excellent introduction to the structure and function of nerve cells and the organization of the brain.

Peters, A., S. L. Palay, and H. deF. Webster. 1976. *The fine structure of the nervous system: The neurons and supporting cells.* Philadelphia: W. B. Saunders Company.
This is an outstanding book on the fine structure of neurons, glia, and other tissues in the nervous system. It contains an informative text and many beautiful electron micrographs as illustrations.

Porter, K. R. and M. A. Bonneville. 1973. *Fine structure of cells and tissues.* 4th ed. Philadelphia: Lea & Febiger.
This is an authoritative book on the fine structure of cells and tissues with excellent electron micrographs and explanations of the structure and function of cellular organelles.

Shepherd, G. M. 1979. *The synaptic organization
of the brain.* 2d ed. New York: Oxford
University Press.

*This is one of the outstanding textbooks in
the neurosciences. Chapters 1 and 2 are
particularly relevant to this chapter. The
first chapter contains a discussion of the
traditional concepts regarding synaptic
organization. The second chapter deals
with the structure of the neuron and with
the various kinds of synapses that have
been described. The remainder of the book
is a detailed analysis of the synaptic
organization of the brain.*

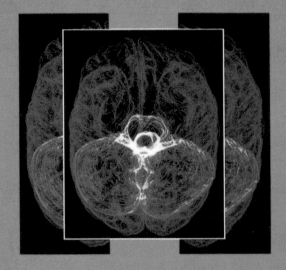

Outline

Introduction

In the previous chapter we discussed the properties and functions of individual nerve cells. However, even the simplest behavior requires the concerted action of many thousands or even millions of nerve cells. In the vertebrate nervous system, neurons are not functionally isolated, but rather seem to work in populations. These populations are often selectively connected by synaptic contact to other populations of neurons in a myriad variety of circuits and systems that make up the information network of the nervous system. Figure 4.1 gives an overview of the entire nervous system in which its two divisions—the **central nervous system** and the **peripheral nervous system**—are illustrated. Included in the central nervous system are the brain and spinal cord. The peripheral nervous system consists of all nervous tissue lying outside these regions. You can think of the central nervous system as the integration center for all behavior, receiving and interpreting sensory information and directing our thoughts and actions. The peripheral nervous system, on the other hand, is required to bring this sensory information from both the external world and the internal environment into the central nervous system. It must also carry the commands of the central nervous system out to the muscles and glands to produce movement, speech, and other behaviors.

Chapter

4

Organization of the Nervous System

nuclei   (nu'kle-i)
ganglia   (gang'gle-ah)
anterior   (an-t're-or)

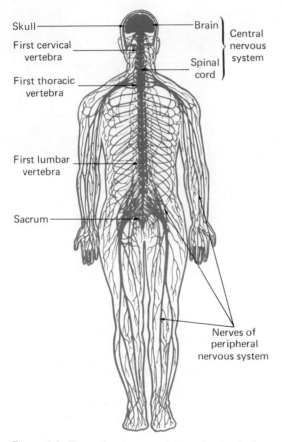

Skull

First cervical
vertebra

First thoracic
vertebra

First lumbar
vertebra

Sacrum

Brain

Spinal
cord

Central
nervous
system

Nerves of
peripheral
nervous system

Figure 4.1 The entire nervous system, showing both
the central nervous system (C.N.S.) and the peripheral
nervous system (P.N.S.). The vertebrae are divided into
groups (cervical, thoracic, lumbar, and sacral), and one
vertebra in each group is labeled.

An enormous amount is known about
how the nervous system is organized, yet much
more remains unknown to challenge scientists
in this important frontier of knowledge. For
the remainder of this chapter you will be introduced to some of the structural organization of the nervous system and some of the
principal features of this remarkable product
of evolution.

Some Basic Vocabulary

Generally, neurons exist in functional populations. Functional groups of neurons may
form layers in the central nervous system, such
as in the cerebral cortex, and may also be
present in small or large groups called **nuclei.**
If the neuron groups occur in the peripheral
nervous system they are termed **ganglia.** The
axons of these neurons leave the region of the
nucleus, or ganglion, to travel sometimes long
distances before reaching their destination.
Upon arrival at this destination, they make
synaptic contact, completing a connection.
Connections occur between groups of neurons
within the central nervous system and between groups of neurons in the central or peripheral nervous system and sensory receptors
or muscles. Axons making up these connections typically travel together in bundles consisting of many fibers. The bundles are called
tracts in the central nervous system and **nerves**
when they occur in the peripheral nervous
system.

Another group of important terms used
regularly in describing the organization of the
nervous system are the directional terms,
which are used to refer to the locations and
positions of structures of the body in relation
to each other. A number of these terms are defined by the illustrations in figure 4.2.

Initially, it is important to note that the
direction specified by a number of important
anatomical terms differs in animals that stand
upright, such as the humans, and those on four
legs. As shown in figure 4.2, structures that are
located toward the head are termed **rostral** or
superior in the upright organism, and those
structures toward the feet are termed **caudal**
or **inferior.** In four-legged animals, structures
located toward the head are termed **rostral** or
anterior, while those toward the tail are termed

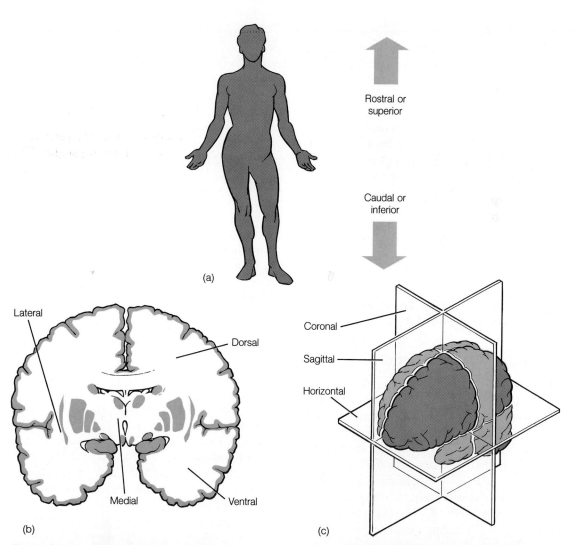

Rostral or
superior

Caudal or
inferior

(a)

Lateral

Dorsal

Medial   Ventral

(b)

Coronal

Sagittal

Horizontal

(c)

Figure 4.2 Directional terms used to define the positions of structures in (a) an upright organism, such as a human, (b) coronal section through the human brain, and (c) the three anatomical planes passing through the human brain.

caudal or **posterior.** Rostral, superior, and anterior are often used interchangeably, as are the terms caudal, inferior, and posterior. **Dorsal** refers to the back or top of an animal, while **ventral** means toward the front or undersurface (fig. 4.2*b*).

In addition to these directional terms, three anatomical planes may be identified—for example, to specify the types of cross sections that are taken through a structure to study its anatomical organization. These are

sagittal   (saj'ı-tal)
stereotaxic apparatus   (ste''re-o-tak'sik)

illustrated in figure 4.2*c*. The **sagittal** plane divides the body or structure contained within it into right and left parts. A common cross section often encountered in this text is the midsagittal section that divides the brain into right and left halves. This plane is also termed the **median** plane. A **frontal,** or **coronal,** plane divides the body into front and back parts and is perpendicular to the sagittal plane. The **horizontal** plane separates the upper and lower parts of the body. Structures toward the median plane of the body are referred to as **medial** while those away from the median plane are called **lateral.** And finally, the terms **proximal** and **distal** are used to refer to the position of structures near or away from the middle of the body, respectively. For example, with respect to the arm, the hand is distal to the elbow and the elbow is proximal to the hand.

Tracing Pathways in the Brain

We noted in chapter 3 that a number of histological techniques may be used to visualize the nerve cell or its processes with the aid of a microscope. The Nissl stain, for example, is used to locate groups of cell bodies in the nervous system since it reacts with the Nissl substance or rough endoplasmic reticulum contained in the cell body. Another classical staining method is the Golgi stain in which the entire neuron, including dendrites, cell body, and a portion of the axon, is stained. The Weigert technique, on the other hand, is used to stain the myelin surrounding axons and so is used to trace the course of axons as they wander through the brain toward their targets. Two classical methods for determining the functional organization of the nervous system involve destruction of selected cell groups or regions where a given cell group sends its axons.

In this section, we will review some of the classical methods used by neuroanatomists to trace neural pathways in the brain. Some of these methods involve the destruction of selected nuclei or the destruction of regions that are believed to receive input from certain nuclei. By studying the neural degeneration that follows, neuroanatomists can verify the axonal connections between brain areas. To understand how this is accomplished, it is necessary to begin with the basic method for operating on the brain.

Stereotaxic Method

The experimental methods for tracing neuroanatomical pathways in the brain require the use of experimental animals. The stereotaxic method enables the experimenter to locate nuclei or axons beneath the surface of the brain. At the heart of this method is the **stereotaxic apparatus,** shown in figure 4.3. The stereotaxic apparatus consists of two basic parts: a

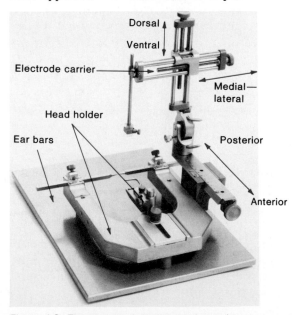

Figure 4.3 The stereotaxic instrument is used to place electrodes in selected regions of the brain.

head holder for holding the animal's head in a precisely determined position; and an **electrode carrier,** used to place electrodes in the brain. Using positioners, the electrode carrier can be moved to any point along three dimensions: **anterior** to **posterior, medial** to **lateral,** and **dorsal** to **ventral.** Once a reference point, or **zero point,** is specified and the animal's head is in the head holder securely, any point within the brain can be specified in terms of its position along the three dimensions with respect to the zero point. For most stereotaxic instruments the zero point is chosen to be a point halfway along an imaginary line between the ears, called the **interaural line.** Since the head holder is designed so that the head of the experimental animal is always placed in precisely the same position, the interaural line and zero point are always in approximately the same place from animal to animal. By use of three-dimensional maps of the brain constructed painstakingly from serial cross sections through the entire brain, any structure within the brain can be located with respect to this constant reference or zero point. Such maps, termed **stereotaxic atlases,** have been made for animals of many species, including the human being.

In order to destroy a particular nucleus or other region of the brain, a wire or **electrode** is connected to the electrode carrier and lowered into the brain during surgery to the appropriate position specified in the stereotaxic atlas. Electric current is then passed through the electrode to destroy the region of tissue surrounding its tip. The electrode is insulated along its length except at the tip where the passage of current is desired. Following the destruction, the animal may be observed and tested to reveal the effects on its behavior of such selective damage. Anatomical techniques then are used to examine the damaged

region (called the **lesion**) of the brain, as well as the fibers connected to the region and the pathways of axons that originate from the region. It should be pointed out that while such techniques sound easy enough, they are often extremely time-consuming and complicated by factors that we have not discussed. For example, a lesion may destroy a particular nucleus and at the same time also damage axons that simply pass through or near the region of damage. In this case, the degenerating fibers may be completely unrelated to the nucleus where damage was intended. Further, if only one branch of an axon is destroyed, which happens where nerve cells send branches of their axons to more than one place, the cell may not show complete degeneration. One way of avoiding the problem of destroying passage fibers with an electrolytic lesion is to use chemical agents that will make a more selective lesion in the brain. Kainic acid, for example, is a highly useful **neurotoxin** that destroys the cell bodies of neurons in the vicinity of its injection into the brain. However, it also leaves intact axons that originate from cells in other parts of the brain but which are only passing through the region.

A great deal of what we know about the organization of the brain and the locations of functional circuits important for behavior was determined from behavioral and anatomical observations of animals with such experimentally produced damage to selected regions of the nervous system. Indeed, the stereotaxic instrument is one of the most common and useful pieces of equipment in the brain-research laboratory. The stereotaxic method is also used to stimulate and record activity from regions beneath the brain's surface.

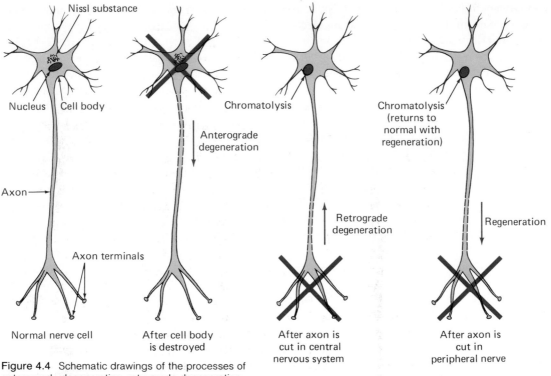

Nissl substance

Nucleus   Cell body

Chromatolysis

Chromatolysis
(returns to
normal with
regeneration)

Anterograde
degeneration

Axon →

Retrograde
degeneration

Regeneration

Axon terminals

Normal nerve cell

After cell body
is destroyed

After axon is
cut in central
nervous system

After axon is
cut in
peripheral nerve

Figure 4.4 Schematic drawings of the processes of anterograde degeneration, retrograde degeneration, chromatolysis, and regeneration in peripheral nerves and the conditions that produce them.

Degeneration Techniques

When the cell bodies in a particular nucleus are destroyed by electrolytic or kainic acid lesions, the axons that originate from those cell bodies begin a process of degeneration termed **Wallerian** or **anterograde degeneration.** After such degeneration has taken place, the brain can be removed, sectioned, and stained so that the pathway originally traveled by the degenerated axons appears as an empty space on the thin sections that are stained to reveal the remaining myelinated axons. Other techniques—for example, the **Marchi method** in which the myelin surrounding degenerating axons is stained dark while leaving all normal axons light—can also be used.

Another degeneration technique involves the destruction of axons. When an axon of a neuron is severed, the cell body from which the axon originates undergoes a series of changes termed **chromatolysis.** In the central nervous system, cutting the axon of a nerve cell also leads to degeneration of the remaining axon and cell body, a process called **retrograde degeneration.** In the peripheral nervous system, axons are capable of regeneration so that when a nerve is severed, the cell body undergoes chromatolysis, but the nerve may regrow and reconnect to the muscle or skin from which it was disconnected. When a nerve or tract is severed, its origin can be determined by looking for the area in which the cells show chromatolysis or in which there is cell loss because of retrograde degeneration. The processes of anterograde and retrograde degeneration, chromatolysis, and nerve regeneration in the peripheral nervous system are illustrated in figure 4.4.

Axonal Transport and Biochemical Neuroanatomy

Within the past two decades, techniques for studying the structure of the nervous system have proliferated enormously, providing a variety of new insights regarding the structure and function of the nervous system. Two significant classes of techniques are the axonal transport and biochemical neuroanatomical methods (Jones and Hartman 1978). These techniques take special advantage of the biochemical and biophysical properties of nerve cells. For example, nerve cells must transport various nutrients and enzymes between the cell body and the distant terminals of the axon. Thus, there is a constant flow of substances from the cell body toward the axon (anterograde transport) as well as from the axon terminals toward the cell body (retrograde transport). In many instances, the cell body or axon terminals take up substances injected into the brain nearby and transport these "markers" down the axon. In some cases, the marker may be a substance that later reacts with a histological stain so that the course of the axon and the placement of its cell body can be identified under the microscope.

One such method that has become popular in recent years is the **horseradish peroxidase** method, which can be used as either a retrograde or anterograde tracing method. The enzyme horseradish peroxidase is injected into

a region of axon terminals and is taken up by the terminals and transported down the axon to the cell body (LaVail and LaVail 1972). When later exposed to the appropriate chemical reagent, the cell bodies may be stained dark brown, blue, or black so that cells sending axons to the injection site can be located in the microscope. When used as an anterograde tracing method, the enzyme solution is injected into a region of cell bodies, and the axons become lightly stained and may be traced to their destinations (Lynch et al. 1974).

In another category of anterograde tracing methods, a radioactive compound can be injected into a region of cell bodies. In many instances, the radioactive compound is an amino acid that is incorporated by the neuron into proteins. The proteins are transported down the axon and slices through the brain are then exposed to photographic emulsion. The radioactivity can be detected in this way since it exposes the photographic plate and leaves light traces wherever it occurs. This method is termed **autoradiography.**

Another important and exciting discovery in neuroanatomical tracing techniques involves the use of a chemical isolated from plants, a lectin termed *Phaseolus vulgaris* leucoagglutinin (Gerfen and Sawchenko 1984). This substance is taken up by nerve cell bodies and dendrites, but unlike some tracing methods, is not absorbed by fibers of passage. Following a simple histochemical treatment and reaction, the tracer can be visualized with both the light and electron microscopes, providing a detailed picture of the sites where a particular pathway terminates as well as a high-resolution view of the ultrastructure of the synaptic contacts made by the pathway as seen in the electron microscope.

In addition to these methods for tracing pathways in the brain, others have been developed that take advantage of the biochemical specificity of neurons. A chemical substance known as a neurotransmitter is released by neurons as a means of communicating with other cells, a process that we will discuss in detail in chapter 6. Some neurotransmitters react with formaldehyde vapor and turn a bright green or yellow when they are later exposed to ultraviolet light. Thus, by using this technique, neuroanatomists actually could see the neurons that contained these fluorescent neurotransmitters and could distinguish them from all other cells in the brain. This technique, first developed in Sweden by Falck and Hillarp (see Falck 1962; Falck et al. 1962), has become known as **histofluorescence** (also see color plate 3).

Histofluorescent staining of several nuclei in the rat brain that contain the transmitter serotonin is shown in figure 4.5. Primarily because of histofluorescent techniques, we now know that the vast majority of neurons containing serotonin are located in a group of nine nuclei along the deep central core of the brain, above the spinal cord but well below the cerebral hemispheres. This nuclear group is termed the **raphe nuclei,** and the neurons in these nuclei send axonal projections to widespread regions of the brain and spinal cord. Histofluorescent staining also has been used to map the location of neurons that contain some other neurotransmitters, including a group of chemicals known as catecholamines. Thus, histofluorescence has allowed neuroanatomists to identify biochemically specific classes of neurons as well as the distribution of their axons.

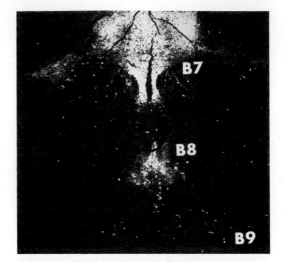

Figure 4.5 Fluorescence stain of neurons in the rat brain containing the neurotransmitter serotonin which occurs in three nuclei labeled B7, B8, and B9, also called the raphe nuclei. In the fluorescent technique used to reveal these biochemically specific neurons, tissue is freeze-dried, which produces the cracks that appear in the tissue.

Advances in molecular biology, particularly the application of methods in immunology, have resulted in even more gains in neuroanatomical methods (Polak and Van Noorden 1984). **Immunocytochemical techniques** are based on the specificity of the reaction between antigens and their corresponding antibodies. Antibodies can be raised in the blood of experimental animals (e.g., rabbits) by injecting them with an antigen (e.g., a foreign protein or peptide) that was obtained from the nerve cells that the investigator wishes to label. In the example shown in figure 4.6, immunocytochemical labeling was done to identify neurons containing the enzyme tyrosine hydroxylase. This enzyme is specific for catecholamines, and thus catecholamine-containing neurons can be seen very

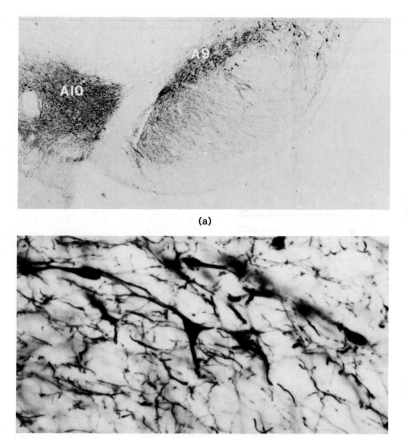

(a)

(b)

Figure 4.6 Dopaminergic neurons of substantia nigra pars compacta (A9) and the ventral tegmental area of Tsai (A10) in the rat immunocytochemically labeled with an antibody to tyrosine hydroxylase. (a) Low-magnification photomicrograph of the ventral mesencephalon showing tyrosine hydroxylase immunoreactive neurons and their processes. (b) Higher magnification photomicrograph of A9 neurons. The very fine, beaded processes are axons.

clearly against a faint and unlabeled background. In these images, the detailed structure of the neuron can be seen not unlike that available with the Golgi method, but with immunocytochemistry, only those neurons with the specific immunological and biochemical identity are labeled. Immunocytochemical techniques are now being used to study the morphology and projections of many classes of chemically specific nerve cells (also see color plates 2 and 3).

In the remainder of this chapter, the structures of the peripheral and central nervous systems, with special reference to human neuroanatomy, will be considered more completely. Keep in mind that much of this information is based on the various research techniques that we have just reviewed.

The Peripheral Nervous System

The major function of the peripheral nervous system is to carry information to and from the central nervous system. Thus, it can be viewed as an important network of communication channels (nerves) bringing information from the body as well as from the outside world and carrying out the commands of the central nervous system in executing various muscular and glandular activities. Peripheral nerves, therefore, can be classified into two basic types: **sensory** or **afferent** nerves, which carry sensory information toward the central nervous system, and **motor** or **efferent** nerves, which carry information away from the central nervous system out to muscles and glands. The majority of peripheral nerves enter and exit from the central nervous system through the spinal cord and are, therefore, termed **spinal nerves.** There are, however, twelve nerves on each side of the body that enter and exit from the brain directly and are therefore called **cranial nerves.**

The Cranial Nerves

Table 4.1 lists the twelve cranial nerves and their functions. These nerves serve the extremely important sensory and motor functions of the head and upper body. For example, the optic nerves (cranial nerve II) connect the

Table **4.1** The Twelve Cranial Nerves and Some of Their Major Functions

Number	Name	Function(s)	Number	Name	Function(s)
I	Olfactory nerve	Sensory fibers from the nose	IX	Glossopharyn- geal nerve	Sensory fibers from the taste buds Motor fibers to muscles of the throat and salivary glands
II	Optic nerve	Sensory fibers from the eyes			
III	Oculomotor nerve	Motor fibers controlling eye muscles	X	Vagus nerve	Sensory fibers from internal organs (e.g., gut) Motor fibers to muscles of the throat and to many internal organs (e.g., heart, blood vessels, gut, tear glands, etc.)
IV	Trochlear nerve	Motor fibers controlling eye muscles			
V	Trigeminal nerve	Sensory fibers from the skin of the head and from the teeth Motor fibers controlling the jaw muscles			
VI	Abducens nerve	Motor fibers controlling eye muscles	XI	Spinal accessory nerve	Sensory fibers from tissues of neck and shoulders Motor fibers to neck and shoulder muscles
VII	Facial nerve	Sensory fibers from the taste buds Motor fibers controlling the muscles of facial expression	XII	Hypoglossal nerve	Motor fibers to muscles of the tongue
VIII	Vestibulo- cochlear nerve	Sensory fibers from the ears			

retinas of the eyes to the brain. The vestibulocochlear nerves (cranial nerve VIII, sometimes called the auditory nerve), bring information into the brain from the ears and the semicircular canals. Destruction of these critical nerves will leave human beings and animal subjects blind or deaf, respectively. The facial nerves (cranial nerve VII) bring sensory information into the brain from the taste buds on the tongue and contain motor nerve fibers that control the muscles of facial expression. The trigeminal nerves (cranial nerve V) also contain both sensory and motor fibers, with sensory fibers bringing information into the brain from the teeth (this is the nerve that is anesthetized by dentists to prevent pain during

work on the teeth), and motor fibers that control the jaw muscles. The positions of entry and exit on the brain for the cranial nerves are shown in figure 4.7.

Somatic and Autonomic Divisions

The peripheral nervous system has two major divisions: the **somatic** division and the **autonomic** division. The **somatic division** carries sensory information to the central nervous system from the skin and musculature and contains motor fibers responsible for bodily movement. The **autonomic division** is responsible for visceral and glandular activity. Much research has centered on this division for many

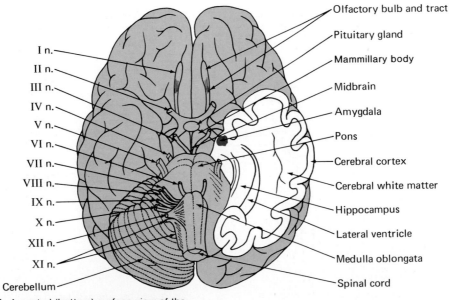

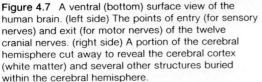

Figure 4.7 A ventral (bottom) surface view of the human brain. (left side) The points of entry (for sensory nerves) and exit (for motor nerves) of the twelve cranial nerves. (right side) A portion of the cerebral hemisphere cut away to reveal the cerebral cortex (white matter) and several other structures buried within the cerebral hemisphere.

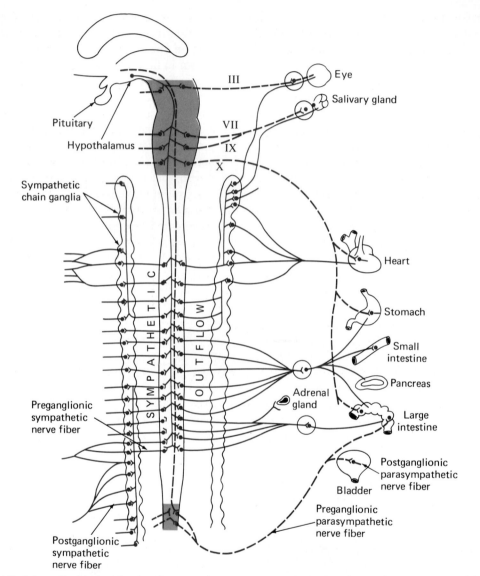

Figure 4.8 Schematic drawing showing the general arrangement of the autonomic nervous system: Sympathetic projections (solid lines) and parasympathetic projections (broken lines) to lower parts of the brain (note that the projections from the hypothalamus to the pituitary gland are omitted); portions of the brain stem and sacral region of the spinal cord from which the parasympathetic preganglionic fibers leave (shaded area); cranial nerves (Roman numerals); sympathetic outflow from the thoracic and upper lumbar regions (labeled); autonomic fibers to organs of the head and trunk (right-hand side); and the sympathetic outflow to blood vessels, sweat glands, and smooth muscle fibers attached to hairs (left-hand side).

years because of its relevance to emotional behavior. A schematic diagram of the autonomic division of the peripheral nervous system is shown in figure 4.8. Studies of the functions of the autonomic division of the peripheral nervous system have revealed that it also has two major divisions that are anatomically and functionally distinct: the **sympathetic branch** and the **parasympathetic branch.** As illustrated in figure 4.8, these two branches of the autonomic division enter and exit from the spinal cord and brain at different places and have different functions. An important anatomical difference between the two branches is that most fibers of the sympathetic division leaving the spinal cord synapse almost immediately in ganglia that lie in a long, interconnected chain called the **sympathetic ganglionic chain.** New axons then arise from the cells in these ganglia to carry information to a variety of target structures such as the heart, salivary glands, and digestive organs. Fibers of the parasympathetic branch do not synapse in a chain of ganglia, but rather synapse on other ganglia that lie near their targets, and new fibers travel short distances to carry this information to the target structures. Thus, **preganglionic** fibers of the sympathetic branch (i.e., fibers that synapse in the sympathetic chain) are generally short, and their **postganglionic** fibers (i.e., axons originating from cells in the ganglia) are fairly long. By contrast, preganglionic fibers of the parasympathetic branch are generally long, and postganglionic fibers are short. A final distinction of particular significance is that these two branches of the autonomic division utilize different chemical transmitter substances in making synaptic contact with their targets. Both sympathetic and parasympathetic preganglionic fibers (i.e., axons of neurons in the spinal cord that synapse in the sympathetic chain or the remote parasympathetic ganglia) are cholinergic, which is to say that acetylcholine is the chemical transmitter in their synaptic endings. However, most postganglionic fibers (those arising in the various ganglia and synapsing onto the target organs or glands) of the sympathetic division are adrenergic, utilizing norepinephrine as their transmitter substance. Postganglionic neurons of the parasympathetic division are cholinergic, like the preganglionic fibers.

The functions of the two branches of the autonomic division are for the most part antagonistic (act in opposition). Activation of the parasympathetic division, for example, slows the heart, increases the production of tears, promotes the activities of the digestive system, and in general acts to conserve energy and promote the vegetative functions of the body. Activation of the sympathetic division, on the other hand, speeds the heart, diverts blood from the digestive organs to the muscles, and in general prepares the body to cope with an emergency or with stress. The sympathetic division also activates the adrenal glands to release **epinephrine** (also called **adrenalin**) into the bloodstream, which complements and increases the effects of the sympathetic branch. The racing heart and other effects of epinephrine released from the adrenal glands are well-known accompaniments of stressful experiences such as automobile accidents. We will have more to say about the autonomic division of the peripheral nervous system in later chapters.

The Central Nervous System

The central nervous system, as we have noted previously, consists of the brain and spinal cord. During embryological development, the nervous system begins as a long, hollow tube along the back of the embryo. As the nervous system develops, the spinal cord maintains the basic tubular organization of the embryonic nervous system, while the brain develops into a large neural mass at the anterior (toward the head) end of the organism, its primitive tubular characteristic becoming extremely distorted. At birth, the original primitive organization of the brain is virtually unrecognizable because of its enormous growth and differentiation. These developmental changes are illustrated in figure 4.9.

Stages in the Development of the Human Brain

Several stages of development of the human brain are illustrated in figure 4.9. Early in the development of the embryo, the entire central nervous system resembles the spinal cord. It is an elongated, segmented tube that quickly begins to change shape and bulge into three major divisions: the **hindbrain,** which is the portion of the brain that will be adjacent to the spinal cord; the **midbrain,** which lies above the hindbrain; and the **forebrain,** which in human beings and other higher mammals gives rise to the bulging cerebral cortex of the fully developed brain. As the developing brain approaches maturity, the three divisions differentiate further, so that the mature brain has

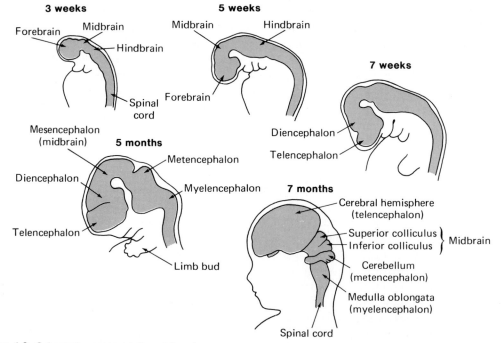

Figure 4.9 Schematic representation of the changes in form of the embryonic and fetal brain.

five major divisions: the hindbrain becomes the **myelencephalon** and **metencephalon;** the midbrain becomes the **mesencephalon;** and the forebrain becomes the **diencephalon** and **telencephalon.**

Studying the development of the brain has provided important clues regarding its organization. Many investigators are now correlating the emergence of various behaviors during development, such as certain sensory, motor, and cognitive skills, to changes that occur simultaneously in the organization of the brain.

The Spinal Cord

A schematic illustration of a cross section through the mature human spinal cord is shown in figure 4.10. Note the basic organization of the spinal cord, a thick tube with a small hollow center called the **central canal.** Also shown in the figure are the places where sensory information and motor information enter and leave the spinal cord respectively.

While the peripheral nerves usually contain both sensory and motor fibers, the two types of information are separated near the spinal cord. Sensory fibers enter the spinal cord by way of large bundles called **dorsal roots,** one dorsal root on each side for each spinal vertebra. The cell bodies from which these sensory nerve fibers originate form ganglia that are contained within spaces in the vertebral bones and are called dorsal root ganglia. The cell bodies of motor nerve fibers are found in the spinal cord and exit from it by way of large bundles termed **ventral roots.** Thus, one of the first principles of organization of the spinal cord (called the Bell-Magendie law after its discoverers as we described in chapter 1) is the segregation of entering sensory and exiting motor information.

The spinal cord is so arranged that neuron cell bodies are located in a butterfly-shaped center portion of the cord, while fibers carrying information to and from different segments of the spinal cord and the brain are located toward the outside. The center portion

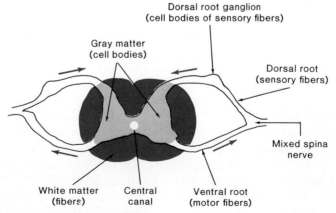

Figure 4.10 A diagrammatic cross section through the spinal cord. Sensory information enters by way of the dorsal roots and motor information exits by way of the ventral roots.

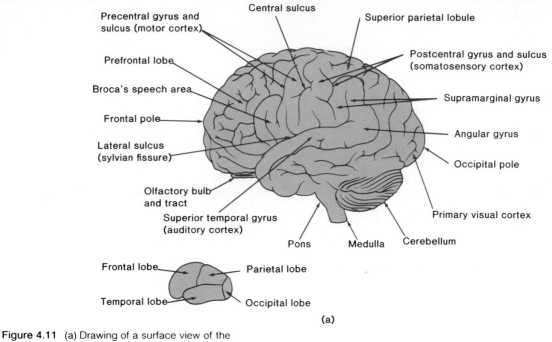

Figure 4.11   (a) Drawing of a surface view of the human brain. (b) Drawing of a midsagittal section through the human brain.

is called gray matter (cell bodies and dendrites as well as some axons are unmyelinated and appear gray in color), whereas the outer area containing nerve fibers is called white matter (myelin appears whitish compared to cell bodies). At the very center of the spinal cord is the central canal, which contains a clear fluid, the **cerebrospinal fluid.**

The spinal cord not only relays information to and from the brain but is also capable of certain types of behaviors independent of the brain—the **spinal reflexes,** some of which involve fairly complicated connections within the spinal cord. It is of particular interest that a great deal of our current theoretical understanding of the ways in which the brain produces behavior depends upon fundamental

assumptions first derived from studying spinal reflexes and the neuronal connections that produce these simple elements of behavior. Spinal reflexes are discussed in chapter 9.

The Brain

The brain forms the greatest bulk of the central nervous system and is responsible for the myriad sensory, motor, and integrative functions that underlie perception, thought, motivation, and behavior.

A surface view of the human brain is illustrated in figure 4.11*a,* along with a schematic view of the four lobes of the cerebral cortex: the **frontal, parietal, temporal,** and **occipital** lobes. Note that the cerebral hemi-

sulcus (sul'kus)
gyrus (ji'rus)

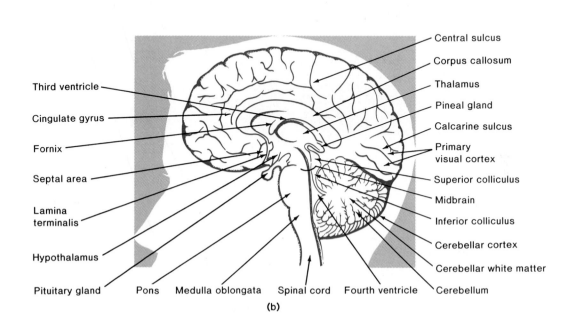

Third ventricle

Cingulate gyrus

Fornix

Septal area

Lamina
terminalis

Hypothalamus

Pituitary gland

Central sulcus

Corpus callosum

Thalamus

Pineal gland

Calcarine sulcus

Primary
visual cortex

Superior colliculus

Midbrain

Inferior colliculus

Cerebellar cortex

Cerebellar white matter

Pons   Medulla oblongata   Spinal cord   Fourth ventricle   Cerebellum

(b)

spheres virtually cover the entire brain, and the cerebral cortex is highly convoluted, consisting of grooves (called **sulci**) that penetrate the hemispheres and of bumps (called **gyri**). Only about one-third of the surface of the cerebral hemispheres is visible, and the other two-thirds are buried within the sulci. Each **sulcus** and each **gyrus** of the brain is named (some of these designations are shown in figure 4.11*a*). Note the cerebellum behind and beneath the cerebral hemispheres. The cortex of the cerebellum is also highly convoluted like the cerebral cortex, but the convolutions are smaller and more regular. In the cerebellar cortex, the protrusions or long bumps are called folia (singular, **folium**), rather than gyri.

A cross section dividing the brain into right and left halves, termed a **midsagittal section,** in which some of the prominent internal structures of the brain are illustrated is shown in figure 4.11*b* and in color plate 1. These structures are discussed in more detail next.

Ventricles of the Brain
As it develops, the brain begins as a tubelike structure with a hollow center. This hollow center becomes extremely distorted as development proceeds, becoming the ventricles of the brain illustrated in the schematic diagram in figure 4.12 and in color plate 4. The ventricles are cavities within the brain and are filled with fluid that is called the **cerebrospinal**

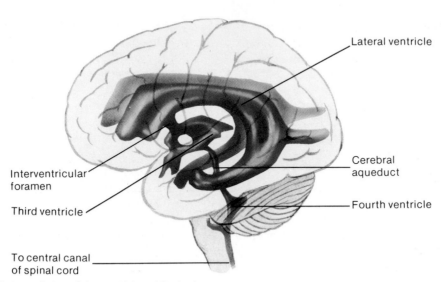

Figure 4.12 Lateral view of the ventricles of the brain.

fluid. This fluid medium of the nervous system acts in part as a shock absorber for the brain and also as a communication channel for nutrients and other substances. The cerebrospinal fluid is manufactured by specialized tissue termed the **choroid plexus,** which is located along the walls of the ventricles. As shown in figure 4.12, there are two large ventricles on either side of the cerebral hemispheres that are called the lateral ventricles. These two large cavities wrap around within the hemispheres to form the anterior and inferior horns of the lateral ventricles. The lateral ventricles are connected to the third ventricle by the **foramen of Monro.** The third ventricle is, in turn, interconnected with the most posterior cavity of the brain, the fourth ventricle, by a narrow tubelike passageway, the cerebral aqueduct.

In addition to the fluid-filled ventricles of the brain, the brain is also protected by its suspension in cerebrospinal fluid that circulates around it. Several membranes also cover the brain, such as the tough outer skin called the **dura mater** and an inner membrane that closely adheres to the surface of the brain, the **pia mater.**

Medulla Oblongata
The spinal cord merges into the brain to form the most posterior (that is, furthest toward the tail of the animal or rear of the brain) division of the vertebrate brain, the **medulla oblongata,** or simply the medulla, as shown in schematic coronal cross sections in figure 4.13a–c. Near the spinal cord, the medulla in cross section resembles the spinal cord very closely. For example, the central canal is still visible at the center of the cross section, with fiber tracts (white matter) running along the outside (e.g., **fasiculus gracilis** and **fasiculus cuneatus, spinocerebellar tracts,** and **spinothalamic**

lemniscus (lem-nis′kus)
pyramidal decussation (pi-ram′ı-dal de′′kus-sa′shun)
tegmentum (teg-men′tum)
peduncle (pe-dung′k′l)

tracts). Just above this level, several prominent nuclei such as the **nucleus gracilis** and the **nucleus cuneatus,** appear. They are synaptic relay nuclei for spinal tracts (fasciculus gracilis and fasciculus cuneatus) carrying touch, pressure, and other sensory information from the skin and body. The nuclei, in turn, send fibers on to higher levels in two prominent fiber bundles called the **medial lemnisci,** one medial **lemniscus** on each side. All tracts connecting the brain with the spinal cord must pass through the medulla.

Other prominent nuclei in the medulla include several that initiate in (motor nuclei) or receive information from (sensory nuclei) cranial nerves (some of the important functions of cranial nerves are outlined in table 4.1 and figure 4.8). One particularly large nucleus that appears in the anterior medulla is the inferior olivary nucleus, the principal projection of which leads to the cerebellum.

Two extremely large bundles of nerve fibers arising in the cerebral hemispheres and traveling to the spinal cord are the pyramids, or the **corticospinal tracts,** important in producing voluntary movement. Note, as is often the case in naming fiber bundles in the nervous system, the term corticospinal is a combination of the word indicating the origin (cortico or cortex) and the word indicating the destination (spinal cord) of the tract. As the corticospinal tracts near the spinal cord, they cross over the midline; therefore, information arising on the left side of the cerebral cortex commands movements on the right side of the body and vice versa. It is for this reason that individuals suffering a stroke or other damage to one side of the cerebral cortex show the effects on the opposite side of the body. The point of crossover is termed the **pyramidal decussation.**

At the core of the medulla is the central and periventricular gray matter, a dense group of cell bodies that surrounds the central canal and forms the floor (called **tegmentum**) of the fourth ventricle. Surrounding this region of gray matter is the **reticular formation,** which makes up the large central region on both sides of the medulla.

Pons and Midbrain

Just anterior to the medulla is the **pons** and in front of it is the midbrain. Lying on top of the pons is the **cerebellum,** which was illustrated in the midsagittal section of the human brain shown in figure 4.11*b.* The cerebellum is involved in motor coordination, and its removal in humans produces uncoordinated, jerky movement. Like the cerebral hemispheres, the cerebellum has a cortex (covering) of gray matter and an underlay of white matter. At the very center of the cerebellum are the deep cerebellar nuclei (not visible in midsagittal section), which serve in part to relay information from the cerebellar cortex to the rest of the brain.

The pons and midbrain are shown in schematic coronal sections in figure 4.13*d–g* (the cerebellum was removed and does not appear here). A number of tracts seen in the medulla are still visible at this level of the brain, including the corticospinal tracts, medial lemnisci, and spinothalamic tracts. Several new fiber bundles appear at this level, including the inferior, middle, and superior **cerebellar peduncles,** which carry information between the cerebellum and the rest of the brain. The word **peduncle** is used here to mean "large bundle of fibers." The three cerebellar peduncles are named for their positions along the brain. The

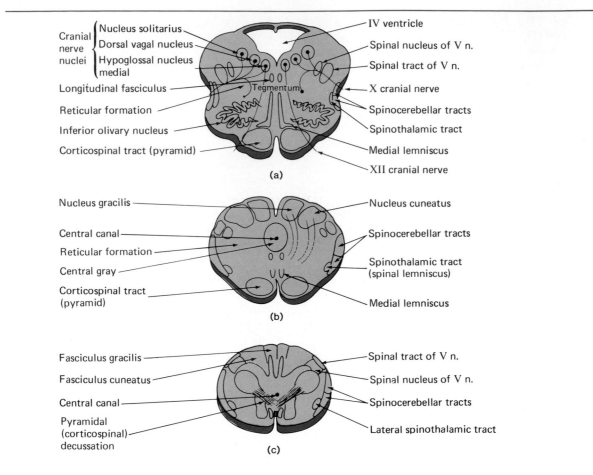

Figure 4.13 Schematic drawings of coronal cross sections of the brain. (a) Section near the top of the medulla. (b) Section in the middle of the medulla. (c) Section through the medulla at a level near the spinal cord. (d) Coronal section through the midbrain. The cerebellum, which lies on top of the pons, is not shown. (e, f, and g) Drawings of coronal sections through the pons.

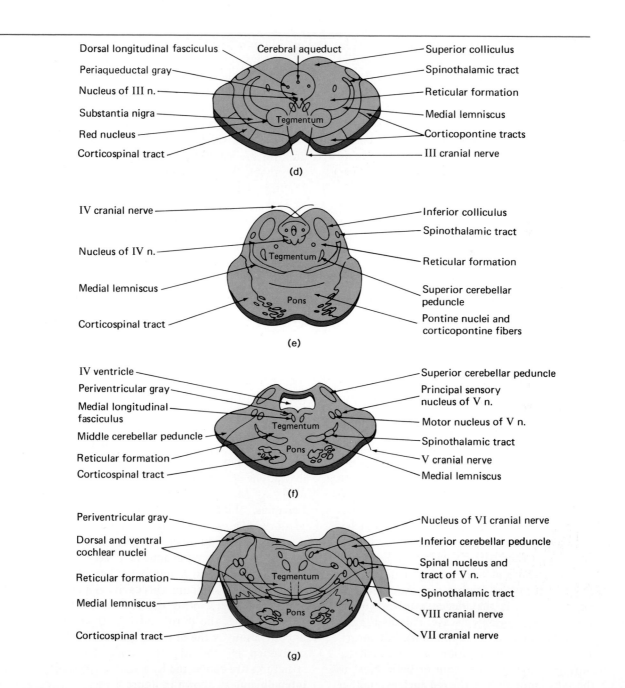

Dorsal longitudinal fasciculus
Periaqueductal gray
Nucleus of III n.
Substantia nigra
Red nucleus
Corticospinal tract
Cerebral aqueduct
Tegmentum
Superior colliculus
Spinothalamic tract
Reticular formation
Medial lemniscus
Corticopontine tracts
III cranial nerve

(d)

IV cranial nerve
Nucleus of IV n.
Medial lemniscus
Corticospinal tract
Tegmentum
Pons
Inferior colliculus
Spinothalamic tract
Reticular formation
Superior cerebellar
peduncle
Pontine nuclei and
corticopontine fibers

(e)

IV ventricle
Periventricular gray
Medial longitudinal
fasciculus
Middle cerebellar peduncle
Reticular formation
Corticospinal tract
Tegmentum
Pons
Superior cerebellar peduncle
Principal sensory
nucleus of V n.
Motor nucleus of V n.
Spinothalamic tract
V cranial nerve
Medial lemniscus

(f)

Periventricular gray
Dorsal and ventral
cochlear nuclei
Reticular formation
Medial lemniscus
Corticospinal tract
Tegmentum
Pons
Nucleus of VI cranial nerve
Inferior cerebellar peduncle
Spinal nucleus and
tract of V n.
Spinothalamic tract
VIII cranial nerve
VII cranial nerve

(g)

corticopontine tracts are also prominent in these sections and carry fibers originating in the cerebral cortex and destined for the pons.

Also notable in the cross sections shown in figure 4.13*d–g* are a number of cranial nerve nuclei sending or receiving information from cranial nerves V, VI, VII, and VIII. The **dorsal** and **ventral cochlear nuclei** are the receiving stations for information arriving from the ears in the vestibulocochlear nerve (n VIII). The fourth **ventricle** is also obvious in the pons, but narrows to become the **cerebral aqueduct** in the midbrain, which connects the fourth ventricle to the third ventricle further anteriorly. The large bulge of the pons obvious in the midsagittal section in figure 4.11*b* consists mostly of axons, including the corticospinal tracts and corticopontine tracts.

In addition to ascending and descending fiber systems that interconnect higher and lower levels of the brain and spinal cord, the midbrain also contains several very large nuclei that are not apparent in sections made at lower levels. On the dorsal surface (top) of the midbrain are prominent bumps called the **inferior** and **superior colliculi,** one of each on both sides of the brain, which are named for their relative positions. The inferior **colliculus** is an important auditory relay station, receiving information from both the superior olivary nuclei and the dorsal and ventral cochlear nuclei. The superior colliculus is a visual relay station and is concerned with a variety of reflexive visual functions and with visual attention. Near the bottom of the midbrain is the **substantia nigra,** a nucleus that degenerates in human victims of **Parkinson's disease.** This disease has a number of different symptoms, but invariably involves deterioration of movement resulting in rigidity or tremor or both. Next to the substantia nigra is the **red nucleus,** another important motor nucleus in the brain that sends its commands to the spinal cord.

On each side, forming the central core of the pons and midbrain, is the **reticular formation**—often called the **pontine reticular formation** in the pons and **midbrain reticular formation** in the midbrain. Thus, the reticular formation creates the central core of the brain stem on both sides all the way from the medulla to the midbrain. We will have more to say about the reticular formation in later chapters, but for now it is of interest to note that this network of cells and fibers is importantly involved in sleep and wakefulness, attention, and other functions. The entire brain stem as seen from a lateral perspective is shown in figure 4.14*a* and from the top when the cerebral hemispheres and the cerebellum are removed in figure 4.14*b.* Several structures visible from these views are labeled. It is particularly instructive to compare the positions of these structures with their positions in the coronal sections shown in figure 4.13 and with their positions in the midsagittal section of the brain shown in figure 4.11*b.*

Thalamus and Hypothalamus

As you ascend to higher levels of the brain, it expands somewhat, as you can see in the illustrations of the brain stem shown in figure 4.14. At the top of the brain stem is the **thalamus,** which is divided into left and right sections. The two sides are interconnected by a large bundle of fibers termed the **massa intermedia.** The cerebral aqueduct becomes the third ventricle, and a number of prominent nuclear groups surround this cavity. The thalamus, therefore, forms the roof and lateral (side) walls of the third ventricle. Below the hypothalamus is the **pituitary gland,** which is controlled by the hypothalamus. The two structures are connected by a stalk termed the **infundibulum** as shown in figure 4.16.

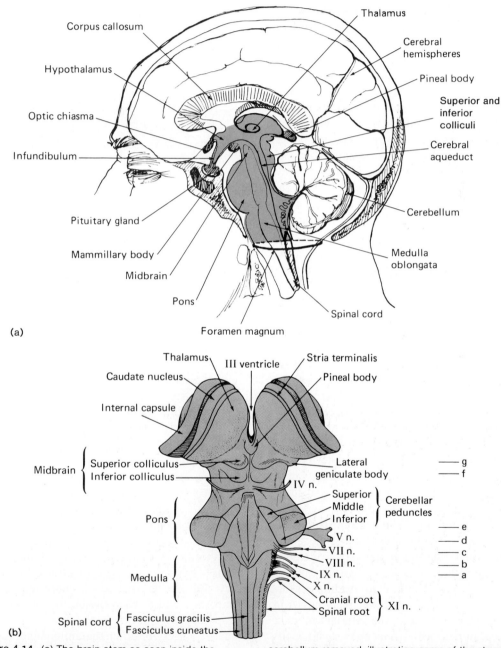

(a)

(b)

Figure 4.14 (a) The brain stem as seen inside the skull from a lateral perspective. Note that it ascends from the spinal cord and lies buried beneath the cerebral hemispheres. (b) Drawing of a dorsal view of the brain stem with the cerebral hemispheres and cerebellum removed, illustrating some of the structures described in the text and shown in coronal or sagittal sections in previous figures. The letters *a* through *g* illustrate the positions of the coronal sections shown in figure 4.13.

The thalamus, illustrated schematically beneath the cerebral hemispheres in figure 4.15 and shown previously with the hemispheres removed in figure 4.14*b,* contains a variety of nuclei, some of which are identified in figure 4.15. The arrows illustrate one of the most important functions of the thalamus, its role as a relay station for information arriving from the sense organs and lower regions of the brain. These incoming fibers make synaptic connections in the thalamus, and the information they carry is transferred by thalamic projections to the cerebral cortex. Most of the nuclei of the thalamus are named in accord with their relative position within the thalamus. The **ventral anterior nucleus,** for example, is near the bottom (ventral) and toward the front (anterior) of the thalamus, and the **dorsomedial nucleus** is on top (dorsal) and toward the midline (medial) of the thalamus.

Some of the nuclei of the thalamus are primarily responsible for relaying sensory information to the cerebral cortex and comprise the specific **sensory relay nuclei.** Sensory information from the retinas, the photoreceptor organs located at the back of the eyeballs, for example, is carried by the optic nerves (cranial nerve II) to the **lateral geniculate nuclei** of the thalamus, one lateral geniculate nucleus being on each side of the brain. After synapse in the lateral geniculate nuclei, visual information is sent by neuron axons in these nuclei to the visual areas of the cerebral cortex located in the occipital lobes. Removal of any one of these structures (optic nerves or tracts, lateral geniculate nuclei, or visual cortex) leaves the human being blind. Auditory information that comes from lower relay nuclei in the brain stem, such as the inferior colliculi, synapses in the **medial geniculate nuclei.** Cells

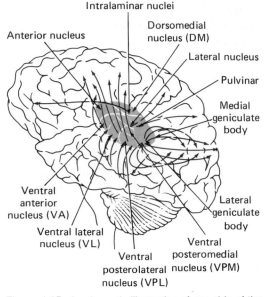

Figure 4.15 A schematic illustration of one side of the thalamus showing some of its connections with the cerebral cortex. Most of the nuclei of the thalamus are named for their relative position within the thalamus.

in these specific sensory relay nuclei of the thalamus send information to auditory areas of the cerebral cortex. Similar nuclei, termed collectively the **ventrobasal complex** because there are several nuclei, relay somatic sensory information such as touch, heat, and pressure. There is also a relay system in the thalamus for the sense of taste, but apparently not for the sense of smell. For the sense of smell, information seems to reach portions of the cerebral cortex without involving a relay through the specific sensory relay nuclei of the thalamus. The anatomical organization of the sensory systems is treated in more detail in chapters 7 and 8 when the brain's processing of sensory information is discussed.

A variety of other thalamic nuclei relay information to regions of the cerebral cortex

hypothalamus (hi''po-thal'ah-mus)
caudate (kaw'dāt)
putamen (pu-ta'men)
globus pallidus (glo'bus pal'ı-dus)

that are not involved in the receipt of specific sensory information, such as the motor cortex and association cortex nuclei that we can call **association nuclei.** Still other nuclei do not send information to the cerebral cortex, but, rather, connect entirely within the thalamus. Called the **intrinsic nuclei** of the thalamus, these nuclei have been implicated, along with a variety of other structures, in the production of sleep and of certain characteristics on the **electroencephalogram** (EEG). A final important point must be made with regard to the thalamus. Much of its function can be said to act as a relay station because it receives information from sensory systems and lower regions of the brain and then appears to relay the information to the cerebral cortex. In addition, some return connections from the cerebral cortex to the thalamus make the relations between the thalamus and the cortex reciprocal. Still other loops between the thalamus and lower structures are known to exist, all of which suggests that the thalamus is not only an important relay station, but also a place where a significant amount of integration of information occurs.

Although it is no larger than a kidney bean, the **hypothalamus,** lying at the base of the brain and forming the floor of the third ventricle, contains many nuclei that are involved in a wide range of behavioral functions. The hypothalamus is critical in such diverse behavioral functions as sexual behavior, hunger, thirst, sleep, maintenance of water and salt balance in the body, and temperature regulation. The hypothalamus controls the pituitary gland and, in part, the autonomic nervous system (see fig. 4.8). Thus, its activities are intimately associated with reproductive behavior, emotional behavior, and myriad functions of the endocrine glands that are

responsive to the hormones released by the pituitary gland (see chap. 11). The hypothalamus and the pituitary gland are illustrated schematically in a sagittal section in figure 4.16. Note that the hypothalamus is connected to the pituitary gland in two ways.

There are neural connections between the hypothalamus and the posterior portion of the pituitary gland (called the posterior lobe). The two structures are also connected by a special system of blood vessels (hypophysial portal system) that exists between the hypothalamus and the anterior portion of the pituitary gland (termed the anterior lobe). Some of the nuclei of the hypothalamus are labeled in figure 4.16. These nuclei and others not shown in this midsagittal view are discussed in greater detail in later chapters.

Cerebral Hemispheres

The cerebral hemispheres, as previous figures indicate, virtually cover the rest of the brain because of their enormous size (see color plates 1 and 4). In addition to their outer covering, the hemispheres comprise several large nuclear groups and layers, the cerebral cortex and its underlying white matter. Buried within the cerebral hemispheres are three large nuclei: the **caudate nucleus, putamen,** and **globus pallidus.** These large nuclei receive information from the cerebral cortex as well as from lower regions of the brain such as the substantia nigra and thalamus. Collectively, the caudate nucleus, putamen, and globus pallidus are termed the **basal ganglia** (see color plate 4). (Sharp readers will note from our vocabulary section that the term "ganglia" is inappropriate for a brain structure; nuclei is the correct term. Unfortunately, the neuroanatomists

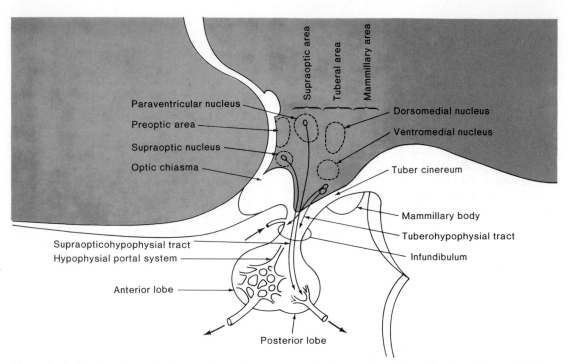

Figure 4.16 A schematic sagittal section through the hypothalamus and pituitary gland illustrating some of the hypothalamic areas and nuclei and their projections to the pituitary. The lateral hypothalamic region is not shown in this section, but would be found behind the ventromedial nucleus in this view.

who first named this structure did not pay much attention to proper terminology.)

The basal ganglia play an important role in movement. Recall, for example, that the substantia nigra, which is involved in the motor impairment seen in Parkinson's disease, sends many of its axons to the basal ganglia. The basal ganglia and their connections in the brain are affected in many motor diseases of the nervous system, several of which will be described in chapter 15. The basal ganglia also appear to play a role in directing or guiding movement according to the sensory information that these structures receive from other brain areas. Thus, the basal ganglia may not be exclusively motor, but rather may be integrative in that they help to shape a particular motor response based on available sensory input.

On one side of the basal ganglia (the inside toward the center of the brain) is the thalamus, while the lateral ventricle is on the outside surface, one lateral ventricle in each hemisphere. Recall that the lateral ventricles are the most distorted derivatives of the hollow center of the tubelike embryonic nervous system, and, like the third and fourth ventricles and the central canal of the spinal cord, are filled with cerebrospinal fluid.

As noted and illustrated previously, the outer layer of the cerebral hemispheres is the highly convoluted cerebral cortex. Beneath it, the cerebral white matter interconnects various regions of the cerebral cortex, the thalamus and other lower regions of the brain. The cerebral cortex is composed of layers of cells and their fibers. Most of the cerebral cortex

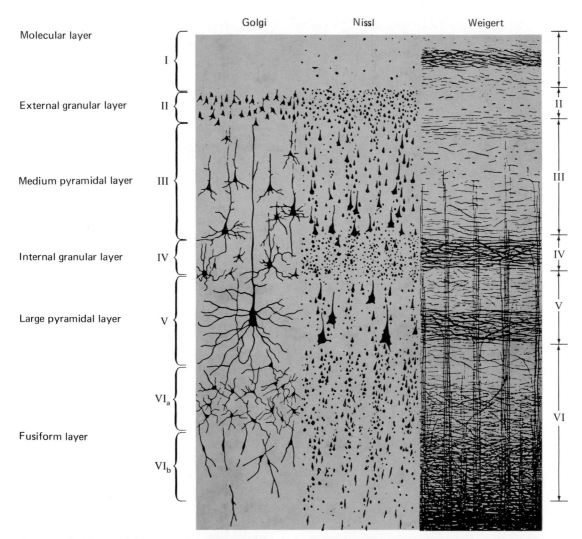

Figure 4.17 A cross section (highly magnified) of the cerebral cortex illustrating its six layers and the cell groups and fibers that comprise them using several different staining methods.

contains six distinct layers, although some regions may have several layers or no layers at all. The cell layers and arrangements of fibers entering or leaving these layers are illustrated in figure 4.17, a highly magnified cross section through the cerebral cortex (actually only about 2 millimeters thick), in which different staining techniques, including the Golgi stain,

the Nissl stain, and the Weigert stain, were used to illustrate different features of the six cortical layers. The thickness of different layers can vary considerably according to the function of the cortical region through which a cross section is taken. Axons from the specific sensory relay nuclei of the thalamus, for example, make synaptic contact with cortical

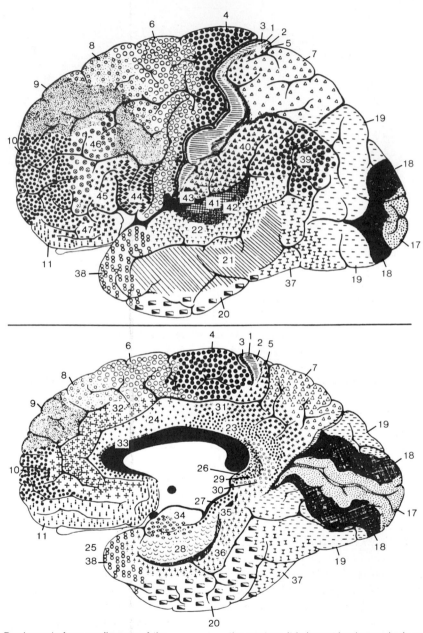

Figure 4.18 Brodmann's famous diagram of the cerebral cortex illustrating regions of the cortex distinguished on the basis of their cytoarchitectonic organization. Although completed around the turn of the century, it is becoming increasingly apparent that these cytoarchitectonic distinctions can be related to the localization of function over the surface of the cerebral cortex.

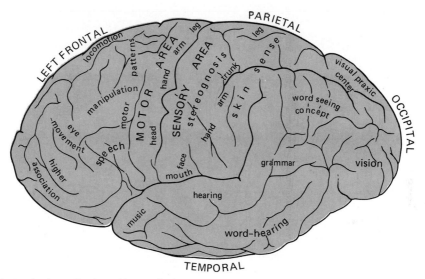

Figure 4.19 Lateral schematic view of human brain showing functional localization (× two-thirds).

cells primarily in layers 3 and 4. Thus, cortical sensory areas tend to have enlarged third and fourth layers when compared to other regions of the cortex. It has been known since before the turn of the century that the functions of the cerebral cortex are, to a significant degree, localized over its surface. Brodmann's early numerical delineation of the cytoarchitectonic variation evident between different regions of the cerebral cortex was particularly prophetic. His early map of the cytoarchitectonic variation over the surface of the cerebral cortex is shown in figure 4.18. By carefully examining differences in the occurrence of different cell types, the thickness of various layers and other features of the cerebral cortex, Brodmann divided it into many numbered regions. Today, findings increasingly indicate this early cytoarchitectonic map corresponds to differences in cellular function localized over the cortical surface.

There can be little doubt that the cerebral cortex is in large measure responsible for the attributes that make us uniquely human, such as the capability to use language and to engage in abstract thought. Thus, an important focus in brain research is to understand the functions of the cerebral cortex and the mechanisms that underlie these important functions. Many aspects of this goal are touched on in later chapters. One particularly fascinating and provocative rendition of the localization of function on the cerebral hemispheres is given in figure 4.19 which is from a classic textbook on neurology. Although it is inaccurate in some respects, this drawing nevertheless gives the feeling of the complexity inherent in human and animal behavior and serves to emphasize the role of the brain, especially of the cerebral hemispheres, in perception, thought, emotion, language, and, indeed, all human behavior.

*Functional Microstructure
of the Cerebral Cortex*

Far from being a homogeneous mass of neurons laid out in a big, convoluted sheet over the hemispheres, the cerebral cortex is actually subdivided into a "mosaic of quasi-discrete space units" (Szentágothai 1978; cf. Eccles 1979). These discrete units are actually semi-independent modules or columns having a width of about 250 microns. It is now apparent that the activities of the nerve cells within one of these discrete modules are related to one another both functionally and anatomically. It is currently believed that there are about 2,500 neurons in a module, and about 1,000 of these are cortical pyramidal cells. In the human neocortex there are approximately four million of these modules (Eccles 1979), so the opportunity exists for vast and complex spatial and temporal patterns of activity among them. Further subdivisions of these modules have also been postulated (Mountcastle 1978). Specific examples of discrete functional modules within the cerebral cortex will be discussed again in several subsequent chapters (chaps. 7, 8, and 9).

An important lesson we have learned in the past decade about the anatomy of the cerebral cortex is that the functional connections of specific regions of the cerebral cortex are not immutable. Rather, connections can be made and broken depending upon the functional demands made on particular regions of the cortex. For example, a certain portion of the cerebral cortex is devoted to receiving sensory information from the hands. Within this area of the neocortex, information from the surface of each digit is received by a different, discrete area. There is a distorted map of the hand where information from each part of it is received. If one of the fingers is amputated, the area previously receiving information from the finger becomes receptive to information from the other fingers surrounding the one that was lost (Merzenich et al. 1984). This kind of reorganization can occur in other sensory modalities and need not involve permanent loss of sensation (Jay and Sparks 1984).

Imaging the Living Brain

The techniques for visualizing the structure of nerve cells and the brain that we have discussed so far can only be used with tissue specimens postmortem, fixed and stained for microscopic examination. Important advances in the fields of biophysics, nuclear medicine, and computer technology have made it possible to obtain images of the brain in living subjects. There are three techniques now available for noninvasive imaging of the living brain. These are **computer-assisted axial tomography** (sometimes termed a CAT scan), **positron emission tomography** (usually called a PET scan), and **nuclear magnetic resonance imaging** (NMR). All three of these imaging methods are based upon computer-assisted reconstruction of many individual images obtained from different planes through the brain. In a CAT scan, the individual images are obtained by passing X rays through the head. A narrow X-ray beam is emitted by a source on one side of the head, and a detector measures the number of X-ray photons that emerge on the other side. This is like a conventional X ray except that many different sections through the brain are obtained.

A PET scan is similar to a CAT scan except that the signal arises from the decay of a radioisotope that has been injected into the patient's circulation (see color plate 8). A distinct advantage of this method is that the radioisotope can be linked to glucose, the

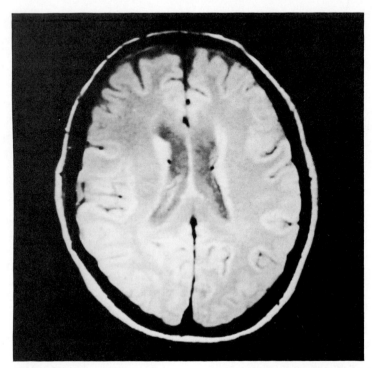

Figure 4.20 One section in the horizontal plane of a
nuclear magnetic resonance image of a patient whose
brain appears normal at this level—about halfway
through the cerebral hemispheres. The dark shapes at
the center are the lateral ventricles. The sulci of the
cerebral cortex are slightly widened due to the
advanced age of this patient (seventy-year-old female).
The white oval border around the image is the scalp
and tissue under it. The interior black border is the
skull.

principal metabolic fuel of the brain. Since the
local utilization of glucose is proportional to
the activity of a given brain region, the ongoing activity can be visualized as the brain
functions. Thus, if the patient is instructed to
listen to music, the region of the cerebral cortex
responsible for receiving and interpreting auditory sensation becomes active and is prom-
inently seen in the PET-scan image. Similarly,
regions of the brain showing abnormal activity, such as epileptic foci, or regions showing
abnormally low activity, such as occurs with
stroke or other brain damage, can be seen
clearly.

In nuclear magnetic resonance imaging,
advantage is taken of the fact that the nuclei
of atoms in the brain respond to magnetic fields
differentially, depending upon their local
atomic environment. By exposing the head to
magnetic fields of different strengths, a
computer-assisted three-dimensional image of
the brain can be obtained. One example of a
section and NMR scan is shown in figure 4.20.
The lateral ventricles, seen as dark shapes toward the center of the brain, are clearly visible
in this image. Also visible are the convolutions
of the cerebral cortex, widened somewhat with
age since this subject was a seventy-year-old
woman.

Summary

The nervous system consists of two divisions: the **central nervous system,** which comprises the brain and the spinal cord, and the **peripheral nervous system,** which includes all nervous tissue outside the central nervous system. A variety of techniques have been developed to study the structure of the nervous system. Experimental methods, such as **retrograde** and **anterograde degeneration** techniques, are used in conjunction with specific lesions of the brain by such neurotoxins as kainic acid to reveal interconnections between various regions of the nervous system. Other means used to trace interconnections include axonal transport methods, such as anterograde or retrograde transport of **horseradish peroxidase,** *Phaseolus vulgaris* **leucoagglutinin,** and **autoradiography.**

The structure of individual nerve cells can be revealed using the Golgi stain. Selective stains have been developed in order to identify neurons having a specific biochemical identity, such as the **histofluorescent** techniques in which neurons containing dopamine, norepinephrine, or serotonin can be identified. More powerful **immunocytochemical** techniques have also been developed in which antibodies to specific neuronal antigens can be used to label specific cell groups.

The peripheral nervous system carries information to and from the central nervous system. It consists of afferent nerves (carrying information toward the central nervous system) and efferent nerves (carrying information away from the central nervous system). **Spinal nerves** enter and exit from the spinal cord, while the **cranial nerves** enter and exit directly from the brain. Bodily sensation and movement utilize the **somatic division** of the peripheral nervous system, whereas glandular and emotional responses are mediated by the **autonomic division.** The autonomic division is further divided into two functional divisions. One of these, the **sympathetic division,** mediates bodily and emotional responses to stress, while the other, the **parasympathetic division,** is involved in processes that conserve bodily and emotional energy.

The central nervous system develops from a primitive, tubelike embryonic nervous system into the brain and spinal cord. Even when fully developed, the central nervous system still maintains this basic tubular organization, although the fluid-filled center of the tube becomes tremendously distorted as different parts of the brain enlarge and change shape. The spinal cord relays information to and from the brain. Incoming information enters through the **dorsal roots,** while outgoing information leaves by way of the **ventral roots.** The central gray matter of the spinal cord provides for neuronal interconnections and mediates the spinal reflexes. The lowest division of the brain, the **medulla oblongata,** is similar in many ways to the spinal cord, with gray matter nearer the center and fibers running along its outer regions. The **pons** also maintains this basic organization, in which the central core of the brain on both sides consists of the reticular formation. A number of important sensory and motor nuclei are found throughout the medulla and pons, including some of the cranial nerve nuclei. Organization of the **cerebellum,** important in motor coordination, is different from that of the brain stem and spinal cord since neuronal cell bodies form a gray-matter covering over the cerebellum and the cerebellar nuclei are contained nearer the center. This type of organization, in which cell bodies form a cover (cortex), is also characteristic of the cerebral hemispheres that are covered by the cerebral cortex. The cerebral cortex consists of layers of cell bodies and associated fibers, with cerebral white matter beneath the cortex. At the center of the hemispheres are the important motor structures, the **basal ganglia.** Information is relayed to the cerebral cortex in part by the **thalamus.** The **hypothalamus,** which lies below the thalamus at the base of the brain, controls the autonomic nervous system and appears to be involved in many "motivated" or "emotional" behaviors. The cerebral cortex is divided into areas according to their cytoarchitecture and function. These regions can be further subdivided into columns or modules, each approximately 250 microns across and each having some anatomical and functional identity. These functional and anatomical units of the cerebral cortex retain a plasticity that allows them to change in response to the sensory and motor demands that are placed on them.

Suggested Readings

Carpenter, M. B. 1985. *Core text of neuroanatomy.* 3d ed. Baltimore: Williams & Wilkins.
This is an excellent paperback textbook of neuroanatomy with special descriptions of clinical syndromes resulting from various forms of brain damage. A very useful book that provides a concise but coherent picture of the organization of the nervous system.

Nauta, W. J. H., and M. Feirtag. 1986. *Fundamental neuroanatomy.* New York: W. H. Freeman.
This paperback text on neuroanatomy is an excellent one written by one of the pioneers in the field of neuroanatomy (Nauta) and an editor for Scientific American *(Feirtag). It is beautifully illustrated and highly informative.*

Netter, F. H. 1953. *The Ciba collection of medical illustrations (Vol. 1, Nervous system).* Summit, N. J.: Ciba Pharmaceutical Co.
Although over two decades old, this is a remarkable collection of illustrations of the human nervous system and various pathologies of the brain, spinal cord, and associated structures whose beautiful illustrations were painted by Dr. Netter, a physician and well-known illustrator.

Noback, C. R., and R. J. Demarest. 1972. *The nervous system: Introduction and review.* New York: McGraw-Hill Book Co.
This is another brief paperback emphasizing the organization of the human nervous system. This book has informative illustrations.

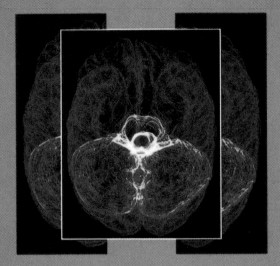

Outline

Introduction

Neurons are electrically excitable cells. Indeed, communication between cells in the brain is electrochemical in nature and can take several different forms. In some cases, the electrical signals produced by nerve cells are large, all-or-none events termed action potentials. The axon of nerve cells is specialized to carry these signals from one site to another in the nervous system. In other cases, the electrical response of a nerve cell is small and is related to the amount of stimulation that the neuron receives. All types of electrical activity in the nervous system depend upon the relative distribution of the electrically charged particles, termed ions, found inside and outside the membranes of nerve cells.

In this chapter, we discuss the basis for the electrical activity of nerve cells. We begin our discussion with a description of the electrical potential that exists across the membrane of nerve cells—the membrane potential. Variations in the membrane potential form the basis for all electrical signals that occur in the nervous system.

Chapter

5

Electrical Activity of the Brain

The Membrane Potential

Neurons, like other animal and plant cells, are electrically charged like a battery. The inside of the nerve cell, and of other cells also, is negatively charged, while the "positive pole" is the outside of the cell, as illustrated schematically in figure 5.1. Just as the voltage of a battery can be measured by means of a voltmeter, the voltage across the nerve cell membrane also can be measured by connecting the inside of the cell to the outside of the cell using a voltmeter (usually an oscilloscope). As shown in figure 5.1, connection is usually accomplished by penetrating the cell with a thin, very sharp **electrode,** which consists of a glass tube filled with salt water so that it conducts electricity. Because of its small size, this device is called a **microelectrode.** Since the potential or voltage exists only *across* the cell membrane—that is, between the inside and the outside of the cell—it is called the **membrane potential.** Although the membrane potential shown in the figure was recorded across the membrane of an axon, the potential also is present across the membranes of cell bodies and dendrites, not just in the membranes of axons. When neurons are not generating electrical impulses, the membrane potential of the neuron is termed the **resting membrane potential.** The resting membrane potential of most neurons is less than 100 millivolts, only one-tenth of a volt, which is quite small compared, for example, to the average flashlight battery of 1.5 volts. The voltage of the resting membrane potential of the neuron shown in figure 5.1 is about 70 millivolts.

The voltage of a battery is produced by the unequal distribution of electrically charged particles, termed **ions,** between the positive and negative poles of the battery. The membrane potential of the neuron also is produced by the

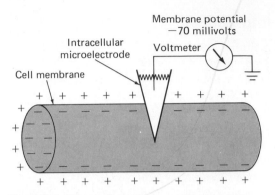

Figure 5.1 Nerve cells possess a resting membrane potential that can be recorded by penetrating the cell with a microelectrode connected to a voltmeter. Although the microelectrode is shown penetrating an axon, the membrane potential can be recorded anywhere across the cell membrane, not just in the axon.

unequal distribution of ions between the inside and the outside of the neuron, as first recognized by Julius Bernstein around the turn of the century (Bernstein 1902). Understanding the mechanisms underlying the resting membrane potential is the key to understanding the significance and basis for the many other electrical signals that can be recorded in the nervous system. Indeed, through evolution, the neuron and muscle cells have become specialized to change their membrane potential in order to generate various types of electrical signals. What are the ions that produce the membrane potential and how does the membrane potential relate to the action potentials produced by neurons and the synaptic transmission between them?

Some of the important ions present inside and outside of nerve cells are shown schematically in figure 5.2, along with an indication of the relative concentrations of these ions on either side of the cell membrane. Note, for example, the several types of ions that are positively charged, such as sodium (Na^+) and

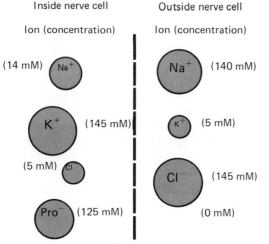

Inside nerve cell
Ion (concentration)

Outside nerve cell
Ion (concentration)

(14 mM) Na⁺

Na⁺ (140 mM)

K⁺ (145 mM)

K⁺ (5 mM)

(5 mM) Cl⁻

Cl⁻ (145 mM)

Pro⁻ (125 mM)

(0 mM)

Cell membrane

Figure 5.2 Some of the ions contained inside and outside the nerve cell. The relative concentrations of the various ions are suggested by the size of the notation indicating each ion species (Na⁺=sodium; K⁺=potassium; Cl⁻=chloride; Pro⁻=protein ions). The approximate concentration of each ion inside and outside the cell is indicated in parentheses. Note that potassium ions exist in high concentration inside the neuron, while sodium and chloride are highly concentrated outside the cell. The large protein ions are found inside the cell.

potassium (K⁺). Other ions, such as chloride (Cl⁻) and the large protein molecules found inside of nerve cells (Pro⁻) possess negative charges. In addition, it is important to note that these ions are not equally distributed across the cell membrane. There is much more sodium in the fluid surrounding nerve cells than there is on the inside of the cells. In contrast, the concentration of potassium ions inside the cell is much higher than it is outside the cell. Finally, it has been determined that the cell membrane allows certain ions to pass through it relatively easily, while it almost completely blocks passage of other ions. The nerve cell membrane, for example, is highly permeable to potassium ions, although not completely

permeable. Thus, these ions pass through the membrane with relative ease. On the other hand, in the resting state the membrane is nearly impermeable to sodium ions and the large proteins found inside the cell. Since the membrane is permeable to some but not all ions, it is called a **semipermeable membrane.** We can understand the importance of these various factors in producing the membrane potential by looking at a simplified example.

Membrane Permeability and Membrane Voltage

Let us assume for the moment that the concentrations of ions on either side of the nerve cell membrane are those shown in figure 5.2, but that the membrane is permeable only to potassium ions. The consequence of this state of affairs is illustrated schematically in figure 5.3a. Because the membrane is permeable to potassium ions, and because many more potassium ions are present inside the cell than outside it, there is a constant tendency for potassium ions to "leak out" of the cell. This process is termed **diffusion** and occurs whenever the cell membrane is permeable to a substance and the concentration of the substance inside the cell is different from that outside the cell. This difference in cell substance is called the **concentration gradient.** In addition, since potassium is electrically charged, its diffusion from inside the membrane to the outside creates an imbalance of electrical charge across the cell membrane. Because of diffusion, a relatively small number of potassium ions leaks out of the cell, making the outside slightly positive and leaving the inside slightly negative. This electrical potential develops until the inside of the membrane is sufficiently negatively charged to the degree that it begins to attract the positively charged potassium ions, thereby

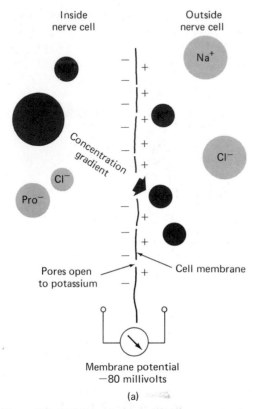

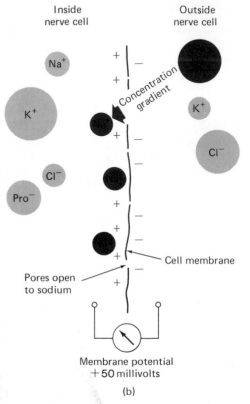

Figure 5.3 (a) If the cell membrane were completely permeable to potassium and impermeable to other ions, the membrane potential would approach the potassium equilibrium potential of approximately −80 millivolts. (b) If the cell membrane were completely permeable to sodium and impermeable to other ions, the membrane potential would approach the sodium equilibrium potential of approximately +50 millivolts.

preventing further movement of potassium to the outside. A kind of equilibrium is created between the force of diffusion that acts to move potassium from the inside to the outside of the cell membrane and the force of the electrical potential that develops across the cell membrane because of this movement. Indeed, this voltage is termed the **equilibrium potential** for potassium. The equilibrium potential for the concentrations of potassium that normally exist across the nerve cell membrane has been calculated and is approximately 80 millivolts negative inside the cell.

It is important to point out that the greater the concentration gradient across the cell membrane, the greater will be the value of the equilibrium potential that develops as a result of it. If the concentrations across the cell membrane were equal, no potential would develop. Thus, the important factor is the concentration gradient rather than the absolute amount of potassium ions.

We have seen that if the cell membrane were permeable only to potassium ions a potential across the cell membrane of approximately 80 millivolts, negative inside—the equilibrium potential for potassium—would develop. Let us now consider a different example in which the membrane is permeable only to sodium ions. As shown in figure 5.3*b*, sodium is highly concentrated outside the cell, but the concentration inside the cell is low. Thus, the situation is now reversed, and the concentration gradient is in the opposite direction, tending to make sodium ions leak *into* the cell. This produces an electrical potential across the cell membrane, but now the inside becomes more positive and the outside more negative. In fact, the equilibrium potential for sodium is approximately 50 millivolts, *positive inside,* as illustrated in 5.3*b*. The two examples shown in figure 5.3 illustrate the effects of a concentration gradient across the membrane for positively charged ions. The same principles apply to negatively charged ions except that the voltage developed is of the opposite sign.

The Nernst Equation

The equilibrium potential for any ion distributed across a semipermeable membrane can be calculated using the simplified equation:

$$E_m = \frac{RT}{zF} \log \frac{[conc.]_{outside}}{[conc.]_{inside}}$$

where E_m represents the voltage that develops across the membrane; R the universal gas constant; T the absolute temperature; z the valence (electrical charge) of the ion; and F the Faraday constant. $[conc.]_{inside}$ is the concentration of a given ion inside the cell, while $[conc.]_{outside}$ is the concentration of that ion outside the cell. This equation is known as the **Nernst equation** and is used to predict the potential that develops across a membrane when the forces acting on a particular ion are at equilibrium. At room temperature $\frac{RT}{zF}$ for

both sodium ions and potassium ions is equal to 58. Thus, we can calculate the equilibrium potentials for sodium and potassium using the Nernst equation and the ion concentrations given in figure 5.2. For potassium (K^+), this would be

$$E_{K^+} = 58 \log \frac{[5]}{[145]}$$

$$E_{K^+} = -84.8 \text{ mV}$$

This value is very close to the actual measured value of the resting membrane potential in most nerve cells. Similarly, for sodium (Na^+) ions, the equilibrium potential would be

$$E_{Na^+} = 58 \log \frac{[140]}{[14]}$$

$$E_{Na^+} = 58 \text{ mV}$$

This corresponds to the approximate height of the action potential when the membrane becomes permeable to sodium ions. Thus, the Nernst equation provides an easy, quantitative method that predicts the approximate membrane potential during different conditions of membrane permeability and reveals which ion species are most likely significant in generating the membrane voltages that occur during rest and during activity.

Each of the ions that we have discussed contributes to some extent to the resting membrane potential, though not equally. The actual resting membrane potential of the neuron is much closer, for example, to the potassium equilibrium potential (85 millivolts, negative inside) than the sodium equilibrium potential (58 millivolts, positive inside). The reason for this discrepancy is that the cell membrane is not very permeable to sodium ions in the resting state, but it is almost completely permeable to potassium ions. Thus, the potassium ions contribute much more to the resting membrane potential than do the sodium ions. If the membrane is impermeable to a particular ion, then that ion cannot contribute to the membrane potential because diffusion cannot take place.

The Action Potential

Although all cells possess membrane potentials, the neuron and muscle cells are specialized. Therefore, the membrane potential can be changed. This capability to alter the membrane potential is what enables neurons to conduct information. The **action potential** represents a temporary, localized change in the resting membrane potential that, because of the specialized nature of the nerve cell membrane, can travel or propagate down the axon of the nerve cell. Action potentials originate in a specialized region of the axon near the cell body. This special region is termed the **initial segment.** Once action potentials are initiated, they travel down the entire length of the axon like the lighted portion of a fuse until they invade the tiny branches of the axon that form synapses. At the synapse the action potential triggers the release of neurotransmitter substance to affect the postsynaptic cell, a process discussed in more detail later. The changes in voltage that occur during the action potential are illustrated in figure 5.4, which shows that the action potential consists of two distinct phases. At the peak of the action potential, the membrane potential has changed from its normal resting value of around 70 millivolts, negative inside, to a value of 50 millivolts, positive inside—a 120 millivolt change. Any change in which the value of the membrane potential becomes less negative inside is termed

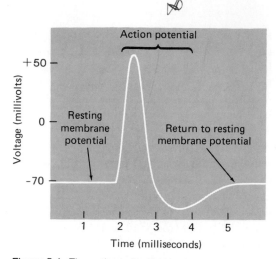

Figure 5.4 The action potential is a temporary change in the membrane potential of the neuron that travels down the axon.

depolarization. Thus, the initial phase of the action potential is a 120-millivolt depolarization. Immediately after this phase, the action potential displays a second phase in which the membrane potential moves back toward the resting value and beyond. Indeed, the membrane potential becomes more negative inside for several milliseconds before returning to the resting value. The second phase, in which the membrane is more than normally negative inside, is called **hyperpolarization.** During hyperpolarization, the cell membrane often reaches 80 (or more) millivolts, negative inside, before returning to the normal resting condition.

Like the resting membrane potential, the action potential is produced by the differential distribution of ions across the cell membrane and the permeability of the membrane to them. In the resting state, the membrane is most permeable to potassium ions and relatively impermeable to sodium ions. Thus, at rest the membrane potential reflects the equilibrium potential for potassium much more than that for sodium. An action potential results when the permeability of the membrane changes. During the first phase of the action potential, the permeability of the membrane to sodium ions increases dramatically. Under these conditions the sodium ions can diffuse into the cell and contribute much more to the membrane potential than when the membrane is at rest. In fact, as shown in figure 5.4, the action potential reaches a peak value of around 50 millivolts, positive inside—very near the equilibrium potential for sodium.

The Giant Axon of the Squid

Many properties of the action potential were discovered during experiments on the giant nerve cells of the squid. Squids possess several of these extremely large nerve cells, two of which are illustrated in figure 5.5a. When confronted with a dangerous obstacle, the squid is capable of propelling itself backward very rapidly. This escape response is controlled by these large neurons.

The axons of these nerve cells, as seen under the microscope and illustrated in figure 5.5b, can be as large as one millimeter in diameter. They can be dissected completely out of the squid, and when placed in a special water bath, they remain alive and function for as long as twelve hours. The substance inside the axon can be squeezed out, like toothpaste out of a tube, and can be replaced with a medium of any chemical constitution. In this way, we can study the effects of removing specific ions, adding special radioactive particles, and so forth. Similarly, a variety of chemical substances can be added to the extracellular bath

to assess the effects of various substances outside the cell. Because the axon is so large, it is unnecessary to use the extremely tiny microelectrodes that are needed to record the electrical activity of small mammalian nerve cells. The substitution of different chemical environments both inside and outside the giant axon of the squid led to the conclusion that the action potential is generated by a breakdown of the cell membrane's barrier to external sodium ions (Na^+). Thus, sodium ions are able to pass into the cell, and subsequently potassium ions (K^+) move out of the cell. It was also shown that following an action potential, an active metabolic pump (**sodium-potassium pump**) forces the excess sodium ions out of the cell and draws potassium ions back into the cell.

Organisms such as the squid have been used as models for understanding phenomena such as the action potential throughout the history of biology and psychology.

Absolute and Relative Refractory Periods

This change in permeability of the nerve cell membrane to sodium ions has been described as an opening of "gates" that cover special channels, or pores, in the membrane through which sodium can pass. During the resting state the gates are closed. When the neuron is sufficiently depolarized, the sodium channels are opened and sodium diffuses through the membrane to contribute to the voltage across the membrane. If the gates were to remain open, however, the voltage across the membrane would remain at about 50 millivolts, positive inside, as noted in figure 5.3b. This does not occur because the membrane has a

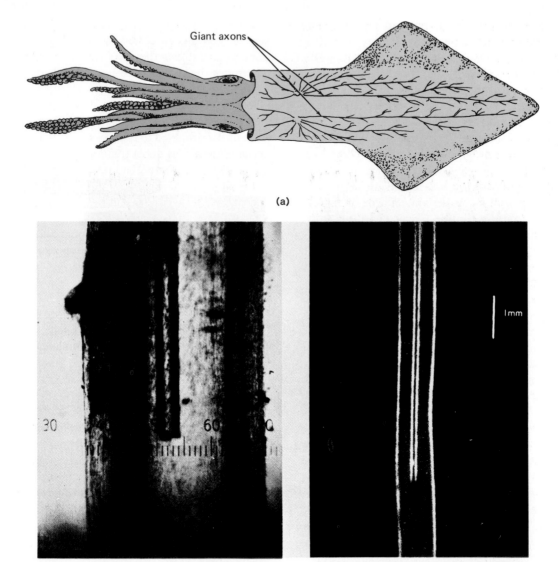

(a)

(b)

Figure 5.5 (a) Giant nerve cells of the squid. The approximate location of two giant nerve cells and their axons is shown from the top of the squid. (b) The photomicrograph illustrates the size of the giant axons. In each case, an electrode is inserted in the axon.

(a) From ''The Nerve Impulse and the Squid'' by Richard D. Keynes. Copyright © 1958 by Scientific American, Inc. All rights reserved.

mechanism that closes the sodium gates when the membrane voltage reaches the peak of the action potential, a process termed **inactivation.** During this brief period the neuron cannot produce another action potential, at least not in that small region of the membrane where the action potential has just occurred. This period is often called the **absolute refractory period,** since even with intense stimulation the neuron is incapable during this time of generating another action potential.

Inactivation of the sodium channels, however, is still not sufficient by itself to account for the second phase of the action potential. Note that the second phase includes a period during which the membrane becomes hyperpolarized. Hyperpolarization occurs because, in addition to the increase in permeability to sodium ions during the action potential, after a short delay a further increase in permeability to potassium ions also takes place. The membrane becomes even more permeable to potassium than during the resting state. However, this change in permeability is slower to develop than the change in sodium permeability, and its effect appears only after the sodium channels have been closed. As noted in figure 5.3*a,* if the membrane were completely permeable to potassium, the membrane potential would approach the equilibrium potential for potassium of about 80 millivolts, negative inside. As shown in figure 5.4, this is precisely what happens to the membrane potential during the second phase of the action potential. During the hyperpolarization phase, the neuron can fire another action potential, but only when more intense stimulation is provided. For this reason, the period is called the **relative refractory period.**

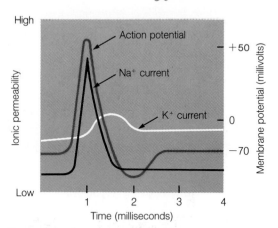

Figure 5.6 The action potential (black line) is produced by an increase in permeability of the membrane first to sodium, allowing it to diffuse into the cell, and then to potassium, allowing it to diffuse out of the cell.

Ionic Currents during the Action Potential

Figure 5.6 illustrates the just described changes in membrane permeability to sodium and potassium ions and the action potentials they produce. First (and most rapidly), an increase in the membrane permeability to sodium occurs and results in diffusion of sodium ions (called the **sodium current**) from outside to just inside the membrane, creating the initial phase of the action potential—**depolarization.** In addition, the permeability to potassium increases more slowly, and therefore diffusion of potassium from inside to just outside the membrane, termed the **potassium current,** occurs. These events cause the second phase of the action potential—**hyperpolarization.** Eventually the membrane permeability to both ions returns to the resting condition.

Electrotonus and Cable Properties

It is important at this point to distinguish between ionic currents, which are produced by changes in the permeability of the cell membrane, and the electric currents, or electrotonus, created by the action potential or any other electrical stimulus. If the membrane of the axon had no channels for ionic current, it would still conduct electricity like a small cable. Under these conditions, however, an electrical stimulus could depolarize the membrane and would be conducted only a short distance down the axon. Because the membrane lacked sodium channels, however, the electrotonic current would dissipate rapidly as a function of the distance it was conducted down the axon. This type of electrical conduction is termed passive and is described by a set of equations originally designed to handle the flow of electricity in undersea communication cables. Hence, these passive properties of neurons are often termed **cable properties.**

The passage of electrotonic current along the axon is related to the resistance the current encounters. Since the resistance through the cytoplasm is much less than the resistance of the membrane of the cell, electrotonic current has a tendency to travel along the inside of the axon rather than leaking out through the membrane. Under certain conditions, the resistance of the cell membrane can be altered, thereby changing the conduction of electrotonus along the axon. If the resistance across the cell membrane decreases, current will tend to leak across the cell membrane and will not travel as far along the inside of the axon. If membrane resistance is increased, electrotonic current can travel further along the length of the axon. This cable property, which describes the length along the axon that can be traveled by electrotonic current, is appropriately termed the **length constant** of the axon.

Action Potential Propagation

When an action potential is initiated, the cable properties of the axon allow the currents created by the depolarizing impulse to be conducted a short distance down the axon. Since this adjacent region of the axon possesses sodium channels that are sensitive to voltage, the electrotonus depolarizes the adjacent region of membrane to threshold, and the sodium

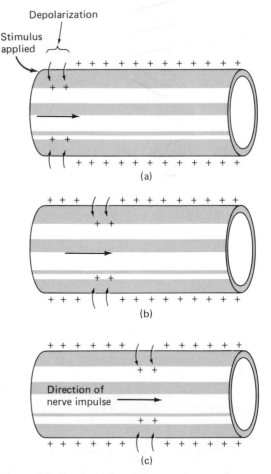

Figure 5.7 Depolarization of the axon by an action potential creates the electrotonus that depolarizes the adjacent region, opens the membrane to sodium ions. The action potential then occurs anew, allowing the action potential to travel down the axon.

gates are opened creating the action potential anew, as shown schematically in figure 5.7. This region then depolarizes the next adjacent region of membrane by electrotonus and the action potential is again initiated. In this way, the action potential propagates down the axon, each region where it occurs serving as an electrical stimulus for the adjacent region until it reaches the axon terminals.

Many neurons in the human nervous system have myelinated axons—that is, the axons are covered by a fatty material called myelin (see chap. 3). Myelin is an electrical insulator that allows electrotonus to be conducted over a much greater distance along the axon because it increases the resistance across the cell membrane, thereby increasing the length constant. In this case, the action potentials occur only at the small gaps in the myelin sheath, the nodes of Ranvier, as illustrated in figure 5.8. Because electrotonic conduction is

virtually instantaneous (the speed of conventional electrical conduction is near the speed of light), conduction between nodes of Ranvier is extremely rapid and vastly increases the speed at which the action potential is propagated down the axon. The action potential occurs only at the nodes of Ranvier, jumping from one node to the next, each one producing electrotonus to depolarize the next node to threshold, the membrane voltage needed to open the sodium gates and create the action potential (see color plate 2). Conduction of action potentials along myelinated axons is termed **saltatory conduction** (from the Latin word *saltare* meaning "to jump"). In the unmyelinated nerve fiber, where the action potential is propagated continuously along the axon, the speed of conduction is often less than several meters per second. In large myelinated axons in which saltatory conduction occurs, the conduction velocity may reach 100 meters per second.

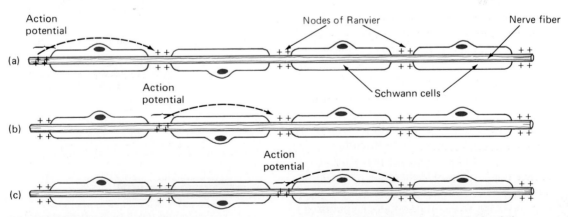

Figure 5.8 In myelinated nerve fibers, the electrotonus created by an action potential at one node depolarizes the next node. Thus, the action potential appears to "jump" from one node of Ranvier to the next. The electrotonic current spreads further

down the inside of the axon due to the insulating property of myelin, creating the appearance of the action potential "jumping" from one node to the next. This greatly increases the speed of action potential propagation.

The Sodium-Potassium Pump

It is important to realize that the actual number of ions that must diffuse across the membrane to produce the resting membrane potential and the action potential is extremely small compared to the number available. Thus, when an action potential occurs, only a virtually insignificant number of ions actually change membrane sides.

Nevertheless, since many neurons are constantly firing action potentials—sometimes thousands within just a few seconds—an excess of sodium ions inside and potassium ions outside of the neuron would eventually accumulate. A special mechanism in the membrane of the neuron, the **sodium-potassium pump,** prevents this from happening. This device pumps sodium out of the cell and potassium back into it. The sodium-potassium pump is actually a biochemical mechanism dependent upon the enzyme sodium-potassium ATPase (see color plate 2). The pump requires metabolic energy to operate, which it obtains by changing ATP into ADP and using the metabolic energy released by this reaction. If the cell is poisoned, the sodium-potassium pump stops and the restoration of ions does not occur. Under these conditions, the membrane potential eventually runs down as sodium accumulates inside and potassium leaks out of the cell. In some neurons, the sodium and potassium pumping action appears to be roughly equal so that the same amount of positive charge moves in either direction across the membrane. In some neurons, however, the sodium-potassium pump can actually pump more sodium out than it pumps potassium in. In this case, there is a net movement of positive ions out of the cell, which creates a slightly more negative membrane interior than otherwise occurs. Such a pump

is termed **electrogenic** since the action of the pump itself generates an electric potential across the membrane.

As mentioned previously, an action potential is usually initiated by the neuron near the cell body in the region of the axon termed the initial segment, near where cell body and axon connect. The action potential then travels or propagates down the axon until it reaches the axon terminal. How is the action potential initiated and propagated? This question could easily be rephrased as What opens the sodium gates and thereby produces the action potential? The answer to this question is that the sodium gates (that is, the permeability of the membrane to sodium ions) are sensitive to depolarization of the membrane. If the membrane is depolarized to a specific level, called the **threshold,** the sodium gates open and the action potential is initiated. Important to remember is that once the action potential is initiated and sodium begins to diffuse into the cell at the initial segment, depolarization of the membrane increases more and more, like an explosion, until the peak of the action potential is reached. The action potential occurring at the initial segment acts like a miniature spark and produces depolarizing currents in adjacent regions of the cell membrane. This depolarization is sufficient to exceed the threshold of the axon just adjacent to the initial segment, producing an action potential in this region.

Synaptic Potentials

We have described the way in which the action potential is propagated. Once it is initiated, the action potential itself creates a depolarization of the neuronal membrane in regions adjacent to where it occurs, termed electrotonus. Depolarization of the adjacent region of the membrane reaches threshold there, and an ac-

tion potential occurs. This explanation also reveals how neurons can be made to fire by means
of synaptic transmission: Their membrane potential must be depolarized to the level of spike
discharge threshold. Excitatory synaptic
transmission works in this way (Eccles 1964).

Excitatory Postsynaptic Potentials

In excitatory synaptic transmission, a chemical transmitter is released from the axon terminal of the presynaptic cell, diffuses across
the synaptic cleft, and attaches to special receptors on the postsynaptic cell membrane in
the region of the synapse. Attachment to these
receptors changes the pattern of ions to which
the membrane of the postsynaptic cell is
permeable, usually by increasing the membrane permeability to sodium ions. The postsynaptic membrane then becomes depolarized.
The potential is a small graded potential whose
size depends upon how many synaptic endings
release transmitter within a short period of
time, usually on the order of tens or hundreds
of milliseconds. If there are many terminals on
the neuron, and if they increase the release of
their transmitter simultaneously, the depolarization of the postsynaptic cell may be sufficient to reach spike discharge threshold in the
region of the initial segment, thus initiating the
action potential to be propagated down the
axon.

Conduction of the postsynaptic potential
occurs by virtue of the cable properties of the
dendrites and cell body. The depolarization is
produced by changes in the permeability of the
postsynaptic cell to various combinations of
ions. This localized depolarization then spreads
out across the cell by means of electrotonic
conduction. If the electrotonus created by the
postsynaptic potential is sufficiently large, the
initial segment is depolarized to its threshold
and an action potential is initiated.

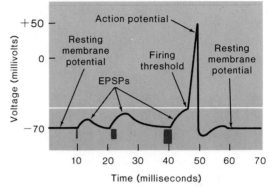

Figure 5.9 Schematic illustrations of excitatory
postsynaptic potentials (EPSPs). The vertical bar
immediately before each EPSP represents the amount
of synaptic activity producing the EPSP. Note that as
the synaptic input increases, the EPSP increases.
When enough synaptic activity bombards the neuron,
the EPSP reaches firing threshold and an action
potential is initiated, as shown on the far right.

The depolarization of neurons produced
by excitatory synaptic transmission is termed
an **excitatory postsynaptic potential** (EPSP),
several of which are illustrated schematically
in figure 5.9. Note that the EPSP can be quite
small. When it is, it is not sufficient to reach
discharge threshold and simply decays within
a period of milliseconds back to the resting
membrane potential. However, if a large
number of synapses operate simultaneously
over the cell's surface, their cumulative effects
result in a phenomenon termed **spatial summation.** In addition, the effects of the synapse
may also accumulate if transmitter is released
several times in rapid succession, an event
called **temporal summation.** In both cases, the
membrane voltage may then reach spike
threshold, and an action potential will be initiated. The action potential is initiated in the
region of the initial segment because this region has a lower threshold than any other portion of the membrane near the synapses. A

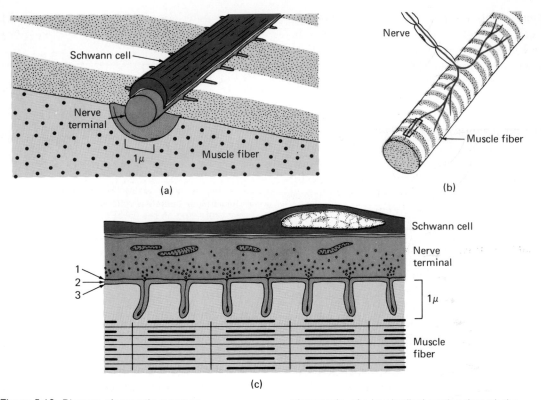

(a)

(b)

(c)

Figure 5.10 Diagram of synaptic structure. Neuromuscular junction of frog: (a) One portion of the junction; (b) general position of endings of motor axon on muscle fibers, showing portion (a) as a small rectangle; (c) schematic drawing from electron micrographs of a longitudinal section through the muscle fiber—(1) terminal axon membrane, (2) "basement membrane" partitioning the gap between nerve and muscle fiber, (3) folded postsynaptic membrane of muscle fiber.

special case of excitatory synaptic transmission, the synapse between nerves and muscles, is described.

The Neuromuscular Junction

Figure 5.10 illustrates one of the most intensely studied of all excitatory synaptic connections: the **neuromuscular junction,** which is between nerve and muscle. Many of the elementary features of synaptic transmission were first discovered by using the neuromuscular junction as the model of this process. For example, the theory that synaptic transmitter substance is stored in and released from synaptic vesicles was confirmed initially in studies of the neuromuscular junction (see Katz 1966). Like excitatory synapses between neurons, chemical transmitter is released from the presynaptic ending of the motor nerve to depolarize the membrane potential of the muscle cell. This depolarization is termed the excitatory postsynaptic potential (EPSP) in neurons and the end-plate potential (EPP) in muscle cells. A fascinating discovery about synaptic transmission using the neuromuscular junction is that transmitter probably leaks out of the presynaptic ending at a slow rate all of the time. This was determined in part by observing that the membrane potential of the muscle cells shows tiny depolarizations even when no action potentials occur in the presynaptic ending. They were appropriately termed **miniature end-plate potentials.** Action potentials in the motor nerve simply increase the amount of transmitter released in order to produce the larger end-plate potentials that lead to muscular contraction.

Inhibitory Postsynaptic Potentials

By depolarizing the postsynaptic cell membrane, excitatory synapses move the membrane potential closer to spike discharge threshold and therefore increase the probability of the postsynaptic cell initiating an action potential. Inhibitory synapses, on the other hand, do the opposite. In postsynaptic inhibition, chemical transmitter is released from the synaptic ending, diffuses across the synaptic cleft, and attaches to receptors on the postsynaptic membrane. However, for inhibitory synapses the pattern of ions to which the membrane becomes permeable is different. Inhibitory synapses usually increase membrane permeability to chloride ions or sometimes to potassium ions. The voltage that results from this change in permeability is hyperpolarization of the postsynaptic cell membrane potential, termed the **inhibitory postsynaptic potential (IPSP)**. Several schematized examples of inhibitory postsynaptic potentials are shown in figure 5.11. This illustration also shows that the IPSPs are graded like the EPSPs and that their size is dependent upon the number of inhibitory synapses that are activated within a brief period of time.

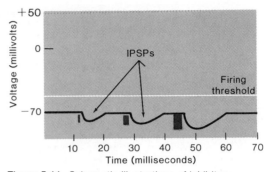

Figure 5.11 Schematic illustrations of inhibitory postsynaptic potentials (IPSPs). The vertical bar immediately before each IPSP represents the amount of inhibitory synaptic activity producing the IPSP. As the amount of inhibitory synaptic activity increases, the IPSP increases (i.e., becomes more negative). The larger the IPSP, the less likely it is that the neuron will fire an action potential.

Much of what we know about excitatory and inhibitory postsynaptic potentials and their relationship to chemical transmission between neurons was first discovered by studying the large motor neurons of the vertebrate spinal cord (e.g., Eccles 1964). The basic principles discovered from studying the synapses onto spinal motor neurons form the basis for understanding synaptic communication throughout the brain. However, important differences also exist between different synapses, even those of the same function. For example, inhibitory synapses in the spinal cord produce IPSPs lasting tens of milliseconds, while in the brain some inhibitory postsynaptic potentials last hundreds of milliseconds. The same is true for different excitatory synapses.

Presynaptic Inhibition

Postsynaptic excitation and inhibition, as the two forms of synaptic transmission that we have been discussing are called, are only two

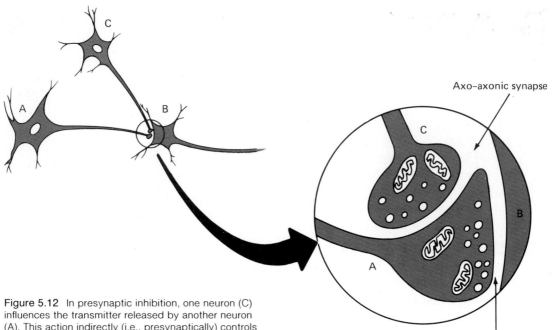

Figure 5.12 In presynaptic inhibition, one neuron (C) influences the transmitter released by another neuron (A). This action indirectly (i.e., presynaptically) controls the activity of neuron B in this schematic diagram.

of many ways that neurons can affect each other (Eccles 1964). **Presynaptic inhibition** is another way in which such control can be exerted. In presynaptic inhibition, one neuron controls the amount of transmitter released by the terminals of another neuron. The axon terminals of one neuron are thought to make synaptic contact with the axon terminals of another neuron, forming an **axo-axonic** synapse as illustrated in figure 5.12. Note that neuron A in figure 5.12 has a strong excitatory synaptic connection with neuron B. When neuron A releases transmitter, it produces a large EPSP in neuron B. However, when neuron C is active, the amount of transmitter released by neuron A is diminished. Thus, the EPSP in neuron B is smaller than it would otherwise be. Neuron C is, in effect, inhibiting neuron B, but only indirectly; hence, the name presynaptic inhibition. This occurs because the action potentials traveling down the axon in neuron A are shunted out through the decreased resistance in neuron A caused by neuron C releasing transmitter onto the terminals of neuron A. For this reason, the sign of the voltage change in neuron A (EPSP or IPSP) is irrelevant, as long as the ionic conductance of the terminals of neuron A is increased. Reducing the amount of transmitter released onto neuron B controls its activity presynaptically. It is also believed that neurons can increase the amount of transmitter released from synaptic endings, a phenomenon termed **presynaptic facilitation.**

Other Electrical Signs of Neural Activity

We have discovered that individual neurons are capable of two basic types of electrical responses: (1) the small, graded changes in the neuronal membrane potential due to inhibitory and excitatory synaptic activity and (2) the all-or-none action potential, termed all-or-none because it either occurs and propagates down the axon or it does not; that is, the action potential is not a graded response. Synaptic potentials and action potentials are usually recorded by penetration of the cell with a fine glass tube filled with a conductive solution, a technique termed **intracellular** (inside the cell) **recording**. Action potentials can be recorded either this way, or fine wire electrodes insulated except at the tip can be moved close to the neuron to record changes in voltage. Since the brain is a conductor (composed mostly of salt water), the voltage of the action potential can be recorded nearby—but outside—the cell that generates it, a technique termed **extracellular (outside the cell) recording.** Examples of intracellularly and extracellularly recorded action potentials from a neuron in the rat brain are shown in figure 5.13.

Multiple-Unit Activity

What must now be stressed is that the brain comprises billions and billions of neurons—neurons that do not work in isolation from one another. Rather, neurons work together in populations. In general, neurons with similar functions exist in groups to form layers or nuclei in the brain. In order to understand the brain it is important to develop ways in which the activity of populations of neurons, that is, **multiple-unit activity,** can also be observed and understood.

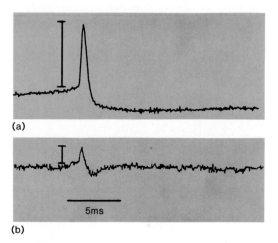

(a)

(b)

Figure 5.13 Action potentials recorded intracellularly (a) and extracellularly (b) from the same neuron from a rat brain. Note that the intracellular action potential is much larger in amplitude than the extracellular action potential and that the intracellularly recorded action potential displays a prominent spike after hyperpolarization that cannot be seen in the extracellular record.

We will see many examples throughout this book that illustrate the value of studying the responses of individual neurons as recorded by microelectrodes in understanding the biological bases of the behavior of organisms. However, since microelectrodes are generally used to record the activity of only one cell at a time, other methods to observe the responses of neuron populations, in some cases consisting of responses generated by millions of neurons responding simultaneously, have been developed. If the recording tip of a microelectrode is enlarged, signals from many neurons can be recorded simultaneously. A recording obtained by means of this technique is called a multiple-neuron or multiple-unit recording and is illustrated in figure 5.14. With the multiple-unit recording technique, the activity of many cells near the microelectrode can be monitored simultaneously and the overall behavior of the population can be studied.

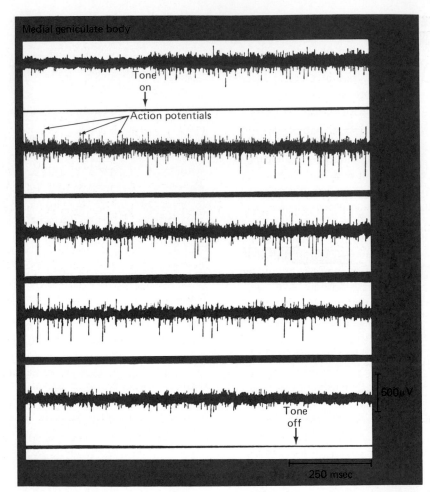

Figure 5.14 A multiple-unit recording from the medial geniculate nucleus of the cat. Cells in this important sensory relay nucleus become more active when a tone is turned on near the animal's ear. The amplitude (height) of the action potentials is determined in part by the size of different cells near the electrode and in part by the distance a cell is from the microelectrode tip.

Changes in multiple-unit activity reveal changes in more than an individual neuron, although changes in the activity of individual members of the population can often be gleaned from multiple-unit recordings (e.g., Verzeano 1974). In figure 5.14, multiple-unit activity was recorded from the medial geniculate nucleus—a nucleus involved in processing auditory signals. The traces show action potentials from a population of neurons that, because these records are squeezed together in time, look like vertical lines or spikes.

The line below each trace shows when a tone was turned on, when it was allowed to increase in intensity, and when it was then decreased to silence. In general, the amplitude of the action potential from any one neuron in the population remains constant provided that the tip of the microelectrode does not move. Thus, the appearance of large action potentials not present before the tone is turned on indicates that additional neurons not responding before the tone are now activated by the sound. As the tone increases in intensity, action potentials of different sizes continue to appear in the record and to drop out as the tone again decreases in intensity. This ability to observe the responses of several neurons simultaneously is a distinct advantage of the multiple-unit recording technique.

Electroencephalogram

Individual neurons in the brain are constantly receiving excitatory and/or inhibitory synaptic input, producing continuous fluctuations in the membrane potentials of billions and billions of neurons. We noted previously that enlarging the size of the recording tip of a microelectrode makes it possible for action potentials from several neurons surrounding the tip to be recorded simultaneously. If the tip of the electrode is enlarged even further—for example, to the size of an ordinary wire—then the combined synaptic potentials from extremely large numbers of neurons can be recorded simultaneously. Such a recording is called an electroencephalogram (EEG). The EEG is probably the best known form of electrical activity recorded in the brain and has been studied for many years in a wide variety of organisms. Indeed, the EEG can be recorded by placing electrodes in contact with

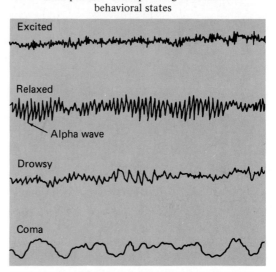

Figure 5.15 EEG patterns corresponding to various behavioral states.

the scalp, a distance several millimeters from the surface of the brain. Since the EEG can be recorded on the scalp without the need for surgery, it is a valuable tool in recording the electrical activity of the human brain.

Figure 5.15 illustrates the characteristics of the electroencephalogram recorded from a human subject under various conditions. In the upper trace, labeled excited, the EEG is relatively flat and has many small, rapid fluctuations in voltage. The EEG of the relaxed human with eyes closed, however, looks quite different. In this case, the EEG voltage fluctuations look much larger and occur more slowly.

These two electroencephalographic records differ in several ways. First is the difference in the amplitude of the waves making up the record. In the alert subject, the amplitude

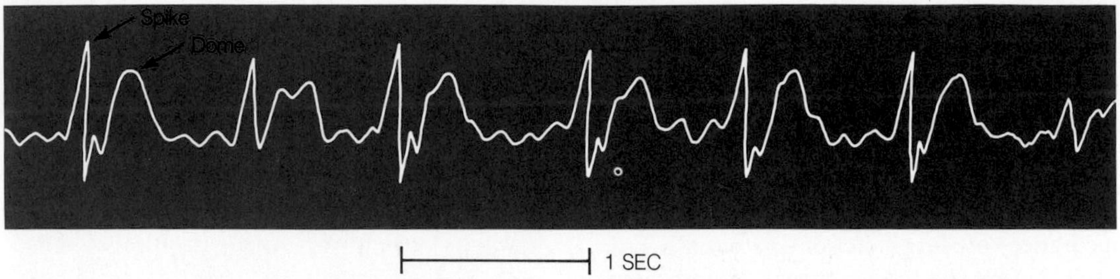

Figure 5.16 The spike-and-dome pattern common in electroencephalograms recorded during epileptic seizures. Sharp, spikelike changes in voltage alternate with large, slow, dome-shaped fluctuations.

(voltage) of the fluctuations is small in comparison with those in the EEG of the drowsy subject. Second, the two electroencephalograms differ with respect to the frequency of changes in voltage. The fluctuations in the EEG of the alert subject are much more rapid than those in the EEG of the relaxed subject. That is, the EEG from the alert subject contains higher frequencies than the EEG from the relaxed subject with the eyes closed. As we will discuss in some detail in a later chapter, the frequency and amplitude characteristics of the EEG can be used to distinguish not only drowsy subjects from alert subjects, but also different stages of sleep and wakefulness. Thus, the EEG is an important index of the subject's state of consciousness.

The EEG is also an important medical diagnostic tool. An abnormality of the brain, for example an area where a tumor is located or which is otherwise damaged, can be determined by placing EEG recording electrodes over different regions of the scalp. Electrodes overlying normal regions of the brain record normal EEG activity, while those placed over regions in which damage is located show abnormal EEG patterns and in some instances, no EEG activity at all. These abnormalities are most prominent over those regions where the damage is most severe and are absent over unaffected areas. An abnormal EEG pattern recorded during an epileptic seizure is shown in figure 5.16. The peculiar pattern of activity overlying the region where the seizure was initiated is shown. This pattern is termed the spike-and-dome pattern because it consists of an EEG characterized by sharp spikelike changes in voltage alternating with large, slower, dome-shaped fluctuations as illustrated in figure 5.16.

It is perhaps important to reveal that even when action potentials in the cerebral cortex have been reduced to a minimum, the brain still displays an EEG, which suggests that much of the activity making up the EEG record consists of synaptic potentials from millions and millions of neurons that are combined electrically by the recording electrode. Thus, the EEG is not simply a multiple-unit record since in multiple-unit recording, action potentials rather than synaptic potentials are recorded. Examination of the two types of records makes this fact evident. The multiple-unit record consists of very fast, spikelike variations (action potentials), while the EEG consists of much slower variations in voltage,

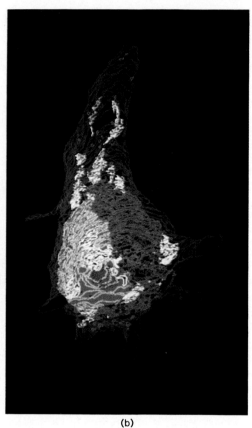

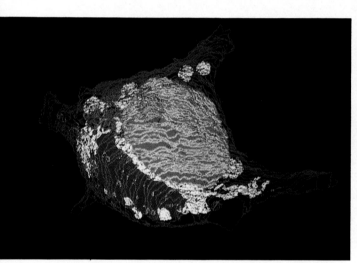

(a)

(b)

Color Plate 5   (a) A computer-assisted three-dimensional reconstruction of a neuron from the cerebral cortex of a patient with Alzheimer's disease. This illustrates a moderately sized neurofibrillary tangle (red) that appears near the nucleus and nuclear membrane (yellow). The small globelike structure (orange) inside the nucleus is the nucleolus. The cellular membrane is drawn (blue); granules of fatty deposits termed lipofuscin (green and brown) can be seen in the cytoplasm of the neuron. (b) A more normal-appearing neuron from the same biopsy sample, illustrating the same color-coded structures as in (a), but lacking a neurofibrillary tangle. The apical dendrite of this pyramidal neuron arises from the soma at the top, and the initial segment of the axon extends out of the bottom at about seven o'clock.

(Illustrations courtesy of Mark Ellisman, Department of Neuroscience, School of Medicine, University of California at San Diego, La Jolla, California.)

ColorPlate 6

(a)

Color Plate 6   Images of the distribution of receptors using receptor autoradiography in which the variations in receptor density have been analyzed and color coded by computer. (a) Receptor distribution of one class of receptors for the neurotransmitter gamma-amino-butyric acid (GABA) in the hippocampus of the rat brain illustrated in cross section. Red signifies the highest density of receptors and yellow signifies an intermediate density. (b) The distribution of opiate receptors in the brain of the guinea pig shown in coronal cross section. (c) The distribution of muscarinic receptors for acetylcholine in the human brain postmortem, illustrated in a cross section of the left cerebral hemisphere. The density of muscarinic receptors is high in the cerebral cortex (the outer portion of the hemisphere) and along the outer border of the image in the cerebral cortex, low in the white matter (dark blue and purple), but is again high in the putamen (near the center of the image). ([a] From Stahl, S. M., K. L. Leenders, and N. G. Bowery. 1986. Imaging neurotransmitters and their receptors in living human brain by positron emission tomography. *Trends in NeuroSciences* 9:241–45. [b] Courtesy of E. B. DeSouza and M. J. Kuhar, National Institute on Drug Abuse, Addiction Research Center, Baltimore, Maryland. [c] From Palacios, J. M., A. Probst, and R. Cortes, 1986. Mapping receptors in the human brain. *Trends in NeuroSciences* 9:284–89.)

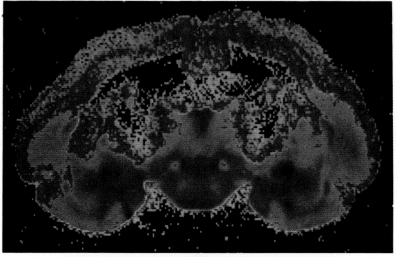

(b)

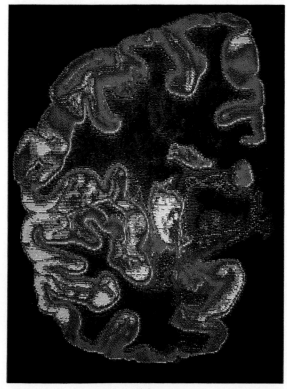

(c)

ColorPlate7

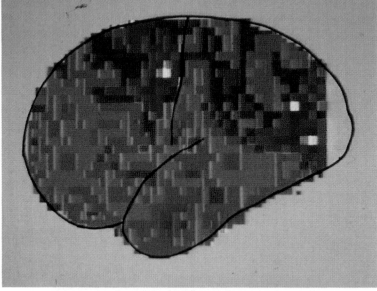

(a)

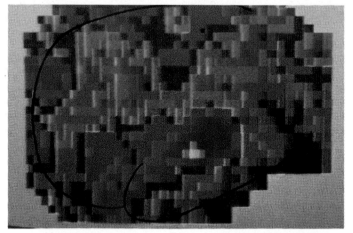

(b)

Color Plate 7 Illustrations of the distribution of blood flow as generated by computer analysis following an injection of a radioactive tracer into the carotid artery. (a) The subject follows a moving object with his eyes. High activity is seen over the occipital lobe of the brain where visual cortex is located. (b) In this image, the subject is listening to speech. High activity occurs

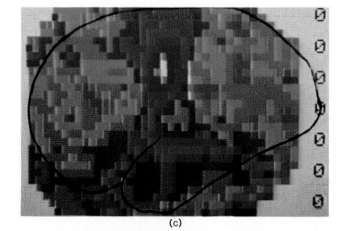

(c)

(d)

over the temporal lobe where auditory cortex is located. (c) The subject moves his fingers on the side of the body opposite to the cerebral hemisphere shown. High activity occurs over motor cortex. (d) The subject counts to twenty, resulting in high activity over the mouth area of the motor cortex and supplementary motor cortex, as well as auditory cortex of the temporal lobe.

(© Niels Lassen)

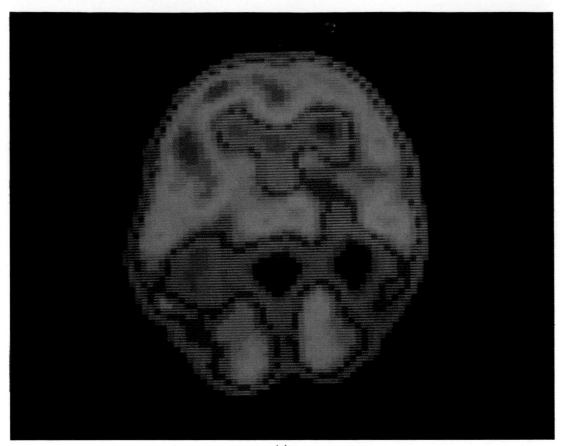

(a)

Color Plate 8 Two methods for depicting the dynamic activity of the living human brain. (a) A positron emission tomography scan (PET scan) of a normal human subject with eyes closed. This illustrates the uptake of radioactively labeled glucose during the application of mild electrical shocks delivered to the forearm. Areas of high glucose uptake, and therefore increased brain metabolism, are indicated by red. (b) PET scan of an unmedicated schizophrenic patient under the same condition as in (a). Note that compared to the normal subject, the schizophrenic patient appears to have much higher glucose uptake in the visual cortex (the bottom of the images) and perhaps lower metabolism in the frontal lobes (toward the top of each image). (c) The amplitude of the P-300 event-related potential in a normal subject (a) and in a schizophrenic patient (b).

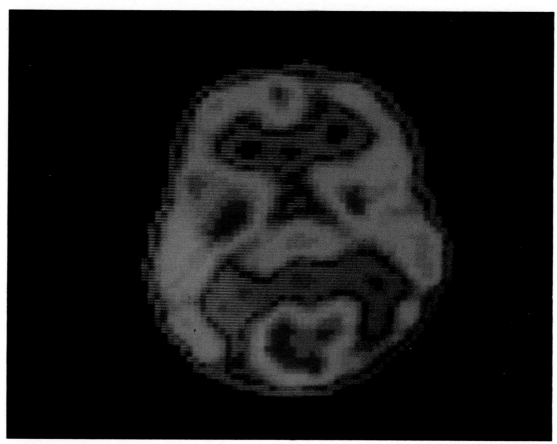

(b)

The P-300 potential was evoked by the occurrence of an
unusual or rarely occurring tone during the repeated
presentation of another tone that was always the same.
Compared to the normal individual, who shows the
maximal amplitude of P-300 at the top of the scalp
(white) and a decreasing amplitude with increasing
distance from this location, the schizophrenic patient (d)
shows very low amplitude over the entire brain,
indicating that the brain's ability to recognize and
respond to novel events is impaired in the patient.
([a] and [b] Courtesy of Dr. Monte Buchsbaum, Department of
Psychiatry and Behavioral Science, School of Medicine,
University of California, Irvine, California. [c] and [d] Courtesy
of Dr. Lewis L. Judd, Department of Psychiatry, School of
Medicine, University of California at San Diego, La Jolla,
California.)

(Continued)

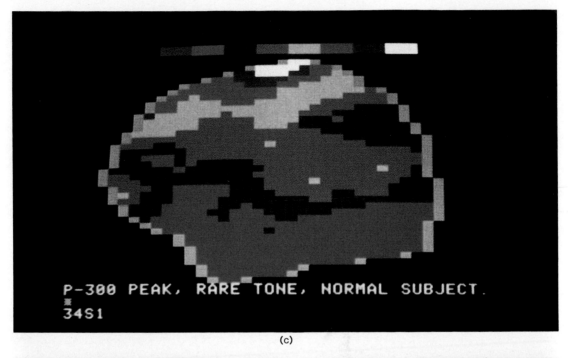

P-300 PEAK, RARE TONE, NORMAL SUBJECT.
34S1

(c)

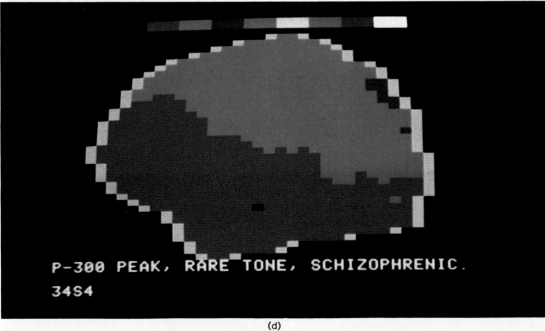

P-300 PEAK, RARE TONE, SCHIZOPHRENIC.
34S4

(d)

including some changes with frequencies of 2 or 3 **hertz** (hertz is a measure of frequency meaning cycles per second).

Evoked Potentials

what elect change happens t outside stimulus

When a large number of neurons is bombarded by synaptic activity simultaneously, as might happen when we are stimulated by a flash of light, changes in the membrane potentials of millions of neurons in specific regions of the brain also occur nearly simultaneously within a fraction of a second after the stimulus. However, since these synaptic potentials are evoked by a stimulus, they occur nearly synchronously. The combined electrical response recorded from this population is termed an **evoked potential** because it is brought about by a stimulus rather than occurring spontaneously. Because the recording electrode adds together synaptic potentials from millions of neurons, the evoked potential is comparatively large like the EEG and can sometimes be recorded from the scalp. In experimental animals, it is often recorded using wire electrodes placed in contact with the surface of the brain. For example, it is possible to record an evoked potential using a large wire placed on the surface of the visual area of the cerebral cortex. An evoked potential as it might look when recorded from the visual cortex of a monkey is shown in figure 5.17. In this experiment the recording electrode is implanted in the brain of the monkey, and the evoked potential will occur in response to a bright flash of light shone into the animal's eyes.

Note that the evoked potential has a number of components. Shortly after the flash of light, the evoked potential reaches a negative peak and then becomes positive, with

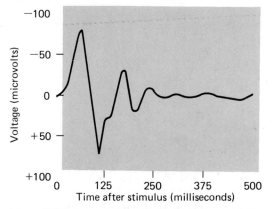

Figure 5.17 A graph showing the evoked potential to a flash of light. The stimulus was delivered at time zero on the graph. The vertical axis shows the voltage changes over time as recorded from the visual area of the cerebral cortex in the monkey.

several subsequent oscillations. The overall magnitude of the evoked potential, as well as the magnitude of each of the components that make up the evoked potential, is influenced by the intensity of stimulation as well as by many other factors of the physical stimulus.

The evoked potential has played an extremely important part in our understanding of the locations of neuronal populations that respond selectively to different stimuli. Indeed, much of what we know today about the locations of brain regions that process visual, auditory, and other modalities of stimulation was first determined by mapping the brain systematically to determine where evoked potentials occur in response to particular types of stimulation. Such a map is illustrated in figure 5.18. In this case, evoked potentials from an auditory stimulus were recorded in a variety of locations on the cerebral cortex of the cat. Note that the evoked potentials are largest in the central region of the portion of cerebral

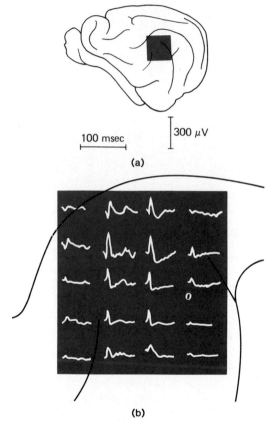

100 msec   300 μV

(a)

(b)

Figure 5.18 An evoked potential map of a region of the surface cerebral cortex of the cat (a). The region is expanded (b) to show where evoked potentials to an auditory stimulus occurred and to indicate their amplitude.

have been made of sensory areas of the cerebral cortex in many other animals, including human beings.

When an electroencephalogram is recorded from the scalp of a human being, potentials evoked by various sensory stimuli are generally too small to be seen. The large changes in voltage of the EEG obscure the small evoked potentials that occur. However, it is possible to obtain records of evoked potentials occurring within the human brain by recording from the scalp and using a computer. This technique is termed averaging. A computer is capable of combining many small signals and thereby extracting the small evoked potential from the larger though *random* EEG record (e.g., Hillyard and Kutas 1983). The technique involves stimulating the subject many times with the same stimulus. Since the EEG occurs spontaneously, it is sometimes positive after the stimulus and sometimes negative. However, the evoked potential, even though very small, is always approximately the same after each stimulus. Adding together the EEG records after many stimulus presentations cancels the random EEG and the evoked potential can eventually be seen.

Averaging has dramatically expanded our ability to record the electrical activity of the human brain since no surgery and minimal risk to subject are involved. Shown in figure 5.19 are averaged evoked potentials recorded from two human subjects under several different conditions of stimulation. For one condition, the stimulus was a checkerboard pattern, while horizontal stripes, a circle, and radial lines were used as the visual stimuli for other conditions. The averaged evoked potentials shown in the figure illustrate several important points. First, in each case four potentials for each stimulus condition are overlaid and illustrate that for a given subject,

cortex indicated by the square. As the electrode is placed farther away from this region, the evoked potentials to the auditory stimulus become smaller. Eventually no evoked potentials can be recorded when the electrode is a sufficient distance away from the active area. Such evoked potential mapping reveals areas of the brain that respond to particular kinds of stimuli. The region shown in figure 5.18 is one of several on the cat's cerebral cortex that process auditory information. Similar maps

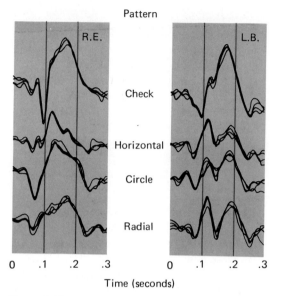

Pattern

R.E.

Check

Horizontal

Circle

Radial

L.B.

0   .1   .2   .3   0   .1   .2   .3

Time (seconds)

Figure 5.19 Averaged evoked responses for two subjects (R.E. and L.B.) to four different visual patterns.

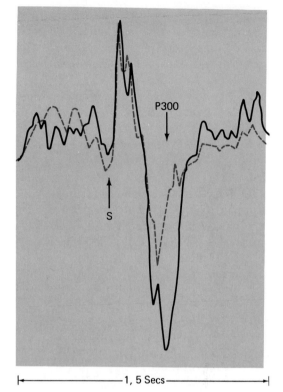

P300

S

|— 1, 5 Secs —|

Figure 5.20 Evoked potentials showing the P300 component. In one case (dashed line), the human subject knew in advance what the stimulus (arrow) would be. In the other condition (solid line), the subject was uncertain what the stimulus would be. In both cases, however, the same visual stimulus, the letter A, was presented to the subjects.

averaged evoked potentials can be quite stable over time, provided that the stimulating conditions remain constant. Second, while definite similarities between the evoked potentials of the two subjects are recorded, distinct individual differences are also apparent. Finally, note that the size and shape of the averaged evoked potential vary as the subjects view different visual patterns.

It has been established that the size and shape of the evoked potential recorded from the scalp of the human subject may vary not only with changes in the physical stimulus, but also with changes in the state of the subject. For example, the evoked potential changes with the state of subject alertness, the familiarity of the subject with the stimulus, and many other similar factors (e.g., Beck 1975; Hillyard and Kutas 1983). Indeed, evidence suggests that certain components of recorded

evoked potentials seem to reflect decision-making processes that occur in the brain. In such cases, the evoked potential is sometimes termed an **event-related potential.**

P300 Potential

An example of an electrical signal related to the decision-making events is the so-called **P300 potential.** As shown in figure 5.20, the P300 signal is a large positive potential that occurs approximately 300 milliseconds after presentation of a stimulus (indicated in the figure by the arrow). In this experiment, the stimulus was a flash of light that illuminated the letter A (Donchin 1975). The evoked potential shown by the dashed line occurred when the subject knew in advance that the stimulus would be the letter A. The solid line shows the evoked potential to the letter A under conditions in which the subject could not accurately predict whether an A or some other letter would appear. The large downward potential occurring about 300 milliseconds after the stimulus is the P300. Note that it is quite different under the two conditions. Even though the same stimulus (letter A) is used to evoke the response, the signal is much larger when the subject is uncertain what the stimulus will be. This potential must, therefore, reflect processes in the brain that are not solely dependent upon the physical characteristics of the stimulus (Kutas and Hillyard 1985).

Contingent Negative Variation

Another interesting example of changes in the electrical activity of the brain that seem to reflect such "psychological" factors rather than the physical characteristics of the stimulus is the contingent negative variation. This potential seems to occur whenever we expect or anticipate an event.

The schematic illustration in figure 5.21 shows the **contingent negative variation** (CNV) discovered by Walter and associates (1964). The contingent negative variation is a slow negative potential that develops over the cerebral cortex in subjects who "expect" some event to occur. In the illustration, presentation of one stimulus—S_1—signals that another

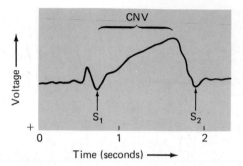

Figure 5.21 The contingent negative variation (CNV) that occurs during the expected event.

stimulus—S_2—is going to occur. During the interval between S_1 and S_2, a slow negative potential occurs that terminates abruptly when S_2 is presented.

This potential does not develop unless the second stimulus is "expected" by the subject and, therefore, seems to reflect the process of expectancy rather than the occurrence of the stimulus per se. Interestingly, the CNV may also occur in anticipation of a voluntary movement (e.g., Kornhuber 1974), which raises the science fiction possibility that it could in some way relate to the process of volition. Such slow potentials also occur in the brains of experimental animals and appear to correlate with a variety of behavioral phenomena (Rowland 1968; Rowland and Dines 1968).

The averaged evoked potential is also being developed for use in diagnostic examination of the human brain. One promising method examines **far-field evoked potentials,** in which the evoked potential recorded from the human scalp is determined by the averaging technique. This is done for many hundreds or thousands of stimulus occurrences. Even the tiniest component of the evoked potential can be extracted and examined using this method. When this is done, a

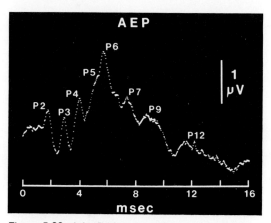

Figure 5.22 A far-field, averaged evoked potential showing various components (P2, P3, etc.), each of which may be attributed to a different stage in the processing of the auditory stimulus by the brain.

complex evoked potential can be recorded in which each component can be related to various steps of processing in the brain (Starr and Achor 1975). For example, the evoked potential depicted in figure 5.22 was recorded from the scalp of a human subject responding to an auditory stimulus consisting of a "click." Each component represents a different stage in the progression of the stimulus into the brain and its sequential passage from the ear to the cerebral cortex (Goff and Allison 1978). Each component is labeled according to its electrical polarity (P means positive), and its position in time (1–12) after the stimulus. P2 represents the electrical activity of the acoustic nerve in response to the stimulus. Successive components represent the response of various nuclei and pathways in the brain where the auditory information is relayed until it finally reaches the thalamus and cerebral cortex. By correlating these various components with specific sites in the brains of experimental animals (Buchwald and Huang 1975)—in which

specific regions may be destroyed and the evoked potential examined to determine which components are affected—inferences can subsequently be drawn regarding sites of brain damage. This is accomplished by recording the far-field evoked response in human patients (Starr 1978).

Evoked Potentials and Neuronal Activity

As we have pointed out, each of the different types of electrical activity that can be recorded from the brain gives us some unique perspective on its operation. In addition, all of these types of electrical activity derive ultimately from changes in the membrane potentials of the billions of individual cells that make up the nervous system. An important object of brain research in this century has been to determine not only how these various types of electrical activity relate to behavior, but also how they relate to each other. For example, how does the activity of an individual neuron in the visual cortex relate to the evoked potentials that occur there in response to visual stimulation? Since both of these events depend in some measure upon synaptic activity, some relationship must surely exist. In fact, it has been established that in many cases the activity of neurons in response to a visual stimulus occurs during specific portions of the evoked potential. Such a relationship is shown in figure 5.23, which shows an evoked potential and the activity of a small population of neurons in the visual cortex of the cat. The two types of responses were recorded simultaneously, so that the timing of both the evoked potential and the action potentials can be compared. Individual action potentials in response to a light flash occurred predominantly

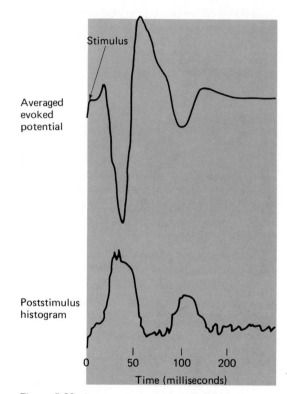

Stimulus

Averaged evoked potential

Poststimulus histogram

0   50   100   200

Time (milliseconds)

Figure 5.23 An average evoked potential (upper trace) compared to a poststimulus histogram showing when neurons fired action potentials over the same time period and to the same stimulus, a light flash. Note that neurons are most likely to fire during the negative-moving (downward) changes in the evoked potential.

during two portions of the evoked potential and can be determined by comparing the upper record (evoked potential) and the lower record (a histogram whose height is determined by the number of action potentials that occur at various times after the stimulus). While such relationships between the evoked potential and the action potentials of individual neurons have

been demonstrated, there is some question as to how stable these are over time (e.g., Vaughan 1969). Indeed, this relationship is one that continues to be the subject of study and evaluation. Such continuing research is important if we are to ultimately understand the relationship of individual neurons to the populations in which they are embedded and the principles by which the activity of such populations produces behavior (MacGregor and Lewis 1977). Similar questions are asked about the EEG and the activity of individual neurons. We know that much of the EEG reflects the combined synaptic potentials occurring in millions of neurons. It is also known, for example, that when the EEG is **desynchronized** (that is, when it is characterized by low-voltage, high-frequency changes as in the alert human record shown in figure 5.15) the activity of neurons in the brain is generally higher than during slower frequency, higher amplitude changes. As we will see in subsequent chapters, each of these types of electrical activity reveals important aspects of the functions of the brain in behavior.

Summary

Neurons are specialized to receive, conduct, and transmit information. The process of conduction involves the generation of **action potentials** by nerve cells that, because of the specialized nature of the nerve cell membrane, can travel or propagate down the axon of the cell to remote destinations. The process of information transmission between cells involves the release of chemical substances (neurotransmitters) from the axon terminals and other portions of the nerve cell to act on other cells with which synaptic contact is made. For both conduction and transmission, certain characteristic electrical signals occur.

The electrical signals that are generated by nervous tissue are based upon the fact that nerve cells, like other cells, act like tiny batteries in which the inside of the cell is negatively charged and the outside of the cell is positively charged. When the nerve cell is at rest—that is, when it is not conducting action potentials—voltage across the cell membrane is termed the **resting membrane potential.** This potential is produced because the electrically charged particles (**ions**) that exist both inside and outside of nerve cells are not equally distributed across the cell membrane. Indeed, much more sodium (Na^+), which is positively charged, is present outside of nerve cells than on the inside. Potassium (K^+), another positively charged ion, is highly concentrated inside nerve cells and less so outside these cells. These differences in concentration are maintained by the **sodium-potassium pump,** which acts to keep sodium outside and potassium inside of the cell.

In the resting state, the membrane of the nerve cell is highly permeable to potassium ions, but not to sodium ions. Thus, potassium ions are able to leak out of the cell by the process of **diffusion,** creating a charge imbalance across the membrane that produces the resting membrane potential. When an action potential is produced, the membrane becomes briefly permeable to sodium so that during this instant, this ion dramatically affects the membrane potential. A subsequent increase in permeability to potassium (even greater than during the resting state) helps restore the membrane to its resting value. These changes in voltage can be estimated using the concentrations of various ions inside and outside the cell with the Nernst equation.

The electrical signs of synaptic activity also occur because of changes in the permeability of the nerve cell membrane to various ions. Secretion of neurotransmitters by presynaptic neurons creates **excitatory** (EPSPs) and **inhibitory** (IPSPs) **postsynaptic potentials** in postsynaptic nerve cells. The voltage across the membrane changes toward (excitatory) or away from (inhibitory) the **threshold** for initiation of an action potential. Synaptic potentials are graded—that is, they depend for their size upon the number of synapses that are active within a short period of time. The action potential, on the other hand, is an all-or-none response. That is, if the membrane potential reaches discharge threshold, the neuron produces an action potential that propagates down the axon. If the threshold is not reached, the action potential does not occur at all. Techniques are available to record action potentials from individual neurons in any region of the brain, and action potentials from a population of neurons can also be recorded. In both instances, since neurons are quite small, electrodes with tiny tips—microelectrodes—are used.

The electroencephalogram, or EEG, represents changes in the membrane potentials of millions of neurons in the brain recorded simultaneously by relatively large electrodes placed in contact with the brain or on the scalp. Several characteristics of the electroencephalogram, such as amplitude and frequency that correlate with levels of sleep and awareness, disease processes in the brain, and other brain functions, have been defined. In addition to these spontaneous electrical changes, signals that result from sensory stimulation, called **evoked potentials,** can be recorded. Evoked potentials have been recorded to reveal the areas of the brain that respond to particular types of stimulation. Use of the averaging technique has also enabled evoked potentials to be recorded from the scalp of human subjects. Such recordings reveal that the electrical activity of the brain is affected not only by physical stimulation but also by other psychological factors such as the affective state of the individual and the uncertainty with which a stimulus occurs. A continuing important aspect of research on the electrical activity of the brain is to determine how these many different electrical signals are related to behavior and to each other.

Suggested Readings

Eccles, J. C. 1973. *The understanding of the brain.* New York: McGraw-Hill Book Co. *This book is an excellent treatment of the basic principles of neurophysiology and synaptic transmission, with an especially informative chapter on motor behavior.*

Kandel, E. R., and J. H. Schwartz, eds. 1981. *Principles of neural science.* 2d ed. New York: Elsevier/North-Holland. *This is a large, modern, and very comprehensive textbook in the neurosciences. Virtually any topic of interest is represented here.*

Katz, B. 1966. *Nerve, muscle, and synapse.* New York: McGraw-Hill Book Co. *This is a fine and proven treatment of the principles of nerve and muscle activity and synaptic communication. Everyone in the neurosciences has probably read or should read this book at one time.*

Kuffler, S. W., J. G. Nicholls, and A. R. Martin. 1984. *From neuron to brain.* 2d ed. Sunderland, MA: Sinauer Associates, Inc. *This is an outstanding elementary textbook in neuroscience; especially informative about the neurophysiological properties of individual nerve cells.*

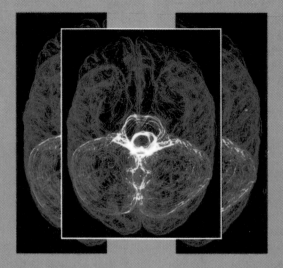

Outline

Introduction

Neurons are designed to communicate. As we mentioned in previous chapters, they accept information from other neurons, integrate it, and then pass a signal on to other cells. Communication between neurons occurs at the **synapse,** a tiny gap or cleft between the membrane of the cell sending the information (the presynaptic cell) and the membrane of the cell receiving it (the postsynaptic cell). Information typically travels across this gap in the form of a specialized chemical substance known as a **neurotransmitter.** The neurotransmitter is released by the presynaptic neuron, and it acts on the postsynaptic cell. This entire process is known as **synaptic transmission,** the subject of this chapter.

No area of neurobiology has grown more rapidly during the past thirty years than the study of synaptic transmission. In the late 1950s, three different chemicals were identified as neurotransmitters in the brain. By the late 1980s, that number had grown to more than three dozen, and most investigators believe that many more remain to be discovered. Why are there so many neurotransmitters? No one really knows. Perhaps different neurotransmitters allow the nervous system to segregate different functions. Neurons involved in the transmission of pain information, for example, may release a different neurotransmitter than neurons involved in transmitting visual information. Perhaps the nervous system needs different neurotransmitters to exert different effects on the receiving cell; some neurotransmitters may act for a relatively prolonged period, some only briefly; other neurotransmitters may inhibit the flow of information, some may facilitate it; and so on.

Chapter

6

Synaptic Transmission and Psychopharmacology

Perhaps the large number of neurotransmitters simply reflects different stages in the evolution of the nervous system. As each brain region evolved, it may have selected its own unique chemical messenger.

There seems to be an element of truth in all of these explanations, but they probably are only part of the story. Whatever the reason for so many neurotransmitters, the fact is that the nervous system could not operate without them. They are the stuff of our sensations, our movements, and our thoughts. Indeed, some of the most profound mental illnesses can be traced to some type of synaptic malfunction.

The importance of neurotransmitters in the normal operation of the nervous system also explains the powerful mind-altering effects of many drugs. As you will see in this chapter, our understanding of how drugs influence behavior is related directly to our understanding of chemical communication between neurons. **Psychopharmacology** is a field of study that deals with the effects of drugs on behavior, and we will explain some of its fundamental principles. We also will discuss some of the major classes of drugs, how these affect behavior, and how these influence synaptic transmission.

Synaptic Transmission

The process of identifying a chemical as a neurotransmitter is not an easy task. The brain is a veritable soup of chemicals, and even though there may be dozens of neurotransmitters, there are many more substances that are not. The decision to identify a particular chemical as a neurotransmitter requires that certain criteria are met, including the following:

1. The chemical must be synthesized or manufactured by the presynaptic neuron. This means that the presynaptic neuron must contain the enzymes necessary for this process as well as the precursor molecule from which the neurotransmitter is assembled.

2. The chemical must be released from the presynaptic neuron in response to electrical stimulation. Such stimulation occurs naturally in the form of an action potential, but it also can be produced artificially by applying electrical current to a stimulating electrode.

3. Once released, the chemical must produce a physiological effect in the postsynaptic cell. The chemical accomplishes this task by interacting with receptors on the postsynaptic membrane.

4. Mechanisms must exist to terminate the effect of the chemical as quickly as possible. One mechanism involves a synaptic enzyme that converts the chemical into a less active form. Another mechanism involves the uptake of the chemical back into the presynaptic neuron where it can be stored for release at another time. Because a chemical can be used repeatedly in this way, the uptake process is known as **reuptake.**

None of these criteria, by itself, is definitive. Simply demonstrating that a chemical is synthesized in a neuron is no guarantee that the chemical will be used as a neurotransmitter. Similarly, the demonstration of release is unconvincing if the chemical produces no physiological effect. The presynaptic neuron may release many substances that have no effect on the postsynaptic cell. But by itself, a postsynaptic effect also is not definitive. Many chemicals, including some found in foods, can evoke a response when applied to a neuron, yet none may be a neurotransmitter. Furthermore, some of these same substances may be inactivated by enzymes or taken up into a neuron. Thus, no compound ever reaches neurotransmitter status by meeting only one of the previously listed criteria. The more criteria that it does meet, however, the more likely that it will be termed a neurotransmitter.

Another important principle concerning synaptic transmission, first formulated in 1952 by Sir Henry Dale, has come to be known as **Dale's Law.** This principle states that if a particular neurotransmitter is released by one of a neuron's synaptic endings, the same chemical is released at all of the synaptic endings of that neuron (Eccles 1982).

Further complicating the picture are some substances that are not neurotransmitters in the classical sense (they do not meet all of the stated criteria), but they are found in the brain and they do exert clear effects on neurons. These substances are called **neuromodulators,** and their existence is the subject of intense interest (e.g., Calne 1979). Some neuromodulators may not have pronounced effects by themselves, but they may enhance the action of certain neurotransmitters. One such substance is ascorbic acid, or vitamin C. Ascorbic acid, also known as ascorbate, is found in high concentrations in the mammalian brain. It is not made here, but is transported into the brain from the blood supply through an active uptake process (Hadjiconstantinou and Neff 1983). When applied in physiological amounts directly onto neurons in certain regions of the forebrain, ascorbate has an excitatory effect on approximately one-third of the cells (Gardiner et al. 1985). Yet when ascorbate is applied along with glutamate, a well-known excitatory neurotransmitter, in the same forebrain region the effects of glutamate are enhanced in almost 70 percent of the neurons, many of which fail to respond to ascorbate alone. These results raise the distinct possibility that certain substances in the diet, like ascorbic acid, can influence neuronal activity, a topic that we will return to when we examine eating behavior. The neuromodulatory actions of ascorbate also appear to be linked to certain behavioral responses, as we will discuss in chapter 15.

Another interesting feature of some neuromodulators is that their effect lasts much longer than that of most neurotransmitters. A typical neurotransmitter, for example, may exert an effect that lasts for only a few milliseconds, whereas some neuromodulators may act for minutes or even days. Most long-acting neuromodulators are hormones, which are released into the bloodstream by specialized glands that we will discuss in later chapters. Such neuromodulators can influence neuronal growth and development.

In the following section, we will review the chemistry of some well-known neurotransmitters. We also will discuss some substances whose synaptic actions have been identified only recently. Many of these substances are still being tested as possible neurotransmitters, but already they are known to exert important effects as neuromodulators. In fact, some chemicals may serve both roles, acting as a neurotransmitter at one synapse and as a neuromodulator at another. We begin our discussion with the classical experiment that started it all.

Neurotransmitters and Neuromodulators

The first demonstration of chemical transmission at a synapse was reported by Otto Loewi in 1921. Loewi had been wrestling with the problem of synaptic transmission since the early 1900s. Some of his colleagues were convinced that synaptic transmission had nothing to do with chemicals; they argued that neurons communicated across the synapse by sending waves of electricity. Loewi, on the other hand, favored the chemical hypothesis. He believed that when an action potential reached the axon terminal, a chemical substance was released, and this chemical—not a wave of electricity—carried information to the postsynaptic cell. After much thought, however, Loewi concluded that it would be impossible to prove his hunch, so he stopped trying. Then, in the middle of a sound sleep on Easter Sunday night almost twenty years after he had abandoned his efforts, the idea for a definitive experiment came to him. He recalls the moment in his autobiography (Loewi 1960). "It was the design of an experiment to determine whether or not the hypothesis of chemical transmission that I had uttered 17 years ago was correct. I got up immediately, went to the laboratory, and performed a simple experiment. . . . " (p. 17). The rest, as they say, is history.

Loewi's experiment involved the vagus nerve, a group of axons that make synaptic contact with the heart. Loewi knew that when the vagus is stimulated, heart rate declines. From this information, he reasoned that if the vagus releases a chemical, then the chemical alone should cause the heart to slow down. To perform this experiment, he operated on two frogs. From one, he dissected the heart with the vagus nerve attached. From the other, he removed only the heart. He placed each heart in a separate fluid-filled chamber where they beat spontaneously (heart muscle does not require neural input to beat). Then he attached stimulating electrodes to the vagus nerve of the first heart and ran a tube from the chamber that contained this heart to the chamber that

contained the second heart. The tube was designed to transfer the fluid that would contain any chemical that might be released by the vagus nerve into the chamber. When he stimulated this nerve, the first heart slowed down as expected. The proof for chemical transmission came when the fluid that had collected during vagal stimulation of the first heart was applied to the second heart. This fluid caused the second heart, which had no neural connections, to slow down just like the first. Thus, the fluid, not the nerve itself, caused the effect. Loewi's experiment is illustrated in figure 6.1. His results convincingly demonstrated that activation of the vagus nerve released a chemical substance. Appropriately, Loewi named this chemical Vagusstoff. Today, we know this chemical as **acetylcholine,** the first substance to be identified as a neurotransmitter. A sum-

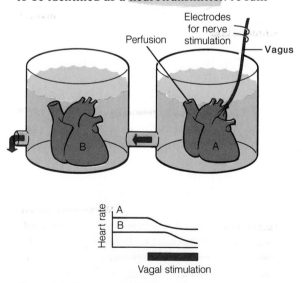

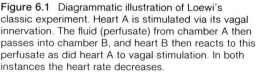

Figure 6.1 Diagrammatic illustration of Loewi's classic experiment. Heart A is stimulated via its vagal innervation. The fluid (perfusate) from chamber A then passes into chamber B, and heart B then reacts to this perfusate as did heart A to vagal stimulation. In both instances the heart rate decreases.

mary of the history of chemical synaptic transmission, written by Sir John Eccles, who shared the Nobel prize in 1963 for his pioneering research on this topic, makes interesting reading and is listed as a suggested reading at the end of this chapter.

Acetylcholine

We now know that acetylcholine is a neurotransmitter at many synapses in the body. Not only is it released by the vagus nerve, but also by the nerves that control most internal organs. It also is released by nerves that make synaptic contact with the skeletal muscles.

These muscles, unlike the heart, are excited by acetylcholine, making this neurotransmitter responsible for the muscular contraction that leads to movement. Acetylcholine is also a neurotransmitter at many synapses in the central nervous system. Neurons that use acetylcholine as a neurotransmitter are called **cholinergic.**

In the brain, the cell bodies of most cholinergic neurons lie in the brain stem reticular formation and in several nuclei in the basal forebrain, as shown in figure 6.2. The axons of these cells either innervate other structures several millimeters away or they travel only a

ACETYLCHOLINE

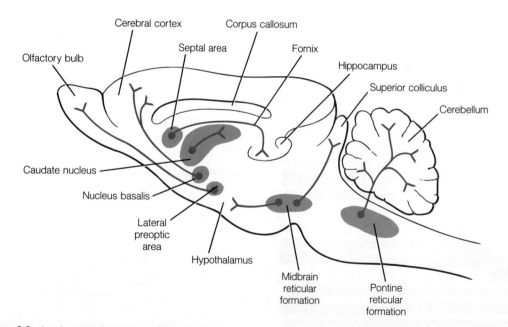

Figure 6.2 A schematic illustration of the major cholinergic neurons as shown in a sagittal section of the rat brain. Points of termination of cholinergic axons are shaded.

short distance and function entirely as inter-neurons. In this case, they terminate on other cells within the same structure. Cholinergic neurons in the septum, for example, send their axons through the fornix to the hippocampus, while cholinergic neurons in the caudate nu-cleus terminate on other caudate cells. Re-cently, some attention has focused on the cholinergic projection from the nucleus basalis (a small cluster of cells between the basal ganglia and hypothalamus) to the cere-bral cortex. These neurons appear to degen-erate in persons suffering from Alzheimer's disease.

Cholinergic neurons synthesize acetyl-choline from two precursors: **choline** and **acetyl-coenzymeA.** Choline, which is made in the liver and which is found in such foods as egg yolk, seeds, and legumes, is transported into cholinergic neurons by an active uptake mechanism. Acetyl-coenzymeA, sometimes abbreviated as **acetyl-CoA,** is made in the mi-tochondria of virtually all cells and partici-pates in many different chemical reactions. In cholinergic neurons, the acetyl portion of the CoA molecule is removed and attached to cho-line to form acetylcholine. The enzyme that promotes this reaction is **choline acetyltrans-ferase,** which, as its name suggests, transfers acetyl to choline (the suffix "-ase" simply identifies this molecule as an enzyme).

After its synthesis, acetylcholine (and other neurotransmitters) is stored in synaptic vesicles. As we discussed in chapter 3, these vesicles are found in large numbers in the pre-synaptic terminal, and when a nerve impulse arrives, calcium ions enter the terminal and the vesicles fuse with the presynaptic membrane and dump their contents into the synaptic cleft. This process is termed exocytosis and is the mechanism of synaptic transmission for many different neurotransmitters. The acetylcholine then diffuses across the synaptic cleft and combines with receptors on the membrane of the postsynaptic cell to produce either an ex-citatory postsynaptic potential (EPSP) or an inhibitory postsynaptic potential (IPSP). Whether the potential is excitatory or inhibi-tory depends entirely on the postsynaptic re-ceptor. Thus, at some synapses, acetylcholine has an excitatory, or depolarizing, effect, whereas at others it has an inhibitory, or hy-perpolarizing, effect. We already have seen this difference at cholinergic synapses onto muscle cells: Heart muscle is inhibited by this neu-rotransmitter, but skeletal muscle is excited.

Once acetylcholine produces its effect on the postsynaptic cell, it must be removed rap-idly from the synapse. Otherwise, it will con-tinue to act on the receptor and thus produce continuous excitation or inhibition. An en-zyme removes acetylcholine by breaking it up into two less active molecules: choline and acetate. Choline is 10,000 times less potent than acetylcholine on postsynaptic receptors, and acetate has virtually no effect. The en-zyme that performs this chemical breakup is **acetylcholinesterase,** an enzyme so powerful that it can degrade 64,000 molecules of ace-tylcholine every second. If you doubt the im-portance of this enzyme, consider that some of the most lethal nerve gases ever developed prevent acetylcholinesterase from working. The result is an excess amount of acetylcho-line in the synapse, causing a prolonged re-duction in heart rate and a simultaneous increase in the contraction of all skeletal mus-cles. The victim goes into violent convulsions and is unable to relax the muscles of the dia-phragm to take another breath. Death is swift and sure.

The choline that is created by the enzymatic breakup of acetylcholine is taken up by the axon terminal where it can be reused to make new molecules of acetylcholine. All of the relevant biochemical events that occur at a cholinergic synapse are summarized in figure 6.3.

For many years, it was believed that the amount of acetylcholine in the brain was controlled very precisely and rigidly. In fact, the level of acetylcholine in neurons was thought to be independent of the amount of choline that might be available. This no longer seems to be true. The level of acetylcholine in the brain actually fluctuates in response to the amount of choline in the diet. Rats fed a diet high in choline, for example, increase their production of acetylcholine in the brain (Cohen and Wurtman 1976). Apparently, cholinergic neurons are able to take up large amounts of choline and then convert this to acetylcholine. The availability of precursor molecules for other neurotransmitters also appears to influence their production (Fernstrom 1981). Thus, the amount of certain neurotransmitters in the brain can be manipulated by the amount of precursor molecules in the diet, offering an exciting new means of treating brain disorders caused by a deficiency of some neurotransmitters (Wurtman, Hefti, and Melamed 1981). In case you are wondering if the acetylcholine deficiency of Alzheimer's disease can be treated this way, the answer appears to be no. The problem in this disease is a degeneration or a loss of function of cholinergic neurons. Thus, even if choline is available in abundant amounts, the machinery required to convert it into acetylcholine no longer works.

The amount of available choline, however, is not the only factor that determines how much acetylcholine a neuron contains. The level of acetylcholine also is controlled enzymatically. Acetylcholinesterase, the same enzyme located on postsynaptic cells to break up acetylcholine in the synapse, also is present in the presynaptic axon terminal where it can destroy any acetylcholine not contained in a synaptic vesicle. If, for example, too much acetylcholine is produced, the vesicles can no longer store it, and it leaks out into the cytoplasm where it becomes vulnerable to acetylcholinesterase. Thus, although a cholinergic

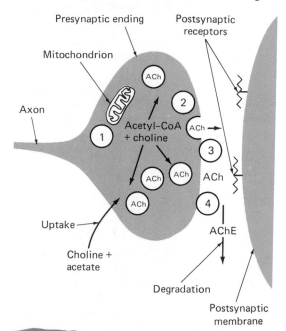

Figure 6.3 The events in cholinergic transmission are depicted schematically. 1. The two compounds, acetyl-coenzymeA (acetyl-CoA) and choline are combined to form acetylcholine, which is stored in synaptic vesicles. 2. The transmitter is released into the synaptic cleft to diffuse across the gap and 3. combine with postsynaptic receptors on the membrane of the postsynaptic cell. 4. The action of the transmitter is terminated by enzymatic degradation in which the enzyme acetylcholinesterase breaks the molecule into two metabolites; choline and acetate. Choline may be taken back up into the cell to be reused.

catecholamines (kat″e-kol-am′in)
norepinephrine (nor″ep-ĭ-nef′rin)
epinephrine (ep″ĭ-nef′rin)

neuron can increase the amount of acetylcholine that it contains by taking up large amounts of choline, the neurotransmitter level will not increase indefinitely. At some point, the vesicles will reach maximal capacity and any additional acetylcholine that is produced will be destroyed. Your brain, therefore, will not be swimming in acetylcholine no matter how many egg yolks or alfalfa sprouts you eat.

Catecholamines

Several different neurotransmitters are classified as **catecholamines.** The term "catecholamine" is derived from two common chemical names: a catechol, which consists of two adjacent hydroxyl groups (—OH) attached to a benzene ring (a ring of six carbon atoms), and an amine, which refers to an NH_2 group (fig. 6.4). There are many catecholamines in the brain, but only three are believed to act as neurotransmitters. Thus, when we refer to catecholamines, we are referring only to these three chemicals. Two of these, **dopamine** and **norepinephrine,** are found in many different brain regions and have been implicated in many different behaviors, as you will see throughout this book. The third catecholamine, **epinephrine,** appears to act as a neurotransmitter in a much smaller population of

neurons. It is confined primarily to the medulla and caudal brain stem, though its role in behavior has not been well defined.

You may recognize epinephrine and norepinephrine by their other names, adrenaline and noradrenaline respectively. Thus, a neuron that contains norepinephrine often is called a noradrenergic neuron, and a neuron that contains epinephrine is known as an adrenergic neuron (sometimes, adrenergic is used more broadly to include both norepinephrine- and epinephrine-containing neurons). Mercifully, there is no mystery to the terminology that applies to the dopamine system; a dopamine-containing neuron is known simply as a dopaminergic neuron.

The cell bodies of most dopaminergic neurons lie in the ventral portion of the midbrain, as shown in figure 6.5. They are divided into three clusters or groups labeled A8, A9,

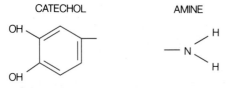

Figure 6.4 The basic elements of a catechol and an amine. Note that the catechol contains two adjacent hydroxyl (—OH) groups on its benzene ring and that the amine consists of a nitrogen atom (N) and two hydrogen atoms (H).

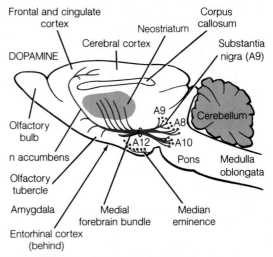

Figure 6.5 A sagittal section through the rat brain schematically illustrating the locations of nuclei that contain dopaminergic cells (A8, A9, A10, A12) and the projections of their axons. Points of termination of dopaminergic axons are shaded. (Note that there is a projection to the entorhinal cortex that does not appear from this angle of view.)

and A10. Two of these groups, A8 and A9, send their axons in a rostral direction to the caudate nucleus and putamen of the basal ganglia. This band of fibers is known as the **nigro-neostriatal pathway,** and it contains more than 70 percent of the dopamine in the brain. It has this name because the A9 group is part of the substantia nigra and the caudate-putamen complex also is known as the neo-striatum. The nigro-neostriatal pathway degenerates in Parkinson's disease, causing a series of movement disorders that we will discuss in later chapters.

Dopaminergic neurons in the A10 group are located just medial to the substantia nigra in a region called the ventral tegmental area. These cells also send their axons rostrally, but they terminate in a large number of limbic and cortical structures. Thus, the dopamine pathway that originates in A10 is called the **mesolimbic pathway,** or more generally the **mesotelencephalic pathway.**

Another group of dopaminergic neurons is located in the hypothalamus. This is the A12 group, which sends its axons ventrally through the median eminence toward the pituitary gland, a structure that we will encounter in later chapters when we discuss hormones.

Noradrenergic neurons are more widely scattered throughout the brain stem, as shown in figure 6.6. Most of their cell bodies are found in groups labeled from A1–A7. Axons from the more caudal groups descend into the spinal cord, although they often branch and ascend to higher structures as well. The more rostral noradrenergic groups—A5, A6, and A7—send their axons toward the midbrain and forebrain where they innervate many structures, including the hypothalamus, cerebral cortex, and hippocampus. Note also that noradrenergic neurons in A6, which is part of a structure known as the **locus coeruleus,** send axon branches into the overlying cerebellum.

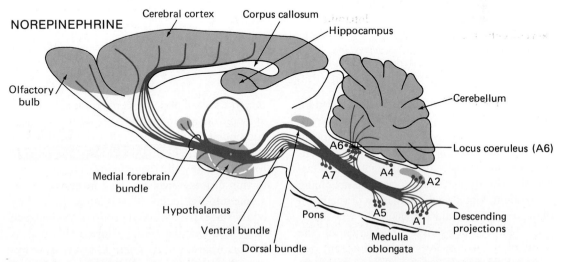

NOREPINEPHRINE

Figure 6.6 A sagittal section through the rat brain schematically illustrating the locations of nuclei that contain norepinephrine cells (A1, A2, A4, A5, A6, and A7) and the projections of their axons. Points of termination of norepinephrine axons are shaded.

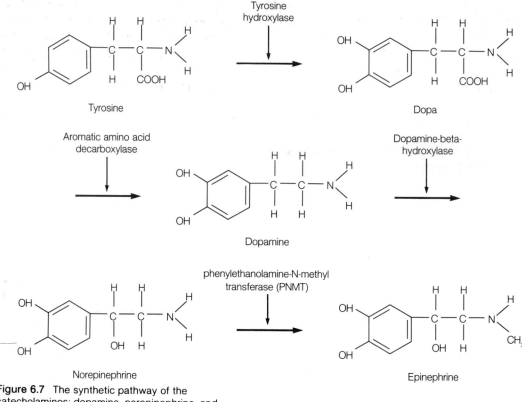

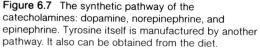

Figure 6.7 The synthetic pathway of the catecholamines: dopamine, norepinephrine, and epinephrine. Tyrosine itself is manufactured by another pathway. It also can be obtained from the diet.

As they ascend toward the forebrain, both dopaminergic and noradrenergic axons travel together in a large band of fibers known as the **medial forebrain bundle.** We will encounter this bundle again in chapter 12, especially the dopaminergic mesotelencephalic component, when we discuss areas of the brain that appear to mediate pleasure or reward.

The synthesis and breakdown of the catecholamines involves many different enzymes. Fortunately, however, many of the enzymes are the same, so you need not learn a completely different set of enzymes for each catecholamine. As you can see in figure 6.7,

the synthesis of dopamine, norepinephrine, and epinephrine are interrelated. All three of these compounds are synthesized from tyrosine, a simple amino acid made in the liver and also found in many different foods. The first step in this process involves the conversion of tyrosine into a catechol. This is accomplished by adding an extra hydroxyl group to the benzene ring. The enzyme that performs this task is known, appropriately enough, as **tyrosine hydroxylase.** It is the rate-limiting enzyme in the synthesis of all of the catecholamine neurotransmitters. This means that it is the slowest step and thus the most vulnerable to disruption. Drugs that block the synthesis of catecholamines are most effective if they interfere with the action of tyrosine hydroxylase.

The compound formed by the addition of the hydroxyl group to tyrosine is dihydroxyphenylalanine, also known in abbreviation as **DOPA.** You may have seen DOPA referred to as L-DOPA in some places; the "L-" simply refers to the isomer DOPA. (Tyrosine, DOPA, norepinephrine, and epinephrine each have two isomers: a left or "L-" form, so called because in solution the molecule will rotate a beam of plane-polarized light to the left; and a right or "D-" form that will rotate a beam of polarized light to the right. In each case, the molecules are exactly the same; one is the mirror image of the other. In the body, most naturally occurring molecules capable of existing in an "L-" or "D-" form typically occur in the "L-" form. Dopamine is unique in that it has no isomer.)

DOPA is rapidly converted to dopamine by the removal of its carboxyl group (—COOH). The enzyme that removes this group is DOPA decarboxylase, also known as **aromatic amino acid decarboxylase.** It has this alternate name because it is a nonspecific enzyme; it removes carboxyl groups from many different aromatic amino acids (those having a benzene ring). Once the carboxyl group is removed, any available hydrogen atom replaces it. Another feature of aromatic amino acid decarboxylase is that it is found in many different cells, not just catecholaminergic neurons. It is present, for example, in other neurons, glial cells, and even in blood plasma. Thus, patients with Parkinson's disease, the result of a dopamine deficiency, can increase dopamine levels in their brains by taking L-DOPA simply because when it reaches the brain, cells containing aromatic amino acid decarboxylase can convert it into dopamine.

In fact, because this enzyme is present in blood, parkinsonian patients must take their L-DOPA along with a drug that inhibits the enzyme in the body's periphery so that the L-DOPA will not be converted to dopamine before it reaches the brain. Dopamine itself cannot be used to treat the disease because, like most neurotransmitters, it does not cross the blood-brain barrier.

In noradrenergic neurons, a third enzyme is present to convert dopamine to norepinephrine. This conversion simply involves adding an hydroxyl group to the first carbon of the side chain. The enzyme involved in this conversion is **dopamine-beta-hydroxylase.** This enzyme, of course, is not present in dopaminergic neurons. The synthesis of epinephrine in adrenergic neurons involves one additional enzymatic step—the addition of a methyl group (—CH^3) to the amine. The enzyme included in this reaction is abbreviated **PNMT.**

All of the catecholamine neurotransmitters are inactivated by the same enzymes. In the axon terminal, the enzyme **monoamine oxidase (MAO)** destroys any catecholamines not stored in synaptic vesicles. Thus, it helps to regulate the amount of catecholamines in neurons in much the same way that acetylcholinesterase regulates the level of acetylcholine in cholinergic neurons. Like the decarboxylating enzyme that we discussed earlier, however, monoamine oxidase is not confined exclusively to catecholaminergic neurons. It is found in the liver, blood plasma, and even other neurons where it performs the much more general function of removing amine groups from many different types of molecules. Thus, any drug that inhibits this enzyme not only will increase the amount of catecholamines in the brain, but also will have widespread effects on other bodily functions.

Catecholamines released into the synaptic cleft are subject to degradation by the enzyme catechol-o-methyl transferase **(COMT).** Unlike acetylcholinesterase, however, COMT is not very powerful. In fact, drugs that inhibit COMT have very little effect on catecholamine transmission or on behavior. But, as we mentioned previously, it is important to remove a neurotransmitter from the synapse. If COMT does not do an effective job, what does? In catecholaminergic neurons, the neurotransmitter is inactivated primarily by reuptake. Once released into the synapse, dopamine, norepinephrine, and epinephrine are taken up again by the presynaptic terminal, where they find their way back into synaptic vesicles and become available for rerelease.

Serotonin

Most of the serotonin in the body is not involved in synaptic transmission. It is found most abundantly in the blood and intestinal tract of virtually every animal species. In fact, serotonin was identified first in the blood,

where it was found to increase the tonus, or contraction, of the muscles surrounding certain blood vessels. Thus, the name **serotonin** reflects the terms from which it originated: blood serum and its tonic effect on the cardiovascular system. Less that 2 percent of the body's serotonin is in the brain, and much of this amount also is associated with the blood supply. Only a tiny fraction is used by neurons as a neurotransmitter. Nevertheless, as you will see later in this chapter and throughout the book, serotonergic neurons play an important role in many different behaviors, including the hallucinatory behaviors produced by psychedelic drugs.

In many respects, the organization of serotonergic neurons in the brain parallels that of norepinephrine. Thus, serotonergic cell bodies are scattered in distinct clusters throughout the brain stem with the more caudal neurons sending their axons into the spinal cord and the more rostral neurons projecting to structures in the midbrain and forebrain. As shown in figure 6.8, groups of serotonergic cell bodies are labeled B1–B9.

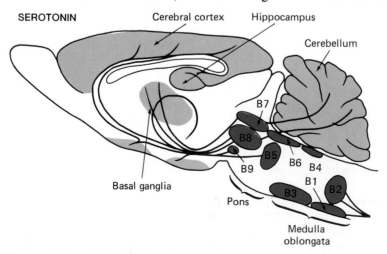

Figure 6.8 The cell groups that contain serotonin and the projections of their axons.

Three of these, B7, B8, and B9, are part of the **raphe nuclei** that innervate the cerebellum, the hypothalamus, parts of the basal ganglia, the cerebral cortex, and the hippocampus.

Serotonin, sometimes abbreviated 5-HT, is formed from **tryptophan,** an amino acid that, unlike tyrosine, cannot be made in the body. Therefore, to maintain an adequate amount of serotonin in the nervous system, we must consume foods rich in tryptophan, including milk and other dairy products, fish, and certain fruits and vegetables. Although tryptophan has a benzene ring, it is devoid of hydroxyl groups and thus is not a catechol. Instead, the benzene ring in tryptophan is attached to another smaller ring called an **indole.** Because tryptophan contains an amine group (—NH2) on its side chain, it is an indoleamine.

The first step in the synthesis of serotonin involves the addition of an hydroxyl group to the fifth carbon atom of the tryptophan benzene ring. This new compound, not surprisingly, is called **5-hydroxytryptophan (5-HT),** and if by now you are becoming wise in enzyme terminology, you may be able to guess that the enzyme that catalyzes this reaction is called **tryptophan hydroxylase.** 5-hydroxytryptophan is converted rapidly to 5-hydroxytryptamine, the chemical name for serotonin. This rapid conversion involves the removal of a carboxyl group (—COOH). The enzyme responsible for this is the same as that which removes the carboxyl group from DOPA—aromatic amino acid decarboxylase. The steps involved in the synthesis of serotonin are summarized in figure 6.9.

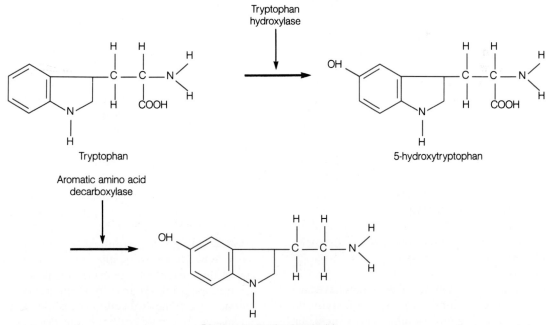

Figure 6.9 The synthetic pathway of 5-hydroxytryptamine (serotonin). Tryptophan is not manufactured in the body; it must be obtained from the diet. Note the indole ring, which is characteristic of serotonin.

Serotonin is inactivated by monoamine oxidase, the enzyme that we mentioned in conjunction with the catecholamines. As with the catecholamines, this enzyme is free to destroy any serotonin in the cytoplasm that is not protected inside a synaptic vesicle. Serotonin released into the synapse is removed by a powerful reuptake mechanism on the presynaptic terminal. This step also parallels the catecholamines in that they too are removed from the synapse by reuptake.

Amino Acids

Although some amino acids serve as precursors for many neurotransmitters, other amino acids may act as neurotransmitters and neuromodulators in their own right. Two of these are **glutamate** (glutamic acid) and **aspartate** (aspartic acid), both of which exert powerful excitatory effects on neuronal activity (Curtis 1974). They are formed in all neurons as part of the normal energy cycle of cells, though some neurons appear to make additional amounts for use as neurotransmitters. Glutamatergic neurons are found throughout the cerebral cortex. They send their axons to the neostriatum and to other subcortical structures. Interneurons in the cerebellum and spinal cord also contain high amounts of glutamate. The highest amounts of aspartate have been found in the thalamus and in the spinal cord. Although enzymes have been found that inactivate these amino acids, they appear to be removed from the synapse primarily by reuptake.

Two other amino acids are believed to act as powerful inhibitory neurotransmitters. One of these, **gamma-aminobutyric acid,** or **GABA,** may be the most ubiquitous neurotransmitter in the brain (Roberts 1986). Between 20–40 percent of all axon terminals in the brain contain GABA. In contrast, less than 5 percent of all synapses are catecholaminergic or serotonergic. GABA-containing, or GABAergic, neurons have been found in dozens of different nuclei from the brain stem to the cerebral cortex. Most of these cells have relatively short axons and act as interneurons.

GABA is formed from glutamate by the enzyme **glutamic acid decarboxylase (GAD).** This reaction also requires vitamin B_6, as does catecholamine biosynthesis. A dietary deficiency of this vitamin actually prevents GABA synthesis. The resulting decline in GABA increases the activity of the nervous system, as you would expect when a major inhibitory neurotransmitter is depleted. One consequence of a decline in GABA or catecholamines can be violent convulsions. This was demonstrated all to sadly several years ago by infants who were fed a baby food that by accident was deficient in vitamin B_6. Over time, the infants began to experience seizures, an effect that was prevented once the deficiency was discovered and corrected. As we will discuss in chapter 12, GABA also has been implicated in anxiety, and many of the drugs that are used to alleviate this condition alter GABA neurotransmission.

Another major inhibitory amino acid is **glycine.** Like GABA, it is found primarily in interneurons, but mainly those in the spinal cord, pons, and medulla (Aprison, Davidoff, and Werman 1970). Relatively little glycine is found elsewhere in the brain. As with the other amino acid transmitters, glycine is formed as part of the normal energy cycle of cells and is removed from the synapse by reuptake. A reduction in glycine transmission also leads to convulsions, but in this case the convulsions are confined primarily to the antigravity muscles of the legs. Such convulsions are caused by **strychnine,** a drug that blocks postsynaptic glycine receptors in the spinal cord.

Neuropeptides

A series of amino acids linked together form a peptide, and there now is abundant evidence that some of these peptides, which we will call neuropeptides, act as neurotransmitters and neuromodulators (see Bloom 1983). Currently, however, we have only sketchy information about their chemistry and synaptic action.

One of the first neuropeptides to be discovered was **substance P,** so named because it originally was isolated in powder form (the "P" stands for powder). Unlike the other neuropeptides, it was found during the 1930s, but at the time no one knew its importance in the nervous system. In fact, forty years passed before its amino acid sequence was identified, and its effects in the central nervous system were not studied until the 1970s. In the brain, substance P has been found in more than a dozen nuclei scattered along the midbrain, pons, and medulla. Substance P also exists in high concentrations in the dorsal horn of the spinal cord, where it appears to be the neurotransmitter released by incoming sensory fibers, especially those that convey pain information. The synthesis and inactivation of substance P remain a mystery, although some evidence indicates that substance P is removed from the synapse by enzymatic degradation rather than by reuptake.

An entire group of neuropeptides, known collectively as **endorphins,** was discovered in the 1970s. They stimulated considerable research because they possess many of the same properties as the opiates, a group of well-known analgesic, or painkilling, drugs such as morphine and heroin. Indeed, the term endorphin means endogenous (internal) morphine. Endorphins consist of chains of between five and thirty amino acids. They have been isolated in many different areas of the brain and spinal cord, and some also are present in the pituitary gland. In many cases, the endorphins are several times more potent than morphine in reducing pain, and for that reason, they have come to be known as the internal opiates of the brain.

Two endorphins, **leu-enkephalin** and **met-enkephalin,** are among the most promising candidates for neurotransmitter status. Both consist of five amino acids; four of these are identical in each molecule. The fifth amino acid is either leucine or methionine (this difference accounts for the prefix "leu" or "met" in their names). These substances are found in many neurons in the limbic system, where they may play a role in the rewarding effects of opiate drugs, and in areas of the brain stem and spinal cord that play a role in pain transmission. They may be formed by enzymes that break up some of the larger endorphin molecules. Enzymes also appear to inactivate the enkephalins once they are released into the synapse. We will consider these neuropeptides again later in this chapter when we discuss the behavioral effects of opiates and narcotic addiction.

Many other neuropeptides also exist in the central nervous system. Some of these occur in extremely small amounts, so small that in order to obtain enough of a sample to analyze their amino acid sequence, investigators have had to collect the brains of hundreds of thousands of animals killed in slaughterhouses to obtain just a few milligrams of a partially purified substance. Is the search worth the effort? Without a doubt. Many of these neuropeptides now have been found to play an important role in the release of hormones and in many other aspects of brain function. Knowledge of the amino acid sequence alone offers hope that some of these molecules can be manufactured in laboratories where they can be tested thoroughly and perhaps used to treat human disorders caused by neuropeptide deficiencies.

Psychopharmacology

Investigators who have been interested in understanding behavior have often used drugs in their research. The use of drugs in behavioral research has accelerated at an enormous rate, resulting in the creation of a specialty that is known both as **psychopharmacology** and as **behavioral pharmacology.** This discipline has been defined as the branch of psychology that utilizes the concepts and tools of both psychology and pharmacology to explore the behavioral actions of drugs (Thompson and Schuster 1968).

Why do investigators interested in brain-behavior relationships use drugs in their research? There are several answers to this question. First, drugs are used as research tools because some pharmacological agents have their principal effect on the nervous system and, therefore, on behavior. These agents can often be used to gain insights into how the nervous system controls various aspects of behavior. Drugs also induce changes in certain interesting behaviors; for example, some drugs alter states of consciousness, others increase activity, and yet others produce symptoms characteristically associated with mental disorders. Compounds that possess these properties enable the investigator to study such behaviors under controlled, experimental conditions and to determine how such effects are produced. Drugs are also studied for more practical reasons. Thousands of new drugs, many of which have behavioral effects, are synthesized each year, and many are produced

specifically for use in the treatment of mental or other disorders. It is necessary to study the mechanisms of action of these compounds, even if they produce unwarranted behavioral side effects, and to assess their therapeutic efficacy. Finally, certain pharmacological agents, collectively referred to as **drugs of abuse,** are sometimes associated with serious behavioral, medical, and social problems. Continued drug use may lead to addiction, physical dependence, and sometimes to life-threatening withdrawal symptoms (if use is abruptly discontinued). These drugs are studied experimentally to gain information about these processes and to find out what to do about their symptoms and problems.

Some Basic Concepts

Drugs have been defined as compounds that by virtue of their chemical structure interact with a specific biological system, such as a cell, in ways that change either the structure or the function of that system. This definition is quite broad. A more restrictive definition is that a drug is a chemical compound that has **selective biological activity.** Here, "selective" refers to the fact that at a low concentration, certain effects of the drug predominate, and "biological activity" refers to the fact that the compound affects a cellular process.

Dose Response and Time Response
Since psychopharmacologists are typically interested in drugs that affect processes in the brain and behavior, these variables are usually the "biological activity" that defines the compounds studied in psychopharmacology. The degree of biological activity produced by a drug depends on many factors, among which is the amount of the compound that is administered. This is called the **dose.** Typically, it is

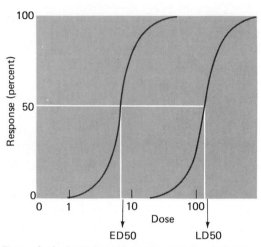

Figure 6.10 Schematic illustration of a dose-response relationship in which the dose of the drug administered is plotted as a function of the percentage of animals that exhibit a response. That dose which produces an effect in 50 percent of the subjects is called the ED_{50} (effective dose for 50%) and that dose which is lethal to half the animals is called the LD_{50} (lethal dose for 50%).

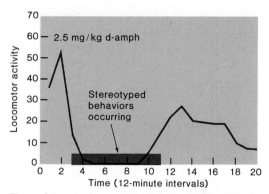

Figure 6.11 A time-response relationship in which the response of a rat to a single dose of amphetamine (2.5 mg/kg) is plotted over time. The behavior being plotted is locomotor activity. It is high initially, but decreases markedly during the occurrence of stereotyped behaviors (shaded bar) one to two hours after drug administration.

important to define the effects of a drug over a range of doses, since both the intensity and qualities of the drug's effects may vary at different doses. The relationship between the effects of a drug and the dose that is administered to an organism is called the **dose-response relationship** depicted in figure 6.10. The response to the drug is graphically plotted on the ordinate, and the dose of the drug is shown along the abcissa. In the most convenient case, the effect of the drug becomes greater with increasing dose, at least over a selected range of doses. However, the dose-response relationship for many drug effects is considerably more complex and may often involve changes in the pattern or kind of behavioral effect that occurs, including toxic effects such as death at high doses. Another important consideration, in addition to the dose-response relationship, is the time after the drug

is administered. Many drugs produce one effect within certain times after they are administered and different effects at other times. This relationship is called the **time-response relationship,** illustrated for the drug amphetamine in figure 6.11.

The curve illustrates the effect of a given dose of amphetamine (2.5 mg of drug per 1 kg of body weight) on the behavioral activity of a rat. If the response of the animal is measured about twenty minutes after the drug is administered, a marked increase in activity will be detected. If this response measure is taken one hour after the drug is given, a marked decrease will be seen. The reason for this reduction in activity is that when the 2.5 mg of amphetamine is given to rats, an increase in locomotor behavior occurs initially. However, after one hour, a different set of behaviors occurs that are typically called **stereotyped behaviors.** In the rat these include licking, grooming, and gnawing. When these behaviors occur, the animal is highly aroused by amphetamine, but does not walk around much!

Interestingly, the time-response relationship for amphetamine is also different for different doses (Rebec and Bashore 1984). Thus, it is important when studying drug effects to consider a range of details in the form of accurate dose- and time-response information.

Administration, Absorption, and Elimination

The response to a drug is also affected by how it is administered, absorbed, metabolized, and ultimately eliminated from the body. Drugs injected into muscle tissue—**intramuscular injection**—are absorbed relatively slowly, while agents injected into a vein—**intravenous administration**—enter the circulation directly. Other methods of administration that govern drug absorption include **ingestion,** in which case the drug is absorbed from the gut or intestines; **intraperitoneal,** in which the agent is injected into the cavity surrounding the viscera; and **inhalation,** in which absorption occurs across the lungs. The rate of absorption also will be determined by how soluble the drug is in water or fat. If, for example, a drug is highly soluble in water but not fat, then it will mix with blood very readily but will have a difficult time crossing cellular membranes, which, as we have seen, have a lipid or fatty component.

The effect of a drug also will depend on how rapidly it can be excreted or metabolized. In some cases, a drug is excreted in the urine, or it is broken down by drug-metabolizing enzymes in the liver and elsewhere. Different tissues may have different rates of elimination, as shown in figure 6.12. The rate of elimination of the drug LSD was determined for the general circulation (bloodstream) and for the fluid filling the brain, cerebrospinal fluid.

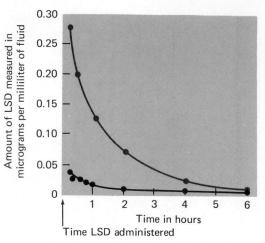

Figure 6.12 Rates of elimination of LSD from blood and from cerebrospinal fluid following a single dose (30 mg/kg) injected directly into the bloodstream of monkeys. The black line represents the rate of elimination of the drug from the bloodstream. The colored line represents the rate of LSD elimination from cerebrospinal fluid.

Those rates are shown in figure 6.12. Since the process of elimination of a drug from the body occurs continuously over a period of time, that point at which one-half of the drug is gone is sometimes chosen to express this variable. This is called the **biological half-life,** which may be expressed in minutes or even days or longer. As shown in figure 6.12, LSD has a half-life in the bloodstream of about an hour. Other important factors that influence the effects of drugs include the species, age, sex, and genotype of the organism.

Agonists, Antagonists, and Receptors

We previously introduced the concept of chemical transmission at the synapse. Many drugs are thought to produce their effects by influencing this important process. Drugs that mimic the action of a particular neurotransmitter molecule (and in so doing increase the effectiveness of transmission at synapses utilizing the neurotransmitter) are sometimes termed **agonists.** Other agents, thought to produce their effects by blocking the action of specific neurotransmitters, are called **antagonists.** Specific receptors located on cell membranes appear to be responsible for many of the actions of drugs and other chemicals on nerve cells. However, receptors for neurotransmitter molecules are only one category of receptors that exist on biological membranes.

Receptors for neurotransmitters and drugs are studied in several ways. For example, the presynaptic cell may be stimulated electrically, and the effects produced by the neurotransmitter released onto the postsynaptic cell are delineated by electrical or biochemical measures. A more recent method developed to study receptors—including both those involved in synaptic transmission as well as those that interact with hormones, drugs, and other substances—is termed **receptor binding,** a technique now in widespread use in studies of drug action on the brain.

In receptor binding a compound is chosen that possesses several important properties. The compound—the **ligand**—must form a very tight chemical bond with the receptor. Secondly, it must be possible to make the ligand highly radioactive by the addition of tritium or other source of radioactivity. When the receptors are isolated by means of a series of biochemical steps, they may be detected by a **scintillation counter** that, in effect, measures the radioactivity associated with the ligand that is still bound tightly to the receptor.

Using receptor binding and other methods, investigators have now measured many of the properties associated with receptors for synaptic transmitters, various other agonists and antagonists, hormones, and drugs. The picture that emerges from this and other evidence is that receptors may be located on or inside nerve cells, glia, and other cells. They are highly dynamic molecules that possess specific molecular properties, are replaced at specific and relatively high rates by the cell, and form an important link between the chemical environment of the brain and body and cellular processes.

Among the first receptors to be characterized by these methods were those for acetylcholine on skeletal muscles. When it is released, acetylcholine binds to receptors located on the membrane of the muscle along the synaptic cleft. This causes changes in the muscle membrane and leads to contraction. One extremely important discovery about receptors is that the number of receptors or their tendency to bind to various ligands, termed their **affinity**, may vary with events that occur at the synapse. For example, when the nerve supply to a muscle is cut and acetylcholine is no longer released onto the muscle membrane, the number of receptors for acetylcholine on the muscle increases dramatically, often appearing in patches of muscle membrane not previously in synaptic contact with the nerve (Sharpless 1975). This increase in sensitivity may be detected by applying acetylcholine directly to the muscle and measuring the resultant response or by receptor binding and other methods. In effect, the muscle becomes supersensitive to acetylcholine and other agonists of this transmitter, a process called **denervation supersensitivity.** We now know that many neurons in the brain and elsewhere respond to denervation in similar ways.

Importantly, in many cases the input to a particular cell need not be destroyed to induce an increase in its sensitivity to agonists. Prolonged administration of antagonists may also produce such effects. Among their other actions, many drugs used to treat psychosis, for example, prevent the action of dopamine at dopaminergic synapses in the brain (Snyder et al. 1974). Prolonged blockade of dopamine receptors, as occurs when these agents are given to animals for long periods of time, produces a marked increase in the number of dopamine receptors in the brain (Burt, Creese, and Snyder 1977). A variety of similar reactions occur for other neurotransmitters and have been implicated in many of the behavioral effects of long-term drug administration.

We already have pointed out that a single neurotransmitter may have quite different effects depending on its postsynaptic target. This difference is due to the fact that different targets may have different receptors. It now is believed that receptors for nearly every neurotransmitter may involve multiple types. Two classes of receptors have been characterized for acetylcholine, for example. These two classes are **muscarinic** and **nicotinic** receptors.

Muscarinic receptors are activated by the drug muscarine, a compound found in some poisonous mushrooms. Muscarinic receptors reside on many internal organs, including the heart, pupils of the eyes, and tear ducts. Eating one of these mushrooms, therefore, will slow the heart (remember that activation of cholinergic receptors on the heart has an inhibitory effect), constrict the pupils, and cause watery eyes. Muscarinic receptors also are located on many nerve cells, which may account for some of the bizarre behavioral effects of certain mushrooms. The antidote is atropine, a drug that blocks muscarinic receptors. By itself, atropine has the opposite effect of muscarine on internal organs: It increases heart rate, dilates the pupils, and drys up the eyes. In fact, atropine's ability to widen the pupils is responsible for its other name, belladonna. (In Italian, *belladonna* means "beautiful woman," and legend has it that in the Middle Ages,

Italian women applied atopine directly to their eyes to dilate their pupils in an effort to make themselves more appealing to male suitors.)

Nicotinic receptors are activated by the drug nicotine, which of course is found in tobacco. These receptors are located on some nerve cells as well as on skeletal muscles (smoking cigarettes can cause a slight muscular tremor, but no one can consume enough nicotine to elicit fatal convulsions since in high amounts nicotine first causes vomiting). Curare is a drug that blocks nicotinic receptors. When taken by itself, curare can cause muscular paralysis. For this reason, many primitives dip their arrow tips in curare to make their weapons much more effective.

Note that at both muscarinic and nicotinic synapses, acetylcholine is the neurotransmitter. But the receptor that responds to acetylcholine is different in each case. Thus, cholinergic receptors on the heart respond to muscarine but not to nicotine, while the reverse is true of skeletal muscle. In fact, it now appears that most neurotransmitters have more than one type of receptor.

Recent technical advances have made it possible to visualize the precise locations of various classes of neurotransmitter and drug receptors in the brain. This is made possible with receptor autoradiography (Kuhar, DeSouza, and Unnerstall 1986). In this method, ligands that bind especially well to the receptor of interest are made radioactive by substitution of one or more of their hydrogen or carbon atoms with the radioactive isotopes tritium and ^{14}carbon. When brain sections are exposed to these radioactive ligands, they bind to their particular class of receptors. When a piece of photographic film or emulsion is placed over the section, the radioactive ligand, still bound tightly to its receptor, exposes the film directly above the location of the receptor.

Because most receptors are not uniformly distributed, the film is exposed in a particular pattern that reflects the density and locations of the receptors.

The image shown in figure 6.13, for example, is an autoradiograph of the distribution density of one class of dopamine receptor in a coronal section through the rat brain. This class of dopamine receptor is referred to collectively as the D_2 dopamine receptor. As can be seen, this receptor is very dense in the neostriatum of the rat brain, but there is virtually no binding in the cerebral cortex. This image is analyzed and enhanced by computer in order to detect slight differences in the binding density. The scale on the right relates the light density in the image to the density of receptors. Areas of high receptor binding are very dark (e.g., dorso-lateral neostriatum and the

olfactory tubercle at the bottom of the brain), while lighter regions have relatively low binding (e.g., there is virtually no binding in cerebral cortex). Color coding of these variations in light and dark produces visual images that are both informative and beautiful, as shown in color plate 6.

Postsynaptic Events in Receptor Activation
Synaptic transmission may affect not only the electrical activity of cells, but also metabolism and other processes in postsynaptic cells. One current theory is that some neurotransmitters, including norepinephrine and dopamine, interact with receptors that are coupled to the enzyme **adenylate cyclase,** which is thought to be physically associated with the receptor molecule (e.g., Greengard 1975). As shown

FMOLS / Mg Protein

900 —

759 —

619 —

478 —

338 —

197 —

56 —

Figure 6.13 An autoradiogram showing the distribution of 3-tritium-labeled spiroperidol, a dopamine antagonist that binds to D_2 dopamine receptor. Binding is very dense in the neostriatum, but there is little receptor binding in the cerebral cortex.

schematically in figure 6.14, interaction of the transmitter with its receptor molecules activates this enzyme, which converts the energy-rich molecule adenosine triphosphate (ATP) to cyclic adenosine monophosphate (cAMP). The accumulation of the cAMP molecule serves as an internal signal to the cell that may affect the properties of its membrane, including its electrical activity and the activity and levels of various enzymes in the cell membrane or its interior (Bloom 1975; Rall 1979). Increases and decreases in the synthesis of particular enzymes in the postsynaptic cell as a result of synaptic activity provide clear evidence for the transsynaptic control of protein synthesis. This is an area of intense research (e.g., Wurtman et al. 1979; Guidotti and Costa 1977).

Cyclic adenosine monophosphate is sometimes called a **second messenger** because it carries the message transmitted by the first messenger, the neurotransmitter molecule. This important concept was first proposed for the effects of hormones on target cells in which cAMP is thought to serve as the second messenger following the interaction of hormones with their receptors (Sutherland 1972).

Some neurons also have receptors for their own neurotransmitters. These receptors, sometimes called "presynaptic" receptors, or **autoreceptors,** participate in a variety of cellular functions. As shown in figure 6.15, autoreceptors are located on the axon terminal and on the soma or dendrites of the neuron releasing the neurotransmitter. Terminal autoreceptors help to control the amount of neurotransmitter released by a nerve impulse (Starke 1980; Tepper, Groves, and Young 1985). When these receptors are activated, for example, an action potential will cause less neurotransmitter release. Apparently, the

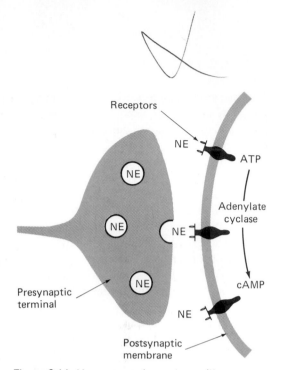

Figure 6.14 Hormones and neurotransmitters may affect cellular metabolism and other cellular processes through the second messenger, cyclic AMP. The enzyme, adenylate cyclase, is activated by the interaction of the neurotransmitter norepinephrine in the schematic example shown above, with its receptor that is associated with the enzyme.

neuron uses these receptors to monitor the amount of neurotransmitter in the synapse, and if some neurotransmitter is present to activate these receptors, the neuron need not release as much. It is as if the neuron is saying, "There already is some neurotransmitter out there, so I'm not going to bother releasing everything that I could." This is a very good example of negative feedback; the neurotransmitter is acting back on the neuron that released it to decrease further release. Similarly, if the terminal autoreceptors are not activated or if they are blocked, the neuron interprets this as little or no neurotransmitter in the synapse. Thus, an action potential under these conditions will cause more neurotransmitter release than normal. Terminal autoreceptors also may regulate neurotransmitter synthesis in the same

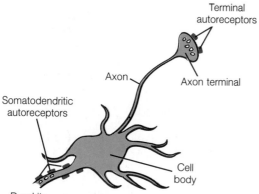

Figure 6.15 Schematic diagram illustrating that some nerve cells are thought to have receptors for their own neurotransmitter. When the transmitter is released from the dendrites or synaptic ending of the cell, it acts back upon these presynaptic receptors for negative feedback control of cellular processes.

way (Roth, Salzman, and Nowycky 1978). If they are activated, neurotransmitter synthesis in the terminal will decline, but if they are blocked or if there is no neurotransmitter in the synapse, synthesis will increase.

Autoreceptors on the cell body or on dendrites help to control the firing rate of the neuron (Groves et al. 1975; Aghajanian and Wang 1978). When a neuron generates an action potential, the impulse not only travels toward the axon terminal, but it also spreads back across the soma and out along the dendrites (in fact, recordings of the electrical activity of single neurons in the brain typically are made from the soma, not from the axon, simply because the cell body is much larger and thus much easier to locate with an electrode). In some neurons, dendrites, like axon terminals, are equipped with synaptic vesicles. As the action potential spreads along the dendrite, the neuron releases its own neurotransmitter onto its own cell body or another dendrite where it can act on autoreceptors,

alter the resting membrane potential of the cell, and play an important role in determining whether the cell will fire another impulse. These autoreceptors tend to inhibit or hyperpolarize the neuron (Grace and Bunney 1985). Thus, they too are part of a negative feedback system; when a neuron generates an action potential, it releases its own neurotransmitter onto itself to reduce the likelihood that it will fire another action potential any time soon. Inhibitory autoreceptors have been identified on many catecholaminergic and serotonergic neurons in the brain.

Drugs that activate these receptors effectively decrease the ability of these neurons to influence postsynaptic activity. Apomorphine, for example, is a dopamine receptor agonist, but at extremely low doses it acts selectively on dopamine autoreceptors and not on postsynaptic dopamine receptors (Skirboll, Grace, and Bunney 1979). Thus, at low doses of apomorphine, the dopaminergic neuron is shut down (both firing rate and release are inhibited), and as a result it no longer can exert any direct effect on the postsynaptic neuron. In fact, postsynaptic cells that normally are inhibited by dopamine actually increase their firing rate with low doses of apomorphine (Rebec and Lee 1982; Rebec 1984). When the dose of apomorphine is increased so that it also stimulates postsynaptic dopamine receptors, this drug inhibits postsynaptic activity.

These results also explain why very low doses of apomorphine have completely different effects on behavior than do high doses. At low doses, apomorphine effectively decreases dopamine neurotransmission because it acts only at autoreceptors. Postsynaptic neurons increase their firing rate because of the lack of dopamine, and the behavioral response is sedation and sleep. At high doses, the drug stimulates postsynaptic receptors and mimics an increase in dopamine neurotransmission. This mimics the action of dopamine, which normally inhibits postsynaptic neurons, and leads to behavioral arousal. In the event you are wondering why in our example an increase in postsynaptic firing rate is associated with sedation and a decrease with arousal, keep in mind that an increase in neuronal activity does not mean an automatic increase in behavior. There are many neurons between a dopaminergic axon terminal and skeletal muscles. Thus, there is ample opportunity for an increase in activity in one group of neurons to be converted to an inhibitory effect on the body's musculature. Do not make the mistake of assuming that every cell in the brain has a direct effect on muscle activity. In most cases, brain neurons are many synapses removed from the spinal neurons that innervate skeletal muscles.

Drugs and Behavior

A number of events in the process of synaptic transmission form the basis for many of the current theories about the actions of various drugs on the brain and behavior. Our discussion of autoreceptors is only one example of this. Some of the other ways that drugs can affect synaptic transmission, and thus behavior, will be discussed in this section. As shown in figure 6.16, drugs can affect the neuronal impulse as it invades the terminal, the uptake and synthesis of transmitters and enzymes or their percursors, the release process, or the interaction of the transmitter with its receptors and degradative enzymes. More general effects of drugs on nerve cells, which also may affect these processes, include inhibiting the cell's ability to manufacture proteins, or other general effects such as influencing respiration and metabolism. Throughout the text we will be concerned with the effects of

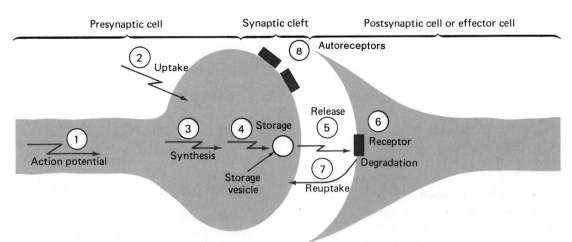

Figure 6.16 Drugs can affect synaptic transmission in a number of ways: (1) by interfering with the action potential as it invades the presynaptic terminal; (2) by interfering with the uptake of the molecules that serve as precursors for the manufacture of the transmitter molecule; (3) by interfering with the synthesis of the transmitter; (4) by interfering with the storage of the transmitter in presynaptic vesicles; (5) by affecting the release of the transmitter; (6) by interacting with the postsynaptic receptor molecule; (7) by affecting the rate at which the transmitter is removed from the synaptic cleft, either by action on degradative enzymes or on presynaptic reuptake mechanisms; and (8) autoreceptors can modulate neurotransmitter release and synthesization. Drugs can also affect synaptic transmission in ways not illustrated.

strychnine (strik'nīn)

picrotoxin (pik''ro-tok-sin)

pentylenetetrozol (pen'tĭ-lēn-tet'rah-zol)

drugs on behavioral processes and the means by which these processes are generated by the brain. In the following paragraphs, we review some of the major classes of psychoactive drugs and how they affect behavior.

Stimulants

Stimulants share a common property: They excite the central nervous system. Different stimulant drugs produce excitatory effects in quite varied ways. Here, we discuss four categories of drugs as central nervous system stimulants: (1) the xanthines, (2) the convulsants, (3) amphetamines, and (4) cocaine.

Xanthines The **xanthines** are the most widely used stimulants because they include the drug **caffeine.** A cup of coffee contains approximately 100 to 150 milligrams of caffeine, which is sufficient to stimulate the nervous system. About the same amount of caffeine is present in a cup of tea and in a one-quart bottle of a cola drink (Ritchie 1975).

Caffeine, as well as the other xanthines, stimulates the heart and increases the tension of skeletal muscles, thus these drugs increase the ability to do physical work while counteracting to a certain extent the effects of fatigue. An important therapeutic action of the xanthines is their ability to relax the smooth muscles of the respiratory system and thus relieve the tense respiratory muscles in asthma sufferers.

One effect of caffeine in the central nervous system is to inhibit the effect of **adenosine,** a naturally occurring compound in the brain known to have depressant effects on behavior (Sattin 1984). An intraventricular injection of adenosine in animals, for example, causes sedation. By blocking this effect, caffeine increases behavioral activity.

Convulsants Convulsant drugs are so named because in sufficiently large doses they produce behavioral convulsions. Central nervous system convulsants include drugs such as **strychnine, picrotoxin,** and **pentylenetetrazol.**

Many of the convulsant drugs appear to produce their excitatory effects by blocking inhibitory systems within the central nervous system. As we have mentioned previously, strychnine acts, in part, by blocking glycine receptors, which inhibit activity in the brain stem and spinal cord. Picrotoxin blocks some inhibitory processes in the brain, especially inhibitory synaptic transmission mediated by GABA. Metrazol appears to excite nerve cells directly, which ultimately results in convulsive discharge. At subconvulsive doses, these drugs produce many of the same effects that xanthines produce.

The convulsants are sometimes referred to as **analeptic drugs** (from the Greek *analēptikos* meaning "to restore"). Clinically, these drugs are sometimes used to "restore" functioning of the central nervous system after it has been depressed by drugs, such as the barbiturates, or by other causes. The analeptic drugs have been used extensively in behavioral research on learning and memory storage processes where subconvulsive doses of convulsant drugs have been shown to facilitate memory storage processes in experimental animals (McGaugh and Krivanek 1970).

Amphetamines The amphetamines have been studied extensively, and we are slowly learning the mechanisms by which they produce their effects. The effects of these compounds are to increase body temperature (hyperthermia), heart rate, and the ability to perform sustained work. The amphetamines diminish the sense of fatigue and produce an elation of mood. Amphetamine has been prescribed extensively, and haphazardly, in the form of diet pills to reduce appetite.

In experimental animals amphetamine increases locomotor activity. At higher doses, it increases the occurrence of the so-called stereotyped behaviors, which in rats include gnawing, sniffing, and compulsive grooming. In humans, amphetamines produce repetitive searching and examining behavior (e.g., dismantling watches, radios, and the like, or longed staring at objects) and motor compulsions (e.g., chewing and licking, moving the same object back and forth, or picking at the skin until it bleeds).

The behavioral effects of the amphetamines appear to be mediated by the action of these drugs on catecholaminergic synaptic transmission. The amphetamines appear to enhance the release of norepinephrine and dopamine from presynaptic neurons and to inhibit the reuptake mechanisms by which these transmitters are removed from the synaptic cleft (Groves and Rebec 1976). Thus, they increase the availability of the catecholamines in the synaptic region. At very high doses, amphetamines appear to affect transmission at serotonergic synapses as well, and when given over long periods of time may cause significant reductions in brain levels of this and other neurotransmitters. Prolonged presence of amphetamines in the brain may produce significant damage to catecholamine neurons (e.g., Ellison et al. 1978).

The amphetamines (and other stimulants such as cocaine) are capable of producing symptoms that are strikingly similar to certain psychotic conditions. Prolonged use of the amphetamines, or sometimes even a single large dose, produces symptoms in humans that are referred to as **amphetamine psychosis.** The similarity between amphetamine psychosis and paranoid schizophrenia has led investigators to propose that studying the former disorder may provide valuable clues to understanding the mechanisms that underlie certain kinds of schizophrenia. This issue is discussed in some detail in chapter 15. Drugs that are used to treat patients with amphetamine psychosis are also very useful in the treatment of schizophrenia (Snyder et al. 1974). These drugs are discussed later in this chapter and in chapter 15.

Cocaine   Cocaine is derived from the leaves of Erythroxylon coca, a plant that is native to Bolivia and Peru. The inhabitants of these areas have long chewed on the leaves of this plant to increase physical stamina.

Today, cocaine is processed either in crystal or powder form. It is a powerful antifatigue drug that also produces feelings of increased mental ability and can result in great excitement and sometimes hallucinatory experiences. Peripherally, the drug increases body temperature and constricts peripheral blood vessels. Centrally, the drug is a neural stimulant. Its central actions are believed to occur because of its effects on noradrenergic and dopaminergic neurons. It appears to inhibit the reuptake of these neurotransmitters, prolonging their life in the synaptic cleft. Therefore, these transmitters are in contact with postsynaptic receptors at higher concentrations and for longer periods of time. The action of both cocaine and the amphetamines on dopaminergic transmission appear to mediate the powerful rewarding effects of these drugs on behavior, as we discuss in chapter 12.

Cocaine has an important local action; namely, it blocks neural conduction when brought into direct contact with nerve fibers. At very low concentrations, it blocks neurotransmission in sensory nerve fibers, which produces a **local anesthetic** action. Its most important medical use is in eye surgery during which a solution of approximately one-half percent anesthetizes the eye (Ritchie et al. 1970). Many local anesthetics are cocaine-like molecules.

Depressants

The **hypnotics** and **sedatives** are classified as depressants since they tend to depress a variety of neuronal functions and to induce drowsiness or sleep. **Barbiturates** are the typical example used to illustrate the actions of hypnotics and sedatives; they are often the major ingredient in prescription "sleeping pills." In addition to a discussion of the barbiturates, this section will include an overview of **alcohol,** the most commonly used and sought after of all central nervous system depressants. Finally, we will discuss **narcotic analgesics,** which although also appropriately classified as central nervous system depressants, have their major medical application as compounds used to relieve pain.

Because of their ready availability and their ability to produce a temporary euphoria, all of these agents are widely abused. The deleterious effects of these drugs on society and the health of chronic users represent a topic of major scientific and social concern.

Barbiturates

The most widespread clinical use of the barbiturates is to induce drowsiness and sleep, although a variety of other applications have also been made. Their depressant action has been used to control convulsions, for example, and they are used frequently to control anxiety. Indeed, a number of nonbarbiturate depressants are used to control anxiety. These include many popular and widely prescribed tranquilizers that go by such well-known trade names as Valium, Librium, and Quaalude. These latter compounds are typically less hypnotic—that is, they do not induce sleepiness as readily—and are preferred for applications in which hypnosis is not desired.

In general, the barbiturates have widespread depressant actions in nerve cells as well as in other cell systems of the body such as the liver and kidney. There is evidence to suggest that this depressant action involves a number of important cellular events, especially synaptic transmission and the excitability of nerve and muscle cells (Harvey 1975). Depending upon the concentration of a particular barbiturate, such agents may depress the excitability of cells so that a greater level of stimulation is required to maintain activity at a normal level. At high concentrations, barbiturates can reduce the release of transmitter substance from presynaptic nerve endings and may also produce an action similar to local anesthetics—conduction of the action potential along nerve fibers is blocked.

The behavioral actions of barbiturates are commonly thought to result, in part, from the depressant actions of the drug on brain systems normally involved in the maintenance of wakefulness and attention. The activity of cells of the reticular formation of the brain, for example, in which a normal level of activity is considered important for the maintenance of attention and wakefulness, is depressed by barbiturates. In general, it is believed that barbiturates have their most marked effects on behaviors dependent upon polysynaptic pathways in the brain, in which activity of a large number of nerve cells is involved and for which many synaptic interconnections exist. It is certainly clear that ongoing behavior of nearly any sort will be affected dramatically by a hypnotic dose of barbiturates.

In general, withdrawal from barbiturates after prolonged use involves hyperexcitability of the nervous system. It is extremely unpleasant, sometimes even life threatening. Reflexes of all sorts become exaggerated, the individual becomes agitated and may experience hallucinations, nightmares, or even convulsions.

It is thought that these symptoms are due, in part, to the reaction of the nervous system to continual depression by barbiturates. The nervous system apparently attempts in a number of ways to compensate for the depressant action of the barbiturates. Nerve cells are thought, for example, to compensate by increasing their level of excitability. While the barbiturate is present, the nerve cell is able to compensate to a degree in the face of being depressed by the drug. When the drug is withdrawn, the nerve cell is more excitable than normal and the symptoms of withdrawal occur until the cells readjust to a state appropriate to the absence of the drug. This process resembles the supersensitivity that develops following pharmacological receptor blockade, or denervation, in which the input to a nerve or muscle cell is removed. The cell becomes more and more excitable in an apparent effort to overcome this loss of input.

Indeed, one prominent theory of physical dependence to barbiturates and other depressant drugs and the occurrence of withdrawal symptoms invokes the concept of supersensitivity. The depressant drug is thought to be analogous to denervation or other processes in which the input to nerve cells is habitually reduced, leading to exaggerated responsiveness following withdrawal (Jaffee and Sharpless 1968).

Other theories of drug dependence emphasize the biochemical processes of nerve cells, especially the synthesis and release of neurotransmitters. If depressants such as barbiturates depress the release of neurotransmitters, it may be that nerve cells attempt to compensate for this effect by an increase in neurotransmitter synthesis or release. When the drug is withdrawn, an excess of transmitter is present leading to the hyperexcitability characteristic of withdrawal (e.g.,

Goldstein and Goldstein 1968). A variety of other processes affected by barbiturates may also show these important compensatory effects and become exaggerated upon withdrawal of the drug.

The phenomena of drug dependence and withdrawal will recur in our discussion of narcotics, which will illustrate these and other factors important in drug addiction.

Alcohol The best known and most widely used and abused central nervous system depressant is ethyl alcohol, which has been used for centuries not only because of its ability to produce intoxication but also as a sedative or hypnotic, an anesthetic, and for many other purposes. Alcohol in sufficient concentrations will kill or produce damage to many biological tissues, including muscle and brain cells. At dopaminergic synapses, alcohol impairs the ability of calcium ions, which are necessary for neurotransmitter release, to enter the axon terminals of dopaminergic neurons (Leslie et al. 1986). The result, therefore, is a decrease in dopamine transmission. Alcohol also is known to interfere with many other neurotransmitters, perhaps also by disrupting the entry of calcium into presynaptic terminals.

The progression of alcoholic intoxication is well known. Initially, alcohol appears to produce an excitatory effect. The individual becomes talkative, inhibitions are reduced, and judgment may be impaired. Performance of skilled motor activities, such as driving, is adversely affected. Later, motor behavior is dramatically affected, the intellect is stunted, normally appropriate controls of behavior and judgment become markedly impaired, and the inebriate may become drowsy or lapse into sleep. Coma is a common sequel to extreme intoxication. All of these consequences depend

upon how each individual absorbs and metab-
olizes alcohol, the person's body weight, the
amount consumed, and other factors, including whether previous drinking has led to
tolerance. Most states now define drunkenness
as the presence of a certain percent of alcohol
in the blood, especially where intoxication becomes a question of legal importance as in
cases of drunken driving and other behaviors
that endanger the drinker or those around him
or her.

For many people, alcoholic intoxication
becomes habitual and leads to alcoholism. The
reasons for the development of alcoholism are
many and complicated, and a number of factors have been identified that appear to increase the risk of alcoholism. These include the
personality of the drinker, his or her familial
history regarding problem drinking, and the
social environment in which the drinker lives
and works, and many others (Schuckit 1979).
For many societies, including American, alcoholism is a problem of enormous proportions, a fact that is well known and highly
publicized.

Narcotic Analgesics   The major medical use
of narcotic or opiate drugs is to produce
analgesia, or relief from pain. When used for
this purpose, the narcotic analgesics have a
unique advantage over other classes of drugs,
such as the general anesthetics used to anes-
thetize patients undergoing surgery. The narcotics can be administered in doses that
produce analgesia without inducing drowsiness and sleep. At high doses, of course, these
drugs do induce sleep. Many narcotic drugs
have been developed, the prototype being
morphine, which is a drug extracted from the
opium poppy. Another well-known and widely

abused opium derivative is heroin, a substance
converted to morphine once it enters the brain.
We will review what is known of the action of
these opiate drugs and the problem of great
concern to society, opiate addiction.

The mechanisms of action of the narcotic analgesics are still poorly understood.
Although drugs such as morphine will produce dramatic relief from chronic pain, this
effect is not so much a reduction in the sensation of pain, even though this does occur to
some degree. Morphine and related opiates
appear to act on the degree to which pain is
appreciated by the individual. Pain can still be
felt, but it is no longer a compelling, bother-
some feeling. Thus, the perception of pain
seems to involve both sensory attributes as well
as our emotional reaction to them. This emotional aspect is most affected by the narcotic
analgesics.

Among the most significant advances in
our understanding of the means by which the
opiates affect the brain is the discovery of specific receptors for opiates in the brain, spinal
cord, and elsewhere to which we have alluded
in previous sections. Using receptor-binding
techniques, investigators have discovered that
opiate drugs interact with specific receptors on
nerve and other cells in the nervous system
(Simon and Hiller 1978). This discovery led,
in large part, to the discovery of the endogenous opiatelike peptides, endorphins, and enkephalins. These are believed to be the
naturally occurring opiates in the brain that
are involved in the regulation of our appreciation of pain and many other functions. Although opiate receptors occur in many parts
of the brain, an unusually high concentration
of these receptors is found in the limbic system

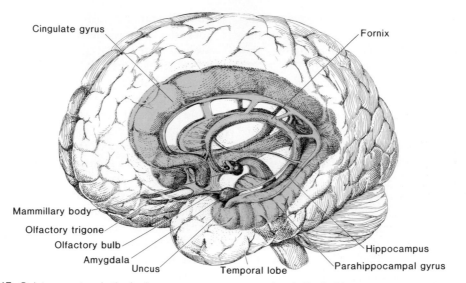

Cingulate gyrus

Fornix

Mammillary body

Olfactory trigone

Olfactory bulb

Amygdala

Uncus

Temporal lobe

Hippocampus

Parahippocampal gyrus

Figure 6.17 Opiate receptors in the brain were identified by measuring the specific binding of radioactively labeled opiate drugs to cell fragments from different brain areas. The largest amount of binding was found in cells from the limbic system (color), a series of evolutionarily primitive regions at the core of the brain that are primarily involved with smelling in lower vertebrates and with the arousal of emotions in humans. The high concentration of receptors in the limbic system suggests it is here that opiates exert their euphoria-producing actions, and also that one internal opiatelike substance or more may play some normal role in modifying emotional component of pain.

(Snyder 1977), which is depicted schematically in figure 6.17. Structures of the limbic system are organized into a complex series of brain circuits apparently responsible for the control and generation of such emotional states as mood. The euphoria-producing effect of opiates is currently believed to involve their action at receptors in the limbic system. High concentrations of the opiate receptors also occur in certain other brain sites and are implicated in the many other pharmacological actions of the narcotics, including nausea, pupillary constriction, changes in body temperature, and constipation.

Psychotomimetic Drugs

Many drugs that we have discussed fit easily into the psychotomimetic drug classification. Amphetamine and cocaine, for example, may produce a psychotic state nearly indistinguishable from paranoid schizophrenia. Thus, they produce effects that mimic psychosis, hence the term **psychotomimetic.** Certain other types of drugs—for example, lysergic acid diethylamide (LSD), psilocybin, mescaline, and marijuana—are categorized as psychotomimetic drugs because they also induce altered states of consciousness, changes in mood and behavior that mimic psychotic behaviors.

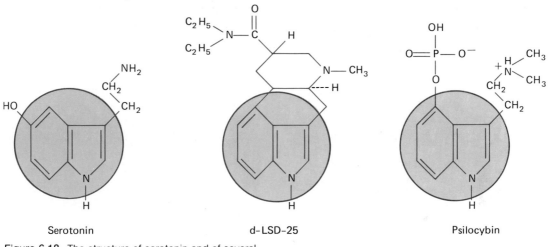

Figure 6.18 The structure of serotonin and of several hallucinogenic drugs. Note the similarities in the structures of these compounds. The indole portion of each is enclosed in the circle.

Lysergic Acid Diethylamide (LSD) Structurally, LSD resembles serotonin, a molecule postulated to have neurotransmitter functions in the central nervous system. Other **hallucinogenic compounds**—psilocybin, for example—also resemble serotonin in structure. The similarities are illustrated in figure 6.18. Chemically, the most interesting quality of LSD is the indole ring, a characteristic common to many hallucinogenic drugs and to serotonin.

The effects of LSD can be divided into three general categories that were summarized by Jacobs and Trulson (1979). These include (1) somatic symptoms such as dizziness, creeping or tingling of the skin, nausea and tremors; (2) perceptual symptoms such as hallucinations and altered time sense; and (3) affective and cognitive symptoms such as rapid mood swings, ranging from severe depression to extreme agitation and anxiety.

The mechanisms of action of LSD have been studied extensively. Gaddum (1953) and Woolley and Shaw (1957) were the first to propose that the central nervous system effects of LSD are mediated by its antagonism of the synaptic action of serotonin. This hypothesis was based on three facts: (1) LSD and serotonin resemble each other in chemical structure; (2) LSD antagonizes the actions of serotonin in certain smooth muscle preparations; and (3) serotonin is a putative neurotransmitter in the central nervous system. This hypothesis soon encountered difficulty because of two very important discoveries. The first discovery was that 2-bromo-LSD (BOL) is as potent as LSD in antagonizing the peripheral effects of serotonin, but it produces few or no behavioral effects. The second discovery was that in some peripheral nervous system sites, LSD mimics the actions of serotonin.

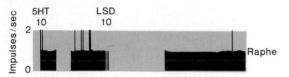

Figure 6.19 (vertical lines) Neuronal firing rates of
cells in the raphe nuclei varying between one and two
action potentials per second. Note that when serotonin
(5-HT) is applied to a cell neuronal activity is inhibited
markedly. Application of LSD also inhibits neuronal
firing. In this example, both 5-HT and LSD were
applied by iontophoresis, a process by which these
compounds are ejected from a glass pipette by
electrical current (10nA in this case). The glass pipette
is part of the electrode that records neuronal activity.

Research on the central nervous system
effects of LSD received major impetus when
Freedman (1961) and Freedman and Giarman
(1962) were able to demonstrate that LSD increases levels of serotonin in the brain. Later,
Aghajanian, Haigler, and Bloom (1972) and
Haigler and Aghajanian (1974) showed that
when LSD is applied directly and in very small
amounts to the serotonergic neurons of the
raphe nucleus of the brain stem, it inhibits
neural firing in this structure. Moreover, BOL
does not have this effect. Effects of LSD on the
firing rates of raphe nuclei cells are shown in
figure 6.19. The current theory of the central
nervous system mechanisms of action of LSD
is that it inhibits the firing of cells in the raphe.
Thus, the net effect of LSD is to remove the
effect of serotonin from many postsynaptic
structures in the brain.

Marijuana   The dried leaves and flowers of
the hemp plant **Cannabis sativa** are called
marijuana. Hashish is the concentrated resin
derived from the flowers of the marijuana
plant. Both marijuana and hashish contain ingredients that produce behavioral effects.

Many of these psychoactive ingredients have
now been identified, the major one being Δ9-
tetrahydrocannabinol. This compound does not
resemble other psychoactive compounds in
chemical structure nor is it similar in composition to any of the known neurotransmitter
molecules. Thus, the mechanisms of action of
this drug remain a mystery.

The effects of marijuana vary from individual to individual and depend in part on
the circumstances surrounding the drug's use.
The effects of the drug become noticeable
within minutes after it is smoked because absorption by the lungs is very rapid. The effects
develop more slowly when the drug is ingested. The effects may persist for considerable periods of time since it is metabolized very
slowly. Its half-life in some individuals has been
estimated to be as high as two days.

Under marijuana's influence, individuals experience a free flow of disconnected
ideas, altered perceptions of time and space,
intense cravings for food, and impulsive behavior. They may talk incessantly, or they may
become quite silent. After very high doses,
hallucinations can also occur. Adverse health
consequences due to marijuana smoking have
been reported occasionally by various authors.
Some of these unfavorable side effects include
damage to nerve cells, the reproductive system,
and other organ systems of the body. However,
many other investigators have been unable to
detect any long-range deleterious effects of the
drug. In an extensive study performed in Jamaica, Rubin and Comitas (1974) were unable to find any evidence to support these
earlier findings.

Pharmacological studies with marijuana
have confirmed that the drug produces mixed
depressant and excitatory effects. For example, marijuana has been shown to enhance

the depressant effects of the barbiturates. On the other hand, this drug has also been shown to potentiate some of the excitatory effects of the amphetamines.

A great deal of research has been conducted on the behavioral effects of marijuana. Much of this research deals with the effects of marijuana on learning and memory storage processes. Nearly all researchers who have studied marijuana's effect on learning and memory have agreed that when it is used, marijuana impairs memory processes, especially those involved in short-term memory and the transfer of information into long-term storage (e.g., Darley et al. 1973). Although some theories have been developed to explain these effects, research concerning the effects of marijuana on health, social behavior, and other aspects of human performance and cognition has not arrived at a definitive conclusion. It is probable that important questions concerning the possible deleterious effects to individual marijuana users will remain unanswered.

Drug Addiction and Conditioning

It has been recognized for many years that the phenomenon of drug dependence may be understood in part as a process of conditioning (e.g., Schuster and Johanson 1973; Thompson and Schuster 1968). Within this theoretical framework the dependence on narcotics, for example, may be regarded as an example of operant behavior in which the use of the opiate drug is reinforced and maintained by the euphoric and other reinforcing characteristics of drug experience. Indeed, animal subjects can be taught to administer opiates and other abused drugs themselves. Using animal models of drug addiction has contributed greatly to our understanding of the process of addiction.

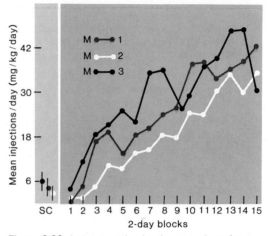

Figure 6.20 Lever pressing by three monkeys for morphine reinforcement. The data at the bottom left (SC) represent the responses made while the animals received saline injections. The rest of the data were obtained during the following thirty days (plotted in blocks of two days) when the animals were injected with morphine. It is important to remember that all injections were contingent upon the monkey's lever-press response.

In a typical experiment, a catheter is implanted into the jugular vein of a monkey. The animal is placed in a restraining chair and is injected with morphine through the catheter on a carefully controlled schedule, usually several injections each day. After a period of time, the actual experiment is begun. A visual or other stimulus and a telegraph key are made available to the animal. Every 4–6 hours, the stimulus light is illuminated, signaling to the monkey that when the telegraph key is depressed, a predetermined dose of morphine is delivered through the jugular catheter. Animals quickly acquire skill in pressing the lever for morphine reinforcement, as shown for three monkeys in figure 6.20. These subjects show both morphine tolerance and physical dependence after administration for periods of one to several weeks (Schuster and Thompson 1969).

This experiment demonstrates that morphine has reinforcing or rewarding properties that can lead to the acquisition of new behaviors. Similar experiments with other drugs have demonstrated that animals will abuse virtually every drug abused by humans (Schuster and Thompson 1969).

The processes of conditioning also may play an important role in the signs of narcotic withdrawal. In experimental animals, for example, a neutral stimulus may acquire the power to produce some of the effects of narcotic withdrawal if it has been present during previous withdrawal episodes (e.g., Goldberg and Schuster 1967). In one study, conditioned narcotic withdrawal signs were produced experimentally in volunteers who were former heroin addicts. In this experiment, O'Brien and associates (1977) presented an odor and sound to the subjects during mild withdrawal from methadone, the replacement drug with which these patients were being treated. In careful monitoring of behavioral and physiological reactions, these researchers demonstrated that following repeated pairing, the noise and odor eventually elicited signs of withdrawal as a conditioned response. Experimental investigations such as this provide objective evidence to support the view that the environment can be significant in maintaining the drug habit and in producing a relapse in former addicts who return to their drug-taking environment after treatment.

Tolerance and Physical Dependence

An extremely important reaction to many drugs is that continued use produces tolerance and dependence. As it relates to habitual drug use, tolerance is the ability to withstand the effects of the drug. Consequently, the user requires higher and higher doses to produce the desired effect. In some cases, this is due to the

fact that the tissue on which the drug acts becomes less sensitive to it. This type of tolerance is called **pharmacodynamic tolerance.** In other cases, more and more of the drug is required to produce its effect because after continual use, the drug is eliminated from the body at higher and higher rates. This type of tolerance is called **drug dispositional tolerance,** an example of which is illustrated for alcohol in figure 6.21. With some drugs, especially the depressants, the development of tolerance is coupled with physical dependence in which withdrawal from the drug after continuous use can produce severe symptoms. During **physical dependence,** the body requires the drug for normal functioning. Thus, when the drug is withdrawn, the body suddenly finds itself without the substance on which it has come to rely and severe withdrawal symptoms develop.

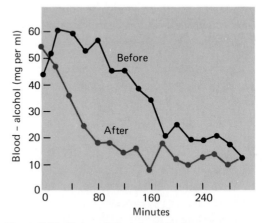

Figure 6.21 Rates of alcohol metabolism as a function of use. (Before) In this experiment subjects were first detoxified and then given an injection of alcohol. The rate of disappearance of the alcohol from bloodstream was then measured. (After) The subjects were next given alcohol daily for a seven-day period and rates of alcohol metabolism were again measured. Note that alcohol is metabolized significantly more quickly after the subjects' seven-day regimen of alcohol.

Physical dependence is very common with repeated use of the narcotic analgesics. During withdrawal, the body responds with symptoms that are the exact opposite of the effects of the drug itself. Table 6.1 contrasts some of the effects of morphine with the signs of withdrawal that follow its repeated use. Note that the depressant effects of morphine are replaced by hyperexcitability and other signs of agitation and arousal. Similar effects occur during withdrawal from heroin, a synthetic type of morphine.

Drugs and Mental Illness

The use of **psychotherapeutic drugs** has revolutionized the treatment of mental disorders of nearly every sort. The development of pharmacological treatment methods for anxiety and psychotic states is usually associated with the introduction of a major tranquilizer, chlorpromazine, which has been found effective in tranquilizing and relieving other symptoms in psychotic patients. Literally hundreds of new

drugs have been developed within the past thirty years for the management of mental illness. In addition to the development of new drugs, a second benefit of the introduction of psychotherapeutic drug treatment has been the intense study of the mechanisms underlying the action of these drugs on the brain. Of course, it is hoped this research will lead to the discovery of new, more effective agents. In addition, finding out which processes in the brain are affected by these drugs may lead to an understanding of the underlying defect in the processes of the brain that initially leads to psychosis. Although the scientific community is a very long way from achieving these important goals, progress has been steady. A great deal is now known about the mechanisms of action of the antipsychotic and anxiety medications. Much of what is known about the effects of psychotherapeutic drugs on the brain will be discussed in chapter 15. Here we will note only briefly that the use of pharmacological treatment methods in the management of mental illness is currently an important focus of research in psychopharmacology. Some contemporary research activity includes the behavioral and biological effects of these pharmacological agents on humans and animals.

In general, drugs used to treat various forms of mental disturbances can be classified into several broad categories that are stated here in accordance with the classes discussed by Byck (1975). These include drugs used to treat schizophrenia and amphetamine psychosis, **antipsychotic drugs.** Chlorpromazine is a prototypical antipsychotic drug. It appears to exert its effects by blocking dopamine receptors in the brain. Drugs used for patients with disorders of affect or mood, including **mood stabilizing** and **antidepressant drugs** (e.g., lithium); and those used primarily for the

Table **6.1** Drug and Withdrawal Effects of Morphine

Drug Effects	Withdrawal Effects
Suppression of autonomic nervous system	Activation of autonomic nervous system (autonomic storm)
Suppression of respiration	Hyperventilation
Suppression of gut movement (constipation)	Intestinal spasms
Analgesia	Acute sensitivity to pain
Fall in body temperature (hypothermia)	Rise in body temperature (hyperthermia)
Euphoria	Dysphoria
Sedation	Insomnia
Suppression of REM sleep (rapid eye movement, or dream sleep)	Increase in REM sleep, nightmares
Pupillary constriction	Pupillary dilation

treatment of anxiety, classified as **antianxiety drugs** (for example, Valium, a member of the benzodiazapine family).

Research on human patient populations has been extensive with many of these drug classes, but even more impressive is the vast array of animal experimentation that has been carried out in an effort to define and quantify the various behavioral actions of these drugs. Basic research concerning the biochemical effects of these agents on the brain has also been highly productive. Based upon this work, a number of theories have been developed concerning the etiology of various forms of mental disturbance. The study of psychoactive drugs, especially those used in the treatment of mental disorders, is a frontier of knowledge. We will review many of these drugs and some of what is known concerning their mechanisms of action in chapter 15 when we discuss disorders of the brain and behavior.

Summary

We have discussed the processes of chemical communication between neurons in this chapter and have developed an overview of the field of **psychopharmacology,** the study of the behavioral actions of drugs.

A number of suspected neurotransmitters and neuromodulators have been identified. One of these, first discovered by Loewi, is **acetylcholine.** This neurotransmitter substance is secreted by the vagus nerve, which exerts inhibitory control over the heart. Acetylcholine now is recognized as a neurotransmitter at many different synapses throughout the body and brain. Other neurotransmitters that have received considerable attention include the **catecholamines, dopamine, norepinephrine,** and **epinephrine.** All of these substances are manufactured by various cell groups in the brain and are secreted onto postsynaptic targets by means of terminals in synaptic contact with postsynaptic cells. A number of the synthetic enzymes used to manufacture the catecholamines are identical, and these transmitters are derived from the same amino acid precursor, **tyrosine.** The release of the catecholamines is controlled by neuronal activity, by biochemical and other feedback processes, and by degradative enzymes contained within the cell terminal. Catecholamines are removed from the synaptic cleft by a process of **reuptake,** a process in which the neurotransmitter is taken up again by the presynaptic terminal where it can be stored for subsequent reuse. **Serotonin,** an indoleamine first found in the blood, is another neurotransmitter that shares some of the same features as the catecholamines.

A number of amino acids also have been regarded as neurotransmitters or neuromodulators. Two of these, **gamma-aminobutyric acid (GABA)** and **glycine,** appear to be uniformly inhibitory, whereas two other amino acids, **glutamate** and **aspartate,** are powerful excitants. All are products of the normal energy cycle of cells. **Neuropeptides** are combinations of amino acids, and a number of these compounds are now believed to function as neurotransmitters and neuromodulators. Among these interesting compounds are the **endorphins** and **enkephalins,** which have pharmacological properties similar to morphine, a powerful opiate drug having analgesic effects. It is thought now that morphine and these endogenous opiate compounds interact with specific receptors on the cell surface or its interior to produce their diverse pharmacological and behavioral effects.

Psychopharmacology, the study of drugs that affect behavior, is a burgeoning field in which the various actions of drugs on behavior and the means by which these actions are achieved are the focuses of interest. In order to study the effects of drugs on behavior, it is important to understand some basic principles of drug action. These include **dose response,** in which the amount of drug administered (dose) is related to its effect, and **time response,** in which the time after a drug is administered significantly determines the action seen. How the drug is administered, absorbed, and eliminated from the body, and the age, sex, and genotype of the organism also may affect the drug response.

In general, the actions of drugs on the brain are conceptualized in terms of their effects on synaptic transmission and other modes of chemical communication between nerve cells and their targets. Some drugs mimic the action of a particular transmitter substance and are termed **agonists,** while others block the action of the neurotransmitter and are termed **antagonists.** Many drugs are thought to interact with specific receptors, and methods such as receptor binding are being used by many investigators to study the properties of these receptors in the brain and elsewhere. Most neurotransmitters appear to act at more than one type of receptor. Acetylcholine, for example, has at least two types of receptors—**muscarinic** and **nicotinic**—which have been distinguished by different cholinergic agonists and antagonists.

Drugs that affect the brain and behavior may be classified in a number of ways. One of these emphasizes the overall behavioral effects of the agent. Stimulants, such as the **xanthines, convulsants, amphetamine,** and **cocaine,** produce predominantly excitatory effects on behavioral processes, though often through quite different mechanisms. Amphetamine and cocaine, for example, tend to increase the

release and/or effectiveness of central catecholaminergic synaptic transmission. The convulsants block inhibitory processes in the brain and, in so doing, cause convulsions when administered in sufficiently high doses. Caffeine, on the other hand, blocks the action of **adenosine,** a naturally occurring compound in the brain that depresses behavior. Depressants, such as the **barbiturates, alcohol,** and the **narcotic analgesics,** produce sedation and sleep, but also through apparently different cellular mechanisms.

The processes of **drug tolerance** and **dependence** are currently conceived as compensatory reactions to the continued use of depressant drugs such that, when the drug is withdrawn, the nervous system is hyperexcitable, leading to the severe withdrawal symptoms charcteristic of physical dependence on these agents. Important behavioral variables such as learning and conditioning also determine, in part, the progression of dependence and the expression of drug-withdrawal signs.

The **hallucinogenic** drugs, such as LSD and psilocybin, have a chemical structure that resembles that of serotonin, and may produce their bizarre behavioral effects by interfering with the action of this neurotransmitter. The effects of **marijuana** vary widely among individuals. This drug produces both depressant and excitatory effects on behavior, and may interfere with many different brain processes. The use of drugs to treat mental disorders has revolutionized psychiatry. An understanding of how the **antipsychotic, antidepressant,** and **antianxiety drugs** act promises to shed new light on the brain mechanisms involved in psychosis. These psychotherapeutic drugs and their actions will be described in later chapters.

Suggested Readings

Cooper, J. R., F. E. Bloom, and R. H. Roth. 1986. *The biochemical basis of neuropharmacology.* 5th ed. New York: Oxford University Press.
This is an excellent paperback book that emphasizes the biochemical mechanisms by which drugs affect the brain.

Eccles, J. C. 1982. The synapse: From electrical to chemical transmission. *Annual Review of Neuroscience* 5:325–39.
An interesting account of the historical development of the research and ideas about chemical synaptic transmission by the Nobel prize-winning neurophysiologist and pioneer in the field of synaptic transmission.

Feldman, R. S., and L. F. Quenzer. 1984. *Fundamentals of neuropsychopharmacology.* Sunderland, MA: Sinauer Associates, Inc.
A serious treatment of both the biochemical and behavioral actions of many psychoactive drugs. This book also provides a detailed discussion of many neurotransmitters and neuromodulators.

Iversen, S. D., and L. L. Iversen. 1981. *Behavioral pharmacology.* 2d ed. New York: Oxford University Press.
Here is a concise, authoritative paperback book that treats both drug mechanisms and their effects on behavior at an understandable level.

McKim, W. A. *Drugs and behavior.* 1986. New York: Prentice-Hall.
A basic introduction to the topic of behavioral pharmacology.

Ray, O. *Drugs, society and human behavior.* 1983. 3d ed. St. Louis: C.V. Mosby.
An outstanding, readable book about commonly used drugs and the social, cultural, and historical factors that relate to drug use, misuse, or abuse. It is a unique integration of information about drugs and drug use. We highly recommend it.

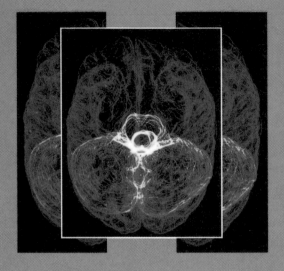

Outline

Introduction

Although the ancient Greeks believed that objects in the world sent faint copies of themselves into human organs of awareness, we now know that all information that we receive comes to us in the form of variations in physical energy. These changes may be patterns of light across our visual space, changes in air pressure that produce our sensations of sound, or other physical events that determine what we feel, taste, and smell.

The basis of our knowledge of the world comes through our senses. This has been the subject of fascination to philosophers, psychologists, physicists, and biologists since antiquity. Why are we aware of certain forms of energy and not others? What are color and pattern? Why do things look the way they do? How do we know that something is real? These are questions intimately bound to our understanding of the function and development of sensory processes. In the past two decades, tremendous progress has been made in understanding how physical energy is transformed into physiological events, and how the nervous system participates in constructing the world that we perceive.

Concepts in Sensory Processing

Our understanding of the biological processes involved in perception can begin with examination of some of the general principles that apply to all senses. For example, all sensation derives from physical stimulation of our sense organs, but not all physical stimulation results in perception. The high pitch of a dog whistle is an example. What we do sense is determined by the characteristics of our sense organs. Thus, a fundamental limitation of

Chapter

7

Sensory Processes: General Concepts and the Visual System

pacinian   (pah-sin'e-an)

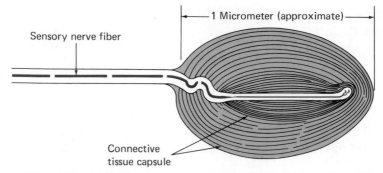

Sensory nerve fiber

1 Micrometer (approximate)

Connective
tissue capsule

Figure 7.1 Diagram of the pacinian corpuscle. Mechanical pressure on the connective tissue capsule is detected by the fine ending of the sensory nerve fiber inside.

sensation in all organisms is the limits of their sensory organs to respond to physical energy. Only in the case of humans has this limitation been overcome by finding means to transform physical events that do not themselves affect our sensory receptors into events that do. Humans can, for example, transform X rays using photographic film into physical variations that are detectable as light. Details of the physical world too small to see with the naked eye can be studied with the aid of the microscope.

Transduction

Stimulation that does affect our sensory receptors must be changed, or transduced, into a form that the nervous system can utilize; namely, action potentials in the cranial and spinal sensory nerve fibers that bring sensory information into the central nervous system. This important step in the process of sensory perception is termed **transduction,** which means changing one form of energy into another. Thus, in all of our senses physical stimulation of sensory receptors results in a series of physical and physiological events that turn physical energy into neural impulses. In some

electrical potential

cases, the sensory receptor and the nerve fiber that carry the information into the central nervous system are part of the same specialized cell. An interesting example of such a case is the **pacinian corpuscle** found in the skin and deep tissues of the body, illustrated in figure 7.1. The pacinian corpuscle consists of a fine branch of a single sensory nerve fiber that is surrounded by a capsule. This capsule consists of many layers of connective tissue resembling the layers of an onion. When the capsule is deformed, for example by mechanical pressure on the skin, the nerve fiber inside the capsule is also deformed. Such deformation depolarizes the membrane potential of the nerve ending and results in an action potential in the sensory nerve that is carried into the central nervous system. The characteristics of the capsule limit the form of physical stimulation to which the fine nerve fiber can respond. Indeed, the elastic properties of the capsule are such that the nerve fiber is deformed only during changes in pressure, not during continuous pressure. Thus, the pacinian corpuscle is specialized to respond to changes in mechanical pressure, and the nerve fiber that responds to this stimulus also carries resulting action potentials into the central nervous system.

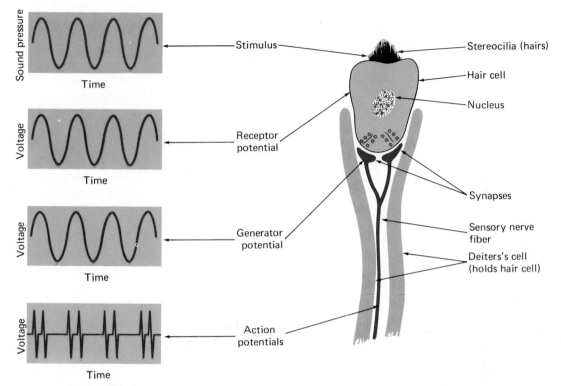

Figure 7.2 Transduction of a sensory stimulus by the auditory receptor cell and the sensory nerve fiber that makes synaptic contact with it. Mechanical stimulation of the hairs on the hair cell results in a receptor potential. Synaptic transmission between the receptor and sensory nerve fiber produces a generator potential in the nerve fiber, which in turn leads to action potentials that are carried into the central nervous system.

In other senses, such as vision and audition (hearing), these processes require more than one specialized cell. For example, stimulation of the auditory receptors, the hair cells of the inner ear, does not produce action potentials in these cells. Indeed, the transduction of such stimulation into neural impulses requires two cells—the receptor cells and the specialized sensory nerve fibers that contact them, as shown in figure 7.2. In this case, sound energy arriving at the ear results in mechanical stimulation of the fine hairs on the auditory receptor cells. This changes the membrane

potential of the receptor, a change termed the **receptor potential.** The receptor potential, like synaptic potentials in the nervous system, is graded and varies with the intensity of physical stimulation. The auditory receptor potential initiates a process of chemical transmission between the hair cell and the nerve fiber with which it makes synaptic contact. This process of chemical transmission then results in depolarization of the nerve fiber, which in turn generates action potentials that are carried by the nerve fiber into the brain. Because the change in membrane potential of the nerve fiber generates action potentials in the sensory nerve, it is called a **generator potential.** Thus, the transduction of sound energy into neural impulses requires a series of events. Initially, a receptor potential occurs in the hair cell due to mechanical stimulation of the hairs on its surface. This in turn results in synaptic transmission between the receptor and the sensory nerve fiber. Depolarization in the nerve fiber, the generator potential, occurs in response to this chemical transmission and produces action potentials that are carried by the nerve fiber into the brain. In the case of the pacinian corpuscle, the receptor potential and generator potential are one and the same. These chains of events initiated by physical stimulation of the auditory hair cell are also illustrated diagrammatically in figure 7.2.

Sensory Coding by the Nervous System

As we have seen, stimulation of sensory receptors eventually leads to action potentials in the sensory nerves that carry these impulses into the central nervous system. Yet, action potentials arising from stimulation of visual receptors produce visual sensations, not sounds. Similarly, stimulation of the pacinian corpuscle leads to sensations of mechanical pressure, but not of light. It must be true, therefore, that the sensory effect of physical stimulation of our sense organs depends not only on stimulation of particular receptors, but also on the specific sensory nerves that are connected to them. This important concept is known as the **law of specific nerve energies** and was first expressed by the famous German physiologist Johannes Müller in the late nineteenth century. You can experience this concept by applying slight mechanical pressure to the outside

of your eyeball (with the eye closed). Although the stimulus is mechanical, it produces visual flashes because nerve fibers stimulated by mechanical stimulation of the visual receptors are specific to the sense of vision. This effect is also termed the concept of **labeled lines.**

Labeled Lines and the Eye of the Newt
A remarkable series of experiments by R. W. Sperry (1956) illustrated the concept of labeled lines. In some of these experiments, the eyes of a newt (salamander) were rotated in their sockets so that they were upside down. Sperry was interested to know what effect such an inversion of the newt's visual world would have and whether the organism's brain could adjust to this alteration. He found that shortly after the operation, the newt acted as though it perceived an upside-down world! For example, when an object was moved upward the newt would follow the object by moving its eyes downward! None of the newts learned to see normally again, even two years after eye rotation. These experiments demonstrate that the optic nerve fibers are labeled for spatial orientation. Those fibers ordinarily receiving information from upper parts of the visual field, for example, are labeled to signify the upper visual field. It is this phenomenon that causes the animal to behave backwardly when these fibers are put on the bottom. These interesting effects are illustrated in figure 7.3.

Labeled Lines and Coding within Lines
The law of specific nerve energies suggests that different qualities of the sensory world are produced by stimulation of different nerve fibers. Each fiber, or line, to the brain is specialized by virtue of the receptors to which it is connected and the regions within the nervous system to which their information is carried. The particular combination of receptor,

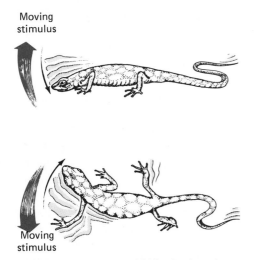

Moving
stimulus

Moving
stimulus

Figure 7.3 A salamander exhibiting backward
behavior following rotation of the eye so that right
becomes left (lower figure) and up becomes down
(upper figure).

nerve fiber, and points of termination of the
nerve in the brain represents a way that the
brain can label, or code, the characteristics of
the external world. In addition, each labeled
line is also capable of coding certain variations
in the energy to which it responds. The visual
receptor, for example, can signal whether a
light stimulus is weak or very intense. The pacinian corpuscle can signal not only the occurrence of a mechanical stimulus, but also
whether the stimulus is repeated and how rapidly repetition occurs. In each case the variations in stimulation are coded by changes in
the number, frequency, or pattern of action
potentials that are carried in the specific sensory nerve fibers connected to these receptors.
An example of this kind of stimulus coding is
shown in figure 7.4.

In this series of experiments by Mountcastle and associates (1967), the action potentials of a single nerve fiber in the arm of a

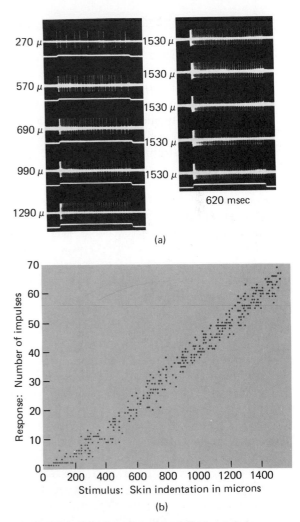

(a)

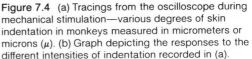

(b)

Figure 7.4 (a) Tracings from the oscilloscope during
mechanical stimulation—various degrees of skin
indentation in monkeys measured in micrometers or
microns (μ). (b) Graph depicting the responses to the
different intensities of indentation recorded in (a).

monkey were recorded during mechanical stimulation of the skin. Note that the nerve fiber responds with a train of impulses to this stimulus, and the frequency of these action potentials is directly related to the degree of skin indentation. This pressure can be very precisely measured in microns of indentation (fig. 7.4*b*). Other nerve fibers may signal similar information, but from other places on the skin.

Coding by Spatial Organization

In the case of nerve fibers carrying sensations from the skin, each line not only carries information about the occurrence and intensity of a touch on the skin, but also relays *where* the stimulus on the body surface occurred. Different nerve fibers convey information about different places, so that together they form a "map" of the body surface. This spatial map of the body surface, with each individual nerve fiber forming one piece, is maintained as the sensory nerve fibers enter the central nervous system to form the central pathways for each of the senses. This general principle of the spatial organization of information within the sensory pathways is termed **receptotopic organization** and represents an extremely important way in which information on stimulus location is coded by the brain. In the **somatosensory system,** which, as you will see, is responsible in part for the sense of touch, the skin represents the receptor surface, and each nerve fiber carries information from a slightly different place on the skin. As these nerve fibers enter the central nervous system, they group to form a specific pathway for the sense of touch. This pathway may involve several synaptic relays, each of which is a particular nucleus or group of nuclei in the brain. Incoming nerve fibers synapse and new neurons carry the information on to higher stations. The relay

nuclei differ for each of the senses, and in some cases different nuclei subserve different sensations within a single sense. In addition, specific regions of the cerebral cortex are set aside to receive sensory information for each of the senses. The map of the sensory surface is maintained throughout these sensory relay stations and the sensory areas of the cerebral cortex.

The spatial map of the body surface in the somatosensory area of the cerebral cortex is shown in figure 7.5. This map indicates that information about touch on a specific part of the body goes to a specific place in the somatosensory cortex. The cross section illustrates where touch information is received for different parts of the body surface. Interestingly, this is not a precise representation of the body surface, but is rather a so-called **topographic representation.** As the figure shows, information from the hands, for example, occupies a larger portion of the cerebral cortex than information from the back, even though the back actually has much more surface area. This is related to the fact that the hands are much more sensitive to touch than the back, and therefore a great deal more information can be gained by touching something with your hands than with your back.

A similar topographic representation of the receptor surface occurs in other sensory pathways. For example, most of the information about an object that we look at comes from the very center of the visual field. It is easy for you to verify this fact by simply noting how much more detail you see when you look directly at something than when it appears in the periphery. Although central vision utilizes only a small percent of the entire receptor surface, the retina, this information occupies approximately 50 percent of the map of the retina in

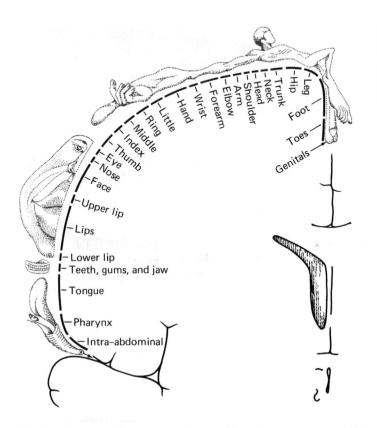

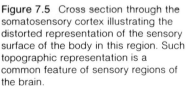

Figure 7.5 Cross section through the somatosensory cortex illustrating the distorted representation of the sensory surface of the body in this region. Such topographic representation is a common feature of sensory regions of the brain.

the visual cortex. Thus, generally speaking, the more information coming from a particular part of the receptor surface, or the more varied and precise that information is, the larger is the area within the central pathways devoted to it.

We have seen that an important way in which the nervous system can preserve information about the location of a stimulus on the receptor surface is by spatial organization. Information is segregated spatially in the form of a map of the receptor surface, distorted according to the different sensitivities of different regions. We will see later that this method of spatial segregation or spatial organization within the nervous system is used

to organize and preserve other types of information as well. However, the spatial organization of information is only one of many ways in which the nervous system analyzes and codes information. Within each of the sensory relay nuclei, sensory information must be analyzed for features other than spatial location. It is important not only to determine where a stimulus occurs, but also to recognize many other details of that stimulus and its relationship to other things. Our understanding of the ways in which these processes take place is developing rapidly and will form the basis for a more detailed discussion of the sensory systems. We begin with a consideration of vision.

sclera   (skle′rah)
aqueous humor   (a′kwe-us hu′mor)

The Visual System

Because it has been studied more extensively than any of the other senses, the sense of vision is where we will begin our more detailed examination of the senses.

The Eye

The vertebrate eye is a remarkable structure designed in many respects like a camera to produce images on a light-sensitive surface. In the case of the camera the surface is photographic film. For the eye, the surface is the retina, which contains the visual receptors. Some of the major structures of the eye and corresponding features of the camera are illustrated in figure 7.6.

The outer surface of the eyeball is composed of a tough tissue called the **sclera,** which at the front of the eyeball becomes the clear outer covering, the **cornea.** Light enters the eye through the cornea, which comprises layers of cells aligned in such a way that they disrupt the passage of light minimally. In the human eye—and in the eye of other terrestrial vertebrates—the cornea is, in fact, the major lens of the eye. It is the most important structure in the eye for bending or refracting the light to form an image on the retina. After entering the cornea, the light passes through a watery substance called the **aqueous humor** and then through the **pupil,** a hole formed by a ring of muscles, the **iris.** (Our eye color is determined by the pigmented (colored) outer layer of the iris.) Changes in the contraction of the iris vary

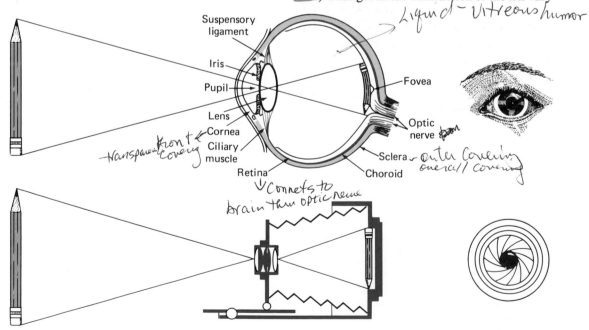

Figure 7.6 The major structural features of the eye and its formation of an image are shown. Similarities of the eye to a camera are illustrated in the lower drawing.

the size of the pupil and thus regulate the amount of light passing through the **lens** behind the iris.

The lens is a layered, onionlike structure in which the inner layers die as new outer layers are formed. The lens is a more or less elastic structure that in mammals such as human beings and rats can change shape slightly to become more rounded or flatter. In all vertebrates, the lens is used to help focus an image on the retina, a process termed **accommodation.** Changes in the shape of the lens are produced by contraction or relaxation of the **ciliary muscles** that are attached to the lens by ligaments termed **zonule fibers.** The lens and the inside layers of the cornea receive their nutrients from the aqueous humor, a fluid very much like blood plasma.

Behind the lens is the **vitreous humor,** a jellylike substance thought to help maintain the shape of the eye and to act as a fluid shock absorber for the eyeball. After passing through this fluid, the light passes through the retina to strike the specialized receptor cells at the back of the retina. The absorption of light by the receptors initiates a complex series of physiological reactions that result in action potentials in the axons of those nerve cells in the retina that form the optic nerve. The optic nerve carries these action potentials into the brain.

The Retina

The image formed by an object such as the pencil in figure 7.6 falls on the receptors at the back of the **retina.** The retina is a complex, multilayered structure with a variety of cell types, as depicted schematically in figure 7.7.

Rods and Cones

The receptor layer of the human retina consists of two classes of cells: **rods** and **cones.** There are approximately 6,000,000 cones and about 125,000,000 rods. These receptor cells are not evenly distributed across the retina. The cones are most dense (approximately 147,000 per square millimeter) and the rods virtually absent in the region termed the **fovea** at the center of the retina (location of the fovea is shown in figure 7.6). The density of cones drops off drastically outside of the fovea and remains low to the peripheral portions of the retina. The rods are greatest in number some distance from the fovea where there are approximately 160,000 in a square millimeter. They, too, then decrease toward the periphery, although more rods than cones exist in the periphery. In the retina, the rods are arranged in well-defined rows with each rod surrounded by six others in a highly regular pattern. The cones are also arranged in a stereotyped pattern (Sterling 1986). Curiously, light must pass through the network of nerve fibers and cells making up the other layers of the retina before it strikes the receptors! It is as if the retina were backward with respect to light entering the eye.

Many other organisms possess this dual-receptor type of retina that we have described for the human eye, although some do not. Some snakes and ground squirrels, for example, have a retina that has only cones. Nocturnal animals, such as the cat and rat, tend to have retinas that are predominantly made up of rods. Diurnal animals typically possess retinas having a high number of cones as well as rods (Walls 1942). The usefulness of this situation for these different groups of animals will become clear as we discuss the features of the rods and cones.

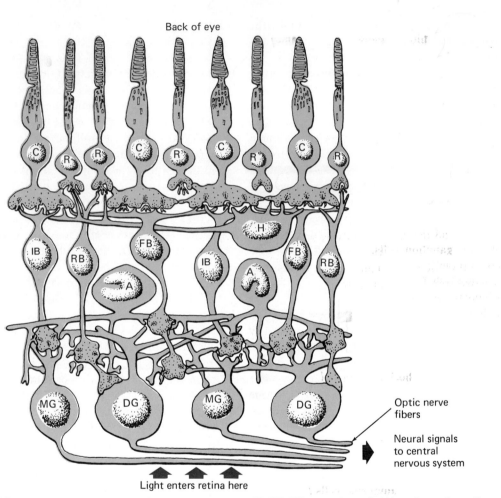

Back of eye

Optic nerve
fibers

Neural signals
to central
nervous system

Light enters retina here

Figure 7.7 The structure of the retina. Shown are rods (R), cones (C), horizontal cells (H), bipolar cells (IB, RB, FB), amacrine cells (A), and ganglion cells (MG, DG).

The rods and cones form synaptic connections with **bipolar cells.** It has become increasingly evident from electron microscopic studies of the retina (e.g., Dowling and Dubin 1984) that different types of bipolar cells are associated with these two different classes of receptors. Rods synapse onto rod bipolar cells (labeled RB in figure 7.7). Typically, many rods synapse onto a single rod bipolar cell. There are three types of bipolar cells associated with cones: flat bipolar cells (labeled FB in figure 7.7) and two different types of so-called invaginating bipolar cells (labeled IB in figure 7.7). The bipolar cells in turn synapse onto the **ganglion cells,** the axons of which make up the optic nerve. Thus, the flow of information through the retina is from receptors to bipolar cells to ganglion cells and then to the brain.

In addition to this vertical arrangement of connections, there are horizontal connections in the retina as well. For example, there are rod and cone **horizontal cells** (labeled H in figure 7.7) that interconnect different rods or cones and can influence the communication between receptor cell and bipolar cell. Horizontal interconnections also occur in the region of the bipolar cell to ganglion cell synapses. These horizontal connections occur by means of the large **amacrine cells** (labeled A in figure 7.7) of which there appear to be many types. In addition to these neuronal interconnections across the retina provided by amacrine and horizontal cells, it has now been established that the receptors themselves are interconnected by means of gap junctions (Sterling 1986). The gap junction between receptor cells allows changes in the membrane potential of one receptor to affect the other directly. Typically, cones communicate to other cones and rods communicate to other rods.

The anatomical organization of the retina presented here is simplified. These five basic retina cell types represent a highly schematic version of retinal anatomy and physiology. Advanced anatomical methods enable investigators to record the activity of retinal elements and then to selectively stain the individual cell from which physiological information has been obtained. Such methods have vastly expanded our understanding of the cellular function and structure of the retina. It is now known that there are many subclasses of the retinal neurons that we have described. Almost fifty different cells representing variations of these basic retinal cell types have been described, each probably having a specialized function in retinal visual processing (Masland 1986; Sterling 1983).

How do these neural elements within the retina affect information about visual patterns? If we consider a pattern of light making up an image across the retina, such as the pencil in figure 7.6, points of light in the image stimulate different receptors. Each receptor sends information about the point of light vertically through the retina from receptor to bipolar cell to ganglion cell. At the same time, this signal is affected by and affects information arising from other points in the pattern by means of the horizontal flow of information across the retina. Again, this flow involves the gap junctions between adjacent receptors and the horizontal and amacrine cells. Thus, the information leaving the retina by means of the 800,000 axons of the ganglion cells is not a simple transmission of the image striking the receptors. Rather, this "neural picture" of the image reflects a great deal of analysis that has already taken place within the retina itself. A number of important vision characteristics can be explained on the basis of a knowledge of the properties of the rods and cones and various other features of the retina.

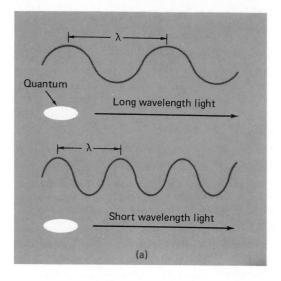

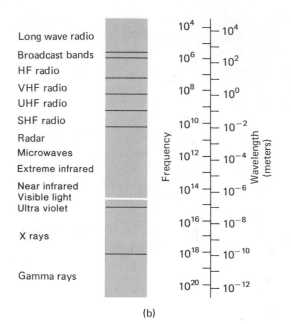

(b)

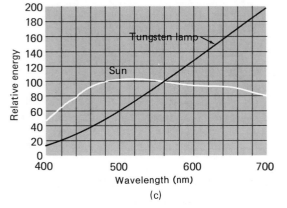

Figure 7.8 Basic properties of light. (a) As a light quantum travels through space at 186,000 miles/second, its energy pulsates according to the curve shown here. The distance between pulsations is the wavelength (λ) of the quantum. Quanta that pulsate more rapidly have shorter wavelengths. (b) The electromagnetic spectrum contains many wavelengths, only a narrow range of which are detected as light. (c) The emission spectra of sunlight (white line) and an incandescent (household) light (black line).

Quanta

The energy emitted from a light source consists of small, wavelike packages of energy termed **quanta** (singular, **quantum**). Because the quanta are wavelike, they can differ from each other in wavelengths, as illustrated in figure 7.8a. While the typical light source usually emits wavelengths over a large portion of the **electromagnetic spectrum,** only a narrow range of wavelengths can be distinguished by the human observer as light, as shown in figure 7.8b. One of the units of measure of a wavelength is the **nanometer,** and wavelengths vary between 400 and 700 nanometers. If a light source emits only a single wavelength of light, it is termed **monochromatic.** As the intensity of a monochromatic light is increased, more quanta are emitted from it per unit of time. The more quanta emitted, the brighter the light will appear. In addition, the wavelength of the monochromatic light generally corresponds to a particular hue or color of light, ranging from violet (about 400 nanometers) to green (about 510 nanometers) to yellow (about 580 nanometers) to red, which has the longest wavelength of visible light (about 700 nanometers). Most lights are not monochromatic, but rather emit many different wavelengths of light at varying levels of energy. The appearance of such a **complex light** depends on which wavelengths are dominant in energy and, as we will discuss in a moment, how sensitive the eye is to each of the different wavelengths emitted by the light. A physical description of the wavelength-power composition of any light

can be described as its **emission spectrum,** illustrated along with various other physical characteristics of light in figure 7.8c.

Scotopic Threshold

Figure 7.9a illustrates one of the elementary features of human vision, the **scotopic threshold curve** (threshold curve for rod vision). This curve is obtained by presenting a monochromatic light to human subjects whose eyes have adapted to the dark. The subject is required to adjust the energy of the light until it is barely detectable. These minimal detectable energies for different wavelengths of light are then used to construct the graph labeled "Rod vision" in figure 7.9a. In order to obtain these minimally detectable values, the subject would have to view the light on that portion of the retina where the rods are most dense—at about 17 degrees of angle off-center, to be more precise.

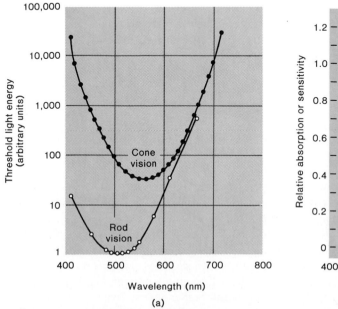

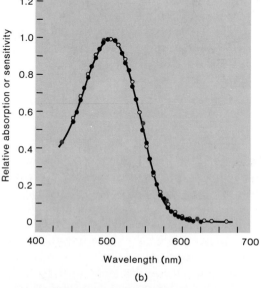

Figure 7.9 (a) Threshold curves for photopic (cone) and scotopic (rod) vision. The lower the threshold, the more sensitive we are to the wavelength. (b) The absorption of light by rhodopsin.

This curve shows that we are not equally sensitive to all wavelengths of light. We require less energy, for example, to detect a light of 505 nanometers (which looks bluish-green) than to detect wavelengths of light longer than this. What is the basis for differential sensitivity?

In order for transduction to occur, light energy must be absorbed by the light-sensitive chemical contained in the receptors, the **photopigment.** The photopigment in rods, called **rhodopsin,** was discovered by Boll in the late nineteenth century. If we measure the amount of light absorbed by rhodopsin for different wavelengths, we discover that the absorption is greatest for 505 nanometers, the wavelength to which we are most sensitive. The absorption curve for rhodopsin is illustrated in figure 7.9*b* for comparison with the scotopic threshold curve. Note that where absorption of light by rhodopsin is best (the highest point on the graph in 7.9*b*), human vision is the most sensitive (the lowest point on the graph in 7.9*a*). Under ideal conditions, we are remarkably sensitive to the presence of light, and require only six to seven quanta of light for a visual sensation to occur (Hecht, Shlaer, and Pirenne 1942).

The chemistry of rhodopsin is now largely understood as is the chain of events occurring when rhodopsin is struck by a photon, culminating in a change in the receptor membrane potential. Rhodopsin is contained in the outer tips of the rods and consists of a combination of chemicals termed retinene— (structurally related to vitamin A) and opsin— a complex protein molecule. When rhodopsin absorbs light, it breaks down into these two components (retinene and opsin), which must be recombined in order to be used again as rhodopsin. In this process, the color of rhodopsin changes from pinkish to pale yellow, a

process termed bleaching. Ultimately, the bleaching of rhodopsin by light leads to a receptor potential. When light strikes a receptor in invertebrates, the membrane of the receptor becomes depolarized as we might expect. However, when light strikes the receptor in a vertebrate retina, the opposite occurs. The receptor potential is a hyperpolarization of the membrane. Thus, in receptors such as those in the human eye, transmitter release from the receptors is greatest in the dark and is reduced by light. In fact, only a single photon of light striking the rod will produce a receptor potential (Sakitt 1972).

The chain of events leading from the breakdown of rhodopsin to the receptor potential is now known to involve the second messenger, cyclic GMP, which amplifies the effect of the rhodopsin breakdown. This second messenger, in turn, controls the membrane permeability of the rod to sodium. It causes sodium permeability to decrease, thus producing an electrogenic hyperpolarization of the receptor membrane potential (Golomb et al. 1985).

Photopic Threshold

A similar **photochemical** process occurs in the cones. The cones differ from the rods in that the opsins combining with retinene vary, whereas all rods contain the same opsin. In fact, there are three different types of cones, each containing one of three different opsins combined with retinene. If we repeat the threshold experiment just described for rods, but now allow the light to fall on the center of the retina where cones are most numerous, the results will be quite different. We will find that, in general, higher energy levels are required to detect the light. This is shown in figure 7.9*a* where the **photopic threshold curve** (i.e., the

scotopic (sko-top′ik)
photopic (fo-top′ik)
Purkinje (pur-kin′je)

211
*Sensory Processes: General
Concepts and the Visual System*

threshold curve for cone vision) lies somewhat above the scotopic curve. Thus, cones are less sensitive to the presence of light than rods.

Why is rod vision more sensitive than cone vision? A number of different factors appear to be responsible for this difference. First, the rods are more sensitive to light than the cones. Another important factor in the sensitivity difference is the way in which these two types of receptors connect to their bipolar cells in the retina. As we noted, several rods may synapse onto a single bipolar cell. Indeed, this **convergence** of inputs from rods onto the bipolar cell increases in the periphery of the retina where many rods may connect to a single bipolar cell. In the periphery of the retina, convergence also occurs for cones, but never to the extent it does for rods. In the fovea a single cone does not share its bipolar cells with other cones. The greater convergence of the rods contributes to their exceptional sensitivity to the presence of light. Although low energy, that is, dim light, may produce only a slight signal from any single rod, many rods converge onto and therefore stimulate the same bipolar cell, and their combined effects are sufficient to stimulate the bipolar cell.

Convergence is an important feature of many structures in the brain and, as it does for rod vision, allows many small signals to be combined into an adequate stimulus where the individual effect of any one signal would not be adequate. Although convergence is an advantage for detecting dim light, it is a disadvantage for recognizing the details of a pattern of light. For example, suppose you are looking at two points of light that are very close together. If these two points of light stimulated a group of rods converging onto a bipolar cell, the effects of the two points of light would sum,

and the signal produced by them could not be distinguished from that produced by a single point of greater intensity. In contrast, if the two points were stimulating cones in the center of the fovea, the difference between the two points and a single point could be distinguished since the cones do not share bipolar cells in this region, and information about each of the two spots is therefore maintained separately through the retina. Since these signals are not combined, very low-intensity lights cannot be detected. Since the cone system displays less convergence than the rod system, it is less sensitive to the presence of light but better suited to resolving the details of an image.

A comparison of the **scotopic** and **photopic** sensitivity curves in figure 7.9*a* shows that with cone vision we are more sensitive to the red end of the spectrum than to the blue end. Under rod vision, on the other hand, we are more sensitive to blue than to red. If you were to view two lights of equal intensity, one red and one blue, with cone vision a red light would appear brighter than a blue one. Under rod vision the opposite would be true; the blue light would be brighter than the red one. This shift in sensitivity between photopic and scotopic vision was first noted by the Czechoslovakian physiologist Purkinje in the nineteenth century and so is called the **Purkinje shift.** We are maximally sensitive to a yellow-green light of 555 nanometers using cone vision as contrasted to a bluish-green light of 505 nanometers for rod vision because the cones and rods contain different photopigments. The relationship between the photopic threshold curve and the absorption of light by the cones is more complex than this relation in rod vision because the photopic curve results from a combination of signals from three different classes of cones having different photopigments. The way in which information is combined from these three classes of cones in the retina also influences the photopic threshold curve.

Dark Adaptation

Adaptation to darkness is another phenomenon that differentiates rod from cone vision. If we were to measure the minimum intensity of light that we can detect at various times after entering a darkened area from the daylight, we would obtain a dark adaptation curve like the one labeled W in figure 7.10.

This curve shows the increase in sensitivity to white light with increasing time in the dark, a phenomenon called **dark adaptation.** Note that the curve is divided into two distinct phases. The initial portion of the curve, lasting about ten minutes, represents an increase in the sensitivity of the cones, whereas the later portion of the curve represents increasing rod sensitivity. This sensitivity can be demonstrated by using a red light for detection. The rods are virtually insensitive to red light, as was shown in the scotopic threshold curve in figure 7.9a. The curve labeled "R" in figure 7.10 shows the results of such an experiment and thus represents adaptation by the scotopic system. The increase in sensitivity of the rod and cone systems, known as dark adaptation, has been attributed in part to the photochemical reaction within the visual receptors. Recall that under high levels of illumination most of the photochemical pigment is broken down. Thus, there is less photochemical to respond (absorb) to the light striking the receptor. If light is removed from the eye, the retinene and opsin recombine, but very little is broken down. As time goes on, then, more photochemical is

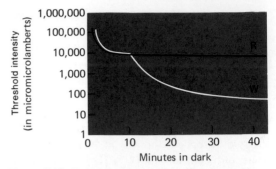

Figure 7.10 Dark adaptation curves. The threshold intensity for detecting red (R) or white (W) light as a function of time in the dark.

available to absorb the light. In addition to this regeneration of photochemicals in the rods and cones, other processes in the receptors and the retina are important in dark adaptation. This fact is known because the increase in sensitivity in darkness is much greater than can be accounted for solely on the basis of an increase in absorption by the receptors. Other retinal elements must, therefore, play a role (Green 1986). For example, it is also known that light falling on one portion of the retina affects dark adaptation on another, separate part of the retina (Rushton and Westheimer 1962). Thus, the photoreceptors cannot be the only retinal cells involved in this process since stimulation of one group of receptors affects adaptation of others. There must, therefore, be horizontal connections in the retina that are involved in dark adaptation.

Color Vision

We noted previously that the rod system does not provide color information. Suppose you view two spots of light, each of the same wavelength, using only rod vision. If one spot is higher in intensity than the other, those rods illuminated by the high-intensity spot will all give a stronger response, while those illuminated by the low-intensity spot will give a weaker response. Now suppose that both spots are equal in energy, but differ in wavelength. Those rods illuminated by a wavelength that is absorbed to a greater extent by rhodopsin will give a greater response. Thus, the same difference in rod response to the two spots of light could mean that the spots differ in wavelength or that they differ in intensity. The rod system cannot, therefore, distinguish wavelength differences from intensity differences.

When you view a spot of light using the cones, the spot illuminates each of the three different types of cones. The sensitivity of these three classes of cones varies in response to different wavelengths of light, as illustrated schematically in figure 7.11. One type of cone (A) absorbs best in the red or long wavelength region of the spectrum; another (B) absorbs best in the green or medium wavelength region; and a third (C) absorbs best in the blue or short wavelength region of the spectrum. The responses of these three types of cones when illuminated by different wavelengths of light are illustrated in figure 7.12. For example, 7.12*a* shows that when we view a light in the red region of the spectrum, the cones maximally responsive to this wavelength give the maximum response, while the other two cone types give minimal responses. If the intensity of this light is varied, the pattern of response from the three cones remains the same. That is, with less intensity, each of the cone types responds less, but the response of the A cones still predominates. Figure 7.12*b* indicates that a different pattern of response is obtained with a green light. Again, varying the intensity of the green light alters the overall

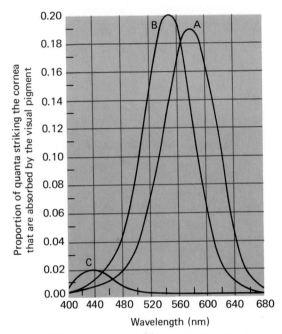

Figure 7.11 Idealized spectral sensitivities of the three color systems of the human retina. Curve A illustrates receptors most sensitive to red, curve B illustrates receptors most sensitive to green, and curve C illustrates receptors most sensitive to blue.

response of the cones, but the green cones still predominate, thus providing the same pattern of response at different intensity levels. Since the cone system produces different patterns of response to different wavelengths, it is capable of distinguishing between changes in intensity and changes in wavelength. However, not all differences in wavelength composition can be discriminated. As shown in figure 7.12*d* and *e*, in the case of yellow light the red and green systems respond equally and to a greater extent than does the blue system. Notice that this pattern of response can be produced by a monochromatic yellow light (fig. 7.12*d*) and by a combination of long (red) and medium (green) wavelengths (fig. 7.12*e*).

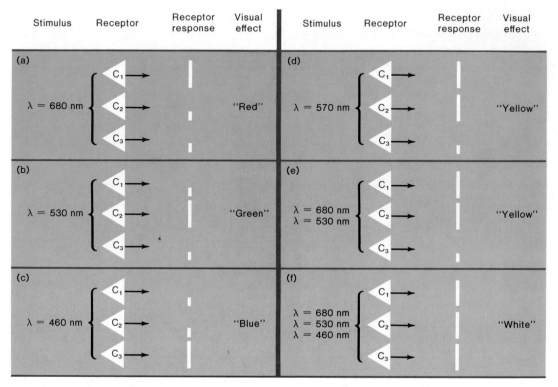

Figure 7.12 Each figure illustrates the response pattern produced by illuminating the three types of cones (C_1, C_2, C_3) with different wavelengths (λ) of light as designated. The visual effect produced by such stimulation is indicated.

Trichromatic Theory

The existence of three different receptor systems for color vision was proposed as the **trichromatic theory** of color vision on the basis of research performed as long ago as three hundred years by such famous figures as Isaac Newton, Hermann von Helmholtz, James Maxwell, and Thomas Young. These scientists found that the color of any spot of light can be exactly matched by some combination of three other lights called **primary lights.** The phenomenon of the three photopigments of the cone system responding differently to the three primary lights accounts for the range of colors that we see.

Opponent Process Theories

Additional evidence is available showing how these three signals are combined as they travel through the retina and how they are coded by the time they reach higher levels of the visual system. DeValois and Jacobs (1968), for example, recorded the responses of single neurons in the lateral geniculate nucleus of the thalamus where the optic tract terminates. They analyzed the responses to different wavelengths of light shown into their subjects' eyes (these subjects were monkeys because their color vision is similar to that of human

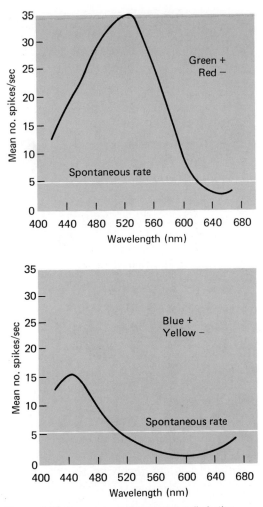

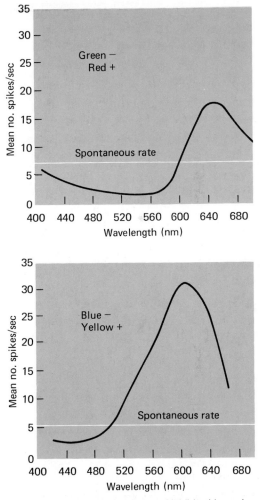

Figure 7.13 Responses of opponent cells in the lateral geniculate nuclei to different wavelengths of light. One class of opponent cells was maximally excited by green wavelengths and inhibited by red, or vice versa (top). Another class was maximally excited by yellow and inhibited by blue, or vice versa (bottom).

beings). One class of neurons in the lateral geniculate nucleus was termed **opponent neurons.** These cells increased their rate of firing maximally to one wavelength and decreased their firing maximally to the presentation of another wavelength, as illustrated in figure 7.13. In one type of opponent neuron, maximum response was to presentation of a green

wavelength, while maximum decrease in firing rate was to a red wavelength. This category of opponent response is abbreviated as follows: green + and red −. Simultaneous presentation of both wavelengths would, in this case, produce no change in response. That is, the responses to green and red oppose each other. Other opponent cells exhibited opposition to yellow and blue wavelengths. The opponent

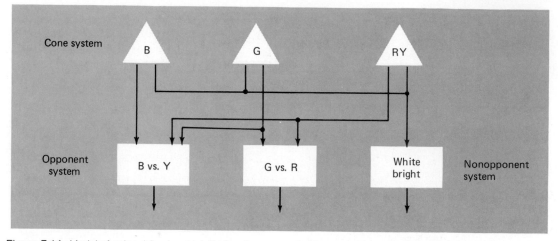

Figure 7.14 Model of color vision in which B absorbs best in blue wavelength region, G absorbs best in green wavelength region, and RY absorbs best in red region. The responses of the three types of cones are fed to an opponent system and to a nonopponent, or white-bright, system. Imagine that the three types of cones are grouped closely in a small area of the retina, and therefore all view the same point of light.

responses of these neurons correspond to another theory of color vision termed the **opponent process theory,** first proposed by Ewald Hering in the nineteenth century.

DeValois and Jacobs observed another major class of cells having responses called nonopponent. One type of nonopponent cell was excited to varying degrees by all wavelengths. In fact, the responses of these types of neurons, when taken as a whole, mirrored the photopic spectral sensitivity curve shown in figure 7.9a. Thus, these cells appear to reflect the differences in brightness that occur in different wavelengths of light.

A descriptive model of color vision that incorporates both the trichromatic and opponent process theories of color vision is given in figure 7.14. In this view, color vision starts with the three cone systems specified by the trichromatic theory. The response patterns of these three classes of receptors are interpreted by higher neural systems in an opponent-process fashion. Thus, the output of the green and red receptor systems interact at a higher level to form the green-red opponent process

system. Similarly, the output of the blue, red, and green receptors interact to form the blue-yellow opponent system. Although you might easily conclude that the higher level systems are located in the lateral geniculate nuclei of the thalamus, similar types of opponent responses have been seen in certain retinal cells, which suggests that these processes are completed entirely within the retina. It now appears that these processes occur as a result of lateral interactions involving the horizontal cells within the retina (DeValois and Jacobs 1984).

Let us examine how this model could account for two specific cases: white and yellow. When a white light is viewed, the responses of the three receptor types are equal. The responses of the red and green receptors completely oppose each other in the green-versus-red opponent system shown in figure 7.14. Therefore, there is no response from the green-versus-red opponent system. Similarly, the "yellow" response produced by the red and green receptors completely opposes the "blue"

Figure 7.15 The three small gray squares illustrate the phenomenon of brightness contrast. Although they are of equal intensity, the squares appear lighter as the background becomes darker.

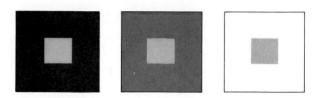

response from the blue receptor. Thus, the only system that has a net response is the achromatic, or white-bright nonopponent system, which simply combines the responses of the three receptor types. Since there is no response from the chromatic system, and since the white-bright system does respond, we see white light. In the case of yellow light, the red-and-green-receptor systems are equally responsive, whereas the blue-receptor system is minimally responsive. Therefore, red opposes green in the green-versus-red opponent system, but red and green also stimulate the blue-yellow system. Since there is only a minimal blue response, yellow predominates in the blue-versus-yellow opponent system, and the visual effect is yellow. The brightness of the yellow is determined by the degree to which the achromatic, or white-bright, system is activated.

The study of color vision provides an excellent example of the interrelations between perceptual, physiological, and physical analyses of visual phenomena. In many cases, scientists studying the relationships between the perception of color and the physics of light were led to postulate physiological mechanisms many years in advance of their actual discovery. In fact, it can be argued that without these previous studies, scientists would not have known what to look for when they began to explore the nervous system.

Pattern Vision

Like the study of color vision, the study of pattern vision reveals relationships between the physical world, our perception of this world,

and the physiological mechanisms that might underlie such a remarkable and fundamental capability. As we discovered for color vision, the initial processes involved in pattern vision occur in the retina. What are the perceptual and physiological processes that are important for pattern vision?

Brightness Contrast

One phenomenon important for pattern vision—**brightness contrast**—is illustrated in figure 7.15. Brightness contrast refers to the fact that brightness in one region of a pattern of light (the square in figure 7.15) is affected by the level of illumination in surrounding regions. What processes might be responsible for this ability of certain pattern regions to influence others? The interaction of different regions can be explained on the basis of the horizontal and lateral interconnections between elements in the retina.

The details of horizontal and lateral interactions in the retina were first explored in lower organisms. Especially revealing was the work of Hartline, Ratliff, and Miller (1961) on the eye of *Limulus*, the horseshoe crab. This remarkable structure is illustrated in figure 7.16. The *Limulus* has a compound eye consisting of many little eyes, or ommatidia. Each **ommatidium** has its own lens and receptors, and the receptors synapse onto a single large neuron—the **eccentric cell**. This cell's axon carries the information into the central nervous system of the animal. In addition, the axons leaving each ommatidium branch to interconnect with other ommatidia, forming what is termed the lateral **plexus.** Note the

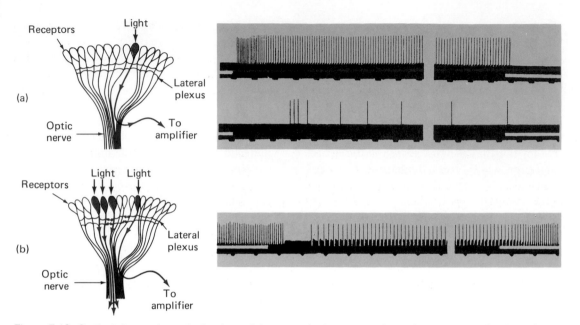

Figure 7.16 On the left are schematic drawings of the eye of *Limulus,* the horseshoe crab, and on the right are tracings showing responses to light stimuli of a nerve fiber connected to its receptor. (a) The upper trace shows the response to high intensity light and the lower trace shows the response to low intensity light. (b) The trace shows that the response of the fiber is markedly reduced when light is shown on a group of receptors nearby.

similarity between such lateral interconnections and the horizontal interconnections that we have described for the vertebrate retina.

Hartline, Ratliff, and Miller recorded from the axons of ommatidia while they were exposed to light. When a single ommatidium was illuminated, as shown in 7.16*a,* the action potentials generated by the eccentric cell increased in frequency. Indeed, the increase in firing was directly related to the intensity of the light shone on the ommatidium. After this step in the experiment, neighboring ommatidia were also exposed to light. When adjacent ommatidia were illuminated, the response of the one ommatidium originally illuminated decreased, as illustrated in 7.16*b.* In other words, the response of one ommatidium depended not only on the excitation produced by its own illumination, but also on the inhibition produced by illumination of surrounding ommatidia. This form of inhibition is termed **lateral inhibition.**

How can the phenomenon of brightness contrast be produced by such a process? Imagine that the square in figure 7.15 illuminates one ommatidium and the surrounding region illuminates other adjacent ommatidia. The ommatidium illuminated by the square is excited by light shining on it. However, its response is inhibited by adjacent ommatidia excited by the surrounding region. The more intense the surrounding illumination, the greater is the inhibition. Thus, the response of the ommatidium to a square of constant intensity, such as the ones in figure 7.15, decreases as the surrounding illumination increases. You can assume that the greater the response, the greater is the brightness. Thus, we have a mechanism that can produce the brightness contrast effects shown in figure 7.15.

It has become clear from studies of the vertebrate retina that similar lateral inhibitory interactions occur. Kuffler (1953), in an extensive series of investigations that recorded from the axons of retinal ganglion cells while the retina was stimulated with small spots of light, found that a given ganglion cell responded to light only over a limited, circular region on the retina. He termed this limited region of the retina the **receptive field** of the ganglion cell. Kuffler noted that the receptive fields of retinal ganglion cells could be subdivided into two regions: the center and the surround. In general, stimulation of these two regions with light produced opposing effects on the response of the ganglion cell. For example, stimulation with light in the center region might produce an increase in ganglion cell activity. Simultaneous illumination of the surround region would then reduce the center response. Thus, center and surround antagonize each other. Note the similarity between the antagonism of center and surround regions of these ganglion cell receptive fields and the lateral inhibitory interactions between adjacent ommatidia in the eye of *Limulus*. In the vertebrate retina, this type of receptive-field organization can be accounted for by the vertical and horizontal flow of information in the retina mentioned earlier. Center responses would be produced by information flowing in vertically oriented cells—the receptor cells, bipolar cells, and ganglion cells. Surround effects would be produced by information relayed in the horizontally oriented elements—the amacrine and horizontal cells. Since there are approximately one million ganglion cells in each retina, it is apparent that the receptive fields for different ganglion cells overlap extensively. This organization of the retina into many overlapping receptive fields is illustrated schematically in figure 7.17.

Mach Bands

A remarkable perceptual effect of the retinal organization is shown in figure 7.18*a*, which illustrates a phenomenon first discovered by Ernst Mach in the nineteenth century. If you look at the pattern of light shown in 7.18*a*, you will perceive near the center of the picture a bright band at point B and a dark band at point D. These are called **Mach bands** (Ratliff 1965). What you see is indicated by the white line in the graph shown in figure 7.18*b*. The heavy black line shown here is the actual physical intensity of light, as measured by a light meter moved along the pattern from left to right. This line also represents the distribution of light intensity across the image of the pattern across your retina. Notice that what you see does not correspond to the physical intensity distribution of the retinal image. The pattern you perceive exaggerates the abrupt transitions in physical intensity across the pattern. Now consider ganglion cells A through D shown in figure 7.18*c*, which are stimulated by points along a horizontal line across the pattern. The receptive field of each ganglion cell is represented by a circle containing a dot. If we compare the responses of ganglion cells A and B, we will find that both of these cells receive the same illumination in the center region of their

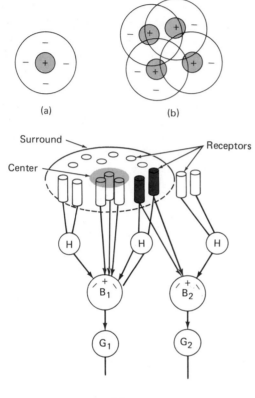

(a)   (b)

(c)

Figure 7.17 Receptive-field organization of retinal ganglion cells. As indicated, the center and surround regions oppose each other (a), and the receptive fields of different ganglion cells overlap considerably (b). Possible neural connections leading to receptive field organization are shown at (c). Receptors in the center region send signals (arrows) to bipolar cells (B), the signals of which are opposed by signals from the horizontal cells (H), which are stimulated by receptors in the surround region. The signal from the bipolar cell to the ganglion cell (G_1) reflects both the positive and negative signals it receives. The shaded receptors show how the receptors in the surround of one ganglion cell (G_1) can form the center of another ganglion cell (G_2).

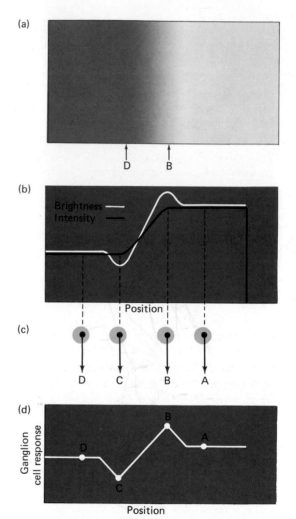

(a)

(b)

(c)

(d)

Figure 7.18 (a) Pattern of light that produces Mach bands, as indicated at D and B. (b) Graph of the physical intensity (black line) and the brightness perceived across the pattern (white line). (c) Receptive fields of some selected ganglion cells that receive light at various points along the pattern. (d) Response or neural picture produced by the ganglion cells.

receptive fields (the dot). However, the surround of ganglion cell B is illuminated partly by a high-intensity region of the pattern and partly by a low-intensity region of the pattern. However, the surround of ganglion cell A is entirely illuminated by the high-intensity region. Thus, center stimulation of ganglion cell B is opposed to a lesser extent than center stimulation of ganglion cell A, as illustrated in the graph, figure 7.18*d*. If we compare the responses of ganglion cells C and D, we note that the centers are equally stimulated by low levels of illumination. However, cell C receives a higher level of illumination in its surround region. Therefore, the center response of ganglion cell C is opposed to a greater degree than the center response of ganglion cell D. This is also illustrated by the graph in figure 7.18*d*.

Thus, the responses of the ganglion cells illustrated by the graph in 7.18*d* resemble very closely what is perceived, illustrated by the white line in 7.18*b*. Our perceptions of patterns of light, then, are imposed upon us in part by the center-surround organization of the retina and in part by the effect of lateral inhibition operating in these receptive fields. While lateral inhibition is used to emphasize certain changes in a pattern of light over space, such as those shown in 7.18*a,* it plays a role in other aspects of vision as well.

X, Y, and W Cells in the Mammalian Retina
Experimental work has suggested several new properties of ganglion cells in the mammalian retina (e.g., Enroth-Cugell and Robson 1966). Three major categories of cells—X, Y, and W—have been proposed so far.

The differences between X and Y cells can be described by using the illustration in figure 7.19. This illustration shows the receptive field of a retinal ganglion cell. Half of the field is evenly illuminated with light, whereas the other half is dark. Now suppose that the illumination were suddenly switched so that the light half were made dark and the dark half, light. An X cell will continue to respond to this change in illumination as before. In other words, provided that the same amount of light is present in the center and surround, the X cell does not distinguish between different locations of illumination. The same switch of illumination, however, provokes a vigorous response in Y cells. Indeed Y cells respond minimally while the light is stationary and markedly during a change in the location of the illumination. For this reason, X cells have been termed **sustained responders,** while Y cells have been called **transient responders.** These differences in response properties suggest that Y cells may be specialized to respond to changes in illumination across their receptive fields; that is, to movement, while X cells

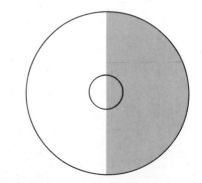

Figure 7.19 Schematic drawing of the receptive field of a ganglion cell of the retina in which half of the field is illuminated by light and the other half is dark.

may represent a group of ganglion cells specialized to detect stationary patterns. Another category of ganglion cells—W cells (Stone and Hoffman 1972)—appear to have more complex receptive fields than those of X and Y cells.

It is interesting that information from X cells appears to be routed exclusively to the visual areas of the cerebral cortex, whereas information from Y cells is projected to both the cerebral cortex and the superior colliculi. Information from W cells projects almost exclusively to the superior colliculi. As we note later,

such an arrangement is consistent with the different functions in vision of the visual cortex and superior colliculi.

The Primary Visual Pathways

In mammals, information from the retina is carried by the fibers of the optic nerve and optic tract to the lateral geniculate nuclei of the thalamus, as illustrated in figure 7.20, which shows the so-called primary visual system. Fibers of each optic nerve make contact with cells of the lateral geniculate nuclei, and these new cells send their axons to the **primary visual**

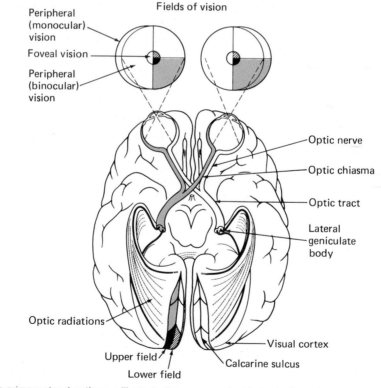

Figure 7.20 The primary visual pathways illustrate the distribution of visual information from the retina on each side to the lateral geniculate nuclei and thence to the visual cortex.

cortex. Note that optic nerve fibers from the right half of each retina go to the right side of the brain, while fibers from the left side of each retina pass to the left side of the brain. Thus, half of each optic nerve must cross over to the other side of the brain. This crossing over takes place at the **optic chiasma.**

Although fibers from corresponding regions of each eye come together at the lateral geniculate nucleus on one side, the information from the two eyes is not combined. Information from the two eyes is sent to alternate layers of the lateral geniculate nucleus. Thus, cells in the lateral geniculate nuclei tend to have monocular responses, that is, they respond to information in one eye only. The responses of lateral geniculate nucleus neurons tend to mirror the responses of the optic nerve fibers from which they receive their information. These cells have concentric, center-surround, receptive fields like retinal ganglion cells, although subtle differences do exist. For example, the extent of surround inhibition is greater for receptive fields of neurons in the lateral geniculate nuclei. The increased surround inhibition is due to small interneurons in the lateral geniculate nuclei that form lateral inhibitory interconnections with cells receiving input from the optic nerve (Levick, Cleland, and Dubin 1972).

The lateral geniculate nuclei are often viewed simply as passive relay stations; that is, simply as stations for transferring visual information from the eyes to the cortex. Actually, the lateral geniculate nuclei may be much more complex. For example, there are descending connections from the visual cortex to these nuclei. In addition, the reticular formation sends projections to them, as do several nuclei in the brain stem. These latter

projections have been implicated by several investigators in the processes of visual attention and dreaming, topics to which we will return later in this book.

It is of interest that the axons of X and Y ganglion cells appear to go to different cell types in the cat and in the primate lateral geniculate nucleus; cells that appear to correspond to X- and Y-type ganglion cells project to different layers in the lateral geniculate nucleus (Bishop 1984). It now appears that the different types of information conveyed by the X and Y cells remain segregated throughout the visual pathways, as if there were two parallel visual systems conveying visual information.

The axons of cells in the lateral geniculate nuclei form two large tracts—the **optic radiations**—as they project to the visual cortex. These axons synapse on cells in layer IV of the visual cortex. Here again, information conveyed by the X and Y systems appears to remain segregated, each system projecting to a different sublayer within layer IV. This visual area corresponds to area 17 in Brodmann's map of the cerebral cortex as described in chapter 4 (fig. 7.21). Cells in area 17 send their information to visual areas 18 and 19. The retina is represented topographically within each of these areas. It should be noted that multiple representation of the receptor surface is a common and important characteristic of other sensory areas of the cerebral cortex.

Receptive Fields in the Visual Cortex

The characteristics of neurons in the visual cortex of a number of experimental animals have been studied by means of micro-electrode-recording techniques. The responses

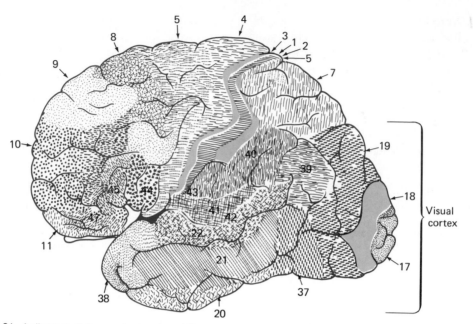

Figure 7.21 A diagram of the cerebral cortex of the human brain showing Brodmann's division of the cortex into numbered areas. The visual cortex corresponds to areas 17, 18, and 19, shown from the outer surface in the drawing.

of individual cells in the areas of the visual cortex are studied while visual stimuli of various sizes and shapes are presented to the eye. The stimuli can usually be moved in any direction, and it is possible to determine with great precision to what in the visual world a given neuron responds. The well-known experimental work of Hubel and Wiesel (1965; 1968; 1977) and Bishop and associates (e.g., Bishop and Henry 1972) exemplify these illuminating experimental techniques. Some of the neurons in layer IV of the visual cortex respond in much the same way as retinal ganglion cells and neurons of the lateral geniculate nuclei. Many others, however, do not have a concentric, center-surround, receptive-field organization. In the classification system of

Hubel and Wiesel, such receptive fields may be **simple, complex, hypercomplex,** and **higher-order hypercomplex.** Several examples of these categories of receptive fields are shown in figure 7.22.

Many cells in layer IV of the primary visual cortex (area 17) possess simple receptive fields. These cells respond very poorly to a spot of light. Their best response occurs when the retina is illuminated with a line or slit of light of particular width, slant or orientation, and place on the retina. In addition, these neurons often respond optimally to such a stimulus when it is *moved* into the appropriate region of the retina from a *particular direction.* Such receptive fields are divided into excitatory and inhibitory regions so that a stimulus produces

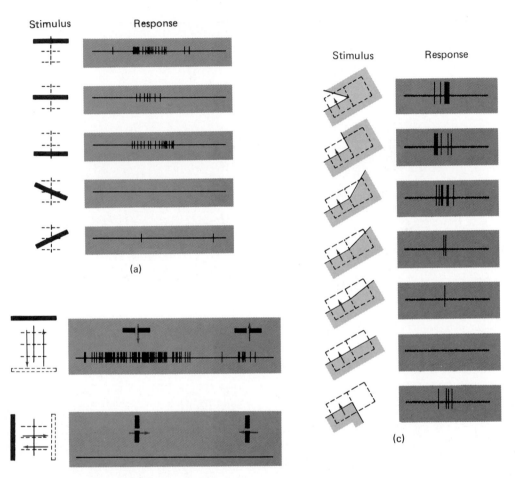

Figure 7.22 Characteristics of the receptive field of some neurons in the visual cortex of the cat. (a) The neuron responds to a horizontal bar in its receptive field. (b) The neuron responds best to downward movement of a horizontal bar and less to upward movement of the same bar and does not respond at all to a vertical bar. (c) The neuron responds best to certain stimulus angles moved into its receptive field, but not to other angles.

the best response when it is aligned within the excitatory region of the receptive field. Cells with complex receptive fields tend to be located in the cerebral cortex somewhat above layer IV and also respond to slit-shaped stimuli. However, for these neurons the stimulus need not be located in a specific place. The proper line-shaped stimulus is effective over a larger region of the retina. For cells with hypercomplex receptive fields, the line stimulus must be of a certain length in addition to the features that are effective for complex receptive fields. Finally, cells with higher-order hypercomplex receptive fields require more elaborate visual stimuli to respond.

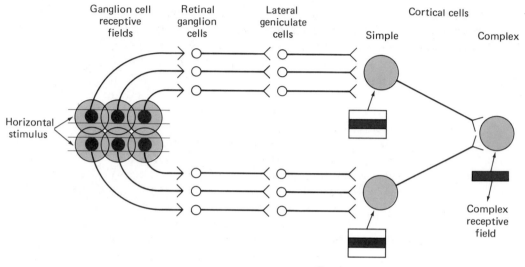

Figure 7.23 A hierarchical model in which cortical neurons with simple receptive fields receive their input from neurons with appropriately aligned concentric, center-surround receptive fields. Cells in the cerebral cortex with simple receptive fields combine their information to produce the more complex receptive fields in the visual cortex.

There has been considerable effort made to discover the neural organization by which these receptive field properties are brought about. Hubel and Wiesel have proposed a hierarchical model in which cells with simple receptive fields receive their input from groups of neurons with center-surround receptive fields. For example, a simple receptive field in which the neuron responds best to a horizontal line would be built out of connections from ganglion cells having center-surround receptive fields alongside one another on a horizontal line as shown in figure 7.23. Similarly, cells with simple receptive fields would combine their information to supply the input to neurons having complex receptive fields, and they in turn would project to cells with hypercomplex receptive fields, and so forth. Hubel and Wiesel found that neurons with simple, complex, and hypercomplex receptive fields of similar orientations tended to be found near one another in the cerebral cortex, suggesting that such a hierarchical arrangement is possible. When a microelectrode was lowered into the cerebral cortex perpendicular to the surface, all of the neurons encountered had receptive fields with similar orientations. This observation led to the view that the cortex is comprised of columns of cells having certain similar properties. One column of neurons might respond best to a vertical stimulus, another to a horizontal line, and so forth. Since the visual cortex is organized topographically, each small region of the retina projects to a small area of the cerebral cortex within which there are many columns. The columns can be specified by the orientations of visual stimuli to which the cells within the column respond.

Although the columnar organization that has been observed in the visual cortex appears to be consistent with the hierarchical model of receptive fields, there is a major controversy over whether the various categories of receptive fields are synthesized by combining simpler types to form more complex types of receptive fields. Some investigators (e.g., Stone et al. 1979; Bishop 1984) have suggested that the receptive fields are a result of parallel inputs, like the X and Y cells discussed earlier, rather than one being a combined version of the other. Currently, it appears that the final picture will be that different receptive fields result from both hierarchical organization and separate parallel inputs.

Columnar Organization

The principle of **columnar organization** is another example of spatial organization of information in the nervous system and will reappear in later discussions of the other sensory systems. In the visual sense, however, properties of the visual world other than the orientation of lines are also coded by means of columnar organization. In area 17, for example, the columns tend to be more sensitive to one eye than to the other, a property termed **monocular dominance.** Using an ingenious technique, several investigators have actually been able to "see" columns containing such monocularly dominant cortical cells, as described in figure 7.24.

The photograph in figure 7.24 illustrates columns of neurons in the visual cortex of the monkey as seen from the top. In order to photograph these neuronal columns, Wiesel, Hubel, and Lam (1974) injected radioactive material into one eye of a monkey. This material was taken up by ganglion cells in the retina and transported up the optic nerve to the lateral geniculate nucleus and then by neurons of the lateral geniculate nucleus to

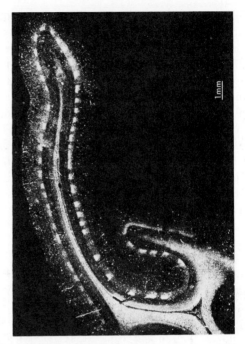

Figure 7.24 Illustrated are columns of neurons in the visual cortex of the monkey as seen from the top.

neurons in the visual cortex. In this way, cortical cells in the visual cortex receiving information from the injected eye became radioactive. When film was exposed to slices of such labeled cortical tissue, radioactive regions could be seen as light spots against a dark background, as illustrated by the photograph. Since only neurons receiving input from one eye were labeled, the investigators could actually see that these neurons do not occur randomly in the cortex, but are organized into the vertical columns exposed in their photographic records. Interestingly, connections between different regions of the cerebral cortex also appear to utilize a columnar principle of organization (Goldman and Nauta 1977).

As we have noted, most neurons in the visual cortex respond to both eyes, although one eye may produce a more dominant response than the other. Some of these cells in area 17 appear to code information regarding the depth of objects obtained from the two eyes. For a scene in depth, the same object often casts an image in slightly different positions on the retinas of the two eyes. This is due to the fact that the two eyes are located in different places on the head and therefore have slightly different angles of view. The amount of difference in the locations of the images on the retinas depends on the depth of an object relative to the point of fixation. This difference in position on the two retinas is called **binocular disparity.**

Different binocular cells in the visual cortex tend to respond best to a particular degree of binocular disparity. One class of binocular disparity neurons is of particular interest. These are the near and far cells (Poggio and Poggio 1984). Far cells have excitatory responses to objects further away than the point of fixation and are inhibited by objects closer to the observer than the point of fixation. Near cells do the opposite. A defect in precisely this type of visual perception is seen in humans. Some individuals are especially poor at locating objects in depth that are nearer than the point of fixation, while others are unable to locate objects further away than the fixation point.

The visual, or striate, cortex is also involved in color vision. As you recall, cells within the lateral geniculate nucleus respond in an opponent-process fashion to color. These cells send this information to the visual cortex. Until recently, it appeared that cells in the visual cortex were not especially selective in their response to color. However, it has now been discovered that there are visual cortical neurons that exhibit an elaboration of color processing. These neurons were located by Horton and Hubel (1980) in a pattern of regularly repeating bloblike structures in layers I and III of visual cortex, stained to reveal the presence

of cytochrome oxidase, a mitochondrial enzyme. These blobs lie within the columns that we have previously described. When the activity of neurons within the blobs was recorded by Livingstone and Hubel (1984), they discovered that neurons within the blobs were not orientation-selective, but rather had a center-surround organization in which opponent color responses could be obtained. Many of these cells were termed double-opponent cells, in which the center region might show excitation to red but inhibition to green, and the surround would have the opposite characteristics. These cells may be coding information regarding more complex aspects of color vision. The double-opponent cell responds well if the center of the receptive field is illuminated with one color and its surround with another. It will not respond if the entire receptive field is illuminated with the same color, since the center and surround oppose each other. It has been suggested that this cell will respond to changes or contrasts in color just as other cells that we have described respond to differences in brightness or brightness contrast. The fact that colors appear different depending upon the colors surrounding them—the phenomenon of color contrast—is well known. The double-opponent type cells may be responsible for the physiological mechanisms involved in the color contrast effect.

Among the remarkable advances in understanding the processing of visual information by the brain has been the realization that there are multiple areas of the cerebral cortex that appear to be involved in visual perception. In general, it is useful to consider that two major visual pathways arise from the primary visual cortex, each destined for a different region of the cerebral cortex and each having a different set of visual functions (Anderson, in press). One of these passes from primary visual cortex to the posterior parietal lobe and is involved in processing spatial functions, including the analysis of motion, selective attention, and visual motor integration. For example, in experiments on monkeys, the activity of neurons in this visual area is particularly influenced by a light stimulus during attentive fixation compared to a relaxed but wakeful state. The responses are altered by the angle of gaze, suggesting that this region of the parietal lobe is involved in visual attention as well as in perception of the location of objects in space relative to head position (Anderson and Mountcastle 1983; Anderson et al. 1985). The other passes ventrally to the temporal lobe and is concerned primarily with color vision and the perception of form and pattern (Anderson 1987; Van Essen 1985). According to Anderson (1987), these ". . . are two largely segregated cortical visual systems, one that includes the inferior parietal lobules concerned with 'where' objects are in the visual environment and the other, including the inferotemporal cortex, interested in 'what' objects are" (cf. Underleider and Mishkin 1982).

It will be beneficial at this point to summarize the important anatomical and physiological properties of the visual system so that their relevance to the process of pattern vision can be made clearer. A pattern consisting of variations in light over space forms an image on the retina. This pattern of light is transduced by the rods and cones into neural signals. The output of the retina, the ganglion cell responses, illustrate that a significant degree of analysis of the image has already taken place at this level. In this neural picture represented by the ganglion cell responses, the process of lateral inhibition has exaggerated differences

or contrasts in the pattern falling on the retina. These differences are increased and modified in the lateral geniculate nuclei, but a topographic representation of the image is still maintained and carried to the visual cortex. Within the cortex, each small region on the topographic map of the retina contains columns of cells. Cells within each column are designed to assess specific sets of features of the visual world, such as lines of a certain orientation and width. In areas 18 and 19 we again encounter columns of cells. However, cells in these areas require more complex or abstract features than simply lines of a specific orientation and width. These neurons also detect the features of binocular disparity, a characteristic necessary to specify the location of objects in depth. This model of sensory processing, if taken to an extreme, might suggest that there must be some ultimate cell at the end of the visual pathway that responds to each unique pattern of visual input. This concept is often amusingly posed as the question, Is there a cell that responds to grandmother's face? Clearly, simple logic reveals that there cannot be an individual cell recognizing each of the infinite variety of patterns each of us sees daily. Thus, if we are to pursue such hierarchical models as that of Hubel and Wiesel we encounter this dilemma. No answers to this question are yet available, but certain possibilities have been proposed. For example, single neurons in the visual cortex could be controlled to respond to one set of features under one circumstance and to another set in other circumstances. For example, the orientation to which cortical cells give their best response can be modified by other sensory inputs, such as that which occurs when the orientation of the body is changed (e.g., Horn and Hill 1969).

Visual Experience and Development of Ocular Dominance Columns

A number of experiments and clinical cases have demonstrated that visual deprivation early in life can have enduring consequences on visual function. Indeed, studies of visual loss early in life in macaque monkeys have established that different visual functions seem to be vulnerable to this experience over multiple, partially overlapping critical periods. For some functions, such as the spectral sensitivity of the rods and cones, the critical period of vulnerability may last from three to six months after birth, but for more complex visual functions, such as spatial vision or resolution, or binocular vision, the critical period during development may be twenty-five months or longer (Harweth et al. 1986).

One important factor is that, at the time of birth for example, ocular dominance columns are only partially formed. Using the method of transneuronal transport and autoradiography, the development of ocular dominance columns has been visualized (LeVay, Wiesel, and Hubel 1981). Figure 7.25 illustrates the progressive development of ocular dominance columns in the macaque monkey for a period ranging from one week to six weeks after birth. As can be seen, the columns are indistinct at one week of age, but become fully developed and distinctive only six weeks after birth. It has been known for some time that the loss of vision in one eye produces a severe and irreversible defect in binocular vision, especially if it occurs early in life. In an attempt to understand the physiological and anatomical factors involved in this loss of visual function and the treatments that might be effective in reversing the loss, LeVay, Wiesel, and Hubel (1981) studied the effect of unilateral eye closure on the development of the visual cortical

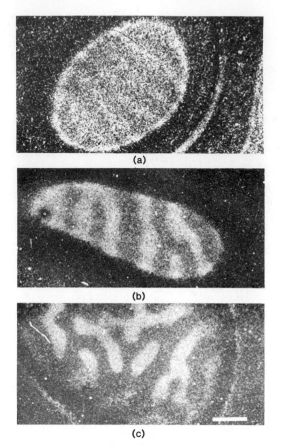

(a)

(b)

(c)

Figure 7.25 The normal development of ocular dominance columns in the macaque monkey studied by autoradiography. The columns are only barely visible at one week of age (a), but become distinctive at three weeks (b), and appear well developed at six weeks of age (c).

columns. Some of their results are shown in figure 7.26. In these experiments, lid closure was produced in macaque monkeys at ages ranging from two days to adult. As shown in the illustration, when the visual cortical columns were examined several months later, it became apparent that deprivation in one eye resulted in an expansion of the columns for the

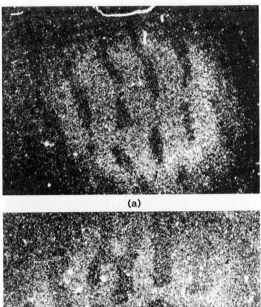

(a)

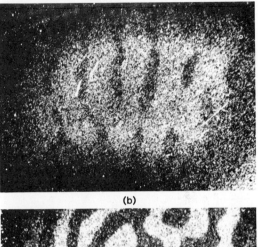

(b)

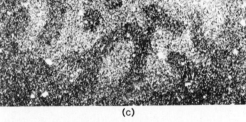

(c)

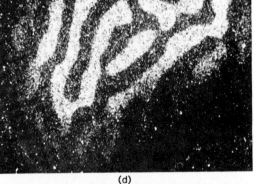

(d)

Figure 7.26 The effects of long-term monocular deprivation begun at two weeks of age (a), five and one-half weeks (b), ten weeks (c), and in the adult (d). The main deadline in susceptibility to the anatomical effects of deprivation occurs between five and one-half to ten weeks of age in the macaque monkey. The effect in the adult animal is indistinguishable from a normal animal.

nonclosed eye and that this effect was most severe in the youngest animals. The procedure did not affect columnar organization in adult animals. If the closed eye were opened so that visual experience became possible, and the previously open eye were closed, the effect of early deprivation could be partially reversed, provided treatment occurred early enough following the original deprivation experience. This kind of work may establish the kinds of anatomical and physiological changes that underlie the malfunction of vision following loss

of sight in one eye and may help to establish programs of remediation that will be used to correct the deficit that occurs.

Visual Experience and Receptive Fields

A variety of other evidence shows that the receptive fields of neurons in the visual cortex can be influenced by experience, especially in infancy. In a demonstration of this effect, Hirsch and Spinelli (1970) raised kittens with specially designed goggles. On one side the kittens saw only vertical stripes and on the other side only horizontal stripes during the first months of life. Whereas in normal cats the visual cortex contains cells responsive to all different orientations, in animals reared with these special goggles a change in response characteristics occurred. Cells responding to input from the eye exposed to vertical stripes tended to respond only to such vertical stimuli. Cells responding to input from the other eye, reared with only horizontal stripes visible, showed a preference for this type of stimulus.

These experiments demonstrate that early visual experience is important in the way that the visual system develops and ultimately in the way that we perceive the world. Indeed, individuals blind at birth who later recover their sight never gain the visual capability of individuals whose vision was normal during development. However, our understanding of the development of vision cannot stop at the characteristics of the classical visual pathway. It is clear, for example, that our analysis of the visible world must also be integrated with our other knowledge and experience and we must be able to respond appropriately to what we see. Indeed, lack of opportunity to move about in the environment can have profound effects on visually guided behavior. Held and Hein (1963) demonstrated this important principle in a series of experiments on kittens. Their experiment is illustrated in figure 7.27.

One kitten was active in the visual environment that as shown in the figure consisted of a cylinder with vertical stripes, while another kitten was passively transported in a gondola due to the motion of the active kitten. The kittens had no prior visual experience, having been reared in dark conditions. After about thirty hours of exposure the active kitten could perform normally in visually guided

tasks such as avoiding a cliff, blinking when an object approached the eye, and so forth. The passive kitten, however, was unable to perform these types of behaviors unless it was later allowed to move about actively. These results demonstrate the necessity for visually guided motor behavior for the normal development of such behavior. Involved in this behavior is a great deal more than simple analysis of the visual stimulus. This analysis appears to be a function of the primary visual system under consideration here, the pathway from the retina to the lateral geniculate nuclei to the visual cortex. However, other attributes of our visual behavior appear to depend on additional visual pathways.

Other Visual Pathways

The schematic diagram in figure 7.28 shows that in addition to the so-called primary visual pathway, two other major visual pathways can be distinguished: the **tectal,** or collicular, and the **pretectal pathways.** Thus, fibers from the optic tracts do not all go to the lateral geniculate nuclei. Some of these fibers project to the **pretectal nuclei.** This system appears to be involved in the control of certain visual reflexes, such as the pupillary reflex and certain eye movements. The tectal pathway, which originates with fibers in the retina projecting to the superior colliculi in the brain stem (the superior colliculi are often called the **optic tectum,** roof), appears to be of major importance for our ability to orient toward a visual stimulus.

The superior colliculi are multilayered structures having superficial, or upper, layers that receive input from both the retina and the visual cortex. The upper layers are topographically organized such that corresponding cortical and retinal signals arrive at the same place. The deep layers of the superior colliculi

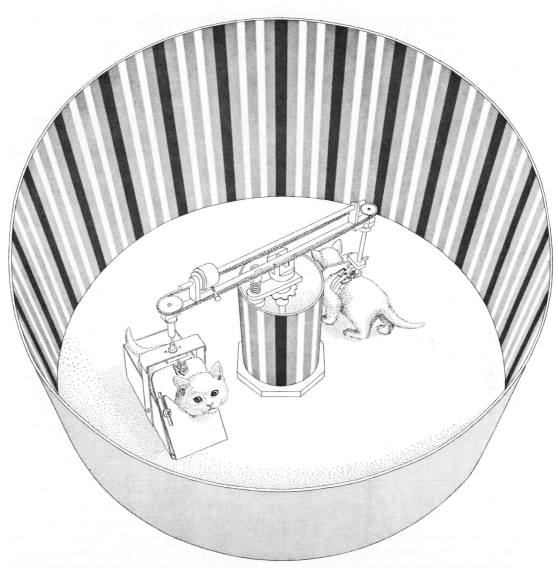

Figure 7.27 Active and passive movements of kittens were compared in this apparatus. The active kitten walked about more or less freely, and its gross movements were transmitted to the passive kitten by the chain and bar. The passive kitten, carried in a gondola, received essentially the same visual stimulation as the active kitten because of the unvarying pattern on the wall and on the center post. Active kittens developed normal sensory-motor coordination, but the passive kittens failed to develop normal sensomotor skills until after they had been freed for several days.

From ''Plasticity in Sensory-Motor Systems'' by R. Held. Copyright © 1965 by Scientific American, Inc. All rights reserved.

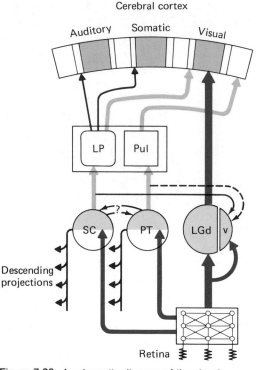

Figure 7.28 A schematic diagram of the visual pathways. Information originates in the retina and projects to the lateral geniculate nuclei (LGd and v), the pretectal nuclei (PT), and the superior colliculi (SC). In the classical visual pathway, information is transmitted to the visual cortex. In the other visual pathways, information passes upward to nuclei of the thalamus (LP and Pul) and thence to various regions of the cerebral cortex. Descending projections to many brain stem nuclei and the spinal cord are also illustrated.

the thalamus and thence to the various sensory and association areas of the cerebral cortex.

The receptive field characteristics of neurons in the superior colliculi are consistent with the view that the superior colliculi control visual orienting and following responses. For example, collicular neurons have large receptive fields compared to those in the visual cortex, which are optimally responsive to stimulus movement. In some animals, such as the cat, these neurons appear to be directionally sensitive (Schiller 1972). Further, these neurons often discharge prior to the execution of eye movements (Wurtz and Goldberg 1971). Based on the deficits produced by experimental damage to the superior colliculi and pretectal regions, Sprague (1972) concluded that these other visual pathways are important in visual spatial orientation and localization, as well as in visual perception and discrimination in mammals. Indeed, the importance of these other visual pathways has also been emphasized by studies of many nonmammalian species that have no visual cortex and in which the tectal and pretectal pathways form major points of termination of the visual pathway (Hodos and Karten 1974; Ingle and Schneider 1970).

It is perhaps important to close our discussion of the visual system by reiterating that the various visual pathways do not operate independently of one another (Hodos and Karten 1974). This important reminder is made obvious by the diagram in figure 7.28. These pathways are interconnected at virtually every level from retina to visual cortex and back. Further, each of these pathways receives descending input from the cerebral cortex, which

receive input from the somatosensory and auditory systems and nonvisual cortical areas. These deep layers send their information to several nuclei in the brain stem involved in the coordination of head and eye movements and to the thalamus at the top of the brain stem illustrated in figure 7.28. The figure also shows that the superficial layers send their signals to reflects the important controlling and integrating actions of this station in the processing of visual information. There is much yet to be discovered about the functions of these many visual regions of the brain and their relationships to other neural systems. The complex interactions portrayed in figure 7.28 at least begin to appear consistent with the richness of visual perception.

Summary

Sensation of the world around us derives from stimulation of our sense organs by physical energy, although not all forms of physical energy can be detected by the human observer. In this chapter, we have described some of the elementary processes by which changes in physical energy affect our sense organs and brain and the relationship of these processes to perception.

Initially, physical energy must be transduced into a form that can be utilized by the brain. The **transduction** of energy by sensory receptors leads to action potentials carried by sensory nerves into the brain. For each of our senses, the afferent nerves code the sensation by changes in the number, frequency, and pattern of impulses transmitted to the brain. In addition to this method of coding information about a physical stimulus, the destination of these fibers in the brain provides another information code, representing the place on the receptor surface where a stimulus occurs. In the visual system, for example, information about where a stimulus occurs is represented by where this information arrives in the visual cortex. The same spatial organization of information occurs in the somatosensory system in which a map of the body surface is represented in the somatosensory area of the cerebral cortex. This is the principle of **topographic spatial organization** and represents only one of the instances in which spatial organization is used by the brain to code information.

Light, visible electromagnetic radiation, which consists of small packets of energy termed **quanta,** is transduced by the **retina.** The process by which an image is focused at the back of the eye is analogous to a camera. A number of cell types are within the retina. The **rods** and **cones** are the receptors and contain the chemical **photopigments** that react with light to initiate the process of transduction. Information about the image is processed extensively within the retina, passing from receptors to **bipolar cells** to **ganglion cells.** The ganglion cells send their axons out the **optic nerve** to carry information into the brain. Interactions between different points in the image also occur in the retina by means of **horizontal** and **amacrine cells.** Among the significant features of vision that can be accounted for on the basis of our knowledge of processes occurring in the retina are the **scotopic** (rod) and **photopic** (cone) threshold curves, **dark adaptation, Mach bands,** and **color vision.** The initial stages of pattern perception also receive an important contribution from the retina in the form of **lateral inhibition,** which enhances contrast between different regions of the pattern.

From study of the responses of single cells at different levels of the visual system, a basic understanding of the biological processes involved in pattern perception has begun to emerge. Ganglion cells in the retina have characteristic responses to light stimulation. Stimulation of a small region of the retina activates these cells. This region, termed the **receptive field,** consists of a small circular center and a somewhat larger surround. Light stimulation in one of these regions may be antagonized by stimulation of the other. The organization of these receptive fields maximizes the usefulness of the process of lateral inhibition. In the lateral geniculate nucleus, where the optic nerve terminates, receptive fields are similar to those of retinal ganglion cells. However, receptive fields of neurons in the visual cortex are elongated or slit shaped and may fall into different categories. The categories of Hubel and Wiesel, for example, are as follows: **simple, complex, hypercomplex,** and **higher-order hypercomplex.** Simple receptive fields are slit shaped, and neurons with such receptive fields respond best to a slit of light of particular width, orientation, and place on the retina. Complex receptive fields are similar, but neurons with these response characteristics may not require that the stimulus be in any particular place on the retina. Hypercomplex and higher-order hypercomplex receptive fields may require certain lengths of lines to respond best, as well as other more elaborate features of visual stimulus such as lines at a specific angle. Within the visual cortex, such receptive fields appear to be organized spatially into columns at right angles to the surface of the brain.

Additional visual pathways include the **tectal,** or collicular, **pathway** and the **pretectal pathway,** both found in the brain stem below the cerebral cortex. These subcortical nuclei and associated pathways appear to be important in visual spatial orientation and localization as well as in visual perception and discrimination. The integration of the subcortical pathways with the primary visual pathway from retina to cerebral cortex occurs by means of interconnections at every level and appears to provide a useful analogy to the richness of visual perception. We have only begun to understand the nature and importance of the biological processes underlying visual perception.

Suggested Readings

Barlow, H. B., and J. D. Mollon, eds. 1982. *The senses.* Cambridge: Cambridge University Press.
A book edited by a well-known sensory physiologist.

Boynton, R. M., ed. 1986. Twenty-fifth Anniversary Issue. *Vision Research* 26, 1986.
An issue of one of the most prominent journals in vision research in which well-known researchers review informally and offer in personal terms the evolution of work in their fields over the last twenty-five years.

Darian-Smith, I., ed. 1984. *Handbook of Physiology: Section I. The nervous system. VIII sensory processes.* Baltimore: Waverly Press.
A major advanced review of our current knowledge of the sensory physiology of vision.

Gregory, R. L. 1970. *The intelligent eye.* New York: McGraw-Hill.
This is an inexpensive paperback with excellent illustrations and clearly written text on visual perception.

Levine, M. W., and J. M. Shefner. 1981. *Fundamentals of sensation and perception.* New York: Random House.
Good, current overview of important issues and ideas in the psychology and physiology of vision.

Marr, D. 1982. *Vision.* San Francisco: W. H. Freeman.
This book is written by a scientist who worked in the fields of vision and artificial intelligence and has had a major impact on current thinking about sensory processing in the visual system.

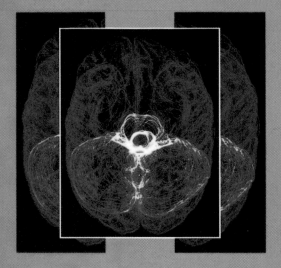

Outline

Introduction

Many of the principles of vision, which we described in chapter 7, also apply to other sensory modalities. In fact, all sensory systems share a common mode of operation: Physical energy is converted into neural energy by specialized receptors, and the resulting neural signals then are coded, analyzed, and interpreted by the nervous system. In this chapter, we begin with the sense of hearing, or audition. The physical stimulus that we preceive as sound is really a series of variations in air pressure that are transduced in the inner ear, an engineering marvel in miniature. From the ear, auditory information follows a tortuous path through the brain stem and eventually reaches a narrow strip of cerebral cortex in the temporal lobe. At each level, the nervous system extracts information and somehow puts it all together to give sound its meaning. The sense of balance, also known as the vestibular sense, is closely linked to the auditory system, as you soon will see. Next, we describe the bodily, or somatic, senses, which require many different receptors to detect many different sensations ranging from temperature and light touch to severe pain. Perhaps more than any other sensory modality, pain has dominated research on sensory systems during the past twenty years, but progress must seem agonizingly slow to millions of people for whom pain has become a chronic and, so far, incurable problem. We also discuss in this chapter the senses that respond to chemical stimuli: the senses of taste and smell.

Chapter

8

Sensory Processes: Audition, Somatic Sensation, Taste, and Smell

Although each of the senses is of fundamental importance in our study of the neural mechanisms underlying behavior, we also must consider how the nervous system integrates these different forms of sensory information. This process, which appears to involve association cortex and other "polysensory systems" throughout the brain, may hold the key to understanding perceptual behavior. It is appropriate, therefore, to conclude this chapter with a discussion of sensory integration.

Audition

If the human ear were any more sensitive to sound, we could hear the random bombardment of molecules in the air and the blood rushing through our heads. To understand how the auditory system works, it is necessary to begin with a brief descrption of the physics of sound. Later, you will see how the auditory system is designed to handle these physical characteristics.

Physical Dimensions of Sound

When you pluck a string on a guitar, the string vibrates back and forth. This vibration causes momentary increases and decreases in air pressure. When the string moves toward your ear, the air in contact with the string is compressed. When the string moves away from your ear, air in contact with the string moves in the opposite direction, creating a region of decompression. These alternating increases and decreases in air pressure travel through the air at the speed of sound (approximately 740 miles per hour) and eventually arrive at the ear, where the **tympanic membrane,** or eardrum, moves back and forth in synchrony with

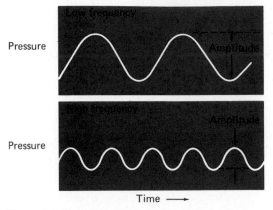

Figure 8.1 Two sine waves representing pure tones of different frequencies and amplitudes. Frequency is a measure of the variations in pressure over time, while amplitude is a measure of the difference between maximum and minimum changes in pressure.

the pulsations of air pressure. You might think that the pulsations of air caused by a vibrating guitar string would be incredibly small, and they are. But they are more than large enough to be heard. In fact, some sounds can be heard when the tympanic membrane vibrates only one billionth of a centimeter.

The simplest pattern of pressure pulsations is that generated by a **pure tone,** or **sine wave,** shown in figure 8.1. One important characteristic of a pure tone is the frequency of the tone, or the number of high to low variations in pressure per second, called cycles. The units of frequency are cycles per second, or hertz (Hz). One low-frequency tone and one high-frequency tone are represented in the graphs provided in figure 8.1. Another important characteristic of pure tones is the degree of change from maximum to minimum pressure, the **amplitude,** or **intensity.** Such pressure changes are typically measured in dynes per square centimeter, a measure of force per unit area. This parameter of sound also is illustrated in figure 8.1.

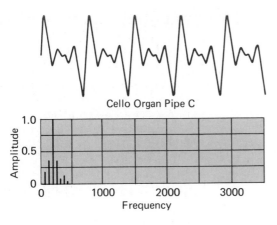

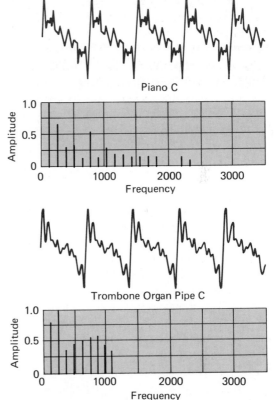

Figure 8.2 Graphs representing complex sounds. When a particular note is played on a musical instrument, a complex tone consisting of a combination of frequencies is generated. The upper tracings show the air pressure changes produced by three instruments playing the same notes indicated, and the lower graphs indicate the frequency composition of the changes.

The physical representation of sounds bears a certain resemblance to that for light. We found in the previous chapter that a light source can be characterized by a spectrum, a combination of wavelengths of particular intensities. Similarly, sounds can be described in terms of their **sound spectrum,** as illustrated in figure 8.2. As just explained, a sound composed of a single sine wave is a pure tone. Other sounds consisting of combinations of frequencies are called **complex sounds** and can be thought of as specific combinations of pure tones.

Humans with excellent hearing can detect air pressure variations in the approximate range of 20 to 20,000 Hz. As the frequency of sound is increased within this range, an increase in the **pitch** of the sound is perceived. The lowest note on a piano (A), for example, corresponds to around 27 Hz and the highest note (C) to about 4,186 Hz. As the **intensity** of a sound of a particular frequency is increased, its loudness increases also. The range of intensities over which we can hear is enormous. Because of this, sound intensities are typically reported in terms of logarithmic units called **decibels.**

As we asked for monochromatic light, we also can ask how sensitive human beings are to pure tones of different frequencies.

timbre   (tim′ber)
ossicles (os′sĭ-k′l)
cochlea   (kok′le-ah)

Figure 8.3 shows that different intensities are required in order for the human listener to detect different frequencies. As shown, we are most sensitive to sounds in the region of 1,000–4,000 Hz, and our sensitivity declines for higher and lower frequencies. This curve indicates that sounds of different frequencies require different amounts of energy in order to be barely loud enough to be heard. Our sensitivity in terms of loudness depends on the frequency of sound in a way that changes with the level of sound intensity. You have probably experienced this phenomenon when listening to music. If you listen to the same piece of music at both high and low volume, you will notice that the bass and treble become much more noticeable at higher volume. Some high-fidelity systems attempt to compensate for this change by providing a loudness control that boosts the bass and treble at low volume.

It also is the case that pitch does not depend solely upon frequency, but upon intensity as well. If the intensity of a low-frequency sound is raised, its pitch decreases. Conversely, if the intensity of a high-frequency sound is raised, its pitch increases.

Typically, the pitch of complex sounds corresponds to the pitch of the lowest frequency component in the sound, called the **fundamental.** Higher frequency components, termed **harmonics,** affect the quality, or **timbre,** of the sound. For example, two musical instruments such as a trumpet and piano playing the same note will generate the same lowest frequency component, or fundamental. However, the higher frequency components, or harmonics, differ as shown in figure 8.2. Harmonics produce the characteristic differences in quality of different instruments. If we were to remove all the harmonics, leaving only the

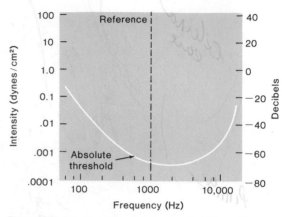

Figure 8.3 The line indicates the threshold intensity required to detect pure tones of different frequencies.

fundamental, a trumpet and piano playing the same note would sound identical.

Now that we have discussed some of the relationships between the physical and perceptual characteristics of sound, it is appropriate to examine how these characteristics are related to the physiological processes of audition in the ear and brain.

The Ear

The tympanic membrane moves back and forth with the variations in the air pressure reaching it. Figure 8.4 illustrates that the tympanic membrane is connected to a series of three tiny bones (malleus, incus, and stapes), the **ossicles,** located within the middle ear. These bones couple the movement of the tympanic membrane to a diaphragmlike membrane, the **oval window.** The oval window, which is illustrated in figure 8.5, is located on a bony, snaillike structure—the **cochlea**—which is the receptor organ for hearing. Figure 8.5 is a schematic diagram of how the cochlea would look if it were uncoiled. The fluid-filled cochlea is divided into upper, middle, and lower chambers

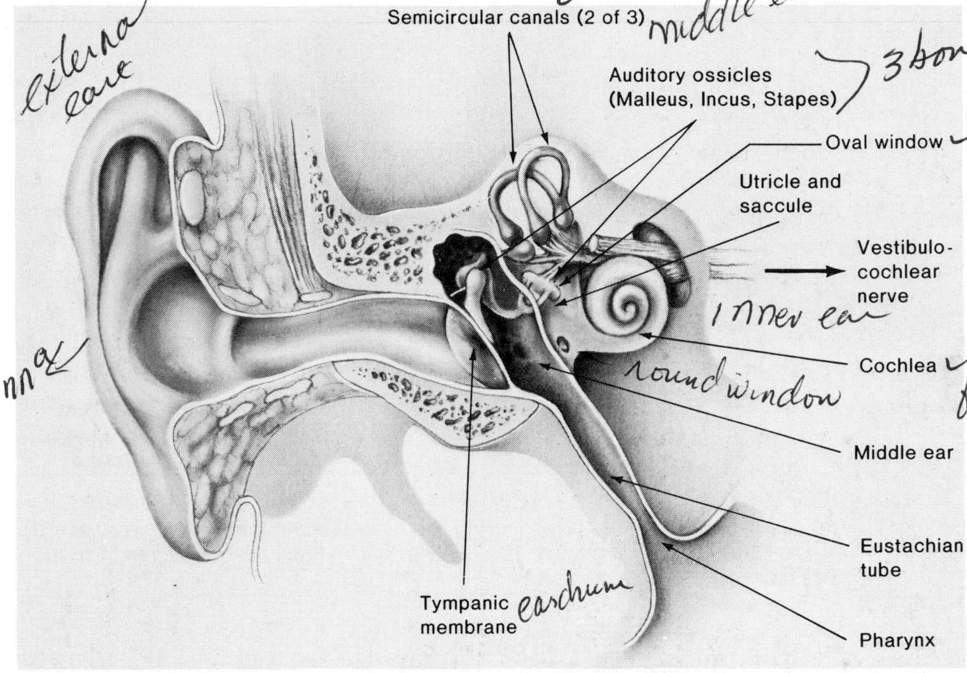
Semicircular canals (2 of 3)
Auditory ossicles
(Malleus, Incus, Stapes)
Oval window
Utricle and
saccule
Vestibulo-
cochlear
nerve
Cochlea
Middle ear
Eustachian
tube
Tympanic
membrane
Pharynx

Figure 8.4 Diagram giving the gross anatomy of the human ear. The bones of the middle ear (malleus, incus, and stapes) transmit vibrations in the tympanic membrane to the oval window of the cochlea.

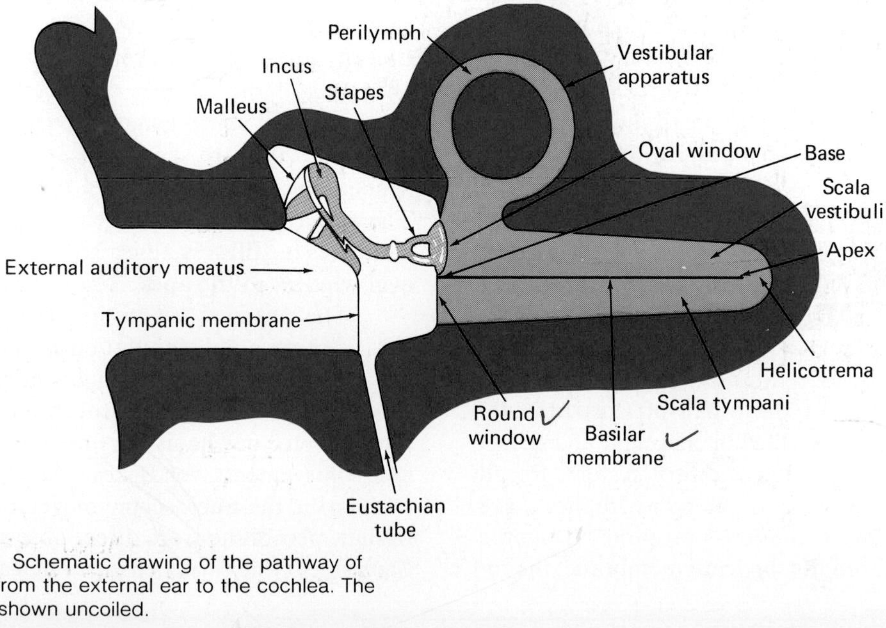
Perilymph
Incus
Malleus
Stapes
Vestibular
apparatus
Oval window
Base
Scala
vestibuli
Apex
External auditory meatus
Tympanic membrane
Helicotrema
Scala tympani
Round
window
Basilar
membrane
Eustachian
tube

Figure 8.5 Schematic drawing of the pathway of vibrations from the external ear to the cochlea. The cochlea is shown uncoiled.

tectorial   (tek-to′re-al)
basilar   (bas′ĭ-lar)
lamina   (lam′ĭ-nah)

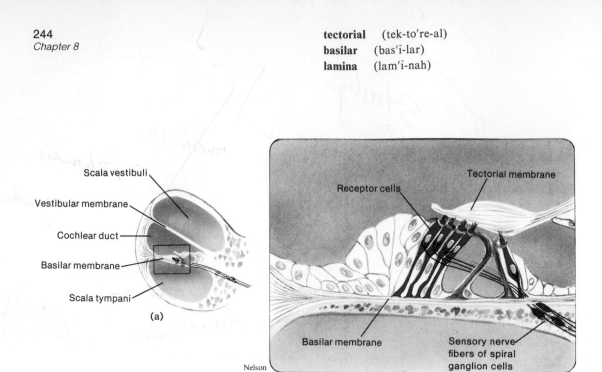

Scala vestibuli

Vestibular membrane

Cochlear duct

Basilar membrane

Scala tympani

(a)

Nelson

Receptor cells

Tectorial membrane

Basilar membrane

Sensory nerve fibers of spiral ganglion cells

(b)

Figure 8.6 (a) Diagrammatic illustrations of the organ of Corti and (b) cross section through the cochlea. The organ of Corti is contained within a fluid-filled duct (scala media) and is bordered above by the tectorial membrane and below by the basilar membrane.

and contains a complex structure called the organ of Corti, illustrated in figure 8.6. Vibrations of the tympanic membrane are conducted by the ossicles to the oval window and create instantaneous pressure changes in the fluid within the cochlea. The pressure changes are transmitted throughout the cochlear fluid and are relieved by the flexibility of another small membrane below the oval window, the **round window.**

The organ of Corti consists of two major structures—the **tectorial membrane,** a rather stiff membrane attached to the bone of the cochlea at one side, and the **basilar membrane.** These structures are shown in cross section in figure 8.6. Between these two membranes are the **hair cells** of the organ of Corti, the receptor cells (described in chapter 7 and shown in figure 7.2) of the auditory system. Recall that the hair cells, as the name implies, have small hairlike extensions that project from the hair cell through a delicate membrane, the **re-**

ticular lamina, and onto the tectorial membrane above. There are two groups of hair cells—the inner and outer hair cells. About 3,400 inner and 12,000 outer hair cells exist in the human ear. Similar to the connections of the rods and cones of the retina, inner and outer hair cells of the cochlea connect to separate populations of **spiral ganglion cells.** These two groups of cells are separated by a structural support, termed the **rods and tunnel of Corti.** The basilar membrane increases in width and decreases in stiffness along its length from the oval window to the apex.

The physical events in the cochlea resulting from sound stimulation are understood largely through the experiments of Georg von Békésy, who pioneered research on the auditory receptor mechanism. Among his remarkable achievements, von Békésy (1960) was able to describe the microscopic movements of the basilar membrane from direct observations of the inside of the tiny cochlea. When a pressure

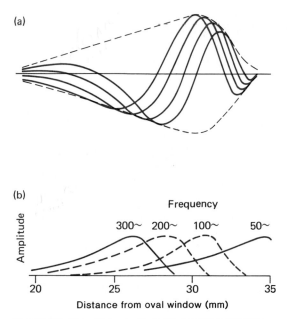

(a)

(b)

Figure 8.7 Traveling waves on the basilar membrane. (a) The graph shows the pattern of deflection as it travels along the basilar membrane, reaches a maximum, and then declines (dotted lines). (b) This graph illustrates that for different frequencies of sound, the maximal amplitude of distortion is reached at different points along the basilar membrane. Note that higher frequencies of sound reach maximum amplitude at shorter distances from the base of the cochlea.

change occurs in the cochlea, the different regions of the basilar membrane flex to a different extent and at a different time, which causes the membrane to distort. The distortion appears to travel away from the round window along the basilar membrane. As the distortion moves, it changes size, reaches a maximum at some point along the membrane depending on the frequency of the sound, and then declines in size after this point, as shown in figure 8.7. As a result of the traveling distortion, the basilar membrane and the hair cells lying on top of it flex in relation to the tectorial membrane. As the basilar membrane moves upward, the tectorial moves upward and to the

side, producing a **shearing movement,** or force, that bends the hairs of the hair cells. It is the shearing, or bending, of the hairs that initiates signals in the hair cells and the auditory nerve. These signals are carried to the brain and are ultimately perceived as sound.

As just noted, the traveling wave, which begins at the oval window, creates a pattern of deflection of the basilar membrane that depends on the frequency of the sound producing it, as shown in figure 8.7. Very high-frequency sounds distort the basilar membrane maximally over a narrow region at its base, near the oval window. As the frequency of sound decreases, the maximal point of distortion moves away from the oval window toward the apex of the basilar membrane, and the area over which this distortion occurs increases. In very low-frequency sounds, the entire membrane is distorted, although maximal distortion occurs nearer the apex.

Detecting the Frequency of Sound

The frequency, or pitch, of a sound is coded by two different mechanisms in the inner ear. As you will see, one mechanism operates exclusively at moderate-to-high frequencies of sound (above 4,000 Hz) and another at low frequencies (under 1,000 Hz). Both mechanisms are used at intermediate frequencies (1,000–4,000 Hz), and accordingly these are the frequencies of sound to which we are most sensitive.

Location on the Basilar Membrane
Hair cells in a given region along the length of the basilar membrane are stimulated most by a frequency of sound that produces the greatest distortion of this same region. Thus, the place of maximal distortion along the basilar membrane may determine the pitch of sound that we hear. This idea, which was first

proposed by von Helmholtz in the nineteenth century, has come to be known as the **place theory of hearing,** or as some pundits would call it, "the pitch is which theory," referring to the fact that the pitch we hear depends on which part of the basilar membrane is distorted the most.

This theory is supported by recordings of the individual axons that make up the auditory nerve. Recall that these axons receive input from hair cells in a particular region of the basilar membrane. Figure 8.8 illustrates how a single axon or fiber responds as the frequency of sound delivered to the ear is varied (Kiang 1965). Note that this cell responds maximally to a certain frequency of sound. Note also that the response of this cell falls off more sharply at higher frequencies than at lower frequencies. This is to be expected given that the pattern of distortion of the basilar membrane is localized more acutely for high-frequency than for low-frequency sounds. We can think of the range of frequencies to which this nerve fiber responds as similar to the receptive field of neurons of the visual system. According to the place theory of hearing, different frequencies of sound correspond to different places of stimulation along the basilar membrane, and they in turn correspond to different nerve fibers having receptive fields in these different places. As the intensity of the sound is increased, holding its frequency constant, the pattern of distortion on the basilar membrane is amplified. Thus, hair cells in this region are stimulated more effectively, and hair cells around this region that did not respond previously may be stimulated now also. This increased stimulation, which results in a greater firing rate of the nerve fibers receiving information from a given place, is presumed to relate to the intensity and therefore to the loudness of sound. Since the amount of dis-

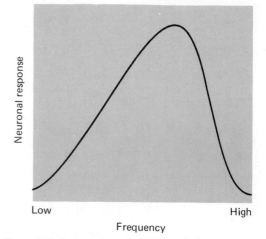

Figure 8.8 Schematic illustration showing how an auditory nerve fiber responds to different frequencies of sound transmitted to the ear.

tortion of the basilar membrane varies for different frequencies of sound, we might expect that those frequencies producing the greatest distortion would be the easiest to detect. Indeed, if the fact that some frequencies are transmitted to the cochlea better than others is taken into account, the magnitude of maximum distortion does relate very well to our thresholds for detecting different frequencies of sound (Zwislocki 1965).

Rate of Neuronal Activity

Distortion of the basilar membrane is not localized for low frequencies of sound because these frequencies distort the entire membrane. The auditory system, therefore, must use another mechanism to detect low frequencies of sound. The mechanism that it uses has come to be known as the **frequency theory of hearing.** It is based on the idea that at low frequencies, auditory neurons generate action potentials at a rate, or frequency, that corresponds to the frequency of the sound. If a 20 Hz sound reaches your ear, it will travel to your brain via the auditory nerve firing at twenty times per

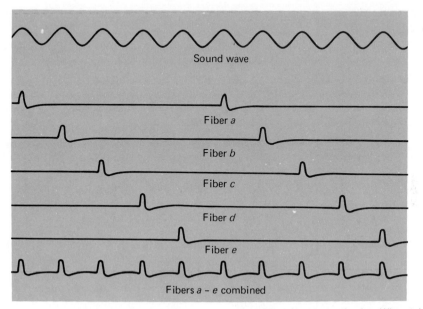

Figure 8.9 A schematic diagram illustrating the volley effect. Individual nerve fibers (*a-e*) fire at different peaks of the sine wave stimulus. When taken together, they convey a higher frequency than any single fiber can convey.

second. Auditory neurons, in other words, faithfully convey the frequency of the sound, much like a telephone wire faithfully conveys information. Thus, the frequency theory is also known as the "telephone theory."

How are auditory neurons able to fire in time with sonic vibrations? At low frequencies, the entire basilar membrane pulsates at the same rate as the frequency of the sound. These pulsations produce bursts of firing in auditory nerve fibers. The firing of auditory neurons in synchrony with the frequency of sound is known as **phase-locking,** a phenomenon that is illustrated in chapter 7 (see fig. 7.2).

Auditory neurons can fire up to about 1,000 times per second, and thus frequencies of sound up to about 1,000 Hz can be coded by the rate of neuronal activity. At higher frequencies, the place theory of hearing begins to take over, though this takeover is not complete until the frequency exceeds 4,000 Hz. The frequency theory still operates between 1,000 and 4,000 Hz, but in a slightly different manner. In this frequency range, several neurons fire during different phases of a tone so that while some fibers are recovering from previous activity, others fire—a continuous process. This is known as the **volley effect** (fig. 8.9). Indeed, when the activity of the entire auditory nerve is recorded, bursts of neuronal activity can be detected that correspond to the frequency of sounds up to 4,000 Hz (Wever and Bray 1930). The volley effect, therefore, extends the range at which the frequency theory operates (Uttal 1973). Above 4,000 Hz, however, the volley effect is exceeded, and the place theory of hearing takes over.

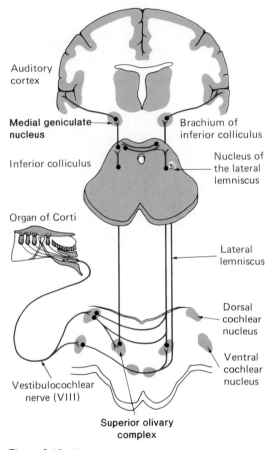

Auditory cortex

Medial geniculate nucleus

Inferior colliculus

Organ of Corti

Brachium of inferior colliculus

Nucleus of the lateral lemniscus

Lateral lemniscus

Dorsal cochlear nucleus

Ventral cochlear nucleus

Vestibulocochlear nerve (VIII)

Superior olivary complex

Figure 8.10 Diagram of the major anatomical pathways of the auditory system.

Adapted with permission from Matzke, H. A. and F. M. Foltz, *Synopsis of Neuroanatomy*, 2d ed. Copyright © 1972, Oxford University Press, New York.

Central Auditory Pathways

The major anatomical pathways from the cochlea to higher centers in the auditory system are illustrated in figure 8.10. Hair cells synapse onto spiral ganglion cells, whose axons form the auditory portion of the vestibulocochlear nerve. From the cochlea, information is carried by the auditory nerve to the **cochlear nucleus** and to several other nuclei in the brain

stem. Information from these centers is carried to the **inferior colliculus,** the **medial geniculate nucleus** of the thalamus, and ultimately to the primary **auditory cortex.** Again, we encounter a similarity between auditory and visual pathways. Recall that in the visual system, important information processing stations include the lateral geniculate nucleus of the thalamus, the superior colliculus in the midbrain, and the primary visual cortex. Several features of the auditory pathways should be mentioned. Note that information from the ears connects to a variety of nuclei in the brain stem before reaching the cerebral cortex. In addition, after the first relay nucleus in the auditory pathways—the cochlear nuclei—information from each ear reaches both sides through connections that cross over from each side of the brain. This bilateral distribution of information is an important feature of sound localization.

Sound Localization

Because we have two ears, we are able to perceive some important information: the location of sound in space. Sound from a single source arriving at the two ears can differ in two ways. Suppose a tone is sounded directly on your right, as shown in figure 8.11a. For higher frequency sounds, the intensity of the sound will be less in the left ear than in the right ear because the sound is blocked by the head before it reaches the left ear. The opposite is true if the tone is sounded on your left. This intensity difference exists only for sounds above about 1,200 Hz. At lower frequencies, the sound can travel around the head without any significant reduction in intensity.

A second source of information about the location of a sound source results from the fact that when a sound must travel further to one ear than to the other, there is a time or phase

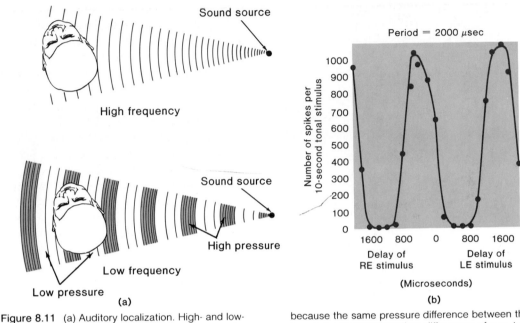

Figure 8.11 (a) Auditory localization. High- and low-frequency sound waves emanating from a source to the right of a person's head are shown arriving at the two ears. Because high-frequency sounds are blocked to some degree by the head (top figure), there is a difference in intensity between the two ears. Low-frequency tones (lower figure) are not blocked, but high- (shaded) and low- (unshaded) pressure variations arrive at the two ears at different times. High-frequency sounds provide ambiguous time information because the same pressure difference between the two ears can represent time differences of one, two, or an undetermined numbers of cycles. (b) Response of a neuron in the inferior colliculus of the cat to various time delays between delivery of a tone to the right and left ears. Numbers on the abscissa (horizontal coordinate) to the left of zero (0) indicate that the tone to the right ear (RE) was delayed, while those on the right show the effects of delay on the left ear (LE).

difference between the arrival of the sound at both ears. Thus, if we imagine the pulsations in air pressure arriving at the two ears when the sound source is nearer one ear than the other, a high-pressure variation will arrive first at the near ear and later at the far ear. Interestingly enough, this source of information is only useful for low-frequency sounds because phase differences become ambiguous when the distance between pulsations of air pressure becomes shorter than the distance between the two ears.

A time difference as small as 30 microseconds between the two ears can be utilized for localization of a sound source. There are many points in the auditory pathways where interactions between the two ears occur. In fact, there is neurophysiological evidence for such binaural interactions at virtually every level where such interaction is anatomically possible, ranging from the **superior olivary complex** (Galambos et al. 1959) to the inferior colliculus and auditory cortex (Rose et al. 1966; Brugge et al. 1964). An example of the response of a neuron in the inferior colliculus of the cat to small differences in timing between tones delivered to the two ears is shown in figure 8.11*b*. Note that the neuron showed

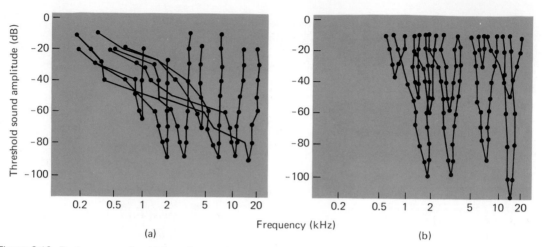

Figure 8.12 Tuning curves, in which each curve illustrates the threshold energy required for a nerve fiber or nerve cell to respond at different frequencies.

(a) Curves from fibers of the auditory nerve; (b) curves from the inferior colliculus.

the greatest response to a time difference of 400 microseconds between the two ears when the tone occurred in the right ear first and a difference of 1,600 microseconds when the tone occurred in the left ear first.

Neurobehavioral evidence suggests that such information is important in the process of auditory localization (e.g., Rosenzweig 1961). Indeed, evidence has shown that unilateral ablation (removal) of the auditory cortex in cats produces severe impairment in the ability to discriminate such differences between the two ears (Cranford et al. 1971).

Coding of Sound by the Brain

Figure 8.12 illustrates one characteristic of the way in which neurons in some of the major auditory relay stations respond to different frequencies of sound. These experiments recorded the activity of single neurons at various levels of the auditory system in response to various frequencies of sound.

Many single neurons in the auditory system respond best—that is, require the least amount of energy to respond—to particular frequencies and are less responsive to other frequencies. Different neurons have different "best frequencies." That is, they are tuned to different frequencies, and for this reason, the curves shown in figure 8.12 are often called **tuning curves.**

Tuning curves exemplify only one of a number of ways in which the auditory system appears to be able to code the frequency of sounds. Another important means by which frequency information can be represented in the auditory pathways is the mechanism of receptotopic organization that was discussed in chapter 7. Like the spatial representation of

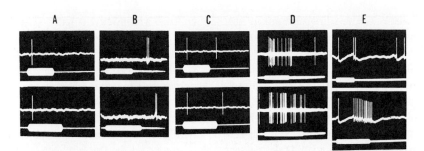

Figure 8.13 Response patterns of the collicular units to tone bursts with their CFs (characteristic frequencies). (A) on type; (B) off type; (C) on-off type; (D) sustained type; (E) intermediate type.

the retina in the visual cortex, there is spatial representation of the basilar membrane over the surface of the auditory cortex (Woolsey 1960). Because various portions of the basilar membrane are differentially activated by different frequencies of sound, there is spatial representation of frequencies in the auditory pathways evident at every level of the auditory system. In some cases the surface of the basilar membrane is represented a number of times within the same nucleus. However, single neurons at these various levels of processing in the auditory pathways do not appear to be specialized simply to code for the frequency of a sound. Indeed, in the auditory cortex, a significant number of neurons do not respond at all to the presentation of a pure tone (Webster and Aitkin 1975). What are the characteristics that will provoke neurons in higher levels of the auditory system, especially in the auditory cortex, to fire?

Extensive experimentation is beginning to unravel the answers to this important question. Some cells at higher levels of the auditory pathways may respond only to the onset

or offset of a tone within a particular frequency range. In a series of experiments in which neurons of the inferior colliculus of the cat were studied, Watanabe and Katsuki (1974) classified the responses that they observed into five categories (fig. 8.13). As shown there, some cells responded only to the onset or offset of a stimulus. Others responded to both onset and offset or showed sustained or intermediate responses. Other investigators have shown that many neurons in the auditory cortex respond best to increases or decreases in the frequency of a tonal stimulus, the **frequency modulation,** rather than to steady tones (e.g., Whitfield and Evans 1965). Still other neurons in the auditory pathways may respond to changes in the intensity of a tone, the **amplitude modulation.**

Many researchers have suggested that, in addition to its physical characteristics, the significance of the auditory stimulus to the organism being studied is of importance (e.g., Webster and Aitkin 1975). In an exciting direction for such work, Funkenstein and associates (1971) have found that some neurons in the auditory cortex of the squirrel monkey are activated most vigorously not by such artificial sounds as tones and clicks, but by species-specific vocalization. In other words, these neurons in the auditory cortex of the squirrel monkey are activated best by the voice of another squirrel monkey! Similar findings have been reported for the auditory cortex of the cat (e.g., Watanabe and Katsuki 1974).

A great deal of interest has been directed toward comparing how the visual and auditory systems analyze information. One point of view is that, as in the visual system, neurons at higher levels of the auditory pathways extract more specific and complex features of the auditory world. However, whereas the scheme by which receptive fields in the visual system can be combined in a hierarchy of increasing complexity, no similarly clear con-

ceptual arrangement yet exists for the auditory system. Part of the problem in developing such a scheme in the study of hearing is that we do not yet understand the nature of the perceptual features of auditory stimuli. However, evidence from auditory cortex damage in experimental animals suggests that the cortical auditory areas, of which there may be as many as six in the cat (e.g., Woolsey 1960), are important in complex auditory discriminations, but are not necessary for distinguishing simple differences in the frequency or intensity of two tones. These areas appear to be essential for discriminating complex tonal patterns (Neff and Diamond 1958; Neff 1961). The effects of removal of the auditory cortex on the ability of cats to discriminate tonal patterns are shown in figure 8.14.

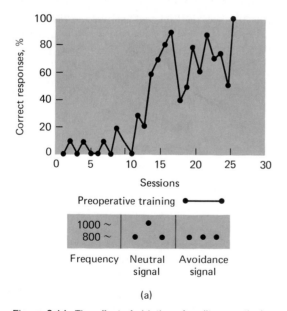

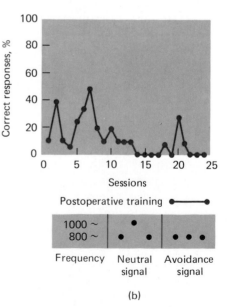

Figure 8.14 The effect of ablation of auditory cortical projection areas on the ability of cats to discriminate tonal patterns. (a) The number of correct responses versus the number of training sessions before the operation. (b) The same responses after the operation. The two stimuli are illustrated below the graphs.

stapedius (stah-pe′de-us)
olivocochlear (ol″ĭ-vo-kok′le-ar)
utricle (u′tre-k′l)
saccule (sak′ul)

253
*Sensory Processes: Audition,
Somatic Sensation, Taste, and
Smell*

Efferent Control

As we noted in chapter 7, sensory systems not only bring information into the central nervous system from their receptors, but in every case also appear to be under descending, or efferent, control; that is, higher centers can control or modify the analysis of incoming information. Nowhere is this important feature of sensory systems more evident than in the auditory system.

One important mechanism of central nervous system control are the middle ear muscles and their control by motor nuclei in the brain stem. Each ear possesses two small muscles—the **stapedius** and **tensor tympani** muscles—which attach to the ossicles. When these muscles contract, they displace the tiny middle ear bones so that coupling between the bones is less efficient. In this way, the middle ear muscles can decrease the transfer of sound from the tympanic membrane to the cochlea. These muscles serve several important functions. For example, they contract during exposure to intense sounds, thereby protecting the delicate inner ear mechanism. They also contract during self-produced vocalization.

Another descending control system appears to originate in or near the auditory cortex and ends in a variety of brain stem auditory nuclei. When stimulated, this pathway appears to inhibit the responsiveness of lower centers (Desmedt 1960). A similar functional system originates in the superior olivary nuclei and is termed the **olivocochlear bundle** (Fex 1962; Rasmussen 1964). As the name implies, this pathway projects to the cochlea and makes contact with the hair cells. Stimulation of this pathway reduces the response of the auditory nerve to sound stimuli (e.g., Galambos 1956), although its function in audition is far from understood. In an interesting experiment, Dewson (1968) found that monkeys in which

the olivocochlear bundle was severed were less able to discriminate certain vowel sounds embedded in white noise (very many frequencies), which suggests that this pathway may be important in detecting signals embedded in background noise. Another experiment by Trahiotis and Elliott (1970) found a similar effect in cats with a damaged olivocochlear bundle. Following such an operation these animals were less able to detect tones interwoven in background noise. Such results suggest that the olivocochlear bundle may be important in adjusting the ratio of auditory signals to the background noise of which they are invariably part. Another interesting possibility is that the descending control systems may be used to alter the transmission of information through the various sensory pathways as a function of experience. We know, for example, that the responses of neurons in the sensory pathways can be modified by a number of experimental treatments, such as increasing or decreasing the level of arousal or alertness of the subject (e.g., Imig and Weinberger 1973) and by various types of conditioning procedures (e.g., Weinberger, Imig, and Lippe 1972; Buchwald, Halas, and Schramm 1965). Such descending control systems have been regarded as possible mechanisms of selective attention.

The Vestibular Sense

The **labyrinth,** or bony structure containing the auditory receptors, also houses the organs of balance, or the **vestibular apparatus.** There are three **semicircular canals** in addition to the **utricle** and the **saccule.** Each of these structures contains sensory cells and associated apparatus that are important for the sense of balance. (See figures 8.4 and 8.5, which depict the anatomy of the human ear.)

endolymph   (en'do-limf)
ampulla   (am-pul'ah)
cupula   (ku'pu-lah)
postrotatory optic nystagmus   (post-ro'ta-tōr''e op'tik nis-tag'mus)
macula   (mak'u-lah)
otolith   (o'to-lith)

It is no mere accident that the organs responsible for our sense of balance and those responsible for hearing are closely associated. They share a common history in evolution, both apparently evolving from ancestral structures in fish that were sensitive to vibration (Van Bergeijk 1967; Wersall and Flock 1965). As in the organ of Corti, the receptor cells of the vestibular system are specialized hair cells. In addition, the fluid-filled vestibular apparatus and cochlea are in part continuous with each other. The components of the vestibular apparatus serve different functions for the organism. The three semicircular canals are oriented in three different planes at right angles to one another. The fluid in the semicircular canals is termed **endolymph.** Near the base of each canal, where it meets the utricle, is an enlargement called the **ampulla.** Each enlargement contains the hair cells and the overlying **cupula,** a gelatinous structure that flexes the hairs on the hair cells when it moves over them. When the head is rotated in one of the three planes of the semicircular canals, the cupula is pushed by the fluid in the canal so that the hair cells are stimulated or inhibited, depending on the direction of acceleration, and the sensation of rotary acceleration occurs. If you are rotated in a chair without any cues to indicate that rotation is taking place (e.g., you are also blindfolded), the sense of rotation is transient and disappears after a constant speed of rotation is established. That is, we sense only rotary acceleration or deceleration. The reason is that the fluid within the semicircular canals moves the cupula only during acceleration or deceleration. At a constant speed of rotation, the fluid eventually becomes stable and no stimulation takes place.

It is possible to stimulate the semicircular canals by pouring warm water in the ear.

Such heat stimulation produces convection currents in the endolymph that move the cupula and thereby stimulate the vestibular receptor cells. The effects of such stimulation include **postrotatory optic nystagmus**—a brief repetitive movement of the eyes back and forth, first rapidly toward the side of stimulation and then more slowly away from it. In addition, a feeling of dizziness occurs similar to that following rapid twirling in a tight circle. This method of stimulation is valuable for medical diagnosis because it is relatively safe, highly effective, and each side can be stimulated individually.

The utricle and saccule are two membrane-bound sacs below the semicircular canals, but still within the bony encasement of the inner ear. Within each of these sacs is a sensory organ—the **macula**—consisting of hair cells, and an overlying gelatinous mass termed the **otolith** into which is embedded a number of small crystals of **calcium carbonate.** When the head is erect, the hair cells of the utricle and saccule are vertical and their otoliths overlie them. The force of gravity or a linear acceleration depresses the otoliths into the stereocilia of the hair cells. Thus, this system detects the absolute position of the head in space, in addition to linear acceleration.

Information from the hair cells of the vestibular apparatus is carried by the eighth cranial nerve (VIII), sometimes called the vestibulocochlear nerve because it also carries the signals from the cochlea. However, fibers of the vestibular portion of the eighth cranial nerve project to the vestibular nuclei in the medulla. Some fibers originating in these nuclei project, in turn, to the occulomotor nuclei in the brain stem to produce optic nystagmus, while still others pass to the spinal cord, reticular formation, cerebellum, and thalamus.

These central destinations of information from the vestibular apparatus underscore the significant role that our vestibular sense plays in balance and motor behavior.

Somatic Sensation

Unlike vision and audition, the stimuli for the somatic, or bodily, senses cannot be specified along any single dimension. In fact, somatic sensation is not a single sense at all, but many qualitatively different senses, each of which may have a different adequate stimulus. In addition, there is a particularly obvious affective or emotional component to some types of somatic sensations, such as the pleasure of certain kinds of touch or temperature and the unpleasantness of pain. As if this were not complication enough, some somatic stimuli sensed by the nervous system never reach consciousness, a phenomenon that seems to apply most often to **proprioception,** which is the sense of the position of the limbs and body in space.

Much research on somatic sensation focuses on the skin, a sensory organ that we often take for granted. When it comes to obtaining information about the environment, we immediately think of the dominant senses of vision and audition. But the skin also serves as an extremely important source of information. This point becomes obvious every time we fumble for our keys or a light switch in the dark. Much more intriguing, however, is the ability of the skin to convey the type of complex information that we typically associate with vision. Consider the Optacon, an optical-to-tactile converter, which is composed of an array of vibrating pins that stimulate the fingertips (fig. 8.15). A sensor converts visual information, such as a letter on a printed page, into a vibrotactile pattern on the fingertip.

Some expert users of this device are able to "read" through their fingertips at rates of up to one hundred words per minute (Craig 1977). It also is possible to use the Optacon to "display" movement (Craig and Sherrick 1982). To begin our discussion of somatic sensation, therefore, it is appropriate to examine the skin and its wide assortment of receptors.

Receptors and Sensations

Among the earliest theories of biological processes in cutaneous (skin) sensation was that of von Frey in the nineteenth century. von Frey capitalized on earlier investigators' observations of so-called **sensory spots** on the skin—small regions of skin where stimulation produces a particular somatic sensation. von Frey developed the view that there are four basic somatic sensations—touch, warmth, cold, and

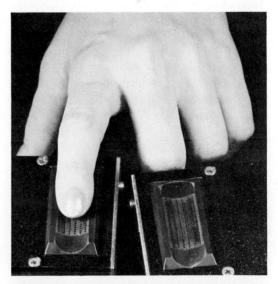

Figure 8.15 Vibrating pins that stimulate the fingertip in different patterns corresponding to visual information. The device responsible for converting visual to tactile information is called the Optacon.

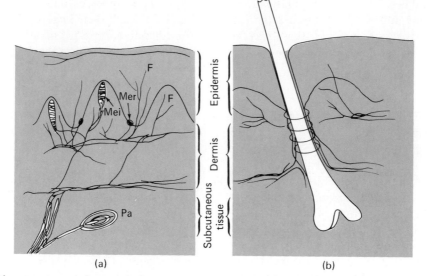

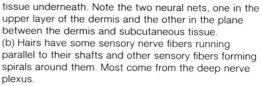

(a) (b)

Figure 8.16 Appearance and placement of some receptor organs of the skin. (a) Free nerve endings (F) are found within and just below the epidermal (outer skin) layer and Meissner's corpuscles (Mei) and Merkel's disks (Mer) at the base of the epidermis. Pacinian corpuscles (Pa) are not usually found within the skin proper, but do occur in the loose connective tissue underneath. Note the two neural nets, one in the upper layer of the dermis and the other in the plane between the dermis and subcutaneous tissue. (b) Hairs have some sensory nerve fibers running parallel to their shafts and other sensory fibers forming spirals around them. Most come from the deep nerve plexus.

pain—based on his careful analysis of the sensitivity of the skin. Influenced by Müller's law of specific nerve energies and the concept of labeled lines discussed in chapter 7, von Frey suggested that each of these basic experiences is due to stimulation of a specific type of receptor in the skin. We now know that von Frey was only partly correct, and more modern theories of somatic sensory coding by the nervous system do not rely on the postulate that the quality of sensation is due solely to the type of receptor that is stimulated. A brief overview of the evidence against the specific receptor theory of von Frey is illuminating.

Since it had been established that somatic sensation is organized as small receptive areas on the skin, von Frey's theory could be tested by finding a particular sensory spot, say a warmth spot, and then examining the region for a specific receptor. Such anatomical analyses were routinely disappointing, and correlation between sensory spots and specific types of receptors was never consistently established. In addition, later investigations showed that von Frey's four basic somatic sensations can be detected from stimulation of the cornea. However, the cornea possessed only one type of receptor, the so-called free nerve ending (e.g., Lele and Weddell 1956). The name of this receptor describes its appearance quite accurately since it is simply a branched end of a sensory nerve fiber. It is the most common type of somatic receptor in the skin. There are other anatomically specialized sensory receptors in the skin, some of which are illustrated in figure 8.16, which shows their approximate placement in different layers of the skin.

These receptors include several types in which the sensitive nerve ending is surrounded by a specialized capsule or other structure, such as Meissner's corpuscles and Merkel's disks or the pacinian corpuscle discussed in chapter 7. A final and compelling bit of evidence suggesting that somatic sensory coding is much more complex than contemplated by von Frey is that modern classifications of somatic sensation identify many sensory experiences that were not included in von Frey's four basic somatic sensations. Sinclair (1967), for example, identified five groups of somatic sensory qualities, and within the so-called contact group alone are the sensations of touch, pressure, vibration, tickle, and tactile paresthesia (pins and needles).

While it is true that specific somatic sensations cannot be correlated one-for-one with specific types of receptors, we already have noted that certain types of receptors do appear to be specialized to transduce certain stimuli. The pacinian corpuscle, for example, is perfectly designed to transduce mechanical pressure on the skin. The nerve endings that wrap around hairs seem specially placed to transmit touch information. What has emerged in more recent attempts to understand the biological processes involved in somatic sensation are theories that combine the special sensitivities of different receptors with the concept of coding by spatial-temporal patterns of activity in the sensory nerve fibers. Some nerves, such as those innervating the cornea, must be able to signal different qualities of sensation even though they do not connect to specialized receptors. On the other hand, some nerves are apparently specialized to transmit certain types of information, such as those ending in pacinian corpuscles.

That certain nerves transmit some types of somatosensory information preferentially is supported by our current understanding of the anatomy and functions of peripheral nerve fibers. Certain types of pain and temperature information, for example, seem to be conveyed by the peripheral nerve fibers having small diameters, while light touch and pressure information is conveyed by larger-diameter nerve fibers. The largest peripheral nerve fibers carry information from the muscle sensory receptors. These detect muscle stretch. However, the distinction between small- and large-diameter nerve fibers is only approximate. Part of the evidence supporting preferential distribution of somatic information according to fiber diameter comes from the effects of local anesthetics. A local anesthetic such as cocaine blocks conduction of action potentials in small-diameter nerve fibers first and in larger fibers later. A related finding is that the first sensations to disappear under local anesthesia are pain and temperature; light touch and pressure disappear more slowly.

Central Pathways and Coding

Now that you know what the skin is able to detect, you can begin to appreciate the diverse information that must be sent to the central nervous system. The route that this information travels and how it is coded are the subjects of this section.

Somatosensory information enters the central nervous system through the cranial nerves, which serve the head and neck, and through the spinal nerves, which serve the rest of the body. Once inside the central nervous system, somatosensory information travels along three different systems, all of which originate in the spinal cord (information from the head and neck joins these systems in the brain stem). These systems are illustrated

lemniscal (lem-nis′kal)
spinoreticulothalamic (spi″no-re-kik′u-lo-thah-lam′ik)

schematically in figure 8.17, and you will note that they get their names from the prominent anatomical structures in each. The **lemniscal system** consists of two separate tracts in the spinal cord—the **dorsolateral pathway** and the **dorsal columns.** It is named after the ribbon-like band of fibers that it forms in the brain stem termed the medial lemniscus (from the Greek, *lemniskos,* meaning "ribbon"). The **spinothalamic system** is so named because it is a direct projection from the spinal cord to the thalamus. The third system shown in figure 8.17, the **spinoreticulothalamic system,** reaches the thalamus via a multisynaptic pathway that

ascends through the spinal cord and the reticular formation.

A common feature of all of these systems is that somatosensory information is crossed; signals arising from one side of the body eventually reach the opposite side of the brain. This feature is especially evident in the lemniscal and spinothalamic systems. In the lemniscal system, the crossing occurs in the lower brain stem. As shown in figure 8.17, axons ascending in the spinal cord synapse in the **lateral cervical nucleus** and the **dorsal column nuclei.** From here, neurons cross to form the medial lemniscus. In the spinotha-

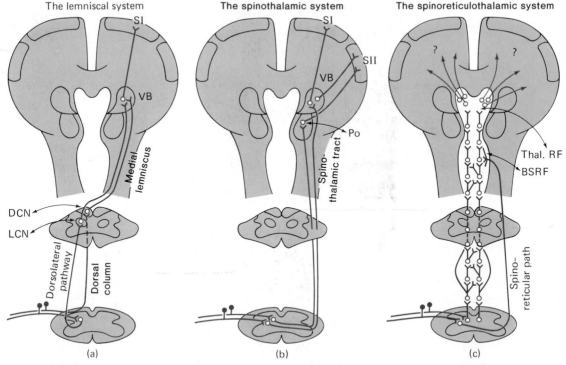

(a)   (b)   (c)

Figure 8.17 Main lines of communication between spinal cord and forebrain involved in somatic sensation. (a) Components of the lemniscal system: the dorsal columns and the dorsolateral pathway. (b) The spincthalamic tracts projecting via two of the nuclear masses of the thalamus to the cerebral cortex. (c) Multisynaptic system of the brain stem and the spinoreticulothalamic system. DCN = dorsal column nuclei; LCN = lateral cervical nucleus; VB = ventrobasal complex of the thalamus; Po = posterior nuclear group; SI and SII = first and second somatic receiving zones of the cerebral cortex; BSRF = brain stem reticular formation; Thal. RF = thalamic reticular formation.

lamic system, axons in the spinal cord cross immediately and then ascend to the thalamus. Somatosensory information also crosses in the spinoreticulothalamic system, but as shown in figure 8.17, axons may cross at several different levels of the spinal cord and brain stem. Moreover, in this system some somatosensory information remains on the same side of the body on which it originated.

The thalamus receives information from all of these systems and then passes it on to higher structures. In each case, however, different thalamic nuclei are involved. The lemniscal system projects to a group of sensory relay nuclei in the thalamus called the **ventrobasal complex.** The spinothalamic system also projects to the ventrobasal complex, but, in addition, innervates another segment of the thalamus—the **posterior nuclei,** often referred to as **Po.** The thalamic destination of the third system is really an extension of the reticular formation known as the **reticular nuclei of the thalamus.**

As in vision and audition, a major function of the thalamus in the somatic senses is to send information to the cerebral cortex. The major receiving area for somatosensory information is known as **primary somatosensory cortex,** or **SI.** Different areas of the body are represented here in direct proportion to their sensitivity to sensory stimuli. The lips and fingers, for example, occupy a large region of SI, which corresponds to the extreme sensitivity of these body parts to light touch. Both the lemniscal and spinothalamic systems send information to SI via the ventrobasal complex. The spinothalamic system also projects to another cortical receiving area known as **secondary somatosensory cortex,** or **SII.** This cortical region, located lateral and slightly posterior to SI, receives input from both the ventrobasal complex and from Po. Presumably, the cerebral cortex also receives infor-

mation from the spinoreticulothalamic system. However, the precise destination of this information in the cerebral cortex is unknown.

These three somatosensory systems appear to code different types of information. Neurons in the lemniscal system are specialized to code light touch, mechanical stimulation, rotation of joints, and deep pressure (Mountcastle 1961; Poggio and Mountcastle 1963). All of these stimuli, however, do not activate all lemniscal neurons. In fact, a given neuron typically responds to only one of these stimuli. A cell in the ventrobasal complex, for example, may respond to light touch but not to bending of the hair on the skin. Thus, different categories of information are coded selectively. Another feature of the lemniscal system is that it organizes information spatially. As one example of this type of organization, the entire surface of the body is mapped onto the SI area of the cortex as well as onto the lower levels of the lemniscal system. Thus, different areas of the body are represented by different fibers, a segregation that is maintained all the way up to the somatosensory cortex. Spatial organization also is evident in another form: neurons responsive to the same type of stimulus are grouped together in small regions (Dykes 1983). A given type of somatic stimulus, light touch for example, is represented by small regions of the ventrobasal complex, with many such small regions scattered throughout this area of thalamus. In somatosensory cortex, neurons that receive information from different types of receptors are organized into columns (Mountcastle 1961). Columnar organization, you will recall, also is a feature of auditory and visual cortex.

In addition, neurons in the lemniscal system have a small receptive field. This means that a given neuron in this system changes its firing rate when a relatively small region of the body is stimulated. Moreover, the receptive

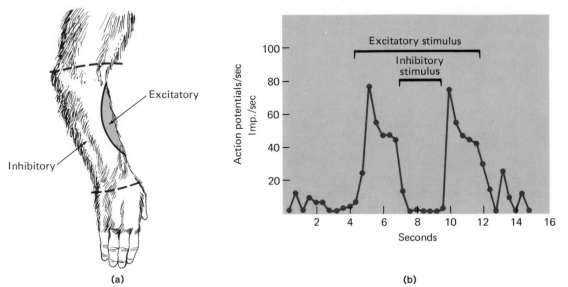

(a)   **(b)**

Figure 8.18 (a) Receptive field of a neuron in the
somatosensory cortex of the monkey; (b) response of
the neuron to tactile stimulation in the excitatory and
inhibitory regions of the receptive field. Note the
opposing effects of stimulation of the inhibitory
surround and the excitatory center.

field is organized into excitatory and inhibitory zones. Figure 8.18 illustrates this type of receptive field and the response of a neuron in the SI region of a monkey. In this example, stroking the monkey's fur in the excitatory portion of the receptive field increases the firing rate of the SI neuron, but if stroking also occurs over the surrounding inhibitory portion of the field, the excitatory effect is blocked (Mountcastle 1961). Moreover, the receptive field can change in response to neural signals that descend from the cerebral cortex (Adkins et al. 1966). An example of this effect is shown in figure 8.19, which is a drawing of the front and back of the left front paw of a cat. The blackened area denotes the receptive field of an SI neuron to light touch under normal conditions. If, however, the touch was preceded by electrical stimulation of the pyramidal tract (a large bundle of axons that carries motor information from the cortex to the spinal cord), the receptive field expanded to include the crosshatched area. It also became responsive

to bending of the hairs in the dotted area. This finding suggests that fibers descending from the cortex can modify the reception and coding of information from the body's surface. As we noted for the auditory system, such efferent control may play an important part in attention and perception.

Neurons in the spinothalamic and spinoreticulothalamic systems are much more difficult to characterize than those in the lemniscal system (e.g., Morse and Vargo 1970; Mountcastle 1961). Some neurons in Po and SII, for example, have small receptive fields, whereas others have receptive fields that are extremely large. Moreover, the receptive fields can be on either side of the body and some can be discontinuous. These unusual receptive fields can be detected in the reticular formation, as shown in figure 8.20. In this example, the activity of neurons in the reticular formation of the rat was recorded while the surface of the skin or the whiskers (vibrissae) were stroked with a probe (Groves et al. 1973).

Figure 8.19 Receptive fields on the forepaw of a cat of a neuron in the somatosensory cortex. Black area shows the extent of the normal receptive field, and crosshatched and dotted areas show expansion of the receptive field when pyramidal tracts are stimulated. Black and hatched areas are sensitive to touch, whereas dotted area is sensitive to bending of hairs.

Figure 8.20 Tactile receptive fields of cells in the reticular formation of the rat responsive to tactile stimulation. While some cells were responsive only to movement of the *vibrissae* (A), others had much larger contralateral (B-D) or less commonly ipsilateral (E) receptive fields. About half of the reticular neurons had receptive fields larger than a third of the body surface (G-I).

Some neurons responded to an extremely limited stimulus, such as touching a single whisker, while others responded to touch over nearly the entire surface of the body or of several discontinuous portions of the body's surface. In addition, some of these neurons also responded to auditory and visual stimuli as well as to touch.

Primarily, however, the spinothalamic and spinoreticulothalamic systems are known for carrying information about temperature and pain. Relatively little is known about the coding of temperature information, but what we do know indicates that it is not a simple process. In fact, the same thermal stimulus can be perceived as either hot or cold depending on the ambient temperature of the skin. If, for example, the skin already is hot, then a warm stimulus will feel cool, but if the same warm stimulus is applied to cold skin, then it will feel hot. Moreover, when a warm stimulus is applied for a prolonged period, we become less responsive to it but more responsive to a cold stimulus. Conversely, prolonged exposure to cold depresses our response to cold but heightens our response to heat. The sensation of temperature, therefore, depends not only on the thermal stimulus but also on the temperature of the skin that comes in contact with the stimulus.

The skin is equipped with different receptors for detecting coolness and warmth. These receptors appear to have separate connections to the brain. In fact, applying a warm stimulus to a cold receptor elicits a sensation of cold. But some receptors have been found that respond to both warm and cold stimuli, indicating that even at the receptor level, the question of thermal sensation has not been resolved. How the brain uses receptor information to code for temperature remains a mystery.

Considerably more is known about the neural mechanisms that underlie pain and the absence of pain, a condition known as **analgesia.** Both of these phenomena are discussed in the next section.

Pain and Analgesia

Pain serves an important survival function. The ability to detect pain is one of the best defenses we have against bodily injury and illness. In some situations, however, an absence of pain is required. When life itself is in danger, for example, it is more important to be able to do what is necessary to survive than to have pain interfere. Accordingly, the body is equipped with mechanisms both for detecting pain and for suppressing it. Although most people are more concerned with the latter, we will begin with former for a simple reason. Before you can understand the mechanisms involved in alleviating pain, you first must understand what generates it.

Neural Basis of Pain

The signals that we interpret as pain appear to arise from free nerve endings. As we mentioned earlier in this chapter, these receptors are located just below the outer layer of skin. They also are found in the cornea of the eye, the internal organs, the pulp of the teeth, and the membranes surrounding bones and muscles. When these tissues are damaged, they release a chemical substance that activates the free nerve endings. The information travels to the central nervous system via two types of fibers: myelinated **A delta fibers,** which conduct impulses at rates of 15–30 meters/second; and thin, unmyelinated **C fibers,** which conduct action potentials at the extremely slow rate of 1–2 meters/second. Both types of fibers join the spinothalamic and spinoreticulothalamic systems, but the difference in conduction times explains why pain often seems to occur in two different waves. A painful stimulus first causes a sharp, localized pain, sometimes called fast pain, followed by a dull, diffuse pain, known as slow pain. Fast pain reflects activity in A delta fibers, whereas slow pain is carried by C fibers.

The perception of pain is mediated primarily by the thalamus (Albe-Fessard et al. 1985). Consider what happens when you smash your toe with a hammer. As shown in figure 8.21, different regions of the thalamus appear to code different aspects of this pain.

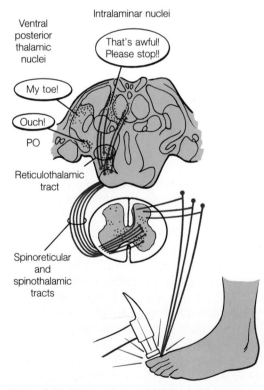

Figure 8.21 A current view of the role of the thalamus in pain sensation.

The information that reaches Po, the posterior nuclei of the thalamus, defines the stimulus as painful (in other words, "Ouch!"). When this information reaches the ventral posterior thalamic nuclei, the painful stimulus is localized (in this example, "My toe!"). Finally, the information reaches the **intralaminar nuclei** of the thalamus, which are located along the midline and which also receive information from the reticular formation. The intralaminar nuclei play a role in elaborating the aversive aspect of the painful stimulus (so you quickly respond, "That's awful! Please stop!" or words to that effect, which we probably could not print here).

The extensive involvement of the thalamus in pain, however, does not rule out a role for other brain structures. All of the thalamic regions associated with pain project to different parts of cerebral cortex. In fact, **parietal cortex** appears to receive a direct pain projection from the ventral posterior nuclei of the thalamus. A complete map of the body's pain receptors appears to exist in this cortical area. Pain at the tip of a finger, for example, corresponds to activity in a very specific region of parietal cortex (Albe-Fessard et al. 1985). Moreover, **prefrontal cortex,** which has close ties with the limbic system, appears to mediate the emotional aspect of pain. Persons with a damaged prefrontal cortex still can perceive pain, but it no longer bothers them.

Some people suffer from pain even when there is no painful stimulus. Amputees, for example, sometimes report pain in limbs that have been amputated, so-called **phantom-limb pain.** Other individuals, who have suffered damage to the peripheral nerves, report pain even after the wound has healed, a condition known as **neuralgia** (*algos* in Greek means "pain"; thus, neuralgia means nerve pain).

How is it possible for the brain to perceive pain even when there is no painful stimulus? Melzack and Wall (1965) argue that the problem lies not with the fibers that carry pain information, but with the fibers that carry other sensory information, such as pressure and touch. In the spinal cord, the nonpain fibers normally excite the **substantia gelatinosa,** a network of interneurons that helps to suppress the flow of pain information up to the brain. In persons suffering from phantom-limb pain and neuralgia, these nonpain fibers appear to be damaged. As a result, the substantia gelatinosa is less active than normal and thus less able to inhibit the pathways that carry pain information. This intriguing model also may explain the analgesic effects of acupuncture. Inserting long needles into specific areas of the body may activate the appropriate sensory fibers, which in turn activate the substantia gelatinosa to reduce the flow of information in certain pain fibers. But the substantia gelatinosa is not the only structure that may play a role in analgesia. As you will see in the next section, the brain also can exert strong control over pain.

Stimulation-Produced Analgesia

Reynolds (1969) first reported that electrical stimulation of specific regions of the brain can produce analgesia in experimental animals. One of these brain regions is the **periaqueductal gray.** This surrounds the cerebral aqueduct in the brain stem and appears to be part of a descending control system that includes the **nucleus raphe magnus** and the gray matter surrounding the third ventricle (Kerr and Wilson 1978; Liebeskind and Paul 1977). When activated, this descending system suppresses pain, and the effect often outlasts the stimulation by many minutes or hours. Under

natural conditions, such a system is not activated easily. Pain, afterall, motivates us to take quick action to relieve an injury. Only under emergency conditions, such as when pain is so intense that survival itself is threatened, does the brain suppress pain. Neurons in this pain-suppression system are thought to act on spinal neurons that conduct pain information into the brain stem (Terman et al. 1984).

Electrical stimulation of the periaqueductal gray is equivalent to an analgesic dose of morphine, one of the most powerful pain-killing drugs known. In fact, direct injections of morphine into the periaqueductal gray also produce analgesia, suggesting that this area of the brain mediates the painkilling effects of morphine (Wei et al. 1975). Indeed, morphine appears to act on specific receptors found not only in the periaqueductal gray, but also in several brain regions that help to control pain (Pert and Snyder 1973; Simon et al. 1973; Terenius 1973). Why is the brain equipped with receptors for morphine? Apparently, the brain contains its own morphinelike substances, a series of peptides that are contained in certain neurons and that suppress pain when released. The chemical structure of morphine allows it to fit into receptors normally occupied by these peptides. Thus, morphine mimics the body's own painkilling system.

Morphinelike Peptides and Pain Sensitivity

The peptides that have a morphinelike effect on pain are called **endorphins,** a term derived from the combination of the words "endogenous morphine." Many different endorphins are known to exist in the brain along with many types of endorphin receptors. Very little is known about most of these endorphin molecules, but two of these—**leu-enkephalin** and

met-enkephalin—were among the first endorphins discovered and thus have received considerable attention. As we mentioned in chapter 6, the enkephalins consist of five amino acids. Four of these amino acids are the same in each; the fifth amino acid is leucine in leu-enkephalin or methionine in met-enkephalin. In the brains of most mammals, met-enkephalin predominates (Bloom 1983). Camels, however, have a high level of leu-enkephalin, though no one knows why. Nor does anyone have a good explanation for why the enkephalins exist in these two forms.

The analgesic actions of the enkephalins and many other endorphins are blocked by **naloxone,** a morphine antagonist. Naloxone binds to endorphin receptors, but does not activate them; it simply prevents the endorphins from acting. By itself, however, naloxone does not cause pain. This means that the enkephalins and endorphins are not released continuously to suppress painful stimuli. They reduce pain only under certain circumstances. As we mentioned, one of those circumstances may be a life-threatening situation. Another may be the power of suggestion. In some people, a placebo—an inert substance—can provide relief from pain if these individuals believe that the substance is medication. This is known as the **placebo effect** and it seems to be mediated in part by an endorphinlike substance because it can be attenuated by naloxone (Levine et al. 1979).

The sites in the central nervous system where the endorphins modulate pain have been pieced together from studies using electrical stimulation of specific pathways and the injection of endorphins directly into specific brain regions. Based on the available data, Frederickson and Geary (1982) propose the model shown in figure 8.22. The periaqueductal gray, designated PAG, is at the center

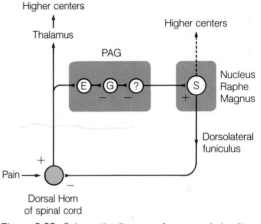

Figure 8.22 Schematic diagram of proposed circuitry in the analgesic effects of morphine, electrical stimulation, and intense stress. PAG=periaqueductal gray; E=enkephalin; G=GABA; ?=neuron whose neurotransmitter remains unknown; S=serotonin; +=excitatory synapse; −=inhibitory synapse.

of the circuit. It consists of three types of neurons: an enkephalin interneuron (E) that inhibits a GABA interneuron (G) that in turn inhibits an output neuron whose transmitter is unknown (?). The PAG output neuron excites serotonin-containing neurons (S) in the nucleus raphe magnus. The S neurons may project to higher centers where they could influence pain, but the main projection is into the spinal cord. The axons of these descending S neurons form a large bundle—the dorsolateral funiculus—that inhibits neurons in the dorsal horn of the spinal cord. These dorsal horn cells are part of the ascending pain pathway. Note that when E is released in the PAG, it inhibits the G inhibitory interneuron. This removes inhibition from the ? neuron, allowing it to excite the descending S neuron. The result is an inhibition of the dorsal horn cells that normally carry pain information to the thalamus.

fires in short burst / inhibitory

This model is informative for several reasons. First, it explains why an injection of morphine into the PAG suppresses pain. Morphine mimics the effect of enkephalin on inhibitory GABA neurons. Thus, PAG output cells are activated, causing an activation of the nucleus raphe magnus and a subsequent inhibition of the pain neurons in the dorsal horn. In fact, when morphine is injected into the PAG, cells in the nucleus raphe magnus increase their firing rate. Second, the model explains why electrical stimulation of the PAG also has an analgesic effect. Such stimulation causes electrical current to spread throughout the PAG, causing an activation of the PAG output neurons. This activation, as we have seen, will act on the nucleus raphe magnus to inhibit dorsal horn cells. This finding is consistent with evidence that a lesion of the dorsolateral funiculus blocks the analgesic effect of PAG stimulation. A third feature of the model is that serotonin plays an important role in the analgesic circuit. If serotonin is depleted from the nucleus raphe magnus or if serotonin receptors are blocked, then neither morphine nor electrical stimulation of the PAG will suppress pain. This is exactly what happens (Akil and Liebeskind 1975; Morhland and Gebhart 1980). In fact, electrical stimulation of the PAG has been used successfully to treat some chronic pain patients, and the analgesic effects of this stimulation are enhanced when the patients receive tryptophan, the precursor of serotonin.

Another aspect of this model is that the circut is activated by the pain pathway itself as it ascends to the thalamus (note the excitatory collateral synapsing onto the enkephalin neuron in the PAG). This suggests that under normal conditions the circuit is active only for brief periods. Thus, if nothing else were involved, the only thing this circuit would accomplish is a change in the firing pattern of the pain pathway. For example, dorsal horn cells would show bursts of activity separated by pauses, with each pause caused by activation of the PAG circuit. In order for the circuit to inhibit pain, it must be active for a prolonged period. Prolonged activation may occur only under highly unusual circumstances, such as taking morphine or artificially stimulating the PAG. Another unusual stimulus could be intense stress, as when we encounter a life-threatening situation. Stress-induced analgesia probably results from the release of **beta-endorphin,** a hormone that is known to be released into the cerebrospinal fluid during stressful events. When the beta-endorphin finds its way to the enkephalin receptors in the PAG, it activates this circuit continuously and thus keeps the dorsal horn cells inhibited. The net result is a suppression of pain.

You may be wondering what this circuit accomplishes under normal circumstances when its only effect is a change in the firing pattern of dorsal horn cells. In this case, it actually may contribute to pain. How? Consider the following evidence. Although the thalamus plays an important role in pain, as we have seen, simple electrical stimulation of this structure does not produce pain. Patients undergoing brain surgery never report pain when their thalamus is stimulated artificially (Mark et al. 1962). Apparently, the pattern of activity coming into the thalamus is critical for signaling pain; a simple excitation produced by a stimulating electrode does not mimic the pain pattern. The PAG circuit may help to provide the critical pattern by making the dorsal horn cells fire in bursts rather than in a continuous fashion. If this bit of speculation is true, it would mean that the same PAG circuit both contributes to the perception and suppression of pain. The critical distinction is simply the amount of time that the circuit is active.

The Chemical Senses: Taste and Smell

In both the senses of taste and of smell, the appropriate stimuli for the receptors are chemical compounds. In the case of smell, these stimuli must be volatile; that is, they must exist in a gaseous state or as a vapor. For taste, the chemicals are generally soluble in water. In addition to this similarity, things that we taste often involve smells. An understanding of the perceptual and biological mechanisms of taste and smell has been especially difficult to achieve because of these similarities between the two senses. Furthermore, in contrast to hearing and vision, where the stimuli can be described relatively precisely in physical terms, stimulation in the gustatory and olfactory systems cannot be so easily specified. However, while progress in understanding the chemical senses is perhaps slower, advancement continues to be made.

Taste

Although not without dissent, there is some general agreement that there exist four basic tastes from which all others are derived: salty, sour, bitter, and sweet. In addition to this categorization of basic tastes, something is known of the requirements that chemicals must have to produce the tastes. For example, sour is produced by hydrogen ions (H^+) found in all acids. However, the degree of sourness does not relate simply to the concentration of hydrogen ions, which suggests that this relationship is a complex one. Alkaloid compounds, basic substances found in plants, generally produce a bitter taste, although other seemingly unrelated compounds may also be bitter. Many bitter and sweet compounds have identical chemical formulas, but differ in the spatial arrangements of their atomic components.

Maximum sensitivity to the four basic tastes is not evenly distributed over the tongue, as illustrated in figure 8.23. Sweet and salty are detected most easily at the tip of the tongue, sour at the sides, and bitter at the back. Within these regions the organs of taste, or taste buds, are located within or near **papillae**—numerous small bumps in the tongue.

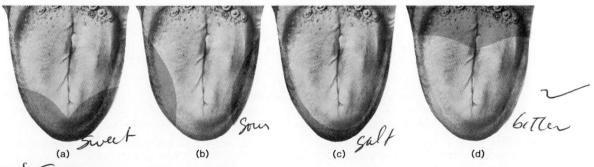

(a)   (b)   (c)   (d)

Figure 8.23 Patterns of taste receptor distribution: (a) sweet receptors; (b) sour receptors; (c) salt receptors; (d) bitter receptors.

The placement of a single taste bud in one of these papillae is illustrated in figure 8.24 and several such taste buds may line a single **papilla.** Each taste bud consists of a group of individual cells. In an ingenious experiment, von Békésy (1966) applied chemical compounds to individual papillae. He observed that each papilla is maximally sensitive to only one of the four basic tastes, a finding that suggests an important receptor correlate of the four basic taste qualities. Further, papillae sensitive to

sour and salty have a rounded shape, while those responsive to bitter and sweet are more pointed.

Each taste bud consists of ten to fifteen individual receptor cells, and it is interesting to note that the life cycle of a single taste receptor cell is only about four or five days. They are replaced by new cells formed from the outer portions of the taste bud. Each receptor possesses microvilli, small extensions that protrude into the pore of the taste bud. Each of

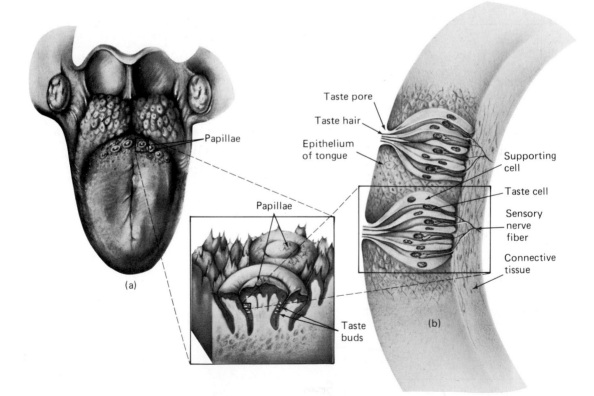

Figure 8.24   (a) Taste buds on the surface of the tongue are associated with nipplelike elevations called papillae; (b) a taste bud contains taste cells and has an opening, the taste pore, at its free surface.

the receptor cells is innervated by one or more fibers of the two cranial nerves, the facial (VII) and glossopharyngeal (IX).

Kimura and Beidler (1961) studied the taste receptors of the rat and hamster utilizing the microelectrode recording technique. They observed that individual receptors were most responsive to one of the four basic tastes. However, there were large variations in the degree of specificity of response. Individual taste receptors within a single papilla differed with respect to which of the four tastes was most effective. The results of these experiments and a number of others have suggested that each receptor cell may be sensitive to all of the basic tastes, but to different degrees. Taste buds responsive to salt, therefore, could contain receptor cells the majority of which are stimulated most effectively by salt, but which are responsive to other taste stimuli as well. Recent biochemical experiments indicate that there may be four different receptor molecules associated with each taste receptor cell, each one receptive for molecules of one of the four basic taste qualities (e.g., Dastoli and Price 1966).

Recordings of activity in the nerve fibers innervating the taste receptors also have been made. Nerve fibers of a branch of the facial nerve, called the **chorda tympani,** innervate the taste receptors toward the front of the tongue, while fibers from the glossopharyngeal nerve innervate the back. Pfaffman (1955; 1959) recorded responses of fibers in the chorda tympani nerve to various taste stimuli applied to the tongue of the rat, cat, and rabbit. He found that single fibers responded to a wide range of

taste stimuli, but appeared to be most sensitive to one of the four basic taste qualities. One fiber, for example, might respond to extremely low concentrations of salt and to somewhat higher concentrations of a sweet substance. Another fiber might have the opposite sensitivities. Because both fibers respond to both qualities, Pfaffman suggests that some higher level of analysis in the brain utilizes a comparison of the responses of different fibers in order to determine which stimulus will be perceived (Pfaffman 1969). This is similar to the situation for color vision in which the relatively broad responses of each of the three different color systems are compared in order to determine which color is perceived.

Taste stimulation is carried by the chorda tympani into the brain stem where the fibers of this and the glossopharyngeal nerve synapse in the **nucleus of the solitary tract.** From this nucleus, fibers project along with the medial lemniscus to the ventrobasal complex, thus forming a close association with the somatosensory lemniscal system. This also suggests that the cortical receiving area for taste is part of SI, the primary somatosensory cortex, although this fact has not been fully established. Neurons in these taste pathways often respond not only to taste, but also to mechanical and temperature stimulation of the tongue (Fishman 1957), which also suggests a functional relationship of some kind between taste and the somatosensory system. Such associations reinforce our everyday experiences in which both the taste and texture of foods may be important in our gustatory experiences.

anosmic   (an-oz'mik)

Smell

Smell is a vital sense for the survival of many organisms, although this is not the case in humans. Many animals and insects use odors to mark territories, to attract mates, to signal sexual receptivity, and for a variety of other communications. In many instances, the receptors for these chemical communicators are highly specific and respond to remarkably low concentrations of them. These chemical messengers are termed **pheromones** and are used by many organisms, including humans.

Pheromones play an important part in communication between members of a given species (Wilson 1965). The fire ant, for example, leaves a chemical trail for other ants to follow when returning from a food source. Infant rats respond to odors emitted by the mother rat. The vaginal secretions of female rhesus monkeys during certain phases of the estrous cycle contain chemical substances that are sex attractants for the males (Michael, Keverne, and Bonsall 1971). Such compounds are also present in abundance around the second week of the human female menstrual cycle (Michael, Bonsall, and Warner 1974). Given the importance of pheromones in the lives of many organisms, it is perhaps not surprising that rendering many animals **anosmic** (loss of sense of smell) produces a variety of other deficits, including disturbances of reproductive behavior (e.g., Murphy and Schneider 1970).

There has been disagreement over whether there is a limited number of fundamental odors in the same sense as there are four basic tastes. An early-century proposal by Henning suggests that there are six primary odors: foul, flowery, fruity, burnt, spicy, and resinous. Another common system is that proposed by Zwaardemaker, a contemporary of Henning, which lists nine basic odors that singly or in combination account for all of the different smells. A more recent model suggests the seven primary odors; these are illustrated in table 8.1, along with chemical examples and familiar substances that illustrate the odors. In addition to the difficulty in specifying basic odors, it has also been difficult to specify the physical characteristics that two or more chemicals must possess in order to

Table 8.1 The Seven Primary Odors, Chemical Examples, and Familiar Substances

Primary Odor	Chemical Example	Familiar Substance
Camphoraceous	Camphor	Moth repellent
Musky	Pentadecanolactone	Angelica root oil
Floral	Phenylethyl methyl ethyl carbinol	Roses
Pepperminty	Menthone	Mint candy
Ethereal	Ethylene dichloride	Dry-cleaning fluid
Pungent	Formic acid	Vinegar
Putrid	Butyl mercaptan	Bad egg

Note: Each of the primary odors is detected by a different receptor in the nose. Most odors are composed of several of these primaries in various proportions.

have identical odors. However, recent revitalization of an ancient theory suggests that odor is determined in some measure by the shape of the odor molecule, the so-called **stereochemical theory of odor** (Amoore, Johnston, and Rubin 1964), the theory postulating the seven basic odors listed in table 8.1. Camphoraceous odors, for example, are believed to be produced by spherical molecules, while musky odors are the result of disk-shaped molecules.

The olfactory receptor cells are embedded in a special region of supporting cells and mucus located in the roof of the nasal passages, a region termed the **olfactory epithelium.** The receptors are actually specialized nerve endings of the first cranial nerve—the **olfactory nerve** (I)—that have fine hairlike extensions, the cilia. These extensions are presumed to possess special receptor sites where, according to the stereochemical theory, different-shaped odor molecules may attach. Each receptor element may possess receptor sites for more than one primary odor.

Recordings of the activity of the extremely fine fibers of the olfactory nerve (e.g., Gesteland et al. 1963) have revealed that these fibers are spontaneously active and may be excited or inhibited by odor stimuli. These investigators reported that different fibers responded selectively to different groups of odors, suggesting that while there is some specificity of response in individual receptors, each possesses a number of receptor sites capable of detecting a variety of different odors. Although Gesteland and associates were able to group the responses into eight different classes

of odor-response categories, there may be a continuum of response characteristics within which no two fibers have absolutely identical response properties. It is, therefore, unclear at this time whether labeled lines exist for different odors from different receptors or whether a higher-level comparator mechanism, similar to that proposed for taste, is involved.

Recordings from the olfactory bulb where the fibers of the olfactory nerve terminate have suggested that different odors may be coded by the place on the olfactory epithelium where they are received. In a classic series of observations Adrian (e.g. 1950; 1953) recorded from the olfactory bulb of the cat during stimulation with different odors. He noted that the anterior region of the olfactory bulb, which receives fibers from the same region of the olfactory epithelium, responded selectively to banana oil and related chemicals. The posterior ventral region of the bulb responded to coal gas and similar compounds. The posterior dorsal region was responsive to carrion (rotten meat) odor. Taken together with other observations, these findings suggest a **place theory of smell** in which receptors in different places on the olfactory epithelium code different odors, not unlike the place theory of hearing in which receptors in different places on the basilar membrane are thought to code different frequencies of sound.

The structure of the **olfactory bulb** is similar in many ways to the structure of the retina (Shepherd 1974). The olfactory bulb receives information directly from the underlying olfactory epithelium and is, therefore, spatially organized with respect to the receptor surface, which is receptotopically organized. It is a layered structure in which both vertically and horizontally oriented cells exist. The vertically oriented cells are the **mitral** and **tufted cells,** which receive information from the olfactory nerve fibers. The horizontally oriented cells are the **periglomerular cells** and the **granular cells,** which provide for lateral interactions between regions of the bulb. Because of this, the olfactory bulb is particularly well designed to analyze the spatial distribution of information over the olfactory epithelium, necessary in a place theory of odor detection.

The question of the code that the brain uses for identification of odors is still wide open, and the place theory will almost surely be significantly modified. Other current evidence and theorizing suggest that the spatial and temporal patterns of arrival of the odor molecules as they dissolve through the mucosa of the olfactory epithelium may be an important feature of the code for odor (e.g., Mozell 1964). In addition, the olfactory bulb generates fascinating rhythmic electrical activity that may also form an important part of the story of how the brain recognizes odors. A further, but not unexpected, complication because of our knowledge of the other senses is that in addition to incoming sensory fibers, there are outgoing efferent fibers reaching the olfactory bulb that must exert some degree of control over information processing in this complex structure.

The output of the olfactory bulb is carried by the axons of the two types of vertically oriented cells, the tufted and mitral cells, and unlike all of the other senses, information does not project to a sensory relay nucleus in the thalamus. Output fibers pass into a variety of structures of the limbic system, including the amygdala and portions of cortex associated with the limbic system. The association of smell and the limbic system reinforces the general view that olfaction and the limbic system are important in aggressive, reproductive, and other emotional behaviors. The importance of smell to the behavior of most organisms and its role in the "emotional brain" also provide important clues to the evolutionary history of the limbic system and the roles it must play in human behavior.

hypothalamus

Polysensory Systems

We have only begun to explore how the brain receives and processes sensory information. Even more must be understood since many structures in the brain are points of convergence of sensory information. Even some relays within individual sensory pathways themselves show this polysensory character. The superior colliculus, for example, contains neurons responsive to visual and auditory stimuli. In some cases, the stimuli must be moving in the same direction from the same region in space, which suggests that the superior colliculi are important in orientation toward moving stimuli (e.g., Wickelgren 1971; Jassik-Gerschenfeld 1966). The reticular formation and many structures in the limbic system also contain neurons that respond to all modalities of stimulation (e.g., Miller and Groves 1977). Perhaps best known for this polysensory characteristic are the association areas of the cerebral cortex, which contain neurons that typically respond to several modalities of stimulation (Thompson, Johnson, and Hoopes 1963; Robertson et al. 1975).

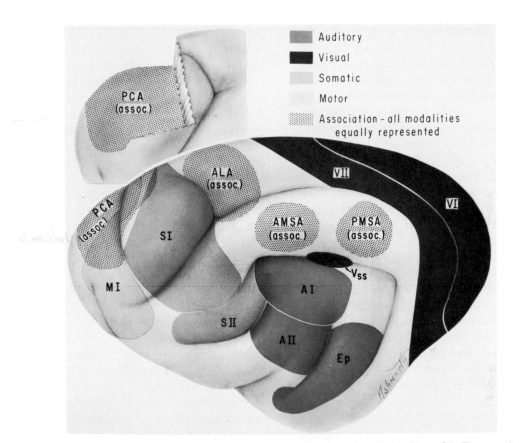

Figure 8.25 Summary diagram of the primary sensory areas and association areas of the cerebral cortex of the cat. The rear of the brain is to the right; the front to the left. Primary sensory areas respond preferentially to one type of sensory message, e.g., visual stimuli (VI, VII, and Vss), auditory stimuli (auditory areas), somatosensory stimuli (SI and SII). The association areas respond to all types of sensory stimulation (PCA = pericruciate association area; ALA = anterior lateral association area; AMSA = anterior middle suprasylvian association area; PMSA = posterior middle suprasylvian association area). The motor cortex is labeled MI.

These areas comprise a significant portion of the surface of the cerebral cortex, as illustrated for the cat brain in figure 8.25.

The functions of the various multimodal structures in behavior are in large measure the topic of much of the remainder of this textbook. A complete understanding of the biological processes underlying perceptual behavior will have to take these structures into account.

Summary

Sound is produced by variations in air pressure that reach the ear. The **pitch** and **loudness** of a sound—its perceptual dimensions—relate to the frequency and amplitude of variations in air pressure. Sound produces vibrations of the eardrum, or **tympanic membrane,** which are carried by the small bones of the inner ear—the **ossicles**—to the oval window of the **cochlea.** There, pressure variations create pressure changes in the fluid-filled cochlea. The pressure variations create distortions of the basilar membrane in the **organ of Corti** that are detected by the auditory receptor cells—the **hair cells.** Sound information then is coded so that cells in the auditory pathways are activated and their patterns of activity are altered. At higher levels of the auditory pathways, such as the **auditory cortex,** neurons may be selectively responsive to complex sounds, such as amplitude and frequency-modulated tones and species-specific vocalizations. Similar receptor mechanisms are involved in the **vestibular apparatus,** which is responsible for the sense of balance and position of the head in space. Changes in the position of the head are detected as fluid movement in the **semicircular canals.**

The bodily sensations differ from auditory and visual stimuli because they cannot be specified along any single dimension. While the early theory of von Frey suggested that specific receptors exist to code specific somatic sensations such as cold, warmth, touch, and pain, it is now known that other forms of coding in the brain are used. There are several different pathways carrying somatosensory information. The **lemniscal system** carries information about mechanical stimulation, such as touch, joint movement, and deep pressure. Information is organized somatotopically at every level of the lemniscal system. The **spinoreticulothalamic** and **spinothalamic systems** have a wider range of properties, including responses to temperature and pain.

Temperature is monitored by warmth and coolness detectors in the skin, although our perception of temperature can vary depending on previous activation of these receptors. Pain is detected by free endings located in the skin and in several internal organs. The thalamus plays a major role in coding pain information. A descending system, which includes the **periaqueductal gray** and the **nucleus raphe magnus,** appears to suppress pain when activated for prolonged periods. This system inhibits dorsal horn cells in the spinal cord, which are responsible for conducting pain information to the thalamus. Important features of this descending system are neurons that release either **enkephalin** or **serotonin.** Both types of neurons are necessary for this system to reduce pain. The system is activated by morphine, by electrical stimulation of the periaqueductal gray, and presumably by a life-threatening or highly stressful situation.

The chemical senses—taste and smell—share the property that the appropriate stimuli for both are chemical compounds. Apparently, specific receptors exist for the basic tastes—salty, sour, bitter, and sweet. Central connections of nerve fibers carrying taste information are the **nucleus of the solitary tract** in the brain stem and the lemniscal pathways just described. The sense of smell, although not important for human survival, is extremely important to the survival of many organisms. Chemical messages called **pheromones** are used to communicate such "smells." There is no generally agreed-upon list of fundamental odors, although classes of odors may possess certain common molecular properties such as shape. This is the basis for the stereochemical theory of odor. The central projections of the olfactory nerve include the olfactory bulb and, ultimately, structures associated with the limbic system.

Important in our understanding of the brain mechanisms of sensation are the association cortex and other regions of the brain that are polysensory; that is, regions where the neurons respond to more than one modality of sensory stimulation.

Suggested Readings

Ludel, J. 1978. *Introduction to sensory processes.* San Francisco: W. H. Freeman. *This book provides a general introduction to the human senses.*

Moller, A. I. 1983. *Auditory physiology.* New York: Academic Press. *This textbook offers a detailed discussion of the auditory system from receptor processes to central coding.*

Sinclair, D. 1981. *Mechanisms of cutaneous sensation.* Oxford: Oxford University Press. *This is a very readable book on the skin senses. It includes chapters on the methods of studying these senses and the biological processes that underlie them.*

Snyder, S. H. 1977. Opiate receptors and internal opiates. *Scientific American* 236: 44–56. *This article summarizes some of the breakthrough research on endorphins and their role in pain suppression.*

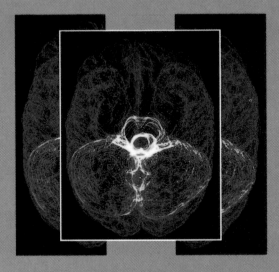

Outline

Introduction

The elaborate neural mechanisms involved in processing sensory information would be useless if we could not act on that information. Our very survival depends on the ability to produce an appropriate response to sensory events, whether they occur internally or in the external world. In this chapter, we discuss these response systems and in so doing lay the groundwork for the rest of this book. All of the behaviors that we discuss in subsequent chapters—from eating to schizophrenia—represent the final output of the nervous system. Thus, we cannot understand behavior completely unless we also understand these output systems.

The output pathways of the nervous system are called **efferents** (from the Latin, meaning "to carry out or away"). These project to glands or muscles. Glands produce chemical secretions that help regulate the body's internal physiology. There are two types of glands: **exocrine glands,** which secrete their chemicals through a duct to specific areas of the body; and **endocrine glands,** which have no ducts, but secrete their products into the bloodstream where they travel throughout the body. Most of the secretions of the exocrine glands are very familiar: They include the oils that coat the skin, the saliva that wets the mouth, the milk released by nursing mammals, and the tears that moisten the inner surface of the eyelids. The endocrine glands also secrete a wide variety of substances, including amino acid derivatives, peptides, proteins, and steroids. These substances are known as **hormones** (in fact, endocrinology refers to the study of hormones), and they provide an important link between the nervous system and various changes in the internal and external environment. The milk that an infant suckles

Chapter

9

Output Systems: Hormones, Muscles, and Movement

from its mother's breasts, the amount of water that we excrete in our urine, the metabolic rate of our cells—all of these and many more events—are controlled by hormones. As you will see in later chapters, hormones also have a profound effect on many different behaviors. In this chapter, we will describe some of the most important hormones and how the nervous system controls their release from endocrine glands.

Muscles, the other target of neural output pathways, are responsible for movement, both internal movement as well as overt bodily movement. Movement occurs when muscle tissue contracts, usually in response to a stimulus from the nervous system. Internal movement is carried out by **smooth muscles** and **cardiac muscles.** Smooth muscles are controlled by the autonomic nervous system, and they also respond to certain hormones. These muscles are involved in such internal processes as constriction of blood vessels, stomach contractions, and bladder control. Cardiac muscles are found only in the heart. They comprise a specialized group of muscles that contract rhythmically even if their nerve supply is cut. Like smooth muscles, however, cardiac muscles also are regulated by neural activity and by some hormones. A third group of muscles, known as **striated muscles,** are responsible for overt movement. Except for the striated muscles that move the eye, tongue, and certain parts of the abdomen, these muscles are attached to bones by means of tendons and move the bones relative to each other. Thus, striated muscles sometimes are called **skeletal muscles.** Striated muscles also are controlled by the nervous system and are sensitive to certain hormones, but because they are responsible for overt movement, the very essence of behavior, we will focus our discussion of muscles on them.

As you read this chapter, keep in mind that the endocrine system and the nervous system constantly interact to regulate behavior. In fact, some endocrine hormones also are released by certain neurons as neurotransmitters. Both systems operate in parallel, but on a different time scale. You can think of the nervous system as controlling the fast-changing activity of the body by producing almost immediate changes in muscles and glands. The endocrine system operates more slowly because it relies on the circulatory system to carry hormones to distant targets.

Hormones

Hormones serve as chemical messengers within the body. They consist of amino acids, which often are strung together to form peptides, and proteins or sterols, which form fat-soluble molecules known as steroids. Hormones work together with the nervous system to control virtually all behavioral and physiological events. In a very real sense, hormones and the nervous system are part of the same process. As you will see in this section, the brain not only releases certain hormones, but is itself a target of hormone action.

The Endocrine Glands

Hormones are produced by the endocrine glands, which release them into the extracellular fluid near capillary beds. From here, they find their way into the general circulation. The endocrine glands are scattered throughout the body, as shown in figure 9.1. You may be surprised to see the brain and heart included as endocrine glands, but indeed these organs do release hormones. The many different hormones secreted by the endocrine glands exert very specific effects on distant target organs.

epinephrine (ep″ĭ-nef′rin)

norepinephrine (nor″ep-ĭ-nef′rin)

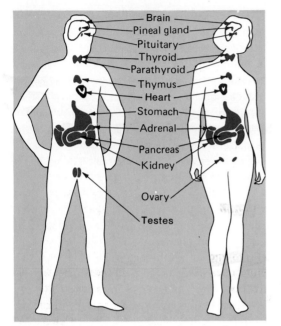

Figure 9.1 The locations of the major endocrine glands in the human male and female.

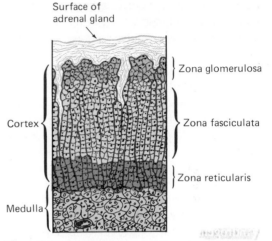

Figure 9.2 The various layers of the adrenal cortex.

In this section, we will review some of the major endocrine glands and the hormones that they release.

Adrenals

The adrenal glands, perched atop the kidneys, are really two separate endocrine glands. An inner gland, known as the **adrenal medulla,** secretes two hormones: **epinephrine** and **norepinephrine.** Both of these hormones, which also are released by some neurons as neurotransmitters, are formed from the amino acid tyrosine. As hormones, epinephrine and norepinephrine have similar effects. They increase heart rate and blood pressure and reduce the flow of blood to the digestive system. They also cause hair to stand on end (piloerection) in furry animals and "goose pimples" in humans. In general, the actions of

these hormones complement the sympathetic division of the autonomic nervous system, which becomes most active in fight-or-flight situations.

The outer gland of the adrenals, the **adrenal cortex,** has entirely different endocrine functions. It produces at least fifty different hormones, all of which are steroids. Only about a dozen of these are active in the body; the rest are converted into an active form when the body needs them. As shown in figure 9.2, the adrenal cortex consists of three cellular layers, each of which produce different types of steroid hormones. The outer layer of the adrenal cortex, the zona glomerulosa, manufactures a group of hormones known as **mineralocorticoids.** These act on the kidney to regulate salt and water balance. The next layer of cells, the zona fasciculata, produces some of the best-known adrenal cortical hormones, the **glucocorticoids.** Cortisone and hydrocortisone belong to this group. These hormones facilitate the breakdown of proteins to provide metabolic energy. They also prepare the body to handle stress and reduce inflammation. Glucocorticoids related to cortisone, for example, are used to treat arthritis, severe allergic reactions, and muscle and joint injuries, all of which involve the inflammatory response.

The third group of adrenal cortical hormones are produced by the zona reticularis. These include the sex hormones, **androgens** and **estrogens,** which also are produced by the reproductive organs. Androgens and estrogens are made in the adrenal cortex of both sexes, but androgens predominate. As you will see in a later chapter, androgens play an important role in the development of male sex organs. Androgens also stimulate the synthesis of some cellular proteins, and thus are responsible for such male characteristics as facial hair and muscular development. The synthesis of new proteins is known as **anabolism;** androgens, therefore, have an anabolic effect. Some athletes, who desire extra muscular development, consume large amounts of anabolic steroids, all of which are chemically similar to androgens (Wright 1982). Unfortunately, the increase in protein synthesis caused by such a practice damages other organs that are involved in protein production, including the liver. Some forms of liver cancer have been traced directly to the use of anabolic steroids. Moreover, because these compounds resemble androgens, they also disrupt normal reproductive functions. Attempts to manipulate the body's physiology beyond its nomal capacity always have a very high price.

Gonads

The reproductive organs, or gonads, are among the most important endocrine glands in the body. As you will see in a later chapter, they not only are responsible for the development and maturation of the sex organs, but they also exert profound influences on behavior. Female gonads, known as **ovaries,** produce a group of sex hormones called estrogens. The corresponding glands in the male—the **testes**—produce androgens. Estrogens are necessary for the development of secondary sex characteristics in females, including growth of the breasts and fat buildup in the hips. Androgens, as we mentioned in our discussion of the adrenal cortex, are responsible for male secondary characteristics.

Thyroid

The thyroid gland is a single organ located in the front of the throat. This gland produces **thyroxine,** an amino acid derivative that contains four atoms of iodine. Thyroxine increases the metabolic rate of cells. An overproduction of this hormone causes high blood pressure, weight loss, and muscular weakness. Insufficient amounts impair cellular metabolism and cause obesity. Too little thyroxine in children leads to **cretinism,** a disorder characterized by a retardation of bone growth, sexual development, and mental ability. The synthesis of thyroxine is controlled, in part, by the amount of iodine in the diet. An iodine deficiency prevents synthesis and causes the thyroid gland to swell in size, forming a **goiter.** The addition of iodine to common table salt has virtually eliminated this disorder in the United States.

Pituitary

A discussion of the endocrine system would not be complete without mention of the pituitary gland, which has been called the "master gland" of the body. The pituitary received this title when some of its hormones were found to control the release of many other hormones. The glucocorticoids, the sex hormones, and thyroxine, for example, are released in response to hormones from the pituitary. As you

hypophysis   (hi-pof′ĭ-sis)

infundibulum   (in″fun-dib′u-lum)

adenohypophysis   (ad″e-no-hi-pof′ĭ-sis)

neurohypophysis   (nu″ro-hi-pof′ĭ-sis)

hypothalamic-hypophyseal   (hi″po-thal′ah-mik-hi″po-fiz′e-al)

soon will see, however, the brain, particularly the hypothalamus, controls pituitary secretions. Thus, the so-called "master gland" itself has a master (Frohman 1980).

The pituitary is a small organ located above the roof of the mouth on the underside of the brain. This location gives the pituitary its other name—**hypophysis**—derived from a Greek term meaning "undergrowth." It is connected to the hypothalamus by a thin stalk known as the **infundibulum.** This stalk attaches to the brain just behind the optic chiasma. In adult mammals, the pituitary consists of two separate and distinct portions: an anterior portion known as the **adenohypophysis,** and a posterior portion known as the **neurohypophysis.** During embryological development, the adenohypophysis arises from tissue that forms the roof of the mouth. This portion of the pituitary gland, therefore, is not of neural origin. In fact, there are no direct neural connections between the hypothalamus and the adenohypophysis. The neurohypophysis, on the other hand, is of neural origin. It grows down from the brain and is connected by nerve cells to the hypothalamus. In some species, the medial portion of the pituitary forms a third division, the **pars intermedia.**

Adenohypophysis   The only means of communication between the adenohypophysis and the hypothalamus is a complex series of blood vessels known as the **hypothalamic-hypophyseal portal system.** In order to control the release of hormones from the adenohypophysis, therefore, the hypothalamus itself must function as an endocrine gland and secrete substances into the blood supply. Indeed, specialized cells in the hypothalamus lie near the portal system and secrete **releasing factors** or **inhibiting factors,** which, as their names suggest, either stimulate or suppress the release of hormones from the adenohypophysis.

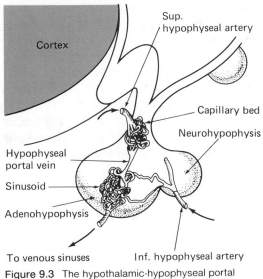

Figure 9.3 The hypothalamic-hypophyseal portal system. It is through this system that the hypothalamus controls the activity of the anterior pituitary. Releasing factors or hormones are "dumped" into veins of the hypothalamus, carried to the pituitary via this system, and there control the release of adenohypophyseal hormones.

There are many different hormones produced by the adenohypophysis, and presumably each of these is controlled by its own releasing and inhibiting factor from the hypothalamus. The circulatory link between the hypothalamus and adenohypophysis is shown in figure 9.3.

Two of the hormones produced by the adenohypophysis act on the gonads and thus are known as **gonadotrophic hormones.** Both of these hormones cause the gonads to release sex hormones. In addition, one of the gonadotrophic hormones, known as **follicle-stimulating hormone,** or **FSH,** promotes the development of the sex cells (sperm or eggs). The other gonadotrophic hormone, **luteinizing hormone,** or **LH,** triggers ovulation in females. Two other hormones from the adenohypophysis also control the secretions of other endocrine glands. **Adrenocorticotrophic hormone,** or **ACTH,** acts on the zona fasiculata cells of the adrenal cortex to stimulate the production and release of the glucocorticoids. The adenohypophysis releases ACTH during injury or other forms of bodily stress. **Thyroid stimulating hormone,** or **TSH,** causes cells in the thyroid gland to secrete thyroxine. TSH also stimulates thyroxine production by causing thyroid cells to multiply and by enhancing their uptake of iodine.

Some hormones released by the adenohypophysis are known for their direct effects on target organs, rather than the release of other hormones. **Growth hormone,** for example, promotes the growth of bones and muscles by increasing the incorporation of amino acids into proteins. Thus, like androgens, it has an anabolic effect (and, yes, some athletes striving for the strength of Goliath take supplements of this hormone, but with the same damaging effects on their livers). Secretions of growth hormone are correlated with the major growth spurts that occur during childhood. An overproduction of this hormone, usually caused by a pituitary tumor, causes severe deformities. If the tumor occurs in children before the bones of the arms and legs have stopped growing, the result is **giantism.** If the disorder occurs later in life when the bones have stopped growing, only the ends of the bones will expand, causing an enlargement of the nose, eyebrow ridges, lower jaw, hands, and feet known as **acromegaly** (from the Greek, meaning "great extremities"). Some individuals who secrete excess amounts of growth hormone as children and as adults suffer from both giantism and acromegaly. Presumably, Maximus I, an early emperor of Rome, was such a victim (Klawans 1982). His

likeness on Roman coins shows the exaggerated facial features characteristic of acromegaly, and historians agree that his height ranged between seven and eight feet. He also had an appetite to match. In a single day he was said to consume seven gallons of wine and thirty or forty pounds of meat. The opposite syndrome, **dwarfism,** is caused by an insufficient production of growth hormone.

Another hormone from the adenohypophysis that influences cellular activity is **prolactin,** or **lactogenic hormone.** This hormone is best known for its role in stimulating the mammary glands of pregnant and nursing mothers to produce milk. (The mammary glands themselves are exocrine glands, and the actual release of milk is controlled by another hormone, as you soon will see.) Prolactin has many other functions, including energy metabolism and bone growth. Thus, this hormone may influence some of the same cellular processes as TSH and growth hormone. Prolactin also plays an important role in parental behavior.

Neurohypophysis Unlike the adenohypophysis, the neurohypophysis receives a rich nerve supply. The cell bodies of these neurons are located in the **supraoptic** and **paraventricular nuclei** of the hypothalamus. They send their axons into the neurohypophysis via the **hypothalamic-hypophyseal tract,** which runs through the infundibulum (fig. 9.4). The neurohypophysis secretes two hormones, but these are not synthesized in the pituitary. Instead, they are made by the neurons in the supraoptic and paraventricular nuclei and then transported to the neurohypophysis down the axons of the hypothalamic-hypophyseal tract. In the neurohypophysis, the hormones collect in axon terminals and are released into the blood supply when the neurons become active. Thus, the manufacture, storage, and release of

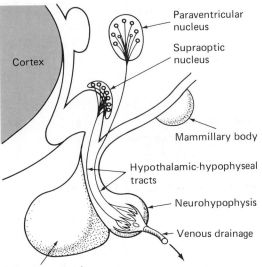

Figure 9.4 The neural connections between the hypothalamus and the posterior pituitary. The posterior pituitary hormones are produced in the paraventricular and supraoptic nuclei of the hypothalamus, carried down the axons of the hypothalamic-hypophyseal tracts, and stored in the cells of the posterior pituitary. The release of these hormones into the general circulation is then triggered by neural activity in the hypothalamus.

hormones in the neurohypophysis is very different from the same processes in the adenohypophysis.

The hormones released by the neurohypophysis exert very different effects. One of these hormones, known as **vasopressin,** or **antidiuretic hormone** (ADH), helps the kidney to reabsorb water and thus prevents dehydration. This substance plays a critical role in drinking behavior, as you will see in a later chapter. The other hormone released from the neurohypophysis, **oxytocin,** acts on the smooth muscles of the mammary glands to help eject milk from the breasts of lactating females. It also is released during labor to aid in expelling the fetus from the birth canal. In both sexes, this hormone helps to increase blood pressure.

Hormone Release Is Controlled by Simple Reflexes

Hormones are released from endocrine glands by a reflexive mechanism. A precise stimulus, arising from inside or outside the body, triggers a change in neural activity that ultimately causes the appropriate hormone to be released from the appropriate endocrine gland. Once the hormone is released and performs its function, its release must be turned off. This is accomplished by additional reflexive mechanisms that again involve both the nervous and endocrine systems. In many cases, the hormone itself acts on the brain to suppress its further release. This effect is reinforced by a neural response from the target organ indicating to the brain that the hormone did its job. Both of these events are examples of **negative feedback,** a process by which the effects caused by a stimulus feed back onto a control center to turn the system off.

Consider the process by which the adenohypophysis releases TSH. This hormone is released when the body needs to increase its metabolism. An effective stimulus for this release is a fall in body temperature. Temperature receptors signal the brain, and the hypothalamus secretes a releasing factor that travels through the hypothalamic-hypophyseal portal system to the adenohypophysis. In response, the adenohypophysis releases TSH into the bloodstream. When TSH reaches the thyroid, thyroxine is released, causing an increase in metabolic activity and a corresponding increase in heat production. This, in turn, causes body temperature to rise. The thyroxine in the blood combines with the rise in body temperature to feed back on the hypothalamus and suppress the further release of TSH from the adenohypophysis. As a result, thyroxine release declines. A schematic illustration of this

284
Chapter 9

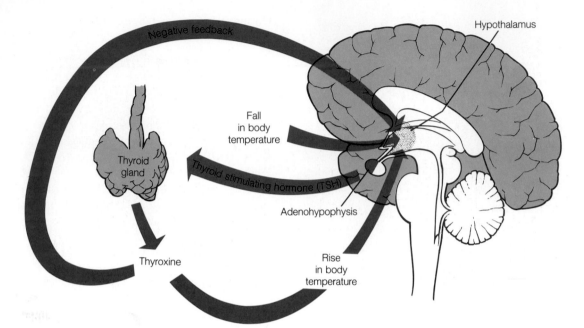

Figure 9.5 Negative feedback systems in the control of thyroxine release. A fall in body temperature triggers the hypothalamus to cause the release of TSH from the adenohypophysis. TSH, in turn, causes thyroxine release from the thyroid gland in the neck. Thyroxine increases body temperature which feeds back on the hypothalamus to stop TSH release. The presence of thyroxine in the blood also feeds back on the hypothalamus to suppress TSH even further.

sequence of events is shown in figure 9.5. Note that both a hormonal and a neural signal feed back to the brain to control hormone release.

In some cases, hormone release is turned off only when a neural signal, not the hormone itself, feeds back to the brain. Milk "let down" in dairy cows and nursing mothers provides an example of this form of negative feedback. The process of milk secretion, which requires the hormone oxytocin, begins when nipples are stimulated. Sensory information travels to the brain and oxytocin-containing cells in the supraoptic, and the paraventricular nuclei become active. This causes the release of oxytocin from nerve terminals in the neurohypophysis.

When oxytocin reaches the breast, it causes milk-producing cells to contract, squeezing out the milk that travels toward the nipples. Oxytocin will continue to be released, however, until the nipple is no longer stimulated. If a high level of oxytocin in the blood alone prevented its further release, then both the dairy farmer and the infant would be disappointed. Thus, oxytocin release continues until enough milk is released to satisfy the individual tugging at the nipple. When the nipple is released, neural activity declines, which signals the hypothalamus to turn off oxytocin release. Of course, milk "let down" is influenced by many factors other than stimulation of nipples. Dairy cows become conditioned to being milked at certain times of the day and will

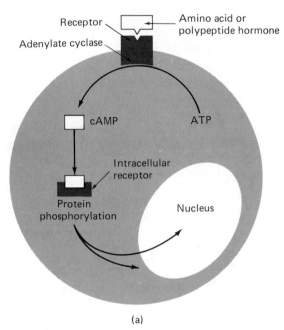

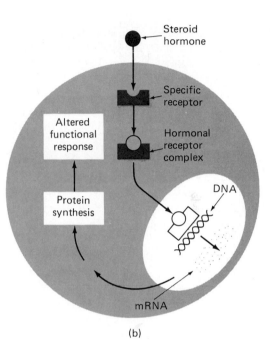

(a)

(b)

Figure 9.6 Two mechanisms by which hormones affect the functioning of cells. (**a**) Proteins and polypeptide hormones interact with receptors on the surface of target cells, increasing the production of cAMP and thus altering cell functions. (**b**) Certain steroid hormones enter target cells and interact with intracellular receptor molecules, thus altering the metabolism of cells.

begin to release oxytocin when the time is right even before the farmer starts the milking process. Emotions also influence milk "let down." Contented cows give more milk than nervous cows. Apparently, the same is true of nursing mothers. The more anxious a woman is about breastfeeding her infant, the more difficulty she will have in doing exactly that.

Hormones Work by Interacting with a Receptor Molecule

In order to produce its effect (release of another hormone or a direct change in cellular function), a hormone must interact with a target cell. This interaction involves receptor molecules located either on the surface or the inside of the target cell (McEwen 1980). In the first case, the hormone does not enter the target cell, but interacts with a receptor molecule on the cell's surface. When this surface receptor is activated, a series of intracellular changes occur that ultimately lead to the appropriate response. Figure 9.6a provides an example of this process, which is common for amino acid, peptide, and protein hormones. As you can see, the hormone interacts with a surface receptor linked to an enzyme known as **adenylate cyclase.** The enzyme then is activated, causing the production of **cyclic AMP,** or cAMP, a compound that acts on other intracellular machinery to produce the desired effect. In the second case, which typically applies to steroid hormones and which is illustrated in figure 9.6b, the hormone enters the target cell directly and combines with an intracellular receptor molecule. This hormone-receptor complex then is transported into the nucleus of the target cell where it alters the transcription of messenger RNA. This, in turn, increases protein synthesis, which ultimately leads to the appropriate response of the target cell.

Muscles

Striated, or skeletal, muscles do their work by pulling, never by pushing. They are attached across joints in such a way that when they contract, they pull on the bone and thus move the body. If you hold your arm out straight and then bend it at the elbow to raise your hand toward your shoulder, a muscle in your upper arm, the biceps, contracts or pulls on the bone in your lower arm and your hand swings upward. To straighten your arm again, a corresponding muscle in your upper arm, the triceps, contracts and pulls the bone down until your arm is straight. This example illustrates another important point about skeletal muscles: They act in opposing pairs. When one muscle contracts, the muscle that moves the bone in the opposite direction must relax. Thus, in our example, when the biceps contracts, the triceps relaxes, and vice versa. No movement is possible without this reciprocal relationship. In this section, we review how muscles work.

Molecular Basis of Muscular Contraction

In order to understand how muscles work (and why they become sore when they work too much), you first must understand their structure. Striated muscles comprise subunits of decreasing size. These subunits, essentially "muscles within muscles," are illustrated schematically in figure 9.7. The largest units are called **muscle fibers.** Each muscle fiber is a single cell formed by the fusion of many different cells and thus contains many nuclei. In short muscles, these fibers extend the entire length of the muscle; in long muscles, the fibers attach to one another. Each individual muscle fiber itself is composed of **myofibrils,** which are about 1 micron in diameter. Both the muscle fibers and the myofibrils that they contain appear to shorten during muscle contractions. The myofibrils, in turn, are composed of thick and thin filaments that lie parallel to each other, also shown in figure 9.7. The thick filaments are made of a protein called **myosin,** and the thin filaments are composed of another protein called **actin.** The thick and thin filaments overlap to form a characteristic banded pattern that gives skeletal muscles their striated (striped) appearance. Each set of bands forms a **sarcomere** that is about 1.6 microns in length when the muscle is at rest. During maximal contraction, the sarcomere shortens by about 50 percent. The thick and thin filaments themselves, however, do not shorten during contraction. Instead, they slide past each other. The thick and thin filaments are connected by tiny **cross-bridges,** which are really molecular extensions of the myosin protein. These myosin cross-bridges break and reform very rapidly as the muscle contracts. This constant reforming and breaking of the cross-bridges converts chemical energy into mechanical energy.

The trigger that causes the thick and thin filaments to slide past each other is calcium. An elaborate network of sacs, or **cisternae,** termed the **sarcoplasmic reticulum** within the muscle contains calcium, which is released when an action potential depolarizes the

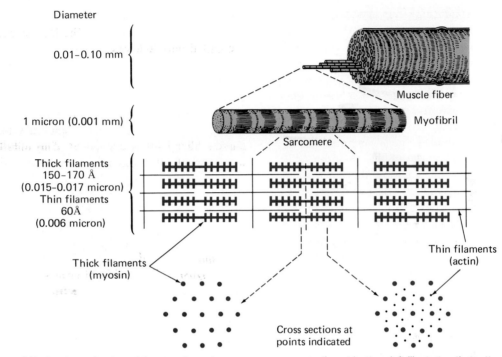

Figure 9.7 A schematic view of the structure of striated muscle at different levels of magnification. Note how the striated pattern is formed by the overlap of thick and thin filaments within each sarcomere. The cross section at bottom left illustrates the pattern of thick filaments at a point where there is no overlap, while that at bottom right indicates how the thin filaments fit in the array of thick ones.

muscle. As calcium is released, it allows the myosin cross-bridges to attach to the actin filaments. The cross-bridges then pivot or swivel, break contact with the actin, and then reattach to the actin further along the filament. In this way, the actin and myosin filaments slide past each other. Muscles that contract very rapidly have a large number of cisternae for the quick release of large amounts of calcium. Muscles that contract more slowly have fewer cisternae and thus less calcium.

Although necessary for movement, calcium does not act alone. Energy is required for the cross-bridges to break and reform. Muscle cells use the energy stored in the energy-rich molecule **adenosine triphosphate, or ATP.** ATP combines with the myosin cross-bridges and promotes the formation of the bond with actin that calcium completes. When the ATP molecule releases its energy, the actin-myosin bond breaks, the myosin protein combines with new ATP, and, in the presence of calcium, forms a new bond further along the actin protein.

The amount of ATP present in striated muscle cells, however, is sufficient only for about 0.5 second of muscular contraction. Where do muscles find the energy to work for longer periods of time? One answer is that muscles store energy in the form of **creatine phosphate.** This molecule can be converted to

ATP very rapidly and thus provides an additional source of energy. But even this supply is exhausted after a few seconds of continuous muscular activity. Additional energy comes from one of two other sources. Muscles will form ATP by **cellular respiration,** a process that involves the oxidative metabolism of carbohydrates. Another source of energy is the anaerobic (without oxygen) metabolism of glucose, known as **glycolysis,** to form ATP. Muscles responsible for slow movements and posture typically depend on cellular respiration for energy, whereas muscles used for fast movements are able to switch from cellular respiration to glycolysis with continued use.

Control of Muscles by Motor Neurons

Skeletal muscles are controlled by **motor neurons.** Their cell bodies lie within the gray matter of the ventral horn of the spinal cord or in various nuclei scattered along the lower part of the brain stem. Motor neurons generally have long axons that pass out of the spinal cord or brain and make synaptic contact with individual muscle fibers. A synapse between a motor neuron and a muscle fiber is highly specialized and is called a **neuromuscular junction.** At the neuromuscular junction, the distance between the axon terminal and the postsynaptic muscle fiber is larger than the typical synaptic distance between two neurons. Moreover, at the point of synaptic contact, the muscle fiber flattens out to form an **end-plate.** The end-plate contains receptors for **acetylcholine,** which is the neurotransmitter released by all motor neurons. Acetylcholine is excitatory at the neuromuscular junction, and the resulting depolarization that occurs in the muscle fiber is called an **end-plate potential.** The end-plate potential leads to an action potential that then travels the length of the

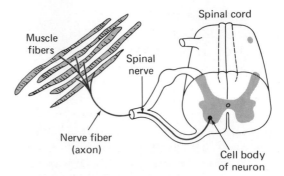

Figure 9.8 Diagram of a motor unit that consists of a single motor neuron and all muscle fibers with which it makes synaptic contact.

muscle fiber. The action potential increases the permeability of the fiber to calcium, which as we have seen, triggers contraction.

Each muscle fiber is controlled by one synaptic ending from the axon of a motor neuron. Such an axon may have just a few (three or four) branches, each contacting one muscle fiber. More commonly, however, motor neurons have as many as one hundred or more axonal branches contacting as many muscle fibers. An individual motor neuron and all muscle fibers with which it makes synaptic contact make up one **motor unit.** A single motor unit is illustrated schematically in figure 9.8. An entire muscle contains several of these motor units.

The number of muscle fibers that are contacted by the axonal branches of a single motor neuron plays an important role in muscle control. Motor neurons that project to the muscles of the hands, for example, have very few axonal branches and thus contact only a few muscle fibers. In this case, therefore, the innervation ratio is relatively high, a fact that permits precise muscular control. In contrast, muscles that do not require very fine control, such as the large muscles that move our legs, have very small innervation ratios. In some leg muscles, each motor neuron may control more than one hundred muscle fibers.

Sore Muscles Are Injured Muscles

Nearly everyone has experienced muscular soreness on the day following some form of excessive physical exertion. Muscles become stiff, and the soreness may persist for two or three days. This condition, which sometimes is accompanied by fever and nausea, appears to be caused by damage to the actin and myosin filaments and the molecular cross-bridges in the muscle itself (Armstrong 1984). In fact, the name for an extreme form of this condition, **exertional rhabdomyolysis,** is derived from a series of Greek terms meaning "breaking of muscle rods." Apparently, high tension in muscles unaccustomed to exercise actually causes structural damage.

For many years, muscle soreness was attributed to an accumulation of metabolic waste products in muscle tissue. This is not the case. The greatest degree of soreness is caused by contractions that require the lowest expenditure of energy and thus produce the fewest waste products. Contractions involved in downhill running, for example, will cause greater soreness than uphill running. Similarly, lowering a weight involves less metabolic activity than lifting a weight, yet lowering will cause more soreness than lifting.

Such statements may seem contradictory, but only because we typically perceive downhill running and lowering weights as requiring very little exertion. In reality, these movements generate the most muscular tension (Bigland-Ritchie and Woods 1976). When we run downhill or lower a weight, our muscles are being lengthened at the same time they are being contracted. This means that fewer motor units are activated at any given moment, and thus the force of contraction is distributed over a smaller cross-sectional area of muscle. The resulting tension can cause structural damage in muscles that are not trained for the particular exercise.

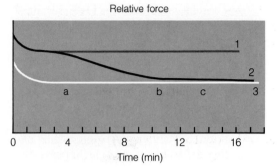

Figure 9.9 Effect of muscle soreness on muscular contraction. Curve 1 shows the force of contraction of well-trained muscle, and curve 2 the response of untrained muscle. Curve 3 is the response of the same untrained muscle on the day after curve 2 was obtained. Thus, curve 3 was made when the muscle was sore. At (a), contractions were very painful, less so at (b), and at (c) the pain had disappeared. Note that despite the loss of pain at (c) muscular contractions remained weak following unaccustomed exercise.

Not surprisingly, when a muscle still is sore from the previous day's exertion, it does not perform well. Part of the explanation, of course, is that we put out less effort when we feel sore. But another reason that performance declines is that the muscle itself, because of damaged filaments and cross-bridges, has a reduced capacity to produce force. Figure 9.9 illustrates this point very clearly. Note that the pain in sore muscles declines as the exercise session continues. After fifteen minutes of vigorous exercise, the muscles that were sore from yesterday's workout are no longer sore, but they continue to exert less force. The decline in muscle soreness during exercise appears to be caused by the release of endorphins (Kelly 1982), which as we have seen in an earlier chapter suppress pain.

Unfortunately, when we stop the exercise, the soreness often returns, and this cycle continues until the muscle tissue is built up through repeated training. No amount of topical liniments, creams, or ointments will speed the healing of sore muscles. Nor can we prevent muscle soreness by warming up before exercise or cooling down afterward. Although warm-ups and cool-downs may protect against muscle tears or tendon damage, they cannot prevent sore muscles when we overexert ourselves.

The best remedy for sore muscles is exercise itself. Muscular soreness in response to vigorous exercise diminishes as the exercise is repeated on a regular basis. Schwane and Armstrong (1983) have shown that vigorous training actually reduces the muscle damage caused by unaccustomed exercise. In fact, if soreness is caused by too much downhill running, it is best relieved by exercise that includes downhill running. Well-trained muscle fibers do not experience soreness.

Do not confuse muscle soreness with pain, however. Pain during exercise is a warning to stop. Further exertion in the face of pain may cause serious injury not only to muscle fibers, but to tendons and joints as well.

Movement

English physiologist Charles Sherrington referred to motor neurons as the "final common pathway" of motor control because all of the factors that influence motor behavior must do so via the motor neurons. These, in turn, control the muscles. In this section, you will see how the spinal cord and the brain control motor neurons and thus control movement.

Spinal Control of Movement

When we stand upright, the force of gravity acts to bend our legs. In so doing, the muscles that we use to keep our legs extended are stretched. This stretching causes the muscles to contract reflexively, and thus we avoid collapsing in a heap. The same reflex is a common part of many routine physical examinations. It is evoked by tapping the tendon just below the kneecap with a small hammer. The tap stretches one of the muscles that extends the leg. This causes the muscle to contract reflexively, and the leg kicks outward. Appropriately, this reflex is called the **stretch reflex,** and it forms the basis of our ability to stand against the force of gravity. In order for this reflex to work, the motor neurons that control the antigravity muscles in the leg must sense that the muscles are being stretched and then react by causing them to contract.

To understand how the motor neurons do their job, you first must understand the neural interconnections that are part of the stretch reflex. These are shown in figure 9.10. Note first that the motor neuron that sends its axons out to the muscle from the spinal cord is called an **alpha motor neuron.** Motor neurons are classified according to their size, and an alpha motor neuron is among the largest in the body. This means that it can conduct information very rapidly: The axon of an alpha motor neuron conducts action potentials at speeds of more than 220 meters/second. The alpha motor neurons synapses onto the muscle fiber at its end-plate region. The muscle fiber itself is known as an **extrafusal fiber,** and, as we have seen, when an action potential speeds along this fiber, it contracts. As more extrafusal fibers contract, the greater is the contraction of the muscle as a whole.

Note also in figure 9.10 that special receptors in the muscle send information back to the alpha motor neuron in the spinal cord. The special receptors are part of a structure called the **muscle spindle organ,** which is attached in parallel to the extrafusal muscle fibers. This means that when the muscle is stretched, the spindle organ is stretched along with it. The spindle organ itself comprises specialized muscle fibers known as **intrafusal fibers.** These fibers extend the length of the spindle, but in their central region they are surrounded by a sensory nerve ending called

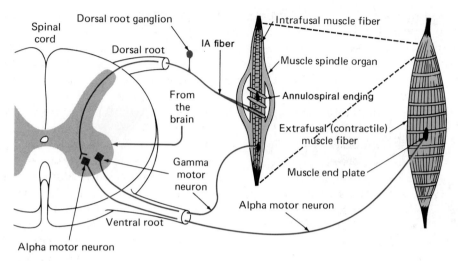

Figure 9.10 Summary diagram of the stretch reflex
and its motor neuron system.

an **annulospiral ending.** As figure 9.10 illustrates, the annulospiral ending gives rise to nerve fibers known as **IA fibers** that travel into the spinal cord and synapse directly onto the alpha motor neuron that controls the same muscle. The sensory fibers and the motor neurons with which they make synaptic contact are the key elements of the stretch reflex. Because they are linked by only one synapse, the stretch reflex also is known as a **monosynaptic reflex.** It is the only monosynaptic reflex in the body. But it is not the only synaptic contact that IA fibers make. As they enter the spinal cord, IA fibers branch to synapse with other neurons, some of which may be part of neuronal loops that also impinge on alpha motor neurons. Thus, even though the basic circuitry for the stretch reflex involves only one synapse, this reflex actually influences many neurons and many synapses. The nervous system, afterall, is a highly integrated structure, and this applies even to simple reflexes.

Like alpha motor neurons, IA fibers conduct information very rapidly. If you doubt the speed at which information travels along

the loop running from the spindle organ through the spinal cord and back to the muscle, try to measure the time that elapses when the tendon below your kneecap is tapped lightly until your leg begins to kick outward. The leg kick seems to occur almost instantly. Actually, about 50 milliseconds elapse (less time than it takes to blink your eye), and during this brief period, several events are taking place. First, the tap on the tendon stretches the muscle (in this case, the quadriceps muscle in your thigh). Stretching the muscle also stretches the intrafusal fibers that are part of the spindle organ. As the spindle is stretched, the annulospiral endings are activated, and nerve impulses travel along the IA fibers into the spinal cord. Here, the IA fibers synapse onto alpha motor neurons, which send impulses to the extrafusal fibers of the muscle. As these fibers contract, the muscle shortens, and your lower leg kicks outward. Try to imagine these events from the diagram shown in figure 9.10.

This same pathway is active whenever we are standing. In this case, gravity stretches

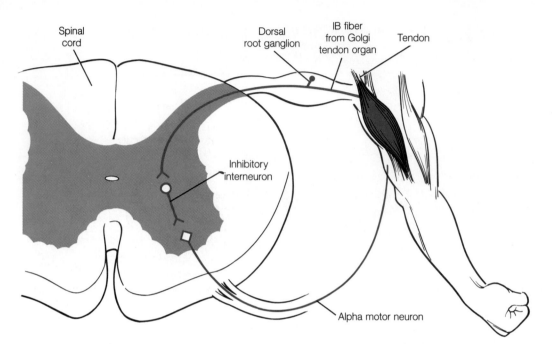

Figure 9.11 Mechanism by which the Golgi tendon organ inhibits further muscular contraction. Note the presence of the inhibitory interneuron, which synapses onto the alpha motor neuron.

our muscles (not only the quadriceps, but several muscles in our legs), and they contract reflexively to keep our legs extended.

Another important feature of the stretch reflex is that it does not require the brain's participation. Even though the brain monitors this reflex and influences its expression (anxiety or nervous tension, for example, enhance the stretch reflex), it still occurs even when the brain is separated from the spinal cord by surgical transection. For this reason, the stretch reflex is termed a spinal reflex. This illustrates that the organization of connections within the spinal cord is critical for movement.

So far, we have focused on only one of these spinal connections: the synapse between IA sensory fibers and alpha motor neurons. There are many more. For example, the muscle spindle organ is equipped not only with annulospiral endings, but also with sensory re-

ceptors that resemble tiny rings or coils. These are called **flower spray endings,** which respond to the same information as the annulospiral endings. The flower spray endings, however, give rise to smaller sensory fibers, known as **II fibers.** These fibers conduct information more slowly than the IAs, and they form complex connections with other neurons in the spinal cord. Thus, II fibers influence alpha motor neurons via several synapses. In addition, alpha motor neurons are controlled by receptors located in the tendons. These receptors are known as **Golgi tendon organs,** and they send their information to the spinal cord via **IB fibers.** These fibers synapse onto small interneurons, which in turn synapse onto alpha motor neurons. The interneurons are inhibitory, and thus when the IB fibers are activated, they will exert an inhibitory effect on alpha motor neurons, as shown in figure 9.11.

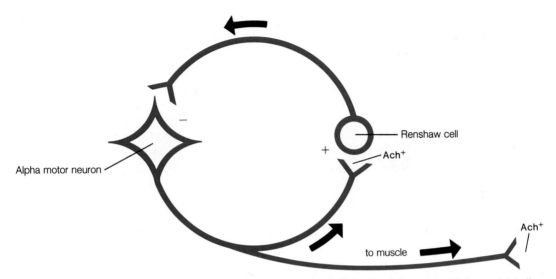

Figure 9.12 The role of the Renshaw cell in regulating the activity of an alpha motor neuron. Note that activity in the motor neuron activates the Renshaw cell, which in turn inhibits the motor neuron (Ach=acetylcholine; +=excitatory synapse; −=inhibitory synapse).

The inhibitory effect of the Golgi tendon organ has an important protective function. You may not be aware of it, but the force that a muscle exerts on its tendons and bones is very high. Some of the large muscles in the leg, for example, can exert a force of almost fifteen hundred pounds, and if all of the striated muscles in your body were strung together so that they could contract in the same direction, they could produce a force of twenty-five tons. Because muscles are so powerful, there is a danger that if they contract too forcefully, they will snap the bones. To prevent this, the Golgi tendon organ is activated when the muscle contracts to the point of doing damage. Thus, the receptors in the Golgi tendon organ have a higher threshold than those in the muscle spindle organ. But when the Golgi tendon organ is activated, the sensory information travels rapidly to the spinal cord (IB fibers conduct information just as rapidly as IA fibers) where interneurons inhibit the alpha motor neurons and automatically prevent further contraction. You could lift more weight by cutting your IB fibers and removing the inhibition that keeps your bones from breaking. But who would want to pay the price?

Alpha motor neurons also are prevented from firing too rapidly by another set of inhibitory interneurons known as **Renshaw cells.** These cells, named after their discoverer, are located in the same area of the spinal cord as the cell bodies of the alpha motor neurons. As shown in figure 9.12, before the axon of the alpha motor neuron leaves the spinal cord, it gives off a branch, or collateral, that turns back toward the Renshaw cell, which in turn forms an inhibitory synapse with the same alpha motor neuron. Thus, as an alpha motor neuron fires, it not only causes muscular contraction, it also increases the amount of inhibition that it receives by activating the Renshaw cell. This means that the faster the alpha motor neuron fires, the more likely that it will inhibit itself.

The inhibition is not prolonged because as soon as the motor neuron stops firing, the Renshaw cell also stops firing, thus removing the inhibition. The Renshaw cell, therefore, allows the motor neuron to rest for a brief period and in that way avoid fatigue. This does not mean, however, that the entire muscle rests. Many alpha motor neurons control a single muscle, and their rest periods are staggered (remember, an entire muscle is made up of several motor units). At any given moment, only the fastest firing alpha motor neurons are subject to Renshaw inhibition. The others continue to operate, but increase their firing rate as they do so and thus become next in line for a rest. By staggering their rest periods, alpha motor neurons can maintain prolonged muscular contraction.

We have seen so far that alpha motor neurons are controlled by IA fibers and by interneurons that receive input from II fibers, IB fibers, and from the alpha motor neurons themselves. Alpha motor neurons also are influenced by sensory input from the skin. You demonstrate this connection every time you withdraw your hand from a painful stimulus. Sensory nerve fibers from the skin convey information to interneurons in the spinal cord. These interneurons then excite the alpha motor neurons controlling the muscles that withdraw the limb. This withdrawal reflex is called the **flexion reflex.** Because more than one synapse is involved between the sensory fiber and the motor neuron, this is a **polysynaptic reflex.** Like the stretch reflex, the flexion does not require any input from the brain.

Additional spinal control of alpha motor neurons comes from opposing groups of muscles. Remember that movement of a limb involves not only contraction of certain muscles, but also relaxation or inhibition of muscles that move the limb in the opposite direction. Thus, all of the sensory fibers from a given muscle that control the alpha motor neuron, which projects back to the same muscle, also control the opposing muscle. For example, IA fibers from the biceps muscle not only excite alpha motor neurons going back to this muscle, but simultaneously inhibit alpha motor neurons that project to the opposing triceps muscle. Similarly, sensory information from the skin that excites the biceps muscle simultaneously inhibits the triceps muscle. Thus, when you unknowingly put your hand on a hot stove, your biceps not only contracts, your triceps also relaxes. As a result, you rapidly withdraw your arm (if both muscles contracted at the same time, your arm would freeze, and in this example, your hand would fry).

This inhibition across opposing pairs of muscles is accomplished by an inhibitory interneuron, as shown in figure 9.13. Note that the sensory information that exerts an excitatory influence on one muscle also synapses on an interneuron that projects to the alpha motor neuron of the opposing muscle. The interneuron is inhibitory. Thus, when the sensory pathway is activated, the interneuron is activated and the opposing alpha motor neuron is inhibited.

Figure 9.14 summarizes the inputs onto alpha motor neurons that we have discussed in this section. The number of inputs seems large. In fact, the number shown here is very limited. We did not include, for example, the inputs that alpha motor neurons receive from other segments of the spinal cord, nor did we mention inputs from the brain. Clearly, each alpha motor neuron is subjected to many influences—some excitatory and some inhibitory—and the balance of the inputs at any one time determines the activity of the alpha motor neuron and thus the state of muscular contraction.

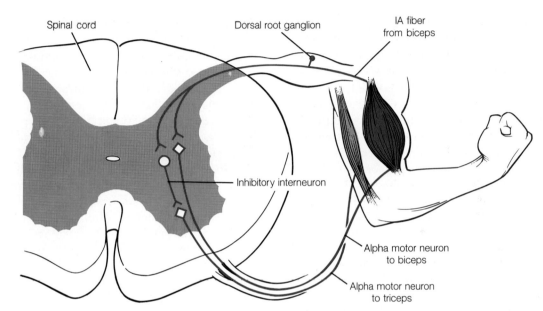

Figure 9.13 Mechanism by which opposing muscles regulate each other. Note in this example that the IA fibers, which excite the alpha motor neuron projecting back to the biceps, simultaneously inhibit alpha motor neurons projecting to the opposing triceps muscle. This inhibition is mediated by an inhibitory interneuron. A comparable circuit allows the triceps to inhibit the biceps.

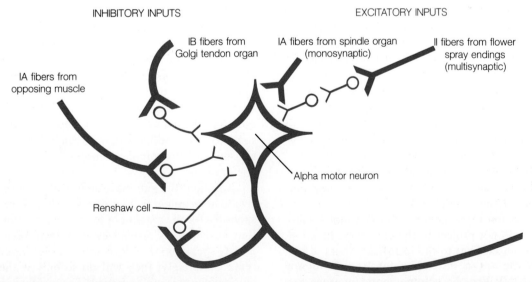

Figure 9.14 A simplified summary of the excitatory and inhibitory inputs onto a single alpha motor neuron in the spinal cord, as described in the text. In reality, each alpha motor neuron receives more than rifteen different types of excitatory and inhibitory inputs.

The organization of connections within the spinal cord is such that the simple act of stepping or walking does not require the participation of higher brain areas. A cat whose brain stem has been severed at the level of the pons will walk on a treadmill if the area below the transection is stimulated electrically (Grillner 1975). In all respects, the stepping movements that the animal displays are similar to those displayed during normal walking. In fact, the transected animal will adjust its walking speed to match the speed of the treadmill. This is a remarkable demonstration because after the operation the animal is in a vegetative state, capable only of breathing. All that is required to activate the walking pattern is a signal from the brain, and in the transected animal the electrical stimulation serves that purpose. This does not mean that the only role of the brain in walking is to get us started. The brain modulates walking in response to sensory inputs (quickening our pace, for example, when we hear someone approaching from behind in a dark alley, or shifting our balance when we try to walk along the deck of a ship in rough seas). The brain also sets the direction of our steps. But the actual contraction and relaxation of opposing muscles in each of the limbs as we walk is handled entirely by the spinal cord.

There is still another system in the spinal cord that is important for movement. This system involves another group of motor neurons known as **gamma motor neurons** (the gamma classification means that they are smaller than the alphas and thus conduct information more slowly). Gamma motor neurons do not project to the extrafusal fibers of the muscle, but to the intrafusal fibers of the spindle organ instead (refer back to figure 9.10). When the gamma motor neurons are active, the ends of the intrafusal fibers will contract. This contraction adds nothing to the force of muscular contraction (the intrafusal fibers are too small to cause any limb movement), but it does stretch the central region of the spindle. As we have seen, when the spindle is stretched, the alpha motor neurons projecting back to the muscle will increase their firing rate.

To appreciate the role that the gamma system plays in movement, consider what happens when a muscle contracts and the gamma motor neurons do not operate. As shown in figure 9.15, the muscle will shorten and the spindle organ will relax. This, in turn, removes the tension from the annulospiral and flower spray endings. As a result, the sensory fibers (the IAs and the IIs) become inactive, and an important excitatory influence on the alpha motor neurons is lost. Thus, the alpha motor neurons will decrease their firing rate, and the muscle will stop contracting. In other words, without the gamma system, we could not maintain muscle contraction. As soon as our muscles contracted, they would begin to relax. But when the gamma system is operating, tension remains on the spindle. As a result, the sensory receptors remain active, the alpha motor neurons continue to fire, and the muscle keeps contracting. Gamma motor neurons, therefore, control the state of tension of the spindle organ and, in that way, control the activity of the alpha motor neurons and the entire muscle.

In fact, the gamma system always is active to a certain extent, and this activity is responsible for the amount of tone or contraction that our muscles display even at rest. Technically speaking, therefore, our muscles never relax completely; they will do so only if the gamma neurons are damaged. The increase in muscular tension that we experience as we

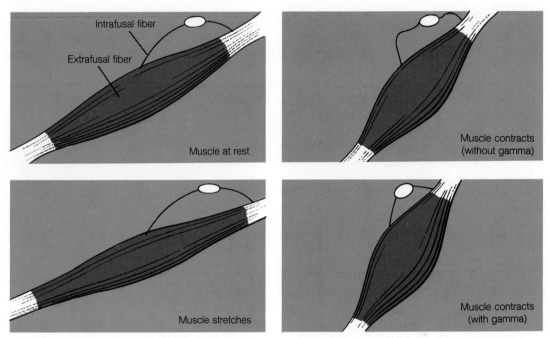

Figure 9.15 Role of the gamma system in maintaining muscular contraction. Because the intrafusal fibers are attached in parallel with the extrafusal fibers, a stretch of the muscle also will stretch the intrafusal fibers and activate sensory endings in the spindle organ that eventually cause contraction. Note, however, that without the gamma system, muscular contraction causes the intrafusal fibers to relax, which in turn will reduce activity in the sensory endings and suppress further contraction. When the gamma system is active, tension remains on the intrafusal fibers, and the muscle continues to contract.

prepare to make a movement also is related directly to activity in the gamma system. By increasing the firing rate of gamma motor neurons, we "bias" our muscles for movement by increasing their overall activity. Thus, the gamma system allows us to anticipate muscle contraction and movement. It also allows us to adjust muscle output automatically if we experience a change in load. Our ability to keep an arm outstretched even if someone places a weight on it is mediated directly by the gamma system.

As you may have guessed, gamma motor neurons are controlled by inputs from the brain. By adjusting activity in the gamma system, the brain plays a direct role in controlling muscular tension. The brain also controls movement by regulating the activity of the alpha motor neurons. Inputs from the brain synapse onto these cells and summate with the spinal inputs to determine the level of alpha activity. The brain, therefore, plays a very direct role in movement, even very simple reflexes. The moment someone promises to pay you a large sum of money if you keep your hand on a hot stove for a few seconds is the moment that this role becomes very obvious. In the following section, we will describe how specific areas of the brain regulate movement.

Control of Movement by the Brain

A large portion of the brain is devoted to movement. As you will see, however, the brain's motor systems arise primarily from circumscribed sites in the cerebral cortex, the basal forebrain, and the brain stem. They work together to control and direct all types of voluntary movement.

Descending Motor Pathways

The brain regulates spinal motor neurons by three major pathways. One of these originates in the cerebral cortex and projects directly to motor areas of the spinal cord. The axons that make up this pathway, known as the **corticospinal tract,** are among the longest in the human body (typically three or four feet). As they descend through the medulla, they are stacked in the form of a pyramid, thus giving this pathway its other name, the **pyramidal tract.** The axons in this tract are crossed: those arising from the right side of cortex cross over to the left side of the nervous system and vice versa. In primates, about 80 percent of the axons cross, or **decussate** (from the Latin, meaning "to cross in the form of an X"), at the lower level of the medulla. The remaining pyramidal fibers that do not decussate in the medulla eventually do so in the spinal cord. Thus, this motor pathway is completely crossed in primates. When you move your left hand, the corresponding area of your right cortex is active. The course of the pyramidal tract from cerebral cortex to spinal cord is shown in figure 9.16.

　　Two other motor pathways are the **rubrospinal tract,** its name derived from the red nucleus (*rubro* in Latin means "red"), and the **reticulospinal tract,** which as its name suggests originates in the reticular formation. The

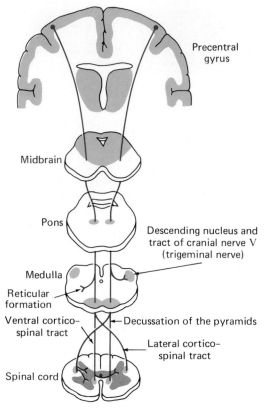

Figure 9.16 Ventral view of the course of the pyramidal tract through the brain and into the spinal cord. Note the axon collaterals to the reticular formation and the crossing or decussation of the pyramids.

Adapted with permission from Matzke, H. A. and F. M. Foltz, *Synopsis of Neuroanatomy*, 2d ed. Copyright © 1972, Oxford University Press, New York.

red nucleus, so called because of the reddish tint of its cell bodies, lies in the ventral portion of the midbrain and receives information from the cerebellum and the basal ganglia, two subcortical areas that play an important role in movement. The reticulospinal tract conveys motor information from the descending reticular formation into the spinal cord. Both tracts and the structures that contribute to them are shown in figure 9.17.

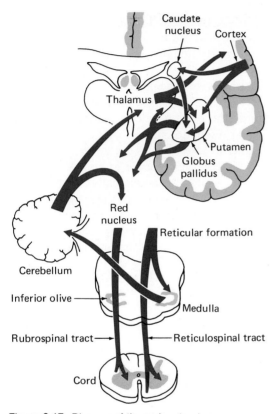

Figure 9.17 Diagram of the major structures
associated with the rubrospinal and reticulospinal
tracts and some of their interconnections.

Adapted with permission from Matzke, H. A. and F. M. Foltz,
Synopsis of Neuroanatomy, 2d ed. Copyright © 1972, Oxford
University Press, New York.

Traditionally, the corticospinal tract has
been regarded as completely separate from the
rubrospinal and reticulospinal tracts. In fact,
it has been treated as an independent motor
system known as the **pyramidal motor system**
because it forms the pyramidal tract. The rubrospinal and reticulospinal pathways are not
part of the pyramidal tract, and thus they have
been lumped together to form a second system,
the **extrapyramidal motor system.** The traditional view of the function of the pyramidal

system is that it mediates voluntary movements, especially those that require precise
control. This view is correct as far as it goes,
but it does not really aid us in distinguishing
between the roles of this system and of the extrapyramidal system. After all, both systems
interact extensively. Axons in the pyramidal
tract, for example, send collaterals that join
both the rubrospinal and reticulospinal tracts.
In addition, structures that contribute fibers
to the extrapyramidal motor system also send
fibers to the thalamus, which in turn projects
to the motor cortex, the origin of the pyramidal system.

It is best to view the functions of the three
descending motor pathways as synergistic. In
primates, each pathway is necessary for normal
movement, but each one makes a unique contribution. Consider what happens when each
of these pathways is damaged separately.
When the corticospinal pathway is destroyed,
lasting deficits occur in the control of fine
movements, especially those involving small
muscle groups in the extremeties. Lesions of
the reticulospinal system, on the other hand,
interfere with the operation of the muscles that
lie along the midline of the body. Rubrospinal-
system lesions produce deficits in the gross
motor control of the limbs. According to Kuypers (1982), who performed many of these
lesion experiments, the reticulospinal and rubrospinal tracts control basic bodily movements as well as corresponding movements of
the limbs. The corticospinal tract amplifies
these functions and adds the capacity to exe-
cute highly fractionated movements of the extremities, including independent movements
of the fingers.

The information contained in the descending motor pathways, of course, must arise
from those brain structures that contribute to

these pathways, including the motor areas of cerebral cortex, the cerebellum, the basal ganglia, and the descending reticular formation. It is in these structures that all types of voluntary movement take shape. They will be examined in turn in the following sections.

Motor Areas of Cerebral Cortex

If certain areas of the cerebral cortex are stimulated by passing electrical current through an electrode placed on the cortical surface, discrete groups of skeletal muscles contract. In fact, if the stimulation is weak enough, stimulation of some electrode locations results in contraction of a single muscle.

By using this stimulation technique both in experimental animals and in humans undergoing brain surgery, investigators have constructed a motor map of the cortex. Figure 9.18 shows that the primary motor area of the cortex is located on the **precentral gyrus,** just across the central sulcus (fissure) from the primary somatosensory cortex discussed in chapter 8.

The various muscle groups of the body are represented topographically along the precentral gyrus, as shown in the cross-sectional diagram in figure 9.19. As you can see, the various parts of the body are represented in order from the toes at the uppermost medial

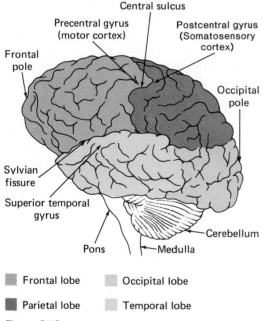

Figure 9.18 A surface view of the brain from the left side showing the location of the primary motor cortex on the precentral gyrus and the somatosensory cortex on the postcentral gyrus.

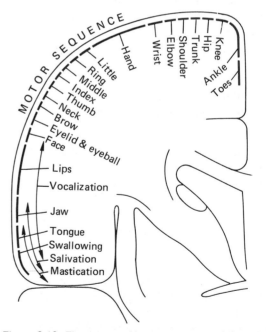

Figure 9.19 The topographic representation of the body on the precentral gyrus in a cross-sectional view. The relative area of motor cortex projecting to the skeletal muscles of each part of the body is indicated by the length of the lines.

portion to the face along the lower side. The most important feature of this diagram, however, is that the area of cortex that controls each set of muscles does not correspond to the relative size of these muscles. Thus, the space on the cortex devoted to the muscles of the hands, lips, fingers, and tongue is far greater than that allotted to the much larger muscles of the trunk, legs, and arms.

The amount of cortex devoted to each muscle group is determined by the precision with which we move these muscles rather than by their sheer size. Although you may not be surprised to learn that the muscles controlling your hands and fingers are under precise control, many people do not think of their lips and tongue as exquisitely precise motor systems, yet they are. Speaking requires very precise muscular control. In fact, language and the use of tools represent two of the most characteristic features of the human species and both are based on the precise motor control made possible by the evolution of the cerebral cortex.

Cellular Anatomy   Primary motor cortex, like all areas of cerebral cortex, consists of six cellular layers. One of the most distinguishing features of primary motor cortex, however, is the fifth cellular layer, which contains the largest cells found anywhere in the cerebral cortex. These cells are called giant **pyramidal cells** for the pyramidlike shape of their cell bodies. They also are known as **Betz cells.** A drawing of some of these cells as they appear when stained by the Golgi method is shown in figure 9.20. Their dendrites extend upward through other cortical layers, and their axons descend through the pyramidal tract and into the spinal cord where many of them form direct monosynaptic connections with motor

neurons. Others terminate on various interneurons in the spinal cord and thus affect motor neurons indirectly through more than one synapse.

The giant Betz cells of the precentral gyrus are not the only neurons that contribute axons to the pyramidal tract. In fact, these cells comprise less than half of this motor pathway. Neurons in several cortical areas contribute axons, including cells in the primary **somatosensory cortex.** Not surprisingly, electrical stimulation of this area also produces discrete movements, even if the precentral gyrus is destroyed. Because many regions of cortex are part of the pyramidal tract, the bodily movements caused by activity in this tract do not arise from a single cortical area.

Just as the pyramidal tract is formed from cells in different parts of cerebral cortex, the axons in this tract influence neurons in many areas of the nervous system in addition to those in the spinal cord. Many of these axons send collaterals to nuclei in the brain stem reticular formation and to sensory relay nuclei in the pons and medulla. Some collaterals also terminate in the nucleus cuneatus and nucleus gracilis, two important relay nuclei in the lemniscal pathways. These connections to incoming sensory relay stations may contribute to the brain's ability to control its own sensory input in a way consistent with ongoing motor activity. You will recall from chapter 8, for example, that stimulation of the pyramidal tract modifies the receptive fields of neurons in somatosensory cortex.

Columnar Organization   More than one hundred pyramidal tract fibers must be active in order to activate a single alpha motor neuron in the spinal cord. Thus, there must be groups

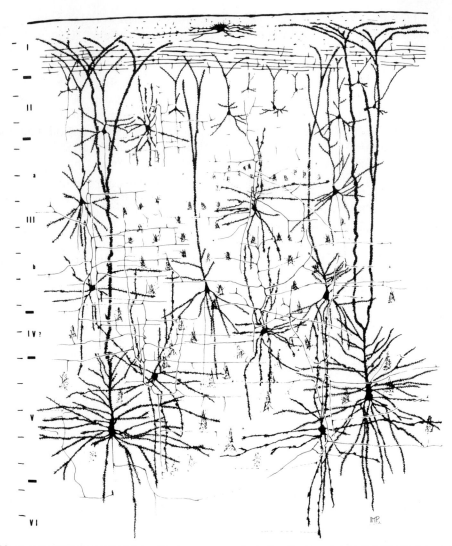

Figure 9.20 A composite drawing of the various neuronal types in the precentral gyrus made from postmortem human brain sections stained by the rapid Golgi technique. Note particularly the many dendrites (dense, fuzzy projections) of the giant pyramidal cells including the long apical dendrite that rises to layer 1 and spreads horizontally. The thin lines descending directly from the pyramidal cell bodies are the axons that become the pyramidal tract. Note their many branches or axon collaterals which provide the basis for the lateral inhibiton discussed in the text.

or colonies of cortical cells whose outputs converge onto a single motor neuron. Moreover, if muscles are to contract in a coordinated fashion, many alpha motor neurons must be activated simultaneously (recall that muscles are made up of many motor units, each innervated by its own alpha motor neuron). For this reason, the colonies of cortical neurons that excite alpha motor neurons of the same muscle overlap one another. This insures that the entire group of alpha motor neurons will be activated and that the muscle will contract smoothly. These functional colonies of cortical neurons are organized into columns, an arrangement termed **columnar organization.** We saw in an earlier chapter that columnar organization plays an important role in areas of cortex involved in sensation and perception. The fact that the motor system uses it as well indicates that the grouping of neurons with related functions into columns is a widespread feature of the cerebral cortex.

Perhaps the most elegant demonstration of columnar organization in primary motor cortex was presented by Asanuma and Rosen (1972). In their experiment, they first lowered a microelectrode into the left-thumb region of the precentral gyrus of a monkey. Then they passed a weak electrical current through the microelectrode and observed the resulting movement of the thumb. Next, they lowered the microelectrode a little further, stimulated, and observed the movement again. By painstakingly repeating this procedure at different points in the cortex about 1 millimeter apart, they were able to construct the map shown in figure 9.21. As you can see, the points that when stimulated caused the same muscle in the thumb to contract are found in a column of tissue roughly perpendicular to the surface of

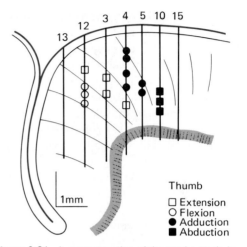

Figure 9.21 A reconstruction of the tracks made by electrodes lowered systematically into the thumb area of the motor cortex of the monkey shown in cross section. The effects of stimulation through the microelectrodes are shown by the symbols and indicate movements of the thumb, as defined in the lower right-hand corner.

the cortex. The size of these columns is such that they each contain hundreds of cortical neurons.

This organization of primary motor cortex into functional groupings illustrates several important points. First, as we mentioned earlier, it allows for the coordinated activation of all neurons that converge onto a single alpha motor neuron. It also allows for the coordinated activation of all columns of neurons that activate the alpha motor neurons of the same muscle. Another interesting feature of columnar organization is that opposing muscles are controlled by adjacent columns, as indicated by the squares and circles in figure 9.21. This feature enables activity in one column to inhibit activity in adjacent columns. Such an arrangement is perfect for muscles because they work in a reciprocal fashion (recall that movement requires both contraction of one muscle and relaxation of the opposing muscle). Thus, when one column is active and one group of alpha motor neurons are active, the column that controls the alpha motor neurons of the opposing muscle is inhibited. The anatomical organization of motor cortex, therefore, contributes elegantly to function.

Functions Evarts (1976) described a series of experiments that provide remarkable insight into how primary motor cortex operates. In these experiments, monkeys were trained to push or pull a handle when it began to shake. Moving the handle as it shook earned them a sip of fruit juice as a reward. In addition, a red or a green light was flashed several seconds before the handle shook. If the light was red, the monkey was to respond by pulling on the handle (flexion of the elbow). If the light was green, the correct response was pushing (extension of the elbow). In either case, the animal had to wait until the handle actually shook before making the response (otherwise, there was no reward). During thousands of repetitions of this paradigm, Evarts and his coworkers used microelectrodes to record the activity of the Betz cells in the precentral gyrus.

What did these investigators find? First, the neurons were almost always active, even when there was no muscle contraction. More importantly, the recordings revealed that these neurons changed their activity in response to the red or the green light almost an entire second before the handle shook and the muscular response occurred. In addition, the way in which neuronal activity changed depended on whether the light was red or green. Thus, simply anticipating a flexion or an extension response elicited different patterns of pyramidal neuron activity. Keep in mind that any

change in cortical activity occurs long before any overt motor response. This means that pyramidal neurons are responding to the intention to move and not just to the sensory feedback that comes from movements already in progress.

These findings also shed some light on the question of why it takes so many active pyramidal cells to discharge an alpha motor neuron. The high threshold of motor neurons to excitation of the pyramidal tract enables the pattern of activity in motor cortex to be adjusted in response to changing conditions (in this case an external signal) without causing an inappropriate movement. You also should keep in mind that even if the pyramidal tract is not active enough to discharge an alpha motor neuron, it still can influence that neuron. Consider what happened when Evarts tested the strength of his monkey's spinal reflexes during the waiting period between the light and the handle shake. If the animal had received a signal that made it want to flex its elbow, then the strength of the reflexes of that limb involving flexors was enhanced, but not the strength of extension reflexes. Similarly, if the animal was waiting to extend its elbow, then extension but not flexion reflexes were enhanced. In short, subthreshold activity in the pyramidal tract has an effect on alpha motor neurons, even if it does not cause them to fire an action potential. Thus, the fairly large amount of pyramidal activity necessary to activate alpha motor neurons does not reflect a lack of efficiency in communication. The motor cortex is not yelling at the spinal cord because of a poor connection! Rather, activity in the cortex can be very effective in regulating the subthreshold excitability of spinal neurons, making them more responsive to other input. Only when the cortex itself wants to drive motor neurons directly are a large number of pyramidal cells required to be active. Apparently, nature has been cautious in committing us to overt movement. Before we can make ourselves move, a large number of cells in the cortex already must have made the decision to do so.

Because the motor cortex is active before movements start, you may wonder if the decision to make a voluntary movement originates there. The answer appears to be no. Kornhuber (1974) recorded electrical potentials from the scalp of human subjects while they voluntarily moved their right index finger at random intervals. He then analyzed the potentials that occurred before movement was produced. His analysis first revealed a widespread negative potential that occurs bilaterally over most of the cerebral cortex about 0.8 second before the subjects move their fingers. This is known as a **readiness potential** and is followed by a similarly widespread positive potential occurring 80–90 milliseconds before movement. Not until about 50 milliseconds before the right index finger actually moves does a **motor potential** appear over the left precentral gyrus. We can conclude, therefore, that the motor cortex is not the only, or even the primary, area of the brain involved in making the decision to initiate a voluntary movement. That decision seems to be made over a much larger area of the cerebral cortex. Presumably, motor cortex acts as a control center that integrates information from diverse areas of the brain before sending movement commands to the spinal cord.

Cerebellum

The cerebellum is located behind the cerebral hemisphere. It is attached to the pons by large bundles of axons known as **peduncles.** As you can see in figure 9.22, the cerebellum is covered by a cortex that is extremely convoluted,

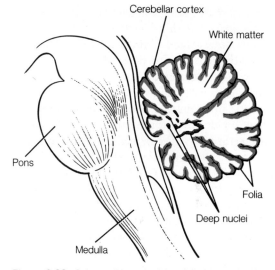

Figure 9.22 Schematic sagittal section through the cerebellum and lower brain stem. Note the outer cortex, inner white matter, and deep nuclei of the cerebellum.

consisting of many regular folds, or **folia.** In fact, the sheer number of folia in such a compact space makes the cerebellum look like a miniature version of the cerebral cortex and gives the cerebellum its name (cerebellum is derived from the Latin meaning "little brain"). Beneath the foliated cortex is the white matter of the cerebellum, consisting of many myelinated fibers that form the peduncles. Buried within the depths of the white matter are **deep cerebellar nuclei.** The cells of these nuclei take complete responsibility for sending information out of the cerebellum to the rest of the brain.

Anatomical Organization   The most striking feature of the cerebellum is its regular geometric pattern. The neuronal elements in each folium are organized in essentially the same pattern throughout the cerebellum. This pattern is centered around a group of neurons known as **Purkinje cells.** Their cell bodies are arranged in a thin sheet about 400 microns below the surface. They give rise to dendrites that branch upward in a single plane, much like an ornate candelabra. If you can envision thousands of these candelabras, each one placed immediately after the other, then you have an idea of how the dendrites of these cells are arranged. An even cruder analogy, but one that we will come back to shortly, is a long line of telephone poles. The axons of Purkinje cells extend in the other direction, down toward the white matter where eventually they synapse onto cells in the deep cerebellar nuclei. Each axon also branches as it leaves the cell body and forms a dense net near the cell body of neighboring Purkinje cells.

The other cells in the cortex of the cerebellum are very small and do not send their axons out to other structures. Thus, they are known as **intrinsic neurons.** One type of intrinsic neuron is the **granule cell.** Large groups of granule cells are located just below the layer of Purkinje cells. Each granule cell has tiny dendrites and a very thin axon that travels up toward the cerebellar surface. As the axon approaches the surface, it divides in two branches, forming the letter T. Each branch runs horizontally along the cortical surface where it becomes known as a **parallel fiber.** Thus, the parallel fibers pass perpendicularly through the plane of the Purkinje cell dendrites, much like wires running from one telephone pole to the next.

Golgi cells comprise another group of intrinsic neurons. Their cell bodies are scattered in the same general region as the granule cells. Their axons branch extensively and terminate on granule cell dendrites. The final type of intrinsic neuron that we will mention is the **basket cell,** located just above the layer of Purkinje cells. Basket cells are known for their curving axons that wrap around Purkinje cell bodies almost like a straw basket.

Input to the cerebellum comes from fibers that pass through the peduncles and wind their way through the white matter to the cerebellar cortex. Some of these axons are very thin and branch extensively as they approach the cortical surface. In this respect, they resemble vines climbing up a garden wall and thus are called **climbing fibers.** They originate in the **inferior olive,** an area of the pons that, in turn, receives input from the cerebral cortex, brain stem, and the spinal cord. Thus, climbing fibers convey information to the cerebellum from all levels of the central nervous system. Another group of axons that projects to the cerebellum is known as **mossy fibers,** so called because they form large mosslike terminals. These fibers arise from nuclei throughout the pons and from the spinal cord. Mossy fibers are much more numerous than climbing fibers, but they, too, carry a wide variety of information.

A three-dimensional section through one of the folia of the cerebellum is shown in figure 9.23. Examples of all of the cell types and inputs, including their unusual shapes, are visible here. The arrows indicate the flow of information.

What type of information does the cerebellum receive? It receives information about all aspects of movement. From the spinal cord, the cerebellum learns about the position of the limbs and the extent of muscular contraction. From the vestibular nuclei of the brain stem, the cerebellum receives information about balance and the position of the head in space. And from the cerebral cortex, the cerebellum learns what type of information the pyramidal system is sending out to the muscles. The cerebellum, therefore, is in an ideal position to regulate and control movement.

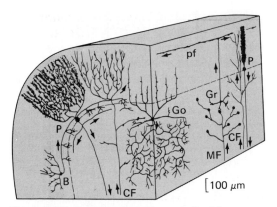

Figure 9.23 Cross section of a cerebellar folium showing the location and relations of neural elements (P=Purkinje cell; B=basket cell; Go=Golgi cell; Gr=granule cell; CF=climbing fiber; MF=mossy fiber; pf=parallel fiber. Arrows indicate the direction of impulse flow).

Adapted with permission from Shepherd, Gordon M., *The Synaptic Organization of the Brain.* Copyright © 1974, Oxford University Press, New York.

If you are impressed by numbers, then you should be impressed by the numbers of the cerebellum. The surface area of the human cerebellum is huge; if it were laid out flat, it would cover about eight square feet. In humans, the cerebellum contains over 14 million Purkinje cells and almost 40 billion granule cells—a lot of telephone poles and a lot of wires. In the next section, we will see how this unusual system of connections works. This is even more impressive.

Functions If there is one area of the brain that acts most like a computer, it is the cerebellum. This structure functions as an error-correcting device for rapid movements. By rapid movements, we mean movements that occur too fast to be influenced by sensory feedback; movements like throwing or hitting a ball are good examples because once such movements begin we are unable to make a midcourse correction. We do not have the luxury,

for example, of monitoring the sensory feedback from our outstretched arm as we try to return a blistering serve from a tennis opponent. Instead, we activate the cerebellum and swing as best we can. In a matter of a few milliseconds, the cerebellum computes the information that it receives on limb and head position, factors this in with information on ongoing movements, and then sends out signals that maintain posture and smooth out muscular contractions. How does the cerebellum do it?

To answer that question, we first must look at how its neurons operate. All of the neurons of the cerebellar cortex are inhibitory except for the granule cells. This means that all excitatory input from the climbing and mossy fibers is converted to an inhibition in, at most, two synapses. Thus, the cerebellum can "reset" itself very quickly whenever the climbing or mossy fibers become active. This feature allows the cerebellum to respond to new input fast enough to control rapid movements. Another important feature of the cerebellar cortex is that the branches of Purkinje cell axons inhibit neighboring Purkinje cells. This means that if a given Purkinje cell is active, it will tend to inhibit the Purkinje cells surrounding it. In addition, these axon branches also inhibit the basket cells, which in turn inhibit the same Purkinje cells. Thus, by inhibiting the inhibitory input that they receive from basket cells, Purkinje cells help to keep themselves active. An active Purkinje cell, therefore, inhibits its neighbors and reinforces its own excitation. Thus, across the cerebellar cortex there will be many islands of activated Purkinje cells separated by surrounding areas of inhibition. The borders of these excitatory and inhibitory zones constantly shift as the cells fight for dominance. These zones of excitation saccades (sah-kād)

and inhibition allow the cerebellum to participate in complex movements, which require the contraction and relaxation of many different groups of muscles.

The main branch of the Purkinje cell axon extends, as we have seen, through the white matter of the cerebellum and synapses onto the deep cerebellar nuclei. This is the only output pathway from the cerebellar cortex, and it, too, is inhibitory. There is no excitatory output from the cerebellar cortex. The deep nuclei, however, are excitatory, and they send projections to various motor areas of the nervous system. These motor areas include the **ventral lateral thalamus,** which projects to the motor cortex, and the **red nucleus** and the **descending reticular formation,** both of which project to motor neurons in the spinal cord. Thus, the cerebellum is part of a neuronal circuit that exerts control over both the pyramidal system and the final common pathway.

The deep cerebellar nuclei also project to the **oculomotor nuclei,** which control the muscles that move the eyeball in its socket. In fact, it is the control that the cerebellum exerts over eye movements that has provided the most insight into its function. When we scan an object or a stationary scene, our eyes do not move slowly, but instead make fast, jerky movements called **saccades.** In short, our eyes dart and stop repeatedly. Persons with cerebellar damage lose control of these movements. They are unable to move and then hold their eyes in precise steps. The cerebellum, therefore, seems to be responsible for both holding and releasing rapid movements.

Control of eye movement is not the only function of the cerebellum. It also times these holding and releasing functions precisely. How? Kornhuber (1975) suggests that it does

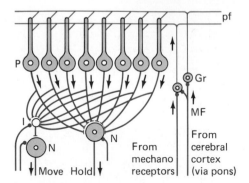

Figure 9.24 A delay-line model for a cerebellar timing circuit (Gr=granule cell; P=Purkinje cell; I=inhibitory interneuron; pf=parallel fibers; N=output neurons of the deep cerebellar nuclei; MF=mossy fiber).

so by acting as a **delay-line timer.** To understand this function of the cerebellum, look at the diagram of cerebellar circuits in figure 9.24. Note that the parallel fibers, which arise from granule cells, excite a long row of Purkinje cells. The length of time between the excitation of the first and last Purkinje cells in the row depends on the length and conduction velocity of the parallel fiber. Because parallel fibers have a length of about 5 millimeters and conduct action potentials as slowly as 0.05 meter/second, delays of 100 milliseconds are possible. If all the Purkinje cells in a row synapse on the same cell in the deep nuclei, that cell can be inhibited continuously for the entire length of time that the parallel fiber is active (up to 100 milliseconds in our example). If, as shown in the diagram, this cell in the deep nuclei is a "hold" cell, then the process of holding movements will be inhibited when the Purkinje cells are active (recall that Purkinje cells are inhibitory). At the same time, these Purkinje cells inhibit an interneuron in the deep nuclei that normally inhibits a "move" cell. This circuit through the interneuron releases its "move" cell from inhibition, and the end result is the release of rapid movement for as long as the Purkinje cells are active. When these cells are silent, which will occur if there is no activity in the climbing or mossy fibers, then the "hold" cell in the deep nuclei will be active, the "move" neuron will be inhibited, and rapid movement will be held in check. All that is required to reset the clock and release rapid movement is some excitatory input onto the granule cells.

In summary, when the Purjinke cells are silent, the output cells of the deep cerebellar nuclei provide a holding signal that inhibits rapid movements. When the Purkinje cells are active, the holding signal is inhibited and movements are released. The timing for these holding and releasing functions is controlled by the parallel fibers, which synapse directly onto rows of Purkinje cells.

This model fits perfectly with clinical observations of patients who have suffered cerebellar damage. When the damage is confined to the deep nuclei, patients at rest display a tremor (resting tremor) presumably because the holding function of the cerebellum is disrupted. Conversely, persons with damage to the cerebellar cortex, which includes the Purkinje cells, display a tremor only when they move (intention tremor). The delay-line function of the parallel fibers is evident in elderly persons suffering from a progressive degeneration of the cerebellum. This illness destroys the thinnest (and therefore the slowest conducting) parallel fibers first. Thus, the first rapid movements affected are the ones of longest duration, and there is a progressive shortening of rapid movements as the disease worsens.

You can demonstrate the opposing roles of the deep nuclei and cerebellar cortex by bringing your finger up to your nose as quickly as possible. The rapid initial movement is controlled by the cerebellar cortex, and the rapid

halt represents the deep nuclei recovering their holding function.

Although the cerebellum is critical for rapid movements, it does not act alone. In fact, it acts closely with the primary motor cortex during a wide variety of movements. When we prepare to initiate a voluntary movement, pyramidal cells in motor cortex change their activity. This change is relayed to the cerebellum, where certain delay lines are activated. The resulting cerebellar time signal is relayed by way of the thalamus back to motor cortex, where commands are sent to the spinal cord. Once the movement begins, the cerebellum receives sensory information from the spinal cord, and this new information will determine which delay lines are activated next (for example, is the limb in the desired place, or is more movement required?).

The cerebellum also appears to interact with primary cortex during complicated-movement learning. At first, when we learn a complicated activity like skiing or riding a bicycle, we perform our movements slowly and deliberately. We seem to think about each movement we make. Eventually, the movements become automatic and require no conscious effort. At this point, the cerebellum has taken over, freeing up the rest of the brain for other activities. This role of the cerebellum is most evident in patients who have suffered cerebellar damage. They report that they must think about each aspect of complicated movements that before the injury seemed completely automatic. Certainly, the enormous number of cerebellar neurons and the regularity of their connections makes the cerebellum especially suited for the automatic control of learned movements, a topic that we will return to in chapter 14.

Basal Ganglia

What the cerebellum is to rapid movements, the basal ganglia are to slow movements. The normal movements of the limbs during walking are the kinds of slow movements controlled by the basal ganglia. In fact, muscles that are not regulated by the basal ganglia are incapable of slow, voluntary movements. The importance of the basal ganglia in such movements was realized initially from observations of patients with Parkinson's disease, a disorder caused by the degeneration of dopamine terminals in the basal ganglia (Kornhuber 1975). This disease is characterized by extreme difficulty in initiating movements, especially the slow, purposeful movements in walking. As you soon will see, however, the basal ganglia do not function simply as a slow-movement generator. Indeed, the complex role of this structure in movement is rivaled only by its complex anatomy.

The basal ganglia consist of three large nuclei buried deep within the cerebral hemispheres on each side of the brain. One of these nuclei has a long curving tail so is called the **caudate nucleus** (from the Latin, meaning "tail"). Immediately adjacent to the caudate nucleus is the **putamen,** which has an oval shape similar to a peach pit (the Latin is helpful here, too, since putamen refers to the part of a fruit that remains as waste). The third component of the basal ganglia is shaped like a globe having very pale markings; hence, it has the name **globus pallidus.** All three structures are laced with myelinated fibers and when cut in cross-section, they have a striped or striated appearance. Because the caudate nucleus and putamen are phylogenetically newer than the globus pallidus, these two structures often are treated as one, and together they are known as the **neostriatum,** or "new striped body." The globus pallidus is the

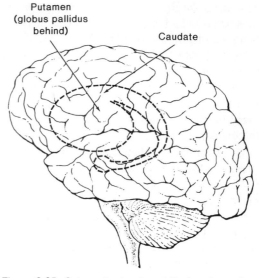

Figure 9.25 Schematic drawing of the basal ganglia including the putamen, globus pallidus, and caudate nucleus. These structures are buried beneath the cerebral cortex in the basal forebrain.

paleostriatum, or "old striped body." The relative location of these structures within the cerebral hemisphere is shown in figure 9.25 (see also color plate 3).

The cellular anatomy of the basal ganglia appears to be much more complex than that of the cerebellum and primary motor cortex. Complexity, of course, is a relative term, and although you may think that the anatomy of the cerebellum is complex, it is at least regular and predictable. As we have seen, each folium with its regular rows of parallel fibers and Purkinje dendrites looks almost exactly like every other folium. Similarly, primary motor cortex is organized into well-defined layers. By contrast, the basal ganglia, especially the neostriatum, have none of these features. There are no distinct layers of cells in the neostriatum, and until recently there was believed to be no obvious pattern to the maze of dendrites and axons that course through this structure. In fact, for many years anatomists treated the neostriatum as a relatively homogeneous mass of neurons that performed relatively simple functions like the control of muscle tone. No one holds this view today, but many improvements in histological and behavioral techniques were necessary before some long-held opinions began to change (see color plate 3*b*).

The turning point began with the observation that inputs to the neostriatum were not distributed uniformly (Kemp and Powell 1971). The major inputs come from the cerebral cortex, and although virtually all areas of cortex send information to the neostriatum, they do so in a distinct pattern. At the very least, this suggests some type of regional specialization within the neostriatum. Recordings of neuronal activity in awake, behaving animals support this idea. Cells in neostriatal areas that receive input from motor cortex, for example, respond vigorously during movement, whereas cells that receive input from other areas of cortex often respond before movement begins or change their activity in a manner that is not linked closely to actual movement at all (Gardiner, Iverson, and Rebec 1986). The presence of such cells contradicts the view of the basal ganglia as a simple motor area. Instead, structures in the basal ganglia may contain assemblies of neurons that are involved in different stages of behavior, including the integration of sensory information that occurs during the preparation of movement (Rolls et al. 1979).

The neostriatum also receives major inputs from the thalamus and the substantia nigra. Thalamic fibers appear to convey sensory and motor information from subcortical structures, including the cerebellum. The nigral projection, on the other hand, may have a more general function. This pathway, which contains dopamine, seems to influence how information is processed in the neostriatum. When dopamine is applied to neostriatal neurons in behaving animals, the response of these neurons to other inputs is enhanced (Rolls et al. 1984). Dopamine causes this enhancement by decreasing spontaneous activity. When spontaneous activity is reduced, the change in firing rate caused by an incoming signal will be much more noticeable and thus more likely to be transmitted through the neostriatum, as shown in figure 9.26. Note that in the absence of dopamine, an incoming signal is virtually buried in ongoing spontaneous activity. When dopamine reduces this background activity, however, the same input signal now appears to be much larger.

This model may be relevant to the impaired ability of Parkinson's disease patients to initiate movement. According to Rolls and co-workers (1984), the lack of dopamine in these patients would increase the noise level in the neostriatum and impair the transmission of important information related to movement, including sensory and motor information from cortical and thalamic inputs. These investigators believe that in the normal situation, dopamine release in different parts of the neostriatum determines which signals are passed through the neostriatum and thus which behavioral responses are emitted. Our choice of movements, therefore, depends on dopamine as a selective enhancer of information transmission through the neostriatum. Parkinsonian patients are deprived of this selection process and, as a result, have a much more difficult time initiating movement. Parkinson's disease and other neurological disorders will be discussed in more detail in chapter 15.

The primary cell type within the neostriatum is known as a **spiny I** cell for the large number of spines that dot its dendrites (Pasik,

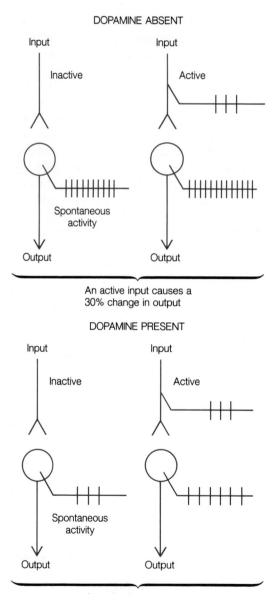

DOPAMINE ABSENT

An active input causes a
30% change in output

DOPAMINE PRESENT

An active input causes a
100% change in output

Figure 9.26 Proposed role of dopamine in enhancing the flow of information through the neostriatum. Without dopamine, an active input causes only a small change above background activity. With dopamine, background activity is reduced, allowing the same input to exert a relatively greater effect.

Pasik, and DiFiglia 1979). It has a rounded cell body with numerous dendrites and a thin axon that gives rise to several branches. The main segment of the axon projects to the globus pallidus and the substantia nigra. Over 95 percent of the neurons in the neostriatum are spiny I cells. The globus pallidus and substantia nigra in turn send axons to that portion of the thalamus that communicates with the precentral gyrus. Thus, information from widespread areas of cortex and thalamus is funneled through the basal ganglia and ultimately relayed to primary motor cortex.

The spiny I cell appears to play a critical role in this funneling process. It receives convergent input from cortex and thalamus as well as from dopamine-containing neurons in substantia nigra. Thus, this cell is situated perfectly to process incoming information and send it on to other structures. Another feature of spiny I neurons is that they interact to form a lateral inhibitory network, illustrated schematically in figure 9.27. The anatomy of this network was discovered by injecting horseradish peroxidase into these cells and then reacting it to cause the entire neuron to turn a dark blue, brown, or black (Wilson and Groves 1980). This procedure makes it possible to visualize these cells under a microscope and to trace their axonal projections. As you can see, each spiny I cell gives off axon collaterals that inhibit neighboring spiny I cells. Like lateral inhibitory interactions in various sensory systems, the lateral inhibitory network formed by spiny I neurons filters incoming signals to refine and sharpen the diffuse information that these neurons receive from other structures (Groves 1983). This arrangement allows incoming sensory and motor information to be molded into a distinct pattern that then can be relayed via the globus pallidus and substantia nigra to the thalamus and then on to motor cortex. In addition, different groups of spiny I

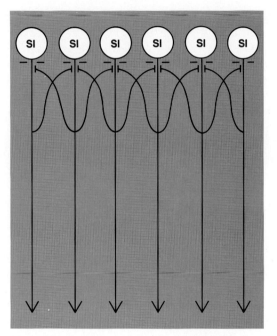

Figure 9.27 Lateral inhibitory network formed by spiny I (SI) cells in the neostriatum. Axon collaterals inhibit neighboring SI cells.

throughout the neostriatum, but may shift from one region to another depending on the overall pattern of information flow through this structure. Interestingly, the distribution of acetylcholinesterase, the enzyme that breaks down acetylcholine, shows an exact spatial correspondence with the dopamine patches in young animals (Graybiel 1983). The uneven distribution of acetylcholinesterase, however, persists even in adults. Zones of low acetylcholinesterase activity in the neostriatum have been termed **striosomes** (Graybiel 1983), and extensive research shows that these correspond to a patchy distribution of other putative neurotransmitters and neuromodulators, even in the adult brain. Figure 9.28, for example, shows the distribution of the neuropeptide enkephalin in the caudate nucleus of the cat. It has now been established that these patches of enkephalin, seen with immunocytochemical staining procedures, are in the same positions as patches of low acetylcholinesterase staining. When these patches are assembled by means of computer-assisted three-dimensional reconstruction from serial sections, a clear three-dimensional latticelike structure is apparent within the caudate nucleus, as illustrated in color plate 3 (Martone et al. 1986).

We still have a great deal to learn about the organization of the basal ganglia. It is not yet clear, for example, how the distribution of spiny I cells corresponds to striosomes, nor is it clear if other cellular and neurochemical zones exist within the neostriatum. One intriguing possibility is that different neurochemical systems, organized into patterns that we do not yet understand, mediate the flow of different types of information. A major research effort is underway to unravel the link between neurochemistry and function in the basal ganglia.

cells may funnel different types of information. Thus, the neostriatum may consist of many different information circuits, all of which may be necessary for the execution of complex movements (Alexander, DeLong, and Strick 1986). The basal ganglia, therefore, are part of a cortical-thalamic loop in which diffuse information is sharpened and eventually funneled to motor cortex where it can be integrated into a specific behavioral pattern.

At the neurochemical level, the neostriatum also appears to be organized into distinct networks. In the neostriatum of young animals, for example, dopamine appears in patches; only in adults does this neurotransmitter show a uniform distribution (Olson, Sieger, and Fuxe 1972). Moreover, as we have seen, the release of dopamine from axon terminals may not occur uniformly

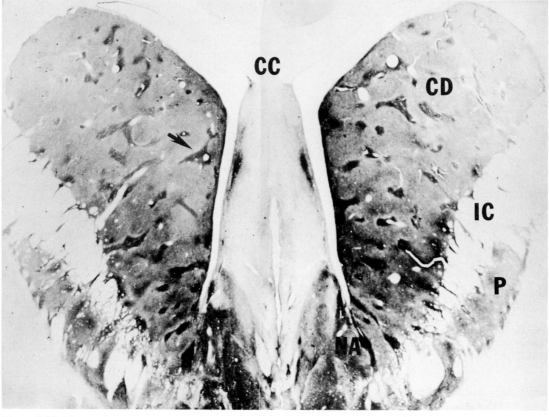

Figure 9.28 The patchy appearance and distribution of the zones showing regions of intense enkephalin staining in the caudate nucleus of the cat brain using immunocytochemical procedures (the patch of enkephalin stain is indicated by the arrow; CC=corpus callosum; CD=caudate nucleus, IC=internal capsule; P=putamen). These patches correspond to the same places in the caudate nucleus known as striosomes, patchy areas low in acetylcholinesterase content. A computer-assisted three-dimensional reconstruction of these patches from serial sections reveals a three-dimensional pattern not apparent in the image of a single section (see color plate 3).

Descending Reticular Formation

A general function of the reticular formation is to integrate information from all levels of the central nervous system. Comprised of more than one hundred nuclei lying in the core of the brain stem from the thalamus to the spinal cord, the reticular formation receives input from every major system of the brain as well as from all incoming sensory modalities. The descending portion of the reticular formation includes those reticular nuclei that send their axons into the spinal cord or to the cranial nerves. Thus, the descending reticular formation is situated perfectly to integrate a wide variety of information and then to use this information to regulate movement.

Consistent with this integrative role, the descending reticular formation receives input from the basal ganglia and cerebellum. In fact, both of these brain areas influence motor neurons via the <u>**reticulospinal tract,**</u> a multisynaptic pathway that originates in the reticular formation. This tract eventually terminates on gamma motor neurons or on spinal interneurons that synapse on alpha motor neurons.

One function of the descending reticular formation is to modulate certain reflexes. The caudal portion of this structure facilitates all stretch reflexes, especially those that involve contraction of the antigravity muscles in the limbs. Rostral areas exert an opposing inhibitory influence. Normally, these areas counterbalance each other and contribute to a normal upright posture against gravity. But if a transection is made between them, then the inhibitory region will be cut off from the excitatory area, and the result is **decerebrate rigidity** in which the legs are reflexively extended.

The descending reticular formation also controls the autonomic motor system, which includes the cardiac muscles and the smooth muscles of the stomach and intestines. The control of these muscles is of obvious importance, and the descending reticular formation has been delegated this responsibility in virtually all vertebrates from amphibians to humans.

Summary

The output, or **efferent,** pathways of the nervous system control the glands and muscles. **Endocrine glands** secrete chemical messengers known as **hormones** that travel through the bloodstream to cause some change in a distant target organ. **Skeletal muscles** move the bones of the body relative to each other and thus are responsible for overt movement.

Endocrine glands are scattered throughout the body. The adrenal glands, located near the kidneys, are really two endocrine glands: an inner medulla and an outer cortex. The **adrenal medulla** releases two hormones that prepare the body for fight or flight. The **adrenal cortex** releases many different hormones that regulate a wide variety of bodily functions, including salt and water balance, stress reactions, and the production of new proteins. The **gonads** are a group of endocrine glands known for their production of sex hormones, which play a critical role in sexual development and behavior. The **thyroid** is an endocrine gland in the throat that releases a hormone to regulate cellular metabolism.

Perhaps the most important endocrine gland is the **pituitary,** or **hypophysis,** located on the underside of the brain. This gland not only controls the release of hormones from many other endocrine glands, but itself is controlled by the hypothalamus. The anterior portion of the pituitary, known as the **adenohypophysis,** releases its hormones in response to chemical signals that travel through a specialized group of blood vessels from the hypothalamus. Hormones from the adenohypophysis act on the gonads, the adrenal cortex, and the thyroid to promote hormone release from these glands. Other hormones from the adenohypophysis regulate the growth of bones and tissues and the production of milk in nursing mammals.

The posterior portion of the pituitary, known as the **neurohypophysis,** has a direct neural connection with the hypothalamus. Hormones produced in the hypothalamus travel via axons into the neurohypophysis where they are released by nerve impulses. One of these hormones promotes water reabsorption by the kidneys and the other is responsible for the ejection of milk from the mammary glands.

The release of hormones from endocrine glands is triggered by precise external or internal stimuli and controlled by simple reflexes. Release is turned off by a **negative feedback** mechanism or by removal of the stimulus that originally triggered release. To produce their effects, hormones interact with receptor molecules located either on the surface or interior of target cells.

Skeletal muscles are composed of increasingly finer subdivisions: fibers, fibrils, and filaments. The proteins **myosin** and **actin** form thick and thin filaments, respectively, that slide past each other during contraction. The thick and thin filaments are connected by crossbridges that break and reform in the presence of calcium and adenosine triphosphate. These bridges are damaged during unaccustomed exercise.

Motor neurons, located in the spinal cord or brain stem, make synaptic contact with individual muscle fibers and control muscular contraction. An individual motor neuron branches several times and thus contacts many muscle fibers. All of the muscle fibers that receive input from one motor neuron comprise a **motor unit.** A single motor unit may consist of as few as three or as many as several hundred muscle fibers innervated by one motor neuron. A high innervation ratio indicates precise muscular control.

Motor behavior is organized, in part, by reflex pathways in the spinal cord. One reflex that involves the spinal cord is the **stretch reflex,** which is really an antigravity reflex. When muscles are stretched, specialized receptors in the muscle spindle organs are activated. This generates action potentials in the large sensory fibers innervating the spindle organs, and these fibers make a direct synaptic contact onto the motor neurons that innervate the muscle. When these motor neurons, known as **alpha motor neurons,** are activated, the muscle contracts. The contraction also relaxes the spindle organs. Inputs from the brain control another group of motor neurons—**gamma motor neurons**—that regulate the spindle organs and in that way regulate further contraction.

Several areas of the brain participate in movement. In the **primary motor cortex** of the precentral gyrus, the body is topographically represented; the area allotted to each segment of the body corresponds not to its size, but to the precision of its muscular control. **Pyramidal cells** in primary motor cortex send their axons through the brain stem and into the spinal cord where they make connections with spinal interneurons and motor neurons. Pyramidal cells are organized into functional columns that both facilitate their coordinated activation and innervate other columns to control antagonist muscles. The activity of pyramidal cells changes prior to the onset of movement, but motor cortex is not the sole source of a decision to move. A **readiness potential** arises over widespread areas of cerebral cortex before movement occurs.

The **cerebellum,** which is connected to the pons, plays an important role in controlling posture and very rapid movements. The cellular anatomy of the cerebellar cortex is striking both for its regularity and the predominance of inhibitory neurons. These features allow the cerebellum to make repeated high-frequency timing computations that are sent via **Purkinje cells** to **deep cerebellar nuclei** and then to other levels of the central nervous system. The cerebellum also may operate as a memory system for well-balanced voluntary movements.

The **basal ganglia** represent another major motor system in the brain. This system consists of the **neostriatum,** which includes the **caudate nucleus** and **putamen,** and the **paleostriatum,** or **globus pallidus.** Although the anatomical organization and functions of the basal ganglia are not as straightforward as those of the cerebellum and motor cortex, it appears that the basal ganglia are involved in slow movements such as walking—a behavior that is severely impaired in patients with Parkinson's disease. This disease is caused by the degeneration of dopamine-containing axon terminals in the neostriatum. The neostriatum also receives a large amount of sensory and motor information from various levels of the nervous system, processes this information, and funnels it on to other structures that eventually communicate with motor cortex. Thus, the basal ganglia system appears to integrate the information that is necessary before actual movement occurs.

Another motor region includes the **descending** portion of the **reticular formation.** Efferents from this system pass to the spinal cord via the reticulospinal tract. The descending reticular formation exerts facilitatory and inhibitory influences on antigravity reflexes and also controls the autonomic motor system, which includes the heart, stomach, and gastrointestinal tract.

Suggested Readings

Alexander, G. E., M. R. DeLong, and P. L. Strick. 1986. Parallel organization of functionally segregated circuits linking basal ganglia and cortex. *Annual Review of Neuroscience* 9: 357–81.
A detailed and up-to-date account of the anatomical circuits of the basal ganglia and their relation to voluntary movement.

Divac, I., and R. G. E. Oberg, eds. 1979. *The neostriatum.* New York: Pergamon Press.
An excellent compilation of information on the anatomy, development, and functions of the most-investigated portion of the basal ganglia. Neurological disorders also are discussed.

Ito, M. 1974. The control mechanisms of cerebellar motor systems. In *The neurosciences: Third study program,* edited by Schmitt and Worden, pp. 293–303. Cambridge, MA: M.I.T. Press.
A thorough account of the mechanisms by which cerebellar circuits regulate movement.

Krieger, D. T., and J. C. Hughes, eds. 1980. *Neuroendocrinology.* Sunderland, MA: Sinauer Associates, Inc.
Articles in this book cover virtually all aspects of the endocrine system from its control by the hypothalamus to its involvement in behavior and psychiatric disorders.

Sherrington, C. S. 1947. *The integrative action of the nervous system.* 2d ed. New Haven: Yale University Press.
A classical monograph on spinal reflexes. Many of the conceptual and experimental foundations for our understanding of motor behavior are in this work.

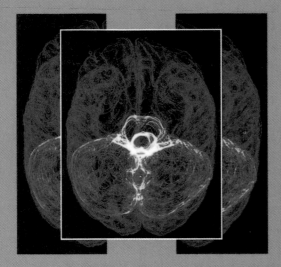

Outline

Introduction

To survive, all animals must maintain their internal environments within very narrow limits. Individual cells are extremely vulnerable to fluctuations in temperature and the supply of nutrients and oxygen. Nerve cells especially are dependent on a stable internal environment. A fluctuation in body temperature of more than just a few degrees can block impulse flow and impair synaptic transmission. So, too, can a disruption in the supply of nutrients or oxygen. If blood flow to the brain is stopped for more than five minutes, permanent brain damage is likely.

The fluid that bathes individual cells—the extracellular fluid—provides the conditions necessary for survival. One-celled animals living in the ocean must rely completely on the surrounding seawater for the elements needed to survive. For these animals, the external environment becomes their extracellular fluid. If they are to stay alive, the proper amount of nutrients and oxygen must be present in the seawater and the temperature must remain relatively constant. When ocean conditions change, the animals must take drastic action or perish. More complex animals carry their extracellular fluid with them as part of their internal environment, and they rely on a wide variety of physiological mechanisms to regulate it with precision. As a result, these animals are less dependent on their external environment for survival. Mammals, for example, are found in just about every area

Chapter

10

Eating Behavior

of the world, even in some very hostile surroundings, and survive quite well. In a very real sense, this ability to maintain a relatively constant internal environment is the key to independence or, as Claude Bernard, the famous nineteenth-century physiologist phrased it, "a free life."

In this chapter and the next, we will focus on the physiological mechanisms that regulate the internal environment. To be effective, these mechanisms must not only coordinate the operation of several different organ systems, but also control the appropriate behavioral response. We drink, for example, when our bodies become dehydrated. Thus, this chapter and the one that follows will deal with behaviors that are motivated or driven by an internal physiological state. Not only do these behaviors have adaptive or survival value, but other behaviors are impossible until our internal needs are met. In fact, complex behaviors like learning and memory may have developed as an extension of basic regulatory behaviors. As animals began to roam the earth and explore new environments, there was a selective advantage for those individuals that could learn and remember new sources of food and water. An understanding of basic regulatory behaviors, therefore, may shed some light on the physiological mechanisms underlying more complex behaviors.

Eating, drinking, and regulating body temperature are all examples of behavior that helps to control the internal environment. In this chapter, we will discuss the physiological mechanisms underlying eating behavior, but first it will be necessary to review some basic properties of regulatory mechanisms.

Homeostasis

The process by which the body maintains a relatively stable internal environment is called **homeostasis** (from the Greek, meaning "standing the same"). Walter B. Cannon coined this term in 1929 to refer to the tendency of animals to keep their internal states at or near a certain "set" level. Although Cannon was a physiologist, his term is applicable to virtually any regulatory device. A classic example of such a device is a thermostat that controls the temperature of a room. The thermostat is responsible for maintaining the room at a certain "set" temperature. When the temperature falls below a critical level, the thermostat detects the change and signals the heating system to start working. As the room warms up and the temperature approaches the "set" temperature, the thermostat turns off the heat. If the thermostat also is connected to an air-conditioning system, then a rise in room temperature would turn on cool air until the temperature again approached the "set" level. In either case, the thermostat is working to keep the room temperature within a very narrow range. The thermostat, therefore, is a homeostatic device.

This example is useful because it illustrates several important points about homeostatic systems. First, there is a **set point,** or some optimal level, that the system tries to maintain. In humans, the optimal level for body temperature is about 98.6° F. There also are optimal levels for blood pH and for the concentrations of sodium, sugar, and many other substances in the blood. Second, the "set" level is maintained by **negative feedback.** In our example of the room thermostat, the rise in temperature that occurs when the thermostat turns on the heating system feeds back onto

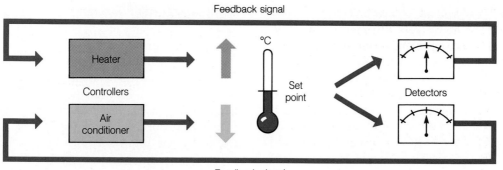

Figure 10.1 Schematic diagram of the basic features of a thermostatically controlled heating and cooling system. A major deviation from set point will turn on one of the temperature controllers, whereas otherwise they are turned off by negative feedback from the detectors.

the thermostat. When the desired temperature eventually is reached, the heating system turns off. The feedback is negative because it opposes the action that started it in the first place. A final point about homeostatic systems is that they must be equipped with a **detector** that is sensitive to deviations from the set point. If the thermostat in our example is unable to detect a change in room temperature, neither warm nor cool air will be turned on regardless of how hot or cold the room actually happens to be. Figure 10.1 illustrates the basic features of a thermostatically controlled heating and cooling system.

In physiological systems, regulation of the internal environment operates according to similar principles. When body temperature deviates from its set point, the body will do what it can to bring the temperature back to normal. Of course, the set point is not really a point but a range. Humans, for example, are not required to maintain an internal temperature of exactly 98.6°F. We would survive quite well at a temperature of 98.4°F or 98.8°F. Our lives would be in danger, however, if our temperature dropped to 90°F or

soared to 106°F. Similarly, the room thermostat also shows some flexibility around the set point. The deviation from the thermostat setting must be substantial (perhaps a half degree or more) before some corrective action is taken. Otherwise, the heating or air conditioning system would be turning on and off constantly with only the slightest change in room temperature. Moreover, like the thermostat, the optimal setting for an internal bodily state can be adjusted depending on the circumstances. During sleep, there is a controlled drop in body temperature. In fact, hibernating animals may lower their body temperature by several degrees.

Not all homeostatic behaviors, however, can be explained completely by the thermostat analogy. Consider eating. Although some deviation from a set point may initiate eating (perhaps nutrient levels in the blood fall below a critical level), a mechanism other than a return to the nutrient set point is responsible for stopping it. This must be the case because several hours are required for food to be digested and for the nutrients to reach the cells in the body. Thus, the body must have some way of monitoring how much is being consumed and then terminating the behavior long before the set point is reached. Certain regulatory behaviors, therefore, require an additional mechanism to tell the body it has had enough—in this case, a satiety mechanism.

Eating

With the possible exception of sex, no other behavior seems to generate more interest and discussion than eating. In scientific literature, eating behavior also receives a large amount of attention. This preoccupation with eating is understandable. Not only is food intake necessary for survival, but public concern about the control of body weight has been increasing steadily for several decades. According to some estimates, one-third of the American population is at least 20 percent above their "ideal" weight, and this condition shows no sign of going away. In fact, the number of obese people in the United States appears to be on the rise. What is most disturbing, however, is that an effective treatment for obesity and many other eating disorders remains elusive. Few people are able to control their weight successfully with drugs or diets, and even those who do are likely to suffer a relapse at some later date.

There is no easy explanation—and thus no simple cure—for eating disorders because the factors that control eating behavior are extremely complex. Until the early 1970s, physiological psychologists tended to emphasize the brain mechanisms that controlled eating behavior and to overlook other physiological systems and processes. Eating was thought to be controlled by hunger and satiety "centers" in the brain. Further research, however, demonstrated the fallacy of this point of view. Different areas of the brain do not function independently of each other; there is considerable communication and interaction. It soon became apparent that all the individual behavioral responses that make up what we call eating behavior could not possibly be controlled by one brain site. Just as important, psychologists have come to realize that the brain does not regulate eating by itself. In fact, several organs in addition to the brain play a critical role in regulating food intake. It is appropriate, therefore, that we begin our discussion of eating behavior with a review of the digestive process (fig. 10.2).

The Process of Digestion

Many physiological and biochemical processes are responsible for digesting the food we eat. In fact, digestion involves the entire alimentary canal. The process begins when food enters the mouth where it is mixed with digestive enzymes in the saliva and is chewed into smaller pieces that can be swallowed. The digestive enzymes initiate the process by which starches are converted into sugars.

Once food is swallowed, the smooth muscles that line the esophagus propel it into the stomach. Here, food is churned and broken into yet smaller pieces. In addition, it is mixed with digestive juices that are secreted by the walls of the stomach. One of the major digestive juices is **hydrochloric acid;** another is the enzyme **pepsin.** Hydrochloric acid acts with the churning stomach to break up food, while pepsin converts proteins into their component amino acids by breaking peptide bonds. A chemist working in a laboratory can break the peptide bonds of proteins by boiling them in

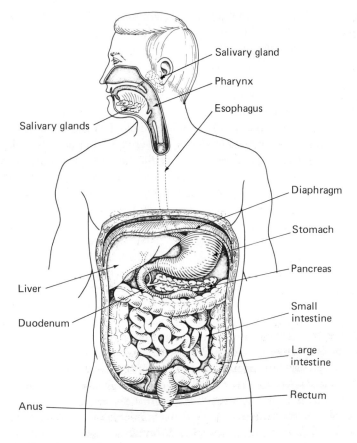

Figure 10.2 The human alimentory canal.

hydrochloric acid at 330° F for about twenty-four hours. Pepsin and other enzymes in our digestive systems can perform the same operation at body temperature in less than three hours.

The stomach's release of digestive juices is controlled by several interacting factors. One of these factors involves branches of the autonomic nervous system that are activated by the odor, sight, and taste of food. These same nerves trigger the release of saliva, and thus are responsible for making our mouths "water"

even before we begin to eat. The autonomic nervous supply to the stomach also is activated by the weight of the food as it settles into the stomach. Finally, there are chemical receptors in the walls of the stomach that are sensitive to various constituents in the food. These chemoreceptors trigger reflex activity mediated via the brain. Thus, the activity of the stomach—churning the food and secreting gastric juices—is controlled by the autonomic nervous system and by complex reflexes.

After a full meal, food may remain in the stomach between two and four hours. The actual time it does so depends, in part, on the kind of food being processed. Carbohydrates and simple proteins pass through the stomach fairly quickly. That is why a person who eats a Chinese dinner of bamboo shoots, bean sprouts, and rice seems to feel hungry only a few hours later. In contrast, fatty or fried foods will elicit a "sticks-to-the-ribs" feeling because they stay in the stomach much longer. Emotions also influence the movement of food through the stomach. Fear, for example, slows down this process, whereas anger speeds it up. In fact, food in a very angry person passes through the stomach much faster than normal, adding a case of indigestion to a person already overwrought with emotion.

The emptying of the stomach is regulated by the sphincter muscle at the lower end of the stomach. The sphincter acts as a valve that opens periodically to allow small quantities of food to pass into the first section of the small intestine, the **duodenum.** At this point, food resembles a liquified amorphous mass, but it is not yet ready to be absorbed into the body. Large drops of fat may still be present, and these must be emulsified into very small particles. The emulsification process begins when chemoreceptors that line the walls of the duodenum detect large fat globules. In response, the duodenum secretes **cholecystokinin,** which in turn causes the gallbladder to release **bile** (in fact, cholecystokinin is derived from a series of Greek root words meaning "movement of bile from the gallbladder"). Bile transforms fat globules into a smooth emulsion. The bile itself is manufactured in the liver and stored in the gallbladder. Another organ, the **pancreas,** also supplies the duodenum with digestive juices. These juices contain enzymes that help to complete the digestion of proteins, starches, and other food components.

Once digestion is complete, the nutrients must be absorbed into the body to enter the bloodstream and lymphatic systems. The absorption process occurs mainly in the small intestine. The inner walls of this organ are covered with tiny fingerlike tentacles called **villi.** These villi greatly increase the surface area of the intestinal wall. In fact, one square inch of intestine holds more than three thousand villi, which are packed together much like the nap of a carpet (the term "villus" is derived from the Latin for "shaggy hair"). Emulsified fats are absorbed through the villi into the lymphatic system, from which they eventually reach the bloodstream (yes, your blood will become creamy for a short time after you eat fatty foods). Other nutrients that pass through the villi are funneled directly into capillaries and then to the **hepatic portal vein** leading to the liver. Thus, the liver is the first destination of nonfatty nutrients. Some of these nutrients are stored in the liver and the remainder pass into the general circulation. Ultimately, they will become part of the body's energy cycle. In turn, this cycle will help to determine when we eat our next meal. To understand the physiological control of eating behavior, therefore, it is important to understand how the body stores and uses the energy derived from food.

Energy Storage and Utilization

A well-balanced meal contains more energy than the body needs at any given moment. If all the energy in a steak dinner were released immediately, we would be dead before we got to the dessert. Body temperature alone would rise by about 70°F. In order for the body to derive the benefits from this or any other meal, it must store the energy contained in nutrients and then dole it out at a rate that adjusts automatically to demand.

The energy in food is derived from three types of nutrients: glucose, amino acids, and fats. Glucose is the principal source of energy for almost all tissues. It is derived from carbohydrates and is metabolized very easily. Amino acids, which are derived from proteins in the diet, are used primarily to manufacture other proteins, but they also serve as a source of energy for the liver. The energy from glucose and amino acids can be used immediately or stored for later use. Fats, on the other hand, are not used immediately. Instead, they are stored in adipose (fatty) tissue where they can be broken down for later use as needed.

After a balanced meal, the level of all three nutrients in the blood is high. They must be absorbed into individual cells, however, before the body benefits. In order for cells to absorb these nutrients, **insulin,** a hormone manufactured in the pancreas, must be present. When insulin is released into the bloodstream, it allows glucose to enter virtually all cells (the brain is one of the few tissues that does not require insulin for this process). Insulin also facilitates the entry of amino acids into muscle for protein synthesis. Thus, without insulin, most tissues cannot metabolize glucose into energy, nor can amino acids be used for protein synthesis.

Insulin also plays a critical role in the storage of nutrients that are not needed immediately for energy. Excess glucose is stored in the form of **glycogen,** an insoluble carbohydrate known as animal starch, and fat (thus, even if you avoid fatty foods, you still can become fat). Both liver cells and muscle cells can convert glucose to glycogen, but only liver cells

convert glucose to fat. Insulin is required for both of these conversions. Likewise, when excess amino acids are available that are not used by the liver (for energy) or by the muscles (for protein synthesis), they are converted into fats and stored in adipose tissue. Fats, whether synthesized from glucose or amino acids or derived from the diet, also require insulin for storage. The sequence of events for storing and utilizing nutrients immediately following a meal are shown in figure 10.3.

The pancreas releases insulin whenever the level of glucose and amino acids in the blood are high. Thus, immediately following a meal, insulin becomes available so that the various tissues and organs of the body can absorb nutrients. Insulin also may be released just prior to or during a meal, even before any nutrients reach the blood. In this case, the autonomic nervous system stimulates the pancreas to secrete insulin, in much the same way that this system also causes our mouths to water once we can see, smell, and taste our food. If the pancreas fails to produce enough insulin, a condition termed **diabetes mellitus** results. Diabetics cannot readily absorb glucose into their cells, and thus depend primarily on fat metabolism for their energy supply (see the following). This is the reason that victims of this disease lose large amounts of carbohydrates in their urine unless they take supplemental injections of insulin. In severe cases, diabetics may require a pancreas transplant. Regardless of how it becomes part of our systems, without insulin, none of us could survive.

Insulin, however, is not released continuously. Once the nutrients from a meal are removed from the blood and stored in various tissues, the body enters another phase of metabolism, also shown in figure 10.3. This phase, which occurs between meals or during fasting, requires the body to utilize the energy that has

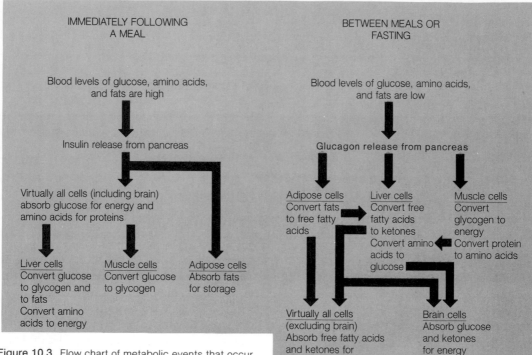

Figure 10.3 Flow chart of metabolic events that occur immediately following a meal and between meals or fasting.

been stored. Thus, instead of forming glycogen and fats, the body now must begin to break these down. At this point, insulin is no longer needed. One of the signals that turns off insulin release is a low glucose level in the blood, which occurs when food has not been eaten recently and there are no nutrients to absorb.

In order to utilize the energy that the body has stored from its previous meals, several substances may be released into the blood to facilitate the breakdown of glycogen and fats. The most important of these factors is **glucagon,** another hormone released by the pancreas. Glucagon release is triggered by the same stimulus that terminates insulin release—low blood glucose. In the presence of

glucagon, glycogen is reconverted to glucose and stored fats are broken down into **fatty acids.** The newly formed glucose will serve as energy only for the brain, however, because only brain cells can take up glucose in the absence of insulin. The rest of the body will get its energy from free fatty acids, although muscle cells also can derive energy from the glycogen stored within them. If fasting is prolonged (more than several hours), the liver converts fatty acids to **ketones,** which can serve as another source of energy for the entire body, including the brain. The body also can extract energy from muscle proteins by breaking them down into amino acids that the liver can convert to glucose. Thus, the brain is assured a supply of energy even during prolonged fasting until all reserves are gone.

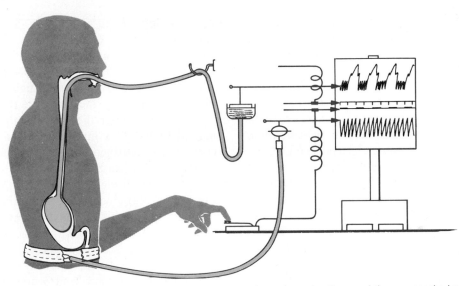

Figure 10.4 This drawing illustrates the experimental setup used by Cannon to show that stomach contractions are correlated with subjective reports of hunger. The subject swallowed a balloon that monitors stomach contractions and then pressed a key whenever hunger was felt. Note from the results that reports of hunger tended to occur just after bursts of stomach contractions.

In summary, different hormones and physiological processes are at work immediately following a meal than are at work during the time between meals or during fasting. In the former situation, energy (in the form of nutrients) is being absorbed and stored, whereas during food deprivation, these processes gradually reverse and stored energy is being broken down and released. It is important to understand both of these processes because as you will see in the following sections they play a critical role in starting and stopping eating behavior.

Bodily Factors that Control Eating

A systematic search for the factors that regulate eating behavior began early in this century. At that time, relatively little was known about the physiology of hunger. The only reliable information was found in a scattering of reports in the medical literature that feelings of hunger originate in the stomach. In the first test of this hypothesis in 1912, Cannon, the physiologist, persuaded human subjects to swallow a balloon that was inflated when it reached the stomach. The balloon was attached to a recording device that monitored stomach contractions. At the same time, the subject pressed a telegraph key to indicate when hunger pangs were felt. Cannon found that stomach contractions and reports of hunger coincided very closely; the former preceded the latter by only a brief period. The procedure that Cannon used in these experiments and an example of his results are shown in figure 10.4.

Cannon argued that stomach contractions did indeed cause the subjective experience of hunger. As you will see, however, such a conclusion was premature. We now know that the stomach is not necessarily involved in "hunger pangs." People that have had their stomachs removed because of cancer or severe ulcers still experience hunger. In fact, these people eat more frequently than normal. Cannon's most valuable contribution in this area was the emphasis he placed on bodily, or non-brain, factors in eating behavior. Since Cannon's day, we have learned a great deal about these factors so that now they are recognized to be as important (and almost as complex) as the brain itself in regulating food intake.

From the Head to the Duodenum

The sight, smell, and taste of food play an important role in controlling eating behavior—perhaps even more than you might think. LeMagnen (1971) found that rats will eat more than three times their normal amount if different flavors are added to their usual food. Apparently, exposure to different tastes stimulates eating. This conclusion is not lost on restaurants that offer a wide variety of appetizers and desserts on their menu. Moreover, taste is influenced by how hungry we are. Sweet-tasting foods are judged to be pleasant by hungry persons, but unpleasant by the same people when they are satiated (Cabanac and Duclaux 1970). Of course, the taste of a substance is determined in large part by its smell, and we all know how the smell of food can influence our appetite.

But all the receptors for regulating food intake are not in the head. This was made very clear by Epstein and Teitelbaum (1962) who trained rats to eat through a tube that was connected directly to the stomach. A liquid diet was delivered to the stomach every time the animals pressed a lever. Even though these animals could not see, smell, or taste their food, they regulated their diet and weight within normal limits. This intragastric feeling procedure has been modified for use in clinical patients, and again food intake was found to be unaffected (Jordan 1969). Thus, the sight, smell, and taste of food may make eating a rich sensory experience (and in that way help to regulate food intake), but they are not necessary for normal eating patterns.

The role of the stomach in eating behavior has raised some controversy over the years, but a clear picture now appears to be emerging as a result of some careful research. An important part of this picture is that the stomach controls the size of a meal that an animal eats. In one of the first experiments that supported this hypothesis, Davis and Campbell (1973) found that the stomach could monitor its contents. These investigators deprived rats of food for four hours and then allowed them to eat their fill of a diet of sweet milk. Next, half the milk was removed from the stomach by suction. Within minutes, the animals began to eat again, and they did not stop until they had consumed almost exactly the same amount of milk as had been removed. Other investigators (Deutsch, Young, and Kalogeris 1978) confirmed these results, lending further support to the idea that food in the stomach provides an important signal for regulating eating behavior.

But how does the stomach monitor its contents? Davis and Campbell suggest that receptors in the stomach are sensitive to distention, or stretch. Thus, when the stomach is distended by incoming food, it signals satiety. If the distention is relieved (as in the previous experiment by sucking out some of the ingested milk), eating resumes. But the stomach does not act simply as a pouch with stretch receptors. If it did, then loading the stomach with nonnutritive bulk should cause satiety. Under these conditions, however, animals continue to eat. Only at the upper limit of stomach capacity does distention shut off eating (Deutsch and Gonzalez 1980). To explain what controls food intake before distention becomes a factor, Deutsch (1983) argues that the walls of the stomach contain receptors that are sensitive to the nutrients in food. He has marshaled considerable evidence to suggest that a stomach filled with dilute nutrients will not exert a strong inhibitory effect on eating, whereas a load of nutrient-rich materials will lead to feelings of satiety. The stomach, therefore, appears to influence the size of a meal mainly by monitoring its nutrient level.

There have been reports that the duodenum also monitors the nutrient content of a meal and is just as important as the stomach in regulating food intake. This hypothesis, however, is not well supported. Most of the evidence favoring involvement of the duodenum is based on injections of food directly into this site. Animals that receive food in this way do indeed stop eating (Campbell and Davis 1974). But we must be careful before we draw any conclusions. Direct injections of undigested food into the duodenum may simply make the animals sick, rather than activate nutrient receptors to terminate eating. If food is allowed to pass rapidly through the stomach without sufficient time for processing, animals will curtail their food intake dramatically (Deutsch, Puerto, and Wang 1977). Yet these same animals will eat normally if given predigested food. Apparently, the duodenum is not prepared to accept whole food; it first must be processed in the stomach. Thus, demonstrating that an animal stops eating after an injection of whole food into the duodenum is not convincing evidence that this organ plays a role in satiety. In fact, when predigested food is injected into the duodenum, no satiety is observed (Puerto et al. 1976). Thus, although strong support exists for the involvement of stomach receptors in the termination of eating, there is no firm evidence that receptors in the duodenum play a similar role.

Substances in the Blood

As we have seen, nutrients absorbed by the small intestine pass immediately to the blood supply, through which they reach the liver and eventually all the other organ systems of the body. Moreover, the hormones that influence the storage and utilization of energy travel through the blood supply to reach their destinations. It is conceivable, therefore, that various constituents in the blood help to regulate eating behavior.

This was demonstrated very convincingly by a group of investigators who transferred blood from well-fed rats to food-deprived rats (Davis et al. 1969). When the hungry animals received the transfusion, their hunger disappeared. This effect could not be explained by the transfusion itself since hunger was suppressed only when well-fed rats donated the blood. Moreover, in order to be effective, the blood had to be taken from the well-fed rats at least forty-five minutes after a meal—the time when the blood begins to accumulate substantial amounts of the nutrients and hormones associated with eating. Blood drawn from well-fed rats immediately after a meal and injected into hungry rats had no effect.

The question of what the blood contains that influences eating behavior has had several answers over the years. In fact, the answer often depended on who was asked. Some investigators focused on glucose. Others emphasized the importance of lipids (fats) or the level of circulating amino acids. More recently, hormonal factors in the blood have received considerable attention. As you will see, none of these factors by themselves can explain why we eat and why we stop eating. But together these factors probably exert a powerful influence on food intake—powerful enough to make a hungry animal stop eating when they enter the blood supply.

Glucose was one of the first blood factors suspected of regulating food intake. Glucose, after all, is the primary nutrient in food and is absolutely essential for the normal operation of the brain. We might expect, therefore, that when blood glucose drops below a critical level we should feel hungry, and this feeling should persist until we eat a meal and raise our blood glucose. Consistent with this view, an injection of insulin can lead to hunger by promoting glucose uptake into storage sites and thereby causing a drop in blood glucose. In contrast, a rise in blood glucose produced by an injection of glucagon leads to satiety. But if the critical factors were simply the level of glucose in the blood, then diabetics, who have abnormally high blood levels of glucose, should never feel hungry. In fact, the opposite is true. Diabetics are hungry most of the time.

To account for the hunger of diabetics without abandoning glucose as an important variable in controlling food intake, Mayer (1955) argued that the critical factor is not the level of glucose in the blood, but its utilization by individual cells. This hypothesis has come to be known as the **glucostatic theory** of hunger. According to Mayer, hunger occurs when glucose utilization is low. Thus, diabetics are hungry because their lack of insulin prevents them from utilizing glucose. Further support for the glucose-utilization hypothesis comes from research with **2-deoxyglucose,** a compound that interferes with carbohydrate metabolism in cells. An injection of 2-deoxyglucose leads to immediate hunger, even in well-fed animals (Smith and Epstein 1969).

The availability of glucose, therefore, seems to be an important factor in regulating food intake. If indeed this is the case, then receptors must exist that are sensitive, if not to glucose, then at least to the utilization of this nutrient. Mayer suggested that such receptors are in the brain. As we shall see, however, the liver appears to be a better candidate, and the receptors themselves appear to respond to more than just glucose.

Glucose is not the only nutrient in the blood supply that is vital for cells. Amino acids are necessary for the manufacture of proteins. Those that are not used in protein synthesis are used as metabolic fuel. Although many amino acids are synthesized by the body, some are not. These essential amino acids must be obtained from the diet. It is reasonable to ask, therefore, if circulating levels of amino acids influence eating behavior.

Some researchers have postulated the existence of amino-acid receptors that control eating. The evidence, however, is very indirect. A meal that is rich in amino acids produces satiety even if blood glucose is very low (Mellinkoff et al. 1956). This finding is interesting, but not especially convincing. Amino acids, like glucose, trigger the release of insulin; thus, blood glucose may be low because the insulin allows it to be absorbed into cells and utilized. It is impossible to know if the amino acids are acting independently of glucose to produce satiety in this study. There also is evidence that animals deprived of amino acids will select amino-acid-rich foods when given a choice. A hunger for amino acids, however, does not necessarily mean that the body is equipped with amino-acid receptors. Such an appetite can be explained by simple learning. Animals deprived of specific nutrients learn to avoid those diets that do not make them feel better. The conclusion of all this research seems to be that amino acids can influence eating behavior, but they may do so indirectly rather than by acting on a specific set of receptors.

Lipids represent another blood-borne nutrient that may control food intake. In fact, Kennedy (1953) developed the **lipostatic theory** of hunger to emphasize the possible role of lipids or some hormone associated with lipids in maintaining a constant body weight over long periods of time. When animals are made obese by some experimental treatment, they tend to return to their normal body weight when the treatment is discontinued (Hoebel and Teitelbaum 1966). When fat is removed from obese animals, they eat excessively until they return to their obese weight (Liebelt, Bordelon, and Liebelt 1973). One way to explain these findings is that the body registers its total amount of fat and controls food intake accordingly.

That some aspect of lipid metabolism can influence food intake has been demonstrated in a study of diabetic rats. Friedman (1978) induced diabetes in rats by damaging the cells of the pancreas that produce insulin. These rats, like all untreated diabetics, must rely on

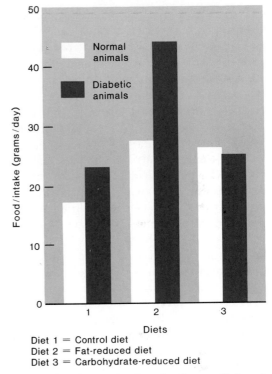

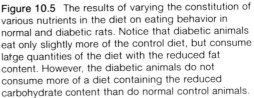

Diet 1 = Control diet
Diet 2 = Fat-reduced diet
Diet 3 = Carbohydrate-reduced diet

Figure 10.5 The results of varying the constitution of various nutrients in the diet on eating behavior in normal and diabetic rats. Notice that diabetic animals eat only slightly more of the control diet, but consume large quantities of the diet with the reduced fat content. However, the diabetic animals do not consume more of a diet containing the reduced carbohydrate content than do normal control animals.

noncarbohydrate sources for energy because without insulin they cannot utilize glucose as a metabolic fuel. Friedman offered both normal rats and the diabetic rats free access to foods that differed in their nutrient content. The results are summarized in figure 10.5. Note that the diabetic rats consumed only slightly more of the control diet than normal rats, but when a reduced-fat diet was offered, the diabetic animals ate substantially more than the normal rats. Evidently, the diabetic rats were much more dependent upon fats for their metabolism, so they compensated for the reduction of fat in the diet by eating more. The reduction of carbohydrates in the third diet had no effect on the diabetics because without insulin they cannot utilize the glucose that is derived from carbohydrates.

Friedman's study has two important implications. First, it demonstrates that the excessive eating normally observed in diabetic rats is due to their increased dependence on noncarbohydrate sources of energy (normal rat chow actually is a high-carbohydrate food). Second, the study suggests that at least one of the signals controlling food intake may be related to the monitoring of fat metabolism. Such monitoring seems to occur because when glucose metabolism is impaired, food intake is influenced heavily by the availability of fats. Of course, the actual signal that the animals respond to may not be related to lipids. As Friedman points out, perhaps the crucial element is the animal's ability to utilize nutrients. Thus, whatever the animal's diet, it may continue to eat until enough useable fuels are consumed to satisfy its metabolic needs. More work is necessary to determine whether blood lipid levels or storage of fats influence food intake directly.

The blood also contains hormones that may influence eating, but this hypothesis has generated some controversy. Some investigators have suggested that cholecystokinin, the hormone released into the duodenum to slow the movement of food through the digestive tract, causes satiety (Gibbs, Young, and Smith 1973; Antin et al. 1975). In fact, animals not only stop eating after an injection of this hormone, they engage in the same kinds of behaviors that they normally show after eating

a meal—a short period of grooming followed by rest and sleep. An obvious conclusion is that receptors in the body monitor the level of cholecystokinin in the blood and then signal the brain to terminate eating when the level rises above a certain point. But there is an alternative conclusion. Deutsch and Hardy (1977) found that if food is paired with the administration of cholecystokinin, rats will avoid that food when it is offered by itself at some later time. In other words, the animals are responding as if the cholecystokinin is aversive. Human volunteers that have been given this hormone often complain of nausea and abdominal cramps (Sturdevant and Goetz 1976). An injection of this substance, therefore, may terminate eating by causing gastric distress. This does not mean, however, that cholecystokinin has no role to play in satiety. The doses of cholecystokinin administered to animals and human subjects may simply be well beyond what is released naturally by the duodenum. Until we know how much cholecystokinin is too much, we cannot rule out a role for this hormone in food intake.

Another interesting piece of information about cholecystokinin is that it exists in certain regions of the brain where it may function as a neurotransmitter. Is brain cholecystokinin related to satiety? This indeed appears to be one of its functions. Direct injections of cholecystokinin into the brain have been reported to suppress eating (Morley 1982). Moreover, genetically obese mice have significantly less cholecystokinin than nonobese littermates (Straus and Yalow 1979). In view of such evidence, it would be a mistake to abandon the search for a direct link between cholecystokinin and satiety.

Other gastrointestinal hormones have been implicated in the regulation of food intake, including **bombesin** and **somatostatin**

(Morley and Levine 1985). These substances, like cholecystokinin, suppress eating when injected into rats. In addition, bombesin suppresses eating in animals when it is applied directly to brain tissue. The same concerns that apply to the research on cholecystokinin, however, also apply to the literature on these other gastrointestinal hormones. Thus, the physiological significance of these hormones for controlling eating remains uncertain.

The Role of the Liver

The liver, the first organ of the body to receive nutrients from digestion, is ideally located to play a role in eating. For many years, however, the liver was regarded primarily as a biochemical factory for storing and breaking down the energy in food. Only recently has the liver received attention as an important controller of food intake.

The first indication that the liver is involved in eating behavior came from evidence that blocking conduction along the vagus nerve, which transmits information between the liver and the brain, reduces eating in hungry animals (Penaloza-Rojas and Russek 1963). This finding is consistent with the notion that the liver monitors the availability of nutrients and signals this information to the brain via the vagus. An important series of experiments emerged from this hypothesis and provided remarkable insight into how the liver could regulate eating behavior.

One of the first issues that had to be resolved in this research is whether the liver really is sensitive to nutrients in food. If it is, then it should be possible to alter eating behavior simply by altering the level of nutrients in the liver. Russek (1971) demonstrated this very point by injecting glucose into different areas of the body. When he injected glucose into the abdominal cavity of hungry animals

(an intraperitoneal injection), they stopped eating, but he did not get this effect when he injected glucose into the jugular vein. The critical difference between these injections is that following an intraperitoneal injection, glucose diffuses into the abdominal cavity where it is taken up primarily by the liver. Glucose injected into the jugular vein, on the other hand, travels throughout the body so the liver receives a much smaller share. Thus, when glucose levels in the liver are high, eating stops. In fact, if glucose is injected into the hepatic portal vein, which goes directly to the liver, then eating also is suppressed in hungry animals (Russek, Lora-Vilchis, and Islas-Chaires 1980).

Note that signals from the liver and signals produced by receptors in the stomach could each play a role in insuring that eating stops when the body has accumulated enough nutrients. If receptors in the stomach alone were responsible for satiety, then we would eat again as soon as the stomach emptied its contents. Since this does not occur very often, there must be other mechanisms that keep eating in check for several hours after a meal. The liver appears to provide one of these satiety signals.

Can the liver also play the opposite role and initiate eating when nutrients are low? To answer this question, Novin, VanderWeele, and Rezak (1973) used 2-deoxyglucose to interfere with the normal metabolism of glucose. An injection of this substance into the hepatic portal vein prevents liver cells from utilizing glucose. Under these conditions, animals eat voraciously. In fact, they begin to eat immediately after the 2-deoxyglucose is injected. These results provide dramatic evidence that the liver can indeed initiate eating when the availability of nutrients (in this case glucose) is low.

Given that the liver is sensitive to nutrients, the question remains as to what aspect of nutrients the liver detects. Apparently, it detects more than just the presence or absence of glucose. An intraperitoneal injection of **pyruvic acid** is even more effective than glucose in suppressing eating behavior. Glucose is converted to pyruvic acid before it is utilized as energy. Similarly, **lactic acid,** a breakdown product of glycogen in muscles, also suppresses eating. (This effect of lactic acid helps to explain why vigorous exercise suppresses appetite. As muscles convert glycogen to glucose for energy, lactic acid is formed as a by-product.) Thus, rather than respond directly to the fuels that the body uses for energy, the liver may respond instead to some by-product of these fuels as they are utilized. This information then is relayed to the brain via the vagus nerve.

Surprisingly, the brain is relatively insensitive to its own nutrient utilization. In fact, if the brain alone is deprived of nutrients, there is no compensatory increase in eating behavior. This was demonstrated in rats by Stricker and colleagues (Stricker et al. 1977). They first injected rats with insulin to lower blood glucose and thereby induce hunger. Next, the rats received fructose, a sugar that can be utilized by the liver, but not by the brain. Thus, these rats have a "hungry" brain (blood glucose levels are low) but a "satiated" liver (the fructose substitutes for glucose). If nutrient receptors in the brain play the most important role in hunger, then these animals should eat, but they do not. Apparently, they obey the satiety signal coming from the liver. In fact, if the signal is abolished by cutting the vagus nerve, these same animals begin to eat.

These results make a strong case for liver control of food intake. They do not mean, however, that the liver operates alone in this task. Consider again the vagotomized rats that received insulin and fructose. These animals have a "hungry" brain, and they do indeed eat when the "satiated" liver is prevented from communicating with the brain via the vagus. Thus, the brain also must be equipped with receptors that monitor nutrients. But because this is not apparent until the vagus is cut, the liver seems to play a predominant role, although by no means the only role, in controlling eating. That eating is regulated by more than just the liver is evident when the vagus nerve is cut in otherwise normal animals. This procedure disrupts eating only temporarily. Eventually, vagotomized animals resume normal eating patterns, even though the liver can no longer transmit neural signals.

Brain Factors that Control Eating

The search for the mechanisms underlying eating behavior has focused on the brain more than on any other organ or system in the body. There are many reasons for this, but consider just one. In figure 10.6, two rats are shown.

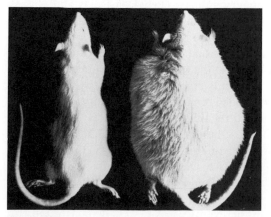

Figure 10.6 Shown are a normal animal and a hypothalamically hyperphagic animal. Note that the hyperphagic rat (right) weighs over two times as much as the normal animal: 290 grams versus 640 grams.

One rat is normal and the other has had a specific region of its hypothalamus destroyed. In a matter of weeks, the brain-damaged rat increased its weight to more than twice that of its normal partner. When this dramatic effect was first reported almost fifty years ago (Hetherington and Ranson 1940), it is no wonder that the brain became the center of attention for investigators interested in the control of food intake.

Most of the early research on the role of the brain in eating became a quest for the location of feeding and satiety "centers"—areas of the brain that could turn eating on and off. Not surprisingly, attention centered on the hypothalamus, where Hetherington and Ranson first placed lesions in the rat brain. Within a relatively short time, separate areas of the hypothalamus were identified that did indeed appear to start and to stop eating behavior. Today, the hypothalamus still receives attention in eating research, but not as the feeding and satiety "center." This notion has been abandoned as physiological psychologists have come to realize that the hypothalamus is but one part of an intricate network of variables that control eating.

An elegant example of a relatively simple network in action was provided by Dethier (1976), who studied eating in the blowfly, a close relative of the common housefly. When this animal is hungry, it flies upwind until it smells food. It then lands and walks about until taste receptors on its feet are activated. The tastier the food, the faster the receptors fire. This firing triggers the extension of the fly's proboscis, through which it feeds and which also contains taste receptors. Different receptors are sensitive to different tastes (salt, sugar, and water). Food is sucked into the proboscis and travels to the stomach. If the food activates only one group of receptors (sugar, for example), the receptors will soon adapt to the taste and stop firing. At this point, the proboscis will retract and the meal will end. If, however, the food contains a variety of tastes, different groups of receptors will remain active. The stomach will continue to fill until it becomes so large that stretch receptors in the walls of the stomach activate the **recurrent nerve,** which signals the brain to inhibit proboscis extension. These inhibitory signals turn off eating.

This entire process very closely resembles a large reflex loop. In fact, if part of this loop is removed, the animal can no longer control its food intake. If, for example, the recurrent nerve is cut, the brain no longer receives an inhibitory signal to stop eating. The proboscis remains extended and the stomach continues to fill. The fly keeps eating until it explodes.

The same fate will not befall the brain-damaged rat in figure 10.6. Rats, like all mammals, depend on many more checks and balances than the fly to regulate eating behavior. As we discussed previously, several different organ systems are involved, each of which works in concert with the brain to regulate food intake. As we shall soon see, the problem with the brain-damaged rat is far more complex than not knowing when to stop eating.

The Ventromedial Hypothalamus and Eating

The area of the hypothalamus that will cause obesity when damaged is known as the ventromedial region. It lies deep in the hypothalamus close to the midline. Rats that sustain lesions of this area display two distinct phases of eating behavior. During the first phase, which begins immediately after the operation and continues for several weeks, the animals eat enormous amounts of food, and they do so ravenously. Excessive overeating is known as hyperphagia. When caused by ventromedial hypothalamic lesions, the response is called **hypothalamic hyperphagia.** Once the animals become obese, however, they enter the second phase, during which the ravenous eating subsides, and they eat only enough food to maintain their new obese weight. The first phase of hypothalamic hyperphagia is referred to as the **dynamic phase,** whereas the subsequent leveling off of both body weight and food intake is the **static phase.** Both phases are illustrated in figure 10.7.

Because damage to the ventromedial hypothalamus produces such a dramatic increase in body weight, it is easy to see how this area came to be regarded as the satiety "center." Hyperphagia is exactly what would be expected if a satiety "center" were damaged. A closer look at hypothalamic hyperphagic rats, however, indicates that they do not behave simply like eating machines. So determined are these animals to maintain their new obese weight that if they are placed on a diet to lose weight, they increase their eating and quickly gain it back as soon as they are taken off the diet. If they are force-fed to gain even more weight, they actually stop eating until

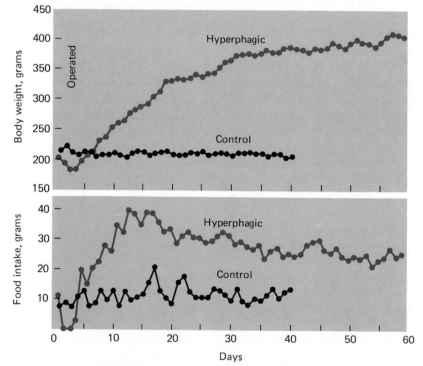

Figure 10.7 Body weight and food intake in control (normal) and hyperphagic (having undergone ventromedial hypothalamic lesions) rats. The data are plotted as functions of time after the placement of bilateral ventromedial hypothalamic lesions.

they return once more to their original obese weight. Thus, they seem to be regulating their body weight at a new, higher level. Another pecularity of these animals is that during the static phase they become very finicky eaters. They prefer soft, palatable food and refuse to eat anything that they do not like. Neither will they work very hard for their food. They prefer to eat no food at all rather than engage in difficult or tedious tasks to obtain it. None of these observations describes an animal whose sole impairment is a damaged satiety "center."

Why then does a rat with a ventromedial hypothalamic lesion behave the way it does? Some aspects of its peculiar behavior may be due to the fact that it is so fat. Curiously, obese humans share the same peculiar behavior patterns as hypothalamic hyperphagic rats (Schachter 1971), yet there is no reason to suspect that these people suffer from a ventromedial hypothalamic lesion (in some cases they do, but this obesity is part of a larger, extremely rare, medical disorder called Froehlich's syndrome). Moreover, normal rats that become fat simply by binging on chocolate chip cookies and candy also refuse to work for their food and become very finicky eaters (Sclafani and Springer 1976). Thus, some of the unusual behaviors of hypothalamic hyperphagic rats seem to be secondary to being fat, rather than any direct effect of the lesion.

But the central question—why does a rat with a ventromedial hypothalamic lesion overeat and gain so much weight?—has not been so easy to answer. The stumbling block for many years has been a preoccupation with the brain as the sole controller of food intake. A proposal by Friedman and Stricker (1976) forces us to reconsider this notion and to regard the brain and body as working together to regulate eating behavior. These investigators propose that rats with ventromedial hypothalamic lesions become obese because they constantly are absorbing and storing their nutrients. Insulin release, which would be required for this process, is in fact elevated following ventromedial hypothalamic lesions (Hustvedt and Lovo 1973). The conversion of glucose into fat also is elevated, while the reverse process—the breakdown and metabolism of fat—is reduced. Because the lesioned animals accumulate fat even when nutrients are not available, they must keep eating just to fulfill their normal energy requirements. In other words, these animals have no more energy available for their tissues than a starving rat. In a sense, these animals are starving because virtually all the nutrients they consume go immediately into storage and are unavailable. We can summarize this entire proposal in the following way: Rats with ventromedial hypothalamic lesions do not gain weight because they overeat; they overeat because they are gaining weight.

This proposal emphasizes the close relationship that must exist between the brain and the rest of the body in order to control food intake and energy metabolism. Under normal conditions, the body communicates energy usage to the brain and the appropriate response is initiated (eat or stop eating). When the ventromedial hypothalamus is damaged, nutrient availability declines, the body signals this change to the brain, and the brain initiates the appropriate response (eat). In addition to causing a chronically high level of insulin in the blood, Powley (1977) points out that ventromedial lesions cause an exaggerated "cephalic reflex" in response to palatable aphagia   (ah-fa'je-ah)

foods. This refers to an excess surge of insulin release (as well as saliva and gastric acid) compared to normal rats. All of these chemical changes combine to increase hunger and to enhance energy storage.

What is it about the ventromedial hypothalamus that damage here produces such dramatic effects? Surprisingly, the answer may have very little to do with the ventromedial hypothalamus itself. Many of the effects associated with ventromedial hypothalamic lesions can be produced by damaging a group of fibers that pass through the general vicinity of the ventromedial hypothalamus (Kapatos and Gold 1973). Lesions that are confined to cell bodies in the ventromedial hypothalamus fail to produce either hyperphagia or obesity (Gold 1973). This means that when the ventromedial hypothalamus is damaged, the critical factor for producing hypothalamic hyperphagia is the destruction of axons that pass through this site. In fact, these axons may not originate in the hypothalamus, although they do appear to terminate there (Gold et al. 1977). Thus, we are faced with the intriguing possibility that another neuronal system interacts with the hypothalamus and makes an important contribution to the hypothalamic hyperphagic syndrome.

The Lateral Hypothalamus and Eating

The ventromedial region is not the only area of the hypothalamus that appears to influence eating. Damage to the lateral hypothalamus produces exactly the opposite effects on food intake. Rats and other animals with lateral hypothalamic damage suffer from **aphagia** (failure to eat) and pronounced weight loss (Anand and Brobeck 1951). In fact, rats will

die of starvation unless they are nursed slowly and painstakingly back to health. Immediately after the lesion, they refuse to eat or drink. They must be fed and watered artificially to be kept alive. Eventually, they will begin to accept wet and very palatable foods (chocolate chip cookies soaked in milk or water, for example) but they still will not drink. Over time, the animals will eat enough wet, palatable foods on their own to sustain life. Only after several months will they begin to drink on their own, and then they do so only when they eat dry food. Epstein and Teitelbaum (1962) divided the recovery from lateral hypothalamic lesions into four discrete stages (fig. 10.8).

In view of what we have learned about the ventromedial hypothalamus, it should come as no surprise that when the pronounced eating deficits of lateral hypothalamic lesions were first reported, the destruction of a feeding "center" was implicated. Nor should it be surprising that subsequent research has shown this notion to be false.

One of the first studies to challenge the notion that feeding behavior is totally dependent on the lateral hypothalamus was conducted by Powley and Keesey (1970). They created lateral hypothalamic lesions in two groups of rats: one group was fed normally and thus was at normal body weight at the time of surgery; the second group was placed on a starvation diet before the surgery, which caused them to lose about 20 percent of their body weight. After the lesion, the normally fed rats showed aphagia and weight loss, as expected. The second group, however, did not. These prestarved rats actually began to eat and to gain weight almost immediately after the lesion. This finding, of course, is incompatible

	Stage I	Stage II	Stage III	Stage IV
	Adipsia, Aphagia	Adipsia, Anorexia	Adipsia, Dehydration–Aphagia	Recovery
Eats wet palatable foods	No	Yes	Yes	Yes
Regulates food intake and body weight on wet palatable foods	No	No	Yes	Yes
Eats dry foods (if hydrated)	No	No	Yes	Yes
Drinks water prandially, survives on dry food and water	No	No	No	Yes
Regulates food intake to dilution, temperature, and deprivation	No	No	No	Yes
Eats in response to glucoprivation	No	No	No	No
Drinks in response to hydrational challenge	No	No	No	No
Eats and drinks despite minimum palatability	No	No	No	No

Figure 10.8 The stages of recovery of animals with lesions of the lateral hypothalamus. The stages of recovery (I through IV) appear at the top of the table, and the behaviors characteristic of the animals at the various stages of recovery are listed in the column at the left of the diagram. Responses of the animals appear within the boxes.

with the view that the lateral hypothalamus functions as a feeding "center." Keesey and Powley (1975) suggest that the lateral hypothalamus maintains a set point for body weight. When this structure is destroyed, a new and lower set point is established. Thus, rats may stop eating after destruction of the lateral hypothalamus not because of a loss of appetite, but because the body is attempting to maintain its weight at a lower set point.

This explanation assumes that food intake is suppressed because these lesions exert a very specific effect—a change in the set point for body weight. Damage to the lateral hypothalamus, however, has effects that go far beyond a change in food intake. Lesions in this site, for example, reduce the response to sensory stimuli, suppress arousal, and attenuate

motor activity (Marshall and Teitelbaum 1974). Thus, the change in eating that follows lateral hypothalamic damage may be part of a larger problem; namely, that these animals have a difficult time performing any type of behavior.

This intuitively appealing hypothesis has gained a considerable amount of support. The first piece of supportive evidence came in 1971 when Ungerstedt demonstrated that damage to the **nigro-neostriatal bundle,** which produces dramatic sensory and motor deficits, also causes aphagia and weight loss. The nigro-neostriatal bundle contains dopamine neurons that originate in the substantia nigra and pass through the lateral hypothalamus before they terminate in certain parts of the basal ganglia, including the neostriatum. It is conceivable, therefore, that lateral hypothalamic lesions produce their effects on food intake by damaging these dopamine neurons. This hypothesis was confirmed when chemical destruction of the nigro-neostriatal bundle with **6-hydroxydopamine,** which spared the cells of the lateral hypothalamus, produced virtually all the symptoms of a lateral hypothalamic lesion, including the finickiness, the reduced activity, and the same four-stage recovery from aphagia (Fibiger, Zis, and McGeer 1973; Zigmond and Stricker 1972).

Other lesions that deplete dopamine in parts of the basal ganglia also disrupt eating. In fact, destruction of dopamine fibers disrupt a broad range of motivated behaviors that include not only eating and drinking, but also maternal behavior and body temperature regulation. Thus, destroying the lateral hypothalamus also destroys a system that exerts a nonspecific activational effect on behavior. When this system is damaged, all behaviors are attenuated. In fact, these behavioral deficits can be reversed temporarily simply by arousing the animals with such nonspecific activators as stimulant drugs or a pinch of the tail (Antelman and Rowland 1975; Stricker and Zigmond 1976).

If the eating impairments reflect a general disruption in behavior, then why do animals recover? Teitelbaum (1971) suggests that recovery from lateral hypothalamic lesions occurs because higher areas of the brain take over the functions formerly served by lower structures—a process called **encephalization.** The study conducted by Teitelbaum and Cytawa (1965), in which they found that a temporary depression of cortical activity caused rats that had recovered from lateral hypothalamic

damage to revert to their aphagic behavior, supports this argument. Control rats with depressed cortical activity did not reduce their food intake. This study supports the notion of a shift in function to a higher site—in this case, the cerebral cortex—following damage to a lower structure.

Another part of the answer to why animals having lateral hypothalamic damage recover is that the remaining dopamine neurons attempt to compensate for the damage. These cells, for example, become more active and release more dopamine (Stricker and Zigmond 1976). Moreover, neurons in the neostriatum increase their sensitivity to dopamine, thereby allowing whatever dopamine is released to have a greater effect (Neve, Kozlowski, and Marshall 1982). Thus, even though many dopamine neurons are destroyed, compensatory changes occur that help to reinstate some level of dopamine function.

There is one more piece of evidence that refutes a lateral hypothalamic eating "center." Zeigler and Karten (1974) found that damage to sensory fibers carrying information from the head and neck—the **trigeminal nerve** and **trigeminal lemniscus**—also produces aphagia followed by a recovery period. During this recovery period body weight is maintained at a new lower level. The reason for focusing on the trigeminal system is that, like the nigro-neostriatal bundle, it courses through the brain in the general vicinity of the lateral hypothalamus. Again, it seems that surgical destruction of the lateral hypothalamus destroys much more than just the lateral hypothalamus. It appears, therefore, that when eating declines following lesions of the lateral hypothalamus, this effect is more likely due to a disruption of motivational, sensory, and motor systems, rather than damage to a structure that specifically controls eating.

If the behavioral deficits associated with lateral hypothalamic lesions are really due to damage of surrounding structures, then an obvious question remains: Does the lateral hypothalamus play a direct role in eating? There is no clear answer. By now, you probably can appreciate the difficulty of studying a structure that lies so close to neuronal pathways controlling motivation, sensation, and movement. Disrupting any of these can disrupt eating. Still, as Grossman (1979) emphasizes, this problem does not preclude the lateral hypothalamus from exercising a very selective influence on eating behavior—an influence that only further research will be able to clarify. Perhaps at present it is best to conclude that if the lateral hypothalamus is involved in food intake, it is only one participant in a complex system that controls a wide range of factors related to eating as well as eating itself.

Before leaving this topic, we also should mention that brain structures outside the hypothalamus may play a role in eating. Damage to some forebrain areas, including the zona incerta or parts of the amygdala, appears to attenuate eating. We do not yet know why such damage has this effect. Perhaps these areas also are a part of a system that exerts a generalized activating effect on behavior or perhaps their functions are more specific. For example, they may play a role in responding to the sensory qualities of food or the coordination of certain mouth or jaw movements. Whatever their role, it should come as no surprise that even rather straightforward behaviors like eating require the coordinated activity of many brain structures.

Eating Disorders Have No Simple Cure

Millions of Americans spend billions of dollars every year for pills, potions, and other paraphernalia to find a cure for their eating problems. But in view of the complexity of the physiological mechanisms controlling food intake, it should come as no surprise that few individuals ever find a complete cure. In one especially discouraging study, the Food and Drug Administration assessed the effects of eleven different appetite-reduction drugs and found that in over ten thousand patients, these drugs produced in one week an effective, average weight loss of about one-half pound (Scoville 1975). Such a small amount does little to uplift the spirits of those looking for a quick cure. In this section, we will review two completely different eating disorders: obesity, the most prevalent eating disorder in Western society, and **anorexia nervosa,** a pathological failure to eat that typically strikes young women.

The first thing to realize about obesity is that there is no shortage of theories to explain it. Theories that emphasize social factors have turned up some interesting facts that seem to be good predictors of the condition. One predictor is that fat parents tend to have fat children (Garn and Clark 1976). This correlation has little to do with genetics, however, because it also holds for adopted children and for house pets. Socioeconomic status, race, and sex also influence body weight, though in a complex way. Black males, for example, get fatter as they move up the socioeconomic scale, while black women get thinner. Overall, white males are fatter than black males, but white females are leaner than black females. All of these observations emphasize the importance of social factors in eating—factors that too often are dismissed in the search for the causes of obesity.

The search for a physiological basis of obesity recently has focused on changes in the chemistry of the brain. This emphasis comes, at least in part, from the dramatic increase in the number of substances that now appear to act as neurotransmitters. Norepinephrine was the first neurotransmitter to be implicated in eating behavior. Grossman (1962) reported that infusion of this substance into the hypothalamus provoked eating in satiated rats. Subsequent research has shown that this effect represents only a small part of the complex chemical machinery that influences food intake. Norepinephrine, for example, both increases and decreases eating; the critical difference is the type and location of adrenergic receptors in the hypothalamus (Leibowitz 1975). Stimulation of alpha-adrenergic receptors in the paraventricular area of the hypothalamus promotes feeding, whereas stimulation of beta-adrenergic receptors in the lateral hypothalamus produces the opposite effect. Many of the drugs used to suppress appetite, the so-called **anorexic drugs,** are believed to act via the beta-adrenergic system. In fact, the anorexic effects of amphetamine and related stimulants are believed to involve beta-adrenergic receptors in the lateral hypothalamus. As we have seen, however, eating involves several different physiological systems, and the role of the lateral hypothalamus in this response is far from settled. Not surprisingly, these drugs are not very effective in controlling food intake over a prolonged period of time.

Some recently developed anorexic drugs increase the release of serotonin. In rats, a depletion of brain serotonin causes hyperphagia and obesity, whereas drugs that enhance the action of serotonin decrease feeding (Hoebel 1977). Serotonin, however, exerts an inhibitory effect on a variety of behaviors, making it difficult to link feeding in any specific way with this neurotransmitter. In fact, some of the anorexic effects of serotonin stimulators may be related to the inhibitory effect of serotonin on the movement of food through the digestive system (Davies et al. 1983).

Some attempts to control eating and the weight gain associated with it involve the development of substances that manipulate the taste of food. Aspartame, more commonly known as NutraSweet®, can substitute for the taste of sugar without the number of calories. A drug that blocks opioid receptors, **naltrexone,** seems to alter the perception of taste. This drug is more effective in reducing the intake of a highly palatable diet than an ordinary one (Apfelbaum and Mandenhoff 1981). This finding is consistent with evidence that endogenous opioids change the incentive value of certain tastes (Morley and Levine 1985). In an interesting bit of speculation, Morley and Levine (1985) suggest that a craving for chili may be related to the rewarding effects of opioids in the brain. This notion is based on the fact that chili contains **capsaicin,** a chemical that releases substance P from nerve terminals. Substance P is found in fibers innervating the tongue and is responsible for the burning taste of chili powder. In response to the release of substance P, there is a compensatory release of opioids in the brain, which have been shown to have rewarding effects on behavior.

As research on the neurochemistry of eating continues, we no doubt will learn of many other substances that can modify food intake. Many more drugs and other treatments for obesity will be based on these findings. But if previous research on the anatomical correlates of eating taught us the danger of thinking in terms of feeding and satiety "centers" in the brain, we should be equally cautious of attempts to find the feeding and satiety "chemicals." The physiological mechanisms involved in eating defy a simple explanation, and when they sometimes fail they will not be cured by a simple drug or dietary manipulation. In fact, there is some reason to question why obesity should be treated at all. When obese patients are put on diets, they compensate by reducing their metabolic rate so that they lose less weight. When nonobese subjects are overfed, they compensate by increasing their metabolic rate. Both of these examples suggest that even during obesity the body defends its weight at some targeted level, making it extremely difficult for any drug or dietary manipulation to be successful. Moreover, Fitzgerald (1981) argues that there are some advantages to being fat. Obese people, for example, are more likely to survive the effects of cancer, and they have a lower rate of suicide than the nonobese. Perhaps with all the emphasis that our society places on the lean body image, obesity has become more of a social problem than a medical one.

In some women, however, the fear of becoming fat is an obsession. These individuals suffer from anorexia nervosa, a very devastating disease characterized by an almost complete cessation of eating. Approximately 0.5 percent of young, white women in North America, Europe, and Australia are afflicted with this condition (it rarely strikes black females). The age of onset is the mid- or late teens. Victims have an almost pathological desire to be extremely thin. They eat only low-calorie foods or refuse to eat at all. Other symptoms include hyperactivity, cessation of menstruation, sleep disorders, difficulty in regulating body temperature, abnormal fear of sexual intercourse, and many other psychiatric problems. Approximately 10 percent of anorexic patients starve to death. A photograph of an anorexic woman is shown in figure 10.9.

The refusal of anorexics to eat resembles the response of animals having lateral hypothalamic lesions. There is no evidence, however, that these patients have any form of brain damage. In fact, their other symptoms are unrelated to a destruction of the lateral hypothalamus (Stricker and Anderson 1980). It seems more likely that hormonal abnormalities are involved since anorexics suffer from extremely low levels of some sex hormones and a decreased synthesis of growth hormone. Still, we cannot be sure if these hormonal difficulties are the cause or the effect of the disease. To date, hormonal treatments have been found to be ineffective in alleviating anorexia nervosa.

Figure 10.9 An anorexic woman.

There is no doubt that psychological conflicts are involved in anorexia nervosa as well. Many of the parents of anorexic women place great emphasis on physical appearance, insisting that their daughters be attractively thin. In addition, the loss of weight may be a way of avoiding sexual intercourse or of rebelling against the parents. Traditional psychotherapeutic techniques, however, also appear to be ineffective in helping anorexic patients.

Males almost never develop anorexia. In fact, some authorities argue that men with this condition are misdiagnosed and suffer instead from brain damage, schizophrenia, or some related disorder (Martin and Dauner 1978). Strangely enough, however, the character, style, and background of some male long-distance runners are remarkably similar to the character, style, and background of the typical woman patient with anorexia (Yates, Leehey, and Shisslak 1983). Many runners demonstrate a preoccupation with food and an unusual emphasis on lean body mass, not unlike anorexic women. In fact, anorexic women, like competitive runners, tend to be compulsively athletic. Yates and colleagues argue that in both cases the goal is to establish an identity or self-image. Clearly, an in-depth psychological study is required to validate this unusual relationship and perhaps to shed further light on anorexia itself.

Specific Hungers

If eating properly is an important part of our health, then the amount of food that we consume is only part of the story. Equally important is what we consume. Yet there has been relatively little research on this aspect of eating behavior. In fact, it was not until 1912 that the first vitamin—vitamin A—was discovered and almost forty years after that before all thirteen of the vitamins needed for complete human nutrition were isolated and identified. Is there some built-in mechanism that triggers an appetite for a specific nutrient when the body's supply runs low? Are the cravings that we sometimes feel for certain foods the body's attempt to satisfy some nutritional deficiency? As you will see, the answers are complicated by factors that go far beyond the physiology of homeostatic mechanisms.

In most cases, we are unable to recognize which foods contain the nutrients that our bodies may need at any given time. There are many examples, but one will suffice. Thousands of people in the Orient died from beriberi, a disease of the nervous system characterized by severe convulsions, before a chemist identified the problem as a thiamine (vitamin B_1) deficiency. No one knew at the time that the practice of polishing rice, which removes the hull, also removes thiamine. Because people are unable to recognize thiamine in their diet, this substance now has become a food additive to insure that a sufficient amount is consumed. Beriberi remains a problem, however, in some areas of the Orient where people continue to consume polished rice and do not have access to enriched foodstuffs.

Rats are no different than people in their inability to detect thiamine. Yet rats will avoid a thiamine-deficient diet and actively seek out new sources of food. How do they do it? Rozin and Kalat (1971) demonstrated that rats can learn to consume diets that provide the nutrients that their bodies need. These investigators maintained rats on a standard laboratory diet and then removed thiamine. As the animals got sick, they ate less and less of their food and even ran away from it. The food became aversive to them. When given a new diet that contained thiamine, the rats ate ravenously. Apparently, the sickness that resulted from eating the thiamine-poor diet prompted the rats to seek out a new source of food.

The behavior of these animals can be explained by conditioned aversion. By associating their illness with their food, the rats developed an aversion to it. In addition, they seemed to form a positive association with a diet that improved their health. This point was demonstrated in another experiment with rats fed a thiamine-deficient diet (Garcia et al. 1967). After several days on the diet, these animals were allowed to drink saccharin, which was followed by an injection of thiamine. The thiamine, of course, restored their health, and thereafter these rats drank more saccharin than normal. They had developed a conditioned preference for the substance that they associated with their improvement.

Humans, too, develop aversions and preferences for food. We all undoubtedly have had experiences when something we ate made us sick, and for some time afterwards we actively avoided that food. Sometimes, however, other factors can override our choice of foods. Social custom is one such factor, and in the southeastern United States it was largely responsible for a strange outbreak of malnutrition during the early part of this century. Both black and white sharecroppers there ate very poorly—mostly grits, greens, and corn mush— but only the white sharecroppers got sick. The difference was even more surprising because both groups cooked their foods exactly the same way: boiling everything for prolonged periods to improve the taste. The whites, however, found it socially unacceptable to drink the cooking water; they threw it away. The blacks, unconcerned about the social stigma attached to cooking water, drank it instead and thus regained all the essential vitamins and minerals that had leached into the water during prolonged cooking.

Our choice of foods, therefore, can be influenced by factors far removed from the physiological needs of the body. In most cases, social factors and learning determine many of our eating habits, not appetites for specific nutrients. There is, however, one essential nutrient that our bodies crave regardless of any other outside influences. Our hunger for sodium, which plays a critical role in regulating the body's fluid supply, is innate. In fact, as we will see in the next chapter, the receptors that are responsible for our appetite for salt appear to be located in the brain itself.

Summary

A stable internal environment is necessary for survival. Individual cells cannot tolerate large fluctuations in their surroundings. **Homeostasis** refers to the tendency of animals to keep their internal environments at or near a certain "set" level. Homeostatic behaviors are motivated or driven by an internal physiological need. In this chapter, we focused on the need to obtain nutrients from food.

To understand the physiological processes that motivate eating behavior, it is necessary to understand how the body stores and utilizes the energy in food. This energy comes from glucose, amino acids, and fats. **Insulin,** which is released by the **pancreas** during and immediately following a meal, is required for the entry of glucose and amino acids into cells (brain cells are unique in that they do not require insulin for this process). In addition, insulin plays a critical role in energy storage.

This hormone helps to convert excess glucose to **glycogen** and fat and to store fat in adipose tissue. People who fail to produce enough insulin suffer from **diabetes mellitus. Glucagon,** another pancreatic hormone, is released between meals and during fasting when blood glucose levels are low. Glucagon facilitates the breakdown of glycogen into glucose and the conversion of fats into free fatty acids.

Eating behavior is regulated by several different organ systems. Sensory factors, that is, the sight, smell, and taste of food, make eating an enjoyable experience, but they are not necessary for normal eating patterns. The stomach appears to play an important role in controlling the size of a meal. This organ is equipped with both nutrient and stretch receptors that help to turn off eating.

Substances in the blood also help to regulate food intake. Glucose has received the most attention in this regard. According to the **glucostatic theory,** hunger occurs when glucose utilization is low. This helps to explain the almost constant hunger of diabetics whose lack of insulin prevents them from utilizing glucose. The amount of amino acids in the blood may provide additional control over eating behavior, but there is little direct evidence for this idea. The **lipostatic theory** emphasizes fat, another blood-borne nutrient, in the control of body weight over long periods of time. The blood also contains **cholecystokinin,** a hormone that may provide a signal to the brain to terminate eating.

The liver not only serves as the primary site for the storage and breakdown of energy in food, but also as a critical organ in the control of food intake. The liver appears to monitor the availability of nutrients and signals this information to the brain via the vagus nerve.

Thus, the liver provides an important satiety signal to turn off eating when nutrients are high and a signal to initiate eating when nutrients are low. Receptors in the liver respond to the presence or absence of glucose as well as to by-products of energy metabolism.

The brain has received the most attention in the control of food intake. Early research suggested that the **ventromedial hypothalamus** represented the satiety "center" of the brain since lesions here caused animals to gain enormous amounts of weight. Subsequent research challenged this idea and indicated instead that ventromedial hypothalamic lesions alter the process by which the energy in food is stored and utilized. When the ventromedial hypothalamus is damaged, the accumulation of fat increases even if food is not available. Any nutrients that are consumed go immediately into fat and become available for use. With ventromedial hypothalamic lesions, therefore, overeating occurs because all the energy in food is being lost to fat, not because a satiety "center" is destroyed. It also is important to keep in mind that many of the effects of ventromedial hypothalamic lesions can be produced by lesions of fibers that pass through the vicinity of the ventromedial hypothalamus. This finding suggests that another neuronal system also may contribute to the overeating associated with ventromedial hypothalamic lesions.

Damage to the **lateral hypothalamus** causes a complete cessation of eating. Animals with lesions in this area will die of starvation unless they are nursed carefully back to health. Despite the devastating effects of lateral hypothalamic lesions, however, the role of this area in eating behavior is far from settled. If animals are forced to lose weight before the lesions, there is no further weight loss afterwards. In fact, prestarved animals actually gain weight after the lesions. Such a finding is incompatible with the notion of a lateral hypothalamic feeding "center." Moreover, the lateral hypothalamus may not even be responsible for the failure to eat and the weight loss that accompanies damage to this area. These same behavioral effects can be produced by destroying the **nigro-neostriatal** bundle, an important dopamine pathway that passes through the lateral hypothalamus. In fact, damage to this pathway not only disrupts eating but produces a generalized disruption of all motivated behavior. Thus, the reduction in eating that accompanies lateral hypothalamic damage can be attributed to the destruction of a separate neuronal system that exerts an activational effect on behavior. Other structures that course through the lateral hypothalamus also may contribute to the behavioral deficits that occur when this area is damaged. Further research will be required to determine how each of the various structures of the brain, including the lateral hypothalamus, regulates food intake.

Eating disorders have no simple cure because eating is regulated by many different neurochemical and physiological processes. Furthermore, obesity, the most common eating disorder in the United States, also is influenced by complex social factors. Not surprisingly, the drugs that are used to treat obesity are not very effective. Nor has an effective treatment been found for **anorexia nervosa,** a disease characterized by an almost complete cessation of eating that strikes young, white females. Hormonal and psychological abnormalities appear to underlie this disorder, although the exact cause of anorexia remains to be determined.

The selection of the foods we eat often has more to do with social custom and learning than an innate desire to balance our nutritional requirements. In most cases, we cannot detect the presence of essential nutrients in food. Conditioning, however, can play a powerful role in dietary selection. Foods that are associated with sickness are avoided, while those that are associated with good health are consumed avidly.

Suggested Readings

Dethier, V. G. 1976. *The hungry fly: A physiological study of behavior associated with feeding.* Cambridge: Harvard University Press.
This book provides an insightful look into the neural mechanisms that control eating in a very simple organism.

Friedman, M. I., and E. M. Stricker. 1976. The physiological psychology of hunger: A physiological perspective. *Psychological Review* 83: 409–31.
The authors of this review discuss hunger from the standpoint of basic biochemical and physiological processes of energy metabolism.

Morley, J. E., and A. S. Levine. 1985. The pharmacology of eating behavior. *Annual Review of Pharmacology and Toxicology* 25: 127–46.
This review summarizes some of the latest information on the neurochemistry of eating and also evaluates some of the drugs used to treat obesity.

Novin, D., W. Wyrwicka, and G. Bray, eds. 1976. *Hunger: Basic mechanisms and clinical implications.* New York: Raven Press.
This edited volume includes articles on many different aspects of eating behavior written by experts in the field. Topics range from basic research with animals to therapies for obesity and anorexia nervosa.

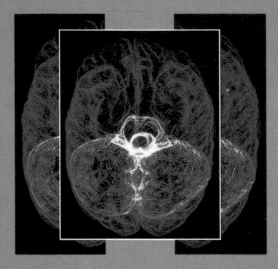

Outline

Introduction

We must perform a wide variety of behaviors in order to maintain a stable internal environment. As we saw in the previous chapter, these homeostatic behaviors are crucial for survival. We also saw that one of these behaviors—the intake of nutrients—is a complex process, influenced by many different factors and controlled by several different organs. The regulation of the body's water supply and internal temperature, which we will discuss in this chapter, are no less crucial for survival. In fact, we can live without food for several weeks, but we cannot survive more than a few days without water, and a change in body temperature of only 10° F can be fatal in a matter of minutes. Like eating behavior, drinking and temperature regulation require the participation of the central nervous system as well as several other organ systems. In a very real sense, physiology and behavior are linked so closely that they are part of one continuous process.

In the first part of this chapter, we will discuss drinking behavior. You soon will see that although fewer variables are involved, water intake, like eating, is controlled by complex physiological systems. We also will discuss what appears to be an innate appetite for sodium, a mineral that plays a critical role in regulating the body's fluid supply. The second part of this chapter will describe how different species regulate their internal temperature and the physiological mechanisms underlying this process. We also will discuss how a small rise in body temperature may be useful in combating disease.

Chapter

11

Drinking Behavior and Regulating Body Temperature

Drinking

Water is the only liquid that our bodies really need. All other liquids that we consume contain other substances as well as large amounts of water. Milk, for example, is almost 90 percent water; the rest is mostly protein, fat, and carbohydrates. Our need for water comes from the fact that we are watery creatures. By weight, we are almost two-thirds water. Our cells require water for virtually all metabolic processes. In addition, water acts as an ideal solvent for sodium, potassium, and chloride ions, making it essential for the conduction of nerve impulses. But because water participates in so many different bodily reactions, it is being lost continuously. Every time we breathe, defecate, and urinate, we are losing water—almost three quarts per day. Sweating can increase this loss to as much as three quarts per hour. Any water loss must be monitored very carefully because the body has no reserve supply. Unlike the nutrients in food, water is not stored for later use. Thus, when a need for water arises, the body has no alternative but to conserve whatever water it possesses and, at the same time, to begin drinking in order to replenish the water that is being lost.

In this section, we will discuss the conservation of water and drinking behavior. As you will see, both are regulated by many of the same physiological mechanisms.

The Distribution of Water in the Body

The water that we consume is absorbed into the body through the large intestine. From there, water finds its way into two general compartments: inside cells (intracellular) and outside cells (extracellular). Approxi-

DISTRIBUTION OF WATER IN THE BODY

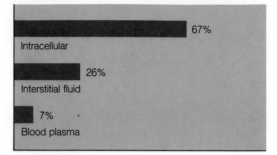

Figure 11.1 Relative sizes of the watery compartments of the body.

mately 67 percent of the body's fluids are contained in the intracellular compartment. The remainder is part of the extracellular compartment, which consists of the interstitial fluid and blood plasma. The interstitial fluid surrounds all cells and accounts for 26 percent of total body water. The remaining 7 percent is found in blood plasma. The relative sizes of the watery compartments of the body are shown in figure 11.1.

All of these compartments are separated by membranes. The walls of blood vessels separate blood from other fluids, and cellular membranes separate the intracellular and interstitial fluids. Membranes play an important role in determining how much water is contained in each compartment. Although water can pass freely through biological membranes, many solutes—chemicals that are dissolved in water—cannot. Whenever one compartment has a greater concentration of solutes than another, water will leave the dilute compartment and enter the concentrated one. In short, membranes help to establish a concentration gradient, and water flows from one compartment to another by osmosis. This process is illustrated in figure 11.2.

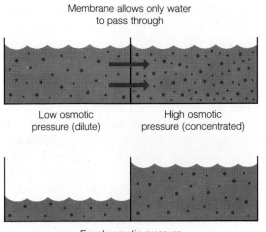

Membrane allows only water
to pass through

Low osmotic
pressure (dilute)

High osmotic
pressure (concentrated)

Equal osmotic pressure

Figure 11.2 Movement of water by osmosis from a
dilute to a concentrated compartment. Water flows
from the dilute to the concentrated compartment (top)
until the osmotic pressure between compartments is
equal.

Sodium chloride (table salt) is an example of a solute that cannot pass easily through membranes. (In most cases, you will recall, cellular membranes are impermeable to sodium ions. Although chloride is able to pass through membranes, it has a negative charge and prefers to remain outside in order to balance the positive charge on sodium.) Normally, the interstitial fluid contains a 0.9 percent solution of sodium chloride, which often is called **isotonic saline.** An injection of isotonic saline has no effect on the body's osmotic gradients because the concentration of solutes does not change. If, however, the concentration of saline exceeds 0.9 percent, then the excess sodium chloride that accumulates in the extracellular compartment will draw water out of cells. This type of saline is called **hypertonic.**

The flow of water out of cells causes intracellular dehydration and can lead to thirst, as we will see later. In the kidney, however, a high concentration of sodium plays an important role in retaining the body's water. Specialized cells in the kidney actually collect sodium and use it to draw water out of the ducts leading to the bladder. The next section focuses on this crucial function of the kidney.

Regulating the Body's Water Supply

Because the need for water is so vital, the body has developed highly effective mechanisms for regulating its supply. Many of these mechanisms seem to converge on the kidney, and for that reason it is necessary to understand how this organ actually works.

The kidney represents the point of contact between the excretory and circulatory systems. Blood flows into the kidney, where it is filtered of wastes, and then returns to the circulation. The kidney sends the wastes on to the bladder, where they are stored as urine for subsequent release to the outside. More than a quart of blood flows through the kidney every two minutes, allowing the body to rid itself of wastes very rapidly. Normally, however, only about 1 percent of what the kidney filters is removed as waste. The remaining 99 percent of the filtrate, which includes water, is returned to the circulation.

The reabsorption of water begins when the filtrate enters the **nephron,** the functional unit of the kidney. As the filtrate passes through the nephron, it enters a long convoluted tubule, an important part of which is the **loop of Henle.** As shown in figure 11.3, this loop consists of a long descending portion and a long ascending portion. Each portion is critical if the body is to retain its water.

Along the descending portion, water flows passively out into the surrounding tissue and sodium moves passively in. Water and sodium flow in these different directions because the surrounding tissue has a high concentration of sodium. Thus, osmotic pressure causes water to flow out and sodium to flow in. As a result, the filtrate is very highly concentrated when it reaches the bottom of the loop—so high, in fact, that in humans the sodium concentration approaches 2 percent. But as the filtrate moves up the ascending portion, an interesting thing happens. Sodium is pumped out of the filtrate into the surrounding tissue. This outward pumping of sodium is an active process (recall that the surrounding tissue already is highly concentrated with sodium, so in order to move sodium out of the ascending loop the kidney must work to pump it out). At the same time, the ascending portion of the loop becomes impermeable to water; this prevents the water in the filtrate from passively following the sodium. Thus, when the filtrate leaves the loop of Henle, it is extremely dilute. This dilute filtrate now enters the distal convoluted tubule, where the membrane once again becomes permeable to water. As a result, water follows its osmotic gradient and flows passively out of the distal convoluted and renal collecting tubule into the surrounding tissue of the nephron. From here, the water enters a bed of capillaries and is returned to the circulation.

At first glance, the process of reabsorbing water may seem more complicated than necessary. After all, the filtrate, which is fairly dilute to begin with, becomes highly concentrated and then becomes dilute again. Why bother with the step of concentrating the filtrate? Refer to figure 11.3 again, as we describe the importance of this step. Note that

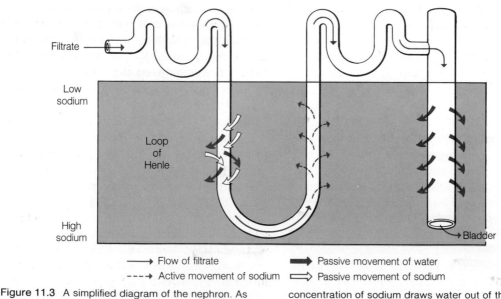

Figure 11.3 A simplified diagram of the nephron. As filtrate moves through the loop of Henle, sodium is pumped out into the surrounding tissue. This high concentration of sodium draws water out of the tubule before it passes on to the bladder.

the concentrated filtrate becomes the source of the sodium that is pumped out of the ascending loop. As more sodium gets pumped out, the osmotic pressure in the region between the ascending loop and both tubules increases. The higher the pressure in this region, the easier it is for water to leave the renal collecting tubule before it has a chance to reach the bladder. Thus, the more concentrated the filtrate becomes, the less water will be lost in the urine.

The concentration of the filtrate depends on the length of the descending loop. The longer that the filtrate travels through this portion of the loop, the more concentrated it becomes. The small amount of water that is lost from the filtrate during this concentration process is a small price to pay for the large amount of water that later will be saved as it passes through the renal collecting tubule. The kangaroo rat, which has one of the longest loops of Henle found in any mammal, also makes the most concentrated urine, an important survival aid for an animal that lives in some of the driest climates on earth.

Efficient though the kidney is at conserving water, neither humans nor kangaroo rats could survive for very long if they depended only on the kidney to prevent excessive water loss in the urine. Of the more than forty-five gallons of fluid that pass through the human kidney each day, more than six gallons of water would be lost in the urine if no other mechanism intervened. Granted, saving about thirty-nine gallons of fluid every day seems like a major accomplishment, and it is, but we cannot afford to lose even six gallons (we normally excrete about two quarts of urine per day). Fortunately, there is another mechanism, and when it works properly we do not have to spend most of our day in the bathroom. This other mechanism involves a hor-

mone that acts on the distal convoluted tubules of the kidney and makes them even more permeable to water. As we have seen, the tissue surrounding these tubules contains a high concentration of sodium, so this change in permeability allows even more water to flow out and to be absorbed into the circulation.

The hormone that increases the permeability of the distal convoluted tubules and thereby decreases water loss in the urine is known as a antidiuretic hormone (ADH) (diuresis refers to an excessive secretion of urine; thus, the hormone that prevents this condition is an antidiuretic). Its real name, however, is arginine vasopressin or, more simply, **vasopressin.** It has this name because in addition to acting on the distal convoluted tubules, it also constricts blood vessels when given in large amounts (this effect leads to an increase in vascular pressure and hence the name).

Vasopressin is released into the blood supply from the **posterior pituitary gland,** which, as we saw in chapter 9, also is known as the **neurohypophysis.** Hormones in the neurohypophysis, including vasopressin, are manufactured by neurons in the hypothalamus and then transported along their axons to axon terminals in the neurohypophysis (embryologically, the neurohypophysis grows out of the hypothalamus). The hypothalamic neurons that manufacture vasopressin are located in the **paraventricular nucleus** and the **supraoptic nucleus.** Thus, when neurons in these hypothalamic nuclei become active, vasopressin is released from axon terminals in the neurohypophysis and then into the circulation. These neurons are activated by two types of stimuli, both of which signal a need for the body to conserve water. One of these stimuli is a reduction in blood volume. As you soon will see, a loss of blood volume is detected by receptors in the heart, which then relay this information to the brain. The brain responds by releasing vasopressin to conserve whatever water the body still has. The other stimulus that triggers the release of vasopressin is intracellular dehydration. If, for example, the extracellular compartment becomes concentrated with solutes, water is drawn out of cells (yes, they actually shrink in size). The paraventricular and supraoptic nuclei respond with an increased firing rate, thereby causing the release of vasopressin to help the kidney conserve water.

The importance of vasopressin in regulating the body's fluid balance is obvious to people suffering from **diabetes insipidus.** In these individuals, the neurohypophysis fails to release vasopressin, and thus their urine is extremely dilute. (Insipid means dull or tasteless, and because the urine of these patients contains so much water, it lacks the tangy flavor of normal urine—or so we are told.) Victims of diabetes insipidus will urinate more than six gallons of fluid in one day unless they receive injections of a pituitary extract that contains vasopressin.

You may have noticed that urinary output also increases after you drink one or two cans of beer. Does alcohol impair vasopressin release? Yes, but that is not why you urinate after drinking only a few beers (the large amount of water in beer causes that). Only during heavy drinking (when blood alcohol approaches 0.1 percent) is vasopressin release impaired enough to cause copious urination. In addition, chronic alcoholism permanently damages the filtering properties of the nephron and seriously impairs the reabsorption of water.

Types of Thirst

The release of vasopressin represents an effort by the body to conserve water. This hormone, however, will not restore water levels to normal. Only drinking can do that. Yet the same mechanisms that are responsible for helping us to conserve water also are responsible for causing us to drink it. Drinking occurs when water is lost from either the intracellular or extracellular compartment. In fact, the primary stimulus for drinking—thirst—originates from either intracellular or extracellular fluid loss.

Loss of Water from the Intracellular Compartment Causes Osmotic Thirst

The craving for water that occurs when fluid flows out of cells is known most commonly as **osmotic thirst** because water leaves the intracellular compartment by osmosis. One of the easiest ways to cause osmotic thirst is to consume a large amount of sodium chloride. Because sodium chloride does not cross cellular membranes very easily, it collects in the extracellular compartment, which, as we have seen, will draw water out of cells by increasing osmotic pressure. As our cells become dehydrated, we experience osmotic thirst.

The factor responsible for osmotic thirst is the loss of intracellular water, not a change in the concentration of solutes. Gilman (1937) made this point very clear by comparing the effects of hypertonic saline and urea on drinking behavior in animals. Hypertonic saline, which is a highly concentrated solution of sodium chloride, does not cross cellular membranes. Thus, an injection of hypertonic saline increases the level of solutes in the extracellular compartment but not in the intracellular compartment. This imbalance causes water to move down its concentration gradient and out of cells. Urea, on the other hand, penetrates cellular membranes easily. An injection of urea, therefore, will increase the concentration of solutes in both compartments. This effect increases osmotic pressure without changing the movement of water. Gilman found that animals will drink vigorously in response to hypertonic saline but not to urea. This experiment shows that cellular dehydration, not a change in osmotic pressure, causes osmotic thirst.

Of course, if cellular dehydration is responsible for osmotic thirst, then any solute that has a difficult time crossing cellular membranes—not just sodium chloride—should draw water out of cells and cause thirst when administered in sufficient concentration. Indeed, this appears to be the case. Sucrose, for example, remains in the extracellular compartment after it enters the body, and, like hypertonic saline, a concentrated sucrose solution causes thirst. You may be interested to know that most concentrated sugar solutions have the same effect. Because the loss of intracellular water causes osmotic thirst, water alone, not some combination of water and solutes, is the best remedy. Thus, increasing the intake of sodium chloride or sucrose will only intensify the loss of water from the intracellular compartment and aggravate osmotic thirst.

Loss of Water from the Extracellular Compartment Causes Volemic Thirst

Thirst produced by a loss of fluid from the extracellular compartment is called **volemic thirst** because the result of such a loss is a reduction in blood volume. The body monitors blood volume very carefully, and when it declines, we experience thirst. The condition of low blood volume that triggers volemic thirst is known as **hypovolemia.**

A deep cut, internal hemorrhaging, and heavy menstrual bleeding all cause volemic thirst. Clearly, each of these examples involves a decline in blood volume. But hypovolemia also can result from a loss of interstitial fluid (water will move from blood plasma to the interstitial fluid if the interstitial fluid declines). Thus, severe diarrhea and sweating, both of which involve a loss of interstitial fluid, also cause volemic thirst.

An important factor makes volemic thirst very different from osmotic thirst: Volemic thirst involves not just the loss of water, but also the loss of salts and other solutes. This means that water can be lost from the extracellular compartment without necessarily drawing water from the intracellular compartment. Thus, the conditions that produce volemic thirst, such as severe bleeding or profuse sweating, do not draw water from inside cells. In fact, there may be a slight movement of water into cells because the loss of salts and minerals actually dilutes the extracellular compartment causing water to move intracellularly. This is why volemic thirst is best relieved by consuming salts and other essential solutes along with water. A person who sweats excessively in very hot conditions loses water as well as salt. Both must be replaced. Drinking large amounts of water alone will cause painful muscle spasms and convulsions, a group of symptoms commonly known as "heat cramps." Salt is the best remedy for this condition. (This does not mean, however, that every time you sweat you should run to the salt shaker. The section on sodium appetite explains why.)

A simple way to produce volemic thirst so that it can be studied experimentally is to inject **polyethylene glycol** under the skin of animals. Polyethylene glycol is a large molecule that cannot cross capillary membranes. Thus, it remains in the interstitial fluid and because of osmotic pressure draws water from the blood.

Thirst Produced by a Combination of Intracellular and Extracellular Water Loss

All of us have experienced at least some of the conditions that produce osmotic or volemic thirst. In many situations, however, the thirst that we experience is caused by a loss of water from both the intracellular and extracellular compartments. This type of thirst occurs whenever we deprive ourselves of water for just a few hours. Under these conditions, there is a decline in both the intracellular and extracellular water supply. The extracellular supply declines because necessary bodily functions, like breathing and urinating, deplete water from the interstitial fluid. Over time, this water loss will increase the salt concentration in the extracellular compartment, which, as we have seen, will cause water to leave the intracellular compartment. The net result of mild dehydration, therefore, is a combination of osmotic and volemic thirst. Since none of us drinks constantly to replace our ongoing water loss, we may experience this combination thirst several times a day. Most commonly, we experience it when we awake from a long period of sleep. Approximately 70 percent of the water that we consume upon waking is used to restore the intracellular supply; the remaining 30 percent restores the extracellular supply.

Neural Control of Drinking

Although the stimuli that produce thirst are understood very well, we cannot say the same for the neural mechanisms that control water intake. At this level, the study of drinking behavior becomes extremely complex. Special receptors are required to monitor the body's water supply, and when a deficit is detected, the information must be sent to special areas of the brain that can integrate it and convert it into a drinking response. As you will see in this section, none of these processes is understood completely. But because of some recent research, we are beginning to gain a new appreciation of how the nervous system controls drinking behavior.

Monitoring the Intracellular Water Supply

Virtually all cells in the body need water. This does not mean, however, that every cell will trigger a thirst signal when it becomes dehydrated. Andersson (1953) demonstrated this point when he began a search in the brain for the receptors that stimulate osmotic thirst, so-called **osmoreceptors.** He infused hypertonic saline, which should cause intracellular dehydration, into different brain regions of animals. Only when the infusions were made into the basal forebrain area near the hypothalamus did the animals drink. Infusions into other brain sites had little or no effect. Was the hypothalamus the site of the osmoreceptors? To find out, Blass and Epstein (1971) improved on Anderson's technique by infusing hypertonic saline into very circumscribed regions of the hypothalamus. They were able to elicit drinking only when infusions were made into the **lateral preoptic area.** This finding seemed to suggest that osmoreceptors indeed were located in the hypothalamus and in a very specific area at that.

The animals that drank in response to these infusions, however, consumed only a few milliliters of water. This is hardly a robust response for rats whose osmoreceptors, if indeed they exist in this region of the brain, must have been stimulated to the maximum by the intracellular dehydration caused by an infusion of hypertonic saline. Osmoreceptors in the lateral preoptic area, therefore, are not a very satisfactory explanation for osmotic thirst. Another problem with the lateral preoptic area is that it lies inside the blood-brain barrier. More recent research indicates that osmoreceptors are located on the outside of this barrier.

The blood-brain barrier consists of capillaries surrounded by a tightly packed layer of cells that prevents large molecules and molecules with a high electrical charge from entering brain tissue. Urea, for example, will not cross the blood-brain barrier, although we saw previously that it will cross cellular membranes. Thus, when urea is injected into the blood supply, it will accumulate on the blood side of the blood-brain barrier and draw water out of the brain, dehydrating it. Yet an injection of urea causes no drinking (Thrasher et

al. 1980). Thus, if osmoreceptors lie in the lateral preoptic area or any other region of the brain inside the blood-brain barrier, they are not very sensitive to osmotic water loss. But we know that an intravenous injection of hypertonic saline or other molecules that cause intracellular dehydration cause vigorous drinking (McKinley, Denton, and Weisinger 1978). The obvious conclusion, therefore, is that osmoreceptors lie outside the blood-brain barrier although the question remains—where?

One possible location is an area of the brain in which the blood-brain barrier is weak. Such an area includes the highly vascularized tissue that borders the third ventricle. As shown in figure 11.4, this area is dominated by two structures: the **subfornical organ,** or **SFO,** and the **organum vasculosum lamina terminalis,** more commonly known as the **OVLT.** Rats

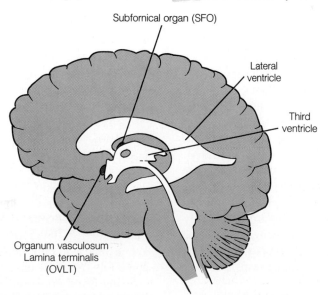

Subfornical organ (SFO)

Lateral ventricle

Third ventricle

Organum vasculosum Lamina terminalis (OVLT)

Figure 11.4 Location of the brain structures near the third ventricle that play a role in drinking behavior.

with SFO lesions fail to respond to hypertonic saline, a finding that would be consistent with the SFO as the site of osmoreceptors. Yet this finding holds only for a relatively mild dose of hypertonic saline. With higher doses, SFO-damaged rats drink as vigorously as normal rats (Hosutt, Rowland, and Stricker 1981). As you will see shortly, the SFO appears to be involved in drinking, but in a much more general way than as the site of osmoreceptors.

Having eliminated the SFO, we now can turn our attention to the OVLT. Thrasher, Keil, and Ramsay (1982) implicated this structure when they disrupted osmotically induced drinking with OVLT lesions. But the OVLT may be only part of the osmoreceptor story. Some drinking still persists in response to osmotic stimuli after OVLT lesions, and when rats with these lesions are left alone and not challenged with hypertonic saline, they regulate their water balance very nicely. Thus, even if the OVLT does contain osmoreceptors, it may not be the only structure that does so. A reasonable conclusion, therefore, is that although osmoreceptors appear to lie outside the blood-brain barrier, they are not confined to any one structure. This possibility has some intuitive appeal because osmotic thirst represents a response to stimuli that under normal circumstances cause intracellular dehydration throughout the body. Thus, the loss of water from cells in a circumscribed area may not provide a signal strong enough to disrupt ongoing behavior and to elicit drinking. Only when signals of intracellular dehydration arise from many sites does the brain pay enough attention to initiate the drinking response.

Monitoring the Extracellular Water Supply

As we have seen, a loss of fluid from the extracellular compartment causes a decline in blood volume. It would seem reasonable,

therefore, that the same mechanism involved in measuring blood volume also provides information about the extracellular water supply and thus plays an important role in volemic thirst.

The body measures blood volume by means of stretch receptors in the left atrium of the heart. These receptors detect the expansion of this chamber as it fills with blood returning from the body. If these receptors play a role in volemic thirst, then it should be possible to elicit thirst simply by reducing the flow of blood to this area of the heart. This is exactly what happens. Fitzsimons (1972) made normal animals drink excessively simply by tying off one of the veins that returns blood to the heart. Apparently, the reduction in blood flow mimics the loss of blood volume that occurs during hypovolemia, and the receptors signal the brain to initiate drinking behavior. In fact, when blood-volume receptors in the left atrium are damaged, the drinking response to hypovolemic stimuli is abolished (Zimmerman, Blaine, and Stricker 1981). Thus, the receptors for volemic thirst are really blood-volume detectors located in the left atrium of the heart.

Are there any other receptors involved in volemic thirst? There is support for this possibility, but as you will see, the evidence involves the production of a chemical substance whose role in drinking is still controversial. The chemical substance is **angiotensin,** which is produced by the same stimulus that causes volemic thirst: a reduction in blood volume. When blood volume declines, the brain immediately tries to counteract this effect by increasing blood pressure. To do this, the brain signals the kidney to secrete **renin,** an enzyme that converts **angiotensinogen,** a substance in the blood, to angiotensin. (There are several forms of angiotensin, each designated with its

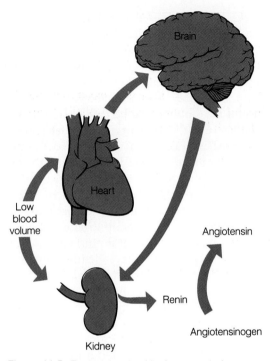

Figure 11.5 Factors involved in the control of angiotensin production.

own Roman numeral from I to III. Because the only form that need concern us is angiotensin II, we will refer to it simply as angiotensin.) The steps involved in the production of angiotensin are summarized in figure 11.5. Note that low blood volume also can act on the kidney directly to begin the process of angiotensin production.

Once in the blood supply, angiotensin constricts blood vessels and thus helps to raise blood pressure. In fact, the term angiotensin is derived from the Greek meaning "blood vessel tension." The increase in blood pressure is critical because the heart cannot function properly when blood volume is low. (This effect of angiotensin is enhanced by vasopressin, another vasoconstrictive agent, that you will

recall also is released by low blood volume.) But does angiotensin also have a role in drinking? Support for this possibility comes from evidence that when angiotensin is injected into the blood supply, drinking is increased (Fitzsimons and Simons 1969). Thus, the angiotensin produced during hypovolemia may contribute to volemic thirst. This intriguing hypothesis received support when Simpson, Epstein, and Camardo (1978) began searching for angiotensin receptors in the brain. They focused their attention on the SFO, a structure near the third ventricle that we encountered in our discussion of osmotic thirst. They found that an injection of angiotensin directly into the SFO causes drinking. This response disappears when the SFO is destroyed or when a drug that blocks the action of angiotensin is injected into the SFO. In another experiment, these investigators made rats hypovolemic by injecting polyethylene glycol into the abdominal cavity. This procedure, which drains interstitial fluid from the extracellular compartment, increases the blood level of angiotensin and at the same time causes volemic thirst. Yet in rats with SFO lesions, the drinking response to polyethylene glycol is reduced dramatically. Taken together, these results suggest that angiotensin plays an important role in volemic thirst and that the SFO mediates this response.

At this stage of our knowledge, however, it is best to be extremely cautious of both conclusions. Regarding the role of angiotensin, Stricker (1978) argues that the amount of angiotensin formed in the blood during hypovolemia is much less than the amount of this substance that must be injected to cause drinking. It is difficult to know, therefore, just how important angiotensin can be in causing volemic thirst under natural conditions. We also must be careful not to focus all of our attention on the SFO. The demonstration that angiotensin injections into the SFO cause drinking is not convincing evidence that this structure acts alone in this response. Because the SFO protrudes into the third ventricle, any substance injected here is likely to leak into the ventricle itself where it can spread to nearby structures. In fact, if angiotensin is injected into the third ventricle and access to the SFO is blocked by a plug of cold cream, angiotensin continues to elicit drinking (Johnson and Buggy 1977). Cold cream applied along the anterior and ventral border of the third ventricle, however, abolishes this response. Lesions of this same region, which includes the OVLT, also reduce angiotensin-induced drinking (Buggy and Johnson 1977). A reasonable conclusion, therefore, is that the OVLT and perhaps structures adjacent to the OVLT are at least as important, if not more so, as the SFO in mediating the response to angiotensin. In addition, evidence that we will present in the following paragraphs suggests that the SFO may play a more important role as a modulator of both osmotic and volemic thirst.

Brain Mechanisms of Thirst

Once receptors detect a need for water—intracellular, extracellular, or both—a thirst signal must travel to the appropriate region of the brain to initiate drinking behavior. As researchers look for this region, they confront many of the same issues that plague the search for areas of the brain that control eating behavior. You will recall that lesions of specific structures abolish food intake, but in most cases this effect is not very specific (many behaviors are affected, not just eating) or the lesion damages axons or fibers of passage (making it difficult to know if the lesioned site

or a site far removed from the lesion is responsible for the behavioral effect). In our chapter on eating behavior, we stressed that the results of any lesion study must be interpreted with caution. We repeat that warning here. This does not mean, however, that no useful information can be gained from lesion studies. On the contrary, when behavior is analyzed carefully, when researchers are aware of the problems of the lesion technique and limit their conclusions accordingly, and when other lines of supporting evidence are available, lesion studies can provide valuable insights into how various brain structures control a given behavioral response. In fact, a recent series of lesion studies have identified areas of the brain that exert very specific influences on water intake. As you will see, these areas appear to form a neural circuit that regulates both osmotic and volemic thirst. When elements of this circuit are damaged, drinking behavior is not abolished, but it is altered in a profound and surprising way.

One component of this circuit is the SFO, a structure that we mentioned previously in connection with angiotensin receptors. Lesions of this structure, you will recall, impair the response of rats to polyethylene glycol or to angiotensin. Hosutt, Rowland, and Stricker (1981) extended these studies and found not only an impaired response to polyethylene glycol, but also to hypertonic saline, a stimulus for osmotic thirst. Moreover, the animals were impaired only when these substances were injected in low concentrations. Abnormally high concentrations of either polyethylene glycol or hypertonic saline produce intense drinking. One effect of SFO lesions, therefore, appears to be an impaired ability to detect or to respond to thirst stimuli. Clearly, the lesions did not abolish drinking; they merely made it more difficult for drinking to occur. Even more surprising, normal drinking could be restored simply by injecting the lesioned animals with caffeine, a stimulant drug. When rats with SFO damage receive caffeine, they drink in response to amounts of either hypertonic saline or polyethylene glycol that previously had been ineffective. In normal animals, caffeine has no obvious effect on drinking. Thus, the SFO appears to be part of a neural system that helps to regulate water intake, perhaps by setting the threshold necessary to elicit this response. When the SFO is damaged, the threshold is much higher and greater stimulation is required to reach it. Caffeine may overcome a higher threshold simply by increasing arousal. The drug makes the lesioned animals more ready to behave, and in that way restores drinking. Of course, it also is possible that caffeine restores drinking by some direct pharmacological action.

Because SFO lesions interfere with both osmotic and volemic thirst, this structure seems to be involved in thirst in a very general way. Lesions of the **zona incerta,** another small nucleus near the third ventricle, also disrupt both types of thirst, and there is no evidence of a diffuse impairment of motor or sensory functions (Rowland, Grossman, and Grossman 1979). It is conceivable, therefore, that a neural circuit exists that exerts a very general control over the drinking response without influencing other aspects of behavior.

The **nucleus medianus,** which receives input from the SFO and lies near the anterior and ventral region of the third ventricle, also appears to be part of such a control system. Lesions of this structure disrupt the normal drinking response to either hypertonic saline or polyethylene glycol (Mangiapane et al. 1983; Gardiner and Stricker 1985a). But these lesions also produce one additional effect: the drinking impairments are present only during daylight hours. At night, rats with nucleus medianus lesions respond normally to hypertonic saline and polyethylene glycol. In fact, about half of the lesioned rats go on a drinking binge at night and consume between two and three times their normal daily amount of water. During the day, these same animals shun liquids. They refuse to drink spontaneously. If they drink at all, unusually high concentrations of substances that cause osmotic or volemic thirst are required.

When Gardiner and Stricker (1985a) discovered these unusual effects, they began a systematic investigation of the role of the nucleus medianus in drinking behavior. First, they tried to determine why the animals drink so much at night. Daily measurements of blood volume, sodium levels, and urination all were within normal range. In fact, there seemed to be no change in any of the systems that regulate bodily fluids, including angiotensin levels. Why, then, do the animals drink excessively? The most reasonable hypothesis seems to be that damage to the nucleus medianus causes a major change in the way that the brain controls water intake.

What kind of change? The fact that the animals drink only at night (or, more precisely, during darkness in the laboratory) provides a clue. Rats are nocturnal animals; they are quiet or asleep during the day. Thus, their response to osmotic or volemic stimuli and their excessive spontaneous drinking occur when they are most aroused. If arousal is the critical factor, then it should be possible to make these animals drink during the day simply by treating them with caffeine, the same procedure that restores drinking in rats with SFO lesions. This is exactly what happens. Under the influence of caffeine, rats with nucleus medianus lesions drink in response to hypertonic saline or polyethylene glycol even during the day (Gardiner and Stricker 1985b). Caffeine has little effect on their drinking behavior at night, when they already are very active. Similarly, caffeine does not alter the drinking behavior of normal animals. Figure 11.6 demonstrates the pronounced effect of caffeine on the daytime drinking of rats with nucleus medianus lesions.

Presumably, the nucleus medianus is another component of a neural circuit that facilitates drinking. When the circuit is damaged, regulation of this response becomes

much more difficult. During the day, when behavioral activity is low, drinking is virtually nonexistent even when there is a need for water. At night or after an injection of caffeine, when behavioral activity is high, drinking resumes and may even become excessive. These results emphasize that drinking is far more than a simple motor response mediated by a "center" for osmotic or volemic thirst. Drinking requires complex control systems that help to fit it into an overall behavioral pattern. The SFO and the nucleus medianus appear to be two important elements in such a system, which undoubtedly includes many other structures as well. Somehow, and we do not yet know how, the brain integrates the information from this and other neuronal systems into the drinking response itself.

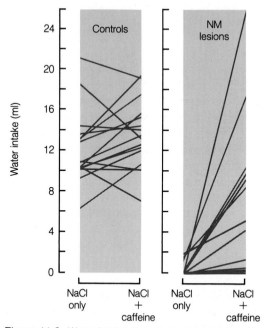

Figure 11.6 Water intake of control rats and rats with lesions of the nucleus medianus. Each line represents the response of individual rats to an injection of hypertonic saline (NaCl only or NaCl and caffeine). Note the dramatic effect of caffeine on the large majority of lesioned rats.

Satiety

Drinking, of course, eventually stops when water supplies are replenished. Because more than fifteen minutes elapse before all the water that we drink is absorbed into the body through the intestines, there must be some mechanism that says we have had enough long before the water actually reaches the intracellular and extracellular compartments. Even people deprived of water for up to twenty-four hours will consume most of the water that they need within the first five minutes that water becomes available. We saw with eating behavior that the satiety response depends on many different organ systems, most of which are part of the alimentary canal. Drinking, too, appears to be terminated by signals arising from receptors outside the brain.

One of the first places to look for a system that monitors water intake and provides a satiety signal is the mouth. After all, this is where water enters the alimentary canal, and neurons in the tongue are known to change their firing rate in response to water. But the mouth alone is not the critical factor. When a tube that leads directly to the stomach is implanted in animals, they learn to press a lever to inject water into the tube. They use this method to regulate their water intake within normal amounts even though no water enters the mouth (Epstein and Teitelbaum 1962). Thus, if the mouth plays any role at all in satiety, it can be bypassed without causing any serious problems. Similarly, the mouth plays a minor role in initiating drinking. A dry mouth may cause us to seek out a source of water, but we do not rely on this stimulus alone to insure that we consume all of the water that we really need.

Still, in some species under certain circumstances the mouth may very well play an important role in satiety. Consider dogs that have been deprived of water for a prolonged period. When allowed to drink, these animals do so ravenously for only a few minutes and then stop, yet they consume almost all of the water that they need. Thus, they know when to stop drinking long before the water is absorbed into the body. In fact, water-deprived dogs will stop drinking even if none of the water reaches the stomach. (A tube that leads from the esophagus and protrudes from the neck is implanted in the animals beforehand. In this condition, all the water they drink lands at their feet.) Rats and primates seem less dependent on feedback from the mouth. When water-deprived, these animals, especially rats, show a more prolonged bout of drinking, which may reflect the time it takes to activate other satiety mechanisms.

The stomach is the next likely place to search for a satiety signal. This organ seems to be more important than the mouth, but again it is not essential. If a noose is tied around the duodenum of rats so that any water that they consume never leaves the stomach, the animals do stop drinking, but they first consume much more than they need (Blass and Hall 1976). Of course, they may stop simply because the stomach becomes distended, but there may be another reason. Novin (1962) found that when water reaches the stomach, even before it has a chance to enter the intestines and be absorbed, cells in the basal forebrain begin to accumulate water. It is as if they anticipate that additional water will arrive soon from the stomach. Despite this unusual effect, the satiety mechanism does not operate normally; the rats with a duodenal noose still drink too much.

Rolls, Wood, and Rolls (1980) examined the role of the duodenum in satiety, and they appear to have found an important source for the termination of drinking. A tube that led directly to the duodenum was implanted in monkeys. When water is injected into the tube, the monkeys stop drinking. You may recall that intraduodenal injections of raw food make animals sick; thus, it becomes important to show that sickness is not the reason that the animals stop drinking when water is injected into the duodenum. With this in mind, the investigators also examined the effects of isotonic saline. If the injections cause some general discomfort, then the animals should stop drinking in response to either water or isotonic saline. If, on the other hand, water alone is the crucial stimulus, then isotonic saline, which matches the body's own level of sodium chloride, should have no effect on water intake. In fact, isotonic saline does not stop drinking, suggesting that the duodenum contains receptors that monitor water intake and provide a strong satiety signal.

There also is a system that terminates drinking when the fluid compartments of the body contain too much water. Even thirsty rats will stop drinking in response to an injection of **hypotonic saline,** which is more dilute than the normal 0.9 percent sodium chloride (Stricker 1969). In this case, the extracellular compartment becomes dilute, and water enters cells by osmosis, causing overhydration. Presumably, receptors respond to this condition, and a signal to stop drinking is sent to the brain.

In short, the signal to turn off drinking is composed of information from several different systems, including relatively minor contributions from the mouth and stomach. Under most circumstances, they all work together to keep water intake within normal limits.

Sodium Appetite

We all need sodium. Virtually every organ system in the body requires sodium to keep operating normally. Moreover, as we saw previously, sodium is essential for the retention of water by the kidneys. Most of us, however, do not need to worry about consuming enough sodium. Typical modern diets contain much more sodium than we really need. Instead of trying to retain it, our bodies are busy trying to excrete the excess. Even the laboratory chow fed to rats contains excess sodium. Because sodium is so readily available, we often do not realize just how crucial it really is. In fact, sodium is so crucial that the body seems to have developed an innate appetite for it.

The absorption of sodium depends on the hormone **aldosterone,** which is released by the outer segment, or cortex, of the adrenal glands. Aldosterone stimulates the sodium pump in the ascending portion of the loop of Henle—an ef-

fect that we have seen allows the kidney to accumulate sodium and in that way reabsorb water. Thus, when the adrenal glands are removed or are not functioning properly, large amounts of both sodium and water will be lost in the urine. Adrenalectomized animals will die unless they have access to salt. As soon as salt becomes available, these animals consume it avidly (Richter 1936). In fact, Nachman (1962) reported that adrenalectomized rats show a strong preference for sodium within fifteen seconds after it is offered. Such an immediate response makes it unlikely that the animals learn to associate the taste of sodium with improved health. Although such learning may explain preferences for other foods, as we saw in chapter 10, no learning is required to consume sodium when the body needs it. Humans, too, appear to have an innate appetite for sodium. Infants born with defective adrenal glands show an almost immediate craving for salt. For one such infant, "salt" became one of the first words of his vocabulary.

We detect sodium by means of salt receptors on the tongue. They let us know immediately if we are consuming sodium. But the receptors that are responsible for triggering sodium appetite appear to lie in the brain itself. Support for this hypothesis comes from research on rats treated with polyethylene glycol (Stricker 1981). You will recall that an injection of this substance depletes the interstitial fluid, which means a loss of water as well as sodium. If animals with a severe sodium loss drink only water, they would simply increase their urinary output and never quench their volemic thirst. Yet, when given a choice, the animals ignore saline at first and prefer water. Only after several hours do the rats begin to drink saline. Why this delay in sodium appetite and how does this implicate the brain?

Sodium appetite is delayed because the body seems to maintain a large store of sodium in the interstitial fluid. Thus, although polyethylene glycol causes some sodium loss, a more immediate effect is the loss of water from blood plasma, which activates blood volume receptors and causes volemic thirst. As the animals drink water, however, their blood volume becomes extremely dilute. This causes even more sodium to be lost from the interstitial fluid, and eventually the sodium store is depleted enough to cause a saline preference. The assumption that the body maintains a large reservoir of sodium seems to be correct. Rats maintained on a sodium-free diet—a special laboratory chow that contains no sodium—respond to a polyethylene glycol injection with a much more rapidly developed preference for saline (Stricker 1981). Presumably, these rats have no sodium reservoir and, therefore, are much more vulnerable to the sodium-depleting effects of polyethylene glycol.

The sodium reservoir may act like a buffer that supplies the brain with normal amounts of sodium despite daily fluctuations in sodium intake and sodium loss. Because of the large amount of sodium in our diets, we probably have a substantial sodium reservoir, making it unnecessary to consume a large amount of salt every time we sweat. Only when the reservoir is depleted and the brain no longer receives its normal supply does it become critical to eat salt. At this point, a sodium appetite will develop. Denton and colleagues (Weisinger et al. 1982) suggested that the critical trigger for sodium appetite was a sodium level reduction in the brain. They reported an immediate increase in sodium appetite in sheep following a reduction in the sodium concentration of the cerebrospinal fluid. Sodium appetite, therefore, seems to develop whenever an insufficient amount of sodium reaches receptor sites in the brain.

Although the brain may trigger sodium appetite, hormonal mechanisms can enhance it. One of these mechanisms involves angiotensin, the hormone produced in response to low blood volume. In many respects, low blood volume presents the same problem as low sodium: too much water is being lost. Not surprisingly, therefore, angiotensin also promotes the release of aldosterone from the adrenal glands. Stricker (1983) found that this release is enhanced at the same time that rats treated with polyethylene glycol begin to prefer saline. Moreover, when the production of angiotensin is increased by drugs, so too is the craving for sodium. In fact, sodium appetite can be produced by an injection of angiotensin directly into the ventricular system of the brain (Fluharty and Epstein 1983). An absence of angiotensin and aldosterone, however, does not impair sodium appetite. Thus, the angiotensin-aldosterone system provides an important regulatory influence on sodium appetite, but these hormones are not responsible for initiating it.

Regulating Body Temperature

For most mammals, including humans, the ability to maintain a stable internal temperature is just as crucial for survival as eating or drinking. Our bodies cannot tolerate large fluctuations in temperature. Proteins begin to unravel and lose their three-dimensional shape at temperatures above 110° F. When the body's temperature drops below 90° F, the integrated activity of the nervous system becomes erratic, and, as a result, behavior itself is impaired. To guard against these extremes, mammals rely on complex physiological mechanisms to maintain their internal temperatures within a fairly narrow range. The optimal temperature range for humans and most other mammals is 98–99° F. Birds also maintain body temperatures within narrow limits, but the optimal range for birds typically begins at temperatures above 100° F. Both birds and mammals generate and store their own heat; thus, they are called **endo-therms** (from the Greek, meaning "internal heat"). Other animals, including most invertebrates and many vertebrates living in water, depend on the external environment to regulate their temperature. These animals are called **ectotherms** (from the Greek, meaning "external heat"). For both types of animals, the regulation of body temperature—**thermoregulation**—provides a classic example of homeostasis in action.

Types of Thermoregulation

Endotherms generate heat with internal metabolic processes. These processes are driven by the utilization of energy stored in food. Utilizing this energy produces heat. When we are resting quietly, almost one-third of the body's heat is produced by the brain (since much of this heat is lost through the top of the head, it is a good idea to keep your head covered when you want to stay warm). During very strenuous activity, the brain's heat production does not change, but the muscles increase their heat production dramatically (muscles are very much like gasoline engines in this respect; both produce about four times as much heat as mechanical work). The body takes advantage of the heat-producing ability of muscles by shivering when the internal temperature drops.

Muscle cells contract out of synchrony at low temperatures causing brief twitches or shivers rather than coordinated movement. Another way to gain heat is to increase the metabolic activity of cells. Cellular metabolism is controlled by **thyroxine,** a hormone released by the thyroid gland in the neck. To stimulate thyroxine release, the anterior pituitary gland, also known as the **adenohypophysis,** secretes thyrotropic, or thyroid stimulating hormone (TSH). TSH circulates in the bloodstream until it reaches the thyroid. Thyroxine then is released and travels throughout the body, causing cells to increase their rate of heat production. The body also creates heat by constricting cutaneous blood vessels. Vasoconstriction reduces heat loss through the skin and concentrates blood near the warm interior of the body. These internal mechanisms of heat gain, summarized in figure 11.7, are controlled by the autonomic nervous system.

These same mechanisms operate in reverse to help the body lose heat. Thus, blood vessels dilate to increase heat loss through the skin, thyroxine release subsides to decrease cellular metabolism, and a major source of body heat, muscle activity, slows down. Of course, if we insist on strenuous physical exertion even in hot surroundings, then we run the risk of overheating. Marathon runners, for example, can elevate their body temperature by more than six degrees if they choose to maintain a fast pace on an unusually warm day.

Sweating provides another means of lowering body temperature. When sweat on the skin evaporates, heat is drawn from the skin, and body temperature declines. Birds and some mammals that do not sweat cool off by increasing their intake of air through the mouth and respiratory tract. As air passes over moist

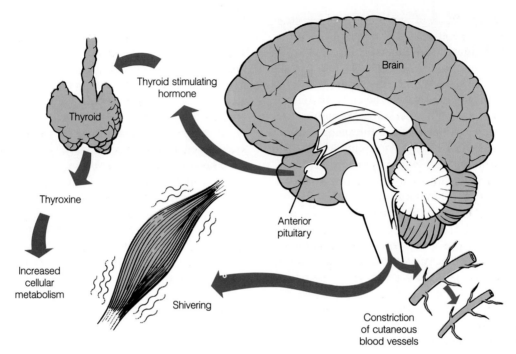

Figure 11.7 Major mechanism of internal heat gain in humans.

respiratory surfaces, it causes evaporative cooling. Thus, pelicans open their beaks and flutter their pouches, while dogs pant heavily.

Ectotherms have almost no direct control over their body temperature. They are at the mercy of their environment. When the temperature is low, these animals are sluggish; as the temperature rises, they become very active. You might think that sheer muscle activity alone would help to keep the internal temperature of these animals high, but this is not the case. Although the muscles in a very active fish generate heat, it is lost very rapidly through the thin walls of the capillaries that surround the gills. In seconds, water, an excellent conductor of heat, draws away whatever heat the ectotherms manage to produce.

For this reason, endotherms living in the ocean must be equipped with thick layers of blubber. Seals, walrus, and whales are able to maintain the typical mammalian body temperature because fat acts as a superb insulator. In fact, whales lose so little heat to their environment that they cannot survive when water temperature rises above 58° F.

Because ectotherms are unable to retain heat, they must move to warm surroundings to raise their body temperature. Lizards and other reptiles are equipped with infrared receptors to detect heat in the environment. These animals seek out warm rocks and expose as much of their bodies as possible to the sun. Butterflies spread their wings to absorb maximal amounts of sunlight. Some butterflies do this so effectively that they can raise their body temperature by more than 10° F in less than a minute. To cool off, ectotherms move to the shade or retreat to water.

Endotherms also use the environment to adjust their body temperature. When hot, for example, we prefer to sit in the shade, rather than in direct sunlight. We would do just the opposite, if we were colder than normal. Most people prefer an ambient temperature of about 72° F. Other mammals may prefer different temperature conditions; an arctic fox, for example, would become very uncomfortable when the temperature rose above 50° F. At their preferred temperatures, endotherms do not need to work as hard in order to maintain a stable internal temperature. Thus, by choosing an optimal environmental temperature, endotherms take some of the load off of their bodies for producing heat. This point becomes especially important for very small animals because the rate of heat loss is related to body size. Small animals lose heat faster than large ones, and thus small endotherms must maintain a higher metabolic rate to keep up their body temperature. A hummingbird weighs less than an ounce, and its metabolic rate is nearly fifty-five times higher than that of a 150-pound human. Because this bird expends so much energy to keep warm, it will starve to death if deprived of food for only a few hours (most people, especially fat ones, can go without food for weeks without starving). Metabolically speaking, therefore, hummingbirds will find life a lot easier in environments that are close to their optimal temperature. In fact, the temperature drop that occurs at night exacts such a high metabolic cost on small birds and many desert rodents that they enter a state of **torpor** to save energy. During torpor, body temperature drops and metabolism slows.

In the hummingbird, torpor is so deep that the animal can be lifted from its nest without showing any sign of protest. When nighttime torpor extends over a prolonged period, animals are said to hibernate. The rationale is the same—to conserve metabolic energy during cold conditions.

Temperature regulation in young animals poses a special problem, especially for endotherms. Many immature birds and mammals are unable to regulate their internal temperatures very well. These animals would freeze to death unless their parents provided extra heat. This often means that parents must spend many hours in the nest transferring their heat to the offspring. What is responsible for such devotion? There may be many reasons why a parent will spend so much time keeping its young warm, but in the rat we need look no further than the mother's own thermoregulatory mechanisms. A nursing rat has a higher than normal body temperature due, in part, to increased levels of prolactin and adrenocorticotropic hormone in her blood. When she comes in contact with cool rat pups in her nest, they draw heat away from her and help to lower her body temperature. The pups, therefore, are doing her just as big a favor as she is doing for them. When the pups warm up, they no longer remove heat from their mother, and she promptly leaves the nest (Leon, Croskerry, and Smith 1978).

Such seemingly cold (pun intended) behavior can be controlled by artificially adjusting the mother's temperature (Woodside, Pelchat, and Leon 1980). In one experiment, a coil of wire was inserted under the mother rat's skin. Electrical current was passed through the wire after she made contact with her litter. The electricity gradually increased her body temperature by several degrees, and she left the nest thirty minutes sooner than normal. If the warming wire was inserted directly into the brain, she left the nest a full fifty minutes sooner than she would without brain stimulation. Thus, when the mother can no longer lower her temperature by staying with her pups, she leaves. Apparently, her body temperature, regulated by mechanisms within her brain, controls the temperature of her litter.

The pups are not completely helpless, however. They rely on an unusual form of group behavior called **huddling** to regulate their temperature when the mother is away from the nest (Alberts 1978). The body temperature of a five-day-old rat pup placed alone in a cool chamber will drop more than 10° F in less than an hour. A group of four pups of the same age placed in the same chamber will lose less than 2° F in an hour and only 5–6° F after four hours. The grouped pups form a huddle (fig. 11.8), and each one moves about in the huddle to raise or lower its temperature. Pups that form the periphery of the huddle lose heat, and over time they work their way to the inside.

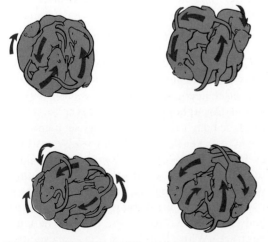

Figure 11.8 Rat pups huddling to regulate body temperature. The pups adjust their position in the huddle to gain or lose heat.

Those pups on the inside move to the periphery as they gain heat. If a cold pup is placed on the top of the huddle, it immediately will sink to the inside to raise its temperature. Huddling declines as the pups grow older. Between thirteen–fifteen days of age, the pups become very good endotherms. By now, they have grown a coat of fur, and they are no longer dependent on their mother or their siblings for warmth. As their eyes open and their motor skills improve, they leave the nest with a mature thermoregulatory system.

In summary, thermoregulation involves a wide variety of autonomic and behavioral responses. Ectotherms, which are unable to retain the heat that their bodies produce, regulate their temperature primarily by behavioral means: sprawling themselves out on a sun-drenched rock to raise their temperature or retreating to an underground burrow to cool off. Endotherms, in contrast, retain their heat fairly well and thus use autonomic responses (shivering, sweating, panting, vasoconstriction, etc.) as well as behavior to control their temperature. Thermoregulation, therefore, is a more complicated process than you might have expected, and you can be certain that such complexity extends to the brain mechanisms that make thermoregulation possible.

Brain Mechanisms of Temperature Control

The autonomic and behavioral responses that together make up the process of thermoregulation are not triggered by a single system in the brain. Instead, many different neural systems seem to be involved, and each one may operate somewhat independently of the others. Consider what happens in mammals when the **preoptic area** of the hypothalamus is destroyed (Satinoff and Rutstein 1970). The autonomic control of thermoregulation disappears. Thus, regardless of the environmental temperature, rats with preoptic damage no longer pant, shiver, or adjust the diameter of their blood vessels. Yet these same animals will continue to regulate their body temperature by behavioral means. They will press a lever, for example, to turn on a heat lamp when they are placed in a cold room.

Apparently, the preoptic area helps to regulate body temperature by coordinating activity in the autonomic nervous system. When a heated probe is placed in the preoptic area, animals will pant or sweat even if they are in cold surroundings. Similarly, if the preoptic area is cooled, animals will shiver, and their cutaneous blood vessels will constrict. There appears to be a thermostat in this area of the hypothalamus that turns on the appropriate autonomic response to raise or lower body temperature (Nelson and Prosser 1981). But the preoptic area does not act alone. If this area is heated at the same time that the skin is cooled, the opposing autonomic responses will cancel each other. Temperature-sensitive receptors in the skin send their information to the brain where it interacts with temperature information from the preoptic area. Thus, although the preoptic area seems to contain a thermostat, it is by no means a thermoregulatory "center."

In fact, data obtained from other areas of the nervous system also could be interpreted as evidence for temperature-sensitive receptors. When the posterior hypothalamus or ventral medulla is heated, for example, rats will engage in grooming behavior to lower their body temperature (Roberts and Mooney 1974). By spreading their saliva over their fur as they groom, rats dissipate heat by evaporative cooling. Even the spinal cord has some capacity for temperature regulation. Spinal animals will attempt to adjust their temperature when placed in warm or cool surroundings, but because the spinal cord does not respond unless body temperature changes by more than 5° F, spinal animals cannot survive for very long in the heat or cold.

What does all this information tell us about the role of the nervous system in thermoregulation? Satinoff (1978) argues that many different neural systems control the many different responses to a change in body temperature. Moreover, she suggests that these systems are arranged in a hierarchical fashion. Thermoregulation in the spinal cord is limited and not very precise, whereas thermoregulatory mechanisms in the hypothalamus respond quickly and keep the body's temperature within fairly narrow limits. In addition, hypothalamic mechanisms coordinate and adjust the activity of all other thermoregulatory systems. Thus, thermoregulation may appear to be controlled by a single process, but in reality multiple interactive systems are involved.

A Little Fever Is Good for You

All of us have experienced the unpleasant effects of fever. The elevated body temperature that often accompanies an illness has been observed throughout history. A fever seems to raise the body's thermoregulatory set point. We begin to shiver and our blood vessels constrict, even at normal room temperatures. Consciously, we comply with these autonomic responses by putting on an extra sweater or hiding under a pile of blankets. It is as if the body has made a decision to increase its temperature. Why should this occur? Fever appears to be one of the most effective means of combating disease.

Kluger (1978) demonstrated this point very convincingly in a study of desert iguanas. Like all lizards, the iguana adjusts its body temperature by moving to warm or cool surroundings. The animals in Kluger's study were housed in a chamber that ranged in temperature from 122° F at one end to room temperature at the other. The iguanas preferred to stay somewhere in the middle, where the temperature closely approximated their natural desert environment. When they were injected with a strain of bacteria that made them sick, however, they spent considerably more time at the hot end of the chamber. They remained there until they had raised their body temperature by 3–5° F. The sick iguanas were giving themselves a fever. The second part of Kluger's study shows why the iguanas acted so. When the sick iguanas were treated with a drug that reduced their fever, more than half of them died. Another group of sick iguanas did not receive the fever-suppressing drug. These animals maintained a fever for several days and survived.

Physicians have recognized the beneficial effects of fever for centuries. Hippocrates, for example, counseled his patients to let their fever run its course rather than to find ways to suppress it. Until the early 1900s, many diseases were treated with an injection of fever-producing bacteria. In fact, it was not uncommon to treat syphilis by injecting the victim with the virus that causes malaria. Although fever did not save these unfortunate individuals, it does seem to help the body defend itself against disease.

Fever is caused by the release into the bloodstream of **endogenous pyrogens** (from the Greek, meaning "internal fire makers"). Apart from elevating body temperature, endogenous pyrogens also increase the production of T cells, a vital part of the immune system. T-cell production increases dramatically even if body temperature rises by only 3° F.

Sickness is not the only stimulus that releases endogenous pyrogens. Vigorous exercise does so as well. Body temperature may remain elevated for up to an hour after long-distance running, perhaps substantiating the claim made by some marathoners that exercise protects them against illness. The protection is marginal at best, however, because even strenuous running elevates the release of endogenous pyrogens to only half the level of that during a fever.

There are many aspects of fever that we still do not understand. It is not clear, for example, why some illnesses cause a fever and others do not. Nor is it clear what mechanisms terminate a fever once an infection ends. In addition, a fever in persons with heart problems can be dangerous. An increase in body temperature of only a few degrees can increase heart rate by as much as 50 percent and put a severe strain on the cardiovascular system. In otherwise healthy individuals, however, a moderate fever appears to be an effective response to disease.

Summary

Drinking and temperature regulation, like all homeostatic behaviors, help the body to maintain a stable internal environment. They are controlled by several different organ systems acting with many neural pathways in the brain.

In order to understand drinking behavior, it is important to begin with some basic information about water supplies in the body. Water is stored in two general compartments separated by membranes. The intracellular compartment includes all the water inside cells; the extracellular compartment includes the fluid that surrounds all cells as well as blood plasma. Water passes easily through cellular membranes, but the amount of water in each compartment is determined by such solutes as sodium chloride, which do not penetrate membranes very easily. When one compartment has a greater concentration of solutes than another, water will move from the dilute compartment to the concentrated one by **osmosis.** Under normal circumstances, the extracellular compartment contains a 0.9 percent solution of sodium chloride.

The body conserves water by returning it to the blood supply before it reaches the bladder. This recycling process is performed by the kidney, which uses sodium to draw water out of the distal convoluted tubules before it has a chance to be lost in the urine. The kidney is aided in this task by **vasopressin,** a hormone released by the posterior pituitary gland in response to low blood volume or intracellular dehydration. People suffering from **diabetes insipidus** fail to produce enough vasopressin and as a result excrete copious amounts of water in their urine.

To replenish our supply of water, we must drink, and we do so in response to two types of thirst. **Osmotic thirst** occurs when a high concentration of sodium or a similar solute draws water from the intracellular compartment. Drinking in this case is triggered by **osmoreceptors** that appear to lie outside the blood-brain barrier. Volemic thirst refers to a loss of water from the extracellular compartment. Because such a loss includes blood plasma, the blood volume receptors in the heart can trigger volemic thirst. These receptors also stimulate the production of **angiotensin,** which may cause drinking by acting on angiotensin receptors in the brain.

Both osmotic and volemic thirst are regulated by a group of forebrain structures that include the **subfornical organ** and the **nucleus medianus.** They lie near the third ventricle and appear to be part of a neural circuit that controls behavioral activation for drinking. Lesions of these structures do not abolish drinking, but instead change the conditions under which animals will drink.

The signal for terminating drinking appears to arise from the duodenum, although the mouth and stomach make some contribution to this signal. Drinking also will stop when the extracellular compartment becomes too dilute.

Not only do we crave water when our supply runs low, but we also appear to have an innate appetite for sodium. Sodium absorption depends on **aldosterone,** a hormone released by the adrenal cortex. **Angiotensin** helps to stimulate aldosterone release. Sodium appetite seems to arise from receptors in the brain, although their precise location remains to be determined.

The control of body temperature is somewhat simpler than the regulation of the body's water supply, but no less important for survival. **Endotherms** such as mammals and birds regulate their internal temperatures by both autonomic and behavioral means. Other animals, called **ectotherms,** are unable to retain heat; they depend almost entirely on their surroundings for normal thermoregulation.

The neural systems that seem to be responsible for thermoregulation are organized in a hierarchy of increasing complexity from the spinal cord to the hypothalamus. Whereas spinal systems are sluggish and not very precise, hypothalamic mechanisms respond quickly and help to maintain temperature within very narrow limits. Although all of the neural systems involved in thermoregulation are capable of operating independently of each other, the hypothalamus seems to have the additional task of coordinating and adjusting their activity to produce an integrated thermoregulatory response.

The rise in body temperature that often accompanies an illness appears to be an effective means of combating disease. Fever, which is caused by the release of **endogenous pyrogens,** improves the survival rate of animals exposed to harmful bacteria and stimulates activity in the body's immune system. Endogenous pyrogens also are released during strenuous exercise, a finding that lends support to the claim that exercise helps to diminish certain types of illness.

Suggested Readings

Andersson, B. 1978. Regulation of water intake. *Physiological Reviews* 58: 582–603.
This comprehensive review focuses on the physiology of osmotic and volemic thirst. Special attention is given to the distinction between osmoreceptors and sodium receptors in the control of water intake.

Cooper, K. E. 1987. The neurobiology of fever: Thoughts on recent developments. *Annual Review of Neuroscience* 10: 297–324.
An up-to-date account of endogenous pyrogens and where they may act in the nervous system to produce fever.

Kluger, M. J. 1978. The evolution and adaptive value of fever. *American Scientist* 66: 38–43.
An entertaining account of the beneficial effects of fever.

Rolls, B. J., R. J. Wood, and E. T. Rolls. 1980. Thirst: The initiation, maintenance, and termination of drinking. In *Progress in psychobiology and physiological psychology,* eds. J. M. Sprague and A. N. Epstein, vol. 9. New York: Academic Press.
This article discusses the physiological mechanisms underlying thirst and the regulation of the body's water supply.

Satinoff, E. 1978. Neural organization and evolution of thermal regulation in mammals. *Science* 201: 16–22.
The author presents a sophisticated discussion of the many neural pathways involved in thermoregulation with a special emphasis on their evolutionary significance.

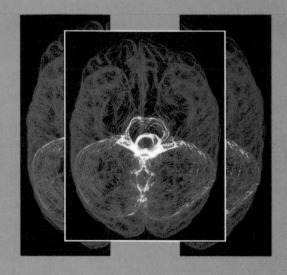

Outline

Introduction

The behaviors that we discuss in this chapter are known for their crowd appeal. Sexual and emotional behaviors always seem to attract attention, whether in our private lives or on television soap operas. More importantly for our purposes, however, these behaviors are regulated and controlled by some very basic motives, the same type of motives that underlie eating and drinking behavior discussed in previous chapters. In fact, you could argue that for many individuals in the industrialized world, the basic need to eat and drink is no longer a critical concern. Sex and emotions, on the other hand, still command considerable attention. Indeed, trying to reach a happy emotional state may be our biggest motive in life. In this chapter we will review the biological mechanisms underlying sexual and emotional behavior.

Chapter

12

Sex and Emotions

Sexual behavior is necessary for the survival of the species. Obviously, if we humans are to survive beyond this generation, we must be able to pass life on to the next. But that is only part of the survival story. Equally important is the fact that each parent provides a unique contribution of genetic material to each of its offspring. This genetic inheritance is combined in the new individual, making that person different from either parent alone. Because the contribution of each parent reflects a random assortment of alternative genes, a single couple in theory can produce an endless number of genetically different offspring (the number actually ends in the trillions, but for many parents even one or two is enough). Thus, except for identical twins, who inherit the same genetic package, all of us are truly unique. This uniqueness helps to perpetuate the species. If all of us were genetically identical, or even close to it, then we would be equally vulnerable to the same diseases, environmental changes, and other natural threats to our survival. A single epidemic could destroy every person on earth. A species with many genetically different individuals, however, is more likely to survive the challenges that Nature throws our way. In addition, as the genetic variability of a species increases, its members are able to establish new ecological niches and thus to stimulate evolution itself.

For many humans, however, sex has become something other than a matter of reproducing the species. Couples engage in sexual behavior even if there is little or no chance of pregnancy. In fact, human sexual behavior seems to be controlled more by cultural and moral influences than by our biological substrates. But, as you will see, biology makes an important contribution, not only to the obvious physical differences between the sexes, but to sexual behavior as well.

Biology also makes an important contribution to our emotions. Galen, the second-century Greek physician, estimated that about 60 percent of his patients suffered from some type of emotional disorder rather than a physical illness. Although this number is approximately the same today, we now know that our emotions are accompanied by distinct physiological changes and that emotional behaviors are an inherent part of our human and biological nature. Emotions, as you will see, are regulated and controlled by distinct chemical and neuronal circuits. The drugs that we often use to control our emotions are strong testimony to this fact. In the section on emotional behavior, we first will discuss the biology of emotions in general terms and then focus on those individual emotions that have generated the most interest and research: anxiety, aggression, and pleasure.

Sexual Development and Differentiation

During the first few weeks after conception, the only distinguishing feature between females and males is the complement of sex chromosomes that they receive from their parents. As we all know, however, there is much more to the sexes than chromosomes. Humans, like all other mammals, are sexually dimorphic (different in form). In this section, we will review the biological processes that are responsible for the development and differentiation of females and males.

The Role of Genetics

At conception, we inherit half of our chromosomes from each of our parents. This genetic endowment includes the sex chromosomes: an X chromosome from the mother and either an X or a Y chromosome from the father. An individual that receives an XX chromosome complement is a genetic female; a genetic male has an XY pair of chromosomes. Because the father can supply either type of chromosome whereas the mother provides only an X, the father determines the genetic sex of the fetus. If a Y-bearing sperm fertilizes an egg, a male will be produced; if an X-bearing sperm is involved, then the result will be a female. In the event you are wondering whether there is a foolproof method of predetermining the genetic sex of the offspring by selecting which type of sperm fertilizes the egg, the answer is no. Several attempts have been made to alter the movement of either X- or Y-bearing sperm in hopes of increasing the chances that only one type of sperm would fertilize the egg. Some of the more unusual methods have included changing the pH of the vagina by flooding it with vinegar or baking soda prior to intercourse. All such attempts at manipulating the genetic sex of the offspring have been unsuccessful.

After conception, both the XX- and XY-fetus develop in the same way until the sixth week of gestation (pregnancy). In fact, both contain an indifferent gonad capable of developing into either female ovaries or male testes. At the beginning of the sixth week, the sex chromosomes will determine which of these structures will take shape. If the fetus is XY, information on the Y chromosome stimulates the indifferent gonads to transform into testes. If, on the other hand, the fetus is XX, the gonads remain indifferent until the twelfth week of life, when they develop into ovaries. Once the ovaries or testes begin to form, the genetic influence on sexual development and differentiation ends. From this point on, a series of hormonal events are set in motion that ultimately will determine the birth of a normal female or male offspring.

The Role of Hormones

Sexual differentiation beyond the formation of ovaries or testes involves the formation of the internal sex organs, as shown in figure 12.1. These organs are formed from tissue contained in every fetus. Thus, early in life all of us had the potential for developing either female or male sex organs. The tissue that forms the female internal sex organs is called the **Müllerian duct.** It is capable of forming the uterus, the inner two-thirds of the vagina, and the fallopian tubes. The male internal sex organs develop from the **Wolffian duct,** which gives rise to the vas deferens, seminal vesicles, and prostate.

One of these two ducts will begin to develop at approximately the twelfth week of gestation. Which one does so will depend on the influence of gonadal hormones. If a genetic male is to develop normally, the testes must secrete **androgens** (from the Greek, meaning "male producers") and a **Müllerian-inhibiting hormone.** Androgens, which are really a group of several hormones, allow the male internal sex organs to develop from the Wolffian duct. The Müllerian-inhibiting hormone, as its name implies, suppresses growth of the Müllerian duct and thus prevents development of the female internal sex organs. Normal masculine development, therefore, depends on the testes to secrete their hormones. Normal female development, on the other hand, requires no hormones from the fetus. The Müllerian duct will grow and the Wolffian duct will recede as part of the natural course of events. It is not even necessary for the female to secrete a Wolffian-inhibiting hormone.

So dependent is the male on his testicular hormones that if these are not present, female internal sex organs will develop even

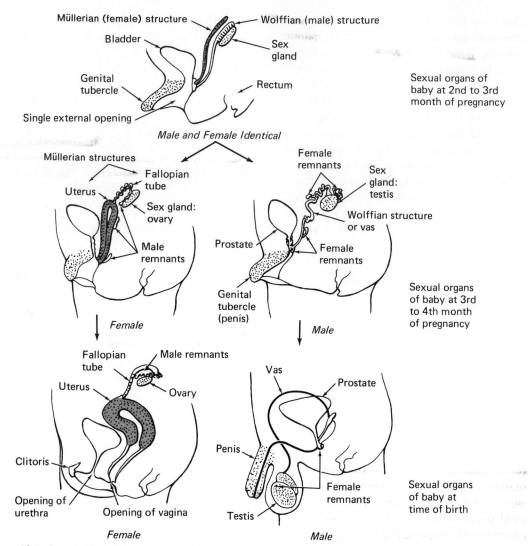

Figure 12.1 Sexual differentiation in the human fetus
is illustrated. Three stages of differentiation of both the
internal and external sexual apparatuses are
illustrated. Note early parallelism of the Müllerian and
Wolffian ducts, from which the internal sexual organs
of both males and females ultimately develop.

though the fetus may carry an XY complement of chromosomes. Moreover, the testes must release their hormones during a relatively short **critical period** in order to insure proper masculine development. Jost (1958) first demonstrated this phenomenon in rabbits. When male rabbits were castrated on the twenty-first day of gestation, they became completely feminized. They failed to develop male sex organs and developed female sex organs instead. When males were castrated on the twenty-third day of fetal development, some masculine differentiation had occurred, but it was incomplete. These rabbits were born with elements of both male and female sex organs. Only when castration occurred after the twenty-fourth day of gestation did differentiation of the internal sex organs proceed normally in the masculine direction. It is as if feminization is destined to occur regardless of genetic sex unless the appropriate hormones are present during the critical period of development to stimulate production of a male. In humans, the critical period of sexual differentiation begins during the twelfth week of pregnancy.

Unlike the internal sex organs, the external genitalia of females and males do not develop from different ducts. The external sex organs arise from tissue capable of assuming either female or male form. But like the internal sex organs, their normal development depends on the presence or absence of androgens. When they are present, the penis, its urethral tube, and the scrotum develop. When they are absent, the corresponding female organs emerge: the clitoris, the labia minora, and the labia majora. Normally, the amount of androgens required to stimulate male development is present only in genetic males. Females

contain small amounts of androgens, which are supplied by their adrenal glands, but usually not in sufficient quantities to alter the course of sexual development. If, however, the adrenal gland should become overactive during the critical period either in the fetus or in the mother a condition termed **congenital adrenal hyperplasia,** then it is likely that the fetus will develop masculinized genitals, even if the genetic sex is female. This condition is known as **pseudohermaphroditism.** A similar anomaly will occur if a pregnant woman consumes drugs that contain large amounts of androgens. In fact, before the role of androgens in sexual development was known, these hormones were administered to pregnant women as a means of preventing miscarriages. This practice, of course, has been discontinued.

Do prenatal androgens also make males the weaker sex? Clearly, the numbers presented in table 12.1 indicate that many more males than females are born, but fewer survive to old age. Of the more than sixty causes of

Table 12.1 The Human Sex Ratio: The Number of U.S. White Males per 100 Females

Stages of Life	Males/100 Females
Four months of embryonic age	107
Birth	106
18 years of age	100
50 years of age	95
57 years of age	90
67 years of age	70
87 years of age	50
100 or more years of age	21

From I. M. Lerner and W. J. Libby, *Heredity, Evolution and Society.* © 1976 W. H. Freeman and Co., New York. All rights reserved. Reprinted by permission.

death listed by the U.S. Census Bureau, fifty-seven have a higher rate among males (Lerner and Libby 1976). Moreover, during childhood, males show a higher incidence of virtually every neurologic and psychiatric disorder (Gualtieri and Hicks 1985). What is it about the male that makes him so vulnerable? A different life-style may have something to do with it. Fighting wars and smoking cigarettes are more common among males. But social patterns alone are not an entirely satisfactory explanation. The number of male embryos aborted or stillborn is higher than that of females, suggesting that the sex ratio may be even more in favor of males at the time of conception. The decline of the male, therefore, seems to begin even before birth. Although there is no widely accepted explanation for this phenomenon, Gualtieri and Hicks (1985) propose that in certain cases the male fetus evokes an immune response from its mother that can damage the fetus and make it more vulnerable to disease and other life-threatening events. Androgens, which are present in large quantities in the male embryo, could elicit this immunoreaction in certain childbearing women. In fact, gonadal hormones are known to influence the immune response (Grossman 1985). Needless to say, the hypothesis that a male fetus actually evokes a damaging immunoreaction from its mother is provocative, but even if this is the case, no one yet has established a clear link between prenatal hormones and male vulnerability.

We do know, however, that during puberty hormones play an important role in the physical development of the sexes. When puberty begins, usually between the ages of eleven and fourteen, the secondary sex characteristics, those which we ordinarily use to distinguish between females and males, finally appear. This process begins when cells in the hypothalamus secrete releasing factors that cause the anterior pituitary gland to produce and release **gonadotrophic hormones.** These hormones are the same in females and males, but they stimulate the gonads to produce and release their own hormones. In females, the gonadotrophic hormones cause the ovaries to produce and release a group of hormones called **estrogens.** The estrogens cause development of the breasts, broadening of the hips, changes in the deposition of body fat, and maturation of the female genitalia. In males, the gonadotrophic hormones cause another surge in the release of androgens from the testes. At this stage of life, androgens are responsible for causing such male characteristics as a deep voice, facial and other bodily hair (and, over time, a receding line of hair on the head), muscular development, and maturation of the male genitalia.

Neither androgens nor estrogens are exclusively male or female hormones. Both sexes produce them. The difference is a quantitative one: males produce more androgens, females produce more estrogens. In fact, the small amounts of androgens that are produced by the adrenal glands are responsible for hair on the female body. In some women, however, the adrenal glands become overactive and secrete large amounts of androgens. When this happens, women begin to experience masculinizing effects. So-called bearded ladies seen in circuses are often victims of overactive adrenal glands. An overproduction of androgens in men will not cause a dramatic change in secondary sex characteristics because these already are present from puberty. But a male

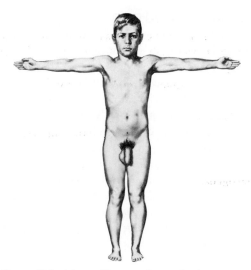

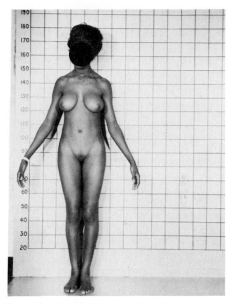

Figure 12.2 A boy with precocious puberty, a condition caused by excess production of adrenocortical hormones. Note the adult appearance of the sexual organs

Figure 12.3 A genetic male with androgen insensitivity syndrome.

child who experiences an androgen surge before puberty will develop male secondary sexual characteristics at an accelerated rate, as shown in figure 12.2. Such cases of **precocious puberty** are rare, but they have been known to cause beards and deep voices in boys that are only four years old.

Although androgens exert a critical influence on sexual development, they do not act alone. The tissues that develop into the male sex organs and that are responsible for the male secondary sex characteristics must be able to detect and then respond to the hormonal message. In rare cases, this does not happen. An XY fetus with normal androgen production will develop the appearance of a female if his tissues are insensitive to androgens. Such a person will have all the external features of a

female, but will be a genetic male with testes (development of testes, you will recall, depends on the XY chromosome complement and not on androgens). Despite their male genetic sex, persons who suffer from **androgen insensitivity** are raised as females. Figure 12.3 shows why.

Sexual Differentiation of the Nervous System

Differences between the sexes are not limited to sex organs or secondary sex characteristics. The nervous system itself is sexually dimorphic. In fact, subcortical structures like the hypothalamus, just like the tissue that forms the internal and external sex organs, are sensitive to androgens during a critical period of development. The critical period for the brain, however, is not the same as the critical period for the sex organs (McEwen et al. 1979). Thus, if circulating androgens are high during one period of development but not another, it is possible to form a male brain in a female body or a female brain in a male body (Arnold and Gorski 1984).

Differences in subcortical brain regions between females and males have been identified throughout the animal kingdom. Consider the preoptic area of the hypothalamus. In rats, for example, a lack of androgens causes a proliferation of dendritic spines (Field and Raisman 1973). The branching pattern of the dendrites in this same region also shows clear sex differences in both rats and monkeys (Greenough et al. 1977; Ayoub, Greenough, and Juraska 1983). Humans, too, have a sexually dimorphic preoptic area. It is more than twice as large in men as in women and contains twice the number of cells (Swaab and Fliers 1985). Such dimorphism may reflect important differences between the sexes as to how neuronal information is received and processed, although it is not clear if these anatomical differences are responsible for differences in sexual behavior.

A discrete group of neurons in the spinal cord, the **bulbocavernosus nucleus,** plays a direct role in sexual behavior by controlling the reflexes of the penis during copulation. This nucleus shows dramatic sexual differences. Adult male rats have approximately two hundred neurons in this nucleus; in females, it contains less than 70. Yet the nucleus is present in both sexes early in development. Atrophy of this nucleus in females is directly related to the absence of androgens (Breedlove and Arnold 1980). Females given androgens during a crit-

ical period of development show an increased number of bulbocavernosus neurons in adulthood. In contrast, males deprived of androgens early in development have the female number of neurons as adults. How do androgens regulate the number of neurons in the bulbocavernosus nucleus? They do so by preventing the death of these cells (Nordeen et al. 1985). As shown in figure 12.4a, cells in this nucleus degenerate as part of normal development. Androgens retard this degeneration process. Figure 12.4b shows the large difference in dying cells between normal males and females early in development. Note that treatment of females with androgens dramatically reduces cell death so that it now approaches the slower rate of males. Androgens may play a similar role in other parts of the nervous system that are sexually dimorphic.

Anatomical differences between females and males also have been observed in the cerebral cortex. In females, the left hemisphere of the cerebral cortex is thicker than the right; in males, the right is thicker than the left. Other evidence that the brains of females and males are different comes from research on the control of hormone release from the anterior pituitary gland. In females, this gland releases gonadotrophic hormones according to a regular cycle. Males release gonadotrophic hormones on a more or less continuous basis (this point has been established for male rats but may not be true of male primates). As you will see, these sexual differences in the release of gonadotrophic hormones do not reside in the pituitary gland, but in the brain regions that control it.

In order to understand the factors that regulate the release of gonadotrophic hormones, it is useful to review this process in females. In primates, the cyclic release of gonadotrophic hormones corresponds to the

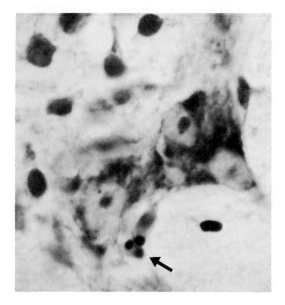

(a)

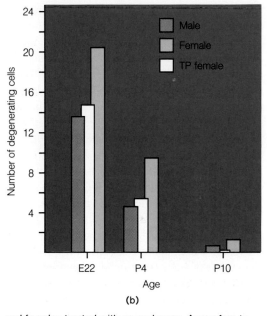

(b)

Figure 12.4 (a) Photomicrograph of bulbocavernosus nucleus in the spinal cord of a rat at the twenty-second day of gestation. The arrow points to a degenerating cell. (b) Numbers of degenerating cells in the same nucleus in normal males, normal females, and females treated with an androgen. Age refers to day of embryonic age (E) or postnatal age (P). Note that at all ages, normal females have more degenerating cells than rats in the other two groups.

menstrual cycle. Other female mammals release these hormones according to an **estrous cycle.** Both cycles are hormonally similar; the only difference is that in the menstrual cycle the uterus sheds its lining.

The Female Cycle

The human female produces between four hundred and five hundred mature eggs, or **ova.** The ova grow out of the ovaries located in the back of the abdominal cavity at about the level of the hips. Approximately every thirty days, one ovum begins to mature. The first step in this process involves the formation of a **follicle,** a layer of epithelial cells around the ovum. This marks the beginning of the menstrual cycle, which is triggered by the release

of **follicle stimulating hormone,** or **FSH,** from the anterior pituitary. FSH is one of two gonadotrophic hormones released by this gland, and as its name suggests, it stimulates the growth of the follicle. In response to FSH, the follicular cells begin to secrete a large number of estrogens. When the estrogens reach the anterior pituitary, they turn off the release of FSH and stimulate the release of the second gonadotrophic hormone known as **luteinizing hormone,** or **LH.** As LH levels rise and FSH levels fall, the follicle reaches maturity. It then is known as a **Graafian follicle** (by now it forms a large bulge just under the ovarian surface). The continued release of LH eventually causes the walls of the follicle to rupture, and a mature ovum is released, a process known as **ovulation.** The ovum finds its way into the fallopian tube and moves toward the uterus where it can be fertilized by a male sperm. Meanwhile, the ruptured follicle forms a yellow mass of tissue called the **corpus luteum** (from the Latin, meaning "yellow body"). Under the influence of LH, the corpus luteum begins to secrete large amounts of **progesterone,** sometimes called the pregnancy hormone because it prepares the wall of the uterus for implantation of the ovum should it be fertilized. If fertilization does occur, the ovum will begin to divide and eventually attach itself to the uterine wall. This is followed by the formation of the placenta, which secretes a series of hormones that prevent menstruation during pregnancy. If fertilization does not occur or if the fertilized ovum does not become implanted in the uterine wall, the corpus luteum will shrink, estrogen and progesterone levels will fall, and the lining of the uterus will slough away— menstruation. A low level of estrogen and progesterone in the blood triggers the release of FSH and the cycle begins again. Figure 12.5 summarizes the major steps in the cycle of the human female.

Mechanisms Controlling the Cyclic Release of Gonadoptrophins

Why does the female pituitary gland release gonadotrophins on a regular cycle? The pituitary gland itself is not responsible. If a female pituitary is transplanted into a male, the gland will begin to secrete gonadotrophins according to the male pattern (continuously). Similarly, if a male pituitary is placed in a female, it will stop secreting gonadoptrophins continuously and secrete them according to the regular female cycle. Thus, the pituitary secretes hormones in a fashion appropriate for the sex of

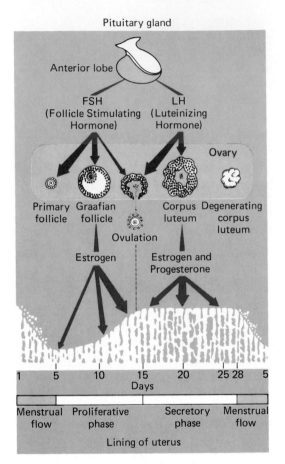

Figure 12.5 The changes in pituitary hormones, ovaries, and uterine wall as a function of the human menstrual cycle are illustrated. The level of the various hormones at the different stages in the cycle is depicted in terms of the width of the arrows. The direction of the arrows indicates cause-effect relations.

the organism, regardless of whether the gland came from a female or male donor.

The gland, however, will not cycle in a female if it is placed too far away from the hypothalamus. Normally, the hypothalamus is linked to the anterior pituitary by a dense vascular bed, and in order for the transplanted gland to become functional, it must be placed close enough to the hypothalamus that blood vessels can regrow. The hypothalamus secretes releasing factors that travel through the vascular bed and cause the pituitary to release its hormones. A cycling female, therefore, has a cycling hypothalamus.

The trigger for this cyclicity is estrogens. In rodents, the brain is organized in such a way that only females respond to these hormones. A high level of estrogens in the blood of female rats will cause the hypothalamus to release luteinizing hormone releasing factor, which in turn will cause LH release from the anterior pituitary. The hypothalamus in a male rat does not cause LH release when estrogens are present. In fact, estrogens have no effect on LH release in male rodents (Mennin and Gorski 1975). Primates, however, present a different story. The brains of female and male primates both secrete luteinizing hormone releasing factor when estrogens are injected, causing both sexes to release LH from the anterior pituitary. Even females exposed to androgens during development, who are born with masculinized genitalia and who show masculinized behavior as adults, still show an LH surge when estrogens rise (Goy 1968). Under normal circumstances, however, male primates are not exposed to high levels of estrogens at regular intervals and thus do not show a cyclic pattern of gonadotrophic hormone release.

Androgens Cause Masculinizing Effects via Estrogens

We have just devoted several pages to androgens as important determinants of masculinity. These hormones and not estrogens appear to make the critical difference. In order to explain how the androgens work, however,

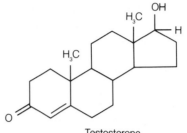

Testosterone

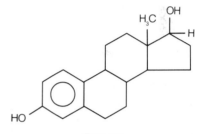

Estradiol

Figure 12.6 Chemical structure of testosterone, a major androgen, and estradiol, an estrogen. Note their overall similarity, but also note the presence of a benzene ring on estradiol.

we now must mention a very surprising fact: Androgens produce at least some of their masculinizing effects by being converted to estrogens. This seems like a contradiction, but as we will explain in the following paragraphs, it is Nature's way of producing at least some male characteristics. We also will tell you why females, who are loaded with estrogens, do not become masculinized.

The first point to realize is that, chemically, androgens and estrogens are very similar. Figure 12.6 shows the chemical structure of testosterone, a major androgen, and estradiol, an estrogen. Note that estradiol has a benzene ring, and testosterone does not. The process of forming a benzene ring on testosterone, a process called **aromatization,** is not very complex; in fact, it occurs in many organs, including the brain. Thus, it is relatively easy for an androgen like testosterone to be converted into an estrogen. Given this fact, we now can discuss what this conversion accomplishes. As you will see, it appears to be important for masculinization of the brain, but the extent of this importance will vary depending on the species.

One role of aromatization in rats is to masculinize the response of the brain to gonadal hormones. Recall that in female rats a high level of estrogens in the blood causes a large increase in LH release from the anterior pituitary. This LH surge does not occur in male rats because of aromatization. When drugs that either block aromatization or block the action of estrogens are administered to male rats during development, they now show the LH surge characteristic of females (Lieberburg, Wallach, and McEwen 1977). Moreover, prenatal females treated with testosterone show masculinization, but not when they are treated with an androgen that fails to undergo aromatization. The conversion of androgens to estrogens, therefore, is essential for organizing a masculine brain.

If this is true, then why are females not masculinized? Surely, they have sufficient levels of estrogens in their body. During fetal development, however, females are protected by a special protein called **alpha-fetoprotein.** This protein binds with estrogens and prevents them from entering *newly formed* cells. Androgens, on the other hand, do not bind to alpha-fetoprotein, and thus are free to enter cells, where they are converted to estrogens. In order for masculinization to occur, therefore, estrogens must be present inside cells. In males,

this is precisely where the estrogens are found; they are converted from androgens intracellularly. In females, estrogens are located extracellularly where they can bind with alpha-fetoprotein and be inactivated. So important is alpha-fetoprotein in females that if they are given more estrogens than their alpha-fetoprotein can handle, then the extra estrogens will enter cells and cause masculinizing effects.

Aromatization occurs not only in developing rats, but also in the human fetus. It is reasonable to ask, therefore, if this process also masculinizes the human brain. The answer seems to be that aromatization may play a role, but in primates other mechanisms are at work as well (MacLusky and Naftolin 1981). In female monkeys, for example, prenatal treatment with an androgen that is not converted into an estrogen also has masculinizing effects. Moreover, although alpha-fetoprotein is present in humans, only a small fraction actually binds to estrogens. Still, this fraction may be important. Women treated with synthetic estrogens, which have a much lower affinity for alpha-fetoprotein than endogenous estrogens, have been reported to give birth to females that showed signs of masculinization (Bongiovanni, DiGeorge, and Grumbach 1959). Thus, the aromatization story may be true for all mammals, but the extent to which it controls sexual differentiation is species dependent.

Sexual Behavior

Adult sexual behavior depends on the complex interaction of numerous factors. This behavior varies greatly in animals of different species, and to state the obvious, it differs in females and males. Beach (1960), a pioneer in research on the factors that influence sexual behavior, argues that in order to understand this behavior completely, you must understand its developmental and environmental determinants as well as its underlying hormonal and neural mechanisms. In the following sections, we will discuss research that focuses on all of these variables.

Developmental and Environmental Influences

Adult sexual behavior typically does not appear until puberty. This does not mean, however, that sexual behavior is not influenced by prepubertal events. On the contrary, events that occur before puberty can exert a dramatic influence on later sexual behavior. Examples of the importance of developmental

factors can be found throughout the animal kingdom, from birds to humans.

Young chaffinches hatch during the early spring and remain in the nest for the next several months. During this time, they hear adult, male birds sing their courtship song to receptive, adult females. By the following spring, the young chaffinches reach sexual maturity, and if they are males, they begin to sing the same song. They are unable to do so, however, if they are raised from birth in a soundproof incubator. No matter how hard they might try (and these birds do try), their song can never duplicate that of normal males (Thorpe 1956). As shown in figure 12.7, the song is flat, phrasing is absent, and it ends on a high note. Birds who sing this song are unable to attract a mate as adults.

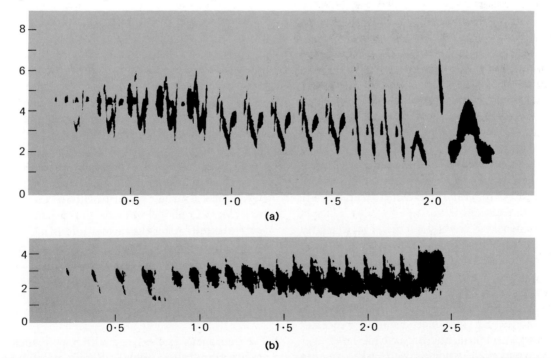

(a)

(b)

Figure 12.7 (a) A sound spectrograph of the mating song of a wild chaffinch. (b) The same song recorded from a chaffinch raised in captivity. Notice the differences in the phraseology and the terminal flourish between the wild and captive bird.

In higher animals, developmental history is even more important in determining adult sexual behavior. Monkeys of both sexes that are reared in conditions of social isolation do not engage in sexual behavior as adults (Harlow 1962). When such animals are placed together, they avoid each other or fight. An important determinant of adult sexual behavior in these animals is the opportunity to engage in infantile or juvenile sexual play. Monkeys that interact with peers during development have no problems engaging in sexual behavior as adults. The human psychiatric literature also is replete with examples of the importance of infantile and juvenile sexual experiences on adult behavior patterns. Even very subtle disturbances in sexual development can have a dramatic impact on adult sexual behavior.

Interactions with environmental stimuli also exert a profound influence on sexuality. Some animals, for example, will secrete a **sex pheromone** that attracts members of the opposite sex by its odor (literally, pheromone means "carrier of excitation"). The scent is highly volatile and specific to the species that emits it. The sex pheromone released by the female silk moth is so powerful that it will attract a male who may be up to two miles away. In fact, he can detect the scent if only forty of his forty thousand olfactory receptors are stimulated.

Monkeys produce a series of volatile fatty acids called **copulins** that have been reported to influence sexual behavior (Michael 1980). Do humans also release a sex pheromone? Little research has been conducted, but one study indicates that certain odors related to sex hormones can influence cognitive processes (Cowley, Johnson, and Brooksbank 1977). Female and male students were asked to rate persons of either sex who were running for a position in student government. The raters were told to base their decisions on data from hypothetical interviews. The raters also were told to wear masks so that their facial expression would be hidden from other raters in the room. The masks actually contained small amounts of copulins or a synthetic androgen. Female raters exposed to copulins gave higher scores to the male candidates, while the synthetic androgen made the male raters prefer female candidates.

Environmental factors also can influence sexual performance. After ejaculation, most male mammals will refrain from sexual activity for a period of time. They may return to copulate with the female again, but there will be an even longer pause before they come back a third time. After several of these episodes, exhaustion will set in, and the male will refuse to copulate until he has a chance to recover. But if the male copulates with a new female after each episode, he will keep up his performance heroically, sometimes doubling the number of ejaculations before exhaustion sets in. This is known as the **Coolidge effect,** and yes, it was named after the former president. Legend has it that President Coolidge and his wife were visiting a chicken farm in the Midwest when his wife wanted to know if just one rooster kept all the hens sexually active. When a farmer confirmed that this was true, Mrs. Coolidge wanted her husband to know about it. After the farmer told Mr. Coolidge, the president asked the farmer to remind Mrs. Coolidge of one important fact: The rooster takes on a different hen each time.

Hormonal Influences

The androgens and estrogens that play such an important role in sexual differentiation and development also play an important role in sexual behavior. As you will see in this section, even human sexual behavior is influenced by these hormones, suggesting that we may not be as free of our biology as we might like to think. For comparative purposes, we will begin our discussion with other mammalian species.

In rodents, sexual behavior is tied very closely to the level of androgens and estrogens circulating in the bloodstream. If a male or female rat is castrated, sexual behavior disappears completely. Supplemental injections of the appropriate hormones in these animals will restore their sexual activity. Cats and dogs also depend on hormones for sexual behavior, but this seems less true for males than for females. Castration, for example, reduces the sexual behavior of male dogs, but by less than 50 percent. Male cats also are affected relatively slightly by castration provided that they have had some sexual experience before the operation. Female cats and dogs show a greater dependence on sex hormones. They will accept males only during that portion of their cycle when the level of estrogens is at its highest (during ovulation). Castration of these females very nearly abolishes sexual behavior.

Primates, on the other hand, are not so closely bound to hormonal influences. Castration of either female or male monkeys reduces, but does not abolish, sexual activity. Still, the reduction in sexual behavior is significant, especially in male primates castrated before puberty. Moreover, female monkeys show more interest in sexual behavior during ovulation, the time when estrogen levels peak. These females, however, do not show any cyclic change in their willingness to engage in intercourse with a male.

Another feature of primate sexual behavior is that hormonal effects vary widely among species. This variability is clearly apparent in studies that have examined the effects of androgens on the sexual behavior of female monkeys. If the adrenal glands are excised, which removes a primary source of female androgens, sexual behavior in ovariectomized rhesus macaques is decreased (Everitt, Herbert, and Hamer 1972), but not in ovariectomized stump-tailed macaques (Baum et al. 1978). Supplemental injections of testosterone in these same animals confirmed these species differences. Thus, the hormone reinstated sexual activity in the rhesus females, but not in the stump-tailed females. Apparently, androgens do influence sexual activity in *some* female primates.

Research on humans paints an even more clouded picture of hormonal influences on sexual behavior, but it would be incorrect to assume that humans are completely free of such influences. Removal of a woman's ovaries (often carried out during surgical removal of the uterus) does not abolish sexual desire. Still, approximately one-third of women who have had this operation report a reduction in sexual behavior (Zussman et al. 1981). In these women, the effect could be related directly to the decline in estrogens caused by the ovariectomy, or it could reflect a secondary effect of the operation (some women, for example, report a reduction in vaginal lubrication that could make intercourse uncomfortable). Another approach in studying the effects of hormones on female sexual activity is to look for a relationship between behavior and the level of estrogens in the blood. Adams, Gold, and Burt (1978) did not measure estrogen levels directly, but they monitored sexual activity (defined as either heterosexual activity or masturbation) during each day of the female

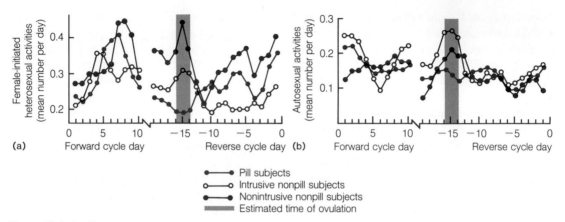

Figure 12.8 (a) Changes in autosexual activity (masturbation and fantasies) and female-initiated heterosexual activity (b) during the monthly cycle. The results are plotted separately for women who use birth control pills, intrusive birth control methods (e.g., diaphragm), or nonintrusive methods (e.g., IUD). Estrogen levels are highest during ovulation.

cycle. They found a peak in sexual activity at midcycle when estrogen levels are known to be highest. These results are shown in figure 12.8.

Again, however, estrogens may not be the only hormones that influence female sexual activity. In some women, androgens also can stimulate sexual desire. Women treated with androgens often report an increased sex drive, whereas removal of the adrenal glands has the opposite effect (Michael 1980).

Men seem to be even more dependent on their sexual hormones than women. Human males, much like males of other species, show a decline in sexual desire and performance after castration. The decline may be less than that in castrated rats, cats, and dogs, but it is still evident. Moreover, treatment with synthetic androgens rapidly restores both sexual drive and function. In otherwise normal males, sexual interest is highest when production of androgens is highest (between the ages of fourteen and twenty-four). Conversely, treatment of male sex offenders with drugs that

block androgen production reduces sexual activity (Berlin and Meinecke 1981).

Because of the clear influence of gonadal hormones on sexual behavior, there have been attempts to determine if a fetus exposed to abnormal levels of these hormones shows excessively strong masculine or feminine behavior later in life. A fairly large sample of such individuals exists because prenatal hormone treatments were common among women whose pregnancies often led to complications (severe bleeding, miscarriages, etc.). For girls born to such women, there is some evidence that prenatal exposure to estrogens and progesterone enhances feminine behavior in childhood and may also increase sexual activity (Ehrhardt et al. 1984). The boys sampled in this study did not seem to be influenced by these hormones. Prenatal exposure to androgens tends to elicit more tomboyish behavior among girls, but no unusual patterns were observed either in childhood sex play or later romantic interests (Money and Ehrhardt 1972). In short, lesbianism did not emerge following early exposure to androgens. Nor did such exposure lead to homosexual behavior in males.

Research on animals, however, indicates that stress placed on the mother during pregnancy causes a reduction in androgen release that may have a feminizing effect on male offspring. Ward (1972) reported that male rats born to mothers exposed to intense stress showed demasculinized sexual behavior as adults. These males failed to copulate with receptive females even after many weeks of testing. Moreover, when males born to stressed mothers were treated with female hormones, they adopted female sexual behaviors more readily than males born to nonstressed mothers. This feminization of male behavior appears to be due to a reduction in androgen release during a critical period of fetal development (Ward 1977). The decreased output of androgens by the male fetus while the mother is under severe stress may be responsible for the change in sexual behavior. Female rats also are influenced by prenatal stress, but in a different way. As adults, they experienced fewer conceptions, suffered more spontaneous abortions, and gave birth to weaker offspring (Herrenkohl 1979).

Maternal stress and the corresponding reduction in androgen release may contribute to male homosexuality, but as we have seen, sexual behavior is influenced by many factors, some of which cannot be duplicated in animals. Moreover, there is no direct clinical evidence for a correlation between fetal stress and homosexuality in humans. Thus, if maternal stress does play a role, it is but one of many factors—physical as well as psychological—that contribute to the child's adult sexual behavior.

Neural Control

The neural mechanisms that regulate sexual behavior are located in both the spinal cord and the brain itself. At the spinal level, sexual behavior is largely reflexive, whereas the brain controls more complex aspects of sexual activity.

Spinal Mechanisms

The reflexes that are an integral part of sexual behavior are controlled by the spinal cord independently of the brain. Stimulation of the genitals in animals can elicit sexual movements and postures even if the brain is severed from the spinal cord (Hart 1967). In fact, penile erections, pelvic thrusting, and seminal emission (ejaculation) have been observed in men who have suffered such damage in accidents (Hart 1978). These people, however, do not experience an orgasm—at least not consciously.

Sexual reflexes normally are held in check by the brain. Stimulation of the genitals in animals, for example, does not elicit sexual responses unless a receptive female is present. Moreover, sexual response is enhanced in animals if activity in the cerebral cortex is suppressed (Clemens, Wallen, and Gorski 1967). Presumably, higher levels of the central nervous system help to control the sexual reflexes wired into the spinal cord.

Brain Mechanisms

The brain region that has received the most attention in the control of sexual behavior is the hypothalamus—specifically, the preoptic area in males and the ventromedial nucleus in females (Malsbury and Pfaff 1974). Lesions of the preoptic area eliminate sexual behavior in male rats. Even subsequent treatment with androgens fails to restore sexual response. If, on the other hand, androgens are injected directly into the preoptic area of normal males, sexual behavior is enhanced. In fact, such injections can restore sexual behavior in castrated male rats. Neurons in the preoptic area actually accumulate testosterone (Pfaff 1968). Considered together, these results indicate that in males this area of the hypothalamus is sensitive to androgens and that when neurons in this area are activated by androgens, sexual behavior is the result. Preoptic damage in females does not abolish sexual response, but it does eliminate the mounting behavior that some female rats occasionally display (Singer 1968).

Female sexual behavior is disrupted by lesions of the ventromedial nucleus, an area that lies just behind the preoptic region (Pfaff 1980). Estrogen has no effect following such lesions. In ovariectomized females, however, direct implants of estrogens into the ventromedial nucleus will initiate sexual behavior. This effect is blocked by implanting drugs that block the action of estrogens (Howard, Etgen, and Barfield 1984). Thus, much like the preoptic area in males, the ventromedial nucleus in females appears to mediate the behavioral response to sex hormones. Ventromedial hypothalamic damage in males has no effect on sexual activity.

Females and males also suffer sexual dysfunction following manipulation of the posterior hypothalamus. This effect, however, may be mediated by a change in hormone release from the anterior pituitary rather than a disruption of a neural pathway controlling sexual behavior.

Other brain regions appear to exert an important modulatory influence on sexual behavior, especially in higher mammals. The temporal lobes, for example, may help to direct attention toward an appropriate sex object. After removal of the temporal cortex and portions of the amygdaloid complex, which lies just beneath the temporal cortex, monkeys become hypersexual and attempt to mate with almost any object in their environment. Similar lesions cause similar effects in cats (Schreiner and Kling 1953). It is unlikely that the temporal lobe or its surrounding structures plays any direct role in sexual behavior because damage here impairs the ability to recognize familiar objects. This impairment, however, explains the inappropriate mounting behavior that follows temporal-lobe damage. In humans, such damage is associated with increased sexual arousal (Blumer 1970). Humans also show abnormal sexual behaviors, not unlike those shown by cats and monkeys, following injury to the temporal cortex (Terzian and Dalle Ore 1955). The brain regions that we have mentioned thus far in our discussion of sexual behavior are located in a fairly circumscribed region near the ventral surface, as shown in figure 12.9.

Another area of the brain important to sexual activity is the neocortex. This should come as no surprise since the neocortex integrates sensory and motor information and plays a critical role in learning, all of which are involved in sexual behavior. Cortical lesions, however, impair sexual behavior to a much greater extent in males than in females. Large lesions of the neocortex dramatically reduce the mounting and copulatory behavior of male rats, whereas females continue to display their receptive posture (Larsson 1964). These results must be interpreted carefully, however, because different behaviors were measured in each case: active, appetitive behavior in males was disrupted, but passive, receptive behavior in females was not. It would

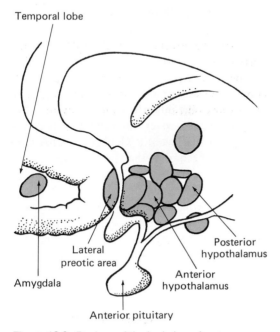

Temporal lobe

Lateral
preotic area

Amygdala

Posterior
hypothalamus

Anterior
hypothalamus

Anterior pituitary

Figure 12.9 Regions of the brain have been implicated in mediating certain aspects of sexual behavior.

be more appropriate to examine the effects of such lesions on the active sexual behaviors of both sexes (in case you are wondering, active sexual behavior by a female rat includes short movements away from the male, ear wiggling, and other inducements). Thus, although cortical lesions seem to reduce the active component of male sexual behavior, we do not know how they influence comparable female behaviors.

The fact that female sexual behavior includes both active and passive components is an important consideration for any study of underlying brain mechanisms. It is conceivable, for example, that the opposing motor predispositions to be active and to stand still require opposing neural responses (Caggiula et al. 1979a). This hypothesis is supported by

what appears to be a different involvement of dopamine neurons in female sexual behavior. A disruption of dopamine neurotransmission suppresses female solicitation, but enhances the passive, receptive behavior (Caggiula et al. 1979b). Thus, the active motor pattern of sexual behavior may require dopamine, whereas the passive pattern of standing still may require a decrease in dopamine activity.

Emotional Behavior

Emotions contribute to the richness of our mental life; they are the stuff of comedy and tragedy. Like many of the other behaviors that we discuss in this book, they involve our entire body: the brain as well as many other organs and glands. It is appropriate, therefore, that we begin our discussion of emotional behavior with a look at the role of our internal physiology.

Autonomic and Endocrine Correlates of Emotion

Emotional experiences often are accompanied by activity in the autonomic and endocrine systems. In fact, one of the first theories that attempted to explain emotional behavior focused on these systems as the primary cause of emotions. This theory, originally formulated nearly one hundred years ago by the American psychologist William James and the Danish physiologist Carl Lange, argues that our experience of emotion comes from an awareness of a change in our internal physiological state. James and Lange pointed out that all emotions are accompanied by certain physiological changes: increases or decreases in blood pressure, heart rate, muscular tension, and so forth. When you experience an emotion, you become aware of these physiological changes. According to the James-Lange theory of emotion, this awareness constitutes the emotion. Thus, if you should come face-to-face with a bear in the woods, you would show fear because you would become aware of your pounding heart, your sweaty palms, and your rapidly running legs.

Many aspects of this theory have intuitive appeal. We all know that our most intense emotions are accompanied by distinct physiological changes. The autonomic nervous system, which regulates our cardiovascular system, the size of our pupils, and other involuntary functions, is very active during emotional behavior. Moreover, different autonomic responses occur during different emotions. Pleasant emotions correspond to an increase in the flow of blood to the limbs, whereas unpleasant emotions have the opposite effect. Pupils are dilated during fear, pain, and excitement, but constricted during a state of pleasant relaxation. There are many other emotional responses that involve the autonomic nervous system. Some of these include sweating of the palms (measured as a change in the galvanic skin response), goose pimples (or hair standing on end in most other mammals), as well as characteristic changes in defecation and urination.

The endocrine system also changes during emotion. In fact, some emotions that persist for prolonged periods are accompanied by fairly dramatic changes in the adrenal glands. The adrenals, an important part of the endocrine system, release a number of substances that help to reinforce the actions of the autonomic nervous system. During rage, for example, the autonomic nervous system accelerates heart rate and also stimulates the adrenals to secrete epinephrine, which causes a further increase in heart rate.

Some aspects of the James-Lange theory also are consistent with experimental evidence. Feedback from the body, for example, does appear to contribute to emotional experiences. Hohman (1966) reported that patients with severed spinal cords show a reduction in the intensity of the emotions they experience. Moreover, the reduction is correlated with the level at which the transection occurred: the higher the transection, the less the bodily feedback and the more flattened the emotional response.

The James-Lange theory, however, cannot hope to explain all aspects of emotional behavior. Some emotions, for example, may persist for prolonged periods of time, but their physiological correlates may be very short-lived. If physiological feedback alone were the answer, then emotions should not outlast the physiological changes. Another problem is that some emotions have a very rapid onset, much more rapid than any change in internal physiology. What enables these emotions to be perceived if they have not yet altered autonomic or endocrine activity? Clearly, there must be more to emotions than our internal physiology. For that reason, other investigators have focused on the brain.

Brain Mechanisms of Emotion

Many different parts of the brain have been implicated in emotional behavior, but no area has received more attention in this regard than the limbic system. In a classic paper published in 1937, Papez (rhymes with "gapes") proposed a circuit of interconnected structures that he thought mediated emotional behavior. As shown in figure 12.10, this circuit includes the hypothalamus, the cingulate gyrus, the hippocampus, and their interconnections. All of these structures form part of the limbic system.

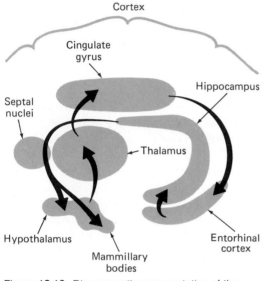

Figure 12.10 Diagrammatic representation of the Papez circuit, proposed to underlie many aspects of emotion. The circuit runs from the hippocampus to the hypothalamus and mammillary bodies, to the anterior thalamus, cingulate gyrus (cortex), and entorhinal cortex, and thence to the hippocampus again.

Papez based his model on an extensive analysis of the clinical and experimental literature available at the time. He observed, for example, that monkeys become tame and docile after lesions of the mammillary bodies of the hypothalamus. He also noted that rabies, a disease characterized by intense emotional symptoms (the term rabies is derived from the Latin, meaning "rage"), was associated with damage in several limbic sites, including the hippocampus.

MacLean (1949; 1970) accepted the role of the limbic system in emotional behavior and spent many years updating and revising Papez's original theory. Apart from providing a more detailed description of the anatomical connections of limbic structures and their role in behavior, MacLean was one of the first investigators to recognize that many of the intense emotional experiences reported by epileptics (such as aggression, fear, or extreme bliss) seemed to occur in patients with an epileptic focus somewhere in the temporal lobe, an area of cortex that includes many underlying limbic structures.

Previous research on animals also indicated that the temporal lobe played an important role in emotional behavior. Kluver and Bucy (1939) reported that a bilateral temporal lobectomy in monkeys produced an extraordinary tameness and loss of fear. These animals apparently had lost the ability to display rage reactions. They also put things in their mouths indiscriminately, accepting foods that previously they had rejected, and they failed to recognize familiar objects, a symptom known as visual agnosia. The monkeys also were hypersexual. They attempted to mate with almost any object in their environment. Collectively, these symptoms constitute the **Kluver-Bucy syndrome,** which has become an important indicator of temporal lobe damage in humans.

One patient suffering from meningoencephalitis exhibited all of the classic Kluver-Bucy syndrome symptoms (Marlow, Mancall, and Thomas 1975). He displayed a flat affect and became remarkably placid. He spent much of his time staring at the television screen, even when the set was off. He thoroughly examined familiar objects placed in front of him as if he were seeing them for the first time. When eating, he tried to consume everything in sight, including the plastic wrapper from a loaf of bread. His sexual behavior also changed. Before his illness, he was vigorously heterosexual, but afterwards he made frequent advances toward other male patients—a change in behavior that prompted his fiancée to break off their relationship. Apparently, the Kluver-Bucy syndrome requires some damage to underlying limbic structures, including the amygdala, and not just the temporal cortex. Patients with temporal lobe damage that spares the amygdala and surrounding structures do not show the syndrome.

Other brain regions also have been implicated in emotional behavior, including the cerebral cortex. Cortical damage in monkeys virtually eliminates social behavior, especially when the damage includes a large area of frontal cortex (Kolb 1984). Frontal cortical damage in humans frequently leads to striking changes in personality. In the following sections, we focus on the mechanisms underlying some very common emotional states.

Anxiety

Many of us have experienced anxiety, the pervading feeling of apprehension or uneasiness that accompanies fearful or stressful events. But unlike fear or stress, anxiety persists even if the real danger is no longer present, and it often occurs in situations that really are not dangerous at all. When it becomes excessive, anxiety contributes to so-called "physical" diseases or at the very least interferes with our ability to function effectively. Anxiety is associated with abdominal distress, headaches, muscular tension, restlessness, and insomnia. It also can contribute to fatigue, irritability, and even some forms of neurosis and psychosis.

To avoid feeling anxious, many people turn to drugs. Since 1970, Americans have filled between 60 million and 100 million prescriptions every year for drugs that alleviate anxiety. Except for alcohol, these drugs are the most frequently used psychoactive substances in the Western world. As you will see in the following paragraphs, research into the actions of these drugs has provided remarkable insight into the neuronal systems underlying this emotion.

Drugs for an Anxious Age

The drugs used to treat anxiety are known as **anxiolytics** (the "-lytic" suffix is derived from the Greek *lysis,* meaning "to dissolve or loosen"; thus, an anxiolytic dissolves or loosens anxiety). The popular press sometimes calls these drugs daytime sedatives or calmatives. Although many different types of anxiolytic drugs have appeared on the market since World War II, by far the most widely used anxiolytics belong to a class of compounds that medical chemists refer to as **benzodiazepines.** The classic benzodiazepine in use today is **diazepam,** which you may recognize by its trade name, Valium (from the Latin, meaning "to be strong and well").

One of the most impressive behavioral effects of the benzodiazepines in animals occurs during what is known as the conflict test (Sepinwall 1983). In this test, a rat is allowed to press a lever that will deliver both a food reward and a shock to the feet. Rats appear very uneasy during this test, and they typically decide not to respond. If they are treated with benzodiazepines, however, the rats begin to press the lever. The benzodiazepines do not increase hunger, nor do they suppress pain. Thus, the drugs seem to be acting directly on the conflict itself. Responding for a reward increases even in the face of punishment. There is no way of knowing, of course, if this means a reduction in anxiety. We certainly cannot ask the animal if it feels less anxious. But all of the benzodiazepines that are effective in this test are helpful in reducing the effects of fear, frustration, and punishment in humans. For this reason, the conflict test is used to screen new drugs suspected of having anxiolytic activity.

Anxiolytics usually are prescribed when a patient feels so anxious that normal daily functioning becomes impossible. They are most helpful in controlling an acute anxiety reaction caused by some transient event that is especially fearful or stressful. One such event is major surgery so anxiolytics often are prescribed as presurgical sedatives. Anxiolytics, however, do not represent a cure for the annoyances, frustrations, and tensions of everyday living. People who use them in this way soon become addicted, much like an alcoholic who drowns life's setbacks in a bottle. For some, Valium has become "dehydrated gin" (Ray 1983). Strong coping mechanisms, rather than habit-forming medication, are the most effective means of dealing with life's anxious moments.

Anxiety May Be Caused by a Peptide in the Brain

The benzodiazepines may not be the perfect panacea for anxiety, but research into their mechanism of action has revealed some startling information about how the brain may generate this emotion. Perhaps the most important breakthrough came with the discovery that certain neurons in the brain actually contain benzodiazepine receptors, sites on the membrane to which the benzodiazepines attach (Braestrup and Squires 1977). The ability of the benzodiazepines to attach to receptors is highly correlated with their anxiolytic activity, suggesting that these drugs exert their behavioral effects by activating these receptors (Tallman et al. 1980). But why should the brain, which has evolved over thousands of years, contain receptors for drugs that have been on the market for less than thirty? Surely, these receptors are not lying dormant, just waiting for us to take our first Valium. On the contrary, benzodiazepine receptors appear to be closely tied to receptors for GABA, a well-known inhibitory neurotransmitter. Normally, the GABA receptor can be suppressed or held in check by a protein called **GABA modulin.** When GABA modulin is active, the synaptic effect of GABA is reduced. The benzodiazepines prevent GABA modulin from acting, and in that way they enhance the synaptic action of GABA (Costa and Guidotti 1979).

If this view of benzodiazepine action is correct, then it raises two intriguing possibilities. First, there may be a naturally occurring benzodiazepine that keeps GABA modulin inactive. If so, this substance would act as the body's own anxiolytic. Second, there may be a naturally occurring substance that stimulates GABA modulin and actually provokes anxiety. In this case, the benzodiazepines would block this anxiety-provoking substance. Evidence for the first possibility is weak. No naturally occurring compound appears to be as effective as the benzodiazepines in attaching to the benzodiazepine receptor and reducing anxiety (Tallman and Gallager 1985). Surprisingly, however, the second possibility is gaining support. Several years ago, Braestrup, Nielsen, and Olsen (1980) showed that it was possible for certain chemicals to inhibit benzodiazepine receptors. If such a chemical could be found in the brain, it would have an effect opposite to that of Valium; it would cause anxiety. The search was on, and investigators at the National Institute of Mental Health soon reported their discovery of an anxiety peptide (Ferrero et al. 1984). The peptide, called **DBI** for diazepam-binding inhibitor, prevents the synaptic action of GABA and, in animal tests, appears to increase anxiety.

Why should the brain produce an "anxiety peptide"? Under certain circumstances anxiety is an entirely appropriate emotion. Feelings of apprehension may help us to avoid an unpleasant situation or to be prepared for it if we cannot avoid it. Only when anxiety becomes excessive does it become a problem. For those times, we may need the benzodiazepines.

Benzodiazepine receptors have been found throughout the brain, but they are especially dense in areas believed to be associated with emotional behavior: the amygdala, frontal cortex, hippocampus, and hypothalamus (see color plate 6). Not surprisingly, DBI follows a similar distribution. GABA is found in these sites as well, but it also is located in many areas of the brain that seem to play no role in emotional behavior. Although both the benzodiazepines and DBI are closely linked to GABA, we still do not understand how a change in GABA neurotransmission changes anxiety. In fact, some drugs that interfere with the GABA receptor directly, rather than with GABA modulin, have little or no effect on this emotion (Sanger 1985). Thus, GABA modulin not the GABA receptor itself, may play the critical role in anxiety. In fact, because GABA modulin is influenced by two widely different compounds—benzodiazepines and DBI—it is conceivable that other substances, probably even other neurotransmitters, can help to regulate anxiety by interacting with this protein. Many researchers, including those employed by drug companies, are busy in their laboratories trying to find and fit the pieces to this chemical puzzle.

Aggression

A precise definition of aggression seems impossible because what we label as aggressive largely depends on the context within which the behavior is observed. A cat killing a mouse may not be considered an aggressive animal, yet the same cat attacking and killing another cat would be considered an aggressive animal by most people. A person selling used cars may use "aggressive" sales tactics and an executive may manage a company "aggressively," but the two words may have very different meanings. Small wonder that people have great trouble defining what they mean by the word aggression.

If we are to study aggression scientifically, we must be able to specify exactly what type of behaviors we are discussing. Moyer (1976) has devised a classification scheme that helps to do exactly that. His classifications are based on the object that is being attacked and on the behaviors exhibited by the attacking organism. Using his scheme, we can distinguish seven different types of aggressive behavior:

1. **Predatory aggression**—observed in carnivores who attack other animals as prey; inasmuch as predators do not appear to display anger during the attack, it seems doubtful that predatory aggression should be considered as aggression at all.
2. **Intermale aggression**—usually occurs in fights over territory or sexual partners.
3. **Fear-induced aggression**—exhibited by wounded animals or animals that have been cornered.
4. **Irritable aggression**—usually caused by discomfort or pain as is the case when two rats in the same cage receive a shock to the feet, then begin to attack each other.

5. **Sex-related aggression**—observed during copulatory behavior in some animals (a male mink, for example, battles the female and eventually subdues her with a bite to the neck).
6. **Maternal aggression**—exhibited by many animals when their young either are threatened or attacked.
7. **Instrumental aggression**—observed in guard dogs that have been conditioned to attack under certain circumstances.

Keep these behaviors in mind as we discuss the physiological mechanisms underlying aggression. As you will see, only a few of these categories have been studied in any detail.

Neural Control

Flynn and his collaborators (Flynn 1967; Flynn et al. 1970) studied the neural systems underlying behaviors that correspond most closely to predatory and irritable aggression. These investigators electrically stimulated various regions of the brain in cats and then observed the response of these animals to rats placed in their cage. Stimulation of the lateral hypothalamus produced predatory aggression, which Flynn calls **quiet-biting attack** for good reason. The cat quietly begins a search of the cage and then suddenly pounces on the rat. Within seconds, the cat delivers fatal bites to the head and neck of the victim and stops as soon as the rat is dead. There is no display of anger or any other emotion; the attack is ruthless and effective. In contrast, stimulation of the medial hypothalamus produced irritable aggression, a response so frought with emotional outbursts that Flynn calls it **affective attack.** The cat arches its back, bares its teeth, hisses and snarls, and, if the stimulation continues, eventually attacks and bites the rat.

Throughout the response, the cat acts as if some irritable stimulus is provoking it into a violent rage. Only after some period of time does it actually go after the rat.

These experiments show that predatory and irritable aggression are very different behaviors and that they are mediated by very different neural circuits. This finding is supported by research on the neurochemical systems underlying aggression (Reis 1974; Valzelli 1981). Treatment with drugs that increase serotonin tends to enhance predatory aggression but reduce affective attack. A rise in norepinephrine, on the other hand, has the opposite effect: an increase in irritable aggression but a decrease in predatory behaviors.

At the midbrain level, both hypothalamic circuits pass through the periaqueductal gray, a circular band of tissue that surrounds the cerebral aqueduct connecting the third and fourth ventricles. When this region is stimulated, both types of aggression appear. Lesions of the periaqueductal gray, on the other hand, block the aggressive behaviors produced by either medial or lateral hypothalamic stimulation (Hutchinson and Renfrew 1966). These results are consistent with evidence that hypothalamic fibers pass through the periaqueductal gray as they travel to lower parts of the brain stem. Thus, stimulation of the hypothalamus also stimulates the midbrain periaqueductal gray.

Is the midbrain involved in aggression or does it simply act as a conduit for hypothalamic fibers? To answer this question, Ellison and Flynn (1968) surgically isolated the hypothalamus from the rest of the brain and then stimulated the midbrain. The stimulation still produced aggressive behavior, although more intense stimulation than normal was required.

It appears, therefore, that the neural circuit for aggressive behavior includes both the hypothalamus and the midbrain, but because removal of the hypothalamus from the circuit does not abolish aggression, this structure is not necessary for its expression. Still, the hypothalamus plays an important modulatory role; it facilitates the response. Without it, the threshold for eliciting aggression increases. The midbrain region, on the other hand, is necessary for aggression; lesions here block the response completely.

The amygdala, an important component of the limbic system, also appears to be part of the aggression circuit. In this case, however, different areas of the amygdala exert different influences. Electrical stimulation of the medial amygdala, for example, inhibits the predatory aggression produced by stimulation of the hypothalamus, yet this same behavior is enhanced following stimulation of the basolateral amygdala (Egger and Flynn 1963). By itself, however, amygdaloid stimulation does not produce predatory aggression, indicating that the amygdala modulates but does not elicit this response. The affective component of attack, which corresponds to irritable aggression, can be produced by amygdaloid stimulation, though this effect is blocked by hypothalamic lesions (Hilton and Zbrozyna 1963). It appears, therefore, that the amygdala exerts its effects on both predatory and irritable aggression via the hypothalamus.

Other brain regions also have been implicated in aggressive behavior, but it is difficult to draw any definite conclusions about their involvement. Consider, for example, the septum, another component of the limbic system. Lesions of the septum in either rats or mice have been reported to increase violent behavior. In rats, however, most signs of aggression subside after a few weeks, and in mice there is reason to doubt that the animals are violent at all. Instead, the animals appear to be hyperemotional; they jump wildly about their cage if provoked, but they do not normally attack. In fact, a mouse with a septal lesion usually will lose a fight with a normal mouse (Slotnick and McMullen 1972). Thus, the septum may exert a very general influence on emotional behavior, perhaps by setting a threshold for its expression, rather than play any direct role in aggression. But even this conclusion may apply only to certain species. In monkeys, septal lesions have no effect on emotional behavior.

Endocrine Control

That the endocrine system influences aggression has been known for a long time. Aggression consistently is related to the level of circulating androgens. In fact, one reason for castrating male farm animals is to make them more manageable or less aggressive. When castrated animals are treated with androgens, their aggressive behavior returns to preoperational levels.

The influence of androgens on aggressive behavior seems to be especially critical during early development. Reinisch (1981) studied aggression in twenty-five boys and girls born to women who had been treated with synthetic androgens during pregnancy. The children were compared to their siblings who were not exposed to excessive androgens. Almost all of the androgen-exposed females scored higher on a standard test of aggression than their unexposed sisters. The results were even more dramatic for the androgen-exposed males. They scored almost twice as high as their normal brothers. One possible explanation for this effect is that the neural systems involved in aggression are present in both sexes, but the extent to which they develop depends primarily on the level of circulating androgens (Edwards and Whalen 1967).

Another hormone implicated in aggression is **adrenocorticotrophic hormone,** or **ACTH.** In order to understand the role of this hormone in aggression, however, it is important to understand the mechanisms controlling its release. ACTH is released into the general circulation by the anterior pituitary gland. Eventually, it reaches the adrenal cortex, where it stimulates the production and release of corticosteroids. When corticosteroid levels in the blood rise, ACTH release declines. Thus, corticosteroids exert an important inhibitory influence on ACTH. Surgical removal of the adrenals, which causes a decline in corticosteroids, produces a chronic elevation of ACTH release from the pituitary. This effect is correlated with a reduction in intermale aggression in mice (Walker and Leshner 1972). When adrenalectomized animals are treated with corticosteroids, aggressive behavior returns to normal. This occurs presumably because the corticosteroid treatment feeds back on the pituitary to inhibit further ACTH release. How can we be sure that ACTH and not corticosteroids exerts the critical influence? Leshner and associates (1973) gave other adrenalectomized mice corticosteroids along with injections of ACTH. This procedure caused a decline in intermale aggression. Because we have seen that corticosteroids restore aggressive behavior in adrenalectomized animals, the decline in this response must be due to the extra ACTH. This hormone, therefore, appears to have antiaggressive effects.

A simple decline in ACTH, however, does not automatically mean that aggression will increase. Androgens also must be present. Castration of male mice will block intermale aggression regardless of what happens to ACTH.

Human Aggression
When humans exhibit violent behavior, efforts usually are made to control it. The rise in violence that has occurred in the United States during the past thirty years has spurred the search for new ways to reduce this behavior. One approach that has received a great deal of attention is the surgical removal of specific areas of the brain in persons who display uncontrolled destructive violence. Hundreds of such operations have been performed throughout the world, and in most of these cases, the amygdala was a favorite target. Narabayashi (1972), a Japanese neurosurgeon, reported on fifty-one violent patients that sustained lesions of the amygdala. He claimed that approximately 85 percent of these patients showed a dramatic reduction in hostility and excitability. Similar results have been reported in this country following surgical or cryostatic (freezing) lesions of the amygdala (Heimberger, Whitlock, and Kalsbeck 1966; Mark, Sweet, and Ervin 1975).

Is such treatment really effective? Sadly, most of the evidence indicates that it is not (Breggin 1975; Valenstein 1973). In many patients, the reduction in violent behavior is short-lived. Thus, initial reports of improvement are no guarantee that the problem is solved. Moreover, there are serious questions about the reduction in violence that these patients supposedly display. Postoperative evaluations of behavior have not been performed very carefully. A loss of hostility, for example, really may reflect a lack of initiative and enthusiasm. In fact, amygdalectomies often cause apathy and listlessness, which can be misinterpreted as a reduction in violent behavior. There are other effects of these lesions as well, including weight gain and an increase in sexual drive.

But the idea that violence reflects a malfunction in a discrete area of the brain has such appeal that it often can color serious investigations into this problem. The story of Charles Whitman, an exmarine who killed fourteen people and then himself at the University of Texas in 1966, is a case in point. Neurosurgeons examining his brain reported finding a walnut-sized tumor in the medial portion of one temporal lobe, an area that lies near the amygdala. This information led to speculation that the tumor may have activated the amygdala and caused this sudden spree of violence. Valenstein (1980), however, points out several problems with this interpretation. First, the location of the brain tumor could not have been known precisely; Whitman's brain was damaged by gunshots and by subsequent mishandling during the investigation. Furthermore, Whitman's violence did not erupt suddenly and spontaneously. He had killed his mother and wife the night before. He also had a troubled childhood and difficult times in the marines. Thus, social, and not biological, factors could explain his violent behavior just as easily. In fact, violence seemed to play a large role in his family's history. Whitman's brother was killed in a barroom brawl.

Scientists know too little about the brain to pinpoint areas that may be involved in violent behavior. If anything, animal research

indicates that emotional behavior is regulated by complex neural circuits, each one of which is modulated by other systems. Most investigators agree that brain surgery for the control of behavioral problems should be used only as a last resort, if at all.

Pleasure: Reward Circuits in the Brain

The discovery of pleasure or reward circuits in the brain came in 1954 when Olds and Milner found that direct electrical stimulation of discrete brain regions could reinforce many different types of behavior in rats. These investigators observed that animals consistently returned to the area of the cage where they had received the stimulation. It seemed as if the animals, in the words of James Olds (1962), were "coming back for more." As shown in figure 12.11*a,* rats rapidly learn to press a lever to receive intracranial stimulation. Figure 12.11*b* illustrates that some animals press the lever at incredibly high rates for prolonged periods.

At about the same time that Olds and Milner first discovered the rewarding effects of brain stimulation, Delgado, Roberts, and Miller (1954) showed that stimulation of certain other brain areas can be aversive. In this case, animals actively avoid receiving the stimulation or even work to turn it off. Cats can learn to terminate a stimulation of certain sites in the brain just as easily as they can learn to terminate electrical shock to the feet. In fact, the aversive stimulus can be powerful enough to establish a conditioned emotional response. Animals receiving aversive stimulation in a particular test chamber, for example, learn to avoid the chamber (Miller 1961). If food is available, the subjects learn to stay away from the food following the aversive stimulus.

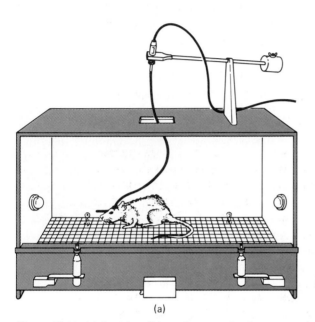

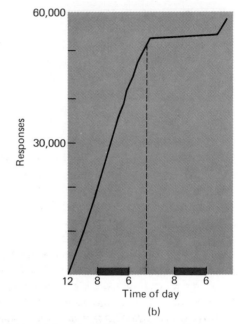

(a)

(b)

Figure 12.11 (a) A rat in a Skinner box pressing for electrical self-stimulation of the brain. (b) Cumulative bar-pressing record of rat shown in (a). The initial steady rise indicates more than 2,000 bar presses per hour night and day (shaded areas) for more than twenty-four hours, followed by a period of sleep (flat area of curve), and then resumption of bar pressing.

Methodology of Intracranial Self-Stimulation

As illustrated in figure 12.12, electrical stimulation of the brain can be carried out with metal electrodes implanted in the brain. The electrodes are insulated along their entire length except for a small portion at the tip. Wires are attached to a small plastic base mounted on the skull and connected to a source of electrical current. The current passes through the electrode to produce a localized excitation of the brain at the uninsulated tip. The subject can control the amount of stimulation delivered to the brain by manipulating a lever or switch in a Skinner box. When the lever is depressed, a short pulse of current passes through the electrode. Thus, the subject must operate the lever repeatedly in order

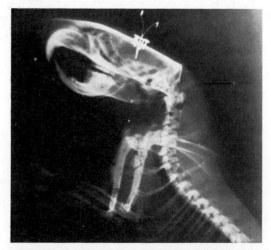

Figure 12.12 X-ray photograph of electrodes implanted in the brain of a rat. The electrodes are held in place by a plastic carrier screwed to the skull and can be used to give an electrical stimulus to the brain.

to maintain the stimulation. This procedure allows the experimenter to obtain an objective measure of the behavior.

The rewarding effect of intracranial self-stimulation acts as a powerful motivator. Rats will endure crossing a highly charged grid in order to press a lever for stimulation, even though they would not cross such a grid for food or other more conventional rewards (Olds 1958). Animals also learn to perform difficult tasks and to navigate complex mazes just to obtain electrical stimulation of the brain (Kling and Matsumiya 1962; Olds 1956). These experiments also illustrate that intra-cranial self-stimulation cannot be explained by simple activation of a motor loop that forces rats to press levers. Animals will engage in al-most all manner of behaviors in order to re-ceive the stimulation.

In some of the early studies done on rats, average rates of bar pressing over time were used as indications of the strength of the re-ward. But if used exclusively, such measures can be misleading because extraneous factors like fatigue and level of arousal often can in-fluence the response (Hodos and Valenstein 1962; Rolls 1975). To avoid this problem, Val-enstein and Meyers (1964) developed a mea-sure of response that does not depend upon the ability of the subject to manipulate a lever, but simply requires the animal to stand on one side of a partitioned box to receive the stimulation. The percent of time spent on the stimulating side then can be used as an index of reward value. Another measure of reward strength that does not depend on the rate of lever pressing involves counting the number of stimulation pulses that are required to keep animals running at maximum speed (Gallistel 1973).

Intracranial self-stimulation has been demonstrated in a wide variety of species, from pigeons to humans. In humans, brain stimu-lation is used primarily as a diagnostic or ther-apeutic procedure. During neurosurgery, for example, various areas of the brain are stim-ulated, and patients, while under local anes-thesia, can report what they feel. This allows the neurosurgeon to learn something about the function of the area that may need treatment. The patients' response leaves no doubt that stimulation can be rewarding. Feelings of in-tense pleasure, well-being, and euphoria often accompany stimulation of sites in the fore-brain. One patient, given a button to press to deliver pulses of intracranial stimulation, made up to four hundred presses per hour for several hours and even passed up attractive trays of food to do so (Bishop et al. 1963).

The Nature of Reward

Given that electrical stimulation of the brain can have rewarding effects on behavior, the question remains: Why is this so? One possi-bility is that brain stimulation is equivalent to such natural rewards as food, water, and sex. This appears to be the case, at least with re-spect to stimulation of certain areas of the hy-pothalamus.

Interaction with Drive States   Along a cir-cumscribed area within the hypothalamus, the rewarding effects of brain stimulation are in-fluenced directly by the hunger of the subject (Olds 1962; Gallistel 1973; Rolls 1975). An-imals with electrodes implanted in the lateral hypothalamic region progressively increase their self-stimulation rate the longer they are deprived of food. If forced to choose between food and brain stimulation reward, hungry rats prefer to stimulate this area to the point of starvation (Routtenberg and Lindy 1965). An injection of insulin, which lowers the level of blood sugar and causes hunger, increases the rate of lateral hypothalamic self-stimulation, whereas glucagon, a hormone that increases blood sugar and reduces eating, has the opposite effect (Balagura and Hoebel 1967). Placing nutrients directly into the stomach, which decreases hunger, also slows lateral hypothalamic self-stimulation (Hoebel 1968). It appears, therefore, that the reward value of lateral hypothalamic stimulation is tied very closely to the reward value of food. Presumably, stimulation of this area mimics the intensity of food reward.

A similar case can be made for other points of stimulation in the hypothalamus and water reward. In the anterior hypothalamus, self-stimulation and drinking can be produced by the same electrode (Mogenson and Stevenson 1966). When the stimulating current is set below threshold, self-stimulation will still occur if water is simultaneously available in the test chamber (Mogenson and Morgan 1967).

The reward value of hypothalamic stimulation can be very specific. Gallistel and Beagley (1971) placed electrodes in two different hypothalamic sites and allowed rats to choose which site to stimulate. As shown in figure 12.13, the animals activated one electrode when hungry and the other electrode when thirsty. Thus, brain stimulation reward can be equivalent to food at one site and to water at another site.

Self-stimulation also can be obtained from the posterior hypothalamus, an area that may play a role in copulatory behavior. Self-stimulation in this region in male rats is enhanced by testosterone (Caggiula 1970). In

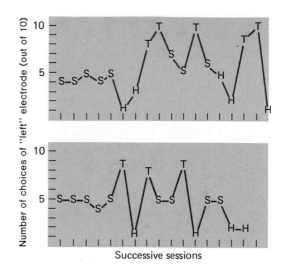

S = Satiated   H = Hungry   T = Thirsty

Figure 12.13 When allowed to choose between two electrode sites for intracranial self-stimulation, the motivational state of the organism can profoundly influence the choice, as shown by these graphs. Thirsty rats (T) show a preference for one electrode placement while the other placement is preferred when the animals are hungry (H). When the rats are satiated, stimulation of either electrode placement is about equally probable.

females, hypothalamic self-stimulation varies with the estrous cycle; response is highest when sexual receptivity is the highest (Prescott 1966).

At some sites outside the hypothalamus, the rate of self-stimulation may not change following the manipulation of hunger, thirst, or sex drives (Olds 1962). Stimulation of these areas may produce positive sensations distinct from any natural reward. The reports of humans who have received stimulation of extra-hypothalamic sites supports this idea.

Stimulation of the septal area in many patients elicits general feelings of joy and euphoria (Sem-Jacobson 1968). Moreover, the emotional condition of the patient at the time of stimulation appears to determine the intensity and quality of rewarding effects (Heath, John, and Fontana 1968). The most intense pleasure responses were obtained from patients suffering deep mental depression or pain. Patients who feel well at the time of stimulation tend to report only mild pleasure. But pleasure may not be the only reason that some persons enjoy brain stimulation. Heath (1963) described one patient who stimulated the brain simply to recall bits and pieces of old memories.

Neural Substrates of Reward

The most powerful rewarding effects of brain stimulation have been obtained from rats implanted with electrodes in the **medial forebrain bundle,** a large system of axons that arise from more than a dozen different nuclei. The axons in this bundle that contain catecholamines, either dopamine or norepinephrine, are suspected of playing an important role in reward because drugs that block catecholaminergic transmission also block the rewarding effects of medial forebrain bundle stimulation (German and Bowden 1974). Moreover, when catecholaminergic neurons are destroyed, brain stimulation reward is abolished almost completely (Breese, Howard, and Leahy 1971).

Although this evidence indicates that catecholamines play an important role in brain stimulation reward, it does not mean that catecholaminergic neurons are activated directly by the stimulation. In fact, when stimulating electrodes are inserted into the medial forebrain bundle, rewarding effects appear to be obtained from activation of noncatecholaminergic neurons. For example, the neurons that support medial forebrain bundle stimulation are heavily myelinated (catecholaminergic neurons are not), and they conduct impulses at a speed that is much too fast for either dopamine-containing or norepinephrine-containing neurons (Gallistel, Shizgal, and Yeomans 1981). Thus, catecholaminergic neurons must lie "downstream" from the point of stimulation; that is, one or more synapses away.

One of these "downstream" catecholaminergic systems is the **mesotelencephalic dopamine pathway.** The cell bodies of these neurons lie in the ventral tegmental area in the midbrain, and their axons ascend through the medial forebrain bundle and then fan out to innervate several limbic structures and parts of the frontal cortex. This pathway has received considerable attention recently because it appears to mediate the rewarding (and presumably addictive) effects of some dangerous drugs of abuse: amphetamine, cocaine, heroin, and morphine.

When allowed to press a lever to obtain intravenous injections of these drugs, rats will respond vigorously—so vigorously that they will neglect everything else, much like some rats responding for brain stimulation reward. The drugs, however, are not activating the noncatecholaminergic neurons in the medial forebrain bundle that support the rewarding effects of electrical stimulation, but rather the mesotelencephalic dopamine pathway that lies "downstream" (Wise and Bozarth 1984).

To understand how these drugs produce their rewarding effects, consider what happens when rats respond to electrical stimulation of the medial forebrain bundle. As we have

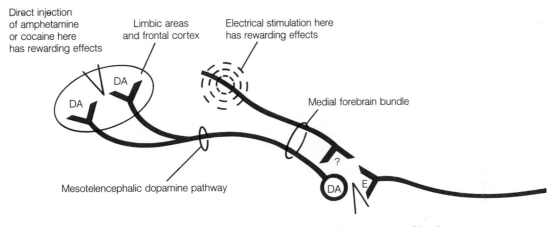

Direct injection
of amphetamine
or cocaine here
has rewarding effects

Limbic areas
and frontal cortex

Electrical stimulation here
has rewarding effects

DA

DA

Medial forebrain bundle

Mesotelencephalic dopamine pathway

?

DA   E

Direct injection of heroin or
morphine here has rewarding effects

Figure 12.14 An apparent reward system in the brain. Note that electrical stimulation directly activates noncatecholaminergic neurons in the medial forebrain bundle, which in turn release an unknown neurotransmitter that activates neurons in the mesotelencephalic dopamine pathway. Certain drugs of abuse engage this reward system by acting at the sites indicated (DA=dopamine; E=enkephalin; ?=unknown transmitter).

seen, the stimulation first activates noncatecholaminergic neurons. These cells synapse in the ventral tegmental area and exert an excitatory effect on dopaminergic neurons, which in turn leads to an increase in dopamine transmission in the forebrain. This circuit is illustrated in figure 12.14. The drugs that we just mentioned act at different points in this circuit, but again the end result is an increase in forebrain dopamine transmission. Amphetamine and cocaine act on dopaminergic axon terminals: amphetamine increases dopamine release, and cocaine blocks dopamine reuptake. In each case, the amount of dopamine in the synapse increases. Heroin and morphine, on the other hand, act on opiate receptors, which increase the firing rate of dopaminergic neurons. The increased activity leads to an increase in dopamine release from axon terminals.

Figure 12.14 also shows that these different drug effects are related directly to reward. Rats will press a lever to receive an injection of amphetamine or cocaine when it is injected into areas that contain mesotelencephalic dopaminergic terminals; they will not do so when the drugs are injected into other brain sites or when dopamine receptors are blocked (Monaco, Hernandez, and Hoebel 1981; Goedders and Smith 1983). Thus, the rewarding effects of amphetamine and cocaine are mediated by dopamine release from axon terminals. In contrast, heroin and morphine produce rewarding effects when they are applied directly to the ventral tegmental area, not to dopaminergic terminal sites (Bozarth 1986). Moreover, the rewarding effects of morphine or heroin are prevented by a blockade of either dopamine or opiate receptors. Thus, unlike amphetamine or cocaine, the opiate drugs are increasing dopamine transmission indirectly by stimulating excitatory opiate receptors in the ventral tegmental area. Their rewarding effects, therefore, can be blocked at this step as well.

If the mesotelencephalic dopamine pathway also is part of the reward system that is activated by electrical stimulation of the medial forebrain bundle, then a blockade of dopamine receptors should prevent the rewarding effects of this stimulation. It does, in fact, do just this (Wise and Bozarth 1984). A blockade of enkephalin receptors, however, does not, suggesting that the medial forebrain bundle is not the source of the excitatory enkephalin input onto these dopaminergic neurons.

Taken together, the results of these experiments indicate that neurons in the mesotelencephalic dopamine pathway are part of a complex reward circuit. They appear to play an important role in brain stimulation reward and in the rewarding effects of certain drugs of abuse. We cannot conclude, however, that dopaminergic neurons actually cause reward. Afterall, they synapse onto limbic and cortical cells, and dopamine must exert an effect on these cells in order to produce rewarding effects. Nor can we conclude that the brain contains only one reward circuit. Brain stimulation reward has been obtained from the cerebellum, dorsal tegmentum, thalamus, and many sites in the telencephalon. Much more research must be done to determine if these different areas are part of one massive reward system or if they are independent of each other. The outcome will have important implications on how we view the role of the brain in reward.

Summary

Sexual and emotional behaviors have stimulated interest and discussion for thousands of years. They also have been the subjects of considerable biological research. In this chapter, we focused on the mechanisms by which internal physiological mechanisms influence and control these behaviors.

The sex chromosomes (XX in females and XY in males) initiate the process of sexual development and differentiation. In females, the sex chromosomes cause an indifferent gonad in the fetus to develop into ovaries. This same gonad develops into testes in a genetic male. Females require no further intervention to develop their internal and external sexual organs. These organs will grow as part of natural fetal development. The male fetus, on the other hand, must release **androgens** from its testes in order to stimulate the growth of the masculine sex organs. The male also must release a substance that suppresses the growth of the female organs.

At puberty, the hypothalamus signals the anterior pituitary gland to release gonadotrophic hormones, which complete the process of sexual development. In females, the gonadotrophic hormones cause the release of **estrogens** from the ovaries. Estrogens are responsible for the secondary sexual characteristics in females. The gonadotrophic hormones in males cause another surge in androgen release from the testes, resulting in male secondary sexual characteristics.

Certain regions of the brain and spinal cord also develop differently in females and males. In the **bulbocavernosus nucleus** of the spinal cord, androgens prevent the cell death that normally occurs during development; thus, males have more than twice as many cells in this nucleus as females. In the hypothalamus, a sensitivity to estrogen in females makes this brain region responsible for the cyclic release of gonadotrophins that occurs during the **estrous cycle.**

Surprisingly, androgens exert some of their masculinizing effects during development by entering cells and then being converted into estrogens. This process, known as **aromatization,** occurs in the brains of all mammals, but seems especially important in rats. Females, which have abundant amounts of estrogens, are not masculinized because a special protein present during development binds with estrogens in the circulation and prevents them from entering cells.

Sexual behavior in adults depends on many factors, including developmental and environmental influences. Infantile and juvenile sexual experiences play an important role in later sexual behavior. Environmental factors may regulate both sexual attractiveness and sexual performance.

Hormones also influence sexual behavior. In females, sexual behavior is associated with a rise in estrogen levels, whereas androgens play the critical role in males. These same influences are present in humans, although they may be moderated somewhat by cognitive and other related influences. In some male animals, homosexual behavior appears to be linked to intense maternal stress, which is associated with a reduction in androgen output from the male fetus. There is no solid evidence, however, that maternal stress is involved in homosexual behavior in male humans.

The neural control of sexual behavior includes reflex mechanisms in the spinal cord and circuits that control more complex aspects of sexual activity in the brain. The brain area that has received the most attention in this regard is the hypothalamus. In males, the **preoptic area** of the hypothalamus is sensitive to androgens and plays an important role in male sexual behavior. In females, the **ventromedial nucleus** of the hypothalamus is sensitive to estrogens and regulates female sexual behavior. Other brain regions, including the temporal lobes, exert an important modulatory influence.

The expression of emotion usually involves the entire body, and one of the first theories of emotional behavior focused on the bodily changes that accompany emotions. The **James-Lange theory** claims that emotions arise from an awareness of the internal physiological changes that accompany certain events. Although feedback from the body may contribute to emotional experience, it is not the sole determiner of emotion. The brain, especially the limbic system and its connections to the temporal lobe, plays an important role.

Research into the brain mechanisms underlying anxiety originated primarily with studies on the actions of the drugs used to treat this emotion. The largest group of antianxiety drugs on the market today, the **benzodiazepines,** appear to enhance transmission at GABA synapses by interacting with a protein called **GABA modulin.** The brain itself appears to produce a peptide that has the opposite effect and may actually induce anxiety.

Aggression, an emotion that is very difficult to define, appears to involve neural circuits that pass through the hypothalamus and midbrain. Different circuits in these brain regions appear to mediate predatory and irritable aggression. The amygdala appears to play an important modulatory role in animal aggression, but its role in humans remains to be elucidated. Hormones, including the androgens and adrenocorticotrophic hormone, appear to have opposite influences on aggression. Androgens appear to be critical for aggressive behavior, whereas adrenocorticotrophic hormone has antiaggression effects.

Specific circuits in the brain also appear to be involved in feelings of pleasure and displeasure. Stimulation of certain brain regions can have powerfully rewarding effects on behavior, whereas stimulation of other regions can have an aversive effect. The rewarding effects of brain stimulation are similar in many respects to conventional rewards such as food, water, and the opportunity to engage in sexual behavior. This is especially true for stimulation sites within the hypothalamus, which also evoke motivated behaviors such as eating, drinking, and copulation. But in many instances, brain stimulation reward does not interact with conventional rewards.

Stimulating electrodes in the **medial forebrain bundle** support very high rates of intracranial self-stimulation. Although drugs that interfere with dopamine transmission block this effect, dopaminergic neurons are not activated directly by the stimulation. Instead, it activates nondopaminergic neurons in the medial forebrain bundle that then synapse onto dopamine-containing neurons in the ventral tegmental area. These neurons, which are part of the **mesotelencephalic dopamine pathway,** send axons to limbic areas and to the frontal cortex. Some widely abused drugs, such as amphetamine, cocaine, heroin, and morphine, appear to produce their rewarding effects by acting in different ways on these dopaminergic neurons.

Suggested Readings

Gallistel, C. R., P. Shizgal, and J. S. Yeomans. 1981. A portrait of the substrate for self-stimulation. *Psychological Review* 88: 228–73.
  This article provides a detailed discussion of the evidence that catecholaminergic neurons are not activated directly by stimulation of the medial forebrain bundle.

Krieger, D. T., and J. C. Hughes, eds. 1980. *Neuroendocrinology.* Sunderland, MA: Sinauer Associates, Inc.
  This edited book is an excellent collection of very readable reviews on the effects of hormones on behavior.

Money, J., and A. A. Ehrhardt. 1972. *Man and woman, boy and girl.* Baltimore, MD: Johns Hopkins University Press.
  This book focuses on the role of hormonal and social factors that influence the development of human sexual behavior. An excellent introduction to the topic.

Tallman, J. F., S. M. Paul, P. Skolnick, and D. W. Gallager. 1980. Receptors for an age of anxiety: Pharmacology of the benzodiazepines. *Science* 207: 274–81.
  The authors provide a detailed description of the molecular actions of the benzodiazepines.

Valenstein, E. S., ed. 1980. *The psychosurgery debate: Scientific, legal, and ethical perspectives.* San Francisco, CA: W. H. Freeman.
The editor has compiled articles from many different experts in the field who discuss the pros and cons of brain surgery to treat various emotional disorders. Special attention is given on the control of human aggressive behavior.

Wise, R. A., and M. A. Bozarth. 1984. Brain reward circuitry: Four circuit elements "wired" in apparent series. *Brain Research Bulletin* 12: 203–8.
This article summarizes the evidence that certain drugs of abuse activate the same reward circuit as electrical stimulation of the medial forebrain bundle.

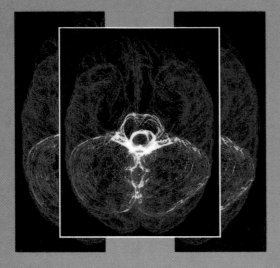

Outline

Introduction

What makes us sleep? and Why do we sleep? are age-old questions. In ancient times, the rhythmic occurrence of sleep and the seasonal or other cyclic variations in the behavior of humans and other organisms were attributed to cosmic and spiritual forces. Today, however, we recognize that the rhythmic occurrence of sleep and other behaviors is determined by the brain even though such cyclic events are often synchronized to external, environmental cues such as sunrise or sunset. Many animals are **diurnal,** such as humans who are active during some portion of the day and sleep at night, while other animals are active during the night, so are **nocturnal,** and sleep or are inactive during the daylight hours.

In this chapter we explore the nature of such cyclic variations in the behavior of humans and other animals; this can be termed **biological rhythms.** The two major categories of sleep—REM and non-REM—will be described as examples of circadian, or about daily, rhythms. We will discuss the relationship of these two categories to the twenty-four-hour day. Research concerning the mechanisms in the brain that might underlie these different states and their rhythmic appearance also will be discussed.

Sometimes disabling disorders of sleep occur in humans and other animals. These will be described, as will some of the attempts to understand and treat these conditions. The important and sometimes deleterious influence of hypnotic drugs (e.g., sleeping pills) as well as the effects that alcohol and other drugs have on sleeping and waking performance, will

Chapter

13

Biological Rhythms and Sleep

be described. Some of the theories and evidence concerning the functions of sleep will complete this introduction to the biology and psychology of this most profound and important facet of human and animal behavior: the alternation of sleep and waking.

Biological Rhythms

Cyclic variations in behavior are pervasive; they occur throughout nature. The alternation between sleep and waking in many organisms represents an important example of a **circadian,** or twenty-four-hour, **rhythm.** The circadian cycle is typically synchronized to external cues, or *zeitgebers*—the "time givers"· of our natural environment. These *zeitgebers* include alarm clocks, sunrise, sunset, and the length of the day. **Circannual rhythms** are those of about a year, and include such examples as the appearance of seasonal mating behaviors in birds and other animals. **Ultradian rhythms** are those having a frequency of more than one cycle per day, while **infradian rhythms** occur with a frequency of less than one cycle per day, such as the approximately weekly or monthly rhythms of estrous in animals and the menstrual cycle in human females.

Circadian Rhythms

It is interesting to note the remarkable extent to which circadian rhythms govern the lives of humans and other organisms (Kripke 1985). Among the curious facts of human behavior rhythms is that even birth and death seem to vary with time of day. Approximately one-third of natural births occur during the early-morning hours at around 3:00 A.M., while death is about 30 percent more common around 5:00 A.M.

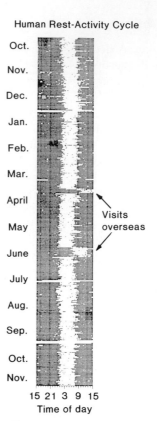

Human Rest-Activity Cycle

Visits overseas

Time of day

Figure 13.1 The rest-activity cycle of a human volunteer, monitored for thirteen months. On two occasions, trips overseas led to a shift in the rhythms corresponding to the change in time zone. Each horizontal line equals one day. Activity is represented by a darkened line, while rest and sleep are light.

The circadian alternation between human sleep and activity is even more evident in figure 13.1, where the activity of a human volunteer was monitored continuously for over 365 consecutive days. Activity can be measured by a special monitor that resembles a wristwatch and can be worn on the ankle or wrist. Each horizontal line in figure 13.1 represents a single twenty-four-hour day, which

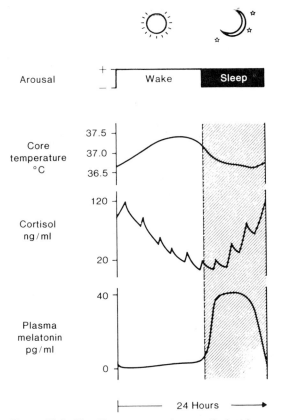

Figure 13.2 Blood hormones, such as cortisol and melatonin, have very large twenty-four-hour rhythms, regulated in part by the light/dark and wake/sleep cycles and in part by such internal rhythms as body temperature.

Compelling evidence for other circadian variations in the physiological function of the brain and body have been measured, such as those depicted in figure 13.2. This illustrates the rhythmic alterations in body temperature, a clear variation of about 1°C within each twenty-four-hour day. The average human subject exhibits the highest body temperature at midafternoon, while body temperature dips to its lowest level during the early morning hours while we are asleep. Blood hormones, such as cortisol (secreted by the adrenal gland) and melatonin (secreted by the pineal gland), illustrate similar cyclicity over the twenty-four-hour day. The level of various neurotransmitters and other brain chemicals and receptors for them, as well as the electrical activity of neurons in the brain, also illustrate the pervasive nature of circadian cycles in the physiological activity and function of the brain.

Free-running Rhythms

Clearly, circadian rhythms are typically tied to external cues, or *zeitgebers,* such as sunrise and sunset. However, even when such cues are not available, human and other organisms continue to spend approximately the same amount of time asleep and awake each day. This has been supported by experimental evidence as depicted in figure 13.3. The spontaneous running activity of a laboratory rat was monitored for about a month before the animal was rendered blind so as to eliminate all visual *zeitgebers.* The rat's behavior was then monitored for about seven months after this experimental manipulation. Note that under

is darkened during activity and is unmarked or light during sleep. Note the remarkably stable circadian appearance of sleep and activity. In at least two instances, travel overseas led to a shift in the subject's rhythmic alternation of sleep and activity, corresponding to the time difference between the different locations.

RAT #23 CP ♀

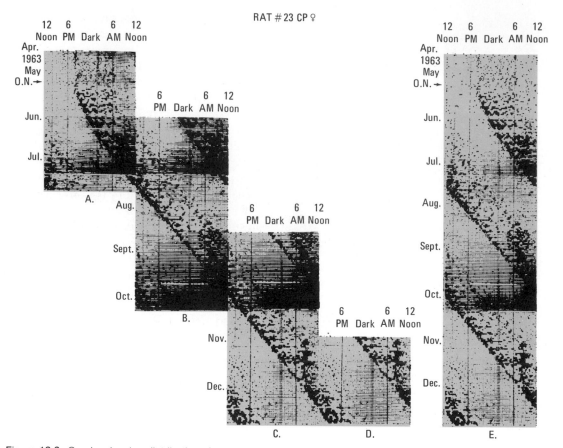

Figure 13.3 Graphs showing distribution of spontaneous running activity of a rat for a period of seven months after it was blinded (O.N.). The months are given on the left of each chart and time of day is indicated at the top. Running activity is indicated by a darkened region on the line that represents each day.

this **free-running condition** (defined by the absence of external cues) the rat still spends approximately the same amount of time each day engaged in running activity and in rest, although the activity starts about twenty minutes later with each twenty-four-hour period. Similar rhythms in the activity and sleep of human volunteers who have been isolated for days or weeks from environmental and social cues in underground caves illustrate that circadian rhythms in behavior are not solely dependent upon or tied to environmental stimuli. Rather, the organization of the brain contains the internal clocks, or oscillators, that regulate the fundamental circadian variation seen in human and animal behavior. An important lesson learned from such experimental evidence is that the free-running circadian clock for sleep and activity in the brain is not actually a twenty-four-hour oscillator. Instead, the free-running circadian clock seems to have

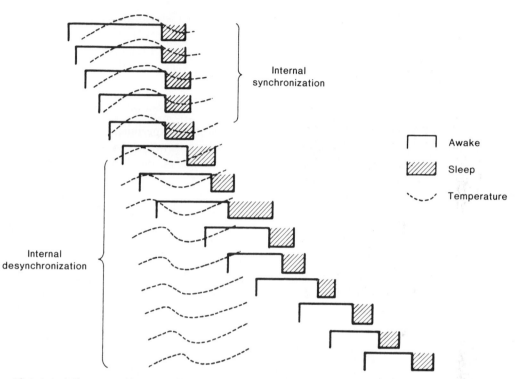

Awake

Sleep

Temperature

Figure 13.4 In isolation, normal human subjects commonly wake and go to sleep a little later each day, but the temperature rhythm continues to peak when the subject is awake (internal synchronization). After a time, some subjects develop sleep/wake cycles that free-run at a different frequency from the temperature rhythm (internal desynchronization).

a somewhat longer cycle than this. In the case of the running activity of a laboratory rat (fig. 13.3), each cycle is longer than it is ordinarily when synchronized to environmental cues. Under such free-running conditions, the natural cycle for human activity and sleep is also longer than the twenty-four-hour environmental cycle of light and darkness.

Desynchronization of Circadian Rhythms

Another important fact that has emerged from the study of animal subjects and human volunteers isolated from circadian cues in the en-

vironment is that circadian rhythms in the body can become **desynchronized** from one another (fig. 13.4). Under the conditions imposed by the isolation experiment shown in figure 13.4, normal human subjects typically wake a little later each day, as do the laboratory rodents who are visually isolated from environmental cues. As shown in figure 13.4, when human volunteers are isolated from the environmental cues that synchronize the rhythmic cycles in body temperature and in sleep, these two circadian rhythms can become desynchronized. The cyclic variation in internal body temperature continues to appear with about a twenty-four-hour cyclicity, while sleep and activity slowly shift out of phase with the temperature cycle. Under this free-running condition, the cycle of sleep and waking closely approximates a twenty-five-hour clock. Since the frequency of the temperature rhythm becomes dissociated from the rhythmic appearance of sleep and other behaviors, it has been suggested that there may be two separate internal clocks that regulate the rhythmic variation in body temperature and the occurrence of sleep. It also has been noted that this internal desynchronization of rhythms may underlie or aggravate various forms of mental illness, such as depression (Wehr and Goodwin 1983). It certainly is apparent that uncoupling circadian rhythms from the external cues that synchronize our twenty-four-hour clocks can lead to serious impairments of behavioral performance and mood, such as the consequences of shift work or the syndrome of jet lag created by traveling from one time zone to another (Johnson et al. 1981).

Neurons as Internal Clocks

Substantial experimental evidence reveals that certain systems in the brain may serve as internal clocks and govern the appearance of circadian and other biological rhythms. Figure 13.5, for example, illustrates the behavior of a "pacemaker neuron" identified in the nervous system of the invertebrate organism *Aplysia,* commonly called the sea hare. In this experiment, the sea hare was removed from its natural environment along coastal tidewaters and exposed to nine successive days of twelve hours of light and twelve hours of darkness. Following this treatment, one ganglion (a collec-

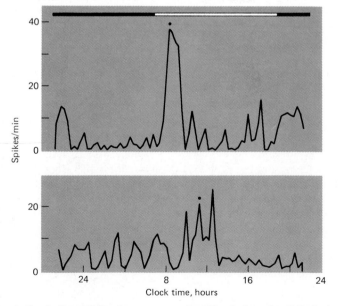

Figure 13.5 A circadian rhythm in the activity of a single neuron taken out of the nervous system of the sea hare (*Aplysia*) recorded for two days. Even when removed from the animal, this neuron shows a circadian rhythm of activity that corresponds to the normal light-dark cycle to which the animal had been exposed.

tion of nerve cells in the nervous system) was removed from the animal and kept in a special water bath. The frequency of action potentials occurring in one neuron was monitored and compared to the light-dark cycle that the organism had previously experienced. Even when isolated from the brain of the animal, this neuron continued to show maximal activity at the time when the light cycle would normally have occurred. A variety of behaviors in the sea hare and other organisms are governed by populations of such neurons serving as internal clocks that regulate the appearance of circadian and other rhythms in behavior. Similar neurons exist in the brains of mammals such as humans to regulate the cyclic variation of behavior.

A striking example of internal clocks in the mammalian brain has been reported in experiments on the brains of animals. Neurons in the **suprachiasmatic nucleus** of the hypothalamus in laboratory animals, for example, illustrate circadian variations in activity like that seen in *Aplysia*. Importantly, if this nucleus in the mammalian brain is destroyed, the rhythmic alternation between sleep and activity is abolished, as shown in the experimental results depicted in figure 13.6. On the left side of this figure, the rhythmic, free-running cycle of sleep and activity in the laboratory rat is easily recognized. On the right side, however, the regular circadian pattern of activity and rest is completely abolished, the result of surgical destruction of the suprachiasmatic nucleus of the hypothalamus. Under these conditions, periods of activity and sleep occur more or less at random throughout the twenty-four-hour day even though the animal still spends approximately the same amount of time asleep during any twenty-four-hour period.

MOTOR ACTIVITY RAT

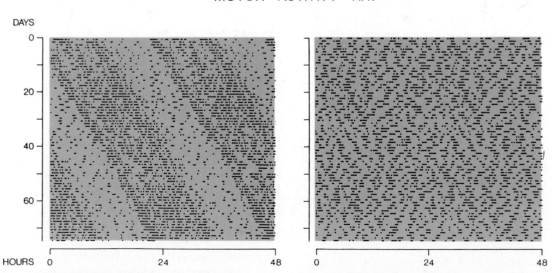

Figure 13.6 The motor activity of a rat under free-running conditions (left side) and following destruction of the suprachiasmatic nucleus of the hypothalamus (right side). Note the disappearance of any rhythmic alternation between rest and activity following the lesion.

Ultradian, Infradian, and Circannual Rhythms

Many biological rhythms have cycles that occur more frequently than every twenty-four hours. These are termed ultradian rhythms. An important example of an ultradian rhythm is the cyclic occurrence of REM sleep, or that phase of sleep during which dreaming occurs. In addition to this approximately ninety-minute cycle of dreaming in human sleep, many other brain and bodily functions exhibit a similar ultradian variation, including blood flow, metabolic rate, oxygen consumption, skeletal muscle tone, and such physiological measures as the electroencephalogram (EEG). (The ninety-minute REM sleep cycle as an example of an ultradian rhythm is discussed in more detail in the next section on the two phases of sleep.)

A very clear example of an infradian rhythm in humans is the female menstrual cycle, which recurs with a frequency of about twenty-seven days. Many well-known physiological, anatomical, and behavioral changes are correlated to and synchronized with the various phases of the menstrual cycle. These include hormonal changes and alterations in the physiology of various glands and organs, in addition to changes in psychological and emotional aspects of behavior.

There is a popular, commercialized belief system, termed biorhythms, that claims that certain rhythms of about twenty-three, twenty-eight, or thirty-three days are triggered at birth and govern our behavior over a lifetime. Like astrology, however, this theory has no scientific validity. Scientific investigations of the influence or occurrence of such biorhythms have been conducted and the results have shown that this theory has no power to explain or predict behavior or the occurrence of accidents, illnesses, or other such phenomena. As Kripke (1985) has stated, scientific investigations of biorhythms such as these have shown that such biorhythm theory is biononsense!

We must mention the circannual rhythms that are omnipresent in the natural world and govern many behavioral and physiological changes over the course of a year's time. Animals living in cold climates adapt to winter by growing a winter coat, storing food, hibernating, or exhibiting other characteristically circannual variations in behavior. The nesting behavior of many birds and the mating rituals of many organisms that appear like clockwork each spring are other profoundly important examples of the circannual variation in nature. In the majority of animals and plants that show these dramatic circannual rhythms, an important determinant or trigger for them is the **photoperiod.** Photoperiod refers to the comparison of day length and night length. A change in the photoperiod signals a change in the seasons. In some organisms, stimulation by light at a certain time during the circadian cycle is critical to the seasonal changes in behavior. Stimulation during a critical interval during the early morning and evening of the lengthening days of spring and summer, for example, is believed to trigger the seasonal rhythm of reproductive behavior in some animals.

Among the most stable and predictable of circadian rhythms is the regular alternation of sleep and waking in humans and other organisms, as we have seen. In the next section we discuss the phases of sleep and the degree to which periodic variations are clearly evident in sleep and waking. It also should become clear from preceding discussions and from descriptions yet to come that various rhythms in nature seem to be intertwined somehow. Ultradian rhythms in the brain and in behavior are seen imposed upon circadian rhythms, while these in turn are affected by infradian and circannual rhythms in the brain and in the environment. Significant questions in this important field relate to the interactions of the internal clocks, or oscillators, that govern these rhythmic variations in behavior and life. How many oscillators are there? Is the timing of events derived from the interaction of several (or perhaps millions) of individual oscillators? Does their interaction lead to the emergence of specific cyclic variations in the brain and behavior of organisms? The rhythm of sleep and waking is one example where significant progress has been made, as we review in the next section.

Two Categories of Sleep

Sleep and waking in mammals illustrate the stable circadian rhythm of behavior. Even within the sleep state, two different categories of sleeping behavior can be recognized. These two categories of sleep, one termed **REM sleep** and the other called **non-REM (NREM) sleep,** are characterized by different behavioral and physiological events.

REM and Non-REM Sleep

The term "REM" is the acronym formed from the words "rapid eye movements." Obviously, such eye movements occur during this category of sleep. During NREM, or non-REM sleep, this behavior is virtually absent. Considerable research is being carried out in order to understand the nature and biological basis of these distinct states (Hauri 1982).

As shown in figure 13.7, the two phases of sleep occur in a regular pattern or cycle in the normal human subject as it does in many other laboratory mammals. Following the transition from waking to sleep in the young adult human subject, there is a progressive change in the physiological and behavioral indicators of NREM sleep such that the subject passes through several levels of NREM sleep in succession. These levels correspond in general to a progression from lighter to deeper sleep. After being asleep for about ninety minutes, the subject again passes through the substages of NREM sleep in reverse order to enter

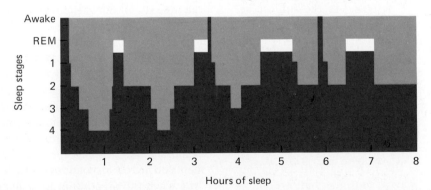

Figure 13.7 Graph depicting sleep pattern in young adults during a normal night of sleep. Note the reduction of NREM sleep during the latter part of the night and the relative increase of paradoxical sleep time.

the first period of REM sleep. It is during REM sleep that most dreaming occurs. Figure 13.7 illustrates that this same cyclic pattern of REM and NREM sleep recurs throughout the night, with a cycle completed in approximately ninety minutes. This is a clear example of an ultradian rhythm. Interestingly, each successive REM episode is somewhat longer, showing that we spend more time in this stage as the night progresses toward morning awakening.

Physiological Indicators of Sleep

In addition to the obvious cessation of most waking behaviors during sleep, research over the past decades illustrates that the different levels of sleep are accompanied by distinct changes in the activity of the brain and body. Among the most convincing evidence for the distinct nature of the phases of human sleep are the changes exhibited by the electroencephalogram, or EEG, during mammalian sleep. Some of these patterns of electroencephalographic activity in the human brain are depicted in figure 13.8. During the awake state, the EEG is characterized by relatively small, rapid fluctuations in voltage, termed a **desynchronized** EEG pattern. As the subject becomes drowsy in the transition from waking to sleep, the EEG amplitude increases and displays regular fluctuations in voltage. Frequencies during this drowsy period range between 8 and 12 Hz (cycles per second). These fluctuations are typically termed **alpha waves.** During the first stage of NREM sleep, the EEG begins to show fluctuations in voltage that range from 3 to 7 Hz; these are termed **theta waves.** As the individual falls deeper into sleep, theta waves continue but are interrupted by occasional **sleep spindles** and **K complexes,** which are intermediate in size and

range in frequency from 12 to 14 Hz. In deep sleep, the EEG is characterized by very large, slow, and regular changes in voltage having a frequency of around 1 or 2 Hz. These large, slow waves are sometimes termed **delta waves** so this stage of deep NREM sleep is sometimes called **delta sleep.** Remarkably, during REM sleep, in contrast to NREM sleep, the EEG is highly active and resembles the low-voltage, high-frequency variations that are characteristic of the awake brain, thus it is sometimes appropriately termed "paradoxical" sleep.

In addition to the electroencephalogram, other physiological variables appear to distinguish wakefulness, NREM sleep, and REM sleep. For example, during the deep stage of NREM sleep (delta sleep), eye movements are virtually absent. Heart rate, blood pressure, and respiration are slowed, but there is still considerable muscle tone in the antigravity muscles, including those of the trunk and neck. During REM sleep, in contrast, heart rate, respiration, and blood pressure become more variable while muscle tone decreases substantially, more so than during NREM sleep. In males, there is full penile erection during REM sleep as well as during the time surrounding the REM episode. In females, clitoral tumescence or vaginal engorgement occurs during REM sleep.

One of the most obvious and characteristic behavioral signs of REM sleep, discovered about thirty years ago, is the rapid eye movement that occurs during this sleep state. These are darting or rolling movements of the eyes that can be seen easily under the closed eyelids of the sleeping subject. These movements do not correspond to the dream imagery even when the dreamer is a participant in the dream action. The eye movements of REM sleep have discontinuous patterns that do not

Awake—low voltage—random, fast

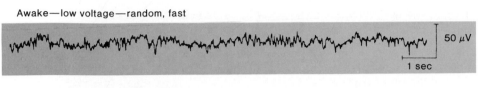

50 μV

1 sec

Drowsy—8 to 12 Hz—alpha waves

Stage 1—3 to 7 Hz—theta waves

Theta waves

Stage 2—12 to 14 Hz—sleep spindles and K complexes

Sleep spindle

K complex —

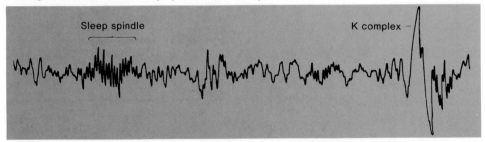

Delta sleep—1 to 2 Hz—delta waves > 75 μV

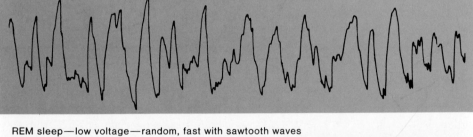

REM sleep—low voltage—random, fast with sawtooth waves

Sawtooth waves   Sawtooth waves

Figure 13.8 Electroencephalographic signs of the various phases of human sleep.

resemble those of normal vision. Moreover, rapid eye movements occur in newborn and decorticate animals lacking the experience or substrate for visual imagery.

Even though dreaming has been associated reliably with REM sleep, many individuals do not remember dreaming. It probably is the case that nearly everyone dreams several times every night, although some are able to recall the dream content more readily than others. In human subjects, the recall of dream content is improved markedly if the individuals are awakened shortly after an episode of REM sleep. Recall declines as time passes after the REM period.

Neural Mechanisms of Sleep and Arousal

One early and widely held theory of sleep and wakefulness was that wakefulness is maintained by sensory input in the cerebral hemispheres. Sleep was seen as a passive result of reduced sensory stimulation. In this view, sleep was the natural state of the brain. More recent evidence, however, shows that both sleep and wakefulness are active processes produced by the brain. While sensory stimulation obviously affects whether we are asleep or awake, sensory stimulation is not the basis for wakefulness and sleep. In this section, we explore some of the regions of the central nervous system implicated in the active processes of sleep and arousal.

Reticular Activating System

Among the early evidence for the passive theory of sleep were the observations of Bremer (1935; 1936). He noted that when the brain of a cat was surgically transected across the midbrain between the inferior and superior colli-

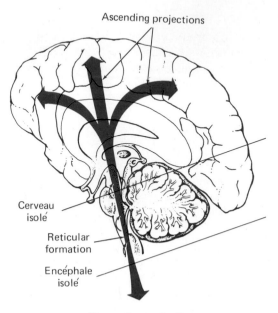

Ascending projections

Cerveau isole

Reticular formation

Encéphale isolé

Descending projections

Figure 13.9 Schematic drawing of the reticular formation. Small arrows along the length of the reticular formation indicate that ascending and descending sensory and motor information is in part relayed to the reticular formation. Large arrows indicate that the reticular formation has widespread influence on the cerebral cortex (ascending projections) as well as on motor activity and spinal reflexes (descending projections). The approximate positions of Bremer's transections of the cat brain are shown at similar position in the human brain.

culi (see fig. 13.9), a continuously sleeping cortical EEG pattern resulted. This transection, termed the *cerveau isolé,* essentially isolates the cerebral hemispheres from all sensory input except from the olfactory and optic nerves. Transection at a lower level, where the brain joins the spinal cord (fig. 13.9), termed the *encéphale isolé,* does not change the normal sleep-wakefulness pattern of the EEG. These results were regarded as support for the theory that sleep results from reduced sensory

input to the _____ vever, later experi____ ___ y destroying the s_____ ___ stem does not pro__ ____ reticular formatio____ ___, does produce con_____ __ et al. 1950).

Moruz____ ____ ____ orted that electric___ ____ ___ ar formation prod____ ____ __e but quiet animal____ ____ __ar formation elici____ ____ ___tation (French 195___ ___ ____ brain stem becam___ ____ ___ **ticular activating sy_____ __ts apparent role _____ ___cephalographic an_____ __l. The continuous s_____ ___ue not to removal of sensory input to the cerebral hemispheres, but rather to removal of the effects of the reticular activating system of the brain stem. This system is depicted diagrammatically in figure 13.9. Note that it projects to the cerebral hemispheres both directly and by way of connections in the thalamus (Robertson, Lynch, and Thompson 1973).

Other regions of the brain also may be regarded as important for behavioral arousal on the basis of other evidence. For example, administration of the drug **atropine** produces a sleeping EEG record, even though the animal is awake and alert (Bradley and Elkes 1953; 1957; Bradley and Key 1958). Since these two indices of arousal can become independent of one another, different mechanisms may underlie them. Furthermore, under some circumstances, animals can gradually recover their normal sleep-wakefulness cycle even after reticular lesions (e.g., Adametz 1959).

Hypothalamus

The pioneering studies of Hess (1957) using electrical stimulation of the brain revealed the importance of the **hypothalamus** in wakefulness and sleep. He discovered that stimulation in the posterior hypothalamus leads to behavioral and physiological signs of activation or arousal. Stimulation in the anterior region of the hypothalamus, on the other hand, leads to cessation of behavior and eventually to sleep. Earlier, Nauta (1946) had shown that destruction of the anterior hypothalamic region caused marked insomnia in experimental animals. Feldman and Waller (1962) found that lesions in the posterior hypothalamus produced continuous behavioral sleep, even though stimulation of the reticular formation produced a desynchronized pattern in the EEG. A wide variety of evidence has thus accumulated to suggest that these opposing regions of the hypothalamus may be important in the balance that we achieve between sleep and arousal. A number of physiological measures have been used to define more precisely the states of arousal, especially measures of autonomic nervous system activity controlled by the hypothalamus.

Basal Forebrain

Electrical stimulation of regions located in the **basal forebrain,** in addition to the anterior hypothalamic region, can lead to cessation of ongoing behavior and the induction of sleep. These regions are the ventral portions of the frontal lobes and the midline thalamus (Sterman and Clemente 1962a; 1962b; 1974). Together, these structures appear to form an important system that normally opposes the

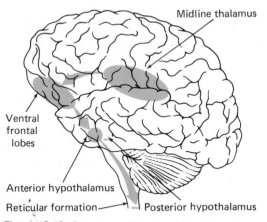

Figure 13.10 Structures of the basal forebrain important in producing sleep. These structures may inhibit the activating effect of the reticular formation and posterior hypothalamus.

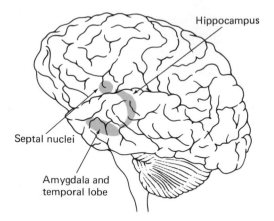

Figure 13.11 Structures in the limbic forebrain implicated in production of slow-wave sleep and inhibitory control of behavioral response.

activating effects of the reticular formation and posterior hypothalamus, as illustrated schematically in figure 13.10. Consistent with the role of these basal forebrain structures in inducing sleep is the neuronal activity in these areas that can be slow during wakefulness and REM sleep, but may then increase with the onset of NREM sleep (Sterman 1972).

Apparently, these regions of the basal forebrain play a role in the production of sleep and in the more general control of behavioral arousal. That is, these and the other regions with which they are connected, such as the basal ganglia, exert a continuous inhibitory control over such acts as spontaneous motor behavior and other signs of behavioral activation in experimental animals. Thus, damage to various regions of the basal forebrain or neostriatum can produce marked reduction in sleep time accompanied by an increase in spontaneous motor activity in a variety of species of experimental animals (e.g., Lynch, Ballantine, and Campbell 1969; Villablanca, Marcus, and Olmstead 1976).

Limbic Forebrain

It has been believed for many years that **limbic system** structures in the forebrain act to inhibit or suppress behavior and arousal (Kimble 1968; Douglas 1967; Dawson, Conrad, and Lynch 1973). Several structures contained within the limbic forebrain are illustrated schematically in figure 13.11, including the **hippocampus,** the **amygdala,** and certain other internal structures of the cerebral hemispheres.

With special reference to sleep and wakefulness, the hippocampus, amygdala, and other limbic forebrain structures appear to inhibit behavioral arousal (Isaacson 1974). Like neuronal activity in the basal forebrain structures, neuronal firing rates in the hippocampus, septal region, and amygdala may be higher during NREM sleep than during other sleep states (Ranck 1973; Jacobs, McGinty, and Harper 1973). During REM sleep, many neurons in the amygdala and hippocampus exhibit quiet activity, as shown in figure 13.12.

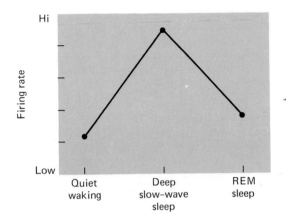

Figure 13.12 Diagram illustrating that neuronal activity in certain cells of the hippocampus and elsewhere may increase during slow-wave sleep as compared with quiet wakefulness or REM sleep.

During NREM sleep, the activity of neighboring neurons in the hippocampus appears to be interrelated, but during wakefulness and REM sleep, neighboring interneuron activity appears to decrease (Noda, Manohar, and Adey 1969). Such evidence suggests that the relationship between the activity of different neurons, as well as between different regions of the brain, may be important in determining whether we are awake, processing information, sleeping, or dreaming.

Lower Brain Stem

In addition to the ascending reticular activating system, numerous cell groups in the lower brain stem (midbrain, pons, and medulla) also appear to be important in the behavioral and physiological signs of wakefulness and sleep (Vertes 1984). For example, Magnes, Moruzzi, and Pompeiano (1961) were able to induce sleep in cats by means of low-frequency stimulation in a circumscribed area of the me-

dulla. Apparently, nuclei in the pons are partly responsible for the transient muscle contractions, rapid eye movements, and PGO spikes (spikelike waves that occur in the pons, lateral geniculate nucleus, and occipital cortex) that occur during REM sleep. Lesions in the pons may abolish all of these signs of REM sleep (Williams, Holloway, and Griffiths 1973). Furthermore, certain neurons of the brain stem, especially of the pons and medulla, show characteristic changes in activity correlated with the onset and offset of REM sleep (Sakai 1985). These have been tentatively identified as cholinergic neurons, or neurons responsive to acetylcholine in the case of REM-on neurons, and possibly serotonergic and/or noradrenergic neurons in the case of REM-off cells (Shiromani and Gillin 1986; Sakai 1985).

In their extensive review of changes in neuronal activity in the brain during wakefulness, NREM sleep, and REM sleep, McGinty, Harper, and Fairbanks (1974) argued that these cell groups of the brain stem may be critical for the normal interaction between different sensory, motor, and other systems in the brain during wakefulness. These systems become uncoupled when behavioral sleep occurs. These dramatic variations in firing rate may be significant in determining the cyclic appearance of various levels of sleep and arousal and accompanying physiological changes.

Neurochemistry of Sleep and Arousal

Naturally occurring chemicals in the central nervous system have long been proposed to exert some influence on the mechanisms of sleep and arousal. Initially, the search for such substances was based on the idea that a sleep-producing toxin accumulates during wakefulness and is dissipated as the organism sleeps.

Legendre and Pieron (1912) reported that injections of cerebrospinal fluid from sleep-deprived dogs directly into the brains of well-rested dogs produced sleep in the rested animals. But these injections caused fever and other complications, making the results difficult to interpret. More recently, sleep induced by electrical stimulation of the thalamus in rabbits was reported to produce a blood-borne substance that causes sleep when some of this blood was injected into other animals (Monnier and Hosli 1964). However, natural sleep cannot be transferred in this way, which suggests that the stimulation procedure itself, not a natural process of the body, is responsible for the sleep-inducing substance. Moreover, Siamese twins who share the same blood supply can sleep independently (Perabo and Kahn 1961). Thus, although the concept of a naturally occurring sleep toxin is attractive, it has not received overwhelming support. Even so, it seems plausible that NREM sleep may involve the action of a naturally occurring sleep substance. Perhaps this is not a blood-borne hormone, but rather some neurochemical that has a highly localized action within the brain and is not carried like a hormone in the circulation. There is substantial research being carried out on sleep-promoting substances in the brain that will promote behavioral sleep when infused into the brain ventricles of laboratory animals (Inoue et al. 1984).

Serotonin and Acetylcholine

The involvement of brain neurotransmitters in sleep and arousal have been investigated extensively. The administration of **parachlorophenylalanine,** a drug that decreases the concentration of serotonin in the brain by inhibiting its synthesis, has been reported to

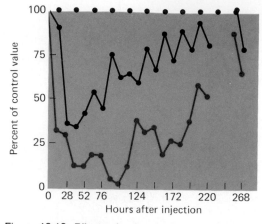

Figure 13.13 Effects of a drug (para-chlorophenylalanine) on percentage of total NREM sleep time (black line) and serotonin levels in the brain (colored line) relative to controls.

cause reduction in NREM sleep time (Jouvet 1969a; 1969b). This relationship is illustrated in figure 13.13. The relative brain levels of several other neurotransmitters appear to be unchanged by this treatment. When serotonin levels in the brain are low, they can be restored by injection of the precursor substance that is converted to serotonin once it enters the brain. Soon after a precursor is administered to serotonin-depleted cats, NREM sleep reappears (Jouvet 1969a). Contradictory evidence for the involvement of serotonin in NREM sleep has come from more recent studies (Gillin et al. 1978). Destruction of the serotonin-rich cell bodies of the raphe nuclei in the brain stem, for example, may not effect a loss of sleep in proportion to the amount of damage to the serotonergic neurons. Further research is needed to resolve this issue.

Biochemical and pharmacological evidence suggests that REM sleep involves changes in synaptic transmission at noradrenergic as well as at cholinergic synapses in the brain. Thus, drugs that block transmission

Interesting recent experiments demonstrate that when the neurotransmitter acetylcholine or related agents that mimic its synaptic action are infused directly into selected regions of the brain stem, various components of REM sleep can be triggered (Shiromani and Gillin 1986). Coupled with evidence from studies of the effect of cholinergic drugs on human sleep, acetylcholine is emerging as an important neurochemical in the brain mechanisms underlying REM sleep.

Norepinephrine and Dopamine

Both electroencephalographic and behavioral arousal require involvement of noradrenergic and dopaminergic transmission. There is considerable evidence showing, for examaple, that stimulant drugs, such as **amphetamine,** may act by affecting noradrenergic and dopaminergic transmission in the brain (Groves and Rebec 1976; Costa and Garratini 1970). As we noted in chapter 4, amphetamine increases the release of norepinephrine and dopamine from nerve endings in the brain and in the peripheral nervous system.

We also saw in chapter 4 that direct infusion of **norepinephrine** or **dopamine** into the ventricles of the brain results in a marked increase in motor activity and other signs of behavioral arousal (Segal and Mandell 1970; Hartmann 1973). In view of the importance of the ascending reticular activating system for electroencephalographic and behavioral arousal, it well may be that noradrenergic neurotransmission produces its behavioral effects in part by increasing the activity of neurons in the reticular formation of the brain (e.g., Aprison et al. 1968). Indeed, amphetamine administration does produce a marked increase in neuronal firing rates in the reticular formation of the rat (e.g., Rebec and

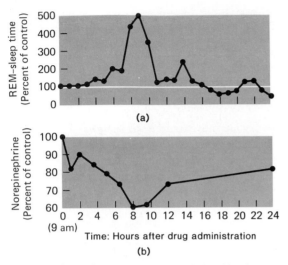

Figure 13.14 Graphs plotting the relationship of percentage of REM sleep time (a) and brain norepinephrine levels (b) following administration of alpha-methylparatyrosine, which inhibits norepinephrine synthesis.

at cholinergic synapses reduce REM sleep. Increasing the effectiveness of cholinergic transmission leads to premature appearance or facilitation of REM sleep in experimental animals as well as in human subjects (Dement, Holman, and Guilleminault 1976; Holman, Elliot, and Barchas 1975; Jacobs, Henricksen, and Dement 1972). Facilitation of noradrenergic transmission appears to reduce REM sleep time (Holman et al. 1975). The results of an experimental study of the relationships between the concentration of norepinephrine in the brain and the appearance of REM sleep is shown in figure 13.14. Note that following treatment with a drug that prevents the synthesis of norepinephrine (13.14*a*), the concentration of this transmitter in the brain declines to a minimal level in about eight hours. The percent of time spent in REM sleep illustrates a perfectly correlated elevation about eight hours after treatment (Hartmann, Bridwell, and Schildkraut 1971).

Groves 1975), and the effect of amphetamine when it is applied directly to these neurons can be mimicked by the application of norepinephrine (e.g., Boakes, Bradley, and Candy 1972).

It is important to note that the mere presence of neurotransmitters in the brain is not a sufficient condition for sleep. Neural organization is also important (Allison 1972). For example, some amphibians that do not show any of the behavioral or electroencephalographic signs of mammalian sleep have relatively high concentrations of serotonin and norepinephrine in the brain. Apparently, such creatures lack the important anatomical structures and neural organization present in the mammalian brain showing REM and NREM sleep.

Sleep Disorders

Sometimes, dramatic alterations in the pattern and occurrence of sleep appear in humans and other animals. In general, these can be classified into several major categories of sleep disorders (Hauri 1982). In one major category, patients complain of not being able to sleep, a predicament termed insomnia. These are the **disorders of initiating and maintaining sleep (D.I.M.S.)** A second major class is the **disorders of excessive somnolence (D.O.E.S.).** In these disorders, patients complain of too much sleep or inappropriate sleepiness. In the disorder termed narcolepsy, for example, the individual may be affected by sudden, uncontrollable attacks of sleepiness. A third major category of problems is the **disorders of the sleep-wake schedule,** which can be either a temporary or a long-lasting condition. Finally,

dysfunctions associated with sleep also occur, such as sleepwalking and sleeptalking. Such dysfunctions are termed **parasomnias.**

Disorders of Initiating and Maintaining Sleep (D.I.M.S.)

Everyone has experienced a night of restlessness and poor sleep. We call such an experience **insomnia,** but it is clear that there are many different psychophysiological causes and life events that can lead to such disorders. Insomnia is characterized by an inability to fall asleep or to stay asleep for the seven to eight hours that most individuals require. The disorders of initiating and maintaining sleep that are derived from life events or stressful situations reflect a condition called **situational insomnia.** This condition is caused by an acute stress, such as an important examination, emotional discord, or other disturbing event, and may become progressively worse.

In many cases, behavioral factors play an important role in the underlying cause of insomnia and its successful treatment. Some of the behavioral factors that seem to be particularly important are poor sleep habits. For example, trying too hard to sleep is commonly a result of stress and tends to exacerbate the problem. Conditioned wakefulness is another behavioral problem maladaptive for initiating and maintaining sleep. Disruption of the sleep-wake rhythm is yet another case in which our behavior makes an important difference in whether we overcome problems in initiating or maintaining sleep.

In these types of sleep disorders, it is frequently helpful for the individual to learn new, more appropriate sleep habits and to attempt some active alteration in the behavior of going to sleep and staying asleep. In the case of conditioned wakefulness, for example, the afflicted individual lies awake in bed, perhaps reading or ruminating about the day's events, worried about not being able to sleep. Some simple but effective ways to overcome such a situation are to go to bed only when sleepy and to do no other type of activity while lying in bed waiting to fall asleep. Moving to another room while awake also changes the environment and reserves the bedroom and bed for those times when it can be associated only with quickly falling asleep. Going to sleep and awakening at a regular time each day also helps to form habits that promote good sleep. As noted by Hauri (1982), poor sleep habits are frequent not only in adults, but also in older infants and toddlers.

Many investigators have seen excellent results from relaxation training and other behavioral techniques that promote bedtime relaxation. Biofeedback, meditation, progressive relaxation, and self-hypnosis have all been used with some success in helping those afflicted with insomnia to acquire better sleep habits and to relax at bedtime so as to promote sleep. In cases where these techniques are not sufficiently effective, sleeping medications may sometimes be prescribed. In general, hypnotic medication, such as barbiturates or benzodiazepines, may be helpful for some forms of insomnia, but they frequently can be a greater liability than expected due to their great potential for addiction and abuse.

The changes in sleeping patterns produced by one type of sleeping pill are shown in figure 13.15. Note that, in addition to the decrease in REM sleep that this barbiturate

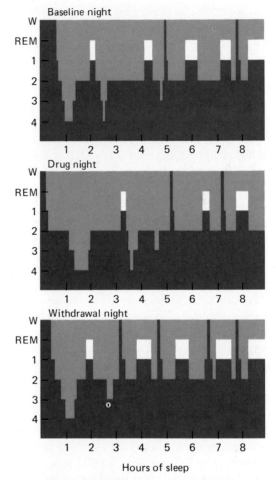

Figure 13.15 Graphs plotting composite sleep patterns of four subjects on three consecutive nights following administration of placebo (baseline night), glutethimide (drug night), and placebo (withdrawal night). Note especially the changes in REM sleep patterns following administration of the drug and subsequent withdrawal

sleeping pill causes (especially evident in the first two-thirds of the night), drug administration lengthens the interval between sleep onset and the first REM period. Following drug withdrawal, there is a rebound increase in REM episodes, which are frequently accompanied by unpleasant nightmares. Such consequences, when coupled with the increased risk of addiction with prolonged use of barbiturate hypnotics, have spurred a concerted effort to find alternative therapies and medications for the treatment of insomnia.

Today, a more commonly prescribed alternative to barbiturates for sleep disorders are the benzodiazepines, also termed **tranquilizers,** with trade names such as Valium. These agents help induce sleep, but apparently also affect the pattern and architecture of sleep (Johnson and Spinweber 1984). These drugs have now been reported to produce impairment of waking performance the next day, inferred from evidence for an anterograde amnesia and a deterioration in daytime psychomotor performance following the use of such agents (Johnson and Chernik 1982). Thus, the prescription and use of medications for insomnia must involve important considerations of special need and related evaluations.

It should be mentioned here that prolonged heroin use may lead to severe disturbances in sleep, and similar effects occur with chronic alcohol abuse. Thus, although sleeping medications may sometimes assist individuals in falling asleep and staying asleep, they, like many other drugs, can alter the distribution of time spent in different phases of sleep and can produce side effects that may be deleterious to effective treatment of disorders in the initiation and maintenance of sleep (Kripke and Gillin 1985).

Sleep Disturbance and Psychopathology

Sleep disturbance often occurs in individuals afflicted with mental disorders. In psychotic disorders, such as schizophrenia, sleep is frequently disturbed. Emotional disturbance is often recognized as the very cause or at least an aggravating circumstance of insomnia. The inability to fall asleep and frequent early morning awakenings are considered part of the symptoms used to identify a depressive disorder. Interestingly, not only is sleep disturbed in people who suffer from a major depression, but the architecture of sleep in those afflicted may also be characteristically changed. An example of such changes is shown in figure 13.16, where polygraphic recordings of normal control subjects are contrasted with similar records from a psychotically depressed patient (Gillin and Borbely 1985). As shown in the figure, several characteristic alterations occur in the sleep of the depressed individual, including a shortened latency to the first REM period of the night; the depressed patient exhibits an abnormally early period of REM sleep. In addition, the earliest REM periods are lengthened relative to the normal night's sleep, and the amount of NREM sleep during the night is less than normal as is total sleep time. The person experiences frequent awakenings during the night as well as early morning awakening. These signs of disturbed sleep in depression may represent a sensitive "marker" of depression or may indicate a vulnerability to depression in people who have not yet experienced the disorder (Wehr and Goodwin 1983).

Based on these characteristic symptoms and on evidence that these individuals also experience other phase advances in circadian rhythms, some theorists have argued that the circadian oscillator responsible for the circadian control of sleep and activity is advanced

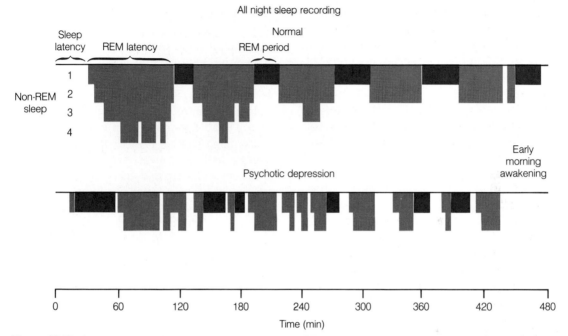

Figure 13.16 All-night polygraphically recorded sleep record from a normal control (upper panel) and from a severely (psychotic) depressed patient (lower panel). Compared with the normal control, the patient shows short REM latency, increased REM duration in the first REM period and in the first half of the night, loss of stage 3 and stage 4 (delta sleep), decreased total sleep time and sleep efficiency, increased awakenings during the sleep period, and increased early morning awake time.

and perhaps is desynchronized in relationship to other bodily and environmental circadian rhythms. There have been several attempts to treat such disorders by resetting the circadian clocks of depressed patients. In these preliminary, experimental treatments, the time for going to sleep and awakening is advanced by several hours or more. In some experiments, patients are awakened and exposed to bright environmental light at critical phases of the sleep cycle. So far, these new approaches in treating neuropsychiatric disorders and disturbances of sleep have produced encouraging results, and additional systematic research is underway in an effort to explore this unconventional treatment in some detail.

Other Conditions Associated with D.I.M.S.

It is known that disorders in the initiation and maintenance of sleep increase as individuals age. Thus, in some sense it is quite normal to experience some increased difficulty with sleep as we grow old. Apart from this commonplace observation, however, there are other conditions that affect sleep and may be more likely to occur in older individuals. Sleep apnea syndromes are one such example (Guilleminault and Dement 1978). In sleep apnea, the sleeping individual experiences a temporary cessation of breathing. Different types of apnea are recognized. In one type, the muscles of the diaphragm operate, but there is an obstruction of

narcolepsy   (nar′ko-lep″se)
cataplexy   (kat′ah-plek-se)
hypnogogic hallucinations   (hip″nah-goj′ik)

the airway and no air is taken into the lungs. In another, the central nervous system does not activate the neurons that drive the muscles necessary for breathing. The cessation of breathing is typically halted when the sleeping individual gasps, snores, or is transiently and reflexively aroused by the lack of oxygen. In some patients, sleep apneas as long as several minutes can occur. Usually, patients with sleep apnea exhibit elements of both central and obstructive apnea. While some success has been achieved in treating obstructive apnea, if the disorder is of central nervous system origin, treatment is not yet available. Individuals suffering from sleep apneas should not consume sleeping pills, alcohol, or other drugs that might exacerbate the condition by adversely affecting the respiratory centers in the brain.

Disorders of Excessive Somnolence (D.O.E.S.)

Disorders of excessive somnolence can frequently appear as the consequence of insomnia. We have noted, for example, that sleep apnea, drug and alcohol abuse, or depression may be associated with poor sleep. As a consequence, daytime sleepiness, napping, and other problems may appear during the hours in which such individuals are awake. In many cases, attempts to overcome sleepiness during the day lead to the use of stimulant drugs, daytime napping, and other circumstances that potentiate the original problem of insomnia. Thus, it is often the case that disorders in the initiation and maintenance of sleep appear at the same time as disorders of excessive somnolence. In some cases, however, the disorder is quite distinctive and severe, is not associated with poor sleep at night, and can be quite threatening to the afflicted individual.

Narcolepsy is a disorder characterized by irresistible, recurrent attacks of sleep along with one or more other symptoms. One such symptom is **cataplexy,** a sudden, dramatic decrease in muscle tone combined with loss of certain reflexes. **Sleep paralysis** is another possible sign of narcolepsy in which the person is briefly unable to move upon falling asleep or awakening. Another possible symptom is **hypnogogic hallucinations**—vivid sensory images at the onset of sleep that generally provide fear and anxiety. These latter conditions are typically associated with REM sleep, but do not occur in REM sleep during a narcoleptic attack. Importantly, the architecture of sleep in narcoleptic patients is abnormal. For example, such patients frequently show a REM period immediately upon falling asleep. This does not happen in the normal, healthy subject, in whom the onset of sleep is characterized by a progression through NREM sleep into the first REM episode.

Treatment of narcolepsy is still limited to providing symptomatic relief, although the underlying cause of this debilitating disorder is sought in experimental laboratories throughout the world. Some help has been provided by a particular breed of dog that shows an increased incidence of narcolepsy. These animals might be running and playing when, like their human counterparts, they suddenly fall asleep, without warning. Studies of the brains of such special subjects, coupled with exploration of the neurophysiological and neuroanatomical basis of sleep in humans and experimental animals, may bring relief to those individuals afflicted with narcolepsy and other debilitating disorders.

Frequently, disorders of excessive somnolence can occur as a result of or as a part of other medical conditions. Some individuals respond to sudden life changes and acute stress by sleeping excessively. In some instances, dis-

somnambulism   (som-nam′bu-lizm)

enuresis   (en′′u-re′sis)

pavor nocturnus   (pa′vor noc-tur′nus)

orders of excessive somnolence occur as part of the symptoms of a psychiatric disorder, as a result of excessive drug abuse, or during drug withdrawal. Careful diagnosis and a thorough knowledge of the individual's medical history often reveal the underlying disorder so that behavioral techniques can be applied to help overcome these conditions.

Disorders of Sleep-Wake Schedule and Parasomnias

We have already noted that shifting the sleep-wake schedule, as occurs in jet lag or shift work, may produce deleterious effects on sleep and mood. The effect of adjusting the sleep-wake schedule can be tolerated by many, although chronic sleep disturbances can result from such changes. In some people, there is a syndrome in which the phase of sleep is significantly advanced or delayed. Such patients do not complain of being unable to sleep; rather, the time at which they must go to sleep or awaken is markedly different from ordinary social norms and practice. In **delayed sleep phase syndrome,** patients may be unable to fall asleep until several hours after their intended bedtime. Some patients with delayed sleep phase syndrome can be successfully treated by a gradual and systematic change in their schedule so that after a period of adjustment they go to sleep and awaken at the appropriate times of day. Often, such systematic behavioral therapy and behavior change yield excellent results.

    We conclude our discussion of sleep disorders by considering parasomnias, behaviors that inappropriately intrude during sleep. Sleepwalking, or **somnambulism, enuresis** (bedwetting), and **pavor nocturnus** (night terrors) are examples of sleep disorders that affect young children almost exclusively. Pavor nocturnus is an especially dramatic event in which

the child awakens screaming and appears intensely afraid, although the episode is typically forgotten by morning. Careful studies of the electroencephalogram reveal that these disorders occur, surprisingly, during NREM sleep and are generally accompanied by body movements and intense physiological activation. Some researchers suggest that these disorders are physiological abnormalities that develop because of an immature central nervous system. Others believe that these behaviors are expressions of emotional conflicts repressed during wakefulness. Almost invariably, children outgrow these episodes, so that the only essential treatment is patience from concerned family members.

The Functional Significance of Sleep

Despite the considerable amount of research dealing with the characteristics and mechanism of sleep, the question remains as to why sleep is necessary. Behavioral and physiological signs of sleep have been observed in reptiles, birds, and mammals. Although they engage in periods of behavioral inactivity, lower vertebrates do not show EEG patterns resembling sleep. These findings have led to speculation that the amount of total sleep time may correspond to the development of the cerebral cortex, especially in mammals. However, the percentage of total time spent asleep in various mammalian species does not correlate with the degree of cortical development. Both rabbits and cats, for example, spend a comparable amount of time asleep, yet they differ considerably in cortical development. In fact, sleep typically tends to be more prominent in mammals with the least endowment of cerebral cortex, such as the opossum and bat (Snyder 1969).

Restorative Function

Before REM sleep was identified, it was assumed that the sleep process as a whole served a restorative function, allowing the body time to recuperate from the daily exertions of wakefulness. This restorative function, however, may be restricted to NREM sleep. Strenuous physical exercise has been shown consistently to increase the amount of NREM sleep time in several different species (Hartmann 1973). In human beings, stage 4 NREM sleep may be especially suited for the restoration process. Physical exertion during wakefulness increases the duration of this sleep stage more than that of any other sleep stage (REM sleep is largely unaffected). In addition, persons selectively deprived of stage 4 sleep for seven consecutive days complained of being physically lethargic and depressed, but no other behavioral changes were evident (Agnew, Webb, and Williams 1967). During gradual sleep reduction from eight hours per night to five hours or less, the total amount of time spent in stage 4 sleep did not show a corresponding decline and even increased slightly, occupying a much greater percentage of total sleep time (Agnew, Webb, and Williams 1964; Johnson and Naitoh 1974). Apparently, NREM sleep (stage 4 sleep, particularly) is a necessary process that facilitates recovery from the fatigue generated during waking.

The significance of REM sleep has been an important question since the discovery that such a stage of sleep can be differentiated. A great deal of speculation has centered on the functions of the dreaming that is most prevalent during REM sleep. Sigmund Freud believed that dreams are highly significant in our mental and emotional affairs and that they provide an outlet for sexual, aggressive, and other types of energies that cannot be acted on in real life. According to Freud, interpretation of dreams can be valuable in understanding the dynamics of our personality and emotions. However, more recent investigations of REM sleep suggest other important possibilities.

In the newborn of virtually every mammalian species, REM sleep dominates total sleep time. Human infants, for example, spend over two-thirds of their daily lives asleep, and at least 50 percent of this time is spent in REM sleep. Total sleep time, and the corresponding amount of REM sleep, declines dramatically early in life, levels off during maturity, and declines again in old age. This age-dependent change in sleeping patterns is illustrated in figure 13.17.

The predominance of REM sleep immediately after birth suggests that this sleep state is important in the development of the immature central nervous system. Some authorities have proposed that REM sleep represents a source of internal stimulation necessary for proper maturation of the brain. Interestingly, premature infants spend an even greater proportion of their time in REM sleep than do other neonates. The requirement for such stimulation apparently declines as the organism matures.

Function in Learning and Memory

The dramatic change in sleep patterns with age has prompted speculation that sleep, especially REM sleep, is in some way connected with memory or learning ability. In the 1960s, Moruzzi proposed that sleep restores synaptic plasticity in the central nervous system and thereby allows memories to be processed and stored. This idea is consistent with the view that the information acquired appears to be

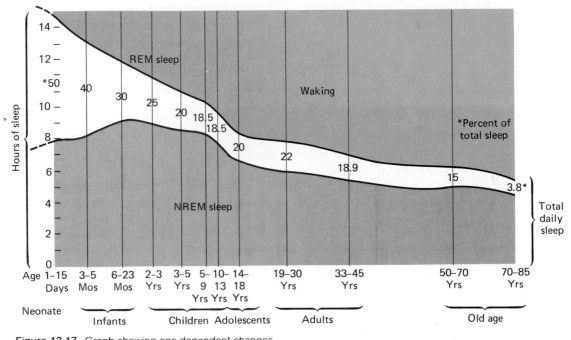

Figure 13.17 Graph showing age-dependent changes in total amounts of daily sleep (NREM and REM sleep) and in percentage of REM sleep.

greatest during childhood, declines to a relatively constant level in adults, and ebbs with the onset of old age.

There are now several lines of evidence suggesting that REM sleep may be important for the memory storage processes, but these remain controversial. The idea that sleep is important for memory storage in human beings has been around for many decades. Generally, human subjects remember more when tested after a period of sleep than after a similar period of wakefulness. Historically, this difference was interpreted in terms of **interference theory.** According to this view, during sleep there is less new learning to interfere with memory than during wakefulness, and therefore more is remembered when sleep intervenes between original learning and recall. Recent experiments on animal subjects suggest that, rather than sleep per se, REM sleep in particular could be important in this effect. However, experiments with human subjects have as yet not shown that selective deprivation of REM sleep interferes with learning or memory storage any more than total sleep deprivation does. Indeed, in one experiment subjects were better able to remember a list of common words following a period of sleep in which NREM sleep was predominant than during a similar period in which REM sleep was predominant (Fowler, Sullivan, and Ek-strand 1973). Further experiments are necessary to determine whether REM sleep is especially important in memory storage and retrieval.

Deprivation of REM Sleep

The effects of REM sleep deprivation have been studied in both animals and human beings. Selective deprivation of REM sleep in human subjects is usually accomplished by waking the subjects whenever rapid eye movements or loss of muscle tone occurs in conjunction with an activated cortical EEG. In both humans and other animals, REM sleep deprivation results in an increased tendency for REM sleep to occur. Following a deprivation period of several nights, there is a **rebound effect** in which the frequency and duration of REM sleep episodes increase. The total time spent in REM sleep increases on recovery nights even when the total amount of sleep is held constant. There appears to be a plateau effect such that after about thirty consecutive days without REM sleep additional deprivation does not result in additional rebound effects. REM sleep deprivation can also produce marked emotional changes. Irritability, anxiety, and lack of concentration appear in human beings during the deprivation period, but the symptoms disappear completely once normal sleep is restored.

Clearly, there is a biological need for both NREM and REM sleep. Hartmann (1973) suggests that the amount of time normally devoted to REM sleep may depend upon certain psychological and behavioral traits. Anxious and worrisome persons appear to require more REM sleep time than do individuals who seem satisfied with themselves and their lives. Thus, REM sleep, in addition to several other possible functions, may have survival value in helping individuals cope with the cares of life. Despite these important clues, however, it is correct to say that sleep researchers still do not know the functions of sleep. This remains an important goal of human understanding.

Summary

Biological rhythms pervade the natural world. The rhythmic alternation between sleep and wakefulness is a **circadian,** or twenty-four-hour, **rhythm** that is ordinarily tied to environmental *zeitgebers,* or "time givers," such as the daily rising and setting of the sun. However, circadian rhythms in body temperature, sleep and activity, the levels of hormones in the blood, and many other variables result from circadian oscillators in the brain and are evident even in situations where they are uncoupled from environmental cues. Under such **free-running conditions,** the circadian rhythms may have longer cycles than the ordinary twenty-four-hour day. Destruction of the **suprachiasmatic nucleus** of the hypothalamus will destroy the normal circadian rhythm of sleep and activity in experimental animals, sometimes leading to a desynchronized condition in which the rhythms of body temperature and the sleep-wake cycle become dissociated from one another. It is believed that this desynchronization of the internal body rhythms can lead to depression or other disorders of behavior and mood in humans, such as the consequences of jet lag and the irregular schedules involved in shift work.

The two phases of human sleep are REM and non-REM (NREM) sleep. These two phases of sleep occur in humans and animals in a regular cycle or pattern during a normal night's sleep. In normal humans, NREM sleep always precedes REM sleep. One complete sleep cycle requires about ninety minutes. It is during REM sleep that most dreaming occurs. Interestingly, the pattern of the EEG during REM sleep resembles the low desynchronized voltage, rapid frequencies seen in the waking EEG. During NREM sleep, the pattern changes to one of slow, large voltages, termed **delta waves.** Many other physiological signs distinguish these two sleep states. During REM sleep there are, in addition to dreaming, rapid movements of the eyes, penile erection in males, and a dramatic decline in muscle tone in the antigravity muscles. Basic research on the brains of experimental animals also suggests that REM and NREM sleep are distinct states, each having identifiable physiological features, and that the occurrence of REM sleep may involve the action of acetylcholine as well as other neurotransmitters. There is currently a search for sleep-promoting substances and neural systems in the brains of experimental animals. Attempts are being made to understand the nature of these biological phenomena.

Part of the rationale for this effort is the attempt to understand and treat sleep disorders. These include **disorders of initiating and maintaining sleep (D.I.M.S.),** which are frequently termed **insomnias. Disorders of excessive somnolence (D.O.E.S.)** also occur and include the dramatic disorder **narcolepsy,** which can be recognized in both humans and animals. Treatment for insomnia includes administration of such sleeping medications as barbiturates or benzodiazepines, as well as attempts to modify maladaptive behaviors. Frequently, poor sleep is aggravated by poor sleeping habits, and attempts to change these poor habits are very helpful. Other conditions

may also include or be associated with disorders of sleep. These include depression and other forms of psychopathology, and sleep apneas or parasomnias, such as **somnambulism** (sleepwalking) and **enuresis** (bed-wetting).

The biological importance, indeed the absolute necessity, for sleep cannot be denied. If deprived of sleep, humans and animals will inevitably show a rebound increase in sleep to make up the deficit. Selective deprivation of REM sleep can produce a selective rebound increase in the amount of REM sleep that occurs on recovery nights. Newborns of many species spend substantially greater amounts of time in REM sleep than NREM sleep. These infants exhibit a tendency for less REM sleep and less total sleep with aging. While there have been suggestions that sleep is important in learning and memory or to restore our minds and bodies after a period of exertion, sleep researchers are still not sure about the functions of sleep. Continued research and effort offer hope to those who suffer from sleep disorders.

Suggested Readings

Hauri, Peter. 1982. *The sleep disorders (Current concepts).* Kalamazoo, MI: Scope Publications.
A fine paperback book that explains the various sleep disorders and the causes of sleep disturbances.
Kripke, Daniel F. 1985. Biological rhythms. In *Psychiatry,* ed. J. O. Cavenar, Jr. Philadelphia: Lippincott.
A modern chapter that explains biological rhythms in animals and in humans. It deals in an especially useful way with the relation of biorhythms to the development and treatment of psychopathology.

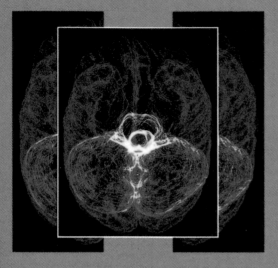

Outline

Introduction

Learning and memory are not things we can see directly. These are processes that we infer from observed changes in the behavior of organisms. In other words, the only way we can identify whether learning and memory have occurred is to observe the performance of an organism and to see it change as a result of the animal's experience. The fundamental question of how the brain and organ systems of the body change as a function of experience is among the most significant questions to challenge human understanding. This question is asked and studied in many different ways and involves the careful study of many different organisms, ranging from bees, insects, and snails to monkeys and humans. In this chapter, we introduce some of the evidence and theory concerning this fundamental ability of humans and other animals.

Initially, we will describe evidence showing that the experience of an organism can modify the structure as well as the function of the brain. Organisms with different levels of experience in the environment show structural changes in the brain. Basic research in biological psychology and the other neurosciences has begun to reveal the nature of the changes that occur in the brain when animals learn and remember. We will describe studies of the biological basis of learning and memory in animal brains, which show that substantial progress has been made in defining the biological mechanisms that underlie some forms of learning, such as habituation and conditioning (Thompson 1986).

Chapter

14

Learning and Memory

Studies of human amnesia and human memory have also made substantial progress (Squire 1987). These, too, will be reviewed. Many patients suffer from memory disorders, the amnesic disorders being dramatic examples (Butters and Miliotis 1985). Although memory storage and retrieval processes probably involve many changes in the brain distributed throughout it, a special role for the temporal lobes and the hippocampus has been established by studies of human memory impairment. Examples of plasticity in the brain suggest numerous brain mechanisms that might underlie memory and related processes of information storage and behavioral change. It is clear that learning and memory do not constitute individual or simple changes in one or two processes in the brain, but rather these probably involve and require many changes in brain structure and function, only some of which are known.

Effects of Experience on the Structure and Function of the Brain

Over the past decades, pioneering experimental evidence on the effects of experience on the brain's structure and function has been produced by Krech, Rosenzweig, Bennett, and Diamond (see Krech 1968; Bennett et al. 1964; 1970) and their many collaborators and students. In their research, laboratory rats were raised in one of three environmental conditions. One condition was called environmental complexity and training, or ECT. These animals were placed in groups in large cages that contained a variety of objects, such as toys, that the animals could play with and explore. The objects were changed every so often to give the animals experience with a wide assortment of objects and toys. In addition, animals reared in this environmental condition were handled, taken out of their cages, and given the opportunity to explore arenas and learn mazes. Every opportunity was used to give these animals exploratory experience and formal training in learning situations. The second condition was called a social control, or SC group. These animals were placed in groups of two in standard laboratory rat cages without an enriched environment. A third control condition was termed isolated control, or IC. These rats were treated in the same way as the SC group, but were housed only one animal to a cage. An illustration of the animals housed in the ECT condition is shown in figure 14.1.

Animals from the three treatment groups were maintained in their respective environments for different periods of time during which certain aspects of the anatomy and biochemistry of their brains were studied (Krech 1968; Bennett et al. 1964; 1970; Mollgaard et al. 1971). It is important to point out that the anatomists and biochemists who did the respective assays did not know the rearing conditions of the animals that they examined. This type of experimental control is called a **blind control experiment,** and its purpose is to ensure that the experimenters cannot introduce bias, albeit unconsciously, into their results. The major findings of these experiments were that certain parts of the cerebral cortex of ECT animals were actually heavier and thicker than those obtained from IC rats. The differences in brain weight and thickness were most apparent when the animals had been put into their respective conditions early in life. There were more glial cells in the cortex of animals in the enriched environment and probably more synapses on individual nerve cells.

Figure 14.1 Living quarters of animals reared in a complex training environment. Notice the many toys in the cage and the fact that the animals are actively exploring their environment and playing with the toys.

In addition to these remarkable differences in the structure of the brain, animals in the ECT condition also exhibited other biochemical differences when compared to the isolated control group. These differences indicate that the experiences of these organisms affected both the structure of the brain and its biochemical composition.

As we might expect, the conditions that produce these differences in the brain also lead to differences in the behavior of animals in these conditions. Greenough (1975) and his associates, for example, studied the brains of experimental mice reared in an enriched environment (EC), in a social control environment (SC), or in an isolated control environment (IC), conditions similar to those just described. After being reared in these conditions, the animals were trained in a maze. Further, the animals were trained on the Lashley III maze under one of two conditions: **massed conditions** of practice giving them three trials per day with a thirty-second intertrial interval, or **distributed conditions** of practice, also giving them three trials per day, but with a two-hour intertrial interval. The number of errors

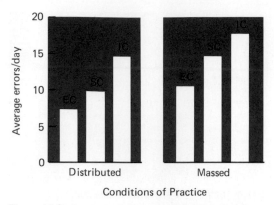

Figure 14.2 Average number of errors made by mice reared in different environments and tested for maze learning under either massed or distributed conditions of training.

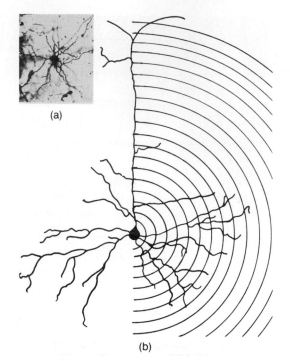

Figure 14.3 (a) Photomicrograph of a nerve cell stained by the Golgi method. (b) Grid of concentric rings in place over the cell in order to analyze the number of dendritic branchings.

the animals made in learning this maze was counted. The results, summarized in figure 14.2, indicate that the animals from the EC condition, when trained under either massed or distributed conditions, made fewer errors in learning the maze than did animals from the other two groups. These results indicate that rearing conditions that affect the anatomy of the brain and its biochemical composition also affect the behavior of animals in learning conditions. It is tempting to speculate that the enriched condition of rearing alters brain function and that this alteration results in improved performance in later learning situations. Caution, however, prohibits us from making such an inference too strongly because we do not know that a large brain *causes* improved performance in mazes, only that the two factors are correlated.

Greenough and associates have also reported on the results of other experiments in which they investigated the effects of experience on other structural changes in the nervous system. (See, for example, Volkmar and

Greenough 1972; Greenough and Volkmar 1973; Greenough 1975.) Using both light and electron microscopes, these investigators have examined the brains of animals given different experiences. Animals used in these experiments were reared in the conditions just described. Later, samples of neurons were obtained from the brains of the animals, and cells were stained using the Golgi method. A photomicrograph of a nerve cell stained by this method is shown in figure 14.3. The Golgi method is especially useful in these types of experiments because it is possible to trace the numerous dendrites of nerve cells and their branches. By placing a grid of concentric rings

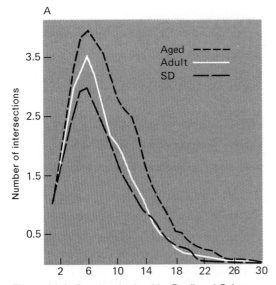

Figure 14.4 Results obtained by Buell and Coleman (1978) in their analysis of dendritic branching in brains from normal adult humans, nondemented aged people, and individuals with senile dementia (SD). The ordinate shows intersections between dendrites, a measure of the complexity of dendritic branching, at different distances from the cell body. Note that dendritic branching was greater in the aged individuals than in normal adults, and the least dendritic branching appeared in the brains from people with senile dementia.

over the cell, as shown in figure 14.3*b,* it is possible to count the number of branchings of the dendrites of such cells. The results showed that the animals in the EC group had significantly higher numbers of dendritic branchings. Since dendrites are important points of communication, the results suggest that the dendrites of the cells from animals reared in complex environments receive significantly more connections than do the dendrites of cells from animals reared in impoverished environments.

Studies of the human brain have also suggested that there may be dendrite growth even in the advanced years of life. In the ex-

periments of Buell and Coleman (1978), brains from elderly but nondemented individuals (average age, 79.6 years) were compared to those of normal adults (average age, 51.2 years) and individuals with senile dementia (average age, 76 years). These investigators used concentric rings to analyze dendritic branching patterns.

Some of their results are shown in figure 14.4. Pyramidal cells from portions of the hippocampal cortex showed more extensive dendritic branching in the nondemented aged brain than in the normal younger adult brain. Individuals with senile dementia displayed the least dendritic branching. These results suggest that the dendrites of some nerve cells may continue to grow and branch throughout life, and that lack of dendritic growth may not characterize the normal aging process. These results also suggest that a deficiency of dendritic branching may characterize the brains of patients with dementia, one hallmark symptom of which is memory impairment.

Studies of animals reared in enriched or impoverished environments suggest that the brain is significantly altered by the environments to which animals are exposed during their lives. Yet such evidence does not establish that changes in the anatomy or biochemistry of the brain are related to particular memories or learning experiences. Other approaches, however, reveal that specific kinds of training or learning situations lead to changes in the activity of neurons in the brain and that such changes occur in selected brain regions or systems believed to play an important part in learning and memory. These neural correlates of learning and memory have begun to clarify the types of changes in the brain that occur during specific types of training and during the development of learning and memory in animal brains.

Neural Correlates of Learning and Memory

For the past several decades, scientists have studied the changes that occur in the nervous system of organisms as they learn and remember. In most cases, such experimental evidence is collected using simple systems or model systems in which simple organisms, such as invertebrates, or portions of the nervous system of more complex animals, such as the spinal cord, are used to define the kinds of alterations that occur in the nervous system during learning and memory. In this approach, simple forms of learning and memory are exhibited by such model systems, and studying the biological processes that underlie the capability for learning and remembering in such models leads to important conclusions concerning the way in which the brain of more complex organisms could change and lead to behavioral alterations that we call learning or memory. Other advantages can also be identified in the simple systems or model systems approach. Some invertebrates, for example the sea snail *Aplysia,* have extremely large nerve cells—so large, in fact, that they can be seen with the naked eye and so can be identified from one subject to the next without difficulty. Their nervous systems also may possess relatively fewer neurons as compared to most vertebrate brains, making an analysis of the neuronal mechanisms of learning and memory in such model systems much less difficult than a similar analysis in a larger, more complex nervous system, such as the mammalian brain. In this section, we will explore several examples of research that has been done using such animal models.

Habituation and Sensitization

Among the most productive models in behavioral neuroscience is the spinal cord of mammals. During the first half of this century, studies by many illustrious figures in neuroscience, such as Sir Charles Sherrington, have probed the organization of the mammalian spinal cord. The results of their efforts have revealed much about the internal organization of the spinal cord, the way in which neurons of the spinal cord are affected by sensory stimulation, and the way these neurons control motor behavior.

Studies of spinal reflexes and simple forms of learning in the surgically disconnected spinal cord have revealed that certain elementary forms of learning can occur entirely within the spinal cord, independent of the brain. Two elementary forms of learning are now known to occur in the isolated spinal cord: **habituation** and **sensitization.** Habituation is defined as a decrease in response to a repetitive stimulus and may, therefore, be regarded as a means by which organisms "learn to ignore" repetitive but inconsequential events in the environment. Sensitization can be defined as an increase in response to a repetitive stimulus, as when an organism encounters a recurring noxious or intense stimulus. In other words, the response of the organism is "sensitized" to a repetitive stimulus and its response becomes progressively stronger rather than weaker. These two simple forms of animal learning do not require that the organism form an association between two stimuli. These represent the simplest and most ubiquitous forms of learning in the animal kingdom. Because they do not require an association to be made between two stimuli, they are sometimes termed **nonassociative learning** (Kupfermann 1975).

Based on extensive experimental analysis of habituation and sensitization in the isolated spinal cord, substantial progress has been made in understanding the neuronal substrates of these simple forms of learning. In a pioneering paper on the properties of habituation and sensitization of the flexion reflex in the isolated spinal cord, Thompson and Spencer (1966) established that habituation and sensitization of the hindlimb flexion reflex resembles habituation of other behavioral responses, even those in intact, behaving animals. The flexion reflex is the reflexive withdrawal of the limb to an intense stimulus. In intact organisms, this reflex occurs, for example, when the foot or hand encounters a painful stimulus and is rapidly and reflexively withdrawn from it. In the case of the spinal cord, this reflex can be elicited in anesthetized animals in which the spinal cord has been transected from the brain. Perhaps more than any other factor, Thompson and Spencer's description of the parallels between habituation and sensitization in the intact animal and in the spinal cord stimulated further work that used the spinal preparation as a model for understanding the neuronal mechanisms that might underlie these simple forms of learning.

Two examples of changes in the activity of spinal interneurons during sensitization and habituation of the flexion reflex in the isolated spinal preparation are illustrated in figures 14.5 and 14.6. In both cases, changes in the reflex response and changes in interneuron activity were recorded simultaneously so that

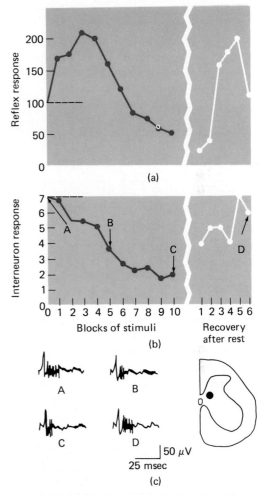

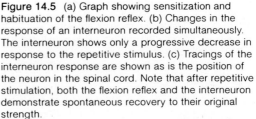

Figure 14.5 (a) Graph showing sensitization and habituation of the flexion reflex. (b) Changes in the response of an interneuron recorded simultaneously. The interneuron shows only a progressive decrease in response to the repetitive stimulus. (c) Tracings of the interneuron response are shown as is the position of the neuron in the spinal cord. Note that after repetitive stimulation, both the flexion reflex and the interneuron demonstrate spontaneous recovery to their original strength.

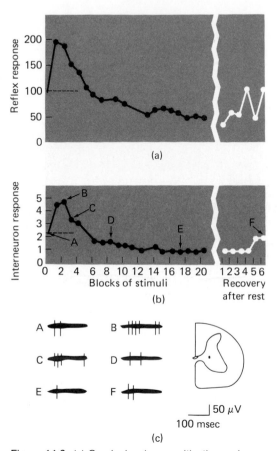

Figure 14.6 (a) Graph showing sensitization and habituation of the flexion reflex. (b) Changes in the response of an interneuron recorded simultaneously. The interneuron shows sensitization followed by habituation. (c) Tracings of the interneuron response and position of the neuron in the spinal cord. Both the reflex response and the interneuron showed spontaneous recovery following a rest, as illustrated to the right of both graphs (a and b).

they could be directly compared. In each case, the reflex response showed an initial sensitization followed by habituation, as illustrated in the top graph (figs. 14.5a and 14.6a) of each figure. However, two different types of changes occurred for different interneurons. In figure 14.5, the interneuron shows only a progressive decrease in response to the repetitive stimulus, even though the reflex shows an initial sensitization. In figure 14.6, the interneuron shows an initial sensitization like the reflex that is followed by a decrease in activity.

On the basis of these and other observations, Groves and Thompson (1970) suggested that the behavioral effect of repetitive stimulation depends on two processes: a sensitization process and an habituation process. These, in turn, were theorized to be due to the two categories of interneurons shown in figures 14.5 and 14.6. On the basis of this analysis of the spinal model system, Groves and Thompson also suggested that similar processes that result in changes in behavior with repetitive sensory stimulation exist in the nervous systems of intact animals. Speculation like this illustrates how analyses of model systems, such as the spinal cord, can be useful in directing the search for neural mechanisms that explain learning in more complicated, intact nervous systems.

Habituation in *Aplysia*

Many diverse invertebrate organisms have been used as models in an attempt to understand some of the biological mechanisms that mediate behavior. *Aplysia* is an especially interesting and productive model system because many of the nerve cells in its nervous

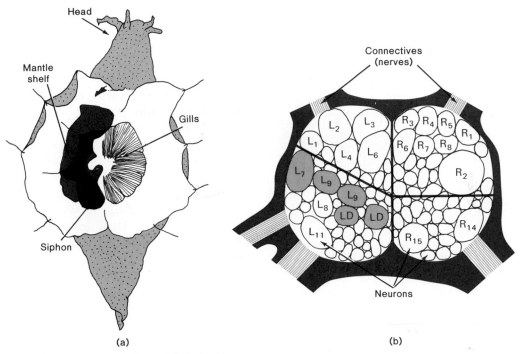

Figure 14.7 (a) Schematic drawing of *Aplysia.* (b) One of the ganglia making up its nervous system. Some of the cells are identified and numbered (L_1, R_1, LD, etc.).

system are large enough to be seen without a microscope. Obvious advantages of this circumstance is that these neurons are easily penetrated with microelectrodes and can be identified from one animal to the next (see fig. 14.7). *Aplysia* shows habituation and sensitization, and a variety of experimental efforts demonstrate that this model system may exhibit both classical and operant conditioning (Carew and Sahley 1986; Cook and Carew 1986).

In an extensive analysis of habituation in *Aplysia,* Kandel and associates (e.g., Kupfermann et al. 1970; Castellucci et al. 1970; Pinsker et al. 1970) not only identified the neurons involved in this simple form of learning, but also developed strong evidence that a synaptic mechanism is the underlying mediator. *Aplysia* and one of the ganglia, the groups of nerve cells that make up its nervous system, are illustrated in figure 14.7. Tactile stimulation near the gills of *Aplysia* causes the

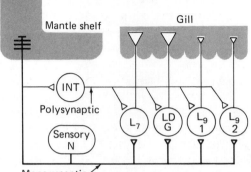

Figure 14.8 Diagram of the pathways in *Aplysia* believed to underlie the gill-withdrawal reflex. Sensory neurons bring information from the siphon and mantle regions directly to motor neurons (L₇ LDG, etc.). These synapses between sensory and motor neurons appear to become less and less effective when activated repeatedly. Other connections to motor neurons occur through interneurons.

organism to withdraw the gills from the stimulus. If the stimulus is repeated, gill withdrawal shows marked habituation so that eventually no withdrawal to the stimulus occurs.

The pathways responsible for this effect are illustrated schematically in figure 14.8. Note that the sensory nerve coming from the siphon and mantle of *Aplysia* connects to motor neurons that send their axons to the gill. It is this monosynaptic connection between sensory and motor neurons that seems to be responsible for habituation of the gill withdrawal response. A connection through an interneuron may be responsible for sensitization. More remarkable yet, Kandel and associates were able to demonstrate that the process in-

volved in habituation is probably some form of depression of excitatory transmission at these synapses. When they repeatedly transmit information to the motor neurons, they become less and less effective, leading to a decrease in the withdrawal response to repetitive stimulation of the mantle. Note that the motor neurons, which are labeled with both letters and numbers, can be identified from one animal to the next, a fact that makes such experiments possible.

As Carew and Sahley (1986) have noted, "The progress achieved over the last 10–15 years in studying a wide variety of forms of learning in simple invertebrate animals is quite striking" (p. 473). In this report Carew and Sahley identify certain common themes that have emerged in the experimental search for the molecular mechanisms underlying learning and memory in the various invertebrate models that have been studied so far. One theme appears to be that "learning (both nonassociative and associative) can be localized to individual neurons and involves alterations of either previously existing synaptic connections or intrinsic cellular properties; in no case have novel synapses or new biophysical properties been induced by learning. The tentative principle then appears to be that certain neurons or groups of neurons are endowed with the capacity for plastic changes, and experience then promotes that change in previously existing circuits" (pp. 473–74). A knowledge of the molecular mechanisms that underlie or promote such plastic change must surely reveal important information regarding the ways in which the mammalian brain learns. It seems likely that such mechanisms may be conserved in the evolution of the brain and behavior and are widespread throughout the animal kingdom. Perhaps these mechanisms form a foundation for understanding the further elaboration and development of structural and functional mechanisms underlying plastic change in the mammalian brain.

Conditioning

In studies of the neural mechanisms underlying habituation and sensitization, recording the activity of individual neurons as learning occurs has provided important insights into where and how the changes in the nervous system that enable organisms to learn and remember occur. Similar approaches have begun to reveal that changes in the activity of neurons in the mammalian brain take place during such complex forms of associative learning as classical and operant conditioning.

In **classical conditioning,** a form of associative learning, an unconditioned stimulus (UCS), which evokes a behavioral response (the unconditioned response, or UCR), is paired with a neutral sensory stimulus that does not evoke the response (termed the CS, or conditioned stimulus). After repeated presentations of the unconditioned stimulus preceded closely in time by the neutral stimulus, the previously neutral stimulus begins to elicit a conditioned response (CR) that is similar to the unconditioned response. An important series of experiments in which the activity of neurons was recorded during classical conditioning has been reported by Thompson and his associates (Thompson 1976; Berger, Clark, and Thompson 1980; Thompson et al. 1983).

In one set of experiments using rabbits, the activity of neurons in the hippocampus, a region of the cerebral cortex that has been implicated in memory storage and retrieval, was studied during classical conditioning of the rabbits' nictitating membrane response. The nictitating membrane is like a "third eyelid" in rabbits and cats that covers the eye reflexively when a sudden stimulus occurs. Using a tone as the conditioned stimulus and an airpuff to the eye as the unconditioned stimulus, these investigators observed a change in the firing pattern of neurons in the hippocampus during the earliest trials of conditioning. This firing-pattern change grew as conditioning progressed and developed into what Thompson (1976) termed "a virtually exact temporal representation of the behavioral response." This change in neuronal firing preceded the behavioral response in time. Poststimulus histograms showing the pattern of neuronal activity that developed during conditioning are given in figure 14.9. Control experiments in which the conditioned stimulus (CS) and the unconditioned stimulus (UCS) were presented, but not paired, indicated that the change in neuronal firing was specific to pairing the CS and UCS, as also illustrated in figure 14.9. Since this response occurred so early in training and continued after the animals were fully trained, Thompson suggested that it may be one of the first events in the formation of memory.

Further careful study by this group has shown that such conditioned changes in the activity of single neurons occur in other regions of the brain during the conditioning experience, especially in the cerebellum

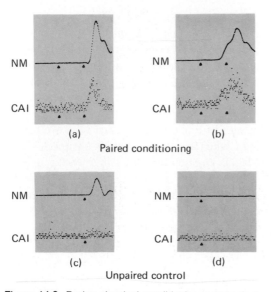

(a)

(b)

Paired conditioning

(c)

(d)

Unpaired control

Figure 14.9 During classical conditioning, neuronal activity in the rabbit hippocampus develops a conditioned response very early in training. (a) An illustration of the average response of the nictitating membrane (labeled NM) appears above and below this, the average response of neurons in a region of the hippocampus (labeled CA1). Both of these show the response as it occurs during the first eight conditioning trials. An upward deflection indicates a response. The first small cursor indicates when the conditioned stimulus (a tone) was presented, and the second cursor shows when the unconditioned stimulus (an air puff) was presented. In (b), the nictitating membrane response is shown as it occurred during the final eight trials of conditioning. A conditioned response is clearly evident since the response of the membrane now occurs even before the unconditioned stimulus is presented. A similar change in neuronal firing, which precedes the unconditioned stimulus and occurs slightly before the onset of the nictitating membrane response is also illustrated. In the lower traces, no conditioned response occurs since the stimuli were not paired in this control experiment. (c) The first eight unpaired control trials. (d) The final eight unpaired control trials. In (c), a nictitating membrane response occurs following presentation of the unconditioned stimulus, but little neuronal firing accompanies this response. When the conditioned stimulus is presented in (d), no membrane or neuronal responses occur.

(Thompson, Berger, and Madden 1983). Indeed, lesions in the deep nuclei of the cerebellum, where such changes can be detected, abolishes the conditioned response, even though the unconditioned response still occurs. This important evidence suggests that changes take place in the cerebellum that are crucial to the development of conditioning. Further research on the neuronal mechanisms of conditioning using these approaches may prove that specific changes in brain structure and formation during associative learning are located in the cerebellum, at least for classical conditioning of this particular response system. Further analyses of this sort will continue to reveal what changes occur and how specific neuronal systems in the brain might be modified during such training (Thompson 1986).

In a pertinent demonstration of the importance of the cerebellum in certain types of learning, Leaton and Supple (1986) have shown that the cerebellum is essential for long-term habituation of the acoustic startle response in rats. This relatively permanent form of nonassociative learning—a decrease in the startle response to a loud noise following repeated presentations of the stimulus lasting for days—is disrupted if a specific portion on the midline of the cerebellum, the cerebellar vermis, is removed. These results, as well as the deficits in classical conditioning that occur following damage to the cerebellum, suggest that this area of the brain may be critical for procedural memory, a general class of memories that will be defined and discussed in more detail later.

Equally interesting and promising research has been done using **operant conditioning** procedures in which a change in behavior or brain activity is reinforced by some rewarding stimulus. This powerful training paradigm represents an extremely important form of learning and conditioning in humans and other animals.

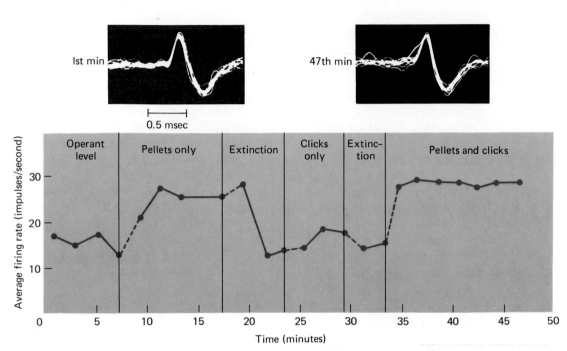

Figure 14.10 Graph illustrating operant conditioning of the firing rate of a single neuron in the motor cortex of the monkey. The operant level illustrates firing rate prior to reinforcement with food pellets, which produced a sustained increase that could be extinguished when reinforcement was withdrawn. Presentation of clicks alone as a feedback signal had no effect, but when combined with a food pellet, reinforcement aided conditioning. Example of the wave form of the action potential at the beginning and end of training are illustrated above the graph.

In a pioneering series of studies, Fetz (1969) studied operant conditioning of single neurons in the motor cortex of monkeys. The results of one experiment are illustrated in figure 14.10. In this experiment, the activity of a single neuron in the motor cortex of an awake monkey sitting in a special primate chair was recorded. Whenever an increase in firing rate occurred, the change was reinforced by giving the animal a food pellet. In some instances, neuronal firing could be increased by as much as 500 percent. As illustrated in figure 14.10, the operant level of firing prior to reinforcement for one cell was around fifteen impulses per second. Presentation of a food pellet occurred whenever the cell fired at rates higher than this baseline rate. This reward produced a marked and sustained increase in firing rate. During extinction, when food pellets were no longer presented, the rate increase could be extinguished. After this, clicks were delivered to the animal when the cell fired in order to provide some sensory feedback so as to determine if sensory feedback alone was responsible for the apparent conditioning effort. Clicks alone did not produce an increase in spontaneous firing rate, but following another extinction period, presentation of clicks and food pellets resulted in rapid conditioning of high-discharge rates for this neuron. Thus, providing sensory feedback to the animal in the form of either an auditory click or a visual stimulus aided conditioning. It is important in such experiments to make certain the same single neuron is being recorded during the entire experiment. Pictures of the wave form of this neuron, shown in figure 14.10, illustrate that it remained constant from the beginning to the end of the experiment. Such evidence indicates that the same neuron was being recorded throughout.

Many experimenters have now reported changes in the electrical activity of single brain cells during conditioning procedures. The results of such experiments make it clear that changes in the electrical activity of the brain during learning and memory are quite widespread. It also has been established that the **engram,** defined as all neural processes involved in the storage of a memory event, involves multiple sites of plastic change in the circuitry of the brain (Woody 1986). As Thompson and his associates (1983) have indicated, nearly every region of the brain where the neurons show learning-induced changes has been found to have some role in learning under appropriate conditions. In addition, such changes may take place in different regions of the brain during different phases of the learning process. It may also be that different types of training rely on different kinds of changes or changes in different regions of the brain, although we do not yet have complete answers to such questions. There is much to be done in the search for the physiological mechanisms underlying learning, particularly at the elementary level of the activity of single neurons.

Neuronal Activity in the Frontal Cortex during Delayed-Response Learning

A final example of changes in nerve cell behavior in animal subjects during learning and memory illustrates that the activity of single neurons may lead to an understanding of memory operation during the performance of complex tasks. One such task that has been studied extensively in animal subjects is the **delayed-response task.** In one common version of this task, the experimental animal, usually a monkey, sits in a cage opposite the experimenter and watches as the experimenter places a raisin, peanut, or other reward under one of several objects on a tray. A screen is then lowered between the animal and the display tray for a specified **delay interval.** Following the delay interval, the screen is raised, the display tray is pushed toward the animal, and it is allowed to make a response. To make a correct response, the animal must remember under which object the reward was hidden, move the object, and retrieve the reward.

In an effort to explore the neuronal changes that might underlie the ability of animal subjects to learn the delayed-response problem and to remember the correct response during the delay interval, Fuster and Alexander (1971) trained monkeys to perform a delayed-response task. Once the animals were well-trained, microelectrodes were implanted in the frontal cortex and in the thalamic nucleus that projects to the frontal cortex, called the **nucleus medialis dorsalis.** An example of the changes in firing of single cells while monkeys performed the delayed response is shown in figure 14.11. Neurons in both the prefrontal cortex and the nucleus medialis dorsalis in the thalamus showed changes in firing frequency during the performance of the delayed-response task. The five cases shown in the figure illustrate that during the presentation of the cue that signaled the onset of the delay period, the activity of these cells was inhibited markedly. During the delay period, when the animals were required to wait prior to responding, the activity of these neurons increased to well above normal levels. In some

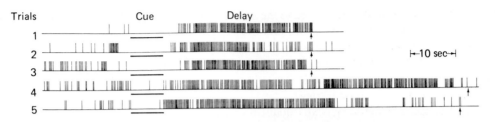

Figure 14.11 Recordings of the firing of a prefrontal cortex neuron (vertical lines) in five consecutive trials of a delayed-response task. Delay intervals were 32, 32, 32, 67, and 65 seconds, respectively, from top to bottom. The cue is indicated by a solid line. The delay interval on each trial follows the cue and ends at the arrow. Note that the neuron fires more during the delay interval than before the trial.

cases, the direction of change was different. However, these experiments illustrate that neurons in the prefrontal cortex and the nucleus medialis dorsalis are modified substantially, particularly during the delay period. Since these changes can be recorded during the delay interval, which is presumably the time during which memory is required and operating, they could be correlates of a short-term memory process operating during the delay interval. These data are also consistent with the well-known effects of prefrontal cortex ablation on the ability of animals to master delayed-response problems. If the prefrontal cortex is removed, the ability to perform the delayed-response task is severely impaired, further suggesting that the processes occurring in the frontal lobe are essential for learning to perform such tasks. Perhaps the frontal lobes contain the neuronal assemblies that permit the animal to remember the correct choice during the delay interval. Frontal lobe disease in patients with verified frontal-lobe lesions is also accompanied by deficits in delayed-response tasks (Freedman and Oscar-Berman 1986).

Human Memory and Amnesia

Careful studies of animal subjects have begun to reveal the changes that occur in the brain as these animals learn and remember. Parallel studies of memory in human subjects, especially those exhibiting memory disorders, have also shown that an important feature of human memory, like that of other animals, is that it consists of distinct processes having different time scales (Norman 1973).

Iversen (1973) identified some of the memory components that are shown in figure 14.12. In this scheme, information is initially stored for a brief period of several hundred milliseconds or less in a **sensory register.** From the sensory register, information is transferred to the **immediate memory** where it may be held for several seconds. **Short-term memory** generally refers to the process in which information is retained over periods of seconds or

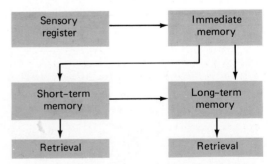

Figure 14.12 Some of the components of memory and possible relationships between them.

hippocampus   (hip''o-kam'pus)

minutes, while **long-term memory** refers to the process of memory storage that spans hours, days, and years. Experimental work has focused for several decades on the distinction between short-term and long-term memory.

Note also that information retrieval is an important aspect of memory. No doubt everyone has experienced the frustrating inability to retrieve an item from memory at a particular moment. In experiments on memory, therefore, it is important to identify whether memory storage or memory retrieval is affected.

Amnesic Disorders and the Limbic System

The division of human memory into short-term and long-term memory was based on information from surgical procedures used to relieve severe epilepsy in human patients. Bilateral surgical removal of the temporal lobes and the hippocampus buried within the temporal lobes on each side of the brain was successful in reducing the severe seizures experienced by these patients. The approximate position of the **hippocampus** within the **temporal lobe** of the human brain is illustrated schematically in figure 14.13. Although this

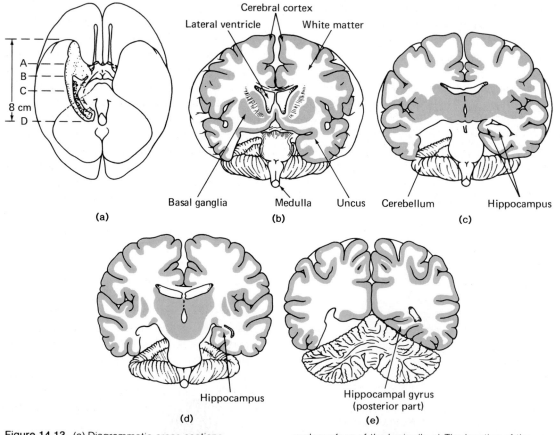

(a)   (b)   (c)   (d)   (e)

Figure 14.13   (a) Diagrammatic cross sections through the human brain illustrating the position of the hippocampus. The upper drawing shows the undersurface of the brain. (b–e) The location of the four cross sections, keyed to the drawing, are shown.

procedure was used effectively in a number of patients, its side effects rapidly precluded further use.

Some of these patients were studied very carefully to determine the nature of these side effects. Although the IQ scores, personalities, and skills learned prior to the operation were not affected by the operation, these individuals could no longer store new information in memory (Scoville and Milner 1957; Milner 1966). They could remember new information for a few seconds, but soon forgot the remembered information, apparently forever, especially if they were distracted. These patients reported that they read the same magazines day after day without ever remembering the

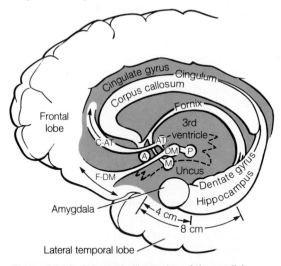

Figure 14.14 Schematic illustration of the medial surface of the hemisphere showing the limbic system, including the medial temporal region (hippocampus, amygdala, dentate gyrus, lateral temporal lobe) and structures along the diencephalic midline (DM = dorsomedial thalamic nucleus, M = mammillary bodies, A = anterior commissure, AT = anterior thalamus, and P = posterior commissure). Also indicated are the pathways interconnecting the dorsomedial nucleus and the frontal cortex (F-DM) and the connection between the anterior thalamus and cingulate gyrus (C-AT). Damage to the medial temporal or midline diencephalic region causes memory dysfunction.

content after they finished. Remarkably, very old memories remained intact so that these individuals had no difficulty in remembering events preceding the operation by many years, such as early childhood memories.

Severe memory defects are a common symptom of damage to a number of structures within the limbic system of the brain (fig. 14.14). These structures include the hippocampus, the amygdala, the dentate gyrus, and the lateral temporal lobe, as well as the various targets of these structures along the midline of the brain stem, such as the dorsomedial nucleus of the thalamus and the mammillary bodies, two nuclei behind the hypothalamus (Butters and Miliotis 1985; Squire 1987).

In general, amnesic disorders can result from damage to the brain by diverse causes. For example, anoxia, nutritional deficiencies, head injuries, cerebrovascular accidents, trauma, or severe alcohol toxicity all can result in severe memory defects. Butters and Miliotis (1985) identify four clinical characteristics typically exhibited by patients suffering from amnesic disorders. The first of these characteristics is that all amnesics have at least some **anterograde amnesia.** This is a condition in which new information cannot be learned and remembered, as we have just described for patients following bilateral surgical operations performed on the temporal lobe. This memory defect is made evident with a simple demonstration. If asked to associate a term from a short list of words with its mate in a second short list, the patient does so only with great difficulty. Whereas a normal individual might take four trials to learn this association, patients with anterograde amnesia might need seventy or eighty trials to learn the same paired-associate list (Butters and Miliotis 1985).

A second defect that amnesic patients frequently exhibit is **retrograde amnesia.** The phenomenon of retrograde amnesia has been of great interest to biological psychologists for many years. The patient, as a result of some type of head injury, suffers a loss of memory for events preceding the traumatic event. A very interesting aspect of the syndrome is that the amnesia is frequently restricted to events that occurred immediately preceding the injury, whereas events that occurred long before the trauma appear to be remembered as well as ever. Such evidence reinforces the view that memory consists in some way of different phases, and that information learned recently is stored differently than information learned earlier.

In 1937, a detailed experimental examination of the phenomenon of retrograde amnesia became possible when **electroconvulsive therapy** was introduced into medical practice as a therapeutic treatment. In electroconvulsive therapy, strong electric current is passed through the brain in order to induce seizures, or convulsions. Although the efficacy and dangers of electroconvulsive therapy still are debated vigorously, the procedure continues to be used and is effective in treating severely depressed patients. Because it also produces memory loss, **electroconvulsive shock** was used as an experimental tool in the study of memory storage processes in human patients as well as in animals.

Zubin and Barrera (1941) conducted one of the first systematic experiments using human subjects and electroconvulsive shock treatments in an effort to learn more about retrograde amnesia and memory processes. In their experiment, patients were taught paired-associate words during an original learning session. After some time, they were asked to relearn this same material. The amount of savings (retained information) was then used as a measure of how much information each subject remembered. The results indicated that there is a significant amount of savings between the original learning session and the relearning trials under normal conditions except when an electroconvulsive shock intervenes between the original learning and the relearning. These investigators found that the shorter the time interval between original learning and the electroconvulsive shock, the greater the amnesic effects. In other words, the severity of amnesia depended upon the time interval between the original learning and the interfering electroconvulsive stimulus.

Duncan (1949) performed a classic experiment using experimental animals that demonstrated that the effectiveness of an electroconvulsive shock in suppressing memory varied as a function of the time interval between the original learning and convulsion. Duncan trained rats in a multiple T-maze, giving the animals one trial per day. The animals were rewarded with food for running through the maze. Various groups of animals were tested, some of which received electroconvulsive shock after each learning trial. The groups given electroconvulsive shock differed in terms of the time interval between running the maze and the administration of the convulsive shock. The results indicated that animals given the electroconvulsive shock shortly after the learning trial performed significantly worse than animals that either did not receive the shock or received the shock long after the learning trial. The data from this experiment are summarized in figure 14.15 and illustrate

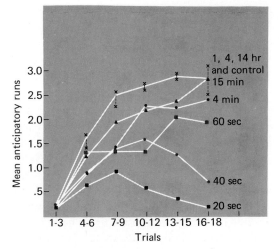

Figure 14.15 The effects of electroconvulsive shock on acquisition of a T-maze task. Animals were given electroconvulsive shock at 20 seconds, 40 seconds, 60 seconds, 4 minutes, and 15 minutes or at 1, 4, or 14 hours after the learning trials. Note that the closer in time the electroconvulsive shock was administered after each learning trial, the poorer the performance.

the period of time over which electroconvulsive shock can affect memory. Keep in mind that these data represent the results of a particular experiment using a particular species of animal in a particular learning situation. Time parameters are known to depend on many variables, including the species used in the study and the learning task employed.

There is an enormous amount of literature on the effects of electroconvulsive shock on memory storage processes. A great deal of this has been summarized in reviews and books on memory (see e.g., Deutsch 1973; McGaugh and Herz 1972; Squire 1987). Several extremely important concepts of memory storage have emerged from this large body of work, as well as from other approaches to be described later. One such concept is the **consolidation theory of memory storage.** The time

following original learning and when an electroconvulsive shock is administered is critical in producing retrograde amnesia. As was stated previously, the greater the time interval between original learning and electroconvulsive shock, the less memory is affected. The progressive memory loss with time interval is called a **retrograde amnesia gradient,** and the existence of this gradient suggests that memory storage is time dependent (McGaugh 1966). In other words, memory does not instantaneously follow learning, but rather some time is required for memory storage to take place. This is referred to as consolidation of memory and forms the basis for the consolidation theory. The consolidation theory is consistent with the view that memory takes at least two different forms: short-term, or recent, memory susceptible to interference by electroconvulsive shock and other treatments and more permanent, long-term memory not easily disrupted by such treatments. However, evidence from studies of human patients suggests that even some long-term memories are susceptible to disruption by electroconvulsive shock. Squire, Slater, and Chace (1975), for example, used a specially designed remote memory test and were able to demonstrate that memories acquired by patients up to three years before may be impaired following electroconvulsive shock treatment.

Evidence such as this suggests that the period during which memories are susceptible to disruption by electroconvulsive shock may extend over a much longer time than previously believed. Even so, some patients exhibit a severe retrograde amnesia lasting even longer than this, such as patients with alcoholic **Korsakoff's syndrome.** This disorder occurs in patients who have been chronic alcoholics for many years and is accompanied by significant pathology of the brain, especially degeneration of certain structures within the limbic system. Such patients may exhibit remote memory loss extending ten years or more and may involve all periods of the patient's life (Butters 1984; Cohen and Squire 1981).

Two other characteristic symptoms frequently exhibited by patients with amnesic disorders are **confabulation** and **intact intellect.** In the case of confabulation, when asked to recall some event from memory, patients may "invent" something to fill in the memory gap. For example, a patient may recall a story or series of events that happened at some time other than that which they are asked to recall.

The fourth characteristic of amnesic patients is that, typically, they have relatively **intact intellectual functions,** as we noted for the epileptic patient who suffered surgical removal of the temporal lobes. Standard intelligence tests reveal that the intelligence and intellectual performance of such patients is equal to normal control subjects when appropriately matched for educational background, socioeconomic class, age, and other important variables (Butters and Cermak 1980).

Memories Evoked by Electrical Stimulation of the Temporal Lobes

Electrical stimulation of the human brain during surgery also indicates that the temporal lobes are important in memory, perhaps as storage and retrieval sites. Among the fascinating early evidence linking the temporal lobe with memory processes were the observations of neurosurgeons who used electrical stimulation of the patient's brain in order to map the locations of various functional regions within this organ. An interesting example of such work is found in the writings of the illustrious Canadian neurosurgeon Wilder Penfield. During his long career at McGill University, Penfield and associates had the opportunity to operate on over four hundred patients, many of whom suffered from tumor of the brain or epilepsy. In their book, *The Cerebral Cortex of Man* (1950), Penfield and Rasmussen describe the effects of electrical stimulation of the temporal lobe in an epileptic patient undergoing brain surgery. Since there are no pain receptors in the brain tissue, electrical stimulation of the brain is carried out while the patient is conscious and able to speak, though under local anesthesia. The description of case J. V. reveals some of the fascinating effects of direct electrical stimulation of the human brain.

Case J. V. The patient was a girl of 14 years who had suffered from epileptiform seizures. . . . Her attacks were characterized by sudden fright and screaming . . . it was learned that during these preliminary periods of fright she invariably saw herself in a scene that she remembers to have occurred at the age of 7 years. . . . She occasionally had nightmares during her sleep, and in the dream the scene was reenacted. . . .

Operation. An osteoplastic craniotomy was carried out under local anesthesia, exposing the posterior half of the right hemisphere . . . the exposed cortex was explored with stimulating electrodes. . . . Stimulation of points on the lateral aspect of the temporal lobe . . . produced in the patient different portions of her "dream". . . . In summary . . . when the cortex was stimulated this neurone pattern referring to the "scene" could be activated from different points, although the cortex surely served as a repository of innumerable other patterns. . . . When the electrodes were held in place for a longer period of time, the hallucinations progressed like a story or memory unfolding. . . . the organization of the temporal cortex is evidently different from that of other areas inasmuch as here alone electrical stimulation . . .

activates acquired synaptic patterns. The fact that it is only in this region that such stimulation produces complex psychical illusions and hallucinations argues for some degree of localization of intellectual function. . . . We have stumbled unexpectedly upon the location of the mechanisms within the humming loom of the mind. (pp. 164–67)

The Hippocampus and Memory Impairment

While several causes of memory impairment have been reported over the years and attributed to hippocampal damage, it has been only recently that clear and convincing evidence for a specific role of the hippocampus in the amnesic syndrome has been obtained. In the case of the famous patient H. M., who underwent a bilateral temporal lobectomy, as well as animal models of amnesic syndromes, damage to the brain typically involves a number of other structures in the temporal lobe in addition to the hippocampus. However, Zola-Morgan, Squire, and Amaral (1986, in press) reported the case of patient R. B., who developed severe amnesia after an episode of ischemia, in which there is a lack of blood to a portion of the brain. During a period of five years before his death, this patient exhibited a marked syndrome of anterograde amnesia with little or no impairment of other cognitive function and relatively little retrograde amnesia. This patient died of congestive heart failure after having undergone a five-year period of careful testing for memory impairment and cognitive function. Permission was given to undertake careful histological examination of this patient's brain, which was acquired within hours of his death at autopsy. This examination revealed that the patient had a restricted bilateral lesion of the hippocampus, which was evident in a region of the hippocampus designated as field CA1 and shown in figure 14.16.

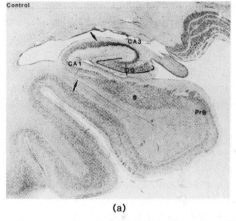

(a)

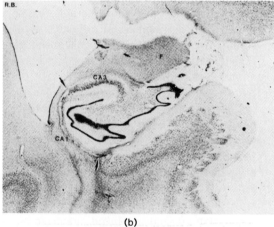

(b)

Figure 14.16 Photomicrographs of thionin-stained, coronal sections through the hippocampal formation of a normal control brain (a) and patient R.B.'s brain (b). R. B. developed an amnesic syndrome in 1978 after an ischemic episode. He died in 1983 at the age of 57. Histological examination revealed a bilateral lesion involving the entire CA1 field of the hippocampus. In the control section, the two arrows indicate the limits of the CA1 field. In R.B.'s brain, the only pathology evident in the hippocampal formation was a complete loss of pyramidal cells from the CA1 field (between the arrows). The amygdala, mammillary nuclei, and mediodorsal thalamic nucleus were normal, and there was no other significant pathology that could reasonably account for the memory impairment (PrS = presubiculum; S = subiculum; CA1 and CA3 = fields of the hippocampus; DG = dentate gyrus; F = fimbria of the fornix).

This region of R. B.'s hippocampus lacked the normal complement of large nerve cells when compared to the normal brain. This evidence has established convincingly for the first time that damage restricted specifically to the hippocampus leads to the characteristic memory impairment that has been described following temporal lobe damage.

Declarative and Procedural Memory

Recent attempts have successfully established that damage to the medial temporal lobe, typically including the hippocampus and amygdala, produce a syndrome of memory impairment in nonhuman primates that is similar to and provides an adequate model of the impairment following comparable brain damage in humans (Mishkin et al. 1982; Squire and Zola-Morgan 1983). The locations of these lesions in the nonhuman primate temporal lobe rule out the other structures that previously had been believed to be involved in the temporal lobe memory impairment. Perhaps even more importantly, careful and creative neuropsychological testing of human amnesics and nonhuman primates with similar brain damage-induced amnesic syndromes have revealed that memory probably exists in at least two distinguishable types or classes, which have been termed **declarative** and **procedural memory** (Squire and Shimamura 1985; Squire 1986; 1987).

The distinction between different classes of memories has been revealed by memory tests involving human patients that exhibit classic memory impairment following temporal lobe damage. In one test, human patients were taught a mirror-reading task in which they were required to read three words that had been reversed, as they would appear in a mirror. The amnesic patients learn this task as well as patients with normal memory, indicating that the deficit in memory that they exhibit is restricted to certain kinds of learning and memory. The amnesic patients improved their mirror-reading skill at a normal rate and maintained a high level of skill even after three months had intervened (Cohen and Squire 1980). This kind of memory is termed **procedural memory** and can be distinguished from those memories that cannot be acquired by such amnesic patients, which are collectively termed **declarative memory.** Sometimes procedural memory is called skill memory to distinguish it from learning and remembering facts and data. These patients could learn and remember the skill of mirror-reading, but might not remember ever having received such training or a specific instance of doing the mirror-reading task. They were unable to recognize familiar words that they had previously learned to read in the mirror-reading task. Thus, motor-skill learning and other kinds of procedural knowledge seem to be preserved in the anterograde amnesic syndrome, while specific knowledge about specific instances that would be remembered by the normal subject is impaired. Procedural memory is sometimes considered the case of "knowing how," while declarative memory is "knowing that." As Squire and Shimamura (1985) have explained

Knowing-how or procedural learning is considered to result in the modification or tuning of existing processing systems, operations, or procedures. This modification changes the way an organism behaves in the world, but without affording to the organism access to its previous experience in the form of specific encounters. . . . Procedural knowledge can be acquired and maintained without the participation of the brain regions damaged in amnesia. . . . By contrast, knowing-that, or declarative memory, refers to all the specific-item information that is measured in conventional tests of memory. (pp. 8–9)

Table 14.1 Properties of Declarative and Procedural Knowledge

Declarative Knowledge	Procedural Knowledge
Stores facts, episodes, and data	Stores skills and procedures
Can be learned in a single trial	Is learned incrementally
Available to many processing systems	Contained within processing systems
Information is modality general	Information is modality specific
Phylogenetically recent	Phylogenetically primitive
Ontogenetically late	Ontogenetically early
Impaired in amnesia	Preserved in amnesia
Accessible to conscious recollection	Inaccessible to conscious recollection

From L. R. Squire, "The neuropsychology of memory" in P. Marler and H. Terrace, (Eds.), *The Biology of Learning.* © 1986 Springer-Verlag, Berlin.

This distinction between two memory systems in the brain and the two kinds of knowledge is illustrated further by the properties of declarative and procedural knowledge listed in table 14.1. This conception and the increased knowledge about two classes of memory and their biological substrates has led to a number of interesting ideas related to amnesia that extend well beyond the domain of memory mechanisms. In one provocative theoretical treatment, for example, Nadel and Zola-Morgan (1984) have suggested that an important tenet of the psychoanalytic theories of Sigmund Freud and others may now yield to a more definitive and parsimonious neurobiological understanding. The tenet is the phenomenon of **infantile amnesia,** to which great significance is attached by Freud and his followers as an example of repressed memories, motives, and sexual desires. Thus, Freud states that during the early years of life, "Most mental experiences and excitations occurring . . . succumb to the infantile amnesia, . . .

which veils our earliest childhood from us and estranges us from it," having noted previously that the memories of early childhood " . . . have never really been forgotten, but were only inaccessible and latent, having become part of the unconscious" (Freud 1938, 286, 178–79). Nadel and Zola-Morgan argue persuasively that the development of the hippocampus in humans and other species seems to relate importantly to the case of infantile amnesia. The hippocampal system underlying the ability to store declarative memory is not mature in humans prior to about two years of life, so there is no substrate for storing declarative knowledge. Hence, what is usually termed infantile amnesia is apparent. This explanation for infantile amnesia does not require the complex theoretic inventions of psychoanalytic theory.

The study of memory and its development reveals that it is not a unitary thing, but rather that there are more than one memory systems and that these various systems become functional only following a postnatal period of neurogenesis—the development of appropriate nerve cells and their connections. As we have seen, the adult hippocampal formation seems to be central to the kinds of learning and memory that are absent in infantile amnesia. Human infants are busy learning motor skills and procedural knowledge, but do not retain declarative knowledge until they reach two or more years of age. Similar distinctions are being drawn concerning the development of memories in infants of other species. Further, in various species studied to date, including humans, the postnatal maturation of the hippocampal region seems to match the time course and development of the ability to learn and retain declarative knowledge (Nadel and Zola-Morgan 1984).

Memory Mechanisms

Over the years, numerous processes and modifications in the brain's structure have been suggested to underlie memory storage. Extensive neurobiological evidence establishes that memory storage may involve many different cellular and subcellular processes and that "Engram formation may be seen to derive from temporal and spatial relationships between electrical and chemical neural events" (Woody 1986, 434). For example, learning and memory in several invertebrate preparations appear to involve changes in the ionic conductance across nerve cell membranes by potassium ions (Carew and Sahley 1986). In addition, in vertebrates, changes in the excitability of neurons in many structures and in pathways involved in production of conditioned responses may be changed (Woody 1986). Even so, because the hippocampus has been so clearly linked to memory processes in humans, especially in studies of the amnesic disorders following hippocampal damage, a special and extensive effort has been devoted to understanding the neurobiology of the hippocampal formation and the cellular processes within the hippocampal system that might underlie its apparent role in the formation of memory (Seifert 1983).

Perhaps more than any other process in the brains of higher vertebrates, the phenomenon of **long-term potentiation** of synaptic transmission following trains of high-frequency stimulation to various excitatory pathways directed to or entirely within the hippocampal formation has been studied extensively. Long-term potentiation is considered a candidate for the cellular processes of plasticity within the hippocampal formation that might underlie or participate in memory storage.

A schematic diagram depicting a cross-section through the hippocampus of the rat, the animal in which most studies of hippocampal long-term potentiation have been carried out, is shown in figure 14.17. The pathway most frequently stimulated in such experiments is the perforant path, which originates in the nearby region of cerebral cortex called the entorhinal cortex. This pathway makes excitatory synaptic contact with granule cells in the dentate gyrus. A brief bout of high-frequency electrical stimulation to this pathway will induce a long-lasting increase in amplitude or duration of the excitatory postsynaptic potentials subsequently evoked in granule cells by individual stimuli (McNaughton 1983). It now has been established that virtually all of the excitatory pathways in the hippocampus show long-term potentiation, such as the perforant pathway from the entorhinal cortex to the dentate gyrus, the mossy fiber pathway from the dentate gyrus to the pyramidal cells within the hippocampus proper, as well as the schaffer collateral pathway that arises as axon collaterals of pyramidal cell axons of the hippocampus to end on other hippocampal pyramidal cells. All of these synaptic connections exhibit a significant potentiation of synaptic transmission—an increase in synaptic strength—following a brief burst of high-frequency stimulation to the presynaptic axons. While some other pathways in the brain also have been shown to exhibit potentiation of synaptic transmission following high-frequency stimulation (e.g., Berger 1984), the phenomenon of long-term potentiation in the hippocampus has captured the imagination of neurobiologists as a potentially significant candidate for a mechanism underlying memory storage (Barnes and McNaughton 1980; Lynch, Halpain, and Baudry 1983).

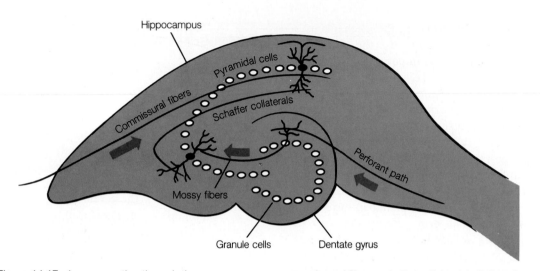

Figure 14.17 A cross section through the hippocampal formation of the rat brain showing the hippocampus and dentate gyrus. The labeled excitatory pathways (perforant path, mossy fibers, commissural fibers, schaffer collaterals) all show long-term potentiation of synaptic transmission following high-frequency stimulation of the presynaptic axons.

The time course of long-term potentiation following perforant path stimulation may be quite lengthy under appropriate conditions, lasting in some cases for days or even weeks (Barnes and McNaughton 1980). A number of mechanisms have been proposed to underlie the long-term potentiation effect, many of which are not mutually exclusive; that is, a number of subcellular and biochemical mechanisms may participate in the long-term potentiation of synaptic transmission. One particularly interesting mechanism involves a change in the structure of the perforant path synapses. This synapse, which is made by the perforant pathway axon onto a dendritic spine, appears to change its shape following high-frequency stimulation. Fifkova and Van Harreveld (1977) stimulated the perforant pathway in the mouse. Following this stimulation, the brain was quickly removed and frozen. Examination of the perforant path synapses revealed that the spines on which these synapses were made appeared to swell slightly. Subsequent experiments by others have also suggested that the shape of the synapse made by perforant pathway axons onto dendritic spines of granule cells in the dentate gyrus changes in response to high-frequency stimulation of the perforant pathway (e.g., Desmond and Levy 1983). An interesting correlation also has been reported between the spatial memory ability of young and old rats and the proportion of synapses in the dentate gyrus having a specific shape (Geinisman, Toledo-Morrell, and Morrell 1986).

Other alterations in the mechanisms of synaptic transmission by the perforant pathway also may be important for the long-term potentiation (Lynch, Halpain, and Baudry 1983). These mechanisms include such processes as increased release of the excitatory neurotransmitter glutamate from the perforant pathway or an exposure of additional postsynaptic receptor sites for released glutamate following potentiating stimulation (e.g., Lynch and Baudry 1984). In an exciting development, two different laboratories have shown that long-term potentiation may involve the association of two stimulation events, reminiscent of associative pairing of stimuli in conditioning. Thus, Larson and Lynch (1986) demonstrated that when a burst of high-frequency stimulation was applied to one input to the hippocampal neurons and a second burst was delivered to a different input to the same target neuron 200 milliseconds later, the second input showed stable potentiation, but not when the second burst of stimulation occurred simultaneously or followed the first stimulus burst by two seconds. Intracellular recordings indicated that the initial burst of high-frequency stimulation extended the normal decay of excitatory postsynaptic potentials evoked 200 milliseconds later. Another group of investigators has observed that the second bout of stimulation or direct depolarization of the postsynaptic target cell may produce this kind of potentiation involving the association of two synaptic events in the same postsynaptic neuron (Sastry, Goh, and Auyeung 1986). You can feel the growing excitement as continued experimental work approaches the goal of understanding the way in which the brain stores information and gives us the memories that characterize the human experience.

Summary

Learning and memory are processes inferred from the performance of organisms. Changes in behavioral performance result from experience; learning and memory are thus said to have occurred. Experience alters the structure and the function of the brain. Rats reared in enriched environments demonstrate increased dendritic branching of nerve cells and increased thickness of the cerebral cortex.

As animals learn, changes in the activity of nerve cells in the brain can be correlated with behavioral performance. The use of model systems has produced substantial information regarding the neuronal mechanisms of such forms of learning as **habituation, sensitization,** and **conditioning.** Habituation and sensitization of the flexion reflex of the acute spinal animal, for example, shows that these simple forms of reflex plasticity are due to changes in the activity of interneurons in the spinal gray matter. An extensive analysis of habituation in the invertebrate organism *Aplysia* has established that habituation is due to the depression of excitatory synaptic transmission. Additional studies of such models suggest that even relatively complex forms of learning can be studied in these model systems, leading to a greater understanding of the molecular basis of learning and memory.

Studies of vertebrate conditioning suggest that a variety of neuronal changes takes place in the brain to mediate conditioning. In one useful model, classical conditioning of the rabbit nictitating membrane has revealed that the cerebellum plays a significant part in the conditioning process. Neuronal activity in the frontal cortex, essential for **delayed-response** learning, correlates with the performance of nonhuman primates during delayed-response tasks.

Careful studies of humans with memory impairments have established that human memory consists of different processes that have different time scales, such as a **sensory register, immediate memory, short-term memory,** and **long-term memory.** Human amnesic disorders illustrate that such human memory impairments typically show signs of **retrograde amnesia, anterograde amnesia,** and **confabulation,** but that such patients have relatively intact intellectual function. The occurrence of retrograde amnesia following **electroconvulsive shock** in animals has established that memories are not formed instantly at the time of learning, but that some period of time is required during which these memories are susceptible to disruption. This has been termed the **consolidation theory of memory,** suggesting that a period of consolidation of the memory trace must follow a learning experience. In humans, this period may extend up to four years or longer following learning.

Classic studies of patients who have had the temporal lobes removed to control severe epilepsy have established that the temporal lobes play an important part in human memory processes. More recent evidence establishes that human patients with brain damage, as well as animal subjects with similar impairments, may exhibit a profound memory disorder following damage specific to the **hippocampus** within the **temporal lobe,** although amnesia may occur following many different kinds of brain injury, especially if damage occurs to the limbic system. Careful studies of such amnesic patients have revealed that only certain classes of memories are impaired by the limbic system damage, especially damage to the temporal lobe. Evidence

such as this has established that the hippocampus and structures related to it are probably important for the formation of **declarative memories** (the memories of specific events and data), rather than **procedural memory** (the memory for skills and procedures). Declarative knowledge is sometimes termed "knowing that" whereas procedural knowledge is sometimes termed "knowing how." **Infantile amnesia,** considered so heavily in psychoanalytic theory, may result from the fact that the hippocampus is not mature until the infant is several years of age and thus there is no substrate for the storage of declarative memory.

Numerous processes have been proposed and investigated as the mechanisms underlying memory, including changes in ionic conductance across nerve cell membranes and changes in nerve cell membrane excitability, as well as accompanying changes in the structure of nerve cells and synapses thought to underlie different forms of learning and memory. The process of **long-term potentiation** in the hippocampus is an instance of plasticity in the brain that has captured the imagination of many investigators because of the evidence for a significant role of the hippocampus in human memory formation. Brief high-frequency electrical stimulation of the perforant pathway or other excitatory synaptic connections in the hippocampal formation produces a prolonged increase in synaptic strength that has been suggested by many to underlie memory formation. Changes in synaptic strength are probably produced by a variety of mechanisms that are the subject of continuing research.

Suggested Readings

Squire, L. 1987. *Memory and brain.* New York:
Oxford University Press.
*An excellent summary of the relationship
of memory to the brain written by one of
the leading authorities on the
neuropsychology of memory and the brain
substrates of human and animal memory.*

Squire, L. R., and N. Butters, eds. 1984.
Neuropsychology of memory. New York:
The Guilford Press.
*An edited volume on the neuropsychology
of memory, including contributions from
over seventy-five leading memory
researchers concerned with both human
and other animal memory and memory
impairment. Contains many chapters on
learning and memory and their
relationship to the brain.*

Teyler, T., ed. 1978. *Brain and learning.*
Stamford, CT.: Greylock Publishers.
*A brief, but excellent, collection of
chapters on the neural mechanisms of
learning and memory.*

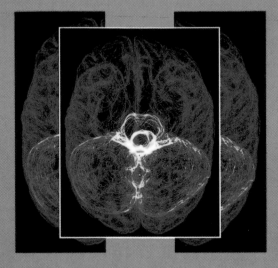

Outline

Introduction

In a report by the National Institute of Medicine requested by the Federal Alcohol, Drug Abuse, and Mental Health Administration the enormity of society's problem of mental illness and addictive disorders is clearly documented (Barchas et al. 1985). For example, the overall prevalence of mental illness and addictive disorders in the United States at any given time is now 15–22.5 percent, which translates to a staggering 30–45 million afflicted people. There are approximately 10 million adults and 3 million children who abuse alcohol, and one measure of alcohol's toll on human lives is that its use is implicated in twenty-eight thousand motor vehicle fatalities each year. Of the ten most expensive medical conditions in the United States, health care involving mental disorders is ranked third, accounting for over 20 billion dollars in health care costs each year (estimated in 1983 dollars). The human toll of these disorders of the brain and behavior is even greater. Suicide is the tenth leading cause of death in the United States, with thirty thousand reported deaths each year. There is a particularly disturbing suicide trend among the youth of America aged fifteen–twenty-four. The suicide rate for this age group rose from 5 per 100,000 young people in 1961 to 13 per 100,000 youth in 1983—an incredible 150 percent increase for this age group. It is now well-known that the tragedy of drug abuse and addiction has touched even the youngest members of our society. These figures concerning mental illness and addictive disorders only touch the surfaces of these enormous problems.

Chapter 15

Disorders of Behavior and the Brain

catecholamines (kat″e-kol-am′in)

The biological basis of behavior has been established with extensive and compelling experimental and clinical evidence, as documented throughout this text. In this chapter, we review some of the progress that has been made in treating and understanding the biological basis for disorders of the brain and behavior. We also will describe some of the exciting discoveries and directions in brain research, which will build the knowledge base that is necessary to develop new and improved methods for treating the manifold disorders of behavior and the brain. We have reason to hope that within our lifetimes treatments will improve sufficiently to allow substantial recovery from many forms of brain damage and mental illness, including improvement in the quality of life of those afflicted, and a return to more normal lives for many who are now disabled, injured, and sometimes institutionalized.

Psychiatric Disorders

Based on the number of admissions to mental hospitals, the most devastating and prevalent forms of major psychiatric disturbance are the **psychoses.** These include the **affective disorders,** which are disorders of mood such as **mania** and **depression,** and **schizophrenia,** a major thought disorder. It is both impressive and disquieting to realize that fully half of the hospital beds in the United States are occupied by psychiatric patients. The incidence of schizophrenia, one of the most serious of mental illnesses, is approximately 1 in 1,000 individuals, which means that about 250,000 Americans suffer from this disorder. One in every ten U.S. residents will require psychiatric help at some time in life, a fact making

it a virtual certainty that a member of your family will have a serious psychiatric problem at some time.

In this section, we review what is known about the biological basis for these serious mental disorders. Initially, we will discuss some of the theories that have been formulated to explain these problems. Considerable progress has been made in relating psychiatric disorders to brain chemistry and other factors in the operation of the brain. We will also review what types of treatment are available for these disorders and how the biological mechanisms underlying them are being studied in animals and humans.

Affective Disorders

Extreme and debilitating fluctuations in mood long have been thought to involve chemical imbalances of the central nervous system. Only recently, however, has a possible relationship between brain neurotransmitter systems and mood states come to light.

Mood and Brain Neurotransmitters

The role of the **catecholamines (norepinephrine** and **dopamine)** in emotional disturbances has been emphasized in a classic theory by Schildkraut and Kety (1967). These investigators noted that drugs that elevate mood and are effective in the treatment of mental depression facilitate catecholaminergic transmission in the brain. Conversely, drugs that produce depression are often used successfully in the treatment of manic behavior. These drugs tend to antagonize the synaptic action of dopamine and norepinephrine.

The types of drugs most often used in the treatment of the various depressive disorders include the **monoamine oxidase inhibitors,** the

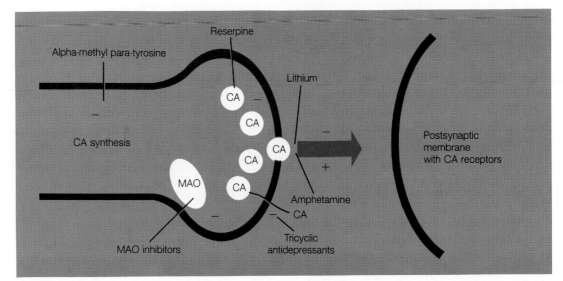

Figure 15.1 Some of the presynaptic drug actions on catecholamine (CA) synaptic transmission that have been used to support the catecholamine theory of mood. Drugs that reduce the strength of synaptic transmission at catecholaminergic synapses depress mood: reserpine, which interferes with catecholamine storage in vesicles and eventually depletes catecholamines; lithium, which inhibits CA release; and alphamethylparatyrosine, which inhibits the synthesis of catecholamines. Drugs that elevate mood include monoamine oxidase (MAO) inhibitors, which prevent the breakdown of catecholamines by inhibiting the action of monoamine oxidase; tricyclic antidepressants, which block the reuptake of the catecholamine back into the synaptic ending; and amphetamine, which facilitates catecholamine release.

tricyclic antidepressants, and the **psychomotor stimulants** (Cooper, Bloom, and Roth 1986). The mechanisms of action of some of these compounds were discussed in chapter 4 and are briefly reviewed here (fig. 15.1). 1. **Monoamine oxidase** is one of the enzymes responsible for the metabolic breakdown of the catecholamines. Inhibitors of this enzyme—the monoamine oxidase inhibitors—presumably make more transmitter available for synaptic release by preventing breakdown of the catecholamines in the brain. 2. The **tricyclic antidepressants,** so named because of their chemical structure and therapeutic action, prevent the reuptake of the catecholamines into presynaptic neurons. **Reuptake** is the major route by which catecholamines are removed from the synaptic cleft in the central nervous system; the tricyclic antidepressants, therefore, increase the levels of the catecholamines in the synaptic cleft. 3. The **psychomotor stimulants** also increase the availability of the catecholamines at the postsynaptic receptor sites and produce a state of excitement or alertness. Amphetamine, this category's prototype drug, appears to promote the release of catecholamines by presynaptic neurons and may also act as both an inhibitor of monoamine oxidase and a catecholamine reuptake blocking agent (Groves and Rebec 1976).

reserpine   (res′er-pēn)
alpha-methylparatyrosine   (al-fah-
meth″il-par′ah-ti-ro′sin)

Drugs that lower the levels of the catecholamines are used in the treatment of manic states. **Reserpine,** for example, depletes the stores of catecholamines in the brain by interfering with the intraneuronal storage of dopamine and norepinephrine. It is an effective behavioral depressant. **Alpha-methylparatyrosine** also produces sedation that is associated with a reduction in catecholamine levels in the brain. This drug blocks the synthesis of dopamine and norepinephrine. Lithium salts, which have also been used in the treatment of **mania** and other disorders, block the release of catecholamines into the synaptic cleft and facilitate their reuptake into the presynaptic terminal. Thus, it is not surprising that mental depression has been equated with a catecholamine deficiency, whereas mania is identified with a catecholamine excess in the brain.

Measurement of catecholamine metabolites, the products of catecholamine degradation, in the urine and cerebrospinal fluids of **manic** and **depressed** patients has been consistent with such hypotheses concerning mood. The relative quantities of these metabolites are used as an index of catecholaminergic activity in the central nervous system. The excretion of norepinephrine metabolites is considerably reduced during periods of depression, whereas it is increased during periods of mania (Schildkraut 1973). These shifts in the secretion of norepinephrine metabolites are probably not a reflection of muscular activity or the degree of movement characteristic of these emotional states since they reliably precede any behavioral shifts by several hours.

Studies of patients with Parkinson's disease, in which dopamine-containing neurons of the brain show a progressive degeneration and disappearance, suggest that dopamine may be an important factor in depression. These individuals as a group tend to be severely depressed, more so than patient populations with other degenerative disorders of the brain. Studies of animals whose brains have been depleted of dopamine indicate that the animals may exhibit a syndrome termed **anhedonia** (Wise 1982) in which stimuli that are normally rewarding lose this hedonic property. One current hypothesis is that the loss of the rewarding qualities of stimuli and events in their environment is related to the severely depressed mood characteristic of many patients with Parkinson's disease (Fibiger 1984).

These experiments do not rule out the real likelihood that other central nervous system neurotransmitters, such as **serotonin,** are involved in the expression of these mood states. The prevalence of serotonergic axon terminals throughout the limbic system, together with the marked changes in mood associated with drugs that alter serotonergic neurotransmission, support the idea that serotonin also might be an important mediator of affective behaviors. Indeed, there is some experimental evidence indicating that manic patients suffer from a deficit in serotonin transmission in the central nervous system (Chase and Murphy 1973). Moreover, some of the drugs used to treat depression, including some popular monoamine oxidase inhibitors and tricyclic antidepressants, are known to increase serotonergic neurotransmission (de Montigny et al. 1984). It even is conceivable that there are at least two different types of depression—one related to a catecholaminergic deficit and one related to a serotonergic deficit.

During the past decade, evidence has been accumulating to suggest that acetylcholine, in addition to the biogenic amines, also may be significant in the etiology of affective disorders. In this hypothesis, mania and depression represent disturbances of the neurochemical balance between norepinephrine and acetylcholine in the brain (Janowsky and Risch 1984). Excessive cholinergic activity—which might occur as a result of increased activity of cholinergic neurons in the brain, increased sensitivity of neurons postsynaptic to them, or other factors—leads to the state of depression. Overactivity in the norepinephrine systems of the brain leads to mania. These two neurochemical systems are in a dynamic state of balance in which any of a number of influences may tip the scale and lead to changes in affect.

These theories represent an advance in conceptualizing the biological basis of psychiatric disorders since they postulate a role for alterations in the balance or interaction of several neurotransmitter systems in the brain. This approach favors both the organizational complexity of the brain and the functional evidence for more than a single neurotransmitter in the mediation of mood and behavior.

Among the recent advances in the treatment of affective disorders is the development of lithium carbonate, a salt of the element lithium. This compound can be effective in stabilizing wide fluctuations in mood, especially the manic phase of manic-depressive psychosis. Several extremely important questions must be addressed in the development of drugs to treat mental disorders, such as whether a new agent produces serious side effects (as many such agents do), and whether these drugs are efficacious only in individuals suffering from a particular disorder. Studies of lithium carbonate's effects on human volunteers are now under way, but research concerning the mechanisms by which lithium affects the brain is in its infancy.

In a series of experiments, Judd and associates (1977a; 1977b) studied the effects of lithium carbonate on human volunteers. They assessed a number of variables, such as affect, mood, and cognitive and motor functions, as well as personality variables, aesthetic judgment, and semantic creativity. Contrary to the belief of many using or prescribing this drug, Judd's study indicated that lithium carbonate has a significant effect on mood, cognitive and motor functions, and other characteristic behaviors of normal people. This drug causes lethargy, loss of interest in interaction with other persons, mental confusion, and marked impairment of certain cognitive and motor functions, especially those requiring an element of timing.

The researchers point out that such studies not only may reveal the possible side effects of such agents, but also may suggest which aspects of cognition and affect are specifically influenced by the drug. This, therefore, will suggest the types of actions significant in the drug's ability to produce therapeutic gain.

Electroconvulsive Therapy
One of the most controversial forms of treatment of mentally ill patients is electroconvulsive therapy, illustrated in figure 15.2. As we observed in chapter 14, this form of treatment was introduced in medical practice during the mid-1930s. Mental patients with all sorts of disorders, including the affective psychoses and schizophrenia, were given this treatment. In its early stages, a wide variety of agents was used to induce the convulsions, including drugs such as pentylenetetrazol (trade name, Metrazol), hormones such as insulin, and electricity. It soon became apparent that not all mental disorders respond to convulsive therapy

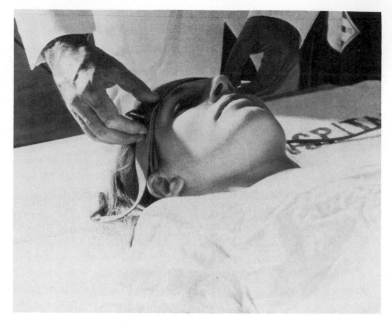

Figure 15.2 Electroconvulsive therapy is disliked by a majority of patients but is now relatively safe and effective in alleviating the symptoms of depression.

equally well. Depressive states were discovered to be most responsive to treatment by these methods. It was also discovered that electrically induced seizures are safer, largely because the stimulus parameters can be controlled within narrow limits of the central nervous system.

While the evidence shows that electroconvulsive therapy is effective in the treatment of depression, this form of therapy has a number of undesirable side effects. Since it must produce a grand mal seizure in the brain in order to be effective (Rich 1985), the seizure could lead to broken bones, amnesia and confusion, and panic following treatment, along with an extreme fear of being treated.

Recent advances in this mode of treatment, however, have minimized the potential for such undesirable side effects. For example, muscle relaxants given routinely before induction of the seizure have significantly reduced the risk of bone fracture. Short-acting barbiturates administered before treatment are reported to reduce the fear of being treated and to alleviate some of the posttreatment confusion (Fink et al. 1974). Thus, the remaining and most serious side effect of electroconvulsive therapy is the amnesia associated with the induction of seizures (Squire 1982). Some investigators have determined that seizures induced unilaterally, especially when the electrode is placed over the nondominant hemisphere, may lead to significantly fewer complaints of amnesia and confusion (Squire and Slater 1983), although the clinical efficacy of unilateral seizures in relieving depressive symptoms is still being debated by individuals engaged in clinical practice.

We do not understand how convulsions relieve depressive symptoms. Convulsions produce a wide variety of peripheral and central nervous system effects, such as activation of the autonomic nervous system, increased secretion of many different hormones by the endocrine organs, release of a host of neurotransmitters in the brain, and changes in the permeability of the blood-brain barrier (Rich 1985). Whether any of these effects, or all of them and more, result in the therapeutic effects of electroconvulsive shock therapy remains to be determined. Research on this question is important because if it were possible to understand the mechanisms underlying the beneficial effects of electroconvulsive therapy, more specific and possibly more effective therapies based on this knowledge could be developed.

Hypothalamic-Adrenal-Pituitary Dysfunction in Depression

Another avenue of exploration in determining the biological correlates and possible mechanisms underlying depression involves measurement of hormonal irregularities in the function of the hypothalamus, adrenal gland, and pituitary. It is currently believed, for example, that a significant number of individuals suffering from depression display a hypersecretion of cortisol from the adrenal cortex. Various investigators have inferred that this abnormal secretion of cortisol results from

an abnormal secretion of ACTH from the pituitary gland, triggered by abnormal activity in those regions of the brain that appear to underlie emotional states; that is, the limbic system (Risch and Janowsky 1985).

Coupled with these ideas is the observation by clinical researchers that in depressed patients, the hypothalamic-adrenal-pituitary system seems to be relatively unresponsive to its normal negative feedback signals. This is apparent in results of the **dexamethasone suppression test,** developed over the past few years as a possible neuroendocrine marker of depressive illness (Whybrow, Akiskal, and McKinney 1984). In this test, patients with depression are given a dose of dexamethasone, a synthetic glucocorticoid (steroid) hormone. In control populations, this agent results in a suppression of cortisol and ACTH secretion by the adrenal gland and pituitary, respectively. In a substantial percentage of individuals who suffer from depression, however, the normal suppression of cortisol and ACTH release does not occur. This kind of evidence suggests that the normal feedback control of cortisol and ACTH secretion does not function properly, and that the brain regions of the hypothalamus and limbic system that control the secretion of ACTH from the pituitary gland are also malfunctioning. This in turn suggests that various neurotransmitter systems that control these functions, such as acetylcholine, norepinephrine, and serotonin, could be responsible. Evidence such as this is beginning to yield a more complete picture of the possible biological systems of the brain and body that malfunction in affective disorders.

Schizophrenia

Without question, schizophrenia is one of the most puzzling psychiatric disorders. Almost one hundred years have passed since the Swiss psychiatrist Eugen Bleuler first coined the term to refer to a discrepancy or split between certain psychological functions (from the Greek **schizo** meaning "split" and **phreno** meaning "mind"). Though almost fifty years have passed since an effective form of drug therapy was introduced, we still do not know what causes schizophrenia. This is especially distressing because schizophrenia is also the most profound psychiatric disorder of our time. It involves a disruption of thought that usually makes normal functioning difficult or impossible. It afflicts over two million Americans, and about half of the available hospital beds for the mentally ill (or about one-quarter of available beds in all U.S. hospitals) are occupied by patients diagnosed as schizophrenic.

Schizophrenia usually begins in young adulthood. Men are most at risk for schizophrenia before the age of twenty-five; women are more likely to develop it after this age. Although schizophrenia can appear suddenly, it often emerges gradually. Patients withdraw into themselves, they experience a loss of identity, and normal daily patterns of eating and sleeping are disrupted. Eventually, full-blown schizophrenic symptoms develop. Hallucinations are common, especially auditory hallucinations ("hearing voices"). The ability to express emotions disappears or is impaired; occasionally emotions are expressed at inappropriate times. Illogical thought patterns or delusions appear. Paranoid delusions are common, and these lead schizophrenics to believe that other people are plotting against them or that unseen forces are controlling their thoughts and actions. To reinforce their delusions, schizophrenics interpret items on radio, television, or in the newspapers as cryptic messages supporting their beliefs.

Schizophrenics also are unable to express themselves clearly. Their speech wanders aimlessly from topic to topic; they are unable to discuss ideas in a logical sequence. Their capacity to process information is slowed and they exhibit attention deficits (Braff 1985). Often, they experience motor disturbances, ranging from a complete state of immobility known as catatonia to frenetic, repetitive behavior accompanied by peculiar mannerisms.

Almost as soon as Bleuler first described schizophrenia, attempts were made to explain it as a biological dysfunction. There have been claims that the brains of schizophrenics suffer from an enzyme abnormality that leads to the production of a substance similar to mescaline, a drug known to cause hallucinations, delusions, and other bizarre experiences (Friedhoff 1973). Some investigators have suggested that toxic metabolites are formed in the brains of schizophrenics, and over time these substances gradually destroy the pleasure systems in the brain and lead to a schizophrenic thought disorder (Stein and Wise 1971). While there is an occasional report that pathology has been detected in the brains of schizophrenic patients, careful studies of the famous Yakovlev collection of schizophrenic brains obtained at autopsy do not indicate that significant brain damage occurs consistently in the schizophrenic brain (e.g., Lohr and Jeste 1986). Finally, there even is evidence that wheat gluten, a substance found in baking flour and cereal grains, may induce schizophrenic symptoms (Singh and Kay 1976). This idea in itself may seem crazy, but some schizophrenics have been known to experience a florid psychosis after eating bread, pastry, or pasta that contains a high amount of wheat gluten.

These examples are only a small sample of the ideas that have emerged to explain the etiology of schizophrenia. They have existed for many years, and most are based on sound experimental evidence. Whether they are correct, even partially correct, remains to be determined. As you can appreciate by reviewing the list of symptoms, schizophrenia is a very complex disorder (in fact, some say that it consists of many different disorders), and it certainly is plausible that many different brain abnormalities are involved (see color plate 8).

One hypothesis of schizophrenia, however, has received more attention and generated more research than all of the others combined. It has been the focal point for the development of new drugs in the treatment of schizophrenia for almost thirty years. Most importantly, although it may not be the sole explanation, this hypothesis points to a major contributory factor in at least some types of schizophrenia. This is the dopamine hypothesis of schizophrenia, and we will review its strongest and weakest points in the following section.

The Dopamine Hypothesis of Schizophrenia
When Carlsson and Lindqvist (1963) proposed that the drugs used to treat schizophrenia, the so-called antipsychotic drugs, blocked dopamine receptors, the stage was set for the dopamine hypothesis of schizophrenia. In simple terms, this hypothesis suggests that schizophrenia is caused by an overactive do-

pamine system. The overactivity could manifest itself in any number of ways. It could involve an abnormal amount of dopamine release from axon terminals or possibly an increase in the sensitivity of postsynaptic dopamine receptors. In the former example, too much dopamine in the synapse overwhelms postsynaptic neurons; in the latter, a normal amount of dopamine has an exaggerated effect. In either case, dopamine neurotransmission is enhanced. The antipsychotic drugs diminish the synaptic action of dopamine by blocking dopamine receptors.

The dopamine hypothesis of schizophrenia is supported by some very substantial evidence. Perhaps the strongest support comes from the remarkably high correlation that exists between the ability of the antipsychotic drugs to bind to dopamine receptors and clinical effectiveness (Seeman 1980). As shown in figure 15.3, those drugs that have the highest affinity for the dopamine receptor are the most potent in treating schizoprenia. Additional support comes from research on drugs that increase dopamine neurotransmission. These drugs actually induce psychotic behavior, even in previously nonpsychotic individuals (Angrist 1983). In fact, amphetamine, a drug that increases the amount of dopamine in the synapse, produces a form of paranoid schizophrenia that so closely resembles the naturally occurring disorder that diagnostic errors are possible. During the 1960s and early 1970s, when amphetamine abuse was at its peak and before the psychotic effects of the drug were widely known, many amphetamine abusers were admitted to mental institutions as paranoid schizophrenics (Smith 1969; Snyder 1973). The same antipsychotic drugs used to treat schizophrenia are used to treat the psychosis produced by amphetamine abuse.

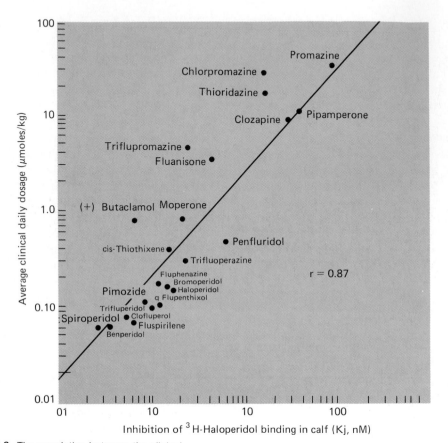

Figure 15.3 The correlation between the clinical potency of antipsychotic drugs in treating the symptoms of schizophrenia and the affinity of these same drugs for binding to the receptor sites in the striatum of the calf brain. The vertical axis shows the potency of the various antischizophrenic drugs as commonly used in clinical practice, while the horizontal axis shows the ability of these same drugs to compete with radioactively labeled spiroperidol, a prototype antipsychotic drug, for the drug binding site. The higher the number on the Y axis, the higher the concentration of drug needed to effectively compete for binding, hence the lower the potency of the drug with respect to its ability to bind to the receptor. The graph shows that clinical potency correlates well with the ability of the various antipsychotic drugs to bind to the receptor in the striatum (calf caudate nucleus and putamen).

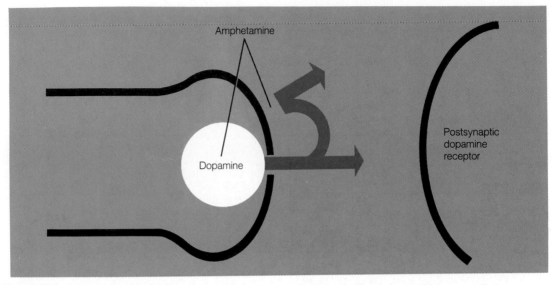

Figure 15.4 Actions of amphetamine at a dopaminergic synapse. By facilitating the release of dopamine and blocking its reuptake into the axon terminal, amphetamine increases the amount of dopamine in the synapse, which means that more dopamine is available to act on the postsynaptic receptor.

Amphetamine enhances dopaminergic neurotransmission by increasing the release of dopamine into the synapse and by blocking its reuptake into axon terminals (fig. 15.4). A series of investigations in animals have confirmed that these actions of amphetamine, rather than its effects on other neurotransmitters, are primarily responsible for its behavioral effects (Cole 1978; Iversen 1977). Lesions or other treatments that destroy the major dopamine pathways in the brain abolish the behavioral response to amphetamine. Furthermore, a direct infusion of this drug into brain areas that receive dopaminergic axon terminals elicits the amphetamine response.

Of course, the behavioral changes produced by amphetamine in animals are not the same as those that occur in human amphetamine abusers. At least we do not think they are. We have no way of knowing, for example, if a rat on amphetamine hears voices or if it thinks that other rats or people are plotting against it. Nor are there known cases of rats scanning newspapers looking for cryptic messages to support their delusions. You might begin to think, then, that the amphetamine response in animals has nothing at all in common with that in humans. But this is not the case. Although we cannot know what is going on inside a rat's head, we can observe its overt movements. Surprising as it may seem, these movements share a common pattern in virtually all mammals, including humans.

The common feature of these movements is that they are highly stereotyped; that is, repetitive and apparently meaningless (Randrup and Munkvad 1974; Rebec and Bashore 1984). Amphetamine, for example, increases motor activity, but the motor activity is highly patterned or stereotyped, not random (fig. 15.5). In addition, these stereotyped

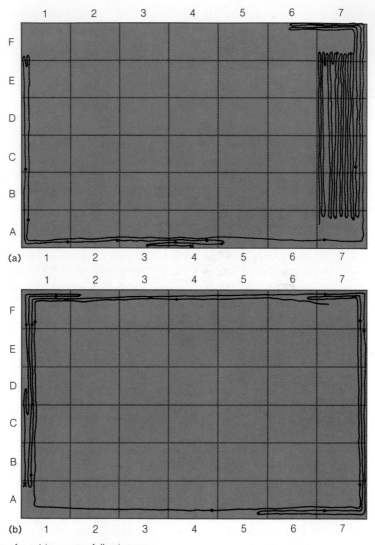

Figure 15.5 Route of a rat in a cage following an injection of amphetamine (a) or a control solution of saline (b). Note that the rat's movement pattern with amphetamine is highly stereotyped with repetitive running back and forth along one wall. Movement of the saline animal, on the other hand, is apparently random along all four walls of the cage.

movements occur in conjunction with searching and examining behaviors. Although different species explore their surroundings in different ways, these are the behaviors that emerge with amphetamine use. Rats rely primarily on snout contact and the sense of smell to explore their environment, and amphetamine produces **stereotyped behavior,** including sniffing, head bobbing, and licking responses in these animals. Primates, on the other hand, rely on sight, and in these animals, amphetamine produces stereotyped eye-hand examination patterns (picking at the skin or at nearby objects) and scanning of the visual field. Humans, too, display a driving investigative behavior with amphetamine use, and often such behavior becomes part of a well-constructed delusion. One amphetamine addict, suspicious of a boyfriend's behavior, admitted, ". . . I looked everywhere for clues, under rugs, behind pictures, and I took things apart. I read magazines looking at periods with a magnifying glass, looking for codes. It would have helped me solve the mystery" (Ellinwood and Sudilovsky 1973, 53).

A remarkable feature of amphetamine-induced stereotyped behaviors is that many of them increase in intensity as use of the drug continues (Rebec and Segal 1980; Eichler, Antelman, and Black 1980). They become focused on particular elements in the environment, and eventually postural abnormalities and fear reactions also develop (Ellison et al. 1978). These behavioral changes are highly reminiscent of the symptoms commonly seen in amphetamine addicts and in paranoid schizophrenics.

With such evidence pointing to a dopamine abnormality in schizophrenia, it might seem as though the mystery of this disorder's cause has been solved. Unfortunately, the dopamine hypothesis of schizophrenia does not cover all the facts. A particularly troubling fact is that there is no direct evidence for a dopamine dysfunction in schizophrenia. The evidence that we just presented is very indirect. It supports a role for dopamine, but it does not actually prove that there is a dopamine abnormality in the brains of schizophrenics. Has anyone actually examined the brains of schizophrenics to see if there is an excess amount of dopamine or an abnormal number of dopamine receptors? Yes, and many investigators have found exactly these changes. But the results are confounded by the use of antipsychotic drugs that by themselves are known to alter dopamine levels and receptors. Thus, it may not be possible to demonstrate unequivocally that a dopamine imbalance occurs in schizophrenia.

Another troublesome finding is that not all schizophrenics are helped by antipsychotic drugs. The critical factor in determining whether a patient responds to drug therapy is the type of symptoms that a patient displays. The antipsychotic drugs are most effective for the treatment of hallucinations, delusions, and persistently bizarre behavior. Patients with impaired emotional expression, poverty of speech, and a general loss of will are not helped by drugs. This finding clearly suggests that there are at least two different types of schizophrenia, and it seems reasonable to propose that only the type that responds to antipsychotic drugs has a dopamine abnormality. Presumably, nonresponsive patients have a different dysfunction. In fact, there is evidence that these patients suffer from enlarged cerebral ventricles (Andreasen and Olsen 1982). Although it is not clear how such a structural abnormality might lead to certain schizophrenic symptoms, it is interesting to note that patients who do respond to antipsychotic drugs are free of gross brain damage, suggesting that their disorder could be limited to a neurotransmitter imbalance (Rebec and Anderson 1986). Thus, if dopamine does play a role in schizophrenia, it may do so only in a limited number of patients.

The dopamine hypothesis of schizophrenia also can be challenged on other fronts. For example, many of the antipsychotic drugs not only block dopamine receptors, they also interfere to varying degrees with the synaptic functions of norepinephrine, serotonin, and acetylcholine. One could make an argument, therefore, for a theory of schizophrenia that also includes these neurotransmitters. Amphetamine, too, acts on other systems in addition to dopamine, and although they may not play the primary role in amphetamine-induced behaviors, they have been shown to influence the intensity of these behaviors.

In conclusion, the dopamine hypothesis of schizophrenia appears to be an oversimplification, and it certainly cannot be considered an established fact. Yet it has stimulated an enormous amount of research on schizophrenia that continues to lead to new findings and new hypotheses. It appears that some combination of the dopamine hypothesis, the role of other neurotransmitters, and the realization that schizophrenia represents more than one disorder will offer the best hope of eventually understanding and curing this disease.

Drug Treatment of Schizophrenia
Although some schizophrenics are not helped by the antipsychotic drugs, many more are. In fact, these drugs are more effective in treating schizophrenia than any other kind of therapy.

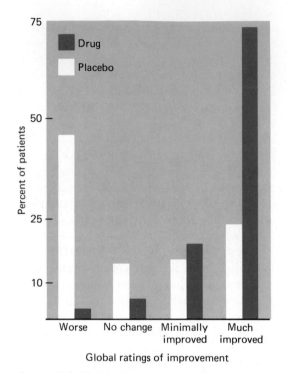

Figure 15.6 Worldwide assessment of improvement in schizophrenic patients following treatment with phenothiazines or placebo during a six-week period.

Their use has enabled many patients who would otherwise be institutionalized for life to function at near-normal levels in society. Figure 15.6 illustrates that in a study conducted by the National Institute of Mental Health, 75 percent of schizophrenic patients benefited substantially from treatment with the antipsychotic drugs during a six-week period. Almost 80 percent of the patients on placebo treatment had to be removed from the study because their condition deteriorated or because they showed no signs or only slight signs of improvement.

Unfortunately, the antipsychotic drugs are not a miracle treatment. Patients who use them must endure some harsh side effects, which in most cases involve motor symptoms and are termed **extrapyramidal side effects.** At first, patients experience a feeling of rigidity and difficulty in initiating movements. These symptoms may disappear, but eventually they are replaced by uncontrollable movements of the upper body, especially the neck and facial musculature. These late-developing motor symptoms known as **tardive dyskinesia** (from the Latin for "late movement disorder"), may persist for years after a patient stops taking the antipsychotic drugs.

These side effects appear to be a direct result of dopamine receptor blockade. The initial feeling of rigidity resembles the symptoms of Parkinson's disease, which is caused by an insufficient amount of dopamine in the basal ganglia. By blocking dopamine receptors, the antipsychotic drugs effectively mimic this condition. In this case, although there is plenty of dopamine, it cannot reach the receptor to produce an effect. Tardive dyskinesia is more difficult to understand, but it too may be related to dopamine receptor blockade. When receptors are blocked for a prolonged period, neurons respond by increasing the production of new receptors. Eventually, enough new receptors are produced so that the antipsychotic drug cannot block all of them. Thus, dopamine can finally get through and because there are more receptors than normal, it has an exaggerated effect. The result is almost the opposite of Parkinson's disease—uncontrollable, spontaneous movements (Jeste and Wyatt 1984). To counteract this effect, the dose of the antipsychotic drug is increased in an effort to block more dopamine receptors. But this works for only a short time until still more dopamine receptors are produced. The patient again increases the dose, and a vicious cycle develops. Note also that the patient cannot afford to stop taking the drug. To do so would mean not only a danger of returning to a full-blown psychosis, but also of developing even more intense uncontrollable movements.

You might wonder why an increase in dopamine receptors does not aggravate schizophrenic symptoms. After all, if dopamine receptor blockade helps to reduce the symptoms in the first place, why do they not return when the number of dopamine receptors increases? This is a fundamental question that so far has no satisfying answer. In fact, some people might point to this question as an additional weakness in the dopamine hypothesis of schizophrenia. Yet without going that far, it seems more reasonable to suggest that we simply do not know enough about tardive dyskinesia or about the factors that cause an increase in dopamine receptors (Baldessarini and Tarsy 1980).

It also is possible that dopamine receptors in the basal ganglia, which are primarily involved in movement, are fundamentally different from dopamine receptors in the limbic system and frontal cortex, which may play a role in the actual thought disorders of schizophrenia. Support for this comes from research on a new line of antipsychotic drugs that are relatively free of motor side effects. These drugs, known as "atypical" antipsychotics, may be more effective in treating brain areas outside the basal ganglia. In fact, neurons in the amygdaloid complex are especially sensitive to these drugs (Rebec et al. 1983; Rebec and Anderson 1986). Even more intriguing is the finding that some of them can be used to treat the tardive dyskinesia caused by the more "classical" antipsychotics (Meltzer and Luchins 1984). In regard to side effects, however, the atypical antipsychotics are not symptom free. Although they do not produce motor difficulties, they have been known to cause heart and liver problems.

Clearly, more research is required not only to develop better antipsychotic drugs but also to determine exactly how the antipsychotics currently used produce their effects. What we have learned recently may be surprising. Consider haloperidol, one of the most prescribed antipsychotic drugs in the United States today. The behavioral effects of this drug in animals are enhanced by pretreatment with ascorbic acid, also known as vitamin C (Rebec et al. 1985). Does vitamin C have an antipsychotic effect? This is a provocative question that has no definitive answer, but consider a few other relevant findings. Ascorbate, the form of vitamin C found in the brain, exists in high concentration in areas that also contain dopamine (Mefford, Oke, and Adams 1981). Multiple injections of amphetamine, which as we have seen cause psychotic behavior in humans, lower the level of ascorbate in the brain (Kamata et al. 1986; Rebec 1986). There also is preliminary evidence that ascorbate levels are lower than normal in the brains of schizophrenics (Adams 1986). Of course, these findings do not mean that low ascorbate causes psychotic behavior. In fact, the opposite may be true: psychotic behavior could cause low ascorbate. Nevertheless, ascorbate seems to have an important neuronal function. The brain maintains an active mechanism for removing it from the blood and for storing it (Spector and Lorenzo 1974), and certain neurons change their firing rate when exposed to it (Ewing et al. 1983; Gardiner et al. 1985). Ascorbate also may regulate the conformation of dopamine receptors and thus alter the ability of antipsychotic drugs like haloperidol to bind to them (Hadjiconstantinou and Neff 1983). We do not yet know enough about ascorbate to understand its role in the brain or its possible link to psychosis, but we do know that dopamine dysfunction alone cannot explain all aspects of schizophrenia or even some of the effects of the drugs used to treat it.

As we noted in chapter 2, schizophrenia is a familial disease. Its incidence in relatives of schizophrenic patients is much higher than its incidence in the general population. In general, the closer the biological relationship of an individual to an affected patient, the greater is the likelihood that that individual will exhibit psychotic symptoms.

The heritability of schizophrenia has been examined extensively in several twin-comparison studies. In these studies, as we saw in chapter 2, a sample of twins is examined for psychopathology and the percentage of twin pairs having the same diagnosis is calculated. This percentage is called a **concordance rate,** and it is consistently higher among monozygotic (genetically identical) twins than among dizygotic twins (no more genetically alike than brothers or sisters). These data suggest that schizophrenia is determined at least partially by genetic factors. Thus, people appear to inherit the neuronal dysfunctions that ultimately lead to schizophrenia.

Not all children of schizophrenic mothers become schizophrenic, however, and the concordance rate among monozygotic twins is not 100 percent. Thus, environmental factors must play some role in the development of this disease. Perhaps the genetic defect is expressed only under certain environmental conditions. Perhaps certain environmental events trigger a schizophrenic outcome in persons who are genetically vulnerable. As Mirsky and Duncan (1986) point out, we must not overlook the familial, social, and community factors that play a role in this disease simply because it appears to have a biological basis.

Neurological and Developmental Disorders

Disorders of the nervous system are typically reflected by symptoms of altered behavior. In the case of psychiatric disorders, although it seems clear that the nervous system is primarily affected, we are as yet unaware of the biological processes that are altered or impaired. In the case of neurological disorders, considerably more is known, and often one of the defining features of the disease or disorder is damage to the nervous system. Throughout the text, we have occasionally discussed disorders of the nervous system and their behavioral manifestations. In nearly all of these instances, brain damage can be detected and related to the behavioral deficits that occur. In this section, we will review several neurological disorders in which progress is being made in identifying affected regions of the brain and for which effective treatments are being sought. In a few cases, treatments have been developed, but are only partly effective, and, sadly, in most cases no effective treatments are available. We will begin with a discussion of epilepsy, a disorder that affects consciousness. Hopefully, our discussion in this chapter will offer both intellectual challenges and optimism for the future understanding and management of this and other serious disorders of the brain and behavior and the human tragedy that they represent.

Seizure Disorders

Epilepsy is a disorder of the brain characterized by transient disturbances of the electrical activity of the brain, sometimes termed seizures. Epileptic seizures occur as a result of diverse causes and may manifest many quite different symptoms. Typically, the term **seizure** reflects the view that these disorders involve an abnormal and synchronous electrical discharge in the brain that originates at a site or focus in the brain that initiates the violent electrical discharge. This then spreads to other regions of the brain in a pattern that is predictable from one episode to another in a given patient. Among the very important issues concerning epilepsy is the nature of events that trigger the convulsive episode and the means by which it is terminated. Equally important is the quest for modes by which epileptic attacks can be controlled. The emphasis continues to be on pharmacological agents that can be used to control the frequency and severity of seizures.

Researchers who have classified epileptic seizures have attempted to represent the clinical patterns of various seizures into a meaningful scheme that emphasizes the clinical manifestations. In doing so, these researchers have realized that the causes are quite diverse (e.g., Goldensohn 1975). They can distinguish four general categories that are further refined to levels beyond the scope of this brief overview.

Partial seizures are those that have a local origin in the brain, which is sometimes referred to as an **epileptic focus.** They may be primarily motor seizures or they may involve sensory and autonomic manifestations. The great English neurologist, John Hughlings Jackson was able to infer the organization of the motor cortex by observing partial seizures involving the motor system. These are now often termed **Jacksonian convulsions.** Typically, these seizures begin as movements of specific groups of muscles. As the electrical discharge spreads from the focus, the seizures involve an orderly progression of other parts of the body. From this progression, Jackson correctly inferred the topographic arrangement of the motor cortex. Partial seizures may also be manifest as primarily sensory in nature, including hallucinations or illusions, or they may occur as intense autonomic reactions or affective symptoms, such as depression or intense fear.

Partial seizures may or may not involve loss of consciousness and may be distinguished from **generalized seizures,** which are typically bilaterally symmetrical and may occur as **grand mal** epileptic seizures. The grand mal is the most familiar type of seizure. The individual may first experience an **aura,** which is a specific sensory or mental experience that heralds the onset of the seizure episode. This is followed by the **tonic phase** of the seizure in which there is an opening of the mouth and eyes, flexion at the elbows, and extension of the legs. Respiration ceases since the respiratory muscles are also in a tonic spasm. Following the tonic phase, the individual may proceed into the **clonic phase** of the seizure in which violent rhythmic contractions of the body musculature occur. In the final phase of the seizure, the individual is still and comatose. After a few minutes, consciousness typically is regained although memory for the events during the seizure is lost.

Another generalized seizure that is familiar to many is the condition termed **petit mal** epilepsy; it also is called **absence.** In this disorder, the seizure is very short and does not typically involve major motor convulsions. There is a brief loss of consciousness during which the individual remains motionless, though abrupt movements of the eyelids, facial muscles, or arms may occur. Petit mal seizure may last only a few seconds. It is the most common seizure affecting children, but in many individuals, the disorder disappears following puberty.

Another common disorder is the unilateral seizure. In this type of seizure, the symptoms occur predominantly or exclusively on one side of the body.

Seizures may occur as a result of stroke, brain damage, tumors, many diseases, and because of adverse conditions of the brain during fetal development. A primary emphasis in understanding epilepsy is to determine how a seizure is initiated and how it stops. Toward this end, there are many experimental models of epilepsy, especially in animals, where a variety of agents may produce an epileptic focus.

For example, it has been known for many years that chemical irritation of brain tissue can lead to the development of an abnormal electrical discharge in the area in which the irritant is applied. Direct electrical stimulation of the cerebral cortex and other regions can also produce seizures. The **kindling effect** refers to the development of seizures following repeated stimulation of certain structures in the depths of the brain, especially the amygdala. Discovered by Goddard (1967), kindling results from extremely low-level electrical stimulation delivered directly through implanted electrodes. It can be administered briefly each day, and at first it appears to have little effect on the brain or on an animal's behavior. After several days or weeks, however, the weak electrical stimulus begins to produce large-scale seizures in the electrical activity of the brain that are eventually accompanied by behavioral seizures. The seizure can also then occur spontaneously.

The mechanisms underlying the generation of seizures such as these have been studied intensively. At the focus of the epileptic seizure, nearly all of the nerve cells are bombarded simultaneously by excitatory or inhibitory synaptic activity, leading ultimately to an intense and sustained depolarization of the cells within the focus. The intense activity resulting from this massive depolarization may

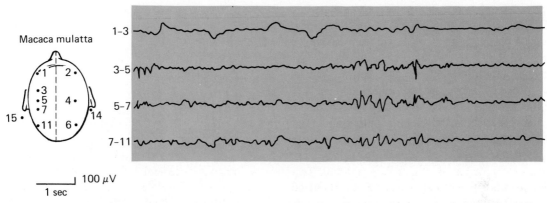

Macaca mulatta

100 μV
1 sec

Figure 15.7 An epileptic focus is present near electrode placement number 3 in the schematic diagram of the monkey cerebral cortex since abnormal spikes characteristic of the epileptic electroencephalogram occur between leads 3 and 5, and 5 and 7. Activity between leads 1 and 3, and 7 and 11 is much less abnormal. The focus was produced by local application of a chemical irritant, alumina gel.

then spread by virtue of the synaptic connections of the cells within the focus to other regions of the brain, resulting in one of the common seizure patterns. The cellular events leading to the initiation and termination of the seizure are still not clearly defined, but may involve both neurons and glia, the accumulation of ions such as sodium or potassium inside or outside the nerve cell, as well as changes in the biophysical properties of the neuronal membrane.

In an attempt to characterize the changes that occur when an epileptic focus is produced, Ribak and associates (1979) produced foci by application of the chemical irritant alumina gel to the cerebral cortex of monkeys. This treatment resulted in characteristic epileptic activity in the cerebral cortex as shown in figure 15.7. When the epileptic focus was studied for the presence of inhibitory synaptic endings containing gamma-aminobutyric acid, it was found that these synapses were mark-edly decreased in number in the region of the focus, suggesting that removal or degeneration of inhibitory synapses might be associated with the development of seizure activity.

The most common treatment of epilepsy is antiepileptic drugs. There are now many drugs marketed in the United States and elsewhere that are used primarily to treat epilepsy. The first of these were the hydantoins, introduced into medical practice in the late 1930s under the trade name Dilantin. Barbiturates were used successfully even before the hydantoins, as were a variety of other compounds in subsequent years. In general, it is believed that drugs that are effective in treating seizures lower the excitability of nerve cells and hence lower the discharge tendency for cells within an epileptic focus and the regions to which it is connected. The exact mechanisms, however, are still the subject of debate and active research.

Surgery also has been used in an effort to remove the offending region of tissue, provided that it is accessible and the disorder is recalcitrant to pharmacological treatment. As research continues, we can be optimistic that continuing improvements in medication and in understanding the biological mechanisms underlying seizure disorders will be made.

Disorders of the Basal Ganglia

Recall that there are three large nuclei buried within the depths of the cerebral hemispheres on each side of the brain. These are the caudate, putamen, and globus pallidus, which together form the basal ganglia. Damage to these nuclei or to systems in the brain to which they are connected has been identified, or is suspected, in several disorders of behavior, including Parkinson's disease, Huntington's disease, as well as a number of other conditions in which the most obvious symptoms are disturbances of motor behavior.

Parkinson's disease is a progressive degenerative disease affecting most clearly the pigmented nerve cells of the human brain, including cell groups in the brain that have been identified as dopamine-containing and norepinephrine-containing nuclei (Hornykiewicz 1966). As the disease develops, the cells in these nuclei slowly degenerate and the patient begins to exhibit the classic symptoms of Parkinson's disease—tremor, rigidity, and bradykinesia. The latter symptom refers to a general slowing of movement.

About two decades ago, a treatment for Parkinson's disease was developed that has been very helpful for many individuals afflicted with this condition (Sachs 1983). It involves the administration of L-DOPA, which, you perhaps will recall from chapter 6, is the

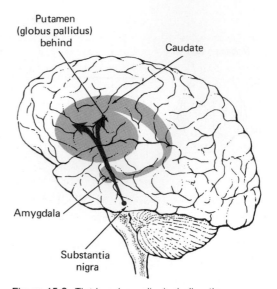

Figure 15.8 The basal ganglia, including the putamen, globus pallidus, and caudate nucleus, and their connection to the amygdala. Degeneration of connections to the basal ganglia from the substantia nigra is involved in Parkinson's disease. Degeneration within the basal ganglia is characteristic of Huntington's disease.

precursor for at least two important neurotransmitters in the brain: dopamine and norepinephrine. The therapeutic efficacy of this treatment has been proven beyond doubt and is believed to derive from the fact that L-DOPA acts to replenish dopamine in a brain that is severely deficient owing to the progressive degeneration of the dopamine-containing neurons in the substantia nigra. This nucleus sends axons to the basal ganglia and is thought to be a region of primary importance for the motor symptoms exhibited by parkinsonian patients (Marsden 1985). This is illustrated schematically in figure 15.8. Many individuals with Parkinson's disease have responded very well to L-DOPA therapy. Recent improvements in this therapeutic method, such as combining L-DOPA with other agents that are thought to affect its conversion to dopamine, have also achieved considerable success.

Even with the almost dramatic success achieved by L-DOPA therapy, many problems remain unresolved, and this form of therapy has both limitations and potentially serious side effects. L-DOPA therapy can produce a psychotic disturbance that is similar to schizophrenia. Even more commonly, L-DOPA therapy can result in uncontrollable movements of the face or arms, disturbances of the gastrointestinal tract, and other problems. Some patients remain unaffected by this treatment, although they are in the minority.

An important scientific issue still unresolved is where L-DOPA is converted to dopamine and how the transmitter is effective. With many dopaminergic neurons gone, it is unclear whether other nerve cells make excess dopamine from the L-DOPA or whether it is converted elsewhere and transported to the basal ganglia in a manner similar to blood-borne hormones. Finally, it should be clear that L-DOPA therapy is helpful in the management of symptoms, but it is not a cure for the disease. Thus, a great deal of research is yet to be done before a completely effective and safe treatment is found or the cause of the progressive damage to the brain is determined and can be arrested.

Huntington's disease, often called Huntington's chorea, is another degenerative brain disease in which the most prominent pathology that occurs is a loss of nerve cells in the basal ganglia, especially the caudate nuclei and the putamen, although degeneration of regions of the cerebellum, the cerebral cortex, and elsewhere is also often noted (e.g., Jeste, Borban, and Parisi 1984). The disorder is an inherited condition that generally affects individuals in the middle and late stages of life.

It has been theorized, on the basis of studies of basal ganglia disorders in both human patients and animal models, that the manifestations of Huntington's disease and Parkinson's disease interact with normal changes associated with aging of the brain. This may partly account for the increase in the motor symptoms seen in these disorders that occurs in middle or late life (Finch, Randall, and Marshall 1981). The most prominent motor symptoms are the severe choreic movements (*chorea* is from the Latin, meaning "dance") that are uncontrollable, involuntary, and typically rapid; complex movements of the head, limbs, and trunk. A progressive dementia also is associated with Huntington's disease, which includes changes in personality and a progressive, severe deterioration of the intellect. Careful studies of the neuropsychological impairments in patients with Huntington's disease illustrate defects in concentration, memory, and manipulation of knowledge and deterioration of conceptual reasoning (Brandt and Butters 1986). Since the degeneration of the brain is most prominent in the basal ganglia, especially the caudate nucleus and putamen, this disorder may demonstrate what has been termed a "subcortical dementia." The memory disorder associated with Huntington's disease appears very early in the course of the illness and consists of deficiencies that are different from those seen in patients with amnesia. Deficits in patients with Huntington's disease include impaired learning and retention of new information, as well as problems with retrieval of previously acquired information. These patients also appear to have deficits in the acquisition of a procedural task, exhibiting a characteristic defect in procedural memory (Martone et al. 1984).

The success in Parkinson's disease management with L-DOPA has prompted similar approaches to control the symptoms of Huntington's disease, although these have been largely unsuccessful. L-DOPA therapy tends to make the choreic movements even worse. An experimental treatment using precursors to the neurotransmitter gamma-aminobutyric acid, or GABA, has also been tried, based on the theory that many neurons of the basal ganglia contain this transmitter substance and replacement of it might lead to improvement in a way similar to L-DOPA replacement therapy in Parkinson's disease. However, initial attempts with this approach have been unsuccessful (Shoulson, Kartzinel, and Chase 1976). The motor symptoms of Huntington's disease, indeed of many movement disorders believed to involve dysfunction of the basal ganglia, are thought to involve the actions of gamma-aminobutyric acid (GABA), dopamine, and acetylcholine, as well as possible unknown actions of numerous recently discovered peptides that coexist with these other more classical neurotransmitter substances. Armed with this knowledge, a variety of new pharmacological strategies for treating movement disorders are now being conceptualized (e.g., Stahl 1986). The most effective treatment for abnormal movements in Huntington's disease is administration of the phenothiazines and related drugs that block dopamine receptors in the brain. Interestingly, these are the same agents that provide symptom control in schizophrenia and a variety of syndromes involving involuntary movements.

Senile Dementia of the Alzheimer's Type

Many degenerative diseases of the brain ultimately can lead to dementia, a progressive and relentless deterioration of personality, intellectual functioning, and memory. It is estimated that around two million older Americans suffer from Alzheimer's disease, the most common form of dementia. Thus, since the population in the United States is getting older, it seems likely that many millions of individuals may be afflicted in future decades (Katzman 1985). Currently, approximately twenty thousand people die of Alzheimer's disease each year (Terry 1986). This disease is difficult to diagnose with certainty in its early stages because the diagnosis requires the identification of symptoms of the disease as well as the brain pathology that is characteristic of the disorder (Terry and Katzman 1983). Symptoms of the disease can include impairments in memory, cognition, language, motor performance, and visual-spatial perception. Since many of these symptoms may signal a variety of diagnoses, the Alzheimer's disease diagnosis typically cannot be completed with assurance until autopsy since it requires an examination of the brain.

Energetic research on the brains of patients with Alzheimer's disease has revealed substantial pathology. As shown in the comparison of a normal brain and a brain from a patient with Alzheimer's disease in figure 15.9, there is considerable cell loss seen as a marked widening of the sulci of the cortical surface and a shrinkage of the cortical gyri. While there is at present no specific biological marker indicative of Alzheimer's disease, Wolozin and associates (1986) have developed a promising

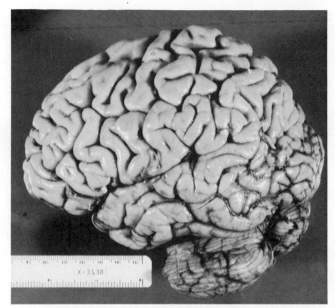

(a)

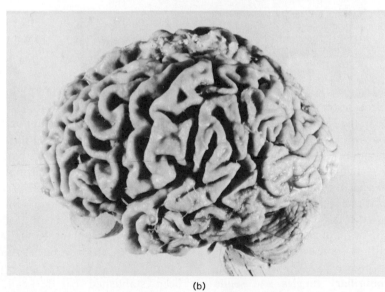

(b)

Figure 15.9 Examples of a normal human brain (a) and the brain of a patient with Alzheimer's disease (b). Note the widening of the sulci and shrinkage of the gyri of the cortex in the case of Alzheimer's disease. Motor cortex and visual cortex are less affected than the rest.

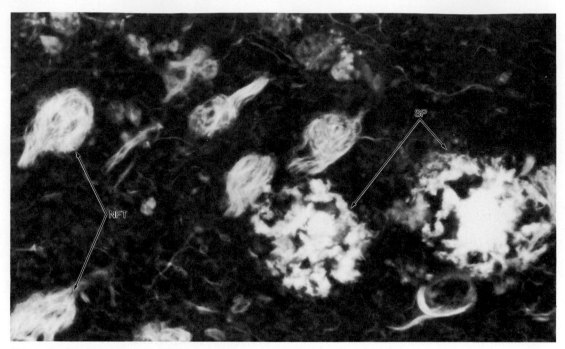

Figure 15.10 Light microscopic images of senile plaques (SP) and neurofibrillary tangles (NFT) from the brain of a patient with Alzheimer's disease.

candidate for such a marker. They have discovered that there appears to be a specific protein concentrated in the brain tissue of patients with Alzheimer's disease that has a molecular weight of approximately 68,000. Only small amounts of this particular protein can be purified from normal brain tissue.

While efforts to develop a diagnostic test for Alzheimer's disease continue, specific pathologies in the brain of such patients have been clearly identified, some examples of which are illustrated in figure 15.10. These pathologies are **neurofibrillary tangles** and **senile plaques** (Terry and Katzman 1983; Price 1986). The neurofibrillary tangles are found in the cytoplasm of neurons in a variety of regions of the brain, especially the cerebral

cortex, but also in certain regions of the brain stem (see color plate 5). In normal nerve cells, delicate threads run throughout the cytoplasm of the cell and are termed **fibrils.** In the neurons of Alzheimer's disease patients, however, these fibrils proliferate, forming an extensive tangle of neurofibrils inside the cell (fig. 15.10). A second sign of pathology is the senile plaque, a dense, spherical body of degenerated nerve cell processes and other material (see fig. 15.10). In addition to portions of degenerated synapses and other nerve cell processes, it has been established that the senile plaques may also contain neurotransmitter or neuromodulator substances, such as the peptide substance P (Armstrong and Terry 1985) or somatostatin (Terry 1986). The existence of somatostatin in senile plaques is considered to be of special importance since neurofibrillary tangles have been identified in neurons of the cerebral cortex that contain this neuropeptide, and a decrease in this substance in the cortex of Alzheimer's disease patients has also been detected (Rossor et al. 1980).

In addition to these two signs of brain pathology in Alzheimer's disease, there is degeneration of several nuclei of the brain stem. With degeneration of cells in these nuclei, there is a corresponding loss of neurotransmitter substances associated with them in areas where axons from these neurons project. A particularly substantial loss of nerve cells occurs in the nucleus basalis of Meynert (Hedreen et al. 1984; Price 1986). This nucleus, near the top of the brain stem below the cerebral cortex, contains cholinergic neurons that supply cholinergic axons to targets in the cerebral neocortex, the amygdala, the hippocampus, and elsewhere. Because of the importance of this group of structures and their potential involvement in memory and other cognitive functions, it is believed that degeneration of these cholinergic neurons may be critical in the memory impairment and possibly other cognitive deficits exhibited by patients with Alzheimer's disease. Initial attempts to administer precursors of acetylcholine or related drugs to patients with the disorder, similar in conception to replacement therapy with L-DOPA in Parkinson's disease, have met with only very limited success.

Although there is no effective treatment for Alzheimer's disease, research on this disorder is now increasing and we can hope that a diagnostic test specific for Alzheimer's disease is on the horizon. Interestingly, about half the cases of the disorder are familial, suggesting that there is considerable heritability for the disease. In addition, the pathology of Alzheimer's disease also appears in adults who

suffer from trisomy 21 or Down's syndrome if they live a long enough life (Terry 1986). Such evidence suggests that an important influence in the disorder may involve a genetic defect. Efforts to identify the pathway by which the pathology and symptoms of Alzheimer's disease develop are an important goal for the future.

Language Disorders and Lateralization of the Cerebral Hemispheres

Language is a characteristically human achievement, and precisely for this reason the study of the cerebral mechanisms of verbal communication has not been a simple task. Despite some remarkable results in teaching chimpanzees to communicate using sign language (Premack 1971) or to use visually coded push-panels for words (Rumbaugh 1977), there are no fully adequate animal models to represent all the aspects of language behavior, including the ability not only to speak but also to understand both the spoken and written word. Although many animals communicate with sounds and gestures, this communication shows no evidence of syntactical organization—the feature of human language that provides the potential to form an infinite number of sentences from a finite number of words and grammatical rules. Much of the evidence regarding the role of specific brain areas in language behavior has been obtained from human beings in abnormal circumstances: brain-damaged persons or patients undergoing brain surgery.

Broca's Area
Careful examination of brain-damaged patients suffering from **aphasia** (loss of language ability) began in the nineteenth century. The first study was reported by Pierre Paul Broca

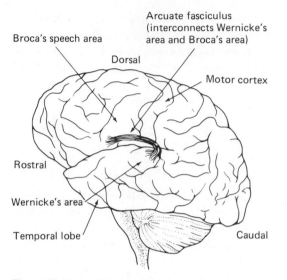

Broca's speech area

Arcuate fasciculus
(interconnects Wernicke's
area and Broca's area)

Dorsal

Motor cortex

Rostral

Wernicke's area

Temporal lobe

Caudal

Figure 15.11 A side view of the human brain illustrating the location of cortical areas involved in language: Broca's area, Wernicke's area, and the arcuate fasciculus.

(1861), a French neurosurgeon. The subject of that study was a patient whose major problem when he was admitted to a hospital was that he could not talk. While in the hospital, he developed an infection and eventually came under the care of Broca. Five days later the patient died. When Broca performed an autopsy on the brain, he discovered a lesion in the third frontal gyrus of the left cerebral hemisphere. Broca concluded that this portion of the brain (fig. 15.11), which later came to be called **Broca's area,** was indispensable in language.

Broca's area is situated immediately adjacent to the region of the motor cortex that is responsible for the movement of the facial muscles. Simple muscle paralysis is not an adequate explanation of the aphasia found among Broca's patients. Damage restricted to the facial area of the motor cortex does not produce

permanent impairment of language ability and causes only slight loss of tonus of the facial muscles. Broca's patients, on the other hand, could utter common words and phrases, such as swear words and simple replies like "yes" or "no." Thus, even though no deficit in intelligence or language comprehension could be detected in the patients, only automatic and frequently used words tended to survive damage to Broca's area.

Wernicke's Area √

Broca's designation of the third frontal gyrus as the speech center supported the then widely accepted notion of precise localization of function within the brain. However, histological techniques have improved, making possible the examination of a broader sample of aphasic patients. Very few persons suffering from aphasia were actually found to have well-localized lesions within Broca's area (Geschwind 1966; Jenkins et al. 1975). Such lesions often encroached on surrounding structures, and damage was also noted in other areas of the brain. Further complicating the issue was the discovery of different types of language disability.

Wernicke (1874), for example, encountered a group of aphasic patients who were capable of speech, but whose sentences were confusing and meaningless. They appeared to have lost all comprehension of language, despite the fact that their hearing ability and intelligence were not impaired. Many of these patients were subsequently found to have had brain damage, not in Broca's area, but in the first gyrus of the left temporal lobe.

Additional studies of aphasia have implicated still other regions of the left cerebral hemisphere, including the **angular gyrus,** the inferior portion of the temporal lobe, and the supplementary motor cortex (Penfield and Roberts 1959).

There appears to be no single area that when damaged is responsible for all types of language disorders. Penfield and Roberts (1959) proposed that in general the closer the lesion is to Broca's area the more the motor components of language behavior are affected, whereas language comprehension suffers most following damage to the more posterior regions of the left cerebral hemisphere. Broca's area and perhaps other restricted regions of the frontal lobe could be essential for the coordination of the numerous muscle groups involved in the production of speech. The integration of auditory and visual input, which underlies language comprehension, might be performed in **Wernicke's area** and other structures in the temporal lobe (Geschwind 1972).

The Arcuate Fasciculus

The **arcuate fasciculus** is illustrated in figure 15.11, where it is shown to consist of a tract that interconnects Broca's and Wernicke's speech areas. More specifically, the arcuate fasciculus interconnects certain regions of the auditory association areas with portions of the motor association cortex, which in turn projects to Broca's area. Patients with damage to this fiber tract and without concomitant damage to either Broca's or Wernicke's area have been studied, and they exhibit an interesting kind of aphasia that has been called **conduction aphasia.**

Patients having conduction aphasia (i.e., Geschwind 1972; 1975) are quite capable of spontaneous speech. If they have an idea and wish to express it, they can do so readily. They also demonstrate that they comprehend spoken language since they readily carry out commands that are given to them verbally. However, they have a great deal of trouble repeating words when asked to do so. Their auditory association cortex is intact and they comprehend the word they are asked to repeat. However,

the auditory association cortex has been disconnected from Broca's area, which is necessary for the production of language. Thus, information from the auditory association cortex reaches Broca's area by other routes, and these patients have difficulty repeating spoken words.

Interestingly, patients with conduction aphasia have little problem reading, identifying, or repeating numbers. Geschwind has suggested that this is the case because numbers are usually associated with the visual and somatosensory cortex. For example, we teach children about numbers by making them count on their fingers. In the case of conduction aphasia, the connections between the visual cortex and Broca's area remain intact, and it is perhaps for this reason that these individuals can repeat numbers. Words, however, are associated with the auditory association cortex; we learn about words by listening to them. Connections between the auditory cortex and Broca's area are damaged in the case of conduction aphasia so these patients cannot repeat words when asked to do so.

In summary, we have discussed three different types of aphasia. We have discussed Broca's area, Wernicke's area, and the arcuate fasciculus. Patients with damage to Broca's area have great trouble pronouncing words, their verbal comprehension is only slightly impaired, and words that can be spoken are used meaningfully. Patients with damage to Wernicke's area have no difficulty with pronunciation; however, their comprehension of the spoken language is very poor. Patients with damage to the arcuate fasciculus have no trouble pronouncing words, their verbal comprehension is only slightly impaired, but they have great difficulties repeating words but not numbers.

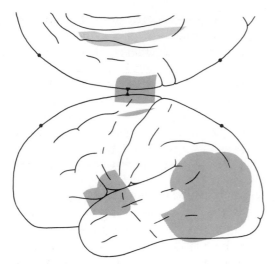

Figure 15.12 Schematic drawing of the cerebral hemispheres. The shaded regions indicate portions of the left cerebral hemisphere that produce disturbances of speech when stimulated electrically.

From Wilder Penfield and Lamar Roberts, *Speech and Brain Mechanisms*. Copyright © 1959 by Princeton University Press and the Literary executors of the Penfield Papers. Figure VIII-14 reprinted with permission of Princeton University Press.

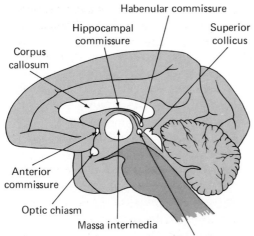

Figure 15.13 Schematic drawing of midline structures sectioned in surgical splitting of brain into right and left halves. Sometimes the cerebellum is also divided in these experiments.

Although the language system in the human brain appears to be much more diffuse than Broca's early studies first suggested, several lines of evidence indicate that language is usually a function of the left hemisphere. In most cases, substantial damage to the right cerebral cortex does not disrupt language behavior. The dominance of the left hemisphere with respect to speech also has been supported by evidence from direct electrical stimulation of the brain. During the course of surgical procedures that require the exposure of brain tissue, the speech areas are mapped to avoid their unnecessary removal. Although vocalization can be elicited by stimulation of the cortical motor areas on either side of the brain, stimulation of the left hemisphere, but not of the right, is effective in disrupting ongoing speech activity in most people (Penfield and Roberts 1959).

Interestingly, stimulation-induced speech disturbances, which involve confusion of numbers, repetition of words, and complete arrest of speech, are elicited primarily from those regions of the left hemisphere that have been implicated in language behavior, including Broca's area, the temporal lobe region, and the supplementary motor area. These areas are shown in figure 15.12. Stimulation of other parts of the left hemisphere has no effect on speech.

The Split Brain

A surgical procedure useful in the study of **lateralization of function** of the cerebral hemispheres, especially language abilities, is the split-brain technique. In this procedure, the fibers that connect the two hemispheres are severed, as shown in figure 15.13. Typically, the large **corpus callosum** connecting the two hemispheres is cut, as are other smaller commissures (interhemispheric tracts). When the

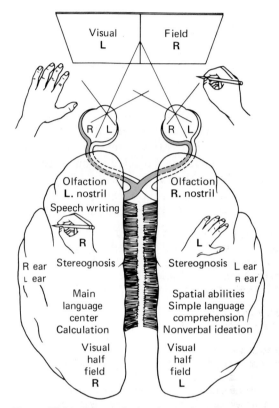

Figure 15.14 Schematic drawing to show the functions separated by surgery for brain disorder. This is a simplified summary combining known neuroanatomy, cortical lesion data, and postoperative testing.

of the brain knowing what the other is doing! It is as if two separate brains were learning independently of each other.

A great deal has been learned about the localization of cerebral function in human beings in whom the corpus callosum has been severed because of surgery for severe epilepsy or other brain disorder (Sperry and Gazzaniga 1967; Sperry 1974). Despite the radical nature of the surgery, split-brain patients behave quite normally under most circumstances. It is possible, however, to place these patients in an experimental situation that takes advantage of the anatomical organization of the central nervous system. As shown in figure 15.14, information entering the right half of the visual field projects to the left occipital lobe, while the right occipital cortex receives information from the left half of the visual field. Tactile sensations are also represented predominantly on opposite sides of the brain. Sensory information from the right side of the body travels to the left side of the brain, and vice versa. This arrangement presents no problem for normal individuals since there are adequate connections between the two halves of the brain. In split-brain patients, however, visual or tactile information reaching one hemisphere may not influence the other. Thus, each side of the brain can be studied as an independent entity.

In studies of this kind, the subject is seated in front of an apparatus, atachistoscope, that flashes visual stimuli to the left or right half of the visual field, as shown in figure 15.15. The patient is prevented from seeing any of the test items on the table or the experimenter in the background. When a picture of a knife is flashed to the right half of the visual field and a pencil to the left, the subject invariably reports that he sees a knife and seems unaware of the pencil.

optic chiasm is also severed (as you will recall from previous chapters), visual input from the right eye is then restricted to the right cerebral hemisphere and input from the left eye to the left cerebral hemisphere.

Using preparations in which the optic chiasm was severed, Sperry (1961) and others demonstrated that animals taught a visual task using one eye were unable to perform the task using the other eye when the trained eye was covered. Even more fascinating, animals can be trained to learn two tasks simultaneously using one eye for each task without one side

Figure 15.15 Experimental apparatus used for testing cerebral language dominance in split-brain patients. While viewing items on a projection screen, the subject (S) is seated in front of a shield that hides the test items, his hands, and the experimenter (E) from view.

Further tests have indicated that these patients are able to speak and write only about objects seen in the right half of the visual field or touched by the right hand. The subjects are unusually silent concerning sensory information that reaches the right cerebral hemisphere. Nevertheless, the right hemisphere seems to be aware of the sensory input, but is unable to provide a verbal or written report. If, for example, the subject is required to identify by touch an object presented either to the left or right half of the visual field, he makes the correct response in each case. Although the right side of the brain may actually have a limited vocabulary, verbal and written expression are largely dominated by the left hemisphere.

Other functions seem to be better suited to the abilities of the right hemisphere, including the ability to arrange spatial patterns

to match samples and to draw simple figures when so instructed. In what may also reflect the different functions of the cerebral hemispheres, the right ear is superior in recognizing spoken words, while the left ear and presumably the right hemisphere are more sensitive to melodies and other nonverbal information (Kimura 1973).

In an interesting extension of the concepts of lateralization of function of the cerebral hemispheres, Ornstein (1972) argued that the relative dominance of one or the other cerebral hemisphere could play a significant role in human consciousness. He notes that human consciousness is often considered **dichotomous** (having two parts). One aspect of consciousness is rational and intellectual, while the other is intuitive and artistic. He notes

The left hemisphere of the cortex which subtends language and mathematics seems to process information primarily in a linear, sequential manner, appropriate to its specialties. The right side of the cortex processes its input more as a 'patterned whole,' that is, in a more simultaneous manner than does the left. This simultaneous processing is advantageous for the integration of diffuse inputs, such as for orienting oneself in space, when motor, kinesthetic and visual input must be quickly integrated. This mode of information-processing, too, would seem to underlie an 'intuitive' rather than an 'intellectual' integration of complex entities. (p. 79)

In a fascinating extension of these concepts, Ornstein argues that differences between the dominance of the right and left hemispheres may provide the basis for differences in thought processes of Western versus Eastern cultures. Western rational thought shows a left-hemisphere dominance while the more intuitive Eastern thought (sometimes termed antirational) reflects a right-hemisphere dominance.

Whatever the fate of such speculation, the importance of the cerebral hemispheres in human behavior cannot be questioned. They govern our perceptions, actions, thoughts, and feelings.

We have only touched on the variety of neurological disorders that affect behavior. It should be clear that scientific progress is being made toward effective treatments and ultimate understanding of the causes of these diseases. The need for further basic research on the brain cannot be overstated. As scientific understanding of the organization and function of the brain continues to expand, treatments based on this increased understanding will continue to be developed and improved. There is considerable hope for the future, but much remains to be done. When we turn to the problem of mental retardation, the tremendous gap in scientific understanding and treatment of disorders of the brain and behavior becomes even more evident, as do the challenges facing those who will make research on the brain their life's work.

Mental Retardation

The *Diagnostic and Statistical Manual of Mental Disorders III* (known as DSM III) of the American Psychiatric Association is the latest version of diagnostic criteria used by psychiatrists and others to define and diagnose mental disorders. In this important diagnostic classification scheme, mental retardation is diagnosed using the following essential criteria: significantly subaverage general intellectual functioning (i.e., an IQ test score of less than 70 points) is associated with deficits or impairments in adaptive behavior and an onset occurring before the age of eighteen. Using such a scheme to classify mental retardation, it is possible to distinguish **mild retardation** (IQ test scores between 55 and 70 on standard IQ

tests such as the Weschler or Stanford-Binet), **moderate retardation** (IQ scores between 40 and 55 points), and **severe retardation** (IQ scores between 25 and 39 points). Most mentally retarded individuals in the United States (perhaps over 90 percent) are only mildy retarded, with estimates of the total population of retarded persons ranging from 1 percent–3 percent of the population, or 2 million–6 million persons. There are currently over two hundred different recognized causes of mental retardation, although these can be grouped into two classes: those having an identifiable organic cause and those in which the etiology is unknown or uncertain (Zigler and Hodapp 1985).

Brain Development and Mental Retardation
Mental retardation can be caused by alterations in the development of the brain brought about by many factors. As we have seen, errors associated with the chromosomes can profoundly affect intellectual development. Similarly, factors in the early environment can, through their effects on the development of the brain, adversely affect development of the intellect. Some of these influences may occur during the prenatal developmental period, while others can be associated with the conditions to which a child is exposed during birth and subsequent development.

Mechanical injuries to the brain can result in mental retardation. Often such injuries occur at birth, although the mother can suffer internal injury during pregnancy that adversely affects the developing fetal brain. Particularly damaging to the developing brain are conditions such as **hypoxemia** (an inadequate supply of oxygen to the brain) and **ischemia** (an inadequate supply of blood to the brain). Nutritional factors, particularly during the developmental period, can have serious effects

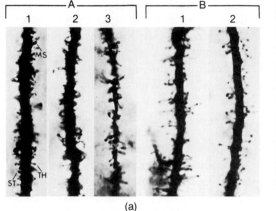
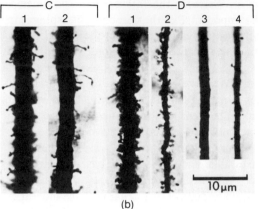

(a)

(b)

Figure 15.16 Characteristic dendrites from pyramidal neurons in the cerebral cortex of (a) normal and (b) mentally retarded children.

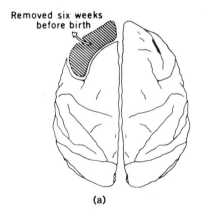

(a)

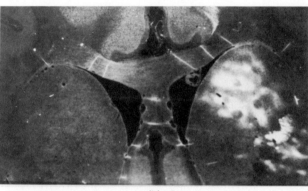

(b)

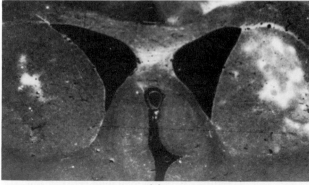

(c)

Figure 15.17 (a) The region of prefrontal cortex removed from the brain of a fetal monkey. (b) A cross section through the caudate nuclei of the left and right hemispheres of a normal monkey as seen under a dark-field illumination. The bright pattern of labeling seen on the right of the brain in (b) is normal, with very little label seen on the opposite side. (c) The brain after 22 weeks following removal of prefrontal cortex on the left side. Note that while there is ordinary dense pattern of labeled axon seen in the ipsilateral hemisphere, there is also no clear label present in the contralateral hemisphere, showing that the projections from prefrontal cortex have grown into the contralateral caudate nucleus as a result of removing prefrontal cortex on one side of the fetal brain. In other words, the brain is rewired following this early lesion.

on an individual and sometimes cause mental retardation. There is fairly compelling evidence to suggest that if maternal nutrition is inadequate, the child's intelligence can be adversely affected. Postnatal malnutrition, particularly protein deficiency, renders children sluggish and listless and lowers their intelligence. It must also be recognized that the intellectual and social performance and motivation of retarded persons can be markedly affected by the social environment that they experience. For example, the repeated experience of failure to achieve will markedly affect the behavior of any person, and this circumstance is more likely to occur in the experience of a retarded individual.

Evidence has been obtained suggesting that mental retardation may be accompanied in some cases by changes in the structure of neurons in the cerebral cortex. Purpura (1974), for example, studied the cerebral cortex of normal and mentally retarded individuals postmortem. Figure 15.16 illustrates the results of some of his observations of cortical tissue stained with the Golgi method. Under A in figure 15.16 are examples of dendrites of neurons in the motor cortex of an apparently normal six-month-old infant. Notice that three different types of processes called **dendritic spines** are identified. They are the mushroom-shaped spines (labeled MS), thin spines (labeled TH), and stubby spines (labeled ST) and are places on the dendrites where the neuron receives axonal endings in the form of synapses. Under B in figure 15.16 are examples of dendrites from neurons in the cerebral cortex of a ten-month-old retarded child. Notice the abnormal number of long, thin spines and the reduced number of thick and stubby spines compared to the normal infant. Under C in figure 15.16 are two examples of dendrites from neurons in the motor cortex of a

three-year-old retarded child. In this case, there are also long, abnormally thin spines with virtual disappearance of other spine types. Finally, under D in figure 15.16 are examples of dendrites from a seven-year-old child (numbers 1 and 2) and a profoundly retarded twelve-year-old child (numbers 3 and 4). Note that the dendrites from the retarded child's brain almost completely lack spines.

In these cases, the development of normal synaptic contacts in the cerebral cortex appears to be disturbed. To a certain extent, the cerebral cortex appears to become more primitive as if the brain had regressed to an earlier stage of development, leading to profound retardation. However, other cases of mental retardation are not accompanied by such dramatic changes in the structure of cortical neurons. Further research is needed to determine why such changes occur in some cases of mental retardation and not in others and what factors govern the normal development of the cerebral cortex and human behavior.

Rewiring the Brain during Development
A fascinating aspect of the developing brain is the process by which nerve cells become interconnected in the myriad variety of circuits that comprise the fully developed brain. Equally interesting is the capacity of the immature brain to rewire itself in the face of injury or disease. This was demonstrated in a remarkable series of experiments on the primate brain by Goldman (1978).

In Goldman's experiments, the prefrontal cortex on one side of the brain was removed from a fetal monkey six weeks before birth. The fetus was then returned to the uterus and allowed to develop to full term. The region of the cortex removed from the fetal brain is shown in figure 15.17.

A few days after the monkey was born, a radioactive amino acid injected into the intact prefrontal cortex on the opposite side of the brain from the undamaged side could be traced by autoradiography. Ordinarily, the prefrontal cortex on the right side of the brain sends axons to the caudate nucleus on the right side, while the left prefrontal cortex connects to the left caudate nucleus. However, when one side of the prefrontal cortex was removed from the fetal brain, the remaining prefrontal cortex formed bilateral connections; that is, connections with the caudate nucleus on the opposite side of the brain in addition to its normal ipsilateral connections. The results are illustrated in figure 15.17.

Studies such as this one suggest that the developing brain has an amazing capacity for rewiring itself in the face of damage. For this reason, the chances of behavior impairment from damage to the brain are less, and recovery is more rapid in young, developing organisms than in aged individuals where the brain is much less capable of such reactive growth and rewiring (e.g., Scheff, Bernardo, and Cotman 1978).

Recovery of Function after Brain Damage

An extremely important practical mission of brain research is to understand the ways in which the brain can adapt to injury. We know that in many cases brain damage produces an initial impairment of behavior from which recovery is possible with time and appropriate care and therapy. In many instances, brain damage in experimental animals produces effects from which considerable recovery is possible, especially in the young. Although little is known concerning the way that the brain recovers from injury, several intriguing possible

mechanisms are being studied extensively (Guth 1974). One such mechanism is **axonal sprouting,** which is the subject of intense experimental work (Raisman 1975).

In one important series of experiments (Lynch et al. 1972; 1975), axons projecting onto cells in one of the layers of the hippocampal formation (which includes the hippocampus and a number of other structures) were destroyed near and along with their cell bodies of origin. However, other inputs to this layer were left intact. The axons that had been destroyed eventually degenerated. Surprisingly, other axons that had not been damaged appeared to "sprout" new branches and make synaptic contact with the areas on the dendrites that had been left vacant by the degenerated axons. The phenomenon of axonal sprouting following brain damage is illustrated schematically in figure 15.18. Remarkably, even axons originating on the opposite side of the brain are able to reinnervate the dendrites vacated by degenerating axons (Steward et al. 1974; 1976). Profound changes in the shape and volume of dendrites also take place very soon after deafferentation (e.g., Rubel and Parks 1975; Benes, Parks, and Rubel 1977). There have now been many demonstrations that such regrowth following brain damage can occur and the mechanisms that guide this brain growth are being determined. An important facet of such brain growth is the discovery that chemical factors, typically called **trophic factors,** which are present in the brain during the recovery process, can facilitate the growth of nerve cells. One such substance is being characterized in some detail and is appropriately termed **nerve growth factor.** It is possible that nerve growth factor is only one of hundreds of such trophic factors present in the brain that are able to facilitate growth and healing after brain injury.

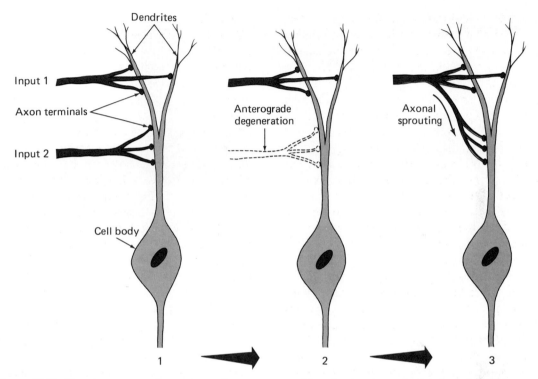

Figure 15.18 The phenomenon of axonal sprouting. One input to the cell is destroyed and degenerates, and the other input sprouts axon branches that connect to the vacated area on the dendrites.

The study of such effects following damage to the nervous system and the mechanisms by which recovery of function is achieved forms an exciting part of contemporary brain research.

Brain Grafting: A Therapy for the Future?

A remarkable technique for achieving recovery after brain damage has been discovered only within the past few years. This method is termed **brain grafting** and has now been successfully used in a number of experiments on animals (Gage and Bjorklund 1986). In this technique, specific portions of the brain from fetal animals are transplanted, or grafted, into the brains of adult animals. The most successful method of grafting fetal brain tissue into the host brain of an adult is illustrated in figure 15.19.

Using this method a portion of the adult animal's brain is destroyed and some functional deficit is revealed upon testing of the animal. These have included destruction of such regions of the rat brain as the dopaminergic substantia nigra, which leads to deficits in motor coordination and, in humans, results in Parkinson's disease. Next, dopaminergic substantia nigra tissue is obtained from a fetal rat brain, or a neonate. The fetal cells are suspended in a fluid medium and injected into the

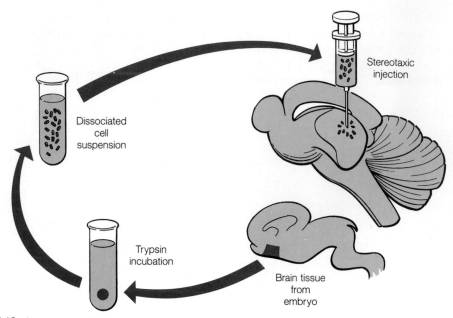

Stereotaxic
injection

Dissociated
cell
suspension

Trypsin
incubation

Brain tissue
from
embryo

Figure 15.19 A common technique used for brain grafting. Brain tissue is obtained from the embryo, incubated with trypsin to dissociate with cells, then injected into the brain of an adult host.

adult brain in the area where their connections are normally made. In the case of the dopaminergic substantia nigra this is the neostriatum, as we have previously seen. After a period of several months, histological and behavioral analyses are made to determine if the grafted cells have grown and have made connections within the host brain and whether there has been any restoration of function following the grafting procedure. Incredibly, the fetal neurons grow and prosper in the host brain, and even more exciting, they appear to facilitate recovery of the functions impaired by the initial damage to the adult animal's brain.

This procedure does not work if adult brains are used for the donor material. This is presumably because, as we have already noted, the fetal, or neonatal, brain cells appear to have a remarkable capacity for growth and development even when transplanted into the adult host. This capacity appears to be lost once the brain has grown into its adulthood.

So far, several exciting demonstrations of recovery of function following such brain grafting have been reported. In the case of the substantia nigra, destruction of this dopaminergic neuron system in the adult leads to impairments of motor behavior. Several months following a brain graft of substantia nigra tissue from the fetal donor, there is substantial recovery of the motor deficit (Gage et al. 1983).

Attempts also have been made to reverse some of the symptoms of aging in the rat. For example, in one series of experiments, hypothalamic tissue from a newborn rat was transplanted into aged female rats. When compared to age-matched controls, the aged female rats showed increased weight of the ovaries and uterus, two signs that the hypothalamic grafted tissue appeared to reverse the normal process of uterine and ovarian aging. Similar experiments have shown that other symptoms of reproductive senescence in aged female rats can be halted and partially reversed in the aged hosts that receive grafted fetal hypothalamic tissue (Rogers et al. 1984).

Perhaps most remarkable of all, preliminary indications are that even deficits in learning and memory abilities can be reversed in the brain-damaged adult by appropriate grafting of fetal brain tissue. Sladek and associates (1984) have reported that grafting of fetal locus coeruleus into the aged adult leads to recovery of the deficit in passive avoidance learning characteristic of aged rodents. Gage and associates (1984) have reported that intrahippocampal grafts of the septal region, which ordinarily projects into the hippocampus, lead to a recovery of the aged adults' ability to negotiate a water maze. This function is impaired in animals following destruction of the septal region, and appears to exhibit recovery after fetal septal tissue is transplanted into the aged brain-damaged adult rat. In an important further demonstration, this recovery was blocked by atropine, which blocks muscarinic cholinergic receptors. This suggests that the recovery effect is mediated by neurotransmission (Gage and Bjorklund 1986). The pathway from the septal area to the hippocampus utilizes cholinergic synaptic transmission.

The field of brain transplantation, or grafting, is in its infancy. Many questions must be resolved. Some of these are important scientific questions, such as the nature of the growth and connections made by the graft in the host brain (Mahalik et al. 1985). Others are legal and ethical questions that must be

resolved by the medical and scientific community along with resolutions developed by society. Even so, the preliminary results of brain grafting offer considerable promise that the tragedy of brain damage and disease, as well as some of the debilitating deficits associated with aging and degeneration of the brain, may be ameliorated by a therapy of the future and that brain research can continue to make an important positive impact on the quality of human life.

Summary

The biological bases of behavior have been established, and it must be that disorders of behavior reflect disorders of brain function. In this chapter we have presented an overview of some of the serious disturbances of behavior that afflict humans, and we have reviewed some of the research that has been carried out to determine the causes of and potential treatments for these disorders.

The major psychiatric disorders have been the subject of considerable research effort. **Affective disorders** and **schizophrenia** are the most prevalent and devastating psychiatric disorders that fill at least half of all hospital beds in this country. Much research has been devoted to looking for disturbances of the chemical environment of the brain. Theories have been formulated in which neurotransmitters, such as the **catecholamines,** are thought to play a prominent role in psychiatric disorders. These efforts include both examination of chemical systems in the brains of animals and humans and studies of the effects of drugs that can be used to treat or produce mental disorders. Drugs used to treat depression, for example, include the **monoamine oxidase inhibitors, tricyclic antidepressants,** and

psychomotor stimulants, all of which are thought to increase the effectiveness of catecholaminergic neurotransmission in the brain. Drugs used to treat mania produce the opposite effect. **Antipsychotic drugs** are believed to block receptors for **dopamine** in the brain, while those that produce psychotic behavior, such as amphetamine, are thought to increase the efficacy of dopaminergic transmission. Antipsychotic drugs have many other effects on the brain, as do psychotomimetic agents, such as LSD. Ultimately, a clearer understanding of the mechanisms of action of these compounds has the potential for considerable improvements in our approach to understanding and treating mental disorders.

Other treatments for psychiatric disorders have also been developed and in some cases are effective. Electroconvulsive therapy is effective in the treatment of depression, especially for those who prove resistant to pharmacological treatment.

Theories of schizophrenia are numerous, but none has proved to be satisfactory. In one theory, schizophrenia is thought to be due to an abnormal immunoglobulin in the blood. Other theories postulate abnormal chemicals in the nervous system or abnormal responses of specific neurotransmitter systems in the brain, such as the dopamine theory. Even with relatively little knowledge of the etiology of psychiatric disorders, pharmacological treatments for psychosis have been developed and the condition of these patients has been markedly improved over the years. In part, psychiatric disorders are thought to involve to a variable degree genetic factors that might lead to the suspected biochemical abnormalities affecting the brain.

An overview of neurological disorders reveals that there are many brain diseases for which altered behavior is the primary symptom. Seizure disorders affect consciousness and may involve serious convulsions of the body musculature, such as grand mal epilepsy. Petit mal epilepsy represents a milder form of the disorder in which conscious awareness is only temporarily halted. Experimental models of epilepsy have led to considerable knowledge concerning the causes of seizures and the means by which they are terminated. The application of chemical irritants to brain tissue can produce an epileptic focus, as can low-level electrical stimulation to certain regions of the brain. Massive electrical discharges in these regions lead to the brain seizure and associated signs involving motor convulsions and a loss of consciousness.

Neurological disorders may affect motor behavior, personality, and the intellect. Parkinson's disease, for example, results in tremor, rigidity, and bradykinesia. Huntington's disease is characterized by uncontrollable movements of the head and limbs, as well as progressive dementia. Advances in the treatment of such progressive, degenerative diseases of the brain have been slow but steady. The advent of L-DOPA therapy resulted in marked improvement in many individuals suffering from Parkinson's disease. Treatments for Huntington's disease are still being sought. Senile dementia of the Alzheimer's type or **Alzheimer's disease** is a progressive disorder of the aged brain that is characterized by a relentless deterioration of the intellect and memory. Pathology of the brain in Alzheimer's disease includes shrinkage of the cerebral hemispheres as well as the appearance of **neurofibrillary tangles** and **senile plaques.**

Effective management of the symptoms of mental retardation and deterioration of the intellect is still an elusive goal. Even in those instances where effective modes of treatment have resulted in improvement in the condition of psychiatric and neurologic patients, there are many limitations. Drug therapy is typically accompanied by unwanted and sometimes debilitating side effects. Surgical treatment is considered irreversible. Even so, basic research on the brain continues, and as new knowledge accumulates concerning the organization and functioning of the brain, clinical applications will continue to emerge so that there is hope for future breakthroughs in the treatment of disorders of behavior and the brain. Recovery of function after brain damage presumably can occur as a result of axonal sprouting and rewiring of existing connections. The technique of brain grafting offers the possibility in the future of a therapy for brain damage and disease.

The cerebral hemispheres are critical for the uniquely human ability to learn and use language. Studies of brain-damaged patients indicate that there are several areas of the cerebral cortex responsible for different language functions, such as language production and language comprehension. Usually, these regions are found in the left cerebral hemisphere, which is therefore termed the dominant hemisphere. Studies of individuals who have had the **corpus callosum** severed, called split-brain patients, also indicate that language and other functions are lateralized in the human brain. Lateralization may play an important part in the nature of human consciousness and experience.

Suggested Readings

Cummings, J. L. 1985. *Clinical neuropsychiatry.* New York: Grune & Stratton.
This book is a modern, comprehensive source for information about neuropsychological impairments and research findings in neuropsychiatry, especially pathology of memory impairment and other cognitive dysfunctions in neurological and neuropsychiatric disorders.

Judd, L. L., and P. M. Groves, eds. 1985. *Psychobiological foundations of clinical psychiatry.* Vol. 3, Sec. 2, *Psychiatry,* ed. J. O. Cavenar, Jr. Philadelphia: J. B. Lippincott.
A modern textbook of biological psychiatry dealing with possible biological factors in the development, manifestation, and treatment of psychiatric illness.

Palmer, G. C., ed. 1981. *Neuropharmacology of central nervous system and behavioral disorders.* New York: Academic Press.
This book, intended for the serious student, provides a series of articles that deal with the neurochemical mechanisms underlying various psychiatric disorders.

Snyder, S. H. 1974. *Madness and the brain.* New York: McGraw-Hill.
A basic introduction to the neurochemistry of mental illness.

Whybrow, P. C., H. S. Akiskal, and W. T. McKinney, Jr. 1984. *Mood disorders: Toward a new psychobiology.* New York: Plenum Press.
A useful text concerned with biological factors in the occurrence and treatment of disorders of mood, such as depression and mania.

Glossary

Pronunciations are from the twenty-fourth and twenty-fifth editions of *Dorland's Medical Dictionary* published by W. B. Saunders Company, in which the following key applies. Unmarked vowels not followed by a consonant are long and those followed by a consonant are short. Long vowels followed by a consonant are indicated by a macron and short vowels ending a syllable by a breve. The syllable *ah* indicates a broader *a*. Primary (') and secondary (") accent marks are used in polysyllabic words, and unstressed syllables are followed by a hyphen. Included in the glossary are the terms in boldface type in the text and other terms in general use in the field of biological psychology.

absolute refractory period
The period after an action potential has been initiated during which the nerve cell cannot be made to fire another action potential.

absorption
The uptake of a nutrient or other chemical compound into the blood and lymphatic fluids.

accommodation
In vertebrates, the automatic adjustment of the eye when focusing on an image in which a change in the shape or position of the lens is required.

acetoxycycloheximide
(as′e-tok-se-si-klo″hek′si-mīd)
A powerful antibiotic used in high doses in experimental animals to inhibit the synthesis of RNA.

acetylcholine (as″e-til-ko′lēn)
A chemical neurotransmitter present in many parts of the body including neuromuscular junctions and the nervous system. It is the transmitter secreted by motor nerves to excite skeletal muscle.

acetylcholinesterase or **AChE**
(as″e-til-ko′lēn-es″ter-ās)
An enzyme that breaks down the neurotransmitter acetylcholine.

acetylcoenzyme A (as″e-til-ko′en″zīm)
A precursor of the neurotransmitter acetylcholine.
It is also the chief precursor of lipids.

ACh
See acetylcholine.

AChE
See acetylcholinesterase.

acid
Any compound which dissociates in solution to
form hydrogen ions (H⁺).

ACTH
See adrenocorticotropic hormone.

actin (ak′tin)
One of the proteins in muscle together with the
protein myosin responsible for muscle contraction
and relaxation. It is also present in nerve cells and
other cells.

action potential
The all-or-none electrical impulse of a nerve cell.
The action potential is a localized, transient
change in the voltage across a cell membrane
propagated down the nerve cell axon where it
triggers release of neurotransmitter.

activation
The over-all level of excitation or arousal of an
organism. Desynchronization (arousal) of an
electroencephalogram is sometimes also called
activation.

acute tolerance
Very rapid tolerance to the effects of a drug, and
sometimes occurs following a single
administration. It also is called tachyphylaxis.

adenine (ad′e-nīn)
A purine base present in nucleic acids (e.g.,
DNA) that codes genetic information.

adenohypophysis (ad″e-no-hi-pof′i-sis)
The anterior lobe of the pituitary gland.

adenosine triphosphate or **ATP**
(ah-den′o-sēn tri-fos′fāt)
A compound made of nucleotides that stores
energy in the form of high-energy chemical
bonds. It is present in all cells.

adenylate cyclase (ah-den′i-lāt si′klās)
An enzyme which converts adenosine
triphosphate to cyclic adenosine monophosphate.

ADH
See antidiuretic hormone.

adipsia (ah-dip′se-ah)
Cessation of drinking; refusal to drink.

adipsic (ah-dip′sik)
Having adipsia.

adrenal cortex (ad-re′nal kor′teks)
The outer portion (covering) of the adrenal gland.

adrenal gland
An endocrine gland located near the kidney.

adrenalin (ad-ren′ah-lin)
A hormone secreted by the medulla (inner
portion) of the adrenal gland. The substance is
also called epinephrine.

adrenal medulla (me-dul′ah)
The inner portion of the adrenal gland.

adrenocorticotropic hormone
(ad-re″no-kor″te-ko-trop′ik)
A hormone secreted by the anterior pituitary
gland that stimulates the adrenal cortex to secrete
steroid hormones.

affective
Pertaining to the feelings and emotion (affect).

affective aggression
The class of aggressive behaviors not related to
food getting (predatory aggression).

affective disorder
A severe mental disturbance characterized by
wide fluctuations in mood, especially mania
(overexcitement, impulsivity, compulsiveness) and
depression (underexcitement; lack of activity and
initiative; feelings of worthlessness, guilt,
apprehension, and despair).

afferent (af′er-ent)
Coming into or toward a structure. Sensory
nerves are afferent nerves because they project
from the periphery into the central nervous
system. It is the opposite of efferent, which means
to project out of or away from a structure.

affinity
The force that allows certain atoms or molecules to combine and stay combined; especially the degree to which a drug combines with a receptor molecule.

agonist (ag'o-nist)
In pharmacology, a compound that mimics the effect of a neurotransmitter at the synapses. Acetylcholine and nicotine are agonists because they mimic each other's effects at the neuromuscular junction, i.e., they both stimulate striated muscle cells. The term also refers to a muscle opposed by another or antagonist muscle.

aldosterone (al''do-stēr'ōn)
Hormone secreted by the adrenal glands rendering the renal collecting tubules more permeable to electrolytes and therefore more permeable to water.

allele (ah-lēl')
One of two or more alternative forms of a gene, usually represented by forms of the same letter, for example, *A* and *a*.

alpha-adrenergic (al'fah-ad''ren-er'jik)
Refers to adrenergic receptors more affected by norepinephrine than by isoproterol and epinephrine. In general use the term refers to excitatory (alpha) adrenergic synapses such as occur in the heart. *See also* beta-adrenergic.

alpha-methylparatyrosine
(al-fah-meth''il-par'ah-ti-ro'sin)
A compound used experimentally to prevent synthesis of catecholamines by nerve cells, which result in eventual depletion of these substances from the brain and elsewhere.

alpha-methyltryptamine
(al-fah-meth''il-trip'ta-min)
A compound used experimentally to inhibit the uptake of serotonin into nerve cells.

alpha motor neuron
One of the large motor neurons in the spinal cord that sends axons out to innervate skeletal muscle.

alpha wave
One of a specific range of frequencies on the electroencephalogram (8–13 hertz) characteristic of relaxed wakefulness. This type of electroencephalogram is also called a synchronized electroencephalogram.

alveolus (al-ve'o-lus) pl. **alveoli**
A general term meaning a small, saclike structure such as occurs in the lungs and mammary glands.

amacrine cell (am'ah-krīn)
A cell in the retina that provides for interconnection across the retina and located between the bipolar and ganglion cell layers.

amino acid (am''ī-no as'id)
One of the fundamental building blocks of proteins consisting of an organic acid to which an amino (NH_2) group has been added.

aminoaciduria (am''ī-no-as''ī-du're-ah)
An excess of one or more amino acids in the urine. A class of genetic disorders is characterized by a defect in metabolism of amino acids.

amino-oxyacetic acid
(am''ī-no-ok''se-ah-se'tik as'id)
A compound used experimentally to increase the levels of gamma-aminobutyric acid (GABA), a suspected inhibitory neurotransmitter.

amniocentesis (am'ne-o-sen-te'sis)
A surgical diagnostic technique in which a sample of amniotic fluid (fluid surrounding the fetus) is taken for analysis of chromosomal and metabolic abnormalities.

amphetamine (am-fet'ah-min)
A stimulant drug believed to work in part by releasing catecholamines from central and peripheral nerve endings.

amphetamine psychosis (si-ko'sis)
A psychotic condition resembling paranoid schizophrenia brought about by continued use of amphetamines.

amplifier
An electronic instrument used to enhance (amplify) small electrical signals.

amplitude
The amount or degree to which something increases or extends. Can also refer to the height of a waveform.

amplitude modulation (AM)
The increase or decrease in the height (amplitude; size) of a wave. Changes in the intensity of a tone are a type of amplitude modulation.

ampulla (am-pul′ah) pl. **ampullae** (am-pul′le)
A small enlargement at the base of each semicircular canal containing hair cells responsible for sensing the position and direction of movement of the head.

amygdala (ah-mig′dah-lah)
An almond-shaped group of nuclei near the tip of the temporal lobe but buried in the center of the lobe on each side of the brain.

amygdalectomy (ah-mig″dah-lek′to-me)
Surgical removal or destruction of the amygdala.

amygdaloid nuclei (ah-mig′dah-loid)
The nuclei making up the amygdala. *See also* amygdala.

anaerobic (an″a-er-o′bik)
Living, growing, or occurring in the absence of free oxygen.

analeptic (an″al-ep′tik)
A compound used to restore function, as, for example, convulsant drugs, which are sometimes used to stimulate the central nervous system after it has been depressed.

analgesia (an″al-je′ze-ah)
Relief from pain.

analgesic (an″al-je′zik)
Having the property of relieving pain; a drug that relieves pain without producing unconsciousness.

androgen (an′dro-jen)
One of a class of hormones produced by the testes; a male sex hormone, for example, testosterone.

angiotensin (an″je-o-ten′sin)
A protein in plasma.

angiotensin II
A substance believed to act on neurons of the hypothalamus to trigger thirst.

angiotensinogen (an″je-o-ten′sin-o-jen)
A protein secreted by the liver that gives rise to angiotensin upon hydrolysis by renin.

animal spirits
A name given to what Descartes believed to be the finest particles of the blood comprising a volatile fluid or gas which filled the brain and the force behind movement.

annulospiral ending (an″u-lo-spi′ral)
A specialized nerve ending wrapped around the muscle spindle organ that responds to stretch; the specialized nerve ending that gives rise to the large IA sensory nerve fibers from muscles.

anosmic (an-oz′mik)
Lacking the sense of smell.

antagonist
In pharmacology, a compound that blocks the action of an agonist. Curare is an antagonist at the neuromuscular junction where acetylcholine is the agonist. It also refers to any muscle opposing the action of another or agonist muscle.

anterior (an-te′re-or)
Toward the head; opposed to posterior.

anterograde degeneration (an′ter-o-grād)
Degeneration of an axon away from the cell body.

Anthropoidea (an″thro-poi′de-ah)
A suborder of primates that includes Old World monkeys, New World monkeys, hominid apes, and man.

antibody (an′ti-bod″e)
A specific protein molecule formed by lymph tissue to interact with a specific antigen (a foreign molecule, bacterium, tissue, etc., which induces the formation of antibodies).

anticholinergic (an″tĭ-ko″lin-er′jik)
Having an effect opposite that of acetylcholine and its agonists; opposed to the action of acetylcholine.

antidiuretic hormone or **ADH** (an″tĭ-di″u-ret′ik)
A hormone of the posterior pituitary gland (neurohypophysis) which increases the absorption of water by the kidney.

antigen (an′tĭ-jen)
Any substance (foreign molecule, cell, tissue, etc.) inducing the formation of antibodies.

antipsychotic drugs (an″tĭ-si-kot′ik)
Any drug used to treat psychosis.

aphagia (ah-fa′je-ah)
Cessation of eating; refusal to eat.

aphagic (ah-fa′jik)
Having aphagia.

aphasia (ah-fa′ze-ah)
Loss of language ability.

Aplysia (a′plizh-e-ah)
The sea hare, a purple or green organism resembling a large shell-less snail and inhabiting coastal tidal waters. The behavioral repertoire and nervous system of this invertebrate have been studied extensively and serve as models for understanding the properties of nerve cells and behavior in vertebrates. *Aplysia californica* is the variety studied most extensively.

apnea (ap-ne′ah)
Transient cessation of breathing.

apomorphine (ap″o-mor′fin)
A drug which mimics the action of dopamine at dopaminergic synapses and hence is a dopaminergic agonist. Its structure closely resembles the structure of morphine. The drug is used to induce vomiting in human beings.

aqueous humor (a′kwe-us hu′mor)
The watery substance in the anterior chamber (outer portion) of the eyeball.

ARAS
See ascending reticular activating system.

arboreal (ar-bo′re-al)
Adapted to live in trees; of or pertaining to trees.

aromatic amino acid decarboxylase (de″kar-bok′si-las)
An enzyme important in the conversion of dopa to dopamine and 5-hydroxytryptophan to 5-hydroxytryptamine (serotonin), as well as in many other reactions.

arousal
The level of excitation or intensity of behavior of an organism. Desynchronization of the electroencephalogram is also called arousal.

arousal response
The increase in alertness and accompanying desynchronization of the electroencephalogram that occurs when a sudden or unfamiliar stimulus is encountered; the awakening from sleep with accompanying changes in the electroencephalogram, etc.

arrest reaction
A momentary cessation of an ongoing behavior.

ascending reticular activating system
The large central portion of the brain stem giving rise to an extensive projection to the forebrain that appears to be importantly involved in the behavioral and physiological signs of wakefulness, activation, etc.; an extensive portion of the brain stem where electrical stimulation produces behavioral and electroencephalographic arousal (activation).

aspartate peptide (ah-spahr′tāt pep′tĭd)
A peptide derived principally from aspartic acid.

astigmatism (ah-stig′mah-tizm)
A visual defect in which the surface of the cornea is irregularly curved.

ataxia (ah-tak′se-ah)
The inability to coordinate bodily movements.

ATP
See adenosine triphosphate.

atropine (at'ro-pin)
In pharmacology, a compound used to block the action of acetylcholine at certain cholinergic synapses in the peripheral and central nervous system; an alkaloid with a variety of clinical uses: to relax various smooth muscles, to increase heart rate, and other anticholinergic effects. The drug especially blocks the action of acetylcholine at muscarinic sites.

audiogenic seizure (aw''de-o-jen'ik)
A convulsion induced by sound.

auditory cortex
See primary auditory cortex.

autonomic division
The portion of the peripheral nervous system responsible for glandular and emotional responses.

autoradiography (aw''to-ra''de-og'rah-fe)
A method to localize radioactively labeled structures by exposing them to a photographic plate.

autosome (aw'to-sōm)
A chromosome other than a sex chromosome.

averaging computer
A machine which extracts small electrical signals embedded in noise.

axo-axonic synapse (aks'o-aks'on-ik)
A synapse between two axons.

axodendritic synapse (aks'o-den-drit'ik)
A synapse between an axon and a dendrite.

axon (ak'son)
The fiber of a nerve cell which carries information (nerve impulses) away from the cell body.

axon hillock
The portion of the nerve cell where axon and cell body connect.

axosomatic synapse (ak''so-so-mat'ik)
A synapse between the axon and a cell body (soma).

Babinski reflex (bah-bin'ske)
Fanning of the toes (dorsiflexion) when the sole of the foot is stimulated.

barbiturate (bar-bit'u-rāt)
One of a class of compounds used to induce sedation or sleep.

basal forebrain
A general term for a group of structures found at the base of the forebrain, especially the ventral frontal lobes, caudate nuclei, and putamen and the midline thalamus. The term is often used when this group of structures is referred to as they appear to function in the production of sleep.

basal ganglia (ba'sal gang'gle-ah)
A large mass of nuclei buried within the cerebral hemispheres and comprised of the caudate nucleus, putamen, and globus pallidus; important in motor behavior.

base
In chemistry, a substance that combines with acids to form salts; the foundation or lowest portion of anything.

basilar membrane (bas'ĭ-lar)
The long membrane in the organ of Corti on which the hair cells are supported and which flexes back and forth during sound stimulation.

basket cell
An interneuron in the cerebellum (and other structures).

behavioral genetics
The field of study concerned with the degree and nature of the heritable causes of behavior.

Benzedrine (ben'ze-drēn)
The trademark for preparations of amphetamine sulfate.

benztropine (benz'tro-pēn)
A drug used in the treatment of Parkinson's disease which is believed to act in part by blocking the reuptake of dopamine into presynaptic terminals; also stimulates certain targets of the parasympathetic division of the autonomic nervous system.

beta-adrenergic (ba′ta-ad″ren-er′jik)
The adrenergic receptors more affected by isoproterenol and epinephrine than by norepinephrine. In general use the term refers to inhibitory (beta) synapses such as occur in blood vessels. *See also* alpha-adrenergic.

beta wave
One of a specific range of frequencies in the electroencephalogram (18–24 hertz) characteristic of a desynchronized electroencephalogram.

Betz cell (betz)
A large pyramidal (pyramid-shaped) cell found in the motor cortex.

bilateral
Having two sides; pertaining to both sides.

binaural (bin-aw′ral)
Pertaining to both ears.

binocular (bin-ok′u-lar)
Pertaining to both eyes.

binocular disparity
The difference in position on the retina of an object seen by the two eyes; especially, the difference in angles of view of the two eyes toward a point in the visual field.

biofeedback
The technique by which biological signals such as heart rate and muscle tension are converted to easily detected stimuli, that is, become perceptible to the senses, and are "fed back" in order to exert conscious mental control over these functions.

biological half-life
The amount of time required to eliminate one-half of a quantity administered.

biological rhythm
The established regularity of a biological process; every 24 hours, yearly, etc.

bipolar (bi-po′lar)
Having two poles. A cell with two processes or extensions originating from the cell body.

bipolar cell
A cell having two processes extending from the cell body; especially, from the cell layer in the retina between the receptor and ganglion cell layers.

bleaching
The process of removing color; especially the chemical reaction that occurs when photopigment absorbs light.

blind control
An experimental method in which the experimenter does not know which experimental treatment different subjects receive.

blood-brain barrier
The mechanism or mechanisms which prevent certain compounds in the general circulation from entering the brain.

brain stem
The structures between the spinal cord and the cerebral hemispheres: medulla, pons, cerebellum, midbrain, hypothalamus, and thalamus.

brain stem reticular formation
See reticular formation.

brightness contrast
The degree to which the brightness of one area of a pattern affects and is affected by the brightness of other, adjacent areas.

brightness discrimination
The training procedure in which an organism learns to distinguish between two or more levels of brightness.

Broca's area (bro′kahz)
The region in the frontal lobes (third frontal gyrus) commonly called the speech center. Damage to the area results in loss of speaking ability.

Brodmann's areas
Regions of the cerebral cortex to which Brodmann assigned a number based on histological appearance, that is, distribution of cell types, thickness of the layer, etc.

bufotenin (bu-fo′te-nin)
A hallucinogenic drug derived from glands in the skin of toads; used in experimental study.

caffeine
A central nervous system stimulant present in coffee and tea; one of the xanthines.

calcium carbonate
A salt crystal made from calcium and carbonic acid.

Cannabis sativa (kan′ah-bis sat′e-va)
The hemp plant from which marijuana is obtained.

cannula (kan′u-lah) pl. **cannulae** (kan′u-le)
A tube for insertion into a body cavity or duct or vessel; used to administer compounds.

carbachol (kar′bah-kol)
A compound that stimulates specific cholinergic receptors in the brain and hence is a cholinergic agonist.

carbamylcholine (kar″bah-mil-ko′lēn)
A drug that stimulates certain cholinergic receptors, especially nicotinic receptors and hence is a nicotinic agonist.

cardiac muscle
Heart muscle.

cataplexy (kat′ah-plek-se)
Sudden, dramatic decrease in muscle tone and loss of certain reflexes.

catecholamine (kat″e-kol-am′in)
One of a class of molecules; especially norepinephrine, dopamine, and epinephrine.

catechol-O-methyltransferase
(kat′e-kol-o-meth″il-trans′fer-ās)
An enzyme that breaks down catecholamines and is believed to be associated with nerve cell membranes as well as with other tissues.

cathode-ray tube
The major component of an oscilloscope.

caudate nucleus (kaw′dāt nu′kle-us)
One of the basal ganglia buried within the cerebral hemispheres.

cell theory
The theory that the fundamental unit of structure and function of living matter is the cell.

cellular respiration
See oxidative metabolism.

central nervous system
The brain and spinal cord.

central sulcus (sul′kus)
The long vertically oriented sulcus on either hemisphere which separates the frontal and parietal lobes of the human brain.

centrifuge (sen′tri-fūj)
Machine for separating particles according to their density. Separation is achieved by spinning the material at high speed so that the particles are subjected to centrifugal force.

centromere (sen′tro-mēr)
The portion of the chromosome at which the spindle is attached during cell division; the point at which the two spiral filaments comprising the chromosome are joined.

cerebellum (ser″e-bel′um)
The large, convoluted structure situated above the pons involved in motor coordination.

cerveau isolé (ser-vo e-so-lay)
A transaction of the brain which isolates the cerebral hemispheres; usually made between the inferior and superior colliculi.

chloroimipramine (klo′ro-i-mip′rah-mēn)
A drug believed to act in part by inhibiting the uptake of serotonin by nerve cells.

chlorpromazine (klōr-pro′mah-zēn)
An antipsychotic drug and major tranquilizer with many effects on the central nervous system, including the ability to interfere with catecholaminergic neurotransmission.

choline (ko′lin)
A precursor of the neurotransmitter acetylcholine. This compound is a vitamin of the B complex contained in many plant and animal products.

choline acetyltransferase (as″e-til-trans′fer-āˉs)
An enzyme that brings about synthesis of the neurotransmitter acetylcholine.

cholinoceptive (ko″lĭ-no-sep′tiv)
Receptive to acetylcholine. Striated muscle cells and some nerve cells are sensitive to acetylcholine, and hence are cholinoceptive.

chorda tympani (kor′dah tim-pan′e)
A branch of the facial nerve that innervates taste receptors on the front part of the tongue.

chromatolysis (kro″mah-tol′ĭ-sis)
A sequence of changes in the cell body of a nerve cell following damage to its axon.

chromosome (kro′mo-sōm)
One of the rod-shaped bodies that assemble during mitosis (cell division) and carry the genetic information (genes).

chronic tolerance
Tolerance to the effects of a drug that develops slowly.

ciliary muscle (sil′e-er″e)
One of the small muscles attached near the lens of the eye which governs the shape of the lens.

circadian rhythm (ser″kah-de′an)
The regular reoccurrence in cycles of approximately 24 hours of activities in biological processes.

cisterna (sis-ter′nah) pl. **cisternae** (sis-ter′ne)
A closed space containing a body fluid.

classical conditioning
An experimental paradigm developed by Pavlov in which a neutral stimulus (the conditioned stimulus) is paired with another stimulus that evokes a response (the unconditioned stimulus and unconditioned response). After pairing, the neutral stimulus acquires the power to evoke a response similar to the one previously evoked only by the unconditioned stimulus. It is sometimes termed pavlovian conditioning.

climbing fiber
One of the excitatory inputs to the cerebellum.

cocaine (ko-kānˉ′)
A local anesthetic. As a stimulant of the central nervous system the drug is believed to work in part by facilitating catecholaminergic neurotransmission in the brain, which leads to behavioral stimulation.

cochlea (kok′le-ah)
The coiled, snaillike bone of the inner ear that contains the receptor organ for hearing.

cochlear nucleus (kok′le-ar)
The first nucleus in the brain system auditory pathways, receiving its input from the auditory nerve (cranial nerve VIII).

codeine (ko′dēˉn)
A narcotic analgesic drug; an opiate.

codon (ko′don)
The unit of genetic material necessary to code for a specific amino acid; especially the three bases needed to code for the synthesis of a given amino acid.

coefficient of genetic determination
A statistic used to estimate the variability of some trait in a population due to genetic factors.

colchicine (kol′chĭ-sin)
A poisonous alkaloid used experimentally to prevent the separation of the double chromosomes during cell division; a compound used to treat gout.

columnar organization
A principle of organization in nervous tissue in which nerve cells having some common property, such as response to a particular feature of a stimulus, are arranged in a cylindrical (columnar) space or column perpendicular to the surface of the cerebral cortex.

comparator
The device in a feedback control system that compares the set point with the error signal.

complex light
Light comprised of two or more wavelengths.

complex receptive field
A receptive field of visual cortical cells as classified by Hubel and Weisel in which neurons respond similarly to those having simple receptive fields, but respond also to direction of movement.

complex sound
A sound consisting of more than a single frequency.

concentration
The amount of a solute (substance) relative to the amount of solvent into which it is dissolved.

concentration gradient
A variation in the concentration of a substance; especially the difference in concentrations of ions across the nerve cell membrane.

concentric
Having a common center such as concentric circles having the same center but differing in diameter.

concordance
In genetics, the occurrence of the same trait in both members of a twin pair; opposed to discordance in which both members do not have the trait.

conditioned alpha blocking
Electroencephalographic arousal response (EEG desynchronization) evoked by a conditioned stimulus as established through classical conditioning.

conditioned response or **CR**
The response evoked by the conditioned stimulus in a classical conditioning paradigm; any response that has become associated to a previously ineffective stimulus through the process of classical conditioning.

conditioned stimulus or **CS**
That stimulus in a classical conditioning paradigm that evokes the conditioned response.

conduction
Propagation of a nerve impulse along a nerve fiber.

conduction velocity
The speed with which an action potential is propagated in a specific direction along a nerve fiber.

cone
One of the cone-shaped light-sensitive cells in the retina.

conjunctiva (kon''junk-ti'vah)
The mucous membrane lining the eyelids and covering the sclera.

consolidation theory of memory
The theory that a memory requires some amount of time after learning before being stored on a permanent basis.

contingent negative variation or **CNV**
A slow, negative change in voltage that develops over the cerebral cortex in subjects who expect or anticipate the occurrence of an event.

contralateral (kon''trah-lat'er-al)
Pertaining to the opposite side.

convergence
Coming together; moving toward a common point.

convulsant
One of a class of drugs that causes convulsions (seizures): strychnine, picrotoxin, Metrazol, etc.

cornea (kor'ne-ah)
The clear outer covering of the eyeball.

coronal section (ko-ro'nal)
A cross section through the brain from side-to-side; also called a frontal section.

corpus callosum (kor'pus kah-lo'sum)
The large bundle of nerve fibers interconnecting the two cerebral hemispheres.

corpus luteum (lu'te-um)
The small, yellowish mass that is produced from the graffian follicle after the follicle has discharged the egg from the ovary.

cortex (kor′teks)
The outer layer of a body or structure.

cortical spreading depression (kor′ti-kal)
Spreading depression over the cerebral cortex.
See also spreading depression.

cranial nerve (kra′ne-al)
A nerve that enters or exits from the brain
directly rather than from the spinal cord;
distinguished from a spinal nerve.

cri-du-chat syndrome (kre-du-shah)
A genetic disorder characterized by severe mental
retardation and a peculiar cry in infancy
resembling that of a cat.

crista (kris′tah) pl. **cristae** (kris′te)
A structure or tissue that projects into a lumen or
forms a ridge or crest.

critical period
A period during development, often relatively
brief, during which and only during which certain
events must take place to ensure proper
development.

crossing-over
In genetics, the exchange of genetic material
between homologous chromosomes.

cross-tolerance
The condition in which tolerance to one drug
produces tolerance to another, but different drug.

cupula (ku′pu-lah) pl. **cupulae** (ku′pu-le)
A small cup-shaped cover over a structure; in this
book, the gelatinous cap overlying the hair cells in
the semicircular canals.

curare (koo-rah′re)
A compound that blocks transmission at the
cholinergic synapses between motor nerves and
striated muscle cells and hence produces muscular
relaxation and eventual paralysis. It is used in
arrow poisons by South American Indians.

cybernetics (si″ber-net′iks)
The science dealing with the study of
information-handling machines such as
calculators and computers and the application of
such knowledge toward an understanding of the
brain.

cytogenetics (si″to-je-net′iks)
The field of study concerned with cellular
mechanisms of heredity.

cytology (si-tol′o-je)
The study of the structure and function of cells.

cytoplasm (si′to-plazm″)
The material inside the cell, but outside the
nucleus consisting of the protoplasm and various
molecules and organelles suspended in it.

cytosine (si′to-sin)
A nitrogenous base in nucleic acids (e.g., DNA).

DA
See dopamine.

dark adaptation
Adaptation of the eyes to vision in the dark or in
reduced illumination.

dark adaptation curve
A graph depicting sensitivity to white light as a
function of increasing time in the darkness.

decarboxylase (de″kar-bok′si-lās)
Any of a class of enzymes that catalyze the
removal of carbon dioxide from certain acidic
molecules.

decibel (des′i-bel)
A unit to express sound intensity experienced as
loudness. Each decibel increase in sound intensity
represents a tenfold increase in sound energy (i.e.,
a logarithmic scale of sound intensity).

decorticate (de-kor′ti-kāt)
To remove all or part of the cortex from an organ
(as from the brain).

decortication
In this book, an experimental preparation having
the cerebral cortex removed.

decussate (de-kus′āt)
To cross over or intersect in the form of an X.

deficiency motivation
An internal condition or state that incites an
organism to seek a particular goal in order to
make up a deficiency (e.g., water deficiency,
nutrient deficiency, etc.).

degradation
The process of degrading or breaking down.

dehydration
The process of removing water from a substance; the condition resulting from extreme loss of water from the body.

delayed-alternation problem
An experimental task in which the subject must wait for a specified interval of time before making a response and in which the correct response on each trial alternates between choices.

delayed-response problem
An experimental task in which the subject must await for a specified interval of time before making a response.

delay interval
The interval between presentation of the stimulus cue and the time when an animal is allowed to respond to the stimulus.

delay-line timing circuit
A series of connections or circuits between nerve cells capable of sustaining activity for a specified period of time or delay interval.

delta wave
One of a specific range of frequencies in the electroencephalogram (1–3 hertz); the slow, high-amplitude wave that occurs during deep sleep.

dendrite (den′drīt)
A fiber or extension from a nerve cell that carries information toward the cell body; also transmits information to other cells in some instances by way of dendrodendritic synapses.

dendritic spine
A small spinelike appendage on the dendrites of some nerve cells generally regarded as a site where synaptic connections occur.

dendrodendritic synapse (den′dro-den-drit′ik)
The synapse between two dendrites.

deoxyribonucleic acid or **DNA**
(de-ok″se-ri″bo-nu-kla′ik)
A large-molecule nucleic acid and a carrier of genetic information. Most DNA is present in the nucleus, consists of a double helix held together by a sugar backbone and alternate links of phosphates, and carries four bases: cytosine, adenine, guanine, and thymine.

deoxyribose (de-ok″se-ri′bōs)
A form of sugar; a constituent of DNA.

depolarization
The change in voltage which renders the cell membrane less polarized; the result of excitatory synaptic transmission. In nerve cells, depolarization is the change in which the inside of the nerve cell membrane becomes more positive.

depressant
An agent that produces depression; especially, a drug that depresses behavior, mood, etc.

depression
A state of extreme underactivity and feelings of worthlessness, guilt, apprehension, and despair.

descending reticular formation
The system of fibers descending from the reticular formation into the spinal cord where they modulate spinal reflexes and various other motor behaviors.

desynchronized
Not synchronized; the change in frequency and amplitude of the electroencephalogram from low frequency and high amplitude (synchronized) to high frequency and low amplitude (desynchronized).

desynchronized pattern
Pattern on an electroencephalogram that shows high-frequency, low-amplitude changes.

Dexedrine (dek′se-drēn)
Trademark for dextroamphetamine preparations.

dextral (deks′tral)
Right-handed.

diabetes insipidus
A metabolic disorder characterized by secretion of large amounts of dilute urine due to damage to the pituitary gland and decrease in antidiuretic hormone.

diazepam (di-az'e-pam)
A minor tranquilizer; trade name Valium.

3, 4-dichloroisoproterenol
(-di-klo''ro-i''so-pro''te-re'nol)
A compound that blocks neurotransmission at beta-adrenergic synapses and hence is a beta-adrenergic antagonist.

dichotomous (di-kot'o-mus)
Dividing into two parts.

diencephalon (di''en-sef'ah-lon)
One of the five major subdivisions of the vertebrate brain; contains the thalamus and hypothalamus.

diffusion
The process of diffusing or spreading out. Diffusion is a passive process not requiring metabolic energy and is significant in the electrical activity generated by nerve cells and other cells.

diisopropylfluorophosphate or **DFP**
(di-i'so-pro''pil-floor''o-fos'fat)
An organophosphate; used experimentally to inhibit the activity of the enzyme acetylcholinesterase. *See also* organophosphates.

3, 4-dimethoxyphenylethylamine
(-di-meth-ok'se-fen'il-eth''il-am'in)
An abnormal metabolite of norepinephrine with psychotomimetic properties reported to occur in higher concentrations in urine of schizophrenics.

dimethyltryptamine (di''meth-il-trip'ta-min)
An hallucinogenic compound derived from a South American plant; theorized to be a possible product of abnormal serotonin metabolism in the brain possibly involved in schizophrenia.

diploid (dip'loid)
Twofold; having two sets of chromosomes; present in all cells except gametes.

dishabituation
An increase in response to habitation stimulus following a change in intensity, frequency, etc., or following the occurrence of a different, often strong, extra stimulus; sometimes called sensitization.

disinhibition (dis''in-hi-bish'un)
The removal of an inhibition; any action that removes an inhibiting influence.

dissociated learning
State-dependent learning.

disulfiram (di-sul'fi-ram)
A compound used experimentally to prevent conversion of dopamine into norepinephrine. As Antabuse, the drug is used clinically in the treatment of alcoholism.

dizygotic (di''zi-got'ik)
Derived from two separate fertilized eggs (zygotes), as dizygotic or fraternal twins.

DMPE
See 3, 4-dimethoxyphenylethylamine.

dominant
Exercising authority or influence over others, especially in social hierarchies; in genetics, the expression of one form of a gene over another; opposed to recessive.

dopamine (do'pah-men)
A suspected neurotransmitter; a catecholamine in certain nerve cells of the mesencephalon, especially the substantia nigra, implicated in Parkinson's disease.

dopamine-beta-oxidase (-ba'tah-oks'i-das)
An enzyme important for conversion of dopamine to norepinephrine in nerve cells, as well as for a variety of other reactions in cells.

dorsal (dor'sal)
Toward the top or back; opposed to ventral.

dorsal column
One of the two large bundles of fibers at the top of the spinal cord adjacent to the midline, fasciculus gracilis and fasciculus cuneatus, that are in part a continuation of certain sensory nerve fibers.

dorsal column nucleus
One of the nuclei at the base of the brain stem where fibers of the dorsal columns terminate.

dorsal root
One of the large fiber bundles entering the spinal cord that carry sensory fibers.

dorsal root ganglion (gang'gle-on)
One of the cell bodies of the dorsal roots.

dorsolateral pathways (dor''so-lat'er-al)
Nerve fiber pathways along the side (lateral) and toward the top (dorsal) of the spinal cord.

dose-response relationship
The relation between the degree of biological activity produced by a compound (drug) and the amount of the compound (dose) administered.

drive
The force activating human behavior; a motive; a physiological need that influences behavior.

Drosophila (dro-sof'ĭ-lah)
A genus of flies; the fruit flies used in genetic research.

drug
A compound which by virtue of its chemical structure interacts with a biological system and causes a change in the structure and/or function of the system; a substance used as a medication.

drug-dispositional tolerance
Lessened susceptibility to the effects of a drug due to continued administration and increased capacity to eliminate the drug from the body.

duplication
See replication.

dynamogenesis (di''nah-mo-jen'e-sis)
The development of energy or force; the non-specific arousing or activating effect originally proposed on the basis of experiments showing increased grip strength with increased sensory stimulation as measured on a dynamometer.

dysphoria (dis-fo're-ah)
The state of feeling unwell or unhappy; restlessness.

eccentric cell (ek-sen'trik)
A specialized cell found in the eye of the horseshoe crab.

ecological isolation
The isolation of different species or groups of organisms because of differences in habitat or mating season.

ED$_{50}$
That dose of a drug which produces an effect in 50 percent of the subjects to whom it is administered.

EEG
See electroencephalogram.

efferent (ef'er-ent)
Projecting away from a structure. Motor nerves are efferent because they project from the central nervous system.

electroconvulsive shock
A strong electrical current applied to the brain, usually through electrodes overlying the scalp, causing convulsions.

electroconvulsive therapy
The use of electroconvulsive shock in treatment of mental disorder.

electrocorticogram (e-lek''tro-kor'ti-ko-gram)
The electroencephalogram recorded from the cerebral cortex.

electrode
A wire or other conductor used to record electrical responses from the brain or to stimulate the brain with electric current.

electroencephalogram or **EEG**
(e-lek″tro-en-sef′ah-lo-gram)
A recording of the spontaneous electrical activity of the brain; especially the activity recorded from the skull in human beings.

electroencephalograph
(e-lek″tro-en-sef′ah-lo-graf)
The machine that records the electroencephalogram.

electrolysis (e″lek-trol′i-sis)
Destruction of tissue by electrical current.

electrolytic (e-lek″tro-lit′ik)
Pertaining to or characteristic of electrolysis. A lesion (area of destruction) made by applying direct current is called an electrolytic lesion.

electromagnetic spectrum
The entire range of electromagnetic radiation from extremely long wavelength waves such as those used in radio transmission, through visible light, to the extremely short wavelengths of X rays and cosmic rays.

electromyogram or **EMG** (e-lek″tro-mi′o-gram)
A recording of the electrical activity of a muscle; a means of detecting muscular activity.

electron (e-lek′tron)
An elementary particle consisting of a negative charge of electricity and forming a part of all atoms.

electron micrograph
A photograph of the highly magnified image formed by the electron microscope.

electron microscope
An electron optical instrument (microscope) in which an electron beam, rather than ordinary lighting, is used to project and observe minute structures.

electroretinogram (e-lek″tro-ret′i-no-gram)
A record of the electrical activity generated by the retina and associated structures when the eye is stimulated with light.

EMG
See electromyogram.

emission spectrum
The physical description of the wavelength and energy composition of a beam of light.

encéphale isolé (en-sa′fal e″so-lay)
Transaction of the brain at the junction of the brain and spinal cord.

endocrine gland (en′do-krin)
A gland that secretes chemical substances into the blood or lymph.

endogenous (en-daj′e-nes)
Naturally occurring, originating internally.

endolymph (en′do-limf)
The fluid of the semicircular canals and the scala media containing the organ of Corti.

endoplasmic reticulum
(en′do-plaz″mik re-tik′u-lum)
An extensive network of membranes found inside of cells that appears to be continuous with or connected to both the outer cell membrane and the nuclear membrane.

endorphins (en-dor′fin)
A class of peptides containing between 15 and 30 amino acids and having many pharmacological properties similar to morphine. It is believed to function as a neurotransmitter, neuromodulator, or hormone.

endotherm (en′do-therm)
See homoiotherm.

engram (en′gram)
Lashley's term for the memory trace.

enkephalins (en-kef′a-lin)
A class of peptides containing a sequence of 5 amino acids and having many pharmacological properties similar to morphine. It is believed to function as a neurotransmitter, neuromodulator, or hormone.

enuresis (en''u-re′sis)
Bed-wetting.

enzyme (en′zīm)
A protein (organic molecule) that catalyzes (facilitates) specific biochemical reactions in living cells.

epinephrine (ep''i-nef′rin)
A hormone secreted by the medulla (central portion) of the adrenal gland; also called adrenalin.

epithelium (ep''i-the′le-um)
The lining or covering of the inner and outer surfaces of the body, blood vessels, ventricles of the brain, etc.

equilibrium potential
The voltage across the cell membrane at which no net transfer of ions occurs. An equilibrium potential may be calculated for any ion which is distributed across the cell membrane and represents a complex state of equilibrium between the effects of the concentration of the substance across the membrane and its electrical charge.

ERG
See electroretinogram.

ergotoxin (er''go-tok′sin)
A poison derived from fungus which acts on the nervous system by blocking neurotransmission at alpha-adrenergic synapses.

error signal
In a feedback control system, the signal that arises when the feedback signal differs from the desired level.

ester linkage (ester bond)
Chemical bond between the phosphate group of one nucleotide and the sugar of an adjoining nucleotide in DNA.

estrogen (es′tro-jen)
A generic term for a class of hormones that produces estrus. In human beings, estrogen is produced in the ovaries, testes, adrenal glands, and placenta and has functions in both men and women. It is responsible for the development of the female sexual characteristics and behaviors.

estrous cycle (es′trus)
The cyclic period of heat in many female animals and associated events such as ovulation, receptivity to a mate, etc.

ethological isolation
The reproductive isolation of different species or groups of organisms because of differences in mating and other behaviors.

eukaryotic cell (u''kar-e-ot′ik)
A cell which contains a nucleus.

euphoria (u-fo′re-ah)
A feeling of well-being, high spirits, etc.

evoked potential
A change in voltage produced (evoked) by a stimulus.

evolutionary adaptation
The process by which traits and functions facilitate survival; especially those traits and functions related to fitness.

excitable cell
A cell that responds to stimulation, such as muscle and nerve cells.

excitatory postsynaptic potential or **EPSP**
The depolarization of a nerve cell resulting from excitatory synaptic transmission.

exocrine gland (ek′so-krin)
One of the glands secreting chemical substances outside of the blood and lymph, especially via a duct.

exotherm (ek′so-therm)
See poikilotherm.

expectancy wave
A negative change in potential that develops over the cerebral cortex when an individual expects an event to occur; also termed the contingent negative variation or CNV.

exteroceptive (eks''ter-o-sep′tiv)
A general term for sensation or stimulation coming from without (outside the body).

extinction
A general term for any process by which something is made to disappear, especially, the gradual waning of a conditioned response that occurs when reinforcement does not follow.

extracellullar (eks″trah-sel′u-lar)
Outside of a cell.

extrafusal
One of the skeletal muscle fibers that perform muscular work, opposed to intrafusal muscle fibers which are specialized to act as sensory receptors.

extrapyramidal motor system
(eks″trah-pi-ram′i-dal)
All structures in the brain involved in motor behavior excluding the pyramidal system.

fasciculus (fah-sik′u-lus) pl. **fasciculi** (fah-sik′u-li)
A general term for a small bundle of fibers such as nerve, muscle, or tendon fibers.

fasciculus cuneatus (ku″ne-a′tus)
The bundle of nerve fibers running in the spinal cord to the nucleus cuneatus, a somatosensory relay nucleus in the brain stem.

fasciculus gracilis (grah-sil′is)
The bundle of nerve fibers projecting in the spinal cord to the nucleus gracilis, a somatosensory relay nucleus in the brain stem.

feedback control
One of the basic concepts of cybernetics in which information about the outcome of an action is fed back and used to control or steer subsequent actions.

fitness
In evolution, the number of offspring an organism leaves to the next generation; successful reproduction.

flexion reflex
The reflexive withdrawal of a limb (flexion) when the skin receives a noxious (e.g., painful) stimulation.

follicle-stimulating hormone (fol′li-k′l-)
A hormone secreted by the anterior lobe of the pituitary gland which stimulates growth and maturation of egg cells in the ovary and with luteinizing hormone stimulates the manufacture of androgens and production of sperm.

follicular phase (fo-lik′u-lar)
That phase of the estrous cycle initiated by the release of follicle-stimulating hormone by the adenohypophysis and ending with ovulation; approximately the first 10–14 days of the human menstrual cycle.

forebrain
The most anterior of three subdivisions comprising the embryonic vertebrate brain; gives rise to the telencephalon and diencephalon.

fornix (for′niks)
A compact bundle of nerve fibers comprising the major output pathway of the hippocampus.

fovea (fo′ve-ah)
A small pit or indentation on the surface of an organ or other structure; especially the fovea of the retina where the fixation point of vision strikes the retina and where visual acuity is greatest.

frequency
The number of times an event occurs during a given period.

frequency modulation or **FM**
The increase or decrease in the frequency of a wave; the change in the frequency (heard as pitch) of a tone.

frequency theory of hearing
The theory that the pitch heard is determined by the frequency of vibration of the basilar membrane and by the frequency of firing in the nerve fibers innervating hair cells on the basilar membrane.

frontal lobotomy (lo-bot′o-me)
A surgical procedure in which connections between the frontal lobes and other regions of the brain are destroyed.

FSH
See follicle-stimulating hormone.

fundamental
The lowest frequency component of a complex sound.

GABA
See gamma-aminobutyric acid.

galvanic skin response (gal-van′ik)
The relatively abrupt change in the electrical resistance and current in the skin occurring when a stimulus, especially an unfamiliar, emotional, or stressful stimulus, is presented.

galvanometer (gal″vah-nom′e-ter)
An instrument for detecting electrical current.

gamete (gam′ēt)
A mature sex cell, either a sperm or an ovum.

gamete mortality
The death of gametes.

gamma-aminobutyric acid or **GABA**
(gam′ah-ah-me′no-bu-tir′ik)
A suspected neurotransmitter in the central nervous system; regarded as an inhibitory transmitter.

gamma-hydroxybutyrate (-hi-drok′se-bu′ti″rāt)
A metabolite of the suspected neurotransmitter GABA.

gamma motor neuron
A small motor neuron of the spinal cord that innervates the intrafusal muscle fiber.

ganglion (gang′gle-on) pl. **ganglia**
A general term for a group of cell bodies located outside the central nervous system.

ganglion cell
One of the cells of the retina that form the optic nerve.

gap junction
A narrow synaptic junction between the membranes of two cells that is frequently the morphological basis for electrical communication between the cells.

gate control theory
A theory of pain in which large sensory nerve fibers form a circuit in the spinal cord which controls information arriving in smaller, pain-carrying fibers.

gender identity
An individual's private feelings about being male or female.

gene (jēn)
The basic biological unit of heredity. The concept of the gene continues to evolve and includes definitions such as a sequence of DNA, a mutational site, etc.

gene pool
The collection of genes in an entire population; specifically, the genetic makeup of a species.

general adaptation syndrome
The sequence of behavioral and physiological changes, especially the hormonal changes, that take place in an individual exposed to severe stress.

generator potential
The graded change in voltage across the membrane of a sensory nerve ending leading to an action potential in the sensory nerve.

genetic code
The sequence of molecules in DNA that carries the genetic information; especially the triplet code, the ordering of bases along the DNA molecule so that groups of three bases code for a specific amino acid.

genotype (jen′o-tīp)
The genetic makeup of an individual or cell.

gill-withdrawal reflex
A reflex in the sea hare *Aplysia* in which the gills are rapidly withdrawn when mechanically stimulated.

glial cell (gle′al)
A nonneural cell that serves a supporting role in the nervous system and is involved in nutritive and other functions.

globus pallidus (glo′bus pal′i-dus)
One of the basal ganglia buried within the cerebral hemispheres.

glucagon (gloo′kah-gon)
A hormone secreted by the pancreas that increases the content of sugar in the blood.

glucocorticoid (gloo''ko-kor'tĭ-koid)
A steriod hormone secreted by the adrenal cortex important in the breakdown of proteins and production of glycogen and sugar.

glucose (gloo'kōs)
A sugar; the main source of energy for the brain.

glucostatic theory of hunger (gloo'ko-stat'ik)
The view that hunger is determined in part by the level of glucose in the blood, especially as detected by certain nerve cells in the brain.

glutamate (gloo'tah-māt)
An amino acid; candidate as a neurotransmitter in the central nervous system.

glycine (gli'sēn)
An amino acid; a suspected neurotransmitter in the central nervous system.

glycogen (gli'ko-jen)
The chief storage carbohydrate in animal tissue. It is stored predominantly in the liver and muscle and broken down into glucose as needed.

glycolysis (gli-kol'ĭ-sis)
The breakdown of sugars into simpler compounds, especially of pyruvate and lactate.

Golgi complex (gol'je)
An extensive membrane system especially prominent in neurons and other cells specialized for secretion of chemical substances; the site where chemical secretions are manufactured or packaged.

Golgi neuron (gol'je)
An interneuron in the cerebellum.

Golgi stain (gol'je)
A histological stain used to stain entire nerve cells including the cell body and all of its extensions (axons and dendrites).

Golgi tendon organ (gol'je)
A specialized sensory receptor found in the tendons of muscles which responds to muscle contraction and stretch.

gonad (go'nad)
A gamete-producing gland; an ovary or testis.

gonadotropin (gon''ah-do-tro'pin)
Any hormone that has a direct effect on the gonads.

go-no go task
An experimental task in which the subject must respond to one stimulus (go) but withhold response to another (no go) stimulus.

graded potential
A potential that may vary in size; in nerve cells, a synaptic potential that varies in amplitude according to the intensity of stimulation.

granule cell
An interneuron in the cerebellum olfactory bulb or elsewhere; any small nerve cell that looks granular under the microscope.

grasping reflex
In infants, the reflexive grasping that occurs when the hand or fingers are stimulated.

gray matter
Neural tissue containing both nerve cells and unmyelinated fibers and having a grayish color, especially in the brain and spinal cord.

growth hormone
A hormone secreted by the anterior lobe of the pituitary gland that stimulates growth.

guanine (gwan'in)
A nitrogenous base in nucleic acids (e.g., DNA).

gustatory (gus'tah-to''re)
Pertaining to the sense of taste.

gyrus (ju'rus) pl. **gyri** (ji'ri)
One of the ridges or convolutions on the surface of the brain.

habituation
The simplest form of learning; a decrease in response to a repetitive stimulus.

hair cell
A cell having small hairlike extensions; especially the receptor cell for hearing in the organ of Corti and in the semicircular canals.

half-life
The time required for elimination of one-half the quantity of a substance or its property.

hallucinogenic (hah-lu''sĭ-no-jen'ik)
Producing hallucinations.

haploid
Having a single set of chromosomes; the gamete number of chromosomes; one-half.

harmonic
A higher frequency component of a complex sound (i.e., above the fundamental).

hedonic tone
A degree of excitation of an individual's emotional or motivational state.

hemicholinium (hem''e-ko-lin'e-um)
A compound that interferes with the synthesis of the neurotransmitter acetylcholine.

herbivore (her'bĭ-vōr)
A plant-eating animal.

heritability
A measure of the degree to which a phenotype is affected by the genotype; the degree to which a specific trait is heritable.

heroin
A narcotic analgesic drug; an opiate.

hertz
The international unit of frequency; equals one cycle per second.

heterozygous (het''er-o-zi'gus)
Having different alleles at a given locus; often represented by two letters, e.g., *Aa* or *aA*.

hexobarbital (hek''so-bar'bĭ-tal)
A barbiturate sedative and hypnotic; a short-acting agent used as an intravenous general anesthetic.

higher-order hypercomplex receptive field
One type of receptive field of visual cortical neurons in the classification of Hubel and Weisel. These cells require more complex or abstract visual stimuli in order to respond than cells with other less complex receptive fields.

hindbrain
The most posterior of the three subdivisions comprising the embryonic vertebrate brain; gives rise to the myelencephalon and metencephalon.

hippocampus (hip''o-kam'pus)
A large, curved structure in the floor of the lateral ventricle consisting principally of a primitive form of three-layered cerebral cortex.

histofluorescence (his''to-flō-res'ens)
A histological method to locate and examine structures of the brain under ultraviolet light; fluorescence produced in the body by administering a substance before X ray or other examination.

hologram (ho'le-gram)
A three-dimensional image produced by interacting light rays.

homeostasis (ho''me-o-sta'sis)
The tendency for the internal state of an organism to be stable and to return to this condition after being perturbed.

homogenization (ho-moj''e-ni-za'shun)
The act or process of homogenizing.

homogenize (ho-moj'e-nīz)
To blend diverse elements into a smooth mixture. Tissues are usually homogenized in a test-tube-shaped vessel using a pestle.

homoiotherm (ho-moi'o-therm)
An organism who maintains body temperature within narrow limits despite changes in environmental temperature; a so-called warm-blooded animal.

homologous (ho-mol'o-gus)
Corresponding in some dimension such as spatial location; entities having similar structures and derived from a common primitive form.

Homo sapiens (ho''mo sa'pe-enz)
The human species.

homozygous (ho''mo-zi'gus)
Having identical alleles at a given locus; often represented by two letters (e.g., *AA* or *aa*).

horizontal cell
One of the cells in the retina interconnecting elements across the retina; especially cells interconnecting different rods and cones and affecting the transfer of information between receptors and bipolar cells in the retina.

hormone
A chemical substance secreted by certain organs and cells, especially cells of the endocrine and exocrine glands; a chemical messenger secreted by one cell to act on another at a distant site.

hybrid
An animal or plant produced from parents who differ in kind, for example, of different genotypes.

hybrid breakdown
The reduction in evolutionary fitness in offspring of certain matings.

hybrid inviability
The inability of offspring of certain matings to stay alive.

hybrid sterility
Matings that result in offspring that cannot reproduce.

hydrogen bond
The bond between two molecules in which a single hydrogen atom is shared by two negatively charged molecules or portions of molecules.

hydroxyindoleacetic acid
(hi-drok″se-in′dol-ah-se′tik)
A product of serotonin metabolism.

5-hydroxytryptamine or **5-HT**
(hi-drok″se-trip′te-mēn)
Serotonin.

6-hydroxydopamine (hi-drok″se-do′pah-mēn)
A compound toxic to nerve cells, especially nerve cells that contain the neurotransmitters dopamine and norepinephrine.

hyperalgesia (hi″per-al-je′ze-ah)
Increased sensitivity to pain.

hypercomplex receptive field
One type of receptive field of visual cortical cells in the classification of Hubel and Weisel. Neurons with these receptive fields respond to features similarly to cells with simple and complex receptive fields, but also require lines of a specific length.

hyperglycemia (hi″per-gli-se′me-ah)
Abnormally increased content of sugar in the blood.

hyperopia (hi″per-o′pe-ah)
Farsightedness; a condition in which the visual image is brought to focus behind the retina.

hyperphagia (hi″per-fa′je-ah)
Eating to excess; overeating.

hyperpolarization
A change in voltage that renders the cell membrane more polarized; in nerve cells, the change in which the inside of the nerve cell membrane becomes more negative; the result of inhibitory synaptic transmission.

hypersomnia (hi″per-som′ne-ah)
Excessive sleepiness.

hyperthermia (hi″per-ther′me-ah)
Abnormally high body temperature.

hypertonic
A biological term to indicate a solution more concentrated than its reference solution; having higher osmotic pressure than a surrounding medium.

hypertrophy (hi-per′tro-fe)
An increase in function or size of a tissue or gland.

hyperventilation (hy″per-ven″tĭ-la′shun)
Abnormally long, rapid, deep breathing.

hypnogogic hallucination (hip″nah-goj′ik)
A vivid sensory image at the onset of sleep that often provokes fear or anxiety.

hypnotic (hip-not′ik)
A drug that induces sleep.

hypokinesia (hi''po-ki-ne′ze-ah)
Abnormal decrease in ability to move.

hypophysis (hi-pof′ĭ-sis)
The pituitary gland.

hypothalamic hyperphagia
See ventromedial hypothalamic syndrome.

hypothalamic-hypophyseal portal system
(hi''po-thal′ah-mik-hi''po-fiz′e-al)
The very extensive network of blood vessels
between the hypothalamus and pituitary gland.

hypothalamus (hi''po-thal′ah-mus)
A group of nuclei near the base of the brain
controlling the pituitary gland and involved in a
variety of behaviors including eating, drinking,
sleeping, and sexual behavior.

hypothermia (hi''po-ther′me-ah)
Lowered body temperature.

hypotonic
A biological term to indicate a solution less
concentrated than its reference solution; having
lower osmotic pressure than a surrounding
medium.

hypotrophy (hi-pot′ro-fe)
A decrease in function of a tissue or gland.

hypovolemia (hi''po-vo-le′me-ah)
An abnormal decrease in volume of the body
fluid.

hypoxemia (hi''pok-se′me-ah)
A deficiency of oxygen in the blood.

ICSH
See interstitial cell-stimulating hormone.

imipramine (ĭ-mip′rah-mēn)
An antidepressant drug believed to act in part by
blocking the reuptake of norepinephrine into the
presynaptic terminals.

immediate memory
The hypothetical memory system in which
information may be held for periods of several
seconds.

immunoglobulin (im''u-no-glob′u-lin)
A blood protein of animals that acts as an
antibody.

inactivation
The cessation or destruction of biological activity;
especially the cessation of sodium ion
permeability occurring during an action potential.

inbred strain
A population of individuals obtained by
inbreeding.

inbreeding
The mating of individuals related to each other
more closely than by chance.

indole ring (in′dōl)
The indole portion of certain molecules; the
molecular structure in which carbon, hydrogen,
and nitrogen form a configuration resembling a
ring.

inferior colliculus (ko-lik′u-lus)
A nucleus in the brain stem auditory pathways
intermediate in the pathway between the cochlear
nucleus and the medial geniculate body.

inferior olive
A nucleus in the brain stem receiving projections
from the spinal cord, brain stem, and cerebral
cortex and projecting to the cerebellum.

inferotemporal cortex
(in''fer-o-tem′po-ral kor′teks)
A region of cerebral cortex lying along the
inferior (lower) portion of the temporal lobe.

inferred process
A process such as memory storage whose
existence is inferred from an observable event
such as a specific behavior.

infrared
Thermal radiation of wavelength greater than the
red end of the visible light spectrum.

infundibulum (in''fun-dib′u-lum)
The stalk connecting the pituitary gland to the
brain.

inhibitory postsynaptic potential or **IPSP**
The hyperpolarization of a nerve cell resulting from inhibitory synaptic transmission.

innervate
To contact or make connection by way of nerve fibers.

innervation
The supply of nerves to a given structure.

innervation ratio
A number describing the density of innervation by motor neurons for a given muscle; especially the number of muscle fibers contacted by a single motor neuron. A low innervation ratio signifies a lack of precise control, while a high innervation ratio indicates considerable precision of control.

insectivore (in-sek′tĭ-vōr)
An insect-eating plant or animal.

insomnia
Inability to sleep.

instrumental learning
A form of learning in which an organism's behavior is instrumental in obtaining a goal.

insulin
A hormone secreted by the pancreas and important in metabolism of carbohydrates, lipids, and amino acids.

intensity
The degree of strength, force, or energy.

interaural line (in″ter-aw′ral)
In stereotaxis, an imaginary line through the head connecting the ears.

interference theory
The view that new learning interferes with old memory, which is partly responsible for forgetting.

internal capsule
A large mass of axons on each side of the brain interconnecting the cerebral hemispheres with structures lower in the brain and spinal cord.

internuncial (in″ter-nun′she-al)
Serving to connect sensory and motor neurons; a synonym for interneuron.

interoceptive
A general term for sensation of stimulation from within (inside the body).

interstitial cell-stimulating hormone or **ICSH** (in″ter-stish′al)
Luteinizing hormone.

intersynaptic filament (in″ter-sĭ-nap′tik)
One of the fine, threadlike extensions that appear to join the presynaptic and postsynaptic cells across the synapse.

intracranial (in″trah-kra′ne-al)
Within the brain.

intrafusal muscle fiber
A muscle fiber specialized to act as a sensory receptor (the muscle spindle organ).

intramuscular
Within muscle tissue.

intraperitoneal (in″trah-per″ĭ-to-ne′al)
Within the peritoneal cavity.

intravenous
Within a vein.

intraventricular (in″trah-ven-trik′u-lar)
Within the ventricles of the brain.

invertebrate (in-ver′te-brāt)
Having no spinal column, that is, a vertebral column and spinal cord.

ion (i′on)
An electrically charged atom or group of atoms.

ionophore (i′o-no-for″)
A pore through which ions flow.

iproniazid (i″pro-ni′ah-zid)
A monoamine oxidase inhibitor preventing the breakdown of catecholamines by the enzyme monoamine oxidase, as well as other reactions. The compound is used as a stimulant.

ipsilateral (ip″sĭ-lat′er-al)
Affecting or being on the same side of the body.

iris
The ring of muscle fibers forming the pupil of the eyeball.

ischemia (is-ke′me-ah)
Deficiency of blood in some part of the body including the brain.

isogenic (i-so-jen′ik)
Having essentially identical genes (e.g., identical twins).

isolating mechanism
A trait or function serving to isolate species from each other in terms of reproduction.

isoproterenol (i″so-pro″te-re′nol)
A drug used to stimulate certain adrenergic receptors in the brain and elsewhere; specifically, a beta-adrenergic agonist; used to stimulate the heart, dilate the bronchia, etc.

James-Lange theory of emotion
The theory that emotions correspond to the peripheral physiological changes that occur when emotions are extant.

karyotype (kar′e-o-tīp)
The chromosomal makeup of the nucleus of a cell; the photomicrograph of a chromosomal arrangement.

kidney
One of the two organs located behind and below the stomach that filter the blood and excrete urine.

kindling effect
The progressive development of seizures following repeated stimulation of certain regions of the brain, especially the amygdala.

Klinefelter's syndrome
A condition associated with an abnormality of the sex chromosomes and characterized by retarded development of the gonads, mental retardation, etc. In this condition the chromosome karyotype is XXY.

Klüver-Bucy syndrome
A constellation of symptoms including the tendency to examine things orally, lack of drive, and hypersexuality that occurs after bilateral temporal lobectomy in which important limbic structures are destroyed.

Korsakoff's syndrome
Severe alcoholic psychosis that includes memory defects, hallucinations, and other symptoms of mental confusion.

labeled-line theory
The concept that specific nerves or pathways carry specific information and exclude other types of information. For example, fibers of the optic nerve carry only visual information, but no information for touch, and are therefore a labeled line for vision.

labyrinth (lab′ĭ-rinth)
A maze of interconnecting canals or spaces; especially the bone-enclosed canals and spaces of the inner ear.

larva pl. **larvae**
A stage in the life cycle of certain organisms (e.g., flies), often wormlike.

lateral
Away from the midline of the body or of a structure; opposed to medial.

lateral cervical nucleus
A small nucleus located in the upper segments of the spinal cord, especially part of the somatosensory system.

lateral geniculate nucleus (je-nik′u-lāt nu′kle-us)
The nucleus in the thalamus responsible for relaying information from the optic tracts to the visual cortex.

lateral hypothalamic syndrome
A constellation of behavioral and physiological changes that occurs when the region in or near the lateral hypothalamus is destroyed on both sides of the brain; the behavioral deficits of aphagia and adipsia, etc.

lateral hypothalamus
The region of the hypothalamus farthest from the midline of the brain.

lateral inhibition
The phenomenon in many neural structures of excitation at one point producing inhibition in adjacent points; in the retina, the phenomenon in which light stimulation at one point on the retina produces inhibition in a surrounding region; a principle of organization of the nervous tissue by which differences in the pattern of input may be enhanced.

lateral plexus
A network of nerve fibers (or lymph vessels, veins) positioned away from the midline (lateral).

lateral reticular nucleus
A nucleus in the reticular formation of the medulla which projects in part to the cerebellum.

law of effect
The dictum credited to Thorndike that the effect of an organism's behavior in part determines its future occurrence, e.g., behaviors that are effective in procuring food or escaping from noxious stimulation tend to recur and those that are not effective tend to decline.

law of independent assortment
Mendel's second law which states that the factors (genes) passed from parent to offspring do so independently of each other.

law of segregation
Mendel's first law which states that each parent possesses two factors (genes) which determine a particular trait and that one of them from each parent (either dominant or recessive) is passed on to the offspring.

law of specific nerve energies
The dictum credited to Johannes Müller that certain nerves are specific to certain types of sensory information; the optic nerve carries information about light but not about touch, sound, etc. *See also* labeled line theory.

LD$_{50}$
That dose of a drug which is lethal to 50 percent of the subjects to whom it is administered.

learned helplessness
A behavioral phenomenon in which prior exposure to noxious stimulation from which escape is impossible leads to inability to later perform responses that are successful in procuring escape.

learning set
A complex learning task in which the subject is given many kinds of discrimination problems to master and is said to form a learning set if the subject is able to master the same kinds of problems later with greater efficiency. Also called learning to learn.

lectin
A general term for substances that cause blood cells to aggregate, or clump together.

lemniscal system (lem-nis′kal)
A series of pathways and structures involved in the reception and analysis of certain bodily sensations, especially light touch; named after the large fiber bundle in the brain stem that forms a part of this system, the medial lemniscus.

lens
A transparent piece of glass or other substance capable of bending (refracting) light; the transparent biconvex body in the eye that is part of the refracting mechanism of the eye. Convex lenses curve outward and concave lenses curve inward.

Lesch-Nyhan syndrome
A rare male sex-linked genetic disorder that results in mental retardation, cerebral palsy, compulsive biting of the lips and fingers, kidney disorders, etc.

lesion (le′zhun)
Abnormal change such as loss of function in an organ due to injury or disease; in this book, especially a region of the brain destroyed by experimental means.

leucine (lu′sin)
An amino acid.

leucotomy
See frontal lobotomy.

LH
See luteinizing hormone.

limbic system (lim′bik)
A general term for a group of structures in the forebrain including the hippocampus and dentate gyrus, cingulate gyrus, the septal region, and sometimes the amygdala. In human beings and many other mammals the limbic system is presumed to be involved in emotional and many other classes of behavior.

linkage
In genetics, a set of genes occurring at different loci on the same chromosome, but tending to act as a single set and to not undergo independent assortment.

lipid (lip′id)
A fat; one of a group of substances including fatty acids, neutral fats, waxes, and steroids that are insoluble in water and soluble in alcohol and similar solvents.

lipofuscin
Any one of a class of pigmented fats.

lipostatic theory of hunger (lip″o-stat′ik)
The view that hunger is regulated in part by the level of a specific chemical that signals the total amount of fat in the body.

lithium (lith′e-um)
A metal; especially the salt of lithium used as a tranquilizer.

lobectomy (lo-bek′to-me)
Removal or destruction of a lobe of the brain; especially frontal lobectomy, an operation in which the frontal lobes or portions of the frontal lobes (e.g., prefrontal lobectomy) are surgically removed or destroyed.

lobotomy
See frontal lobotomy.

locus (lo′kus) pl. **loci** (lo′si)
The specific site of a gene on a chromosome.

locus coeruleus (se-ru′le-us)
A nucleus in the brain stem near the midline comprised mostly of noradrenergic nerve cells.

long-term memory
A general term for memory lasting for a long period of time, for example, hours, days, or years.

lordosis (lor-do′sis)
A characteristic arching of the back and sideward movement of the tail by the receptive female rat in response to mounting by the male.

loudness
The subjective experience of sound intensity, heard as loud, soft, etc.

LTH
See luteotropic hormone.

luteal phase (lu′te-al)
The phase of the estrous cycle during which the corpus luteum develops; approximately the last half of the human menstrual cycle.

luteinizing hormone or **LH** (lu′te-in-iz″ing)
A hormone secreted by the anterior lobe of the pituitary gland which stimulates ovulation, the growth of the corpus luteum, and the testes to produce androgens.

luteotropic hormone or **LTH** (lu″te-o-trop′ik)
A hormone secreted by the anterior pituitary gland which functions to maintain the corpus luteum in some species and in the production and secretion of milk by the mammary glands; sometimes called prolactin.

lysergic acid diethylamide or **LSD**
(li-ser′jik as′id di-eth′il-am-id)
A powerful hallucinogenic drug.

lysosome (li′so-sōm)
One of the small bodies containing digestive enzymes seen with the electron microscope in many types of cells.

Mach band
One of the bands of light and dark that occur at the juncture of specific patterns of changing light intensity.

macula (mak′u-lah) pl. **maculae** (mak′u-le)
The small sensory organ within the utricle and saccule consisting of hair cells and overlying otolith.

mammary gland (mam'er-e)
One of the two glands that in female mammals are situated on the breast and secrete milk to nurse the newborn.

mammilothalamic tract (mam''mil-o-thah-lam'ik trakt)
A bundle of nerve fibers projecting from the mammillary bodies to the thalamus.

mania (ma'ne-ah)
Overexcitement, impulsivity, compulsiveness; a state of extreme excitement or agitation.

manic-depressive psychosis
A severe mental disturbance characterized by wide fluctuations in mood between mania (overexcitement, impulsivity, compulsiveness) and depression (extreme underexcitement, feelings of worthlessness, guilt, apprehension, and despair).

Marchi (mar'ke)
A histological method of staining the myelin around axons of nerve cells undergoing degeneration.

mecamylamine (mek''ah-mil'ah-min)
A compound that antagonizes neurotransmission at nicotinic cholinergic synapses and hence a nicotinic antagonist; used as an antihypertensive drug.

mechanical isolation
The reproductive isolation of species or groups of organisms because of differences in location, size, shape, etc., of the sexual organs.

medial
Toward the midline of the body or a structure; opposed to lateral.

medial forebrain bundle
A large, relatively diffuse bundle of primarily ascending nerve fibers passing near the midline of the brain between the brain stem and cerebral cortex; a common site for intracranial self-stimulation.

medial geniculate nucleus (je-nik'u-lāt)
The sensory relay nucleus in the thalamus responsible for relaying auditory information to the cerebral cortex.

medial lemniscus (lem-nis'kus)
A large band of ascending nerve fibers carrying somatosensory information through the brain stem.

median eminence
The portion of the hypothalamus which lies just above the infundibulum at the base of the hypothalamus.

meiosis (mi-o'sis)
The process of cell division by gametes (sperm and ova); also called reductional division of cells.

melanin (mel'ah-nin)
Dark pigment of the skin and other tissues.

melanocyte-stimulating hormone or **MSH** (mel'ah-no-sīt-)
A hormone secreted by the anterior lobe of the pituitary gland which controls skin pigmentation.

melatonin (mel''ah-tōn'in)
A hormone manufactured in the pineal gland that may be important in sexual development and other physiological and behavioral functions.

membrane potential
The voltage difference that exists across the semipermeable cell membrane.

memory trace
The hypothetical entity or process that underlies the ability to remember; also called engram.

meprobamate (me-pro'bah-māt)
A minor tranquilizer with various trade names (e.g., Miltown, Equanil).

mescaline (mes'kah-lin)
A poisonous alkaloid with hallucinatory properties.

mesencephalon (mes''en-sef'ah-lon)
The midbrain and one of the five major subdivisions of the vertebrate brain.

mesolimbic pathway
A group of dopamine-containing neurons with cell bodies in the ventral segmental area whose axons ascend to the forebrain, especially structures in the limbic system.

mesotelencephalic pathway
The major dopamine pathway in the brain that includes the nigro-neostriatal bundle and the mesolimbic pathway. Portions of the mesotelencephalic pathway are involved in reward.

messenger RNA or **mRNA**
A fraction of RNA; specifically, the RNA that carries genetic information from the nucleus to the cytoplasm.

metabolism
The physical and chemical processes by which cells maintain life; especially the processes of anabolism (by which foods are built up into protoplasm) and catabolism (by which substances are broken down into simpler ones with the release of energy for cellular work).

metabolite
A substance produced by metabolism. *See also* metabolism.

metencephalon (met″en-sef′ah-lon)
One of the five major subdivisions of the vertebrate brain.

methadone (meth′ah-dōn)
A narcotic analgesic drug; an opiate.

methamphetamine (meth″am-fet′ah-men)
A central nervous system stimulant; a form of amphetamine.

microelectrode
One of the very thin wires or glass capillary tubes filled with a conductive solution used to record the activity of single nerve cells or small populations of nerve cells.

microsome (mi′kro-sōm)
A fraction of cellular material consisting of endoplasmic reticulum and ribosomes obtained by centrifugation.

microtome (mi′kro-tōm)
An instrument used to slice very thin sections of tissue for microscopic observation.

midbrain
The middle of three subdivisions comprising the embryonic vertebrate brain; also called the mesencephalon to which it gives rise during development.

mineralocorticoid (min″er-al-o-kor′ti-koid)
A class of hormones secreted by the adrenal cortex important in maintaining appropriate levels of sodium, chloride, and bicarbonate ions in the body.

mirror focus
An abnormal region of the cerebral cortex that develops in correspondence to a region on the opposite side of the brain stimulated to produce a localized region of seizure activity; a model for possible mechanisms underlying memory.

mitochondrion (mi″to-kon′dre-on) pl.
mitochondria
A small, spherical or rod-shaped organelle in the cytoplasm of cells. Mitochondria are responsible for the energy-producing reactions of cells (cellular respiration).

mitosis (mi-to′sis)
The process of cell division by somatic cells (i.e., not gametes or sex cells); also called equational division.

mitral cells (mi′tral)
One of two vertically oriented cell types in the olfactory bulb that receives information from the olfactory nerve fibers.

model system
Any organism or experimental preparation that can be studied as a model for various phenomena or processes in other organisms; especially, a system useful as a model for understanding human behavior and the biological mechanisms that underlie it.

molecular genetics
The field of study concerned with the physical nature (molecular structure) of genes and their functions in cell division, etc.

molecule (mol′e-kūl)
An aggregation of two or more atoms.

monoamine oxidase (mon″o-am-in ok′sĭ-dās)
An enzyme that breaks down catecholamines and is believed to occur inside nerve terminals as well as in nonnervous tissue; also catalyzes the conversion of 5-hydroxytryptamine (serotonin) to its metabolite, 5-hydroxyindolacetate.

monoamine oxidase inhibitor
Any compound that prevents (inhibits) the catalytic action of monoamine oxidase, i.e., any drug that prevents the breakdown of catecholamines by monoamine oxidase; a class of drugs used to treat depression.

monochromatic light (mon″o-kro-mat′ik)
Light having a single wavelength.

monocular (mon-ok′u-lar)
Pertaining to one eye.

monocular dominance
Dominance of response of one eye over response of the other eye.

monomer (mon′o-mer)
A simple molecule capable of combining into repeating units to form larger units (polymers).

monosynaptic
Relayed through only one synapse.

monozygotic (mon″o-zi-got′ik)
Derived from the same fertilized egg (zygote); as identical twins.

Moro's reflex
In infants, a reflexive, outward, embracing motion of the arms following a sudden noise or other startling stimulus.

morphine (mor′fēn)
A narcotic analgesic; an opiate.

morphological (mor″fo-loj′ĭ-kal)
Pertaining to the shape, form, or structure (morphology) of plants and animals.

morphology (mor-fol′o-je)
The science or study of the shape, form, or structure of plants and animals.

mossy fiber
One of the excitatory inputs to the cerebellum.

motive
A state that brings about behavior; especially, the force that incites individuals to behave in certain ways, and especially to seek certain goals.

motoneuron (mo″to-nu′ron)
See motor neuron.

motor neuron
One of the neurons having their cell bodies in the brain and spinal cord, with axons that leave the central nervous system to innvervate various muscles, organs, and glands; especially, the motor neurons of the spinal cord that innervate striated muscle as well as other target structures; neurons carrying information away from the central nervous system.

motor unit
An individual motor neuron and all muscle fibers with which it makes synaptic contact.

Müllerian duct (mil-e′re-an)
The feminine portion of the primitive sexual structures of the developing embryo.

Müllerian inhibiting substance or **MIS**
A hormone secreted by the testes during early development preventing the development of the Müllerian ducts.

multiple unit activity
The electrical discharges produced by a population of nerve cells; the activity of two or more nerve cells.

multipolar
Having many poles; a cell with many extensions projecting from the cell body.

muscarine (mus′kah-rin)
A substance in mushrooms that stimulates certain cholinoceptive targets in the peripheral and central nervous system; a highly poisonous alkaloid compound.

muscarinic
Responsive to muscarine; denotes receptors for acetylcholine that are also affected by muscarine.

muscle fiber
The structural unit of muscle. Each muscle fiber is a single cell formed by the fusion of many cells and hence contains a number of nuclei. In short muscles the fiber may extend the entire length of the muscle, while in longer muscles, fibers attach to one another.

muscle spindle organ
A special receptor in muscles which signals degree of stretch; sometimes termed the intrafusal muscle fiber.

myelencephalon (mi''el-en-sef'ah-lon)
The most posterior of the five major subdivisions of the vertebrate brain.

myelin (mi'e-lin)
The white, fatty substance surrounding many nerve cell axons.

myofibril (mi''o-fi'bril)
One of the smaller fibers making up the individual muscle fibers and comprised of thick and thin protein filaments of actin and myosin.

myopia (mi-o'pe-ah)
Nearsightedness; a condition in which the visual image is brought to focus in front of the retina.

myosin (mi'o-sin)
One of the proteins in muscle which together with the protein actin is responsible for muscle contraction and relaxation; also present in nerve cells and other cells.

nalorphine (nal-or'fēn)
A compound that antagonizes the action of opiates and hence an opiate antagonist.

nanometer (na''no-me'ter)
One-billionth of a meter; equal to 10 Ångstrom units.

narcolepsy (nar'ko-lep''se)
A disorder of sleep characterized by recurrent, irresistible attacks of sleep.

narcotic analgesic
A compound derived from opium that produces behavioral depression and sleep (narcosis) and relieves pain (analgesic), for example, morphine, heroin, codeine, and methadone.

natural selection
The survival of individuals and their offspring who are better equipped to adapt to their environment and to reproduce.

N-dimethyltryptamine (-di-meth''il-trip'tah-mēn)
A powerful hallucinogenic compound having certain structural similarities to the neurotransmitter serotonin.

NE
See norepinephrine.

negative reinforcement
Any stimulus or situation whose removal tends to increase the occurrence of a response.

neocortex (ne''o-kor'teks)
The six-layered dorsal region of the cerebral cortex presumed to be the most advanced type of cortex.

nerve
One of the bundles of nerve fibers found outside the central nervous system that conveys impulses to and from the nervous system or other parts of the body.

neurasthenic insomnia (nu''ras-then'ik)
A disorder of sleep characterized by subjective reports of inability to fall asleep easily and difficulty in staying asleep.

neurilemma (nu''ri-lem'mah)
The insulating sheath that wraps around nerve fibers in the peripheral nervous system; also called the myelin sheath.

neuroblastoma (nu''ro-blas-to'mah)
A type of cancerous nerve cell. These cells are often grown in tissue culture for scientific investigation.

neurohumor
Any chemical substance secreted by nerve cells; any chemical substance in the body that affects nerve cells.

neurohypophysis (nu''ro-hi-pof'ĭ-sis)
The posterior lobe of the pituitary gland.

neuromuscular junction
The synapse between nerve cells and muscle.

neurotransmitter (nu″ro-tranz-mit′er)
The chemical substance released by one nerve cell to act on another at the synapse; the chemical by which nerve cells transmit information.

nicotine (nik′o-tin)
A compound present in some plants, especially tobacco leaves; one of a number of alkaloid compounds found in plants considered poisonous and used as insecticides. This substance stimulates certain cholinoceptive targets such as striated muscle.

nicotinic
Pertaining to nicotine or nicotinic acid. Especially receptors affected by acetylcholine, and nicotine, for example, receptors in striated muscle, are said to be nicotinic.

nictitating membrane (nik′ti-tāt″ing)
A special membrane present in the eye of many animals such as cats and rabbits capable of covering the eye in response to a puff of air or other stimulus causing blinking.

nigro-neostriatal bundle (ni″gro-ne″o-stri-a′tal)
A bundle of axons originating in the substantia nigra of the mesencephalon and terminating in the neostriatum on the same side of the brain. This pathway utilizes dopamine as a neurotransmitter and is eventually destroyed in patient's with Parkinson's disease.

Nissl stain
A histological stain which reacts primarily with the Nissl substance of cells.

Nissl substance
A portion of the reticulum in the cytoplasm of nerve cells; also called chromatin granules, Nissl bodies, etc.

nodes of Ranvier (rahn-ve-a)
Small areas along the myelin sheath surrounding nerve cell axons.

nonassociative learning
Learning that does not require formation of an association between two stimuli; refers to such forms of learning as habituation and sensitization, in which stimulus pairing is not involved.

nonopponent cell
A functional category of DeValois and Jacobs of neurons in the lateral geniculate nucleus. This type of neuron is excited or inhibited to varying degrees by different wavelengths of light.

nonoxidative metabolism
A type of metabolism that does not require oxygen or glycolysis; also called anaerobic metabolism.

norepinephrine (nor″ep-ĭ-nef′rin)
A molecule secreted by the adrenal medulla and by certain neurons. Norepinephrine is the neurotransmitter used by postganglionic fibers of the sympathetic division of the autonomic nervous system and by numerous groups of noradrenergic nerve cells in the brain.

nucleolus (nu-kle′o-lus) pl. **nucleoli**
A small, round dense body within the nucleus that contains RNA.

nucleoplasm (nu′kle-o-plazm)
The watery substance of the nucleus in which many molecules are suspended; the material between identifiable structures in the nucleus of a cell.

nucleotide (nu′kle-o-tīd)
The compound consisting of a sugar, a phosphate, and a base that forms the basic structural unit of DNA.

nucleus (nu′kle-us) pl. **nuclei** (nu′kle-i)
The central mass in most cells that controls all cellular function and contains the genetic material DNA.

nucleus cuneatus (ku″ne-a′tus)
A somatosensory relay nucleus in the brain stem near the junction of the brain and spinal cord; a nucleus of the lemniscal system.

nucleus gracilis (gra-sil′is)
A somatosensory relay nucleus in the brain stem near the junction of the medulla and spinal cord; a nucleus of the lemniscal system.

nucleus of the inferior olive
See inferior olive.

nucleus medialis dorsalis (nu′kle-us me-de-al-is dor-sa′lis)
A nucleus of the thalamus having connections with the hypothalamus and other subcortical regions, the cerebral cortex and other thalamic nuclei.

nucleus pontis (nu′kle-us pon′tis)
Cell groups in the pons which receive projections from cerebral cortex and send axons to the cerebellum through the middle cerebellar peduncle.

occipital (ok-sip′i-tal)
Pertaining to the occipital bone.

oculomotor nucleus
One of the nuclei in the brain stem that gives rise to fibers of the oculomotor nerve and innervates certain muscles of the eye.

oddity problem
A type of learning set; an example of concept formation in animals. The subject must learn to choose the odd object of any set of three objects in which two are the same.

olfactory (ol-fak′to-re)
Pertaining to the sense of smell.

olfactory bulb
The bulblike extension of the olfactory tract on the undersurface of the frontal lobe.

olfactory epithelium (ep′′i-the′le-um)
The special layer of cells and mucus located in the roof of the nasal passages.

olfactory nerve
One of the nerves of smell consisting of about 20 bundles arising in the olfactory epithelium.

oligodendroglia (ol′′i-go-den-drog′le-ah)
The cells that wrap around axons in the central nervous system, insulating them with myelin.

olivocochlear bundle (ol′′i-vo-kok′le-ar)
A descending pathway of the auditory system arising from the superior olive and terminating in the cochlea and important in the efferent control of auditory input.

ommatidium (om′′ah-tid′e-um) pl. **ommatidia**
An element of the compound eye of the horseshoe crab *Limulus*. Each ommatidium has its own lens and groups of receptor cells.

omnivorous (om-niv′o-rus)
Feeding on both animal and plant substances.

ontogenetic (on′′to-je-net′ik)
Relating to ontogeny, that is, to the development or life cycle of a single individual.

ontogeny (on-toj′e-ne)
The development or life cycle of a single individual.

operant conditioning
A training procedure in which a response (the operant) is consistently followed with reinforcement (e.g., a reward).

opponent neuron
A functional category of DeValois and Jacobs of neurons in the lateral geniculate nucleus. This type of cell responds maximally to one wavelength of light and maximally decreases firing rate to another wavelength of light.

opponent process theory
Hering's theory of color vision in which different color systems oppose one another.

opsin (op′sin)
A complex protein molecule which is one of the constituents (precursors) from which rhodopsin (photopigment in rods) is made.

optic chiasma (ki-as′mah)
That place where some fibers of the optic nerves cross over to the other side of the brain.

optic nystagmus (nis-tag′mus)
Rapid, involuntary movements of the eyes.

optic tract
The bundle of nerve fibers inside the central nervous system that originates in the retina of the eye and is an extension of the optic nerve.

oral
Pertaining to the mouth.

organ of Corti (kor-te)
The receptor organ for hearing located in the cochlea.

organelle (or''gan-el)
Any of the small structures contained within a single cell such as the mitochondrion.

organophosphate
One of many experimental compounds that inhibits the activity of the enzyme acetylcholinesterase and thus prevents the degradation of acetylcholine at synapses.

orienting reaction
A set of physiological and behavioral changes that occurs when a sudden or novel stimulus is encountered including orientation of the head toward the source of the stimulus, desynchronization of the electroencephalogram, etc.

orienting reflex
See orienting reaction.

oscilloscope (o-sil'o-skōp)
An electronic instrument that displays electrical potentials.

osmoreceptor (oz''mo-re-cep'tor)
A receptor that responds to osmotic pressure.

osmosis (os-mo'sis)
The movement of water or other solvent by means of osmotic pressure.

osmotic pressure (os-mot'ik)
The tendency for water or other solvent to move from a region of low concentration to a region of higher concentration when the two are separated by a semipermeable membrane which allows solvents but not solutes to pass.

ossicle (os'sī-k'l)
A bone, especially one of the three small bones of the middle ear, the malleus, incus, and stapes.

otolith (o'to-lith)
The small, cup-shaped, gelatinous cap overlying the hair cells in the maculae of the utricle and saccule.

oval window
A small membrane on the cochlea to which the stapes, one of the bones of the middle ear, is connected and which it vibrates during sound stimulation.

ovary (o'vah-re)
The female gonad; the gland that produces egg cells (ova).

overnight decrement
The decrease in performance in responding to electrical stimulation of the brain that occurs from one day's training to the next.

oxidative metabolism
Metabolism that requires oxygen; sometimes called cellular respiration.

oxytocin (ok''se-to'sin)
A hormone manufactured by cells of the hypothalamus and stored in the posterior lobe of the pituitary gland. This hormone causes the smooth muscles of the uterus to contract and releases milk from the mammary glands.

pacemaker neuron
Any neuron that functions to trigger a regular, cyclic event such as breathing, heartbeat, certain brain waves, etc.

pacinian corpuscle (pah-sin'e-an)
A specialized sensory receptor that responds to mechanical pressure.

pancreas (pan'kre-as)
An endocrine gland located behind the stomach. It secretes insulin and glucagon in addition to a variety of digestive enzymes.

papilla (pah-pil'ah) pl. **papillae** (pah-pil'e)
A small nipple-shaped projection or elevation on tissue.

para-chlorophenylalanine or **p-CPA**
(par''ah-klo''ro-fen''il-al'ah-nīn)
A compound used experimentally to reduce levels of serotonin in the brain and elsewhere. This substance inhibits the activity of the enzyme tryptophan hydroxylase.

paradoxical sleep
See rapid eye movement sleep.

parasomnia (par″ah-som′ne-ah)
A disorder of sleep in which behaviors that would normally occur during wakefulness (e.g., walking, talking) occur during sleep.

parasympathetic branch
The portion of the autonomic division of the peripheral nervous system responsible for the conservation of energy; enters or exits from the cranial and sacral regions of the spinal cord.

parasympatholytic (par″ah-sim″pah-tho-lit′ik)
Any agent that counteracts or acts opposite to the actions of the parasympathetic division of the autonomic nervous system; especially opposes the effects of acetylcholine at synapses in the parasympathetic division.

parasympathomimetic
(par″ah-sim″pah-tho-mi-met′ik)
Any agent that mimics the actions of the parasympathetic division of the autonomic nervous system; especially an agent that mimics the effects of acetylcholine at synapses of the parasympathetic division.

parathyroid gland (par″ah-thi′roid)
An endocrine gland located near the thyroid gland that secretes parathormone, a hormone important in the metabolism of phosphorous and calcium.

paraventricular nuclei (par″ah-ven-trik′u-lar)
Nuclei in the dorsal hypothalamus near the walls of the third ventricle, important in the control of the pituitary gland.

parenteral (par-en′ter-al)
Not by way of the alimentary canal but rather by some other route, for example, injection into muscle, subcutaneous tissue, or intraperitoneal cavity.

pargyline (par′je-lin)
A compound used to inhibit the activity of the enzyme monoamine oxidase and hence a monoamine oxidase inhibitor; used as an antihypertensive medication.

Parkinson's disease
A disturbance of motor behavior characterized by rigidity, tremor, and inability to initiate voluntary movements.

pars intermedia (pars in″ter-me′de-ah)
The part in between; especially the pars intermedia of the pituitary gland.

partial reinforcement
Reinforcement given less often than every time the operant (behavioral) response occurs.

parturition (par″tu-rish′un)
The act or process of giving birth.

passive avoidance
An experimental task in which the subject can avoid an aversive stimulus by not responding (i.e., being passive).

pathogen
A microorganism or substance that produces disease.

pathological
Having or pertaining to disease or abnormality.

pavor nocturnus (pa′vor noc-tur′nus)
"Night terrors"; frightening dreams that awaken young children in apparent terror, but that are generally not remembered subsequently.

peduncle (pe-dunk′l)
A large bundle of nerve fibers.

pellet (pel′et)
The sediment at the bottom of a centrifuge tube containing particles of highest weight or density; to be distinguished from the remaining portion, the supernatant.

pentylenetetrazol (pen′ti-lēn-tet′rah-zol)
A convulsant drug; trade name, Metrazol.

peptide (pep′tīd)
A compound consisting of a group of two or more amino acids. Some peptides are believed to function as hormones or neurotransmitters.

periaqueductal (per″e-ak″we-duk′tal)
Around or surrounding the small opening between the third and fourth ventricles.

periglomerular cells (per″ĭ-glo-mer′u-lar)
One of the horizontally oriented cells in the olfactory bulb responsible for interactions between different regions of the olfactory bulb (lateral interactions).

perikaryon (per″ĭ-kar′e-on)
That portion of the nerve cell body, or soma, surrounding the nucleus.

perilymph (per′ĭ-limf)
The fluid surrounding the membranous sac containing the organ of Corti and fluid-filled semicircular canals. In the cochlea perilymph occurs in the scala vestibuli and scala tympani.

peripheral nervous system
All nervous tissue lying outside the brain and spinal cord.

periventricular
Around or surrounding the ventricles of the brain.

perseveration of central sets (per-sev″er-a′shun)
The term used by Mishkin to describe the deficit in monkeys following damage to the frontal lobes; a syndrome in which the animal appears to find it difficult to change behavior from one situation to the next.

PGO wave
One of the large, spikelike waves that occurs in the electroencephalogram as recorded from the pons, lateral geniculate nucleus, and occipital cortex during REM sleep.

pH
The symbol denoting the acidity or alkalinity of a solution. pH of 7 is neutral (not acidic nor basic), while values above are progressively more alkaline (basic) and below are progressively more acidic.

pharmacodynamic tolerance
Tolerance to the effects of a drug due to a decreased response of cells to the agent; opposed to drug dispositional tolerance where increased elimination of the drug produces tolerance to its effect.

phase-locking
Occurrence of an event with regularity at a specific phase of a sine wave.

phenomenon, pl. **phenomena**
Any fact or occurrence that is apparent to the senses and thus can be described, measured, etc.

phenothiazine (fe″no-thi′ah-zēn)
One of a class of antipsychotic drugs with a variety of effects on the central nervous system, especially the ability to block dopaminergic receptors in the brain.

phenotype (fe′no-tīp)
A measurable trait or characteristic; the visible properties of an organism as determined both genetically and environmentally.

phenylalanine (fen″il-al′ah-nīn)
A naturally occurring amino acid.

phenylalanine hydroxylase (hi-drok′si-lās)
The enzyme that catalyzes conversion of the amino acid phenylalanine to the amino acid tyrosine; a liver-specific enzyme.

phenylketonuria or **PKU** (fen″il-ke″to-nu′re-ah)
A heritable metabolic disorder in which the amino acid phenylalanine is not metabolized properly.

phenylpyruvic acid (fen″il-pi-ru′vik)
An abnormal metabolite of phenylalanine in individuals with phenylketonuria.

pheromone (fer′o-mōn)
A volatile chemical produced by an animal that serves as a stimulant especially to individuals of the same species.

phosphocreatine (fos″fo-kre′ah-tin)
A molecule used as a source of energy for muscle contraction.

photochemical
A chemical that reacts with light or other radiation.

photopic (fo-top′ik)
Pertaining to vision in bright light; refers to the light-adapted eye; cone vision.

photopic threshold curve
A graph depicting the lowest energy levels for different wavelengths of light just detectable using photopic (high illumination) vision.

photopigment
A light-sensitive chemical substance in visual receptor cells.

photoreceptor
A receptor cell that responds to light.

phrenology (fre-nol′o-je)
The study of the surface features of the skull as being indicative of personality and intellectual characteristics.

phylogenetic (fi″lo-je-net′ik)
Pertaining to evolutionary development.

phylogeny (fi-loj′e-ne)
The evolutionary development of a species or other group of organisms.

physical dependence
The state in which an individual depends upon a drug to prevent the severe physiological reactions that occur with abstinence; the condition in which an individual experiences withdrawal reactions when a drug is abruptly discontinued.

physostigmine (fi″so-stig′min)
A compound used as an acetylcholinesterase inhibitor to prevent degradation of acetylcholine at synapses; an alkaloid compound extracted from certain plant seeds to produce meiosis (pupillary contraction); also called eserine.

picrotoxin (pik″ro-tok′sin)
A convulsant drug believed to act in part by blocking certain inhibitory processes in the central nervous system, especially presynaptic inhibition.

pilocarpine (pi″lo-kar′pin)
A compound that facilitates neurotransmission at certain cholinergic synapses; specifically, an agonist at muscarinic cholinergic synapses and hence a muscarinic agonist; used in ophthalmology.

pineal gland (pin′e-al)
A small gland located near the center of the brain above and behind the thalamus. The pineal gland contains high concentrations of serotonin and melatonin.

pitch
The subjective experience of sound frequency heard as high, low, etc.

pituitary gland (pĭ-tu′ĭ-tār″e)
A small gland located at the base of the brain beneath the hypothalamus and above the roof of the mouth; the master endocrine gland of the body. *See also* hypophysis.

place theory of hearing
The theory credited to Helmholtz that the place along the basilar membrane activated by a particular sound determines the pitch heard.

place theory of smell
A theory that the place where odors activate the olfactory epithelium determines the kind of smell perceived.

plasma
The fluid part of blood.

pleasure center
Any region of the brain in which electrical stimulation is rewarding; a region of the brain for which experimental animals work to procure direct electrical stimulation.

plexus (plek′sus)
A general term for a network of nerves, lymph vessels, or veins.

poikilotherm (poi-kil′o-therm)
An organism whose body temperature varies with that of the environment; a cold-blooded animal.

polydipsia (pol″e-dip′se-ah)
Excessive or abnormal thirst.

polygenic (pol″e-jēn′ik)
Determined by many different genes.

polyribosome (pol″e-ri′bo-sōm)
A complex or aggregation of ribosomes as they are brought together along the messenger RNA molecule; the site of protein synthesis in cells.

polysensory
Pertaining to more than a single sense; especially, regions of the brain where sensory response is to more than one modality of stimulation.

polysome (pol′e-sōm)
See polyribosome.

polysynaptic (pol″e-sĭ-nap′tik)
Characterized by more than a single synaptic connection.

polyurea (pol″e-u′re-ah)
Excessive secretion of urine.

pons
The region of the brain stem between the medulla and midbrain.

pontogeniculooccipital waves
See PGO waves.

positive reinforcement
Any stimulus or situation that tends to increase the occurrence of a response.

posterior
Toward the tail; situated in back of or affecting the back part of a structure; opposed to anterior.

posterior nuclei
A group of nuclei in the posterior region of the thalamus believed to be in part responsible for relaying certain types of bodily sensations, for example, pain; especially this region in the brain of the cat.

postganglionic
Pertaining to nerves that originate in the ganglia of the autonomic division of the peripheral nervous system to terminate on various target organs; opposed to preganglionic.

postmating barrier
A factor leading to failure of reproductive success including gamete mortality, hybrid inviability, hybrid sterility, and hybrid breakdown.

postparturient (post″par-tu′re-ent)
After giving birth.

postrotatory optic nystagmus
(post-ro′ta-tōr″e op′tik nis-tag′mus)
Rapid, involuntary movement of the eyes that occurs after rotation of the head and body or other stimulation affecting the vestibular apparatus.

postsynaptic cell
The cell which receives information across the synapse, opposed to presynaptic cell.

postsynaptic inhibition
The process of synaptic transmission in which the synaptic transmitter substance released by one cell hyperpolarizes the membrane potential of another cell.

postsynaptic web
A collection of fine, threadlike filaments present in the postsynaptic membrane beneath the synapse.

potassium current
The flow of potassium ions through the cell membrane.

precentral gyrus (ji′rus)
The region of primary motor cortex (in front of the central sulcus) in the human brain.

precursor
In biological processes, a chemical or other substance from which another substance is formed.

predatory aggression
The class of aggressive behaviors related to food getting (predation).

prefrontal cortex
The most anterior portion of the frontal lobes.

preganglionic
Nerve fibers of the autonomic division of the peripheral nervous system that project from the brain or spinal cord to the ganglia of the autonomic division; opposed to postganglionic.

premating barrier
An obstacle to procuring access to a mate including ecological isolation, ethological isolation, and mechanical isolation; a barrier to reproduction between different populations.

preparturient (pre″par-tu′re-ent)
Before giving birth.

presynaptic cell
The cell which transmits information across the synapse; opposed to the postsynaptic cell.

presynaptic inhibition
The process by which one cell regulates the amount of excitatory synaptic transmitter substance that another cell releases onto a third neuron; a decrease in activity of one cell produced by the presynaptic action of another cell.

pretectal nucleus (pre-tek'tal)
One of the nuclei in the brain stem in front of the optic tectum which forms a part of the visual system.

primary auditory cortex
The region of the cerebral cortex presumed responsible for the analysis of sounds, for example, the frequency composition of a melody; the highest level in the auditory pathways, the region to which the medial geniculate nuclei of the thalamus project, etc.

primary light
One of the three colors of light which when combined in varying proportions produces all other colors.

primary somatosensory cortex
(so-mat'o-sen'so-re)
A complex of regions of the cerebral cortex, especially the postcentral gyrus, believed to be responsible for the receipt of various types of bodily sensations such as touch, pressure, etc.; the region of the cerebral cortex to which the nuclei of the ventrobasal complex project.

primary visual cortex
The region of the cerebral cortex presumed responsible for the analysis of visual information; the highest level of the visual pathway; the region of the cerebral cortex to which the lateral geniculate nuclei project.

primary visual system
The visual pathways and structures from the retina to the lateral geniculate nuclei and on to the visual cortex.

Primates
The highest order of mammals, including man, apes, monkeys, and lemurs.

principle of equipotentiality
The principle established by Karl Lashley stating that within limits different regions of the cerebral cortex have equal potential for memory storage.

principle of mass action
The principle established by Karl Lashley stating that within limits, the amount of cerebral cortex destroyed by a lesion determines the degree of resulting deficit, rather than the specific region destroyed.

progesterone (pro-jes'ter-ōn)
The hormone produced by the corpus luteum, adrenal cortex, and placenta, whose function is to prepare the uterus for implantation of the fertilized egg.

prokaryotic cell (pro''kar-e-ot'ik)
A cell which does not contain a nucleus.

prolactin (pro-lak'tin)
See luteotropic hormone.

Prosimii (pro'sime''ī)
A suborder of Primates including tree shrews, lemurs, lorises, and tarsiers.

protein (pro'te-in)
A complex organic molecule consisting of sequences of amino acids. Proteins are the principal constituents of cells, especially their structural elements.

psilocybin (si''lo-si'bin)
A powerful hallucinogenic compound isolated from certain poisonous mushrooms.

psychopharmacology (si''ko-fahr''mah-kol'o-je)
The field of study that utilizes concepts of psychology and pharmacology to explore the behavioral actions of drugs.

psychosis (si-ko'sis)
A severe mental disturbance that includes some loss of contact with reality and sometimes delusions, hallucinations, and disorders of the thought processes.

psychosurgery
Brain surgery performed to alter or relieve behavioral or psychological symptoms.

psychotomimetic (si-kot″o-mi-met′ik)
Being able to induce the characteristics of psychosis; a property of some drugs.

pupil
The opening at the center of the iris through which light passes into the eyeball.

pure tone
A sound consisting of a single frequency.

Purkinje cell (pur-kin′je)
One of the large neurons with extensive dendritic fields in the cortex of the cerebellum.

Purkinje shift
The change in sensitivity to certain wavelengths of light occurring between photopic (light-adapted) and scotopic (dark-adapted) vision.

puromycin (pūr-o-mi′sin)
A powerful antibiotic used in high doses to inhibit protein synthesis in the brain and elsewhere in experimental animals.

putamen (pu-ta′men)
One of the basal ganglia buried inside the cerebral hemispheres.

pyramidal (pi-ram′ĭ-dal)
Shaped like a pyramid.

pyramidal decussation (de″kus-sa′shun)
The region where the fibers of the pyramidal tracts cross the midline of the brain stem.

pyramidal system
The motor system of the brain originating in the cerebral cortex and descending by way of the pyramidal tracts to the brain stem and spinal cord.

pyramidal tract
The long bundle of axons arising from the cerebral cortex (especially the motor cortex) and projecting downward to the brain stem and spinal cord.

pyrogen (pi′ro-jen)
A fever-inducing substance.

quantum (kwon′tum) pl. **quanta**
In the quantum theory one of the very small units into which many forms of energy are subdivided; a small, wavelike package of light energy.

raphe nucleus (ra′fe)
Any of the group of nuclei along the midline of the brain stem that contain the neurotransmitter serotonin.

rapid eye movement sleep or **REM**
The stage of sleep during which rapid movements of the eyes occur, accompanied by a desynchronized electroencephalogram, loss of muscle tone, frequent twitches of the limbs, and a number of other physiological events; the stage of sleep during which most dreaming is presumed to take place.

rare-male advantage
The reproductive success achieved in certain populations by males with rare characteristics.

rate-limiting
Any factor or variable that limits the speed of a reaction or process.

rebound effect
An effect or process that follows another and is generally opposite in direction.

receptive field
A general term for the region of a receptor surface or of the stimulus field to which a given neuron responds; especially the effective region of stimulation on the retina or in the visual field to which a retinal or other cell responds when the region is stimulated appropriately.

receptor
A molecule or portion of a molecule with which other molecules combine; especially, a molecule or group of molecules on the surface of cells with which specific substances such as drugs, neurotransmitters, and antigens interact.

receptor potential
A graded change in voltage across the membrane of a sensory receptor cell in response to physical stimulation.

receptotopic organization (re-sep''to-top'ik)
A spatial organization similar to a receptor surface; for example, the visual cortex shows a point-for-point representation of the retina and hence is receptotopically organized.

recessive
Tending to recede or to be subordinate; in genetics, a gene not expressed in the phenotype because of the presence of another, dominant form of the gene; opposed to dominant.

red nucleus
A prominent nucleus in the midbrain important in motor behavior.

reductional division
The process of cell division (meiosis) by which the number of chromosomes is halved in each daughter cell.

refract
To cause to deviate; to determine ocular power of the eye.

refraction
The deviation of light when it passes from one medium to another.

reinforcement
A stimulus or situation that increases the occurrence of a behavior; the process by which certain responses become strengthened or modified when they are consistently associated with specific goals.

relative refractory period
The period after an action potential has been initiated during which the nerve cell can be made to fire, but only to more intense stimulation.

releasing factor
Any chemical substance that acts on cells of the anterior lobe of the pituitary gland to trigger or inhibit the release of a hormone.

REM rebound
An increase in the time spent in Stage-1 REM sleep following a period of deprivation of this sleep stage.

REM sleep
See rapid eye movement sleep.

renin (re'nin)
An enzyme secreted by the kidney especially in response to low blood pressure.

replication
The process of duplicating or reproducing, as in the synthesis of duplicate DNA during cell division.

reserpine (res'er-pēn)
A drug used as a tranquilizer and antihypertensive derived from the plant *Rauwolfia* presumed to act in part by blocking the intraneuronal storage of catecholamines.

resting membrane potential
The membrane potential of a nerve cell not producing action potentials.

reticular formation (re-tik'u-lar)
The central core of the brain stem on both sides of the brain; important in mediating sleep and wakefulness and modulating various motor behaviors.

reticular lamina (lam'i-nah)
A delicate membrane in the organ of Corti through which the hairs of the auditory receptor cells project.

reticulospinal tract (re-tik''u-lo-spi'nal)
A bundle of nerve fibers originating in the reticular formation and terminating in the spinal cord; part of the extrapyramidal motor system.

retina
The light-sensitive layered structure at the back of the eyeball responsible for the transduction of light energy; the place where visual images are focused in order to be perceived.

retinene (ret'i-nēn'')
One of the chemical constituents (precursors) from which rhodopsin (photopigment in rods) is made.

retrograde amnesia
Loss of memory for events that occurred previous to the disease or trauma causing the injury.

retrograde amnesia gradient
The relation between memory loss and time of administration of an electroconvulsive shock or other amnesia-producing treatment; the greater the time interval between learning and treatment, the less the memory loss.

retrograde degeneration
Degeneration of a nerve cell body following destruction of its axon; degeneration toward the cell body.

reuptake
A general term for the return of neurotransmitters to the nerve cell from which they were released.

reuptake mechanism
The means by which neurotransmitters are removed by the presynaptic nerve cell into the synaptic terminal where they are presumed to be used again; the general process of uptake (taking up) of materials into the cell.

reverberatory (re-ver′b′ra-tor″e)
Pertaining to action by reverberation; in this book, especially neuronal signals circulating through a network of excitatory interconnections and tending to maintain cellular activity.

rhodopsin (ro-dop′sin)
The light-sensitive chemical substance in rod receptor cells of the retina; rod photopigment; also called visual purple.

ribonucleic acid or **RNA** (ri″bo-nu-kla′ik)
The large molecule that controls protein synthesis and is similar in composition to deoxyribonuleic acid (DNA) except that it contains the base uracil instead of thymine. RNA is synthesized by DNA to carry the genetic information specified by the genetic code out of the nucleus into the cytoplasm of the cell.

ribosome (ri′bo-sōm)
A small, dark, spherical body where protein synthesis takes place; ribosomes may be attached to the endoplasmic reticulum or suspended in the cytoplasm.

rods
One of the rodlike cells in the retina; a class of receptor cells.

rods and tunnel of Corti
The cartilagenous supports and the space that they enclose in the organ of Corti.

rooting reflex
In infants, the turning of the head toward the side of stimulation in response to a touch on the cheek.

rostral (ros′tral)
Toward the head or front; anterior.

round window
A small flexible membrane located on the cochlea which relieves the instantaneous changes in pressure that occur inside the cochlea during sound stimulation.

rubrospinal tract (roo″bro-spi′nal)
A bundle of nerve fibers originating in the red nucleus and terminating in the spinal cord; part of the extrapyramidal motor system.

rut
The period during which male deer, goats, camels, etc., are sexually aroused.

saccade (sah-kād′)
A rapid, involuntary, jerky movement of the eye that occurs as the point of fixation changes.

saccadic eye movement (sa-kad′ik)
See saccade.

saccule (sak′ul)
A general term meaning "little sac"; a portion of the inner ear that contains sensory cells important for the sense of balance; the smaller of two baglike regions of the inner ear.

sagittal section
A cross section through the longitudinal axis of the brain.

saltatory conduction (sal′tah-to″re)
The propagation (conduction) of action potentials down a myelinated axon. Conduction of action potentials appears to jump from one node of Ranvier to the next.

sarcomere (sar'ko-mēr)
The unit of length of a myofibril, consisting of about 1.6 micrometers in resting muscle and comprised of the distance between Z bands (the stripes on striated muscle formed by overlapping thick and thin filaments).

satellite cell
A nonneural cell such as the cells forming the myelin sheath; also called glia or glial cell.

schedule of reinforcement
The arrangement of contingencies between an animal's behavioral response and delivery of reinforcement.

schizophrenia (skiz''o-fre'ne-ah)
The most common category of mental illnesses characterized by peculiar thought disorders, withdrawal from reality, and sometimes delusions, hallucinations, etc.

Schwann cell (shvon)
One of the cells wrapped around nerve fibers in the peripheral nervous system that forms the neurilemma or myelin sheath.

scintillation counter (sin''tǐ-la'shun)
A piece of equipment which measures emission of radioactivity.

sclera (skle'rah)
The tough outer tissue of the eyeball.

scopolamine (sko-pol'ah-mēn)
A compound that interferes with neurotransmission at certain cholinergic synapses. Specifically, this compound blocks transmission at muscarinic cholinergic synapses and hence is a muscarinic antagonist.

scotopic (sko-top'ik)
Pertaining to vision in dim light; refers to the dark-adapted eye; rod vision.

scotopic threshold curve
The lowest energy level at which varying wavelengths of monochromatic light can be just detected.

sedative
A drug that produces sedation, that is, soothes, calms, decreases agitation, etc.

selective biological activity
The action of a drug at low concentration in which one of its effects predominates.

selective breeding
The mating of individuals who are phenotypically more similar than other individuals in a population.

self-stimulation
Electrical stimulation by an organism of its own brain; especially, a rat pressing a bar to receive electrical stimulation of the brain.

sella turcica (sel'ah tur'si-ca)
The small depression in the skull above the roof of the mouth in which the pituitary gland is situated.

semicircular canal
One of the three small, bone-enclosed, fluid-filled circular canals at right angles to each other forming part of the inner ear; especially the vestibular apparatus.

semipermeable membrane
A membrane that allows certain substances to pass through (permeate) but hinders other substances from doing so.

sensitization
An increase in response to a repetitive stimulus; any increase in sensitivity to a stimulus; sensitization not due to stimulus pairing (stimulus association).

sensory register
The hypothetical brief sensory memory system in which sensory input is retained for a period of several hundred milliseconds.

sensory relay nuclei
Nuclei in the thalamus that relay sensory information to sensory areas of the cerebral cortex.

sensory spot
A small region of the skin that responds to a particular kind of stimulus such as cold.

septal area
Refers to the septal nuclei and the many nerve fibers passing through this region.

septal nucleus
Any of the small group of nuclei at the top of the brain stem which forms an important source of projections to the hippocampus; hence, part of the limbic system.

serotonin (ser″o-to′nin)
A suspected neurotransmitter substance secreted by certain groups of neurons in the brain, especially the raphe nuclei.

set point
In a feedback control system, a desired level, for example, the temperature setting on a thermostat.

sex chromosome
One of the two chromosomes involved in sex determination; represented by the letters X and Y.

sham rage
The rage reaction of animals whose cerebral cortex has been removed; an undirected rage response.

shearing movement
A scissorslike movement in which two edges move past one another.

short-term memory
A general term for memory that lasts for a short period of time, that is, from a few seconds to a few minutes.

signal-to-noise ratio
The strength of a particular stimulus or event (the signal) in relation to the other stimuli or events in which it is embedded (noise).

simple receptive field
One type of receptive field of visual cortical cells in the classification of Hubel and Weisel. Neurons with these receptive fields respond best to a slit or line of light of particular width, orientation, and place on the retina.

simple system
A less complex organism or experimental preparation that is more amenable to analysis of behavioral or physiological phenomena than are complex, intact animals.

sine wave (sīn)
Represents periodic oscillation or sequential cycle beginning at zero, increasing to a maximum value, falling through zero to a minimum value, and finally returning to zero.

sinistral (sin′is-tral)
Related to the left; left-handed.

situational insomnia
A disorder of sleep characterized by inability to fall asleep and/or stay asleep because of an emotionally charged or stressful situation.

skeletal muscle
A muscle attached to the skeleton and involved in bodily movement. *See also* striated muscle.

sleep apnea (ap-ne′ah)
A brief cessation of breathing during sleep.

sleep-induction insomnia
Difficulty in falling asleep.

sleep-maintenance insomnia
Difficulty staying asleep.

sleep paralysis
Inability to move upon falling asleep or upon awakening.

sleep spindle
A burst of waves in the electroencephalogram in the frequency range of 10–14 hertz that occurs during light sleep (especially stage 2 sleep).

slow-wave sleep
Deep sleep in which the electroencephalogram is characterized by large, relatively slow delta waves in the frequency range of 1–3 hertz; delta-wave sleep.

smooth muscle
Involuntary muscle; lines the blood vessels, certain glands, etc.

sodium current
The flow of sodium ions through the cell membrane.

sodium-potassium pump
A mechanism in the nerve cell membrane which moves ("pumps") sodium from inside to outside and potassium from outside to inside across the cell membrane.

solubility
The state of being soluble; the degree to which a substance will dissolve in a given amount of another substance.

solute (so'lūt)
A substance dissolved in a solvent.

solvent
A liquid that is capable of dissolving.

soma (so'mah)
The cell body of a nerve cell.

somatic division (so-mat'ik)
The portion of the peripheral nervous system responsible for bodily sensation and movement.

somatic sensation
A sensation of the body such as cold, warm, pain, touch, vibration, etc.

somatosensory (so-mat''o-sen'so-re)
Pertaining to the bodily senses such as touch, pressure, temperature, pain, etc.

somatosensory cortex
See primary somatosensory cortex.

somnambulism (som-nam'bu-lizm)
Sleepwalking.

sound spectrum
The frequency and energy (intensity) composition of a sound.

spatial summation
Summation in which the effects of many synaptic inputs over the surface of a cell are added together.

speciation
The formation of species.

species
A class of organisms possessing similar characteristics; subordinate to genus and superior to subspecies or variety.

species specific
Characteristic of a particular species; having a characteristic interaction or effect (said of a drug, etc.).

specific hunger
Hunger that is specific for a particular type of food or nutrient; especially hunger that develops for a nutrient that has been absent from the diet.

spectrum (spek'trum) pl. **spectra**
A range of frequencies of wavelengths, sound, etc.

spinal reflex
Any reflex mediated by connections entirely within the spinal cord.

spinocerebellar tract (spi''no-ser''e-bel'ar)
A bundle of nerve fibers in the spinal cord projecting to the cerebellum.

spinoreticulothalamic system
(spi''no-re-tik'u-lo-thah-lam'ik)
A series of pathways and structures believed to be responsible in part for analyzing certain types of bodily sensations such as pain.

spinothalamic system
A series of pathways and structures believed to be responsible in part for analyzing certain types of bodily sensations such as temperature.

split-brain preparation
A surgical operation in which certain pathways interconnecting the cerebral hemispheres are severed.

spontaneous recovery
The increase in a conditioned response when some amount of time elapses after it has been extinguished; the increase in strength of an habituated response following an interval during which the habituation stimulus is withdrawn.

spreading depression
Depression of function of nervous tissue after application of salt solution that spreads from the site of application to adjacent tissue and may last for a considerable time.

stapedius (stah-pe'de-us)
One of the small muscles of the middle ear.

state-dependent learning
Learning in which complete recall depends upon the physiological state of the organism at the time learning takes place.

stereochemical theory of odor
A theory of the detection of odor that states that configuration and other physical features of the odor molecule determine its effect on the receptor and the quality of the odor.

stereotaxic apparatus (ste″re-o-tak′sik)
An instrument used to locate structures in the brain for implantation of electrodes, making lesions, etc.

stereotyped behavior
A general term for certain behavior that is repetitious, similar within a species, and typically involves investigatory, grooming, and other highly repetitive movements and patterns.

steroid
Any of a class of compounds including many hormones having a specific ringlike molecular structure. Many sex hormones are steroids.

stimulant
An agent that produces stimulation, excitation, etc.; especially, a drug that stimulates behavior.

stochastic (sto-kas′tik)
Pertaining to skillful conjecture; involving random variables; by extension, statistical analysis.

stretch reflex
The reflexive shortening (contraction) of a muscle when it is stretched slightly; the myotatic reflex. The knee jerk reflex is a stretch reflex.

striated muscle (stri′āt-ed)
One of the muscles used in bodily movement and expression; especially, a muscle cell with a striped appearance; voluntary muscle; skeletal muscle.

strychnine (strik′nīn)
A convulsant drug; a powerful alkaloid which affects the nervous system in part by blocking certain types of postsynaptic inhibition.

subcortical (sub-kor′tĭ-kal)
Pertaining to any portion of the brain below the cerebral cortex, especially the brain stem.

subcutaneous
Under the skin.

substantia nigra (sub-stan′she-ah ni′grah)
A nucleus near the base of the brain in the mesencephalon. A portion of the substantia nigra contains nerve cells that utilize dopamine as their neurotransmitter and have been implicated in Parkinson's disease.

subthreshold
A stimulus that is not of sufficient energy to be detected; any stimulus that does not reach the threshold for initiation of an action potential by a neuron.

sulcus (sul′kus) pl. **sulci** (sul′si)
A general term for a depression or groove in the surface of the brain.

sulcus principalis (prin″sĭ-pahl′is)
A sulcus in the brain of the macaque monkey over the frontal lobes.

supernatant (su″per-na′tant)
Located above or on top of something; the material remaining above the sediment or pellet after centrifugation.

supraoptic nucleus (su″prah-op′tik)
A nucleus in the hypothalamus which sends projections to the pituitary gland.

sympathetic branch
The portion of the autonomic division of the peripheral nervous system which is responsible for mobilization of energy in response to stress.

sympatholytic (sim″pah-tho-lit′ik)
Any agent that counteracts or acts opposite to the actions of the sympathetic division of the autonomic nervous system, especially that of noradrenergic effects at postganglionic fibers of the sympathetic division.

sympathomimetic (sim″pah-tho-mi-met′ik)
Any agent that mimics the action of the sympathetic division of the autonomic nervous system, especially that action at noradrenergic postganglionic synapses of the sympathetic division.

synapse (sin′aps)
The functional connection between nerve cells or between nerve cells and their targets (e.g., muscle cells, etc.).

synaptic cleft (sĭ-nap′tik kleft)
The small space between the presynaptic and postsynaptic cell membrane; the space across a synapse.

synaptic potential
An electrical potential produced by the events of synaptic transmission; a graded voltage change occurring as a result of synaptic transmission.

synaptic transmission
The process of chemical communication between nerve cells in which the presynaptic cell secretes the chemical and the postsynaptic cell responds to it; the transmission of information across the synapse.

synaptic vesicle (ves′ĭ-k′l)
A small spherical or irregularly shaped body in the presynaptic ending which contains the chemical neurotransmitter. Synaptic vesicles are thought to release their contents into the synaptic cleft.

synaptosomal fraction (sĭ-nap′to-sō′mal)
The fraction of nervous tissue resulting from centrifugation that contains synapses.

synchronization
In this book, having the property of acting together or simultaneously and refers to the large-amplitude, simultaneously occurring waves of the electroencephalogram that appear to represent changes in the membrane potential of many nerve cells. These waves are synchronous.

synergistic (sin′′er-jis′tik)
Acting together. Muscles cooperating in the same movement act synergistically.

tachycardia (tak′′e-kar′de-ah)
Excessively rapid action of the heart.

Tay-Sachs disease (ta-saks)
A genetic disorder especially prominent among European Jews, characterized by progressive development of mental retardation, blindness, paralysis, etc.

tectal (tek′tal)
Pertaining to the roof of a structure; especially the optic tectum, the roof of the midbrain.

tectorial membrane (tek-to′re-al)
A stiff membrane of the cochlea attached at one side and into which project the hairs of the auditory receptor cells.

tegmentum (teg-men′tum)
An anatomical covering; the part of the cerebral peduncle in back of the substantia nigra.

telencephalon (tel′′en-sef′ah-lon)
The most anterior of the five major subdivisions of the vertebrate brain; it contains the cerebral hemispheres.

temporal lobe syndrome
The constellation of behavioral and other changes that occurs when the temporal lobes are removed or extensively damaged; especially the memory deficit that occurs following such removal.

temporal summation
Summation in which the effects of synaptic inputs spaced closely in time are added together.

tensor tympani
One of the small muscles of the middle ear.

testis (tes′tis) pl. **testes** (tes′tēz)
The male gonad; the gland that produces sperm.

testosterone (tes-tos′ter-ōn)
A hormone produced by the interstitial cells of the testes important in the development of male sexual characteristics and behavior.

△9-tetrahydrocannabinol
(-tet′′ra-hi′′dro-ka-nab′ĭ-nol)
An active ingredient of marijuana.

thalamus (thal′ah-mus)
A large group of nuclei at the top of the brain stem containing sensory relay nuclei, association nuclei, and intrinsic nuclei.

therapeutic index
In pharmacology, the margin of safety for a compound stated in the ratio of the ED_{50} to the LD_{50}.

thermodynamics
The science dealing with the relations of heat and mechanical energy.

thermoregulation
The regulation of temperature; especially the regulation of body temperature.

theta wave (tha'tah)
One of a specific range of frequencies in the electroencephalogram (4–7 hertz); especially, the pattern of activity characteristic of the electroencephalogram of the hippocampus and indicative of behavioral arousal or activation.

threshold
The point at which a stimulus is of just sufficient intensity to produce a response; in nerve cells, the membrane voltage at which action potentials are initiated.

thymine (thi'min)
A nitrogenous base in nucleic acids such as DNA.

thyroid gland (thi'roid)
One of the endocrine glands located near the front and base of the neck.

thyrotropic hormone (thi''ro-trop'ik)
A hormone secreted by the anterior lobe of the pituitary gland that stimulates the thyroid gland; sometimes called thyroid-stimulating hormone, thyrotropin, or TSH.

thyroxine (thi-rok'sin)
The hormone secreted by the thyroid gland, important for rate of cellular metabolism, etc.

timbre (tim'ber)
The quality of sound in terms of the experience of its frequency and energy composition.

time-decay process
A process that decays or fades with time.

tolerance
The state in which repeated use of a drug leads to a lessened effect of the same dose; the condition in which continual use requires a higher dose to produce the same effect.

topographic representation
An inexact spatial representation of certain surface or other features; especially, the spatial representation of certain sensory and motor information in the brain.

tract
A bundle of nerve fibers within the central nervous system.

tranquilizer
Any of a number of drugs used to quiet an individual's emotional state, acting to calm the person. Minor tranquilizers are used in treating neuroses, while major tranquilizers are used to treat psychotic symptoms.

transcription
The process by which RNA is made from DNA.

transduction
The action or process of changing (transducing) one form of energy into another form of energy; especially sensory receptors changing physical energy into neural activity.

transfer RNA or tRNA
A type of RNA involved in the transfer of amino acids onto messenger RNA in the process of protein synthesis.

translation
The process by which proteins are made from the information coded in RNA.

transmission
The process by which one nerve cell communicates with another across the synapse.

tremor
Involuntary trembling or quivering; shaking.

trichromatic color theory (tri''kro-mat'ik)
A theory of color vision in which three separate primary color systems respond and interact to code color information; the Young-Helmholtz theory.

tricyclic antidepressant (tri-sik′lik)
A class of drugs used to treat depression; especially a group of compounds with a three-ringed (tricyclic) molecular structure used to treat some forms of depression and presumed to act in part by blocking the reuptake of catecholamines into presynaptic endings.

trigeminal lemniscus (tri-jem′ĭ-nal lem-nis′kus)
The central fiber projection of the trigeminal nerve.

trigeminal nerve
The fifth cranial nerve.

trisomy (tri′so-me)
The presence of an extra or third chromosome rather than the normal pair.

trisomy 21
A congenital abnormality characterized by an extra chromosome 21, increased susceptibility to disease, severe mental retardation, high infant mortality, etc.; Down's syndrome.

true breeding
Production of offspring identical to the parents for most traits.

tryptophan (trip′to-fān)
An amino acid; especially a precursor in the synthesis of serotonin.

tryptophan hydroxylase (hi-drok′sil-ās)
An enzyme that converts tryptophan to 5-hydroxytryptophan in the synthesis of serotonin.

TSH
See thyrotropic hormone.

tufted cell
A cell belonging to one of two vertically oriented cell types in the olfactory bulb that receive information from the olfactory nerve fibers.

tuning curve
A graph depicting the lowest sound pressure level (intensity) needed to produce a neuronal response for a range of frequencies of sound.

Turner's syndrome
A congenital abnormality characterized by a defective or absent second sex chromosome, undifferentiated gonadal development, and other defects.

tympanic membrane
A thin, stiff membrane separating the inner and middle regions of the ear that functions in the reception of sound waves by vibrating at the frequency of pulsations produced by a sound source; the eardrum.

tyrosine (ti-ro′sin)
An amino acid synthesized from the naturally occurring amino acid phenylalanine and important in synthesis of catecholamines.

tyrosine hydroxylase (hi-drok′sil-ās)
An enzyme that catalyzes the conversion of tyrosine to dopa, the precursor to the catecholamines and presumed to be rate-limiting in the synthesis of catecholamines.

unconditioned response or **UR**
The response evoked by an unconditioned stimulus in a classical conditioning paradigm; any response that can be evoked by a stimulus in the absence of conditioning.

unconditioned stimulus or **US**
The stimulus in a classical conditioning paradigm that evokes the unconditioned response (opposed to the conditioned stimulus).

uncus
The anterior end of the parahippocampal gyrus.

unipolar (u″ni-po′lar)
Having one pole; a cell with only one process or extension projecting from the cell body; especially a nerve cell.

uracil (u′rah-sil)
A nitrogenous base found in nucleic acid (RNA).

utricle (u′tre-k'l)
A small sac or baglike structure; the portion in the inner ear containing sensory cells important in maintaining balance.

vagus nerve (va′gus)
The tenth cranial nerve arising from the medulla to innervate the larynx, lungs, esophagus, heart, and most organs of the abdomen.

vasopressin (vas″o-pres′in)
A hormone secreted by the pituitary gland that increases blood pressure and decreases flow of urine.

ventral
Pertaining to the undersurface or bottom; opposed to dorsal.

ventral root
The large fiber bundles leaving the spinal cord carrying the axons of motor neurons.

ventricle
A cavity within the brain or other structure.

ventrobasal complex
A group of nuclei in the thalamus responsible for relaying somatosensory information to the cerebral cortex.

ventromedial hypothalamic syndrome
A constellation of behavioral and physiological changes that occurs when the region of the ventromedial nucleus of the hypothalamus is destroyed; especially the hyperphagia and obesity that such treatment produces.

ventromedial hypothalamus
The region at the base of and near the midline of the hypothalamus; especially the ventromedial nuclei of the hypothalamus.

vertebrate
Having a spinal column, that is, a vertebral column and spinal cord.

vestibular apparatus (ves-tib′u-lar)
The organs of balance including the semicircular canals, utricle, and saccule on each side in the labyrinth.

viscera (vis′er-ah) sing. **viscus** (vis′kus)
The internal organs of the body; especially those located in the great cavities of the body such as the heart, the liver, etc.

visual agnosia (ag-no′se-ah)
The inability to recognize familiar objects by sight; a disturbance in recognition of visual stimuli.

visual cortex
See primary visual cortex.

visual field
The entire field of view; everything visible at a given fixation.

vitreous humor (vit′re-us)
The jellylike substance inside the eyeball behind the lens thought to help maintain the shape of the eyeball.

volatile (vol′ah-til)
Tending to evaporate rapidly; used especially in reference to substances in a gaseous or vaporous state that act as stimuli for the senses of taste and smell.

volley effect
The aggregate of nerve impulses when firing out of phase, or alternately, in which the combined frequency is twice that of two neurons firing singly, three times that of three neurons firing singly, etc.

wavelength
The distance between the peak of a wave and the peak of the succeeding wave; wavelengths of light are perceived as color or hue.

Weigert stain (vi′gert)
A histological stain that reacts with the myelin surrounding nerve cell axons.

Wernicke's area (ver′nĭ-kez)
A region of the temporal lobe responsible in part for language comprehension.

white matter
Neural tissue consisting mostly of myelinated nerve fibers with a whitish color underlying the gray matter of the brain or collected in nerves.

withdrawal symptom
A physiological and behavioral reaction, sometimes severe, that takes place when drug use is abruptly terminated.

Wolffian duct (woolf′e-an)
The masculine portion of the primitive sexual structures of the developing embryo.

xanthine (zan′thēn)
One of a class of stimulant compounds such as caffeine.

yohimbine (ho-him′bēn)
A compound that blocks neurotransmission at alpha-adrenergic synapses and hence an alpha-adrenergic antagonist.

zero point
The arbitrarily chosen point within the brain which serves as a reference for all other points in the stereotaxic method.

zonule fiber (zōn′ul)
One of the small ligaments that attach the ciliary muscles to the lens of the eye.

zygote (zi′gōt)
A cell formed by the union of two gametes (male and female); the fertilized ovum.

References

Adametz, J. H. 1959. Rate of recovery of function in cats with rostral reticular lesions. *Journal of Neurosurgery* 16: 85–98.

Adams, D. B., A. R. Gold, and A. D. Burt. 1978. Rise in female-initiated sexual activity at ovulation and its suppression by oral contraceptives. *New England Journal of Medicine* 299: 1145–50.

Adams, R. N. 1986. Ascorbate distribution patterns in human brain. In Workshop on Ascorbate: A vitamin as neuromodulator. Society for Neuroscience 16th Annual Meeting, 12. ed. G. V. Rebec.

Adkins, R. J., R. W. Morse, and A. L. Towe. 1966. Control of somatosensory input by the cerebral cortex. *Science* 153: 1020–22.

Adrian, E. D. 1950. The electrical activity of the mammalian olfactory bulb. *Electroencephalography and Clinical Neurophysiology* 2: 377–88.

Adrian, E. D. 1953. Sensory messages and sensation: The response of the olfactory organ to different smells. *Acta Physiologica Scandinavica* 29: 5–14.

Aghajanian, G. K., H. J. Haigler, and F. E. Bloom. 1972. Lysergic acid diethylamide and serotonin: Direct actions on serotonin-containing neurons. *Life Science* 11: 615–22.

Aghajanian, G. K., and R. Y. Wang. 1978. Physiology and pharmacology of central serotonergic neurons. In *Psycopharmacology: A generation of progress,* eds. M. A. Lipton, A. DiMascio, and K. F. Killam. New York: Raven Press.

Agnew, H. W., Jr., W. B. Webb, and R. L. Williams. 1964. The effects of stage four sleep deprivation. *Electroencephalography and Clinical Neurophysiology* 17: 68–70.

Agnew, H. W., Jr., W. B. Webb, and R. L. Williams. 1967. Comparison of stage four and 1 REM sleep deprivation. *Perceptual and Motor Skills* 24: 851–58.

Agranoff, B. W., R. E. Davis, L. Casola, and R. Lim. 1967. Actinomycin-D blocks formation of memory of shock-avoidance in goldfish. *Science* 158: 1600–1601.

Akil, H., and J. C. Liebeskind. 1975. Monoaminergic mechanisms of stimulation-produced analgesia. *Brain Research* 94: 279–96.

Albe-Fessard, D., K. J. Berkeley, L. Kruger, H. J. Ralston, and W. D. Willis. 1985. Diencephalic mechanisms of pain sensation. *Brain Research Reviews* 9: 217–96.

Alberts, J. R. 1978. Huddling by rat pups: Multisensory control of contact behavior. *Journal of Comparative and Physiological Psychology* 92: 220–30.

Alexander, G. E., M. R. DeLong, and P. L. Strick. 1986. Parallel organization of functionally segregated circuits linking basal ganglia and cortex. *Annual Review of Neuroscience* 9: 357–81.

Allison, T. 1972. In *The sleeping brain,* ed. M. H. Chase, 1–7. Los Angeles: University of California Brain Research Institute.

Amoore, J. E., J. W. Johnston, Jr., and M. Rubin. 1964. The stereochemical theory of odor. *Scientific American,* 210: 42–49.

Anand, B. K., and J. R. Brobeck. 1951. Localization of a feeding center in the hypothalamus of the rat. *Proceedings for the Society of Experimental Biological Medicine* 77: 323–24.

Andersen, R. A. 1987. The role of the inferior parietal lobule in spatial perception and visual motor integration. In *Handbook of physiology.*

Andersen, R. A., C. Asanuma, and W. M. Cowan. 1985. Callosal and prefrontal associational projecting cell populations in area 7A of the macaque monkey: A study using retrogradely transported fluorescent dyes. *Journal of Comparative Neurology* 232: 443–55.

Andersen, R. A., and V. B. Mountcastle. 1983. The influence of the angle of gaze upon the excitability of the light-sensitive neurons of the posterior parietal cortex. *Journal of Neuroscience* 3: 532–48.

Andersson, B. 1953. The effect of injections of hypertonic NaCl solutions in different parts of the hypothalamus of goats. *Acta Physiologica Scandinavica* 28: 188–201.

Andersson, B. 1978. Regulation of water intake. *Physiological Review* 58: 582–603.

Andreasen, N. C. and S. Olsen. 1982. Negative v. positive schizophrenia. *Archives of General Psychiatry* 39: 789–94.

Angrist, B. 1983. Psychoses induced by central nervous system stimulants and related drugs. In *Stimulants: Neurochemical, Behavioral and Clinical Perspectives,* ed. I. Creese. New York: Raven Press.

Antelman, S. M., and N. Rowland. 1975. Hyperphagia in normal rats and recovery of behavioral deficits in rats with lateral hypothalamic lesions: Stress-induced effects related to the nigrostriatal dopamine system. *Psychosomatic Medicine* 37: 81.

Antin, J., J. Gibbs, J. Holt, R. C. Young, and G. P. Smith. 1975. Cholecystokinin elicits the complete behavioral sequence of satiety. *Journal of Comparative and Physiological Psychology* 89: 784–90.

Apfelbaum, M., and A. Mandenoff. 1981. Naltrexone suppresses hyperphagia induced in the rat by a highly palatable diet. *Pharmacology, Biochemistry, and Behavior* 15: 89–91.

Aprison, M. H., T. Kariya, J. N. Hingtgen, and M. Toru. 1968. Neurochemical correlates of behaviour: Changes in acetylcholine, norepinephrine, and 5-hydroxytryptamine concentrations in several discrete brain areas of the rat during behavioural excitation. *Journal of Neurochemistry* 15: 1131.

Arbuthnott, G. W., T. J. Crow, K. Fuxe, L. Olson, and U. Ungerstedt. 1970. Depletion of catecholamines in vivo induced by electrical stimulation of central monoamine pathways. *Brain Research* 24: 471–83.

Armstrong, D. M., and R. D. Terry. 1985. Substance P immunoreactivity within neuritic plaques. *Neuroscience Letters* 58: 139–44.

Armstrong, R. B. 1984. Mechanisms of exercise-induced delayed onset muscular soreness: A brief review. *Medicine and Science in Sports and Exercise* 16: 529–38.

Arnold, A. P., and R. A. Gorski. 1984. Gonadal steroid induction of structural sex differences in the CNS. *Annual Review of Neuroscience* 7: 413–42.

Asanuma, H., and I. Rosen. 1972. Topographical organization of cortical efferent zones projecting to distal forelimb muscles in the monkey. *Experimental Brain Research* 14: 243–56.

Axelrod, J., R. O. Brady, B. Witkop, and E. V. Evarts. 1957. The distribution and metabolism of lysergic acid diethylamine. *Annals of New York Academy of Sciences* 66: 435–43.

Ayoub, D. M., W. T. Greenough, and J. M. Juraska. 1983. Sex differences in dendritic structure in the preoptic area of the juvenile macaque monkey brain. *Science* 219: 197–98.

Balagura, S., and B. Hoebel. 1967. Self-stimulation of the lateral hypothalamus modified by insulin and glucagon. *Physiology and Behavior* 2: 337–40.

Baldessarini, R. J., and D. Tarsy. 1980. Pathophysiological basis of tardive dyskinesia. In *Long-term effects of neuroleptics,* eds. F. Cattabeni, G. Racagni, P. F. Spano, and E. Costa, 451–61. New York: Raven Press.

Banker, G. A. 1980. Trophic interactions between astroglial cells and hippocampal neurons in culture. *Science* 209: 809–10.

Barchas, J. D., H. Akil, G. R. Elliot, R. B. Holman, and S. J. Watson, 1978. Behavioral neurochemistry: Neuroregulators and behavioral states. *Science* 200: 964–73.

Barchas, J. D., G. R. Elliott, P. A. Berger, P. R. Barchas, and F. Solomon. 1985. The ultimate stigma: Inadequate funding for research on mental illness and addictive disorders. *American Journal of Psychiatry* 142 (Supplement), 6–41.

Barnes, C. A., and B. L. McNaughton. 1980. Spatial memory and hippocampal synaptic plasticity in middle-aged and senescent rats. In *The psychobiology of aging: Problems and perspectives,* ed. D. Stein, 253–72. Amsterdam: Elsevier.

Baum, M. J., A. K. Slob, F. H. DeJong, and D. L. Westbrook. 1978. Persistance of sexual behavior in ovariectomized stumptailed macaques following dexamethasone treatment or adrenalectomy. *Hormones and Behavior* 11: 323–47.

Beach, F. A. 1940. Effects of cortical lesions upon the copulatory behavior of male rats. *Journal of Comparative Psychology* 29: 193–239.

Beach, F. A. 1960. The snark is a beejum. *American Psychologist* 35: 1–18.

Beck, E. C. 1975. Electrophysiology and behavior. *Annual Review of Psychology* 26: 223–62.

Békésy, G., von. 1960. *Experiments in hearing.* New York: McGraw-Hill.

Békésy, G., von. 1966. Taste theories and the chemical stimulation of single papillae. *Journal of Applied Psychology* 21: 1–9.

Benes, F. M., T. N. Parks, and E. W. Rubel. 1977. Rapid dendritic atrophy following deafferentation: An EM morphometric analysis. *Brain Research* 122: 1–13.

Bennett, E. L., M. C. Diamond, D. Krech, and M. R. Rosenzweig. 1964. Chemical and anatomical plasticity of the brain. *Science* 146: 610–19.

Bennett, E. L., M. R. Rosenzweig, and M. C. Diamond. 1970. Time course of effects of differential experience on brain measures and behavior in rats. *Molecular approaches to learning and memory,* ed. W. L. Byrne. New York: Academc Press.

Berger, T. W. 1984. Long-term potentiation of hippocampal synaptic transmission affects rate of behavioral learning. *Science* 224: 627.

Berger, T. W., G. A. Clark, and R. F. Thompson. 1980. Learning-dependent neuronal responses recorded from limbic system brain structures during classical conditioning. *Physiological Psychology* 8: 155–67.

Berlin, F. S., and C. F. Meinecke. 1981. Treatment of sex offenders with antiandrogenic medication: Conceptualization, review of treatment modalities, and preliminary findings. *American Journal of Psychiatry* 138: 601–7.

Bernstein, J. 1902. Untersuchungen zur Thermodynamik dor bioelektrischen Ströme. *Pflugers Arch. Physiol.* 92: 521–62.

Bigland-Ritchie, B., and J. J. Woods. 1976. Integrated electromyogram and oxygen uptake during positive and negative work. *Journal of Physiology* (London) 260: 267–77.

Bishop, M. P., S. T. Elder, and R. G. Heath. 1963. Intracranial self-stimulation in man. *Science* 140: 394–95.

Bishop, P. O. 1984. Processing of visual information within the retinostriate visual system. In *Handbook of physiology: Section I. The nervous system. VIII sensory processes,* ed. I. Darian-Smith, 341–424. Baltimore: Waverly Press.

Bishop, P. O., and G. H. Henry. 1972. Striate neurons: Receptive field concepts. *Investigative Ophthalmology* 11: 346–54.

Blass, E. M., and A. N. Epstein. 1971. A lateral preoptic osmosensitive zone for thirst in the rat. *Journal of Comparative and Physiological Psychology* 76: 378–94.

Blass, E. M., and W. G. Hall. 1976. Drinking termination: Interactions among hydrational, orogastric, and behavioral controls in rats. *Psychological Review* 83: 356–74.

Bloom, F. E. 1975. The role of cyclic nucleotides in central synaptic function. *Review of Physiology, Biochemistry and Pharmacology* 74: 1–103.

Bloom, F. E. 1983. The endorphins: a growing family of pharmacologically pertinent peptides. *Annual Review of Pharmacology and Toxicology* 23: 151–70.

Blumer, D. 1970. Hypersexual episodes in temporal lobe epilepsy. *American Journal of Psychiatry* 126: 1099–1106.

Boakes, R. J., P. B. Bradley, and J. M. Candy. 1972. A neuronal basis for the altering action of (+)-amphetamine. *British Journal of Pharmacology* 45: 391–403.

Bongiovanni, A. M., A. M. DiGeorge, and M. M. Grumbach. 1959. Masculinization of the female infant associated with estrogenic therapy alone during gestation: Four cases. *Journal of Clinical Endocrinology and Metabolism* 19: 1004–11.

Bozarth, M. A. 1986. Neural basis of psychomotor stimulant and opiate reward: Evidence suggesting the involvement of a common dopaminergic system. *Behavioural Brain Research* 22: 107–16.

Bozarth, M. A., and R. A. Wise. 1983. Neural substrates of opiate reinforcement. *Progress in Neuro-Psychopharmacology and Biological Psychiatry* 7: 569–75.

Bradley, P. B., and J. Elkes. 1953. The effect of atropine, hyoscyamine, physostigmine, and neostigmine on the electrical activity of the brain of the conscious cat. *Journal of Physiology* (London) 120: 14.

Bradley, P. B., and J. Elkes. 1957. The effects of some drugs on the electrical activity of the brain. *Brain.* 80: 77–117.

Bradley, P. B., and B. J. Key. 1958. The effect of drugs on arousal responses produced by electrical stimulation of the reticular formation of the brain. *Electroencephalography and Clinical Neurophysiology* 10: 97–110.

Braestrup, C., M. Nielson, and C. E. Olsen. 1980. Urinary and brain B-carboline-3-carboxylates as potent inhibitors of brain benzodiazepine receptors. *Proceedings of the National Academy of Sciences* (USA) 77: 2288–92.

Braestrup, C., and R. F. Squires. 1977. Specific benzodiazepine receptors in rat brain characterized by high-affinity (3H)-diazepam binding. *Proceedings of the Nat. Acad. Sci. USA* 74: 3805–9.

Braff, D. L. 1985. Attention, habituation, and information processing in psychiatric disorders. In *Psychiatry--Vol. 3, Section 2: Psychobiological Foundations of Clinical Psychiatry,* ed. J. O. Cavenar, Jr. Philadelphia: Lippincott.

Brandt, J., and N. Butters. 1986. The neuropsychology of Huntington's disease. *Trends in NeuroScience* 9: 118–20.

Brazier, M. 1959. The historical development of neurophysiology. In *Handbook of physiology,* edited by Field, *Section I: Neurophysiology.* Washington, D.C.: American Physiological Society.

Breedlove, S. M., and A. P. Arnold. 1980. Hormone accumulation in a sexually dimorphic motor nucleus of the rat spinal cord. *Science* 210: 564–66.

Breese, G. R., J. L. Howard, and J. P. Leahy. 1971. Effect of 6-hydroxydopamine on electrical self-stimulation of the brain. *British Journal of Pharmacology* 43: 255–57.

Breggin, P. R. 1975. Psychosurgery for the control of violence: A critical review. In *Neural bases of violence and aggression,* eds. W. Fields and W. H. Sweet. St. Louis: Warren Green.

Bremer, F. 1935. Cerveau isolé et physiologie du sommeil. *Comptes Rendus des Searces Societe de Biologie, Paris* 118: 1235–42.

Bremer, F. 1936. Nouvelles recherches sur le mecanisme du sommeil. *Comptes Rendus des Searces Societe de Biologie, Paris* 122: 460–64.

Broca, P. 1861. Remarques sur le siege de la faculté du langage articule, suivies d'une observation d'aphemie (perte de la parole). *Societe Anatomique de Paris, Bulletin et Memoire* 6: 330–57.

Brodmann, K. 1907. Die Kortexgleiderung des Menschen. *Journal fur Psychologie und Neurologie* 10: 231–46.

Brugge, J. F., N. A. Dubrovsky, and J. E. Rose. 1964. Some discharge characteristics of single neurons in cats' auditory cortex. *Science* 146: 433–34.

Buchwald, J. S., E. S. Halas, and S. Schramm. 1965. Progressive changes in efferent unit responses to repeated cutaneous stimulation in spinal cats. *Journal of Neurophysiology* 28: 200–15.

Buchwald, J. S., and C. M. Huang. 1975. Far-field acoustic responses: Origins in the cat. *Science* 189: 382–84.

Buell, S. J., and P. D. Coleman. 1978. Dendritic growth in the aged human brain and failure of growth in senile dementia. *Science* 206: 854–56.

Buggy, J., and A. K. Johnson. 1977. Preoptic-hypothalamic periventricular lesions: Thirst deficits and hypernatremia. *American Journal of Physiology* 233: R44–R52.

Burt, D. R., I. Creese, and S. H. Snyder. 1977. Antischizophrenic drugs: Chronic treatment elevates dopamine receptor binding in brain. *Science* 196: 326–28.

Butters, N. 1984. The clinical aspects of memory disorders: Contributions from experimental studies of amnesia and dementia. *Journal of Clinical Neuropsychology* 6:17–36.

Butters, N., and L. S. Cermak. 1980. *Alcoholic Korsakoff's syndrome: An information-processing approach to amnesia.* New York: Academic Press.

Butters, N., and P. Miliotis. 1985. Amnesic disorders. In *Clinical Neuropsychology,* eds. K. Heilman and E. Valenstein, 403–51. New York: Oxford University Press.

Byck, R. 1975. Drugs and the treatment of psychiatry disorders. In *The pharmacological basis of therapeutics,* 5th ed. eds. L. S. Goodman and A. Gilman, 152–200. New York: Macmillan Publishing Co., Inc.

Cabak, V., and R. Najdanovic. 1965. Effects of undernutrition on physical and mental development. *Archives of Disease in Childhood* 40: 532–34.

Cabanac, M., and P. Duclaux. 1970. Obesity: Absence of satiety aversion to sucrose. *Science* 168: 496–97.

Caggiula, A. R. 1970. Analysis of the copulation-reward properties of anterior hypothalamic stimulation in male rats. *Journal of Comparative and Physiological Psychology* 70: 399–412.

Caggiula, A. R., J. G. Herndon, R. Scanlon, D. Greenstone, W. Bradshaw, and D. Sharp. 1979. Dissociation of active from immobility components of sexual behavior: implications for CA involvement in sexual behavior and sensorimotor responsiveness. *Brain Research* 172: 505–20.

Caggiula, A. R., and H. Szechtman. 1972. Hypothalamic stimulation: A biphasic influence on copulation of the male rat. *Behavioral Biology* 7: 591–98.

Calne, D. B. 1979. Neurotransmitters, neuromodulators, and neurohormones. *Neurology* 29: 1517–21.

Campbell, C. S., and J. D. Davis. 1974. Licking rate of rats is reduced by intraduodenal and intraportal glucose infusion. *Physiology and Behavior* 12: 357–65.

Carew, T. J., and C. L. Sahley. 1986. Invertebrate learning and memory: From behavior to molecules. *Annual Review of Neuroscience* 9: 435–487.

Carlsson, A., and M. Lindqvist. 1963. Effect of chlorpromazine and haloperidol on formation of 3-methyoxytyramine and normetanephrine in mouse brain. *Acta Pharmacologia et Toxicologia* 20: 140–44.

Casey, K. L. 1971. Responses of bulboreticular units to somatic stimuli eliciting escape behavior in the cat. *International Journal of Neuroscience* 2: 15–28.

Castellucci, V., H. Pinsker, E. Kupfermann, and E. R. Kandel. 1970. Neuronal mechanisms of habituation and dishabituation of the gill-withdrawal reflex in *Aplysia*. *Science* 167: 1745–48.

Chase, T. N., and D. L. Murphy. 1973. Serotonin and central nervous system function. *Annual Review of Pharmacology* 13: 181–97.

Christensen, B. M., and E. R. Perl. 1970. Spinal neurons specifically excited by noxious or thermal stimuli: Marginal zone of the dorsal horn. *Journal of Neurophysiology* 33: 293–307.

Clavier, R. M., and A. Routtenberg. 1974. Ascending monoamine-containing fiber pathways related to intracranial self-stimulation. *Brain Research* 72: 25–40.

Clemens, L. G., K. Wallen, and R. Gorski. 1967. Mating behavior: Facilitation in the female cat after cortical application of potassium chloride. *Science* 157: 1208–9.

Cohen, E. L., and R. J. Wurtman. 1976. Brain acetylcholine: Control by dietary choline. *Science* 191: 561–62.

Cohen, N. J., and L. R. Squire. 1980. Preserved learning and retention of pattern-analyzing skill in amnesia: Dissociation of knowing how and knowing that. *Science* 210: 207–10.

Cohen, N. J., and L. R. Squire. 1981. Retrograde amnesia and remote memory impairment. *Neuropsychologia* 19: 337–56.

Cole, S. O. 1978. Brain mechanisms of amphetamine-induced anorexia, locomotion, and stereotypy: A review. *Neuroscience and Biobehavioral Reviews* 2: 89–100.

Cook, D. G., and T. J. Carew. 1986. Operant conditioning of head waving in *Aplysia*. *Proc. Natl. Acad. Sci. USA* 83: 1120–24.

Cooper, J. R., F. E. Bloom, and R. H. Roth. 1986. *The biochemical basis of neuropharmacology,* 5th ed. New York: Oxford University Press.

Costa, E., and A. Guidotti. 1979. Molecular mechanisms in the receptor action of benzodiazepines. *Annual Review of Pharmacology and Toxicology* 19: 531–45.

Cowley, J. J., A. L. Johnson, and B. W. L. Brooksbank. 1977. The effect of two odorous compounds on performance in an assessment-of-people test. *Psychoneuroendocrinology* 2: 159–68.

Cox, B. M., K. E. Opheim, H. Teschemacher, and A. Goldstein. 1975. A peptidelike substance from pituitary that acts like morphine. Purification and properties. *Life Sciences* 16: 1777–82.

Crabbe, J. C., A. Kosobud, and E. R. Young. 1983. Genetic selection for ethanol withdrawal severity: Differences in replicate mouse lines. *Life Sciences* 33: 955–62.

Craig, J. C. 1977. Vibrotactile pattern perception: Extraordinary observers. *Science* 196: 450–52.

Craig, J. C., and C. E. Sherrick. 1982. Dynamic tactile displays. In *Tactual perception: A sourcebook,* eds. W. Schiff and E. Foulke. Cambridge: Cambridge University Press.

Cranford, J., R. Ravizza, I. T. Diamond, and I. C. Whitfield. 1971. Unilateral ablation of the auditory cortex in the cat impairs complex sound location. *Science* 172: 286–88.

Creese, I., and S. H. Snyder. 1977. Brain neurotransmitter and drug receptors. In *Medicinal Chemistry V.* Amsterdam: Elsevier Scientific Publishing Company 135–53.

Crow, T. J. 1972. A map of the rat mesencephalon for electrical self-stimulation. *Brain Research* 36: 265–73.

Crow, T. J., P. J. Spear, and G. W. Arbuthnott. 1972. Intracranial self-stimulation with electrodes in the region of the locus coeruleus. *Brain Research* 36: 275–87.

Cuello, A. C., T. M. Jessell, I. Kanazawa, and L. L. Iversen. 1977. Substance P: Localization in synaptic vesicles in rat central nervous system. *Journal of Neurochemistry* 29: 747–51.

Curtis, D. R. 1974. Amino acid neurotransmitters and the brain. *Medical Journal of Australia* 2: 723–31.

Darley, C. F., J. R. Tinklenberg, W. T. Roth, L. E. Hollister, and R. C. Atkinson. 1973. Influence of marijuana on storage and retrieval processes in memory. *Memory and Cognition* 1: 196–200.

Dastoli, R. F. and S. Price. 1966. Sweet-sensitive protein from bovine taste buds: Isolation and assay. *Science* 154: 905–7.

Davies, R. F., J. Rossi, J. Panksepp, N. J. Bean, and A. J. Zolovik. 1983. Fenfluramine anorexia: A peripheral locus of action. *Physiology and Behavior* 30: 723–30.

Davis, J. D., and C. S. Campbell. 1973. Peripheral control of meal size in the rat: Effect of sham feeding on meal size and drinking rate. *Journal of Comparative and Physiological Psychology* 83: 379–87.

Davis, J. D., R. J. Gallagher, R. F. Ladove, and A. J. Turausky. 1969. Inhibition of food intake by a humoral factor. *Journal of Comparative and Physiological Psychology* 67: 407–14.

Dawson, R. G., L. Conrad, and G. Lynch. 1973. Single and two-stage hippocampal lesions: A similar syndrome. *Experimental Neurology* 40: 263–77.

DeDuve, C. The lysosome. 1963. *Scientific American* 208: 64–72.

DeFries, J. C., and J. P. Hegmann. 1970. Genetic analysis of open-field behavior. In *Contributions to behavior-genetic analysis: The mouse as a prototype,* eds. G. Lindzey and D. D. Thiessen. New York: Appleton-Century-Crofts.

DeFries, J. C., and G. E. McClearn. 1970. Social dominance and Darwinian fitness in the laboratory mouse. *American Naturalist* 104: 408–11.

DeFries, J. C., and G. E. McClearn. 1972. Behavioral genetics and the fine structure of mouse populations: A study in microevolution. In *Evolutionary biology,* eds. T. Dobzhansky, M. K. Hecht, and W. C. Steere, vol. 5. New York: Appleton-Century-Crofts.

DeFries, J. C., and R. Plomin. 1978. Behavioral genetics. *Annual Reviews of Psychology* 29: 472–515.

Delgado, J. M., W. W. Roberts, and N. E. Miller. 1954. Learning motivated behavior by electrical stimulation of the brain. *American Journal of Physiology* 179: 587–93.

Dement, W., R. B. Holman, and C. Guilleminault. 1976. Neurochemical and neuropharmacological foundations of the sleep disorders. *Psychopharmacology Communications* 2: 77–90.

de Montigny, C., P. Blier, and Y. Chaput. 1984. Electrophysiologically-identified serotonin receptors in the rat CNS. *Neuropharmacology* 23: 1511–20.

DeRobertis, E., W. N. Nowinski, and F. A. Saez. 1965. *Cell biology.* 4th ed. Philadelphia: Saunders.

Desmedt, J. E. 1960. Neurophysiological mechanisms controlling acoustic input. In *Neural mechanisms of the auditory and vestibular systems,* eds. G. L. Rasmussen and W. F. Windle. Springfield, Il.: Charles C. Thomas.

Desmond, N. L., and W. B. Levy. 1983. Synaptic correlates of associative potentiation/depression: An ultrastructural study in the hippocampus. *Brain Research* 265: 21–30.

Dethier, V. G. 1976. *The hungry fly: A physiological study of the behavior associated with feeding.* Cambridge: Harvard University Press.

Deutsch, J. A., ed. 1973. *The physiological basis of memory.* New York: Academic Press.

Deutsch, J. A. 1983. Dietary control and the stomach. *Progress in Neurobiology* 20: 313–32.

Deutsch, J. A., D. W. Adams, and R. J. Metzner. 1964. Choice of intracranial stimulation as a function of delay between stimulations and strength of competing drive. *Journal of Comparative and Physiological Psychology* 57: 241–43.

Deutsch, J. A., and M. F. Gonzalez. 1980. Gastric nutrient content signals satiety. *Behavioral and Neural Biology* 30: 113–16.

Deutsch, J. A., and W. T. Hardy. 1977. Cholecystokinin produces bait shyness in rats. *Nature* 266: 196.

Deutsch, J. A., A. Puerto, and M. L. Wang. 1977. The pyloric sphincter and differential food preferences. *Behavioral Biology* 19: 543–47.

Deutsch, J. A., W. G. Young, and T. J. Kalogeris. 1978. The stomach signals satiety. *Science* 201: 165–67.

DeValois, J. E., and G. H. Jacobs. 1984. Neural mechanisms of color vision. In *Handbook of physiology: Section I. The nervous system. VIII sensory processes,* ed. I. Darian-Smith, 425–55. Baltimore: Waverly Press.

DeValois, R. L., and G. H. Jacobs. 1968. Primate color vision. *Science.* 162: 533–40.

Dews, P. B., and W. H. Morse. 1961. Behavioral pharmacology. *Annual Review of Pharmacology* 1: 145–74.

Dewson, M. H., III. 1968. Efferent olivocochlear bundle: Some relationships to stimulus discrimination in noise. *Journal of Neurophysiology* 31: 122–30.

Diamond, M. C., R. E. Johnson, and J. Ehlert. 1979. A comparison of cortical thickness in male and female rats—Normal and gonadectomized, young and adult. *Behavioral and Neural Biology* 26: 485–91.

Donchin, E. 1975. Brain electrical correlates of pattern recognition. In *Signal analysis and pattern recognition in biomedical engineering,* ed. B. F. Inbar. New York: Halsted Press.

Donchin, E., and D. B. Lindsley. 1969. *Average evoked potentials: Methods, results and evaluations.* Scientific and Technical Information Division, Office of Technology Utilization, National Aeronautics and Space Administration, NASA SP-191. Washington, D.C.: U.S. Government Printing Office.

Douglas, R. J. 1967. The hippocampus and behavior. *Psychological Bulletin* 67: 416–22.

Dowling, J. E. 1967. The site of visual adaptation. *Science* 55: 273–76.

Dowling, J. E., and M. W. Dubin. 1984. The vertebrate retina. In *Handbook of physiology: Section I. The nervous system. VIII sensory processes,* ed. I. Darian-Smith, 317–39. Baltimore: Waverly Press.

Duncan, C. P. 1949. The retroactive effect of electroshock on learning. *Journal of Comparative and Physiological Psychology* 42: 32–44.

Dykes, R. W. 1983. Parallel processing of somatosensory information: A theory. *Brain Research Reviews* 6: 47–115.

Eccles, J. C. 1964. *The physiology of synapses.* New York: Springer-Verlag.

Eccles, J. C. 1973. *The understanding of the brain.* New York: McGraw-Hill.

Eccles, J. C. 1979. *The human mystery.* New York: Springer-Verlag.

Edwards, D. A., and R. E. Whalen. 1967. Hormonal determinants of the development of masculine and feminine behavior in male and female rats. *Anatomical Record* 157: 319–20.

Egger, M. D., and J. P. Flynn. 1963. Effect of electrical stimulation of the amygdala on hypothalamically elicited attack behavior in cats. *Journal of Neurophysiology* 26: 705–20.

Ehrhardt, A. A., H. F. L. Meyer-Bahlburg, J. F. Feldman, and S. E. Ince. 1984. Sex-dimorphic behavior in childhood subsequent to prenatal exposure to exogenous progestogens and estrogens. *Archives of Sexual Behavior* 13: 457–77.

Eichler, A. J., S. M. Antelman, and C. A. Black. 1980. Amphetamine stereotypy is not a homogeneous phenomenon: Sniffing and licking show distinct patterns of sensitization and tolerance. *Psychopharmacology* (Berlin) 68: 287–90.

Ellinwood, E. H., Jr., and A. Sudilovsky. 1973. Chronic amphetamine intoxication: Behavioral model of psychoses. In *Psychopathology and psychopharmacology,* eds. J. O. Cole, A. M. Freedman, and A. J. Friedhoff. Baltimore: Johns Hopkins University Press.

Ellisman, M. H., and K. R. Porter. 1980. Microtrabecular structure of the axoplasmic matrix: Visualization of cross-linking structures and their distribution. *Journal of Cell Biology* 87: 464–79.

Ellison, G. D., M. Eison, H. S. Huberman, and F. Daniel. 1978. Long-term changes in dopaminergic innervation of caudate nucleus after continuous amphetamine administration. *Science* 201: 276–78.

Ellison, G. D., and J. P. Flynn. 1968. Organized aggressive behavior in cats after surgical isolation of the hypothalamus. *Archives Italiennes De Biologie* 106: 1–20.

Enroth-Cugell, C., and J. G. Robson. 1966. The contrast sensitivity of retinal ganglion cells of the cat. *Journal of Physiology* (London) 187: 517–52.

Epstein, A. N., and P. Teitelbaum. 1962. Regulation of food intake in the absence of taste, smell, and other oropharyngeal sensations. *Journal of Comparative and Physiological Psychology* 55: 753–59.

Evarts, E. V. 1976. Brain mechanisms in motor control. *Life Sciences* 15: 1393–99.

Ewing, A. G., K. D. Alloway, S. D. Curtis, M. A. Dayton, R. M. Wightman, and G. V. Rebec. 1983. Simultaneous electrochemical and unit recording measurements: Characterization of the effects of D-amphetamine and ascorbic acid on neostriatal neurons. *Brain Research* 261: 101–8.

Falck, B. 1962. Observations on the possibilities of the cellular localization of monoamines by a fluorescent method. *Acta Physiologica Scandinavica* 56: Supplementum 197: 1–25.

Falck, B., N. Hillarp, G. Thieme, and A. Torp. 1962. Fluorescence of catecholamines and related compounds condensed with formaldehyde. *Journal of Histochemistry and Cytochemistry* 10: 348.

Feinberg, I. 1969. Effects of age on human sleep patterns. In *Sleep: Physiology and pathology,* ed. A. Kales. Philadelphia: Lippincott.

Feldman, S. M., and H. J. Waller. 1962. Dissociation of electrocortical activation and behavioral arousal. *Nature* 196: 1320–22.

Fernstrom, J. D. 1981. Dietary precursors and brain neurotransmitter formation. *Annual Review of Medicine* 32: 413–25.

Ferrero, P., A. Guidotti, B. Conti-Tronconi, and E. Costa. 1984. A brain octadecaneuropeptide generated by tryptic digestion of DBI (diazepam binding inhibitor) functions as a proconflict ligand of benzodiazepine recognition sites. *Neuropharmacology* 23: 1359–62.

Fetz, E. E. 1969. Operant conditioning of cortical unit activity. *Science* 163: 955–57.

Feuchtwanger, E. 1923. Die Funktionen des Stirnhirns. In *Monographienaus dem gesamtgebiete der psychiatrie.* Berlin: Springer.

Fex, J. 1962. Auditory activity in centrifugal centripetal cochlear fibres in cat. *Acta Physiologica Scandinavica* 55: Supplementum 189.

Fibiger, H. C. 1984. The neurobiological substrates of depression in Parkinson's disease. *Canadian Journal of Neurological Sciences* 11: 105–7.

Fibiger, H. C., A. P. Zis, and E. G. McGeer. 1973. Feeding and drinking deficits after 6-hydroxydopamine administration in the rat: Similarities to the lateral hypothalamic syndrome. *Brain Research* 55: 135–48.

Field, P. M., and G. Raisman. 1973. Structural and functional investigations of a sexually dimorphic part of the rat preoptic area. In *Recent studies of hypothalamic function: Symposium proceedings,* ed. Alberta Calgary.

Fifková, E., and A. Van Harreveld. 1977. Long-lasting morphological changes in dendritic spines of dentate granular cells following stimulation of the entorhinal area. *Journal of Neurocytology* 6: 211–30.

Finch, C. E., P. Randall, and J. F. Marshall. 1981. Aging and basal gangliar functions. *Annual Review of Gerontology and Geriatrics* 2: 49–87.

Fink, D. J., and H. Gainer. 1980. Axonal transport of proteins: a new view using in vivo covalent labeling. *Journal of Cell Biology* 85: 175–86.

Fink, M., S. Kety, J. McGaugh, and T. A. Williams. 1974. *Psychobiology of convulsive therapy.* New York: Halsted Press.

Fishman, I. Y. 1957. Single fiber gustatory impulses in the rat and hamster. *Journal of Cellular and Comparative Physiology* 49: 319–34.

Fitzgerald, F. T. 1981. The problem of obesity. *Annual Review of Medicine* 32: 221–31.

Fitzsimons, J. T. 1972. Thirst. *Physiological Reviews* 52: 468–561.

Fitzsimons, J. T., and B. J. Simons. 1969. The effect on drinking in the rat of intravenous infusion of angiotensin, given alone or in combination with other stimuli of thirst. *Journal of Physiology* (London) 203: 45–57.

Flourens, P. 1864. *Psychologie comparee.* 2d ed. Paris: Garnier Fréres.

Fluharty, S. J., and A. N. Epstein. 1983. Sodium appetite elicited by intracerebroventricular infusion of angiotensin II in the rat: II. Synergistic interaction with systemic mineralocorticoids. *Behavioral Neuroscience* 97: 746–58.

Flynn, J. P. 1967. The neural basis of aggression in cats. In *Neurophysiology and emotion,* ed. D. C. Glass. New York: Rockefeller University Press.

Flynn, J. P., H. Vanegas, W. Foote, and S. Edwards. 1970. Neural mechanisms involved in a cat's attack on a rat. In *The neural control of behavior.* eds. R. E. Whalen, R. F. Thompson, M. Verzeano, and N. M. Weinberger. New York: Academic Press.

Fouriezos, G., and R. A. Wise. 1976. Pimozide-induced extinction of intracranial self-stimulation: Response patterns rule out motor or performance effects. *Brain Research* 103: 377–80.

Fowler, M. J., M. J. Sullivan, and B. R. Ekstrand. 1973. Sleep and memory. *Science* 179: 302–4.

Fox, C. F. 1972. The structure of cell membranes. *Scientific American* 226: 30–38.

Frederickson, R. C. A., and L. E. Geary. 1982. Endogenous opiod peptides: Review of physiological, pharmacological and clinical aspects. *Progress in Neurobiology* 19: 19–69.

Freedman, D. X. 1961. Effects of LSD-25 on brain serotonin. *Journal of Pharmacology and Experimental Therapeutics* 134: 160–66.

Freedman, D. X. and N. J. Giarman. 1962. LSD-25 and the status and level of brain serotonin. *Annals of New York Academy of Sciences* 96: 98–106.

Freedman, M., and M. Oscar-Berman. 1986. Bilateral frontal lobe disease and selective delayed response deficits in humans. *Behav. Neurosci.* 100: 337–42.

French, J. D. 1957. The reticular formation. *Scientific American* 196: 54–60.

Freud, S. *A general introduction to psychoanalysis.* 1938. Garden City, NY: Garden City Publishing Co.

Friedhoff, A. J. 1973. Biogenic amines and schizophrenia. *Biological psychiatry,* ed. J. Mendels. New York: Wiley.

Friedman, M. I. 1978. Hyperphagia in rats with experimental diabetes mellitus: A response to a decreased supply of utilizable fuels. *Journal of Comparative and Physiological Psychology* 92: 109–17.

Friedman, M. I., and E. M. Stricker. 1976. The physiological psychology of hunger: A physiological perspective. *Psychological Review* 83: 409–31.

Frohman, L. A. 1980. Neurotransmitters as regulators of endocrine function. In *Neuroendocrinology,* eds. D. T. Krieger, and J. C. Hughes. Sunderland, MA: Sinauer.

Fuller, J. L., and W. R. Thompson. 1978. *Foundations of behavior genetics.* St. Louis: C. V. Mosby.

Funkenstein, H. H., P. G. Nelson, P. Winter, Z. Wollberg, and J. D. Newman. 1971. Unit responses in the auditory cortex of awake squirrel monkeys to vocal stimulation. In *Physiology of the auditory system,* ed. M. B. Sachs. Baltimore: National Educational Consultants.

Fuster, J. M., and G. E. Alexander. 1971. Neuron activity related to short-term memory. *Science* 173: 652–54.

Gaddum, J. H. 1953. Antagonism between LSD and 5-hydroxytryptamine. *Journal of Physiology* (London), 15: 1–15.

Gage, F. H., and A. Bjorklund. 1986. Cholinergic septal grafts onto the hippocampal formation improve spatial learning and memory in aged rats by an atropine-sensitive mechanism. *Journal of Neuroscience* 6: 2837–47. (a)

Gage, F. H., and A. Bjorklund. 1986. Neural grafting in the aged rat brain. *Annual Review of Physiology* 48: 447–59. (b)

Gage, F. H., A. Bjorklund, U. Stenevi, S. B. Dunnett, and P. A. T. Kelly. 1984. Intrahippocampal septal grafts ameliorate learning impairment in aged rats. *Science* 225: 533–36.

Gage, F. H., S. B. Dunnett, U. Stenevi, and A. Bjorklund. 1983. Aged rats: Recovery of motor impairments by intrastriatal nigral grafts. *Science* 221: 966–69.

Galambos, R. 1956. Suppression of auditory nerve activity by stimulation of efferent fibres to the cochlea. *Journal of Neurophysiology* 19: 424–37.

Galambos, R., and H. Davis. 1943. The response of single auditory nerve fibers to acoustic stimulation. *Journal of Neurophysiology* 6: 39–58.

Galambos, R., J. Schwartzkopff, and A. Rupert. 1959. Microelectrode study of superior olivary nuclei. *American Journal of Physiology* 197: 527–36.

Gallistel, C. R. 1966. Motivation effects in self-stimulation. *Journal of Comparative and Physiological Psychology* 62: 95–101.

Gallistel, C. R. 1973. Self-simulation: The neurophysiology of reward and motivation. In *The physiological basis of memory,* ed. J. A. Deutsch. New York: Academic Press.

Gallistel, C. R., and G. Bealey. 1971. Specificity of brain stimulation reward in the rat. *Journal of Comparative and Physiological Psychology* 76: 199–205.

Gallistel, C. R., P. Shizgal, and J. S. Yeomans. 1981. A portrait of the substrate for self-stimulation. *Psychological Review* 88: 228–73.

Garcia, J., F. R. Ervin, C. H. Yorke, and R. A. Koelling. 1967. Conditioning with delayed vitamin injections. *Science* 155: 716–18.

Gardiner, T. W., M. Armstrong-James, A. W. Caan, R. M. Wightman, and G. V. Rebec. 1985. Modulation of neostriatal activity by iontophoresis of ascorbic acid. *Brain Research* 344: 181–85.

Gardiner, T. W., D. A. Iverson, and G. V. Rebec. 1986. Regional responses to amphetamine in the neostriatum and nucleus accumbens of awake behaving rats. *Society for Neuroscience Abstracts* 12: 514.

Gardiner, T. W., and E. M. Stricker. 1985. Hyperdipsia in rats after electrolytic lesions of nucleus medianus. *American Journal of Physiology* 248: R214–R223. (a)

Gardiner, T. W., and E. M. Stricker. 1985. Impaired drinking responses of rats with lesions of nucleus medianus: Circadian dependence. *American Journal of Physiology* 248: R224–R230. (b)

Gardner, E. 1968. *Fundamentals of neurology.* 5th ed. Philadelphia: Saunders.

Garn, S. M., and D. C. Clark. 1976. Trends in fatness and the origins of obesity. *Pediatrics* 57: 433–56.

Geinisman, Y., L. Toledo-Morrell, and F. Morrell. 1986. Loss of perforated synapses in the dentate gyrus: Morphological substrate of memory deficit in aged rats. *Proc. Natl. Acad. Sci. USA* 83: 3027–31.

Gerfen, C. R., and P. E. Sawchenko. 1984. An anterograde neuroanatomical tracing method that shows the detailed morphology of neurons, their axons and terminals: Immunohistochemical localization of an axonally transported plant lectin, *Phaseolus vulgaris* Leucoagglutinin (PHA-L). *Brain Research* 209: 219–38.

German, D. C., and D. M. Bowden. 1974. Catecholamine systems as the neural substrate for intracranial self-stimulation: A hypothesis. *Brain Research* 73: 381–419.

Geschwind, N. 1966. Carl Wernicke, the Breslau School and the history of aphasia. In *Brain function,* ed. E. C. Carterette. Berkeley: University of California Press.

Geschwind, N. 1972. Language and the brain. *Scientific American* 226: 76–83.

Geschwind, N. 1975. The apraxias: Neural mechanisms of disorders of learned movements. *American Scientist* 63: 188–95.

Gesteland, R. C., J. Y. Lettvin, W. H. Pitts, and A. Rojas. 1963. Odor specificities of the frog's olfactory receptors. In *Olfaction and taste,* ed. V. Zotterman, part I. New York: Macmillan.

Geyer, M. A., D. S. Segal, and A. J. Mandell. 1972. Effect of intraventricular infusion of dopamine and norepinephrine on motor activity. *Physiology and Behavior* 8: 653–58.

Gibbs, J., R. C. Young, and G. P. Smith. 1973. Cholecystokinin elicits satiety in rats with open gastric fistulas. *Nature* 245: 323–25.

Gibson, W. E., L. D. Reid, M. Sakai, and P. B. Porter. 1965. Intracranial reinforcement compared with sugar water reinforcement. *Science* 148: 1357–59.

Giese, A. C. 1968. *Cell physiology.* Philadelphia: Saunders.

Gillin, J. C., and A. A. Borbely. 1985. Sleep: A neurobiological window on affective disorders. *Trends in NeuroSciences* 8: 537–42.

Gillin, J. C., W. B. Mendelson, N. Sitaram, and R. J. Wyatt. 1978. The neuropharmacology of sleep and wakefulness. *Ann. Rev. Pharmacol. Toxicol.* 18: 563–79.

Gilman, A. 1937. The relation between blood osmotic pressure, fluid distribution and voluntary water intake. *American Journal of Physiology* 120: 323–28.

Ginsburg, B., and W. C. Allee. 1942. Some effects of conditioning on social dominance and subordination in inbred strains of mice. *Physiological Zoology* 25: 485–506.

Goddard, G. V. 1967. The development of epileptic seizures through brain stimulation at low intensity. *Nature* 214: 1020.

Goeders, N. E., and J. E. Smith. 1983. Cortical dopaminergic involvement in cocaine reinforcement. *Science* 221: 773–75.

Goff, W. R., and T. Allison. 1978. The functional neuroanatomy of event related potentials. In *Event-related brain potentials in man,* eds. E. Callaway, P. Tueting, and S. H. Koslow, 1–79. New York: Academic Press.

Gold, R. M. 1973. Hypothalamic obesity: The myth of the ventromedial nucleus. *Science* 182: 488–90.

Gold, R. M., A. P. Jones, P. E. Sawchenko, and G. Kapatos. 1977. Paraventricular area: Critical focus of a longitudinal neurocircuitry mediating food intake. *Physiology and Behavior* 18: 1111–19.

Goldberg, S. R., and C. R. Schuster. 1967. Conditioned suppression by a stimulus associated with nalorphine in morphine-dependent monkeys. *Journal of Experimental Analysis of Behavior* 10: 235–42.

Goldensohn, E. S. 1975. The classification of epileptic seizures. In *The nervous system,* ed. D. B. Tower, vol. 2. The clinical neurosciences. New York: Raven Press.

Goldman, P. S. 1978. Neuronal plasticity in primate telencephalon: Anomalous projections induced by prenatal removal of frontal cortex. *Science* 202: 768–70.

Goldman, P. S., and W. J. H. Nauta. 1977. Columnar distribution of cortico-cortical fibers in the frontal association, limbic, and motor cortex of the developing rhesus monkey. *Brain Research* 122: 393–414.

Goldstein, A. 1976. Opioid peptides (endorphins) in pituitary and brain. *Science* 193: 1081–86.

Goldstein, A., L. Aranov, and S. M. Kalman. 1969. *Principles of drug action.* New York: Harper & Row.

Goldstein, A., and D. B. Goldstein. 1968. Enzyme expansion theory of drug tolerance and physical dependence. *Research Publications of Association for Research in Nervous and Mental Disorders* 46: 265–78.

Golomb, B., R. A. Andersen, K. Nakayama, D. I. A. MacLeod, and A. Wong. 1985. Visual thresholds for shearing motion in monkey and man. *Vision Research* 25: 813–20.

Goodman, L. S. and A. Gilman. 1974. *The pharmacological basis of therapeutics,* 4th ed. New York: Macmillan Co.

Gottesman, I. I., and J. Shields. 1982. *Schizophrenia: The epigenetic puzzle.* Cambridge: Cambridge University Press.

Goy, R. W. 1968. Organizing effect of androgen on the behaviour of rhesus monkeys. In *Endocrinology of human behaviour,* ed. R. P. Michael, London: Oxford University Press.

Grace, A. A., and B. S. Bunney. 1985. Low doses of apomorphine elicit two opposing influences on dopamine cell electrophysiology. *Brain Research* 333: 285–98.

Gray, E. G. 1959. Axo-somatic and axo-dendritic synapses of the cerebral cortex: An electron microscope study. *Journal of Anatomy* 93: 420–33.

Graybiel, A. M. 1972. Some extrageniculate visual pathways in the cat. *Investigative Ophthalmology* 11: 322–32.

Graybiel, A. M. 1983. Compartmental organization of the mammalian striatum. In *Progess in brain research: Molecular and cellular interactions underlying higher brain functions* 58, eds. J. P. Changeux, J. Glowinski, M. Imbert, and F. E. Bloom. Amsterdam: Elsevier.

Green, G. D. 1986. The search for the site of visual adaptation. *Vision Research* 20: 1417–29.

Greengard, P. 1975. Cyclic nucleotides, protein phosphorylation and neuronal function. In *Advances in cyclic nucleotide research,* eds. G. Drummond, P. Greengard, and G. Robison, 585–602. New York: Raven Press.

Greenough, W. T. 1975. Experimental modification of the developing brain. *American Scientist* 63: 37–46.

Greenough, W. T., C. S. Carter, C. Steerman, and T. J. DeVoogd. 1977. Sex differences in dendritic patterns in hamster preoptic area. *Brain Research* 126: 63–72.

Greenough, W. T., and F. R. Volkmar. 1973. Pattern of dendritic branching in complex environments. *Experimental Neurology* 40: 491–504.

Grillner, S. 1975. Locomotion in vertebrates: central mechanisms and reflex interaction. *Physiological Reviews:* 55: 247–304.

Grossman, C. J. 1985. Interactions between the gonadal steroids and the immune system. *Science* 227: 257–61.

Grossman, S. P. 1962. Direct adrenergic and cholinergic stimulation of hypothalamic mechanisms. *American Journal of Physiology* 303: 872–82.

Grossman, S. P. 1979. The biology of motivation. *Annual Review of Psychology* 30: 209–42.

Groves, P. M. 1983. A theory of the functional organization of the neostriatum and the neostriatal control of voluntary movement. *Brain Research Reviews* 5: 109–32.

Groves, P. M., S. W. Miller, M. V. Parker, and G. V. Rebec. 1973. Organization by sensory modality in the reticular formation of the rat. *Brain Research* 54: 207–24.

Groves, P. M., and G. V. Rebec. 1976. Biochemistry and behavior: Some central actions of amphetamine and antipsychotic drugs. *Annual Review of Psychology* 27: 97–128.

Groves, P. M., and R. F. Thompson. 1970. Habituation: A dual-process theory. *Psychological Review* 77: 419–50.

Groves, P. M., C. J. Wilson, S. J. Young, and G. V. Rebec. 1975. Self-inhibition by dopaminergic neurons. *Science* 190: 522–29.

Gualtieri, T., and R. E. Hicks. 1985. An immunoreactive theory of selective male affliction. *Behavioral and Brain Sciences* 8: 427–41.

Guidotti, A., and E. Costa. 1977. Trans-synaptic regulation of tyrosine 3-monooxygenase biosynthesis in rat adrenal medulla. *Biochemical Pharmacology* 26: 817–23.

Guilleminault, C., and W. C. Dement. 1978. *Sleep apnea syndromes.* New York: Alan R. Liss.

Guth, L. 1974. Axonal regeneration and functional plasticity in the central nervous system. *Experimental Neurology* 45: 606–54.

Hadjiconstantinou, M., and N. H. Neff. 1983. Ascorbic acid could be hazardous to your experiments: A commentary on dopamine receptor binding studies with speculation on a role for ascorbic acid in neural function. *Neuropharmacology* 22: 939–43.

Hahn, J. R. 1974. Somesthesis. *Annual Review of Psychology* 25: 233–46.

Haigler, H. J., and G. K. Aghajanian. 1974. Lysergic acid diethylamide and serotonin: A comparison of effects on serotonergic neurons and neurons receiving a serotonergic input. *Journal of Pharmacology and Experimental Therapeutics* 188: 688–99.

Ham, Arthur W. 1974. *Histology.* 7th ed. Philadelphia: Lippincott.

Harlow, H. F. 1962. The heterosexual affectional system in monkeys. *American Psychologist* 37: 1–9.

Hart, B. L. 1967. Sexual reflexes and mating behavior in the male dog. *Journal of Comparative and Physiological Psychology* 66: 388–99.

Hart, B. L. 1978. Hormones, spinal reflexes, and sexual behaviour. In *Determinants of sexual behaviour,* ed. J. B. Huthinson. Chichester: Wiley & Sons.

Hartline, H. F., F. Ratliff, and W. H. Miller. 1961. Inhibitory interaction in the retina and its significance in vision. In *Nervous inhibition,* ed. E. Florey. New York: Pergamon Press.

Hartmann, E. L. 1973. *The functions of sleep.* New Haven: Yale University Press.

Hartmann, E. L., T. J. Bridwell, and J. J. Schildkraut. 1971. Alpha-methylparatyrosine and sleep in the rat. *Psychopharmacologia* 21: 157–64.

Harvey, J. A., ed. 1971. *Behavioral analysis of drug action.* Glenview, IL: Scott, Foresman.

Harvey, J. A., and C. E. Lints. 1971. Lesions in the medial forebrain bundle: Relationship between pain sensitivity and telecephalic content of serotonin. *Journal of Comparative and Physiological Psychology* 74: 28–36.

Harvey, S. C. 1975. Hypnotics and sedatives: The barbiturates. In *The pharmacological basis of therapeutics,* eds. L. S. Goodman and A. Gilman. 5th ed., 102–23. New York: Macmillan Publishing Co.

Harweth, R. S., E. L. Smith, G. C. Duncan, M. L. J. Crawford, G. K. von Noorden. 1986. Multiple sensitive periods in the development of the primate visual system. *Science* 232: 235–38.

Hauri, P. 1982. *The sleep disorders.* 2d ed. Kalamazoo, MI: Upjohn Co.

Hayat, M. A. 1986. *Basic techniques for transmission electron microscopy.* Orlando, FL: Academic Press.

Heath, R. G. 1963. Electrical self-stimulation of the brain in man. *American Journal of Psychiatry* 120: 571–77.

Heath, R. G., S. B. John, and C. J. Fontana, 1968. Studies by stereotaxic techniques in patients. In *Computers and electronic devices in psychiatry,* eds. N. Kline and E. Laska. New York: Grune & Stratton.

Heber, R. A. 1959. A manual of terminology and classification on mental retardation. *American Journal of Mental Deficiencies* 64: (Monogr. Suppl.). (Rev. ed., 1961. Modifications in the manual on terminology and classification in mental retardation 65: 499–500).

Hecht, S., S. Shlaer, and M. H. Pirenne. 1942. Energy, quanta and vision. *Journal of General Physiology* 25: 819–40.

Hedreen, J. C., R. G. Struble, P. J. Whitehouse, and D. L. Price. 1984. Topography of the magnocellular basal forebrain system in human brain. *Journal of Neuropathology and Experimental Neurology* 43: 1–21.

Heimburger, R. F., C. C. Whitlock, and J. E. Kalsbeck. 1966. Stereotaxic amygdalotomy for epilepsy with aggressive behavior. *Journal of American Medical Association* 198: 165–69.

Heimer, L. 1970. Selective silver impregnation of degenerating axoplasm. In *Contemporary Research Methods in Neuroanatomy,* eds. W. J. H. Nauta and S. O. E. Ebbesson, New York: Springer-Verlag.

Held, R., and A. Hein. 1963. Movement-produced stimulation in the development of visually guided behavior. *Journal of Comparative and Physiological Psychology* 56: 872–76.

Hess, W. R. 1957. *The functional organization of the diencephalon.* New York: Grune & Stratton.

Heston, L. L. 1970. The genetics of schizophrenia and schizoid disease. *Science* 167: 249–56.

Hetherington, A. W., and S. W. Ranson. 1940. Hypothalamic lesions and adiposity in the rat. *Anatomical Record* 78: 149–72.

Heuser, J. E., and T. S. Reese. 1979. Synaptic-vesicle exocytosis captured by quick-freezing. In *The Neurosciences, Fourth Study Program,* eds. F. O. Schmitt and F. G. Worden. Cambridge, MA: M.I.T. Press.

Hillyard, S. A., and M. Kutas. 1983. Electrophysiology of cognitive processing. In *Annual Review of Psychology,* eds. M. R. Rosenzweig and L. W. Porter, 33–61. Palo Alto, CA: Annual Reviews, Inc

Hilton, S. M., and A. W. Zbrozyna. 1963. Amygdaloid region for defense reactions and its afferent pathway to the brain stem. *Journal of Physiology* (London) 165: 160–73.

Hirsch, H. V. B., and D. N. Spinelli. 1970. Visual experience modifies distribution of horizontally and vertically oriented receptive fields in cats. *Science* 168: 869–71.

Hodgkin, A. L., and A. F. Huxley. 1952. A quantitative description of membrane current and its application to conduction and excitation in nerve. *Journal of Physiology* (London) 117: 500–544.

Hodos, W., and H. J. Karten. 1974. Visual intensity and pattern discrimination deficits after lesions of the optic lobe in pigeons. *Brain, Behavior and Evolution* 9: 165–94.

Hodos, W., and E. S. Valenstein. 1962. An evaluation of response rate as a measure of rewarding intracranial stimulation. *Journal of Comparative and Physiological Psychology* 55: 80–84.

Hoebel, B. G. 1968. Inhibition and disinhibition of self-stimulation and feeding. *Journal of Comparative and Physiological Psychology* 66: 89–100.

Hoebel, B. G. 1977. Pharmacologic control of feeding. *Annual Review of Pharmacology and Toxicology* 17: 605–21.

Hoebel, B. G., and P. Teitelbaum. 1966. Weight regulation in normal and hypothalamic hyperphagic rats. *Journal of Comparative and Physiological Psychology* 61: 189–93.

Hohman, G. W. 1966. Some effects of spinal cord lesions on experienced emotional feelings. *Psychophysiology* 3: 143–56.

Holman, R. B., G. R. Elliott, and J. D. Barchas. 1975. Neuroregulators and sleep mechanisms. *Annual Reviews of Medicine* 26: 499–520.

Horn, G., and R. M. Hill. 1969. Modifications of receptive fields of cells in the visual cortex occurring spontaneously and associated with body tilt. *Nature* (London) 221: 186–88.

Hornykiewicz, O. 1966. Dopamine (3-hydroxytyramine) and brain function. *Pharmacological Review* 18: 925–64.

Horton, J. C., and D. H. Hubel. 1980. Cytochrome oxidase stain preferentially labels intersections of ocular dominance and vertical orientation columns in macaque striate cortex. *Society for Neuroscience Abstracts* 6: 315.

Hosobuchi, Y., J. Rossier, F. E. Bloom, and R. Guillemin. 1979. Stimulation of human periaqueductal gray for pain relief increase immunoreactive B-endorphin in ventricular fluid. *Science* 203: 279–81.

Hosutt, J. A., N. Rowland, and E. M. Stricker. 1981. Impaired drinking responses of rats with lesions of the subfornical organ. *Journal of Comparative and Physiological Psychology* 95: 104–13.

Howard, S. B., A. M. Etgen, and R. J. Barfield. 1984. Antagonism of central estrogen activity by intracerebral implants of tamoxifen. *Hormones and Behavior* 18: 256–66.

Hsia, D. Y. Y. 1970. Phenylketonuria and its variants. In *Progress in Medical Genetics,* eds. A. G. Steinberg and A. G. Bearn. New York: Grune and Stratton.

Hubel, D. H., and T. N. Wiesel. 1965. Receptive fields and functional architecture in two nonstriate visual areas (18 and 19) of the cat. *Journal of Neurophysiology* 28: 229–89.

Hubel, D. H., and T. N. Wiesel. 1968. Receptive fields and functional architecture of the monkey striate cortex. *Journal of Physiology* (London) 195: 215–43.

Hubel, D. H., and T. N. Wiesel. 1970. The period of susceptibility to the physiological effects of unilateral eye closure in kittens. *Journal of Physiology* (London) 206: 419–36.

Hubel, D. H., and T. N. Wiesel. 1977. Functional architecture of macaque monkey visual cortex, *Proceedings of the Royal Society, London, B.* 198: 1–59.

Hughes, J. 1975. Isolation of an endogenous compound from the brain with pharmacological properties similar to morphine. *Brain Research* 88: 295–308.

Hustvedt, B. E., and Lovo, A. 1972. Correlation between hyperinsulinemia and hyperphagia in rats with ventromedial hypothalamic lesions. *Acta Physiologica Scandinavica* 84: 29–33.

Hutchinson, R. R., and J. W. Renfrew. 1966. Stalking attack and eating behavior elicited from the same sites in the hypothalamus. *Journal of Comparative and Physiological Psychology* 61: 300–17.

Imig, T. J., and N. M. Weinberger. 1973. Relationships between rate and pattern of unitary discharges in the medial geniculate body of the cat in response to click and amplitude-modulated white-noise stimulation. *Journal of Neurophysiology* 36: 385–97.

Ingle, D., and G. E. Schneider. 1970. Subcortical visual systems. *Brain, Behavior, and Evolution* 3: 1–352.

Inoue, S., K. Honda, Y. Komoda, K. Uchizono, R. Ueno, and O. Hayaishi. 1984. Differential sleep-promoting effects of five sleep substances nocturnally infused in unrestrained rats. *Proc. Natl. Acad. Sci. USA* 81: 6240–44.

Isaacson, R. L., T. Jessel, and I. Kanazawa. 1976. Release and metabolism of substance P in rat hypothalamus. *Nature* 264: 81–83.

Iversen, L. 1974. *The limbic system.* New York: Plenum.

Iversen, S. D. 1973. Brain lesions and memory in animals. In *The physiological basis of memory,* ed. J. A. Deutsch, New York: Academic Press.

Iversen, S. D. 1977. Neural substrates mediating amphetamine responses. In *Cocaine and Other Stimulants,* eds. E. H. Ellinwood and M. M. Kilbey. New York: Plenum Press.

Iversen, S. D., and L. L. Iversen, 1975. *Behavioral pharmacology.* New York: Oxford University Press.

Jacobs, B. L., S. J. Henricksen, and W. C. Dement. 1972. Neurochemical bases of the PGO wave. *Brain Research* 48: 406–11.

Jacobs, B. L., D. J. McGinty, and R. M. Harper. 1973. Brain single unit activity during sleep-wakefulness—a review. In *Brain unit activity during behavior,* ed. M. I. Phillips. Springfield, Il: Charles C. Thomas.

Jacobs, B. L., and M. E. Trulson. 1979. Mechanisms of action of LSD. *American Scientist* 67: 396–404.

Jacobs, P. A., M. Brunton, M. M. Melville, R. P. Brittain, and W. F. McClemont. 1965. Aggressive behavior, mental sub-normality, and the XYY male. *Nature* 208: 1351–52.

Jaffe, J. H. 1975. Drug addiction and drug abuse. In *The pharmacological basis of therapeutics,* eds. L. S. Goodman and A. Gilman. 5th ed., 284–324. New York: Macmillan Publishing Co.

Jaffe, J. H., and S. K. Sharpless. 1968. Pharmacological denervation supersensitivity in the central nervous system: A theory of physical dependence. *Proceedings of Association for Research on Nervous and Mental Disorders* 46: 226–46.

Janowsky, D. S., and S. C. Risch. 1984. Adrenergic and cholinergic balance and affective disorders. *The Psychiatric Hospital* 15: 163–71.

Jasper, H. H., and T. L. Sourkes. 1983. Nobel laureates in neurosciences: 1904–1981. *Annual Review of Neuroscience,* eds. W. M. Cowan, E. M. Shooter, C. F. Stevens, and R. F. Thompson, vol. 6. Palo Alto, CA: Annual Reviews, Inc.

Jassik-Gerschenfeld, D. 1966. Activity of somatic origin evoked in the superior colliculus of the cat. *Experimental Neurology* 16: 104–18.

Jay, M. F., and D. L. Sparks. 1984. Auditory receptive fields in primate superior colliculus shift with changes in eye position. *Nature* 309: 345–47.

Jenkins, J. J., E. Jimenez-Pabon, R. E. Shaw, and J. W. Sefer. 1975. *Schull's aphasia in adults.* New York: Harper & Row.

Jenner, P., C. Pycock, and C. D. Marsden. 1978. The effect of chronic administration and withdrawal of amphetamine on cerebral dopamine receptor sensitivity. *Psychopharmacology* 58, 131–36.

Jeste, D. V., L. Barban, and J. Parisi. 1984. Reduced Purkinje cell density in Huntington's disease. *Experimental Neurology* 85: 78–86.

Jeste, D. V., and R. J. Wyatt. 1984. *Neuropsychiatric movement disorders.* Washington, D.C.: American Psychiatric Press.

Johnson, A. K., and J. Buggy. 1977. A critical analysis of the site of action for the dipsogenic effect of angiotensin II. In *International symposium on the central actions of angiotensin and related hormones,* eds. J. P. Buckley and C. Ferrario. Oxford: Pergamon Press.

Johnson, L. C. 1973. Are stages of sleep related to waking behavior? *American Scientist* 61: 326–38.

Johnson, L. C. 1982. Sleep deprivation and performance. In *Biological rhythms, sleep, and performance,* ed. W. B. Webb, 111–41. John Wiley & Sons.

Johnson, L. C., and D. A. Chernik. 1982. Sedative-hypnotics and human performance. *Psychopharmacology* 76: 101–13.

Johnson, L. C., and P. Naitoh. 1974. The operational consequences of sleep deprivation and sleep deficit. *North Atlantic Treaty Organization Advisory Group for Aerospace Research and Development* 193: 1–43.

Johnson, L. C., and C. L. Spinweber. 1984. Benzodiazepine activity: Day-time effects and the sleep EEG. *Clinical Neuropsychopharmacology* 7: 820–21.

Johnson, L. C., D. I. Tepas, W. P. Colquhoun, and M. J. Colligan. 1981. *Biological rhythms, sleep and shift work*. New York: SP Medical and Scientific Books.

Jones, E. G., and B. K. Hartman. 1978. Recent advances in neuroanatomical methodology. *Ann. Rev. Neuroscience* 1: 215–96.

Jordan, H. A. 1969. Voluntary intragastric feeding: Oral and gastric contributions to food intake and hunger in man. *Journal of Comparative and Physiological Psychology* 68: 498–506.

Jost, A. 1958. Embryonic sexual differentiation. In *Hermaphroditism, genital anamolies, and related endocrine disorders*, eds. H. W Jones and W. W. Scott. Baltimore: Williams and Wilkins.

Jouvet, M. 1969. Biogenic amines and the states of sleep. *Science* 163: 32–41. (a)

Jouvet, M. 1969. Neurophysiological and biochemical mechanisms of sleep. In *Sleep: Physiology and pathology*, ed. A. Kales Philadelphia: Lippincott. (b)

Judd, L. L., B. Hubbard, D. S. Janowsky, L. Y. Huey, and P. A. Attewell. 1977. The effect of lithium carbonate on affect, mood, and personality of normal subjects. *Archives of General Psychiatry* 34: 346–51. (a)

Judd, L. L., B. Hubbard, D. S. Janowsky, L. Y. Huey, and K. I. Takahashi. 1977. The effect of lithium carbonate on the cognitive functions of normal subjects. *Archives of General Psychiatry* 34: 355–57. (b)

Kamata, K., R. L. Wilson, K. D. Alloway, and G. V. Rebec. 1986. Multiple amphetamine injections reduce the release of ascorbic acid in the neostriatum of the rat. *Brain Research* 362: 331–38.

Kapatos, G., and R. M. Gold. 1973. Evidence for ascending noradrenergic mediation of hypothalamic hyperphagia. *Pharmacology, Biochemistry, and Behavior* 1: 81–87.

Katz, B. 1966. *Nerve, muscle, and synapse*. New York: McGraw-Hill.

Katzman, R. 1985. Research frontiers in Alzheimer's disease. Distinguished faculty lecture, 21 February at University of California, San Diego.

Keesey, R. E., and T. L. Powley. 1975. Hypothalamic regulation of body weight. *American Scientist* 63: 558–65.

Kelleher, R. T., and W. H. Morse. 1968. Determinants of the behavioral effects of drugs. In *Importance of fundamental principles in drug evaluation*, eds. D. Tedeschi and R. Tedeschi. New York: Raven Press.

Kelly, D. D. 1982. The role of endorphins in stress-induced analgesia. *Annals of the New York Academy of Science* 398: 260–70.

Kemp, J. M., and T. P. S. Powell. 1971. The site of termination of afferent fibres in the caudate nucleus. *Philosophical Transactions of the Royal Society*, series B262: 413–27.

Kennedy, G. C. 1953. The role of depot fat in the hypothalamic control of food intake in the rat. *Proceedings of the Royal Society*, series B140: 578–92.

Kent, E., and S. P. Grossman. 1969. Evidence for a conflict interpretation of anomalous effects of rewarding brain stimulation. *Journal of Comparative and Physiological Psychology* 69: 381–90.

Kerr, F. W. L., and P. R. Wilson. 1978. Pain. *Ann. Rev. Neuroscience* 1: 83–102.

Kety, S. S. 1974. Biochemical and neurochemical effects of electroconvulsive shock. In *Psychobiology of convulsive therapy*, eds. N. Fink, S. Kety, J. McGaugh, and T. A. Williams. Washington, D.C.: V. H. Winston.

Kiang, N. Y. S. 1965. Stimulus coding in the auditory nerve and cochlear nucleus. *Acta Oto-Laryngologica* 59: 186–200.

Kimble, D. P. 1968. Hippocampus and internal inhibition. *Psychological Bulletin* 70: 285–95.

Kimura, D. 1973. The asymmetry of the human brain. *Scientific American* 228: 70–78.

Kimura, K., and L. M. Beidler. 1961. Microelectrode study of taste receptors of the rat and hamster. *Journal of Cellular and Comparative Physiology* 58: 131–39.

Klawans, H. L. 1982. *The medicine of history*. New York: Raven Press.

Kling, J. W., and Y. Matsumiya. 1962. Relative reinforcement values of food and intracranial stimulation. *Science* 135: 668–70.

Kluger, M. J. 1978. The evolution and adaptive value of fever. *American Scientist* 66: 38–43.

Kluver, H., and P. C. Bucy. 1939. Preliminary analysis of the temporal lobes in monkeys. *Archives of Neurology and Psychiatry* 42: 979–1000.

Kolb, B. 1984. Functions of the frontal cortex of the rat: A comparative review. *Brain Research Reviews* 8: 65–98.

Kornhuber, H. H. 1974. Cerebral cortex, cerebellum, and basal ganglia: An introduction to their motor functions. In *The neurosciences: Third study program,* eds. F. O. Schmitt and F. G. Worden. Cambridge, MA.: M.I.T. Press.

Kornhuber, H. H. 1975. Cerebral cortex, cerebellum, and basal ganglia: An introduction to their motor functions. In *The neurosciences: Third study program,* eds. F. O. Schmitt and F. G. Worden. Cambridge, MA: M.I.T. Press.

Krech, D. 1968. Brain chemistry and anatomy: Implications for behavior therapy. In *Mind as a tissue,* ed. D. C. Rupp. New York: Harper & Row.

Kringlen, E. 1967. *Heredity and environment in the functional psychoses: An epidemiological clinical twin study.* Oslo: Universitetsförlaget.

Kripke, D. F. 1985. Biological rhythms. In *Psychiatry,* ed. J. O. Cavenar, Jr., vol. 3. Philadelphia: Lippincott.

Kripke, D. F., and J. C. Gillin. 1985. Sleep disorders. In *Psychiatry,* ed. J. O. Cavenar, Jr., vol. 3. Philadelphia: Lippincott.

Kuffler, S. W. 1953. Discharge patterns and functional organization of mammalian retina. *Journal of Neurophysiology* 16: 37–68.

Kuhar, M. J., E. B. Souza, and J. R. Unnerstall. 1986. Neurotransmitter receptor mapping by autoradiograph and other methods. *Annual Review of Neuroscience* 9: 27–59.

Kupfermann, I. 1975. Neurophysiology of learning. *Annual Review of Psychology* 26: 367–91.

Kupfermann, I., V. Castellucci, H. Pinsker, and E. R. Kandel. 1970. Neuronal correlates of habituation and dishabituation of the gill withdrawal reflex of *Aplysia. Science* 167: 1743–45.

Kutas, M., and S. A. Hillyard. 1985. Event-related potentials and psychopathology. In *Psychiatry,* ed. J. O. Cavenar, Jr. Philadelphia: Lippincott.

Kuypers, A. 1982. A new look at the organization of the meter system. In *Anatomy of descending pathways to the spinal cord; Progress in brain research* 57, eds. A. Kuypers and H. Martin, 381–403.

Larson, J., and G. Lynch. 1986. Induction of synaptic potentiation in hippocampus by patterned stimulation involves two events. *Science* 232: 985–88.

Larsson, K. 1964. Mating behavior in male rats after cerebral cortex ablation: II. Effects of lesions in the frontal lobes compared to lesions in the posterior half of the hemispheres. *Journal of Experimental Zoology* 155: 203–14.

LaVail, J. H., and M. M. LaVail. 1972. Retrograde axonal transport in the central nervous system. *Science* 176: 1416–17.

Leaton, R. N., and W. F. Supple. 1986. Cerebellar vermis: Essential for long-term habituation of the acoustic startle response. *Science* 232: 513–15.

LeBouef, B. 1974. Male-male competition and reproductive success in elephant seals. *American Zoologist* 14: 163–76.

Legendre, R., and H. Pieron. 1912. Recherches sur le besoin de sommeil consecutif a une veille prolongée. *Zeitschrift Allg. Physiol.* 14: 235–62.

Leibowitz, S. F. 1975. Amphetamine: Possible site and mode of action for producing anorexia in the rat. *Brain Research* 84: 160–65.

Lele, P. P., and G. Weddell. 1956. The relationship between neurohistology and corneal sensibility. *Brain* 79: 119–54.

LeMagnen, J. 1971. Advances in studies on the physiological control and regulation of food intake. In *Progress in physiological psychology,* 4, eds. E. Stellar and J. M. Sprague. New York: Academic Press.

Leon, M., P. G. Croskerry, and G. K. Smith. 1978. Thermal control of mother-young contact in rats. *Physiology and Behavior* 21: 793–811.

Lerner, I. M., and W. J. Libby. 1976. *Heredity, evolution and society.* San Francisco: W. H. Freeman.

Leshner, A. I., W. A. Walker, A. E. Johnson, J. S. Kelling, S. J. Kreisler, and B. B. Svare. 1973. Pituitary adrenocortical activity and intermale aggressiveness in isolated mice. *Physiology and Behavior* 11: 705–11.

Leslie, S. W., J. J. Woodward, R. E. Wilcox, and R. P. Farrar. 1986. Chronic ethanol treatment uncouples striatal calcium entry and endogenous dopamine release. *Brain Research* 368: 174–77.

LeVay, S., T. N. Wiesel, and D. H. Hubel. 1981. The postnatal development and plasticity of ocular-dominance columns in the monkey. In *The organization of the cerebral cortex.* eds. F. O. Schmitt, F. G. Worden, G. Adelman, and S. C. Dennis. Cambridge, MA: M.I.T. Press.

Levick, W. R., B. G. Cleland, and M. W. Dubin. 1972. Lateral geniculate neurons of the cat: Retinal inputs and physiology. *Investigative Ophthalmology* 11: 302–10.

Levine, J. D., N. C. Gordon, and H. L. Fields. 1979. The role of endorphins in placebo analgesia. In *Advances in brain research and therapy,* eds. J. J. Bonica, J. C. Liebeskind and D. Albe-Fessard, vol. 3. New York: Raven Press.

Liebelt, R. A., C. B. Bordelon, and A. G. Liebelt. 1973. The adipose tissue system and food intake. In *Progress in physiological psychology,* eds. E. Stellar and J. M. Sprague. New York: Academic Press.

Lieberburg, I., G. Wallach, and B. S. McEwen. 1977. The effects of an inhibitor of aromatization (1,4,6 androstatariene-3,17-dione and an anti-estrogen (C1628) on in vivo formed testosterone metabolities recovered from neonatal rat brain tissues and purified cell nuclei. Implications for sexual differentiation of brain. *Brain Research* 128: 176–81.

Liebeskind, J. C., and L. A. Paul. 1977. Psychological and physiological mechanisms of pain. *Ann. Rev. Psychol.* 28: 41–60.

Liebman, J. M., and L. L. Butcher. 1974. Comparative involvement of dopamine and noradrenaline in rate-free self-stimulation in the substantia nigra, lateral hypothalamus and mesencephalic central gray. *Naunyn-Schmiedeberg's Archives of Pharmacology* 284: 167–94.

Lindsley, D. B., L. H. Schreiner, W. B. Knowles, and H. W. Magoun. 1950. Behavioral and EEG changes following chronic brain stem lesions in the cat. *Electroencephalography and Clinical Neurophysiology* 2: 483–98.

Livingstone, M. D., and D. H. Hubel. 1984. Anatomy and physiology of a color system in the primate visual cortex. *Journal of Neuroscience* 4: 309–56.

Loewi, O. 1921. Uber humorale Ubertragbeit Herznervenwirkung. *Archives fuer die Gesamte Physiologie des Menschen und der Tiere* 189: 239–62.

Loewi, O. 1960. An autobiographic sketch. *Perspectives in Biological Medicine* 4: 2–35.

Loh, H. H., L. F. Tseng, E. Wei, C. H. Li. 1976. B-Endorphin is a potent analgesic agent. *Proc. Natl. Acad. Sci. USA* 73: 2895–98.

Lohr, J. B., and D. V. Jeste. 1986. Cerebellar pathology in schizophrenia? A neuronometric study. *Biological Psychiatry* 21: 865–75.

Lynch, G. S., P. Ballantine, and B. A. Campbell. 1969. Potentiation of behavioral arousal following cortical lesions and subsequent recovery. *Experimental Neurology* 23: 195–206.

Lynch, G. S., and M. Baudry. 1984. The biochemistry of memory: A new and specific hypothesis. *Science* 224: 1057–63.

Lynch, G., C. Gall, P. Mensah, and C. W. Cotman. 1974. Horseradish peroxidase histochemistry: A new method for tracing efferent projections in the central nervous system. *Brain Research* 65: 373–80.

Lynch, G., S. Halpain, and M. Baudry. 1983. Structural and biochemical effects of high frequency stimulation in the hippocampus. In *Neurobiology of the hippocampus,* ed. W. Seifert, 253–64. London: Academic Press.

Lynch, G. S., D. A. Matthews, S. Mosko, T. Parks, and C. W. Cotman. 1972. Induced acetylcholinesterase-rich layer in the rat dentate gyrus following entorhinal lesions. *Brain Research* 42: 311–18.

Lynch, G. S., G. Rose, C. Gall, and C. W. Cotman. 1975. The response of the dentate gyrus to partial deafferentation. In *Golgi centennial symposium,* ed. M. Santini. New York: Raven Press.

McClearn, G. E. 1959. The genetics of mouse behavior in novel situations. *Journal of Comparative and Physiological Psychology* 52: 62–67.

McClearn, G. E. 1960. Strain differences in activity of mice: Influence of illumination. *Journal of Comparative and Physiological Psychology* 53: 142–43.

McClearn, G. E., and J. C. DeFries. 1973. *Introduction to behavioral genetics.* San Francisco: W. H. Freeman.

McClearn, G. E., and R. Kakihana. 1981. Selective breeding for ethanol sensitivity: SS and LS mice. In *The development of animal models as pharmacogenetic tools,* eds. G. E. McClearn, R. A. Deitrich, and V. G. Erwin. Washington: NIAA Monograph, 147–59.

McEwen, B. S. 1980. The brain as a target organ of endocrine hormones. In *Neuroendocrinology,* eds. D. T. Krieger and J. C. Hughes. Sunderland, MA: Sinauer.

McEwen, B. S., P. G Davis, B. Parsons, and D. W. Pfaff. 1979. The brain as a target for steroid hormone action. *Annual Review of Neuroscience* 2: 65–112.

McGaugh, J. L. 1966. Time-dependent processes in memory storage. *Science* 153: 1351–58.

McGaugh, J. L., and M. J. Herz. 1972. *Memory consolidation.* San Francisco: Albion.

McGinty, D. J., R. M. Harper, and M. K. Fairbanks. 1974. Neuronal unit activity and the control of sleep states. In *Advances in sleep research,* ed. E. Weitzman. New York: Spectrum Publishing.

MacGregor, R. J., and E. R. Lewis. 1977. *Neural modeling.* New York: Plenum Press.

McKinley, M. J., D. A. Denton, and R. S. Weisinger. 1978. Sensors for antidiuresis and thirst—Osmoreceptors or CSF sodium detectors? *Brain Research* 141: 89–103.

MacLean, P. D. 1949. Psychosomatic disease and the visceral brain: Recent developments bearing on the Papez theory of emotion. *Psychosomatic Medicine* 11: 338–53.

MacLean, P. D. 1970. The limbic brain in relation to the psychoses. In *Physiological correlates of emotion,* ed. P. Black. New York: Academic Press.

MacLusky, N. J., and F. Naftolin. 1981. Sexual differentiation of the central nervous system. *Science* 211: 1294–1303.

McNaughton, B. L. 1983. Activity dependent modulation of hippocampal synaptic efficacy: Some implications for memory processes. In *Neurobiology of the hippocampus,* ed. W. Seifert, 233–52. London: Academic Press.

Magnes, J., G. Moruzzi, and O. Pompeiano. 1961. Synchronization of the EEG produced by low frequency electrical stimulation of the solitary tract. *Archives Italiennes des Biologie* 99: 33–67.

Mahalik, T. J., T. E. Finger, I. Stromberg, and L. Olson. 1985. Substantia nigra transplants into denervated striatum of the rat: Ultrastructure of graft and host interconnections. *Journal of Comparative Neurology* 240: 60–70.

Malsbury, C., and D. W. Pfaff. 1974. Neural and hormonal determinants of mating behavior in adult male rats. In *Limbic and autonomic nervous system research,* ed. L. DiCara. New York: Plenum.

Mangiapane, M. L., T. N. Thrasher, L. C. Keil, J. B. Simpson, and W. F. Ganong. 1983. Deficits in drinking and vasopressin secretion after lesions of the nucleus medianus. *Neuroendocrinology* 37: 73–77.

Margules, D. L. 1969. Noradrenergic rather than serotonergic basis of reward in dorsal tegmentum. *Journal of Comparative and Physiological Psychology* 67: 32–35.

Mark, V. H., F. R. Ervin, and P. I. Yakovlev. 1962. The treatment of pain by stereotaxic methods. *Confina neurologica* 22: 238–45.

Mark, V. H., W. Sweet, and F. Ervin. 1975. Deep temporal lobe stimulation and destructive lesions in episodically violent temporal lobe epileptics. In *Neural bases of violence and aggression,* eds. W. S. Fields and W. H. Sweet. St. Louis: Warren Green.

Marlowe, W. B., E. L. Mancall, and J. J. Thomas. 1975. Complete Kluver-Bucy syndrome in man. *Cortex* 11: 53–59.

Marsden, C. D. 1985. Defects of movement in Parkinson's disease. In *Clinical neurophysiology in parkinsonism,* eds. P. J. Delwaide and A. Agnoli, 107–15. Elsevier.

Marshall, J. F., and P. Teitelbaum. 1974. Further analysis of sensory inattention following lateral hypothalamic damage in rats. *Journal of Comparative and Physiological Psychology* 86: 375–95.

Martin, M., and I. Dauner. 1978. Anorexie bei Knaben—zu ihrer differenzialdiagnose. *Zeitschrift fur Kinder- und Jugendpsychiatrie* 6: 117–30.

Martone, M., N. Butters, M. Payne, J. T. Becker, and D. S. Sax. 1984. Dissociations between skill learning and verbal recognition in amnesia and dementia. *Archives of Neurology* 41: 965–70.

Martone, M., P. M. Groves, S. J. Young, and D. M. Armstrong. 1986. Three-dimensional reconstructions of a striosomal network in the caudate nucleus of adult cats. *Soc. Neuroscience Abstracts* 12: 1543.

Masland, R. H. 1986. The functional arthitecture of the retina. *Scientific American* 255: 102–11.

Mayer, D. J., and J. C. Liebeskind. 1974. Pain reduction by focal electrical stimulation of the brain: An anatomical and behavioral analysis. *Brain Research* 68: 73–93.

Mayer, J. 1955. Regulation of energy intake and the body weight: The glucostatic theory and the lipostatic hypothesis. *Annals of the New York Academy of Science* 63: 15–43.

Mefford, I. N., A. F. Oke, and R. N. Adams. 1981. Regional distribution of ascorbate in human brain. *Brain Research* 212: 223–26.

Mellinkoff, S. M., M. Frankland, D. Boyle, and M. Greipel. 1956. Relation between serum amino acid concentration and fluctuations in appetite. *Journal of Applied Psychology* 8: 535–38.

Meltzer, H. Y., and D. J. Luchins. 1984. Effect of clozapine in severe tardive dyskinesia: A case report. *Journal of Clinical Psychopharmacology* 4: 286–87.

Melzack, R., and P. D. Wall. 1965. Pain mechanisms: A new theory. *Science* 150: 971–79.

Mendell. L., and P. D. Wall. 1975. Responses of single dorsal cord cells to peripheral cutaneous unmyelinated fibres. *Nature* 206: 97–99.

Mendelson, J. H., S. Stein, and N. K. Mello. 1965. Effects of experimentally induced intoxication and metabolism of ethanol-1-^{14}C in alcoholic subjects. *Metabolism* 14: 1255–61.

Mennin, S. P., and R. A. Gorski. 1975. Effects of ovarian steroids on plasma LH in normal and persistent estrous adult female rats. *Endocrinology* 96: 486–91.

Merrenkohl, L. R. 1979. Prenatal stress reduces fertility and fecundity in female offspring. *Science* 206: 1097–99.

Merzenich, M. M., R. J. Nelson, M. P. Stryker, M. S. Cynader, A. Schoppman, and J. J. Zook. 1984. Somatosensory cortical map changes following digit amputation in adult monkeys. *Journal of Comparative Neurology* 224: 591–605.

Michael, R. P. 1980. Hormones and sexual behavior in the female. In *Neuroendocrinology,* eds. D. T. Krieger and J. C. Hughes. Sunderland, MA: Sinauer Associates.

Michael, R. P., R. W. Bonsall, and P. Warner. 1974. Human vaginal secretions: Volatile fatty acid content. *Science* 186: 1217–19.

Michael, R. P., E. B. Keverne, and R. W. Bonsall. 1971. Pheromones: Isolation of male sex attractants from a female primate. *Science* 172: 946–47.

Milby, K., A. Oke, and R. N. Adams. 1982. Detailed mapping of ascorbate distribution in rat brain. *Neuroscience Letters* 28: 15–20.

Miller, N. E. 1961. Learning and performance motivated by direct stimulation of the brain. In *Electrical stimulation of the brain,* ed. D. E. Sheer. Austin: University of Texas Press.

Miller, S. W., and P. M. Groves. 1977. Sensory evoked neuronal activity in the hippocampus before and after lesions of the medial septal nuclei. *Physiology and Behavior* 18: 141–46.

Milner, B. 1966. Amnesia following operation on the temporal lobes. In *Amnesia*, eds. C. W. M. Whitty and O. L. Zangwill. London: Butterworth.

Mirsky, A. F., L. E. DeLisi, M. S. Buchsbaum, O. W. Quinn, P. Schwerdt, L. Siever, L. Mann, H. Weingartner, R. Zec, A. Sostek, I. Alterman, V. Revere, S. D. Dawson, and T. Zahn. 1985. The Genain quadruplets: Psychological studies. *Psychiatry Research:* in press.

Mirsky, A. F., and C. C. Duncan. 1986. Etiology and expression of schizophrenia: Neurobiological and psychosocial factors. *Annual Review of Psychology* 37: 291–319.

Mirsky, A. F., and C. C. Duncan-Johnson. 1985. Nature versus nurture in schizophrenia: The struggle continues. *Integrative Psychiatry:* in press.

Mishkin, M., B. J. Spiegler, R. C. Saunders, and B. L. Malamut. 1982. An animal model of global amnesia. In *Alzheimer's disease: A report of progress in research,* eds. S. Corkin, K. L. Davis, J. H. Growden, E. Usdin, and R. J. Wurtman. New York: Raven Press.

Mogenson, G. J., and C. W. Morgan. 1967. Effects of induced drinking on self-stimulation of the lateral hypothalamus. *Experimental Brain Research* 3: 111–16.

Mogenson, G. J., and J. A. F. Stevenson. 1966. Drinking and self-stimulation with electrical stimulation of the lateral hypothalamus. *Physiology and Behavior* 1: 251–54.

Mollgaard, K., M. C. Diamond, E. L. Bennett, M. R. Rosenzweig, and B. Lindner. 1971. Qualitative synaptic changes with differential experience in rat brain. *International Journal of Neuroscience* 2: 113–28.

Monaco, A. P., L. Hernandez, and B. G. Hoebel. 1981. Nucleus accumbens: Site of amphetamine self-injection: Comparison with the lateral ventricle. In *Neurobiology of the Nucleus Accumbens,* eds. R. B. Chronister and J. F. De France. Brunswick, MN: Haer Institute for Electrophysical Research.

Money, J. 1968. Cognitive deficits in Turner's syndrome. In *Progress in human behavior genetics,* ed. S. G. Vandenberg. Baltimore: Johns Hopkins University Press. (a)

Money, J. 1968. *Sex errors of the body: Dilemmas, education, counseling.* Baltimore: John Hopkins University Press. (b)

Money, J. and A. A. Ehrhardt. 1972. *Man and woman, boy and girl.* Baltimore: Johns Hopkins University Press.

Monnier, M., and L. Hosli. 1964. Humoral regulation of sleep and wakefulness by hypnogenic and activating dialysable factors. *Progress in Brain Research* 18: 118–23.

Moore, R. Y., R. K. Bhatnager, and A. Heller. 1971. Anatomical and chemical studies of a nigro-neostriatal projection in the cat. *Brain Research* 30: 119–35.

Morhland, J. S., and G. F. Gebhart. 1980. Effect of selective destruction of serotonergic neurons in nucleus raphe magnus on morphine-induced antinociception. *Life Sciences* 27: 2627–32.

Morley, J. E. 1982. The ascent of cholecystokinin (CCK)—From gut to brain. *Life Sciences* 30: 479–93.

Morley, J. E., and A. S. Levine. 1985. The pharmacology of eating behavior. *Annual Review of Pharmacology and Toxicology* 25: 127–46.

Morse, R. W., and R. A. Vargo. 1970. Functional neuronal subsets in the forepaw focus of somatosensory area II of the cat. *Experimental Neurology* 27: 125–38.

Moruzzi, G., and H. Magoun. 1949. Brain stem reticular formation and activation of the EEG. *Electroencephalography and Clinical Neurophysiology* 1: 455–73.

Mountcastle, V. B. 1961. Some functional properties of the somatic afferent system. In *Sensory communication,* ed. W. A. Rosenblith. Cambridge, MA: M.I.T. Press.

Mountcastle, V. B. 1967. The problem of sensing and the neural coding of sensory events. In *The neurosciences,* eds. G. Quarton, T. Melnechuk, and F. Schmitt. New York: Rockefeller University Press.

Mountcastle, V. B. 1978. An organizing principle for cerebral function: The unit module and the distributed system. In *The Neurosciences Fourth Study Program.* M.I.T. Press.

Mountcastle, V. B., and T. P. S. Powell. 1959. Central nervous mechanisms subserving position sense and kinesthesis. *Bulletin of Johns Hopkins Hospital* 105: 173–200. (a)

Mountcastle, V. B., and T. P. S. Powell. 1959. Neural mechanisms subserving cutaneous sensibility, with special reference to the role of afferent inhibition in sensory perception and discrimination. *Bulletin of Johns Hopkins Hospital* 105: 201–32. (b)

Moyer, K. E. 1976. *The psychobiology of aggression.* New York: Harper & Row.

Mozell, M. M. 1964. Olfactory discrimination: Electrophysiological spatio-temporal basis. *Science* 143: 1336–37.

Mulder, A. H., J. Wemer, and C. D. J. de Langen. 1979. Presynaptic receptor mediated inhibition of noradrenaline release from brain slices and synaptosomes by noradrenaline and adrenaline. In *Presynaptic receptors, advances in bioscience,* eds. S. Z. Langer, K. Starke, and M. L. Dubocovich, vol. 18, 219–24. Oxford: Pergamon Press.

Murphy, M. R., and G. E. Schneider. 1970. Olfactory bulb removal eliminates mating behavior in the male golden hamster. *Science* 167: 302–4.

Nachman, M. 1962. Taste preference for sodium salts by adrenalectomized rats. *Journal of Comparative and Physiological Psychology* 55: 1124–29.

Nadel, L., and S. Zola-Morgan. 1984. Infantile amnesia: A neurobiological perspective. In *Infant memory,* ed. M. Moscovitch, 145–72. New York: Plenum Press.

Narabayashi, H. 1972. Stereotaxic amygdalectomy. In *The neurobiology of the amygdala,* ed. B. Eleftheriou. New York: Plenum.

Nauta, W. J. H. 1946. Hypothalamic regulation of sleep in rats: An experimental study. *Journal of Neurophysiology* 9: 285–316.

Neff, W. D. 1961. Neural mechanisms of auditory discrimination. In *Sensory communication,* ed. W. A. Rosenblith. New York: Wiley.

Neff, W. D., and I. T. Diamond. 1958. The neural basis of auditory discrimination. In *Biological and biochemical bases of behavior,* eds. H. G. Harlow and C. N. Woolsey. Madison: University of Wisconsin Press.

Nelson, D. O., and C. L. Prosser. 1981. Intracellular recordings from thermosensitive preoptic neurons. *Science* 213: 787–89.

Neutra, M., and C. P. LeBlond. 1969. The Golgi apparatus. *Scientific American* 220: 100–107.

Neve, K. A., M. R. Kozlowski, and J. F. Marshall. 1982. Plasticity of neostriatal dopamine receptors after nigrostriatal injury: Relationship to recovery of sensorimotor functions and behavioral supersensitivity. *Brain Research* 244: 33–44.

Newman, E. A. 1986. High potassium conductance in astrocyte endfeet. *Science* 233: 453–54.

Nicol, S. E., and I. I. Gottesman. 1983. Clues to the genetics and neurobiology of schizophrenia. *American Scientist* 71: 398–404.

Nicoll, R. A., C. Schenker, and S. E. Leeman. 1980. Substance P as a transmitter candidate. *Annual Review of Neuroscience* 3: 190–227.

Noback, C. R., and R. J. Demares. 1972. *The nervous system: Introduction and review.* New York: McGraw-Hill.

Noda, H., S. Manohar, and W. R. Adey. 1972. Spontaneous activity of the cat hippocampal neurons in sleep and wakefulness. *Experimental Neurology* 24: 217–31.

Nordeen, E., K. Nordeen, D. Sengelaub, and A. P. Arnold. 1985. Androgens prevent normally-occurring cell death in a sexually dimorphic spinal nucleus. *Science* 229: 671–73.

Norman, D. A. 1973. What have the animal experiments taught us about human memory? In *The physiological basis of memory,* ed. J. A. Deutsch. New York: Academic Press.

Nottebohm, F. 1984. Birdsong as a model in which to study brain processes related to learning. *Condor* 86: 227–36.

Novin, D. 1962. The relation between electrical conductivity of brain tissue and thirst in the rat. *Journal of Comparative and Physiological Psychology* 55: 145–54.

Novin, D., D. A. VanderWeele, and M. Rezek. 1973. Hepatic-portal 2-deoxy-D-glucose infusion causes eating: Evidence for peripheral glucoreceptors. *Science* 181: 858–60.

O'Brien, C. P., T. Testa, T. J. O'Brien, J. P. Brady, and B. Wells. 1977. Conditioned narcotic withdrawal in humans. *Science* 195: 1000–1002.

Olds, J. 1956. Runway and maze behavior controlled by basomedial and forebrain stimulation in the rat. *Journal of Comparative and Physiological Psychology* 49: 507–12.

Olds, J. 1958. Self-stimulation of the brain. *Science* 127: 315–24.

Olds, J. 1961. Differential effects of drive and drugs on self-stimulation at different sites. In *Electrical stimulation of the brain,* ed. D. E. Sheer. Austin: University of Texas Press.

Olds, J. 1962. Hypothalamic substrates of reward. *Physiological Review* 42: 554–604.

Olds, J., and P. Milner. 1954. Positive reinforcement produced by electrical stimulation of the septal area and other regions of the rat brain. *Journal of Comparative and Physiological Psychology* 47: 419–27.

Olds, M. E. 1975. Effects of intraventricular 6-hydroxydopamine and replacement therapy with norepinephrine, dopamine, and serotonin on self-stimulation diencephalic and mesencephalic regions in the rat brain. *Brain Research* 98: 327–42.

Olson, L., A. Seiger, and K. Fuxe. 1972. Heterogeniety of striatal and limbic dopamine innervation: Highly fluorescent islands in developing and adult rats. *Brain Research* 44: 283–88.

Ornstein, R. E. 1972. *The psychology of consciousness.* San Francisco: W. H. Freeman.

Palade, G. E. 1953. An electron microscope study of the mitochondrial structure. *Journal of Histochemistry and Cytochemistry* 1: 188.

Palay, S. L. 1967. Principles of cellular organization in the nervous system. In *The neurosciences: A study program,* eds. G. C. Quarton, T. Melnechuk, and F. O. Schmitt. New York: The Rockefeller University Press.

Palay, S. L., and V. Chan-Palay. 1977. General morphology of neurons and neuroglia. In *Handbook of Physiology,* eds. J. M. Brookhart and V. B. Mountcastle. *Section 1: The Nervous System.* Bethesda, MD: American Physiological Society.

Papez, J. W. 1967. *Comparative neurology.* New York: Hafner.

Pasik, P., T. Pasik, and M. DiFiglia. 1979. The internal organization of the neostriatum in mammals. In *The Neostriatum,* eds. I. Divac and R. G. E. Oberg. New York: Pergamon.

Penaloza-Rojas, J., and M. Russek. 1963. Anorexia induced by direct current blockade of the vagus nerve. *Nature* 200: 176.

Penfield, W., and T. Rasmussen. 1950. *The cerebral cortex of man: A clinical study of localization of function.* New York: Macmillan.

Penfield, W., and L. Roberts. 1959. *Speech and brain mechanisms.* Princeton, NJ: Princeton University Press.

Perabo, F. E., and A. U. Khan. 1961. Conjoined twins. *Helv. Paediat. Acta.* 16: 850.

Pert, C. B., A. M. Snowman, and S. H. Snyder. 1974. Localization of opiate receptor binding in synaptic membranes of rat brain. *Brain Research* 70: 184–88.

Pert, C. B., and S. H. Snyder. 1973. Opiate receptor: Demonstration in nervous tissue. *Science* 179: 1011–13.

Pfaff, D. W. 1968. Autoradiographic localization of radioactivity in the rat brain after injection of tritiated sex hormones. *Science* 161: 1355–56.

Pfaff, D. W. 1980. *Estrogen and brain function.* New York: Springer-Verlag.

Pfaffmann, C. 1955. Gustatory nerve impulses in rat, cat and rabbit. *Journal of Neurophysiology* 18: 429–40.

Pfaffmann, C. 1959. The afferent code for sensory quality. *American Psychologist* 14: 226–32.

Pfaffmann, C. 1969. *Olfaction and taste, Part III.* New York: Rockefeller University Press.

Pinsker, H., V. Castellucci, I. Kupfermann, and E. R. Kandel. 1970. Habituation and dishabituation of the gill-withdrawal reflex of *Aplysia. Science* 167: 1740–42.

Plomin, R. J., J. C. DeFries, and G. E. McClearn. 1980. *Behavioral genetics.* San Francisco: W. H. Freeman.

Poggio, G. F., and V. B. Mountcastle. 1963. The functional properties of ventrobasal thalamic neurons studied in unanesthetized monkeys. *Journal of Neurophysiology* 26: 775–806.

Poggio, G. F., and T. Poggio. 1984. The analysis of stereopsis. *Annual Review of Neuroscience.* Palo Alto, CA: Annual Reviews, Inc., 379–412.

Polak, J. M., and S. Van Noorden. 1984. *An introduction to immunocytochemistry: Current techniques and problems.* London: Oxford University Press.

Porter, K. R., and M. A. Bonneville. 1973. *Fine structure of cells and tissues.* Philadelphia: Lea & Febiger.

Porter, K. R., A. Claude, and E. F. Fullam. 1945. A study of tissue culture cells by electron microscopy. *Journal of Experimental Medicine* 81: 233–54.

Postman, L. 1962. *Psychology in the making.* New York: Alfred A. Knopf.

Powley, T. L. 1977. The ventromedial hypothalamic syndrome, satiety, and a cephalic phase hypothesis. *Psychological Review* 84: 89–126.

Powley, T. L., and R. E. Keesey. 1970. Relationship of body weight to the lateral hypothalamic feeding syndrome. *Journal of Comparative and Physiological Psychology* 70: 25–36.

Premack, D. 1971. Language in chimpanzees? *Science* 172: 808–22.

Prescott, R. G. 1966. Estrous cycle in the rat: Effects on self-stimulation behavior. *Science* 152: 796–97.

Price, D. L. 1986. New perspectives on Alzheimer's disease. *Annual Review of Neuroscience* 9: 489–512.

Puerto, A., J. A. Deutsch, F. Molina, and P. L. Roll. 1976. Rapid rewarding effects of intragastric injection. *Behavioral Biology* 18: 123–34.

Purpura, C. 1974. Dendritic spine "dysgenesis" and mental retardation. *Science* 186: 1126–27.

Quartermain, D., and D. Webster. 1968. Extinction following intracranial reward: The effect of delay between acquisition and extinction. *Science* 159: 1259–60.

Raisman, G. 1975. Neuronal plasticity in the septal nuclei. In *Golgi centennial symposium proceedings,* ed. M. Santini. New York: Raven Press.

Rall, T. W. 1979. General regulatory role of cyclic nucleotides in hormone and neurohormone action. In *The Neurosciences Fourth Study Program,* eds. F. O. Schmitt and F. G. Worden, 859–64. Cambridge: M.I.T. Press.

Rall, W., G. Shepherd, T. Reese, and M. Brightman. 1966. Dendro-dendritic synaptic pathway for inhibition in the olfactory bulb. *Experimental Neurology* 14: 44–56.

Ranck, J. B. 1973. Studies on single neurons in dorsal hippocampal formation and septum in unrestrained rats. Part I. Behavioral correlates and firing repertoires. *Experimental Neurology* 41: 461–531.

Randrup, A., and I. Munkvad. 1974. Pharmacology and physiology of stereotyped behavior. *Journal of Psychiatric Research* 11: 1–10.

Rasmussen, G. L. 1964. Anatomic relationships of the ascending and descending auditory systems. In *Neurological aspects of auditory and vestibular disorders,* eds. W. S. Fields and R. R. Alford. Springfield, Il.: Charles C Thomas.

Ratliff, F. 1965. *Mach bands: Quantitative studies on neural networks in the retina.* San Francisco: Holden-Day.

Ray, O. 1983. *Drugs, society, and human behavior.* St. Louis: C. V. Mosby.

Rebec, G. V. 1984. Auto- and postsynaptic dopamine receptors in the central nervous system. In *Neuroreceptors in Health and Disease,* eds. J. Marwaha and W. Anderson. Basel: Karger.

Rebec, G. V. 1986. Long-term amphetamine administration: Changes in the firing rate of monoaminergic neurons and the release of ascorbate. In *Inactivation of hypersensitive neurons,* ed. N. Chalazonitis. New York: Alan R. Liss.

Rebec, G. V., and G. D. Anderson. 1986. Regional neuropharmacology of the antipsychotic drugs: Implications for the dopamine hypothesis of schizophrenia. *Behavioral Assessment* 8: 11–29.

Rebec, G. V., and T. R. Bashore. 1984. Critical issues in assessing the behavioral effects of amphetamine. *Neuroscience and Biobehavioral Reviews* 8: 153–59.

Rebec, G. V., J. M. Centore, L. K. White, and K. D. Alloway. 1985. Ascorbic acid and the behavioral response to haloperidol: Implications for the action of antipsychotic drugs. *Science* 227: 438–40.

Rebec, G. V., J. Gelman, K. D. Alloway, and T. F. Bashore. 1983. Cataleptogenic potency of the antipsychotic drugs is inversely correlated with neuronal activity in the amygdaloid complex of the rat. *Pharmacology, Biochemistry, and Behavior* 19: 759–63.

Rebec, G. V., and P. Groves. 1975. Differential effects of the optical isomers of amphetamine on neuronal activity in the reticular formation and caudate nucleus of the rat. *Brain Research* 83: 301.

Rebec, G. V., and E. H. Lee. 1982. Differential subsensitivity of dopaminergic and neostriatal neurons to apomorphine with long-term treatment. *Brain Research* 250: 188–92.

Rebec, G. V., and D. S. Segal. 1980. Apparent tolerance to some aspects of amphetamine stereotypy with long-term treatment. *Pharmacology, Biochemistry and Behavior* 13: 793–97.

Reinisch, J. M. 1981. Prenatal exposure to synthetic progestins increases potential for aggression in humans *Science* 211: 1171–73.

Reis, D. J. 1974. Central neurotransmitters and aggression. In *Publications of the association for research in nervous and mental disease,* 52, ed. S. H. Frazier.

Reynolds, D. V. 1969. Surgery in the rat during electrical analgesia induced by focal brain stimulation. *Science* 164: 444–45.

Ribak, C. E., A. B. Harris, J. E. Vaughn, and E. Roberts. 1979. Inhibitory, GABAergic nerve terminals decrease at sites of focal epilepsy. *Science* 205: 211–14.

Rich, C. L. 1985. Electroconvulsive therapy. In *Psychiatry—Vol. 3, Sec. 2: Psychobiological Foundations of Clinical Psychiatry,* ed. J. O. Cavenar, Jr. Philadelphia: J. B. Lippincott.

Richter, C. P. 1936. Increased salt appetite in adrenalectomized rats. *American Journal of Physiology* 115: 155–61.

Risch, S. C., and D. S. Janowsky. 1985. Limbic-hypothalamic-pituitary-adrenal axis dysregulation in melancholia. In *Psychiatry—Vol. 3, Sec. 2: Psychobiological foundations of clinical psychiatry.* ed. J. O. Cavenar, Jr. Philadelphia: J. B. Lippincott.

Ritchie, J. M. 1975. Central nervous system stimulants: The xanthines. In *The pharmacological basis of therapeutics,* eds. L. S. Goodman and A. Gilman. 5th ed. New York: Macmillan.

Ritchie, J. M., P. J. Cohen, and R. D. Dripps. 1970. Cocaine, procaine, and other synthetic local anesthetics. In *The pharmacological basis of therapeutics,* eds. L. S. Goodman and A. Gilman. 4th ed. London: Macmillan.

Ritter, S., and L. Stein. 1974. Self-stimulation in the mesencephalic trajectory of the ventral noradrenergic bundle. *Brain Research* 81: 145–57.

Roberts, E. 1986. GABA: The road to neurotransmitter status. In *Benzodiazepine/GABA Receptors and Chloride Channels: Structural and Functional Properties,* 1–39. New York: Alan R. Liss.

Roberts, W. W., and R. D. Mooney. 1974. Brain areas controlling thermoregulatory grooming, prone extension, locomotion, and tail vasodilation in rats. *Journal of Comparative and Physiological Psychology* 86: 470–80.

Robertson, R. T., G. S. Lynch, and R. F. Thompson. 1973. Diencephalic distribution of ascending reticular systems. *Brain Research* 55: 309–22.

Robertson, R. T., K. S. Mayers, T. J. Teyler, L. A. Bettinger, H. Birch, J. L. Davis, D. S. Phillips, and R. F. Thompson. 1975. Unit activity in posterior association cortex. *Journal of Neurophysiology* 38: 780–94.

Rogers, J., G. E. Hoffmann, S. F. Zornetzer, and W. W. Vale. 1984. Hypothalamic grafts and neuroendocrine cascade theories of aging. In *Neural transplants: Development and function,* eds. J. R. Sladek, D. M Gash, 205–22. New York: Plenum Press.

Rolls, B. J., R. J. Wood, and E. T. Rolls. 1980. Thirst: The initiation, maintenance, and termination of drinking. In *Progress in psychobiology and physiological psychology,* 9, eds. J. M. Sprague and A. N. Epstein. New York: Academic Press.

Rolls, E. T. 1975. *The brain and reward.* New York: Pergamon.

Rolls, E. T., S. J. Thorpe, M. Boytim, I. Szabo, and D. I. Perrett. 1984. Responses of striatal neurons in the behaving monkey. 3. Effects of iontophoretically applied dopamine on normal responsiveness. *Neuroscience* 12: 1201–12.

Rolls, E. T., S. J. Thorpe, S. Maddison, A. Roper-Hall, A. Puerto, and D. Perrett. 1979. Activity of neurons in the neostriatum and related structures in the alert animal. In *The Neostriatum,* eds. I. Divac and R. G. E. Oberg. New York: Pergamon.

Rose, J. E., J. F. Brugge, D. J. Anderson, and J. E. Hind. 1967. Phase-locked response to low-frequency tones in single auditory nerve fibers of the squirrel monkey. *Journal of Neurophysiology* 30: 769–93.

Rose, J. E., N. B. Gross, C. D. Geisler, and J. E. Hind. 1966. Some neural mechanisms in the inferior colliculus of the cat which may be relevant to localization of a sound source. *Journal of Neurophysiology* 29: 288–314.

Rosenzweig, M. R. 1961. Auditory localization. *Scientific American* 205: 132–42.

Rossor, M. N., P. C. Emson, C. Q. Mountjoy, M. Roth, and L. L. Iversen. 1980. Reduced amounts of immunoreactive somatostatin in the temporal cortex in senile dementia of Alzheimer type. *Neuroscience Letters* 20: 373, 377.

Roth, R. H., P. M. Salzman, and M. C. Nowycky. 1978. Impulse flow and short-term regulation of transmitter biosynthesis in central catecholaminergic neurons. In *Psychopharmacology: A Generation of Progress,* eds. M. A. Lipton, A. DiMascio, and K. F. Killam. Raven Press: New York 185–98.

Routtenberg, A., and J. Lindy. 1965. Effects of the availability of rewarding septal and hypothalamic stimulation on bar-pressing for food under conditions of deprivation. *Journal of Comparative and Physiological Psychology* 60: 158–61.

Routtenberg, A., and C. Malsbury. 1969. Brain stem pathways of reward. *Journal of Comparative and Physiological Psychology* 68: 22–30.

Rowland, N., S. P. Grossman, and L. Grossman. 1979. Zona incerta lesions: Regulatory drinking deficits to intravenous NaCl, angiotensin, but not to salt in the food. *Physiology and Behavior* 23: 745–50.

Rowland, V. 1968. Cortical steady potential (direct current potential) in reinforcement and learning. In *Progress in physiological psychology,* eds. E. Stellar and J. Sprague, vol. 2. New York: Academic Press.

Rowland, V., and G. Dines. 1968. Cortical steady potential shift in relation to the rhythmic electrocorticogram and multiple unit activity. In *Bioelectric recording techniques. Part A. Cellular processes and brain potentials,* eds. R. F. Thompson and M. M. Patterson. New York: Academic Press.

Rozin, P., and J. W. Kalat. 1971. Specific hungers and poison avoidance as adaptive specializations of learning. *Psychological Review* 78: 459–86.

Rubel, E. W., and T. N. Parks. 1975. Organization and development of brain stem auditory nuclei of the chicken: Tonotopic organization of n. magnocellularis and n. laminaris. *Journal of Comparative Neurology* 164: 411–34.

Rubin, V., and L. Comitas. 1974. *Ganja in Jamaica. A medical anthropological study of chronic marijuana use.* The Hague: Mouton.

Rumbaugh, D. M., ed. 1977. *Language learning by a chimpanzee: The Lana Project.* New York: Academic Press.

Rushton, W. A. H., and G. Westheimer. 1962. The effect upon the rod threshold of bleaching neighbouring rods. *Journal of Physiology* 165: 318–29.

Russek, M. 1971. Hepatic receptors and the neurophysiological mechanisms controlling feeding behavior. In *Neurosciences research* 4, eds. S. Ehrenpreis and O. C. Solnitzky. New York: Academic Press.

Russek, M., M. C. Lora-Vilchis, and M. Islas-Chaires. 1980. Food intake inhibition elicited by intraportal glucose and adrenaline in dogs on a 22-hour fasting/2-hour feeding schedule. *Physiology and Behavior* 24: 157–61.

Sachs, O. 1983. *Awakenings.* New York: A. E. Dutton.

Sakai, K. 1985. Neurons responsible for paradoxical sleep. In *Sleep: Neurotransmitters and neuromodulators,* ed. A. Wauquier et al., 29–42. New York: Raven Press.

Sakitt, B. 1972. Counting every quantum. *Journal of Physiology* 223: 131–50.

Sanger, D. J. 1985. GABA and the behavioral effects of anxiolytic drugs. *Life Sciences* 36: 1503–13.

Sastry, B. R., H. W. Goh, and A. Auyeung. 1986. Associative induction of posttetanic and long-term potentiation in CA1 neurons of rat hippocampus. *Science* 232: 988–90.

Satinoff, E. 1978. Neural organization and evolution of thermal regulation in mammals. *Science* 201: 16–22.

Satinoff, E., and J. Rutstein. 1970. Behavioral thermoregulation in rats with anterior hypothalamic lesions. *Journal of Comparative and Physiological Psychology* 71: 77–82.

Sattin, A. 1984. Adenosine receptors: some behavioral implications for depression and sleep. In *Neuroreceptors in health and disease,* eds. J. Marwaha and W. Anderson. Basel: Karger.

Schachter, S. 1971. Some extraordinary facts about obese humans and rats. *American Psychologist* 26: 129–44.

Scheerenberger, R. C. 1964. Mental retardation: Definition, classification, and prevalence. *Mental Retardation* 1: 432–41.

Scheff, S. W., L. S. Bernardo, and C. W. Cotman. 1978. Decrease in adrenergic axon sprouting in the senescent rat. *Science* 202: 775–78.

Schildkraut, J. J. 1973. Norepinephrine metabolism in the pathophysiology and classification of depressive and manic disorders. In *Psychopathology and pharmacology,* eds. J. O. Cole, A. M. Freedman, and A. J. Friedhoff. Baltimore: Johns Hopkins University Press.

Schildkraut, J. J., and S. S. Kety. 1967. Biogenic amines and emotion. *Science* 156: 21–30.

Schiller, P. H. 1972. The role of the monkey superior colliculus in eye movement and vision. *Investigative Ophthalmology* 11: 451–60.

Schlesinger, K., W. Boggan, and D. X. Freedman. 1968. Genetics of audiogenic seizures: II. Effects of pharmacological manipulations of brain serotonin, norepinephrine and gamma-amino-butyric acid. *Life Sciences* 7: 437–47.

Schreiner, L. H., and A. Kling. 1953. Behavioral changes following rhinencephalic injury in the cat. *Journal of Neurophysiology* 16: 643–59.

Schuckit, M. A. 1979. *Drug and Alcohol Abuse.* New York: Plenum Medical Book Co.

Schuckit, M. A. 1985. Trait (and state) markers of a predisposition to psychopathology. In *Psychiatry,* ed. J. O. Cavenar, Jr. Philadelphia: J. B. Lippincott.

Schuster, C. R. 1970. Psychological approaches to opiate dependence and self-administration by laboratory animals. *Federation Proceedings* 29: 2–5.

Schuster, C. R., and C. E. Johanson. 1973. Behavioral analysis of opiate dependence. In *Opiate addiction: Origins and treatment,* eds. S. Fisher and A. M. Freedman. Washington, D.C.: V. H. Winston.

Schuster, C. R., and R. Thompson. 1969. Self-administration of a behavioral dependence on drugs. *Annual Review of Pharmacology,* 9: 483–502.

Schwane, J. A., and R. B. Armstrong. 1983. Effect of training on skeletal muscle injury from downhill running in rats. *Journal of Applied Physiology* 55: 969–75.

Sclafani, A., and D. Springer. 1976. Dietary obesity in adult rats: Similarities to hypothalamic and human obesity syndromes. *Physiology and Behavior* 17: 461–71.

Scott, J. W. 1967. Brain stimulation reinforcement with distributed practice: Effects of electrode locus, previous experience and stimulus intensity. *Journal of Comparative and Physiological Psychology* 63: 175–83.

Scoville, B. 1975. Review of amphetamine-like drugs by the Food and Drug Administration. In *Obesity in perspective,* Part 2, ed. G. A. Bray. Washington, D.C.: U.S. Government Printing Office.

Scoville, W. B., and B. Milner. 1957. Loss of recent memory after bilateral hippocampal lesions. *J. Neurol. Neurosurg. Psychiat.* 20: 1121.

Searle, L. V. 1949. The organization of hereditary maze-brightness and maze-dullness. *Genetic Psychology Monographs* 39: 279–325.

Seeman, P. 1980. Brain dopamine receptors. *Pharmacological Reviews* 32: 222–313.

Segal, D. S. 1975. Behavioral characterization of d- and l-amphetamine: Neurochemical implications. *Science* 190: 475–77.

Segal, D. S., C. McAllister, and M. A. Geyer. 1974. Ventricular infusion of norepinephrine and amphetamine: Direct versus indirect action. *Pharmacology, Biochemistry, and Behavior* 2: 79–86.

Segal, D. S., and A. J. Mandell. 1970. Behavioral activation of rats during intraventricular infusion of norepinephrine. *Proceedings of National Academy of Sciences* 66: 289–93.

Seiden, L. S., N. W. Fischman, and C. R. Schuster. 1975. Long-term meth-amphetamine induced changes in brain catecholamines in tolerant rhesus monkeys. *Drug and Alcohol Dependence* 1: 215–19.

Seifert, W. 1983. *Neurobiology of the hippocampus.* London: Academic Press.

Sem-Jacobsen, C. W. 1968. *Depth-electrographic stimulation of the human brain and behavior: From fourteen years of studies and treatment of Parkinson's disease and mental disorders with implanted electrodes.* Springfield, IL: Charles C. Thomas.

Sepinwall, J. 1983. Behavioral studies related to the neurochemical mechanisms of action of anxiolytics. In *Anxiolytics: Neurochemical, behavioral, and clinical perspectives,* eds. J. B. Malick, S. J. Enna, and H. I. Yamamura. New York: Raven Press.

Shah, S. A. 1970. Report on the XYY chromosomal abnormality. U.S. Public Health Service publication number 2103. Washington, D.C.: U.S. Government Printing Office.

Sharpless, S. K. 1964. Reorganization of function in the nervous system—use and disuse. *Annual Review of Physiology* 26: 357–88.

Sharpless, S. K. 1975. Supersensitivity-like phenomena in the central nervous system. *Federation Proceedings* 34: 1990–97.

Shepherd, G. M. 1974. *The synaptic organization of the brain: An introduction.* New York: Oxford University Press.

Sherrington, C. 1940. *On man and his nature.* London: Cambridge University Press.

Shiromani, P. J., and J. C. Gillin. 1986. Cholinergic regulation of REM sleep: Basic mechanisms and clinical implications for affective illness and narcolepsy. In *Neurobiology of acetylcholine,* eds. N. J. Dun and R. L. Perlman. Plenum Press.

Shoulson, I., R. Kartzinel, and T. N. Chase. 1976. Huntington's disease: Treatment with dipropylacetic acid and gamma-amino-butyric acid. *Neurology* 26: 61–63.

Simon, E. J., and J. M. Hiller. 1978. The opiate receptors. *Annual Review of Pharmacology and Toxicology* 18: 371–94.

Simon, E. J., J. M. Hiller, and I. Edelman. 1973. Stereospecific binding of the potent narcotic analgesic (^{3}H) etorphine to rat brain homogenate. *Proc. Natl. Acad. Sci. USA* 70: 1947–49.

Simpson, J. B., A. N. Epstein, and J. S. Camardo. 1978. The localization of dipsogenic receptors for angiotensin II in the subfornical organ. *Journal of Comparative and Physiological Psychology* 92: 581–608.

Sinclair, D. 1967. *Cutaneous sensation.* London: Oxford University Press.

Singer, J. 1968. Hypothalamic control of male and female sexual behavior in female rats. *Journal of Comparative and Physiological Psychology* 66: 738–42.

Singer, S. J., and G. L. Nicolson. 1972. The fluid model of the structure of cell membranes. *Science* 175: 720–31.

Singh, M. M., and S. R. Kay. 1976. Wheat gluten as a pathogenic factor in schizophrenia. *Science* 191: 401–2.

Skirboll, L. R., A. A. Grace, and B. S. Bunney. 1979. Dopamine auto- and postsynaptic receptors: Electrophysiological evidence for differential sensitivity to dopamine agonists. *Science* 206: 80–82.

Sladek, J. R., D. M. Gash, and T. J. Collier. 1984. Noradrenergic neuron transplants into the third ventricle of aged F344 rats improve inhibitory avoidance memory performance. *Society for Neuroscience Abstracts* 10: 772.

Slotnick, B. M., and M. F. McMullen. 1972. Intraspecific fighting in albino mice with septal forebrain lesions. *Physiology and Behavior* 8: 333–37.

Smith, D. E. 1969. Physical vs. psychological dependence in intolerance in high dose methamphetamine abuse. *Clinical Toxicology* 2: 99–103.

Smith, G. P., and A. N. Epstein. 1969. Increased feeding in response to decreased glucose utilization in the rat and monkey. *American Journal of Physiology* 217: 1083–87.

Snyder, F. 1969. Sleep disturbance in relation to acute psychosis. In *Sleep: Physiology and pathology,* ed. A. Kales. Philadelphia: Lippincott.

Snyder, S. H. 1973. Amphetamine psychosis: a "model" schizophrenia mediated by catecholamines. *American Journal of Psychiatry* 130: 61–67.

Snyder, S. H. 1980. Brain peptides as neurotransmitters. *Science* 209: 976–83.

Snyder, S. H., S. P. Banerjee, H. I. Yamamura, and D. Greenburg. 1974. Drugs, neurotransmitters and schizophrenia. *Science* 184: 1243–53.

Snyder, S. H., and R. Simantov. 1977. The opiate receptor and opioid peptides. *Journal of Neurochemistry* 28: 13–20.

Somjen, G. 1972. *Sensory coding in the mammalian nervous system.* New York: Appleton-Century-Crofts.

Spector, R., and A. V. Lorenzo. 1974. Specificity of ascorbic acid transport system of the central nervous system. *American Journal of Physiology* 226: 1468–73.

Sperry, R. W. 1956. The eye and the brain. *Scientific American* 194: 48–52.

Sperry, R. W. 1961. Cerebral organization and behavior. *Science* 133: 1749–57.

Sperry, R. W. 1974. Lateral specialization in the surgically separated hemispheres. In *The neurosciences: Third study program,* eds. F. O. Schmitt, and F. G. Worden. Cambridge, MA: M.I.T. Press.

Sperry, R. W., and M. S. Gazzaniga. 1967. Language following surgical disconnection of the hemispheres. In *Brain mechanisms underlying speech and language,* eds. C. H. Millikan and F. L. Darley. New York: Grune & Stratton.

Sprague, J. M. 1972. The superior colliculus and pretectum in visual behavior. *Investigative Ophthalmology* 11: 473–81.

Squire, L. R. 1982. Human memory: Neuropsychological and anatomical aspects. *Ann. Rev. Neurosci.* 5: in press.

Squire, L. R. 1986. Mechanisms of memory. *Science* 232: 1612–19.

Squire, L. R. 1987. *Memory and brain.* New York: Oxford University.

Squire, L. R., and A. P. Shimamura. 1985. Learning and memory. In *Psychiatry,* ed. J. O. Cavenar, Jr.

Squire, L. R. and P. C. Slater. 1983. Electroconvulsive therapy and complaints of memory dysfunction: A prospective three-year follow-up. *British Journal of Psychiatry* 142: 1–8.

Squire, L. R., P. C. Slater, and P. M. Chace. 1975. Retrograde amnesia: Temporal gradient in very long-term memory following electroconvulsive therapy. *Science* 187: 77–79.

Squire, L. R., P. C. Slater, and P. L. Miller. 1981. Retrograde amnesia following ECT: Long-term follow-up studies. *Archives of General Psychiatry* 38: 89–95.

Squire, L. R., and S. Zola-Morgan. 1983. The neurology of memory: The case for correspondence between the findings for humans and the non-human primate. In *The physiological basis of memory,* 2d ed., ed. J. A. Deutsch. New York: Academic Press.

Stahl, S. M. 1986. Neuropharmacology of movement disorders: Comparison of spontaneous and drug-induced movement disorders. In *Movement disorders,* eds. N. S. Shah and A. G. Donald, 1–36. New York: Plenum Press.

Stark, P., and E. S. Boyd. 1963. Effects of cholinergic drugs on hypothalamic self-stimulation response rates of dogs. *American Journal of Physiology* 205: 745–48.

Starke, K. 1980. Presynaptic receptors and the control of noradrenaline release. *Trends in Pharmacological Science* 6: 268–71.

Starr, A. 1978. Sensory evoked potentials in clinical disorders of the nervous system. In *Ann. Rev. Neurosci.,* eds. W. M. Cowan, Z. W. Hall, and E. R. Kandel, vol. 1, 103–27. Annual Reviews, Inc., Palo Alto.

Starr, A., and L. J. Achor. 1975. Auditory brain stem responses in neurological disease. *Arch. Neurol.* 32: 761–68.

Stein, L. 1964. Self-stimulation of the brain and the central stimulant action of amphetamine. *Federation proceedings* 23: 836–50.

Stein, L. 1969. Chemistry of purposive behavior. In *Reinforcement and behavior,* ed. J. T. Tapp. New York: Academic Press.

Stein L., J. D. Belluzi, S. Ritter, and C. D. Wise. 1974. Self-stimulation reward pathways: Norepinephrine versus dopamine. *Journal of Psychiatric Research* 11: 115–24.

Stein, L., and C. D. Wise. 1971. Possible etiology of schizophrenia: Progressive damage to the noradrenergic reward system of 6-hydroxydopamine. *Science* 171: 1032–36.

Stein, L., and C. D. Wise. 1974. Serotonin and behavioral inhibition. In *Advances in biochemical psychopharmacology,* eds. E. Costa and P. Greengard. New York: Raven Press.

Sterling, P. 1983. Retinal microcircuitry. *Annual Review of Neuroscience.* Palo Alto, CA: Annual Reviews, Inc., 149–85.

Sterman, M. B. 1972. In *The sleeping brain,* ed. M. H. Chase. Los Angeles: University of California Brain Research Institution.

Sterman, M. B., and C. D. Clemente. 1962. Forebrain inhibitory mechanisms: Cortical synchronization induced by basal forebrain stimulation. *Experimental Neurology* 6: 91–102. (a)

Sterman, M. B., and C. D. Clemente. 1962. Forebrain inhibitory mechanisms: Sleep patterns induced by basal forebrain stimulation in the behaving cat. *Experimental Neurology* 6: 103–17. (b)

Sterman, M. B., and C. D. Clemente. 1974. Forebrain mechanisms for the onset of sleep. In *Basic Sleep Mechanisms,* eds. O. Petre-Quadens and J. Schlag. New York: Academic Press.

Stern, C. 1973. *Principles of human genetics.* 3d ed. San Francisco: W. H. Freeman.

Stevens, C. F. 1966. *Neurophysiology: A primer.* New York: John Wiley & Sons.

Steward, O., C. W. Cotman, and G. Lynch. 1974. Growth of a new fiber projection in the brain of adult rats: Reinnervation of the dentate gyrus by the contralateral entorhinal cortex following ipsilateral entorhinal lesions *Experimental Brain Research* 20: 45–66.

Steward, O., W. F. White, C. W. Cotman, and G. Lynch. 1976. Potentiation of excitatory synaptic transmission in the normal and in the reinnervated dentate gyrus of the rat. *Experimental Brain Research* 26: 423–41.

Stone, J., B. Dreher, and A. Leventhal. 1979. Hierarchical and parallel mechanisms in the organization of visual cortex. *Brain Research Reviews* 1: 345–94.

Stone, J., and K. Hoffmann. 1972. Very slow-conducting ganglion cells in the cat's retina: A major, new functional type? *Brain Research* 43: 610–16.

Straus, E., and R. S. Yalow. 1979. Cholecystokinin in the brains of obese and nonobese mice. *Science* 203: 68–69.

Stricker, E. M. 1969. Osmoregulation and volume regulation in rats: Inhibition of hypovolemic thirst by water. *American Journal of Physiology* 217: 98–105.

Stricker, E. M. 1978. The renin-angiotension system and thirst: Some unanswered questions. *Federation Proceedings* 37: 2704–10.

Stricker, E. M. 1981. Thirst and sodium appetite after colloid treatment in rats. *Journal of Comparative and Physiological Psychology* 95: 1–25.

Stricker, E. M. 1983. Thirst and sodium appetite after colloid treatment in rats: Role of the renin-angiotensin-aldosterone system. *Journal of Comparative and Physiological Psychology* 97: 725–37.

Stricker, E. M., and A. F. Anderson. 1980. The lateral hypothalamic syndrome: Comparison with the syndrome of anorexia nervosa. *Life Sciences* 26: 1927–34.

Stricker, E. M., N. Rowland, C. F. Saller, and M. I. Freidman. 1977. Homeostasis during hypoglycemia: Central control of adrenal secretion and peripheral control of feeding. *Science* 196: 79–81.

Stricker, E. M., and M. J. Zigmond. 1976. Recovery of function following damage to central catecholamine-containing neurons: A neurochemical model for the lateral hypothalamic syndrome. In *Progress in psychobiology and physiological psychology,* 6, eds. J. M. Sprague and A. N. Epstein. New York: Academic Press.

Sturdevant, R. A., and H. Goetz. 1976. Cholecystokinin both stimulates and inhibits human food intake. *Nature* 261: 713–15.

Sutcliffe, J. G., R. J. Milner, J. M. Gottesfeld, and W. Reynolds. 1984. Control of neuronal gene expression. *Science* 225: 1308–15.

Sutherland, E. W. 1972. Studies on the mechanism of hormone action. *Science* 177: 401–8.

Swaab, D. F., and E. Fliers. 1985. A sexually dimorphic nucleus in the human brain. *Science* 228: 1112–15.

Szentágothai, J. 1978. The neuron network of the cerebral cortex: A functional interpretation. *Proceedings of the Royal Society* (London) series B201: 219–48.

Tallman, J. F., and D. W. Gallager. 1985. The ABA-ergic system: A locus of benzodiazepine action. *Annual Review of Neuroscience* 8: 21–44.

Tallman, J. F., S. M. Paul, P. Skolnick, and D. W. Gallager. 1980. Receptors for the age of anxiety: Pharmacology of the benzodiazepines. *Science* 207: 274–81.

Teitelbaum, P. 1971. The encephalization of hunger. In *Progress in physiological psychology.* 4, eds. E. Stellar and J. M. Sprague. New York: Academic Press.

Teitelbaum, P., and J. Cytawa. 1965. Spreading depression and recovery from lateral hypothalamic damage. *Science* 147: 61–63.

Tepper, J. M., P. M. Groves, and S. J. Young. 1985. The neuropharmacology of the autoinhibition of monoamine release. *Trends in Pharmacological Sciences* 6: 251–56.

Terenius, L. 1973. Stereospecific interaction between narcotic analesics and a synaptic plasma membrane fraction of rat cerebral cortex. *Acta Pharmacologica et Toxicologica* 32: 317–20.

Terenius, L. 1980. Endogenous peptides and analgesia. *Annual Review of Neuroscience* 3: 190–227.

Terenius, L., and A. Wahlstrom. 1975. Search for an endogenous ligand for the opiate receptor. *Acta Physiologica Scandinavica* 94: 74–81.

Terman, G. W., Y. Shavit, J. W. Lewis, J. T. Cannon, and J. C. Liebskind. 1984. Intrinsic mechanisms of pain inhibition: Activation by stress. *Science* 226: 1270–77.

Terry, R. D. 1986. Normal aging of the brain and Alzheimer's disease. Distinguished faculty lecture, 20 March at University of California, San Diego.

Terry, R. D., and R. Katzman. 1983. Senile dementia of the Alzheimer type. *Annals of Neurology* 14: 497–506.

Terzian, H., and G. Ore Dalle. 1955. Syndrome of Kluver and Bucy reproduced in man with bilateral removal of the temporal lobe. *Neurology* 5: 373–80.

Thiessen, D. D. 1972. *Gene organization and behavior.* New York: Random House.

Thompson, R. F. 1976. The search for the engram. *American Psychologist* 31: 209–27.

Thompson, R. F. 1986. The neurobiology of learning and memory. *Science* 233: 941–47.

Thompson, R. F., T. W. Berger, and J. Madden, IV. 1983. Cellular processes of learning and memory in the mammalian CNS. *Annu. Rev. Neurosci.* 6: 447–91.

Thompson, R. F., L. A. Bettinger, H. Birch, P. M. Groves, and K. S. Mayers. 1969. The role of synaptic inhibitory mechanisms in neuropsychological systems. *Neuropsychologia* 7: 217–33.

Thompson, R. F., R. H. Johnson, and J. J. Hoopes. 1963. Organization of auditory, somatic sensory, and visual projection to association fields of cerebral cortex in the cat. *Journal of Neurophysiology* 26: 343–64.

Thompson, R. F., and W. A. Spencer. 1966. Habituation: A model phenomenon for the study of neuronal substrates of behavior. *Psychological Review* 173: 16–43.

Thompson, T., and C. R. Schuster. 1968. *Behavioral pharmacology.* Englewood Cliffs, NJ: Prentice-Hall.

Thorpe, W. H. 1956. *Learning and instinct in animals.* London: Methuen.

Thrasher, T. N., C. J. Brown, L. C. Keil, and D. J. Ramsay. 1980. Thirst and vasopressin release in the dog: An osmoreceptor or sodium receptor mechanism? *American Journal of Physiology* 238: R333–R339.

Thrasher, T. N., L. C. Keil, and D. J. Ramsay. 1982. Lesions of the organum vasculosum of the lamina terminalis (OVLT) attenuate osmotically-induced drinking and vasopressin secretion in the dog. *Endocrinology* 110: 1837–39.

Tissot, R. 1975. The common pathophysiology of monoaminergic psychoses: A new hypothesis. *Neuropsychobiology* 1: 243–60.

Trahiotis, C., and D. N. Elliott. 1970. Behavioral investigation of some possible effects of sectioning the crossed olivocochlear bundle. *Journal of Acoustical Society of America* 47: 592–96.

Trulson, M. E., and B. L. Jacobs. 1979. Long-term amphetamine treatment decreases brain serotonin metabolism: Implications for theories of schizophrenia. *Science* 205: 1295–97.

Tryon, R. C. 1940. Genetic differences in maze-learning ability on rats. *Yearbook of National Society for the Study of Education* 1: 111–19.

Tsou, K., and C. S. Jang. 1964. Studies on the site of analgesic action of morphine by intracerebral micro-injection. *Science Sinica* 13: 1099–1109.

Underleider, L. G., and M. Mishkin. 1982. Two cortical visual systems. In *The analysis of visual behavior,* eds. R. J. W. Mansfield, and M. A. Goodale, 549–86. Cambridge, MA: M.I.T. Press.

Ungerstedt, U. 1971. Adipsia and aphagia after 6-hydroxydopamine induced degeneration of the nigro-striatal dopamine system. *Acta Physiologica Scandinavica* 82, s367: 95–122. (a)

Ungerstedt, U. 1971. Stereotaxic mapping of the monoamine pathways in the rat brain. *Acta Physiologica Scandinavica.* Supplementum 367. (b)

Uttal, W. R. 1973. *The psychobiology of sensory coding.* New York: Harper & Row.

Vale, W., and M. Brown. 1979. Neurobiology of peptides. In *The Neurosciences Fourth Study Program,* eds. F. O. Schmitt and F. G. Worden, 1027–41. Cambridge, MA: M.I.T. Press.

Valenstein, E. S. 1966. The anatomical locus of reinforcement. *Progress in Physiological Psychology* 1: 149–90.

Valenstein, E. S. 1973. *Brain control: A critical examination of brain stimulation and psychosurgery.* New York: Wiley & Sons.

Valenstein, E. S. 1980. Historical perspective. In *The psychosurgery debate: Scientific, legal, and ethical perspectives,* ed. E. S. Valenstein. San Francisco: W. H. Freeman.

Valenstein, E. S., and B. Beer. 1964. Continuous opportunities for reinforcing brain stimulation. *Journal of Experimental Analysis of Behavior* 7: 183–84.

Valenstein, E. S., V. C. Cox, and J. W. Kakolewski. 1967. Polydipsia elicited by the synergistic action of a saccharin and glucose solution. *Science* 157: 552–54.

Valenstein, E. S., and W. J. Meyers. 1964. Rate-independent test of reinforcing consequences of brain stimulation. *Journal of Comparative and Physiological Psychology* 57: 52–60.

Valzelli, L. 1981. Aggression and violence: A biological essay of the distinction. In *Aggression and violence,* eds. L. Valzelli and L. Morgese. Milan, Italy: Edizioni Saint Vincent.

Van Bergeijk, W. A. 1967. The evolution of vertebrate hearing. In *Contributions to sensory physiology,* ed. W. Neff, vol 2. New York: Academic Press.

Van Essen, D. C. 1985. Functional organization of primate visual cortex. In *Cerebral cortex,* eds. A. Peters, and E. G. Jones, 239–329. New York: Plenum Press.

Vaughan, H. G., Jr. 1969. The relationship of brain activity to scalp recordings of event-related potentials. In *Average evoked potentials: Methods, results and evaluations,* eds. E. Donchin and D. B. Lindsley. Scientific and Technical Information Division, Office of Technology Utilization, National Aeronautics and Space Administration, NASA No. SP-191. Washington, D.C.: U.S. Government Printing Office.

Vertes, R. P. 1984. Brainstem control of the events of REM sleep. *Progress in Neurobiology* 22: 241–88.

Verzeano, M. 1974. The study of neuronal networks in the mammalian brain. In *Bioelectric recording techniques,* eds. R. F. Thompson and M. M. Patterson. New York: Academic Press.

Vierck, C. J., Jr. 1974. Tactile movement detection and discrimination following dorsal column lesions in monkeys. *Experimental Brain Research* 20: 331–46.

Villablanca, J. R., R. J. Marcus, and C. E. Olmstead. 1976. Effects of caudate nuclei or frontal cortex ablations in cats. II. Sleep-wakefulness, EEG, and motor activity, *Experimental Neurology* 53: 31–50.

Volkmar, E. R., and W. T. Greenough. 1972. Rearing complexity affects branching of dendrites in the visual cortex of the rat. *Science* 176: 1445–47.

Volpe, E. P. 1979. *Man, nature, and society.* Dubuque, IA: Wm. C. Brown Publishers.

Wald, G. 1950. Eye and camera. *Scientific American* 183: 32–41.

Wald, G. 1964. The receptors for human color vision. *Science* 145: 1007–17.

Wald, G., P. K. Brown, and I. R. Gibbons. 1963. The problem of visual excitation. *Journal of Optical Society of America* 53: 20–35.

Walker, W. A., and A. I. Leshner. 1972. The role of the adrenals in aggression. *American Zoologist* 12: 652.

Wall, P. D. 1972. Somatosensory pathways. *Annual Review of Physiology* 34: 315–36.

Walls, G. L. 1942. *The vertebrate eye.* Bloomfield Hills, MI: Cranbrook Institute of Science.

Walter, W. G., R. Cooper, V. J. Aldridge, W. C. McCallum, and A. C. Winter. 1964. Contingent negative variation: An electric sign of sensorimotor association and expectancy in the human brain. *Nature* 203: 380–84.

Ward, I. L. 1972. Prenatal stress feminizes and demasculinizes the behavior of males. *Science* 175: 82–84.

Ward, I. L. 1977. Sexual diversity. In *Psychopathology: Experimental models,* eds. J. D. Maser and M. E. P. Seligman. San Francisco: W. H. Freeman.

Watanabe, T., and Y. Katsuki. 1974. Response patterns of single auditory neurons of the cat to species-specific vocalization. *Japanese Journal of Physiology* 24: 135–55.

Webster, W. R. and L. M. Aitkin. 1975. Central auditory processing. In *Handbook of psychobiology,* eds. M. S. Gazzaniga and C. Blakemore. New York: Academic Press.

Wehr, T. A., and F. K. Goodwin. eds. 1983. *Circadian rhythms in psychiatry.* Pacific Grove, CA: Boxwood Press.

Wei, E., and H. Loh. 1976. Physical dependence on opiate-like peptides. *Science* 193: 1262–63.

Wei, E., S. Sigel, and E. L. Way. 1975. Regional sensitivity of the rat brain to the inhibitory effects of morphine on wet shake behavior. *Journal of Pharmacology and Experimental Therapeutics* 193: 56–63.

Weinberger, N. M., T. J. Imig, and W. Lippe. 1972. Modification of unit discharges in the medial geniculate nucleus by click-shock pairing. *Experimental Neurology* 7: 829–40.

Weisinger, R. S., P. Considine, D. A. Denton, L. Leksell, M. J. McKinley, D. R. Mouw, A. F. Muller, and E. Tarjan. 1982. Role of sodium concentration of the cerebrospinal fluid in the salt appetite of sheep. *American Journal of Physiology* 242: R51–R63.

Wernicke, C. 1874. Der aphasische symptoencomplex. Max Cahn and Weigert, Breslau.

Wersall, J., and A. Flock. 1965. Functional anatomy of the vestibular and lateral line organs. In *Contributions to sensory physiology,* ed. W. D. Neff, vol. 1. New York: Academic Press.

Wever, E. G., and C. W. Bray. 1930. The nature of the acoustic response: The relation between sound frequency and frequency of impulses in the auditory nerve. *Journal of Experimental Psychology* 13: 373–87.

White, C. 1969. Discussion in *Average evoked potentials: Methods, results and evaluations,* eds. E. Donchin and D. B. Lindsley. Scientific and Technical Information Division, Office of Technology Utilization, National Aeronautics and Space Administration. Washington D.C.: U.S. Government Printing Office.

Whitfield, I. C., and E. F. Evans. 1965. Responses of auditory cortical neurons to stimuli of changing frequency. *Journal of Neurophysiology* 28: 655–72.

Whybrow, P. C., H. S. Akiskal, and W. T. McKinney. 1984. *Mood disorders: Toward a new psychobiology.* New York: Plenum Press.

Wickelgren, B. G. 1971. Superior colliculus: Some receptive field properties of bimodally response cells. *Science* 173: 69–72.

Wiesel, T. N., D. H. Hubel, and D. M. K. Lam. 1974. Autoradiographic demonstration of ocular-dominance columns in the monkey striate cortex by means of transneuronal transport. *Brain Research* 79: 273–79.

Williams, H. L., F. A. Holloway, and W. J. Griffiths. 1973. Physiological psychology: Sleep. *Annual Review of Psychology* 24: 279–316.

Wilson, C. J., and P. M. Groves. 1980. Fine structure and synaptic connections of the common spiny neuron of the rat neostriatum. A study employing intracellular injection of horseradish peroxidase. *Journal of Comparative Neurology* 194: 599–615.

Wilson, C. J., P. M. Groves, and E. Fifková. 1977. Monoaminergic synapses, including dendrodendritic synapses in the rat substantia nigra. *Experimental Brain Research* 30: 161–74.

Wilson, E. O. 1965. Chemical communication in the social insects. *Science* 149: 1064–70.

Wimer, R. E., and C. C. Wimer. 1985. Animal behavior genetics: A search for the biological foundations of behavior. *Annual Reviews of Psychology* 36: 171–218.

Wise, C. D., B. D. Berger, and L. Stein. 1973. Evidence of alpha-noradrenergic reward receptors and serotonergic punishment receptors in the rat brain. *Biological Psychiatry* 6: 3–21.

Wise, R. A. 1978. Catecholamine theories of reward: A critical review. *Brain Research* 152: 215–47.

Wise, R. A. 1982. Neuroleptics and operant behavior: The anhedonia hypothesis. *Behavioral and Brain Sciences* 5: 39–89.

Wise, R. A., and M. A. Bozarth. 1984. Brain reward circuitry: Four circuit elements "wired" in apparent series. *Brain Research Bulletin* 12: 203–8.

Witkin, H. A., S. A. Mednick, F. Schulsinger, E. Bakkesstrom, K. O. Christiansen, D. R. Goodenough, K. Hirschorn, C. Lundsteen, D. R. Owen, J. Philip, D. B. Rubin, and M. Stocking. 1976. Criminality in XYY and XXY men. *Science* 193: 547–55.

Wolozin, B. L., A. Pruchnicki, D. W. Dickson, and P. Davies. 1986. A neuronal antigen in the brains of Alzheimer patients. *Science* 232: 648–50.

Woodside, B., R. Pelchat, and M. Leon. 1980. Acute elevation of the heat load of mother rats curtails maternal nest bouts. *Journal of Comparative and Physiological Psychology* 94: 61–68.

Woody, C. D. 1986. Understanding the cellular basis of memory and learning. *Annu. Rev. Psychol.* 37: 433–93.

Woolley, D. W., and E. N. Shaw. 1957. Evidence for the participation of serotonin in mental processes. *Annals of New York Academy of Sciences* 66: 649–59.

Woolsey, C. N. 1960. Organization of cortical auditory system: A review and a synthesis. In *Neural mechanisms of the auditory and vestibular systems,* eds. G. L. Rasmussen and W. F. Windle. Springfield, Ill.: Charles C Thomas.

Wright, J. E. 1982. *Anabolic steroids and sports.* Natick, MA: Sports Science Consultants.

Wurtman, R. J., F. Hefti, and E. Melamed. 1981. Precursor control of neurotransmitter synthesis. *Pharmacological Reviews* 32: 315–34.

Wurtman, R. J., M. A. Moskowitz, and H. N. Munro. 1979. Transynaptic control of neuronal protein synthesis. In *The Neurosciences Fourth Study Program,* eds. F. O. Schmitt and F. G. Warden, 893–909. Cambridge: M.I.T. Press.

Wurtz, R. H. and M. E. Goldberg. 1971. Superior colliculus cell responses related to eye movements in awake monkeys. *Science* 171: 82–84.

Yates, A., K. Leehey, and C. M. Shisslak. 1983. Running—An analogue of anorexia? *New England Journal of Medicine* 308: 251–55.

Zeigler, H. P., and H. S. Karten. 1974. Central trigeminal structures and the lateral hypothalamus syndrome in the rat. *Science* 186: 636–37.

Zigler, E., and R. M. Hodapp. 1985. Mental retardation. In *Psychiatry,* ed. J. O. Cavenar, Jr. Philadelphia: Lippincott.

Zigmond, M. J., and E. M. Stricker. 1972. Deficits in feeding behavior after intraventricular injection of 6-hydroxydopamine in rats. *Science* 177: 1211–14.

Zimmerman, M. B., E. H. Blaine, and E. M. Stricker. 1981. Water intake in hypovolemic sheep: Effects of crushing the left atrial appendage. *Science* 211: 489–91.

Zola-Morgan, S., L. R. Squire, and D. G. Amaral. 1986. Human amnesia and the medial temporal region: Enduring memory impairment following a bilateral lesion limited to field CA1 of the hippocampus. *J. Neurosci.*

Zubin, J., and S. E. Barrera. 1941. Effect of electric convulsive therapy on memory. *Proceedings of Society for Experimental Biology and Medicine* 48: 596–97.

Zussman, L., S. Zussman, R. Sunley, and E. Bjornson. 1981. Sexual response after hysterectomy-oophorectomy: Recent studies and reconsideration of psychogenesis. *American Journal of Obstetrics and Gynecology* 140: 725–29.

Zwislocki, J. 1965. Analysis of some auditory characteristics. In *Handbook of mathematical psychology.* eds. R. D. Luce, R. R. Bosh, and E. Galante, vol. 3. New York: Wiley.

Credits

Illustrators

Rolin Graphics

Figs. l.4, 2.16, 4.2a–c, 5.6, 5.16, 6.1, 6.2, 6.4, 6.5, 6.7, 6.9, 6.15, 8.21, 8.22, 9.5, 9.9, 9.11, 9.12, 9.13, 9.14, 9.15, 9.22, 9.26, 9.27, 10.1, 10.3, 11.1, 11.2, 11.3, 11.4, 11.5, 11.6, 11.7, 11.8, 12.4*b*, 12.6, 12.8, 12.14, 13.16, 14.14, 14.17, 15.1, 15.4, 15.5, 15.19.

Illustrations

Chapter 2

Figs. 2.3 and 2.4 From Schlesinger, Kurt and Philip M. Groves, *Psychology: A Dynamic Science.* © 1976 Wm. C. Brown Publishers, Dubuque, Iowa. All Rights Reserved. Reprinted by permission. **Figs. 2.5, 2.6, 2.7, 2.8, and 2.10** From Volpe, E. Peter, *Biology and Human Concerns,* 3d ed. © 1975, 1979, 1983 Wm. C. Brown Publishers, Dubuque, Iowa. All Rights Reserved. Reprinted by permission. **Fig. 2.9*b*** From *Principles of Human Genetics,* Third Edition, by Curt Stern. Copyright © 1973 W. H. Freeman & Co., New York. Reprinted by permission. **Fig. 2.11** From Hsia, D. Y.-Y, "Phenylketonuria and its variants" in A. G. Steinberg and A. G. Bearn, (Eds.), *Progress in Medical Genetics, Vol. 7.* © Grune & Stratton, Inc., Orlando, Florida. Reprinted by permission. **Fig. 2.16** From *Psychology in the Making,* by Leo Postman. Copyright © 1962 by Alfred A. Knopf, Inc. Reprinted by permission of the publisher. **Fig. 2.17** From Nicol, S. E. and I. I. Gottesman, "Clues to the genetics and neurobiology of schizophrenia" in *American Scientist, 71,* 398–404, 1983. Data from Gottesman and Shields, 1982. Copyright © 1983 Sigma XI—Scientific Research Society of North America. Reprinted by permission.

Chapter 3

Fig. 3.1 Descriptions adapted from Giese, A. C., *Cell Physiology.* © 1968 W. B. Saunders Co., Philadelphia. Reprinted by permission. **Figs. 3.1, 3.8, 3.11, and 3.12** From Volpe, E. Peter, *Biology and Human Concerns,* 3d ed. © 1975, 1979, 1983 Wm. C. Brown Publishers, Dubuque, Iowa. All Rights Reserved. Reprinted by permission. **Fig. 3.2** From Hole, John W., Jr., *Human Anatomy and Physiology,* 3d ed. © 1978, 1981, 1984 Wm. C. Brown Publishers, Dubuque, Iowa. All Rights Reserved. Reprinted by permission. **Figs. 3.6 and 3.7** From Mader, Sylvia S., *Inquiry Into Life,* 4th ed. © 1976, 1979, 1982, 1985 Wm. C. Brown Publishers, Dubuque, Iowa. All Rights Reserved. Reprinted by permission. **Fig. 3.9*b*** From Mader, Sylvia S., *Inquiry Into Life,* 3d ed. © 1976, 1979, 1982 Wm. C. Brown Publishers, Dubuque, Iowa. All Rights Reserved. Reprinted by permission. **Fig. 3.10** From Singer, S. J. and G. L. Nicolson, "The fluid model of the structure of cell membranes" in *Science,* 1972, *175,* 720–731. © 1972 American Association for the Advancement of Science, Washington, D.C. Reprinted by permission. **Fig. 3.16** From DeRobertis, E. D. P., et al., *Cell Biology,* 4th ed. © 1968 W. B. Saunders Company, Philadelphia, Pa. Reprinted by permission. **Fig. 3.19** From Groves, P. M. and S. J. Young in J. O. Cavenar, Jr., (Ed.), *Psychiatry, Vol 3,* Chapter 42. Copyright 1986 J. B. Lippincott Company, Philadelphia. Reprinted by permission. **Fig. 3.20** From Hole, John W., Jr. *Human Anatomy and Physiology,* 4th ed. © 1978, 1981, 1984, 1987 Wm. C. Brown Publishers, Dubuque, Iowa. All Rights Reserved. Reprinted by permission.

Chapter 4

Fig. 4.1 From Ham, Arthur W., *Histology,* 7th ed. © 1974 J. B. Lippincott Company, Philadelphia. Reprinted by permission. **Figs. 4.7, 4.11, 4.13, 4.14*b*, 4.15, and 4.16** Modified from Noback, C. R. and R. J. Demarest, *The Nervous System: Introduction and Review.* Copyright © 1972 by McGraw-Hill, Inc. Used with permission of McGraw-Hill Book Company. **Figs. 4.8 and 4.9** From Gardner, E., *Fundamentals of Neurology,* 5th ed. © 1968 by W. B. Saunders Co., Philadelphia, Pennsylvania. Reprinted by permission. **Fig. 4.12** From Hole, John W., Jr., *Human Anatomy and Physiology,* 4th ed. © 1978, 1981, 1984, 1987 Wm. C. Brown Publishers, Dubuque, Iowa. All Rights Reserved. Reprinted by permission. **Fig. 4.14*a*** From Hole,

measured with lights of different hues" in *The Journal of General Physiology, 30,* 423–437, 1947. Reproduced by permission of Rockefeller University Press. **Fig. 7.11** From Wald, George, "The receptors for human color vision" in *Science, 145,* 1964, 1007–1016, fig. 4.4, September 1964. Copyright © 1964 by the American Association for the Advancement of Science. Reprinted by permission. **Figs. 7.12, 7.14, 7.15, and 7.17** From Schlesinger, Kurt and Philip M. Groves, *Psychology: A Dynamic Science.* © 1976 Wm. C. Brown Publishers, Dubuque, Iowa. All Rights Reserved. Reprinted by permission. **Fig. 7.13** From DeValois, R., et al., "Analysis of response patterns of LGN cells" in *Journal of the Optical Society of America, 56,* 966–977, 1966. Reprinted by permission. **Fig. 7.16** From Ratliff, F., *Mach Bands.* © 1965 Holden-Day Publishing, San Francisco. Reprinted by permission. **Fig. 7.18*a* and *b*** From Cornsweet, Tom N., *Visual Perception.* © 1970 Academic Press, Inc. Reprinted by permission. **Fig. 7.20** Modified from Noback, C. R. and R. J. Demarest, *The Nervous System: Introduction and Review.* Copyright © 1972 by McGraw-Hill, Inc. Used with permission of McGraw-Hill Book Company. **Fig. 7.21** Used with permission of Macmillan Publishing Co., Inc. from *Comparative Neurology* by J. W. Papez. Hafner Press, 1967. **Fig. 7.22*a* and *b*** From Hubel D. and T. N. Wiesel, *Journal of Physiology, 160,* 1962, figs. 7 and 8, pp. 120 and 121. Reprinted by permission of Cambridge University Press. **Fig. 7.22*c*** From Hubel, D. and T. N. Wiesel, *Journal of Neurophysiology, 28,* 1965, fig. 9, p. 245. Reprinted by permission of the American Physiological Society. **Fig. 7.28** From Graybiel, Ann M., "Some extrageniculate visual pathways in the cat" in *Investigative Opthamology, 11,* 1972, 322–332. © 1972 C. V. Mosby Company, St. Louis. Reprinted by permission.

Chapter 8

Fig. 8.2 From H. Fletcher, *Speech and Hearing.* © 1953 Bell Telephone Laboratories, Inc. Reprinted by permission of Wadsworth Publishing Co., Belmont, California. **Fig. 8.3** From Fletcher, Harvey and W. A. Munson, "Loudness: Its definition, measurement, and calculation" in *Journal of the Acoustical Society of America, 5,* 82–108, 1933. Reprinted by permission of the American Institute of Physics. **Figs. 8.4, 8.6, 8.23, and 8.24** From Hole, John W., Jr., *Human Anatomy and Physiology,* 4th ed. © 1978, 1981, 1984, 1987 Wm. C. Brown Publishers, Dubuque, Iowa. All Rights Reserved. Reprinted by permission. **Fig. 8.5** From von Békésy, G. and W. A. Rosenblith, "The mechanical properties of the ear" in S. S. Stevens, (Ed.), *Handbook of Experimental Psychology.* © 1951 John Wiley & Sons, New York. Reprinted by permission. **Fig. 8.7** From von Békésy, G., *Journal of the Acoustical Society of America, 19,* 1947, 452–460, and *25,* 770–785, 1953. Reprinted by permission. **Fig. 8.9** From Wever, E. G., *Theory of Hearing.* Copyright © 1949 John Wiley & Sons, Inc., New York. Reprinted by permission of the author. **Fig. 8.11*a*** From Schlesinger, Kurt and Philip M. Groves, *Psychology: A Dynamic Science.* © 1976 Wm. C. Brown Publishers, Dubuque, Iowa. All Rights Reserved. Reprinted by permission. **Fig. 8.11*b*** From Rose, Jerzy E., et al., "Some neural mechanisms in the inferior colliculus of the cat which may be relevant to localization of a sound source" in *Journal of Neurophysiology, 29,* 288–314, 1966. © 1966 American Physiological Society. Reprinted by permission. **Fig. 8.12** From Katsuki, Y., "Neuromechanisms of auditory sensations in cats" in W. A. Rosenblith, *Sensory Communication.* © 1961 Massachusetts Institute of Technology, Cambridge, Massachusetts. Reprinted by permission. **Fig. 8.13** From Watanbe, T. and Y. Katsuki, "Response patterns of single auditory neurons of the cat to species-specific vocalization" in *Japanese Journal of Physiology, 24,* 135–155. © 1974 Center for Academic Publications, Tokyo, Japan. Reprinted by permission. **Fig. 8.14** From Diamond, I. and K. Chow, "Biological Psychology" in *Psychology: A Study of Science,* Vol. 4, edited by S. Koch. Copyright © 1962 by McGraw-Hill, Inc. Used with permission of McGraw-Hill Book Co. **Figs. 8.16 and 8.17** From Somjen, George, *Sensory Coding in the Mammalian Nervous System.* Copyright © 1972 Plenum Publishing Corporation, New York. Reprinted by permission. **Fig. 8.18** From Mountcastle, V. P. and T. P. S. Powell, "Neural mechanisms subservice cutaneous sensibility, with special reference to the role of afferent inhibition in sensory perception and discrimination" in *Bulletin of the Johns Hopkins Hospital, 105,* 201–232, 1959. © 1959 Johns Hopkins University Press. Reprinted by permission. **Fig. 8.19** From Adkins, R. J., et al., "Control of somatosensory input by the cerebral cortex" in *Science, 153,* 1020–1022, fig. 1, 26 August 1966. Copyright © 1966 by the American Association for the Advancement of Science. Reprinted by permission. **Fig. 8.20** From Groves, Philip M., et al., "Organization by sensory modality in the reticular formation of the rat" in *Brain Research, 54,* 207–244, 1973. © 1973 Elsevier/North-Holland Press, Amsterdam, The Netherlands. Reprinted by permission. **Fig. 8.21** From Albe-Fessard, D., et al., "Diencephalic mechanisms of pain sensation" in *Brain Research Reviews, 9,* 217–296, 1985. © Elsevier Biomedical Press, Amsterdam. Reprinted by permission. **Fig. 8.22** From Frederickson, R. C. A. and L. A. Geary, "Endogenous opioid peptides: Review of physiological, pharmacological and clinical aspects" in *Progress in Neurobiology, 19,* 19–69, 1982. Copyright © 1982 Pergamon Press, Inc., New York. **Fig. 8.25** From Thompson, R. J., R. H. Johnson, and J. J. Hoopes, "Organization of auditory somatic, sensory and visual projection to association fields of cerebral cortex in the cat" in *Journal of Neurophysiology, 26,* 343–364, 1963. © 1963 American Physiological Society. Reprinted by permission.

Chapter 9

Figs. 9.3 and 9.4 From Jacobson, Stanley, "Hypothalamus and autonomic nervous system" in B. A. Curtis, S. Jacobson, and E. M. Marcus, (Eds.), *An Introduction to the Neurosciences.* © 1972 W. B. Saunders Company, Philadelphia. Reprinted by permission. **Fig. 9.6**

From McEwen, B. S., "Tne brain as a target organ of endocrine hormones" in D. T. Kreiger and J. C. Hughes, (Eds.), *Neuroendocrinology.* © 1980 HP Publishing Co., New York. Reprinted by permission. **Fig. 9.7** From Bloom, W. and Fawcett, D. W., (Eds.), *Textbook of Histology.* © 1968 W. B. Saunders, Philadelphia. Reprinted by permission. **Fig. 9.8** From Basmajian, J. V., "Electromyography: Single motor unit training" in *Bioelectric Recording Techniques: Part C. Receptor and Effector Processes,* R. F. Thompson and M. M. Patterson, (Eds.). Fig. 5.1, p. 139, 1974. Copyright © 1974 Academic Press, Inc., Orlando, Florida. Reprinted by permission. **Fig. 9.9** From Armstrong, R. B., "Mechanisms of exercise-induced delayed onset muscular soreness: A brief review" in *Medicine and Science in Sports and Exercise, 16,* 529–538, 1984. Copyright © 1984 Williams & Wilkins Company. Reprinted by permission. **Fig. 9.10** Figure 12.16 (page 387) from *Foundations of Physiological Psychology* by Richard F. Thompson. Copyright © 1967 by Richard F. Thompson. Reprinted by permission of Harper & Row Publishers, Inc. **Fig. 9.19** From Rasmussen and Penfield, "Further studies of the sensory and motor cerebral cortex of man" in *Federation Proceedings, 6,* 452–460, 1947. Reprinted by permission. **Fig. 9.20** From Marin-Padilla, M., "Prenatal and early postnatal ontogenesis of the human motor cortex: A golgi study. I. The sequential development of the cortical layers" in *Brain Research, 23,* 167–183, 1970. © 1970 Elsevier/North-Holland Biomedical Press, Amsterdam, The Netherlands. Reprinted by permission. **Fig. 9.21** From Asanuma, H. and I. Rosen, "Topigraphical organization of cortical efferent zones projecting to distal forelimb muscles in the monkey" in *Experimental Brain Research, 14,* 243, 257, 1972. © 1972 Springer-Verlag, New York, Inc. Reprinted by permission. **Fig. 9.24** From Kornhuber, H. H., *The Neurosciences: Third Study Program.* Copyright © 1975 Massachusetts Institute of Technology, Cambridge, Massachusetts. Reprinted by permission.

Chapter 10
Fig. 10.2 From Mader, Sylvia S., *Inquiry Into Life,* 4th ed. © 1976, 1979, 1982, 1985 Wm. C. Brown Publishers, Dubuque, Iowa. All Rights Reserved. Reprinted by permission. **Fig. 10.4** From Schlesinger, Kurt and Philip M. Groves, *Psychology: A Dynamic Science.* © 1976 Wm. C. Brown Publishers, Dubuque, Iowa. All Rights Reserved. Reprinted by permission. **Fig. 10.5** From Friedman, Mark I., "Hyperphagia in rats with experimental diabetes mellitus: A response to a decreased supply of utilizable fuels" in *Journal of Comparative and Physiological Psychology, 92,* 109–117, 1978. Copyright © 1978 American Psychological Association. Reprinted with permission of the author. **Fig. 10.7** Reprinted from 1961 *Nebraska Symposium on Motivation,* edited by M. R. Jones, by permission of University of Nebraska Press. Copyright © 1961 by the University of Nebraska Press. **Fig. 10.8** From Epstein, A. N., "The lateral hypothalamic syndrome: Its implications for the physiological psychology of hunger and thirst" in *Progress in Physiological Psychology, Vol. 4,* E. Stellar and J. Sprague, eds. © 1971 Academic Press, Inc., Orlando, Florida. Reprinted by permission.

Chapter 11
Fig. 11.6 From Gardiner, T. W. and E. M. Stricker, "Impaired drinking responses of rats with lesions of nucleus medianus: Circadian dependence" in *American Journal of Physiology, 248,* R224–230, 1985. Copyright © 1985 American Physiological Society. Reprinted by permission. **Fig. 11.8** From Alberts, J. R., "Huddling by rat pups: Multisensory control of contact behavior" in *Journal of Comparative and Physiological Psychology, 92,* 220–230, 1978. Copyright, © 1978 American Psychological Association. Reprinted by permission of the author.

Chapter 12
Fig. 12.1 From Money, J. and A. A. Erhardt, *Man and Woman, Boy and Girl.* Copyright © 1972 Johns Hopkins University Press, Baltimore, Maryland. Reprinted by permission.

Fig. 12.4*b* From Nordeen, E. J., K. W. Nordeen, D. R. Sengelaub, and A. P. Arnold, "Androgens prevent normally occurring cell death in a sexually dimorphic spinal nucleus" in *Science, 229,* 671–673, 16 August 1985. Copyright © 1966 by the American Association for the Advancement of Science. Reprinted by permission. **Fig. 12.5** From Volpe, E. Peter, *Biology and Human Concerns,* 3d ed. © 1975, 1979, 1983 Wm. C. Brown Publishers, Dubuque, Iowa. All Rights Reserved. Reprinted by permission. **Fig. 12.7** From Thorpe, W. H., *Learning and Instinct in Animals.* Copyright © 1956 Metheun Publishers, London. Reprinted by permission. **Fig. 12.8** From Adams, D. B., A. K. Gold, and A. D. Burt, "Rise in female-initiated sexual activity at ovulation and its suppression by oral contraceptives" in *New England Journal of Medicine, 299,* 1145–1150, 1978. Copyright © 1978 Massachusetts Medical Society. Reprinted by permission. **Fig. 12.11** From Olds, J., "Self-stimulation experiments and differential rewards" in H. H. Jasper, et al., (Eds.), *Reticular Formation of the Brain.* Copyright © 1958 Little, Brown & Co., Boston. Used by permission of the publisher, the editor, and the Henry Ford Hospital.

Chapter 13
Fig. 13.1 From Borbely, Alexander, *Das Geheimnis des Schlafs.* © 1984 Deutsche Verlags-Anstalt GmbH, Stuttgart. Reprinted by permission. **Figs. 13.2 and 13.4** From Kripke, D. F., "Biological Rhythms" in J. O. Cavenar, Jr., (Ed.), *Psychiatry, Vol 3,* Chapter 59. Copyright © 1986 J. B. Lippincott, Philadelphia. Reprinted by permission. **Fig. 13.3** From Richter, Curt P., "Sleep and activity: Their relation to the 24-hour clock" in *Sleep and Altered States of Consciousness,* S. S. Kety, E. V. Evarts, and H. L. Williams, (Eds.). Copyright © 1967 Association for Research in Nervous Mental Disease, New York. Reprinted by permission. **Fig. 13.5** From Strumwasser, Felix, "The demonstration and manipulation of a circadian rhythm in a single neuron" in *Circadian Clocks,* J. Aschoff, (Ed.), p. 445. Copyright © 1965 ASP Biological and Medical Press, North-Holland Division, Amsterdam, The Netherlands. **Fig. 13.6** Courtesy

Tobler, I. and Borbely, A. A., unpublished. **Fig. 13.7** From Berger, R. J., "The sleep and dream cycle" in A. Kales, (Ed.), *Sleep: Physiology and Pathology.* Copyright © 1969 J. B. Lippincott Company, Philadelphia. Reprinted by permission. **Fig. 13.8** From Peter Hauri, *Current Concepts™: The Sleep Disorders.* Copyright © 1982 The Upjohn Company, Kalamazoo, Michigan. Reprinted by permission. **Fig. 13.9** From Schlesinger, Kurt and Philip M. Groves, *Psychology: A Dynamic Science.* © 1976 Wm. C. Brown Publishers, Dubuque, Iowa. All Rights Reserved. Reprinted by permission. **Fig. 13.12** From Ranck, J. B., "Studies on single neurons in dorsal hippocampal formation and septum in unrestrained rats. I. Behavioral correlates and firing repertoires" in *Experimental Neurology, 41,* 461, 531, 1973. Copyright © 1973 Academic Press, Inc., Orlando, Florida. Reprinted by permission. **Fig. 13.13** From Jouvet, M., "Biogenic amines and the states of sleep" in *Science, 163,* 32–41, figs. 1, 2, 3, January 1969. Copyright © 1969 American Association for the Advancement of Science. Reprinted by permission. **Fig. 13.14** From Hartmann, E. L., T. J. Bridwell, and J. J. Schildkraut, "Alphamethyl-paratyrosine and sleep in the rat" in *Psychopharmacologia, 21,* 157–164, 1971. Copyright © 1971 Springer-Verlag, New York. Reprinted by permission. **Fig. 13.15** From Kales, A., E. J. Malmstrom, M. B. Scharf, and R. T. Rubin, "Psychological and biochemical changes following use and withdrawal of hypnotics" in A. Kales, (Ed.), *Sleep: Physiology and Pathology.* © 1969 J. B. Lippincott Company, Philadelphia. Reprinted by permission. **Fig. 13.16** From Gillin, J. C. and A. Borbely, "Sleep: A neurobiological window on affective disorders" in *Trends in Neurosciences, 8,* 537, 1985. © 1985 Elsevier Biomedical Press, Amsterdam. Reprinted by permission. **Fig. 13.17** Reprinted with permission of Macmillan Publishing Company from *Sleep: An Experimental Approach* by Wilse B. Webb. Copyright © by Wilse B. Webb.

Chapter 14

Fig. 14.2 Data adapted from Greenough, W. T., "Experimental modification of the developing brain" in *American Scientist, 63,* 37–46, 1975. Reprinted by permission, *American Scientist,* Journal of Sigma XI, The Scientific Research Society of America. **Fig. 14.3b** From Greenough, W. T., "Experimental modification of the developing brain" in *American Scientist, 63,* 37–46, 1975. Reprinted by permission, *American Scientist,* Journal of Sigma XI, The Scientific Research Society of America. **Fig. 14.4** From Buell, S. J. and P. D. Coleman, "Dendritic growth in the aged human brain and failure of growth in senile dementia" in *Science, 206,* 854–856, fig. 1A, 1979. Copyright © 1979 American Association for the Advancement of Science. Reprinted by permission. **Figs. 14.5 and 14.6** From Groves, P. M., et al., "Habituation and sensitization of spinal interneuron activity in acute spinal cat" in *Brain Research, 14,* 521–525, 1969. Copyright © 1969 Elsevier/North-Holland Biomedical Press, Amsterdam, The Netherlands. Reprinted by permission. **Fig. 14.7** From Kandel, E. R., V. Castellucci, H. Pinsker, and I. Kupferman, "The role of synaptic plasticity in the short-term modification of behavior" in G. Horn and R. H. Hinde, (Eds.), *Short-term Changes in Neural Activity and Behavior.* Copyright © 1970 University Press, London. Reprinted by permission. **Fig. 14.8** From Kupferman, I., V. Castellucci, H. Pinsker, and E. Kandel, "Neuronal correlates of habituation and dishabituation of the gill-withdrawal reflex in *Aplysia*" in *Science, 167,* 1743–1745, fig. 1, 27 March 1970. Copyright © 1970 American Association for the Advancement of Science. Reprinted by permission. **Fig. 14.9** From Thompson, Richard F., "The search for the engram" in *American Psychologist, 31,* 209–227, 1976. Copyright © 1976 American Psychological Association. Reprinted by permission of the author. **Fig. 14.10** From Fetz, Eberhard E., "Operant conditioning of cortical unit activity" in *Science, 163,* 955–957, fig. 1, 28 February 1969. Copyright © 1969 American

Association for the Advancement of Science. Reprinted by permission. **Fig. 14.11** From Fuster, J. M. and G. E. Alexander, "Neuron activity related to short-term memory" in *Science, 173,* 652–654, fig. 3, 13 August 1971. Copyright © 1971 American Association for the Advancement of Science. Reprinted by permission. **Fig. 14.12** From Iverson, S. D., "Brain lesions and memory in animals" in *The Physiological Basis of Memory,* J. A. Deutsch, (Ed.). Copyright © 1973 Academic Press, Inc., Orlando, Florida. Reprinted by permission. **Fig. 14.13** From Scoville, W. B. and B. Milner, "Loss of recent memory after bilateral hippocampal lesions" in *Journal of Neurology, Neurosurgery, and Psychology, 20,* 11–21, 1957. Copyright © 1957 British Medical Association, London. Reprinted by permission. **Fig. 14.14** From L. R. Squire, "The neuropsychology of memory" in P. Marler and H. Terrace, (Eds.), *The Biology of Learning.* © 1986 Springer-Verlag, Berlin. **Fig. 14.15** From Duncan, C. P., "The retroactive effect of electroshock on learning" in *Journal of Comparative Physiological Psychology, 42,* 32–44, 1949. Copyright © 1949 American Psychological Association.

Chapter 15

Fig. 15.5 From Randrup, Axel and I. Munkvad, "Pharmacology and physiology of stereotyped behavior" in *Journal of Psychiatric Research, 11,* 1–10, 1974. Copyright © 1974 Pergamon Press, Inc. Reprinted by permission. **Fig. 15.6** From Davis, J. M., "Recent developments in the drug treatment of schizophrenia" in *American Journal of Psychiatry, 133,* 208–214, 1976. Copyright © 1976 by the American Psychiatric Association. Reprinted by permission. **Fig. 15.8** From Ribak, C. E., A. B. Harris, J. E. Vaughn, and E. Roberts, "Inhibitory, GABAergic nerve terminals decrease at sites of focal epilepsy" in *Science, 205,* 211–214, 1979. Copyright © 1979 American Association for the Advancement of Science. Reprinted by permission. **Fig. 15.12** From Wilder Penfield and Lamar Roberts, *Speech and Brain Mechanisms.*

Copyright © 1959 by Princeton University Press and the Literary executors of the Penfield Papers. Figure VIII-14 reprinted with permission of Princeton University Press. **Fig. 15.13** From Sperry, R. W., "Some developments in brain lesion studies of learning" in *Federation Proceedings, 20,* 606–616, 1961. Reprinted by permission. **Figs. 15.14 and 15.15** From Sperry, R. W., "Lateral specialization in the surgically separated hemispheres" in *The Neurosciences: Third Study Program,* F. O. Schmitt and F. G. Worden, (Eds.). Copyright © 1974 Massachusetts Institute of Technology. Reprinted by permission. **Fig. 15.17** From Goldman, P. S. "Neural plasticity in primate telencephalon: Anomalous projections induced by prenatal removal of frontal cortex" in *Science, 202,* 768–770, 1978. Copyright © 1978 American Association for the Advancement of Science. Reprinted by permission.

Photos

Chapter 1
Figs. 1.1 and 1.2 Historical Pictures Service, Inc., Chicago; **Figs. 1.3 and 1.7** Bettmann Archive, Inc. **Fig. 1.8** Historical Pictures Service, Inc., Chicago. **Fig. 1.9** Courtesy of M. E. Olds.

Chapter 2
Fig. 2.1 J. C. DeFries, Institute of Behavioral Genetics, University of Colorado. **Fig. 2.2** B. LeBouef, Department of Biology, University of California, Santa Cruz. **Fig. 2.12** Upjohn Company and Margery Shaw, M.D. **Fig. 2.13** Money, John: *Sex Errors of the Human Body: Dilemmas, Education, Counseling.* © 1968 The Johns Hopkins University Press. **Fig. 2.14** © Digamber S. Borgaonkar. **Fig. 2.15** Upjohn Company and Margery Shaw, M.D.

Chapter 3
Fig. 3.3 © Martin M. Rotker/Taurus Photos. **Fig. 3.4** © Janice Juraska. **Fig. 3.5** Groves, P. M. and Wilson, C. J.: Fine structure of rat locus coeruleus, *Journal of Comparative Neurology,* 1980, *193,* 844–852. **Fig. 3.6** Jensen, W. A. and Parks, R. B.: *Cell Ultrastructure.* © 1967 Wadsworth Publishing Company, Inc., Belmont, CA. **Fig. 3.7a** © Keith Porter. **Fig. 3.9a** © Gordon F. Leedale/Biophoto Associates. **Fig. 3.14** Courtesy of Dr. S. F. Sawyer. **Fig. 3.15** Wilson, C. J., Groves, P. M., Kitain, S. T. and Linder, J. C.: Three-dimensional structure of dendritic spines in the rat neostriatum. *Journal of Neuroscience 3:* 393–398, 1983. **Fig. 3.17** Courtesy of Charles J. Wilson, University of Tennessee, from Groves, P. M. and Young, S. J.: Neurons, networks and behavior (chapter 12) in Cavenar: *Psychiatry,* vol. 3. © 1986 Lippincott, Philadelphia. **Fig. 3.18** In Wilson, C. J., Groves, P. M. and Fifková, E. *Experimental Brain Research 30:* 161–174, 1977. **Fig. 3.20b** © J. D. Robertson; **Fig. 3.21** Wilson, C. J.: Neuronal organization of the rat neostiatum. University of Colorado, Boulder, unpublished doctoral thesis, 1979.

Chapter 4
Fig. 4.3 David Kopf Instruments, Tujunga, CA. **Fig. 4.5** © Mark A. Geyer, University of California, San Diego. **Fig. 4.6a and b** © F. H. Gage, University of California, San Diego. **Fig. 4.20** © Terry Jernigan, Ph.D., Department of Psychiatry, University of California, San Diego, School of Medicine, La Jolla, CA.

Chapter 5
Fig. 5.5b From A. Hodgkin and R. Keynes: Experiments on the injection of substances into squid giant axons by means of a microsyringe. *Journal of Physiology 131,* 1956, pp. 592–616. Cambridge University Press. **Fig. 5.22** © Truett Allison, Veterans Administration Hospital, West Haven, CT.

Chapter 6
Fig. 6.13 © John Marshall, Ph.D., Department of Psychobiology, University of California, Irvine.

Chapter 7
Fig. 7.4a From Mountcastle, V. B.: The problem of sensing and the neural coding of sensory events. In M. Quarton et al.: *The Neurosciences.* © 1967 Rockefeller University Press. **Fig. 7.24** From Hubel, D. H. and Wiesel, T. N.: Functional architecture of macaque visual cortex. © 1977 *Proceedings of the Royal Society, London B. 198:* 1.59. **Figs. 7.25 and 7.26** From LeVay, S., Wiesel, T. N. and Hubel, D. H.: in Schmitt, F. O., Worden, F. G., Adelman, G. and Dennis, S. G.: *The Organization of the Cerebral Cortex.* © 1981 MIT Press.

Chapter 8
Fig. 8.15 © James C. Craig, Indiana University.

Chapter 9
Fig. 9.28 Courtesy of Maryann Martone.

Chapter 10
Fig. 10.6 © Philip Teitlebaum. **Fig. 10.9** © Robert Eckert/EKM-Nepenthe.

Chapter 12
Fig. 12.3 © John Money, Ph.D. **Fig. 12.4a** Nordeen, E. J., Nordeen, K. W., Sengelaub, D. R. and Arnold, A. P.: *Science,* vol. 229, pp. 671–673, 16 August 1985/ © AAAS. **Fig. 12.12** From Olds, James: Pleasure centers in the brain. *Scientific American,* October 1956.

Chapter 14
Fig. 14.1 Courtesy of Dr. David Krech. **Fig. 14.3** From Greenough, W. T.: Experimental modifications of the developing brain. *American Scientist,* 1975, *63,* 37–46. **Fig. 14.16a and b** From Squire, L. R.: *Science 232:* 1618/ © 1986 AAAS.

Chapter 15
Fig. 15.2 Courtesy of The National Institute of Mental Health. **Figs. 15.9 and 15.10** © Dr. Robert Terry, Department of Neurosciences, University of California, San Diego, School of Medicine. **Fig. 15.16** Purpura, D. P.: *Science 186:* 1126–1127, figure 10, 20 December 1974/ © AAAS. **Fig. 15.17b and c** Goldman, P. S.: *Science 202:* 768–770, figures 1 and 2/ © 1978 AAAS.

Name Index

Subject Index